Lecture Notes in Computer Science 3347

R.K. Ghosh   Hrushikesha Mohanty (Eds.)

Distributed Computing and Internet Technology

First International Conference, ICDCIT 2004
Bhubaneswar, India, December 22-24, 2004
Proceedings

Volume Editors

R.K. Ghosh
IIT Kanpur, Department of Computer Science and Engineering
Kanpur, India
E-mail: rkg@cse.iitk.ac.in

Hrushikesha Mohanty
University of Hyderabad, Department of Computer and Information Sciences
Hyderabad, India
E-mail: hmcs@uohyd.ernet.in

Library of Congress Control Number: 2004116532

CR Subject Classification (1998): D.1.3, C.2.4, D.2, F.2, H.3, H.4, D.4.6, K.6.5

ISSN 0302-9743
ISBN 3-540-24075-6 Springer Berlin Heidelberg New York

Springer is a part of Springer Science+Business Media

springeronline.com

Printed in Germany

Typesetting: Camera-ready by author, data conversion by Scientific Publishing Services, Chennai, India
Printed on acid-free paper SPIN: 11366805 06/3142 5 4 3 2 1 0

Program Chairs' Message

This volume contains the papers presented at the 1st International Conference on Distributed Computing and Internet Technology (ICDCIT 2004), December 22–24, 2004. The Conference was held in Bhubaneswar, the capital city of Orissa and the city of a thousand temples. It was hosted by the Kalinga Institute of Industrial Technology (KIIT).

We received 211 contributed papers from researchers in 15 countries across the world. With the help of a strong international program committee that comprised 48 members and four track chairs, Vijay Kumar (Distributed Computing), Sanjay Madria (Internet Technology), Indrakshi Ray (System Security) and Abhik Roychoudhury (Software Engineering), we offered an excellent technical program. Each of the submitted papers was reviewed by two reviewers and by at least one program committee member. Every effort was made to include the papers of the highest quality in the technical programme. Less than 23% of the contributed papers were selected for presentation after the review process. As the conference is a focused one, we had to be selective and had to return even some good papers. We are confident that this volume will attest to the technical quality of the conference.

The presentations were grouped under four tracks, namely Distributed Computing, Internet Technology, Software Engineering, and System Security. Distributed Computing track presentations were organized into three different sessions with first and second sessions each having two parallel sittings. The papers in the Distributed track report results on several important problems like leader election, modeling, protocols and performance, distributed transaction processing, and information dissemination. The Internet Technology track was comprised of three sessions with the second session having two parallel sittings. The track included papers about some recent problems on application development using Internet technologies, related protocols, information retrieval, and service delivery in the Internet environment. The Software Engineering track consisted of two sessions with the second session having two parallel sittings. This track contained some interesting papers on formal modeling, generating systems from specifications, requirements engineering, distributed program analysis and program reusability. The System Security track had three sessions; the second and third sessions had two parallel sittings each. The track contained papers on interesting issues in systems security. Several hot topics like intrusion detection and access control were in the second session. Some security issues pertaining to conventional and ad hoc computer networks were also presented in this session. The third session addressed the issues in the design of secured systems. The papers discussed anonymity in mobile commerce, and techniques of steganography and cryptography for achieving secured services. The preconference activities included tutorials and a workshop. The workshop on Data Mining, Security and Other Applications was organized by Prem Uppuluri (University of Missouri-

Kansas City) and Ashok Srivastava (NASA Ames Research Center, USA). The tutorials were on security issues in distributed systems and enterprise resource planning.

We take this opportunity to thank various people and organizations who contributed to make this conference a grand success. Our heartfelt thanks to the track chairs whose full cooperation and technical assessments were crucial to achieve this high level of quality even in the first edition of the conference. The full participation of the program committee members and the reviewers made it possible to complete the peer-review process in time. We are extremely thankful to them. We would like to thank our advisors and general chair for having confidence in us. Our special thanks go to A. Samanta and P.K. Mishra of KIIT for their support and encouragement in organizing this conference. We gratefully acknowledge the financial and logistic support extended by KIIT in hosting this conference. The All India Council of Technical Education (AICTE), Government of India, New Delhi provided a generous grant-in-aid for organizing ICDCIT. We thankfully acknowledge AICTE's support. We are thankful to Springer for its cooperation in publishing the proceedings in such a short time. We are also thankful to our parent departments, Department of Computer Science and Engineering, IIT Kanpur and Department of Computer and Information Sciences, University of Hyderabad, for providing infrastructural support to carry out the editorial work. We thank Krithi Ramamritham and Pradeep Khosla for agreeing to deliver the lectures in the plenary sessions. We also extend our thanks to Susil Jajodia, Bharat Bhargava and Vijay Kumar for agreeing to deliver the track keynote addresses and Satish Chandra and Sharma Chakravarthy for agreeing to deliver the invited talks. All the talks focused on the themes of the conference and were well appreciated and thought provoking.

We would like to thank all the authors and attendees for making this conference a grand success. We sincerely hope that the three-day program of ICDCIT 2004 provided a platform to researchers for further academic interactions and collaborations. We plan to make the ICDCIT conference an annual event with the support of KIIT and the cooperation of Springer. We hope the ICDCIT proceedings in the coming years will report exciting research results in hot topics in computer science and engineering.

December 2004

R.K. Ghosh
Hrushikesha Mohanty

General Chair's Message

The convergence of computing, communication and control is setting the research agenda for the coming years. Distributed computing and Internet technology are two important in this issues. The series of international conferences on Distributed Computing and Internet Technology (ICDCIT 2004) was initiated to provide a forum for researchers around the world. It was indeed a great honor and privilege for me to welcome all the participants to ICDCIT 2004, held in the historical cultural city of Bhubaneswar.

A true measure for a conference is the material being presented and also the participation. I was extremely delighted to see a wealth of material represented here that can be broadly categorized into the following tracks: (i) Distributed Computing, (ii) Internet Technology, (iii) Software Engineering, (iv) System Security. In addition to these tracks, various tutorials were dedicated to Web mining, intrusion detection, enterprise resource planning and distributed secured systems. Gauging the impact of the convergence of computing, communications and control on science and on society is very difficult. This conference is a forum that shall attempt not only to comprehend the impact but also reshape it. It was a delight to see the enthusiastic participation of researchers from a large number of countries. The most interesting feature was that the conference was held in a purely academic environment of a typical college in India that naturally attracted a large number of students from Orissa and other parts of India.

I would like to thank the plenary speakers Krithi Ramamritham, IIT, Bombay and Pradeep Khosla, CMU. In addition, I thank all the keynote speakers of various tracks for joining us in making the conference a success.

I would like to thank R.K. Ghosh and H. Mohanty for compiling such an excellent program. I would like to thank all the PC members, especially the track chairs who did excellent work.

It is a pleasure to thank the Kalinga Institute of Industrial Technology (KIIT), Bhubaneswar who took the brunt of the organization of ICDCIT 2004. My special thanks go to A. Samanta, Chancellor, and P.K. Mishra, Pro-chancellor, KIIT (Deemed University) for all the organizational efforts, and also to the innumerable dedicated volunteers who were responsible for the organization of the conference. Finally, I thank Springer for having accepted to bring out the proceedings in their LNCS series.

December 2004 R.K. Shyamasundar

Conference Organization

Advisory Committee

General Chair
R.K. Shyamasunder, TIFR, Mumbai, India

Advisors
Chris George, UNU/IIST, Macau, China
Gautam Barua, IIT Guwahati, India
Achyuta Samanta, KIIT, Bhubaneswar, India
M. Bhattacharjee, KIIT, Bhubaneswar, India

Program Committee

Program Chairs
R.K. Ghosh, IIT, Kanpur, India
Hrushikesha Mohanty, University of Hyderabad, India

Track Chairs
Distributed Computing:
Vijay Kumar, University of Missouri-Kansas City, USA
Internet Technology:
Sanjay K. Madria, University of Missouri-Rolla, USA
Systems Security:
Indrakshi Ray, Colorado State University, USA
Software Engineering:
Abhik Roychoudhury, National University of Singapore, Singapore

Program Committee Members

Distributed Computing Track
Albert Burger, Heriot-Watt University, UK
Ashok N. Srivastava, NASA Ames Research Center, USA
Bharat Bhargava, Purdue University, USA
Deendayal Dinakarpandian, University of Missouri-Kansas City, USA
Evaggelia Pitoura, University of Ioannina, Greece
Gi-Chul Yang, Mokpo National University, South Korea
Lein Harn, University of Missouri-Kansas City, USA
Margaret H. Dunham, Southern Methodist University, USA
Panos Chrysanthis, University of Pittsburgh, USA
Prem Uppuluri, University of Missouri-Kansas City, USA
Raj Kannan, Louisiana State University, USA
Sharma Chakravarthy, University of Texas at Arlington, USA
Yugyung Lee, University of Missouri-Kansas City, USA
Vijay K. Garg, University of Illinois, Chicago, USA
Vijay Vaishnavi, Georgia State University, USA

Internet Technology Track

Dheeraj Bhardwaj, IIT Delhi, India
Gajanan Chinchwadkar, Sybase Inc., USA
Gi-Chul Yang, Mokpo National University, South Korea
Kajal Claypool, University of Massachusetts, Lowell, USA
Kalpdrum Passi, Laurentian University, Canada
Leszek Lilien, Purduev University, USA
Mukesh Mohania, IBM Research Lab, India
N.L. Sarda, IIT Mumbai, India
Neelima Gupta, University of Delhi, India
Pabitra Mitra, IIT Kanpur, India
Sourav Bhowmick, NTU, Singapore
S.K. Gupta, IIT Delhi, India
Shiyong Lu, Wayne State University, USA
Takahiro Hara, Osaka University, Japan

Software Engineering Track

Bikram Sengupta, IBM Research Lab, India
Gopal Gupta, University of Texas, Dallas, USA
Giorgio Delzanno, University of Genoa, Italy
Jin Song Dong, National University of Singapore, Singapore
Kung-Kiu Lau, University of Manchester, UK
Rushikesh K. Joshi, IIT Mumbai, India
Shaoying Liu, Hosei University, Japan
Supratik Mukhopadhyay, NASA IV&V Center, USA
Zhiming Liu, UNU/IIST, Macau, China

System Security Track

Aditya Bagchi, Indian Statistical Institute, India
Brajendra Panda, University of Arkansas, USA
Csilla Farkas, University of South Carolina, USA
Duminda Wijesekera, George Mason University, USA
Elena Ferrari, University of Insubria at Como, Italy
Elisa Bertino, Purdue University, USA
Indrajit Ray, Colorado State University, USA
Pierangela Samarati, University of Milan, Italy
Ravi Mukkamala, Old Dominion University, USA
Sabrina De Capitani di Vimercati, University of Milan, Italy
Vijayalakshmi Atluri, Rutgers University, USA

Workshop Organizers

Workshop on Data Mining, Security and Other Applications

Co-chairs

Ashok N. Srivastava, NASA Ames Research Center, USA
Prem Uppuluri, University of Missouri-Kansas City, USA

Organizing Committee

Organizing Chair
P.K. Mishra, KIIT, Bhubaneswar, India

Finance Chair
Dhanada K. Mishra, KIIT, Bhubaneswar, India

Scholarship Chair
Atul Negi, University of Hyderabad, India
M.M. Gore, IIIT-Allahabad, India

Host Institution
Kalinga Institute of Industrial Technology, KIIT, Bhubaneswar, Orissa, India

List of Referees

Debopam Acharya
Vijayalakshmi Atluri
A. Badia
Aditya Bagchi
Gautam Barua
Cory Beard
Elisa Bertino
Bharat Bhargava
Sourav Bhowmick
S. Biswas
Albert Burger
Sudip Chakraborty
Sharma Chakravarthy
B.D. Chaudhary
Gajanan Chinchwadkar
Panos Chrysanthis
Soon Ae Chun
Kajal Claypool
A.R. Dani
Pradipta De
Giorgio Delzanno
Deendayal Dinakarpandian
Jin Song Dong
Margaret H. Dunham
Mohamed Eltoweissy
Csilla Farkas
Eduardo Fernandez
Elena Ferrari
Michael Gertz
R.K. Ghosh
K. Gopinath
M.M. Gore
Ehud Gudes
Gopal Gupta
S.K. Gupta
Arobindo Gupta
R.C. Hansdah
Takahiro Hara
Lein Harn
Chittaranjan Hota
Chin-Tser Huang
Amit Jain
Rushikesh K. Joshi
Vamsi Kambhampati
Raj Kannan
Ng Wee Keong
Vijay Kumar
Sukhamay Kundu
Kung-Kiu Lau
Yugyung Lee
Ninghui Li
Leszek Lilien
Shaoying Liu
Zhiming Liu
Peng Liu
Shiyong Lu
Sanjay Madria
Rajib Mall
Nasir Memon
Pabitra Mitra
Hrushikesha Mohanty
Mohammed Moharrum
Ken Moody
Supratik Mukhopadhyay
Ravi Mukkamala
Glen Nuckolls
Martin Olivier
S.P. Pal
Brajendra Panda
Kalpdrum Passi
Evaggelia Pitoura
Nayot Poolsappit
Nitin Prabhu
Ashish Raniwala
Indrakshi Ray
Indrajit Ray
Sibabrata Ray
Abhik Roychoudhury
Pierangela Samarati
N.L. Sarda
Bikram Sengupta
Anna Squicciarini
Ashok N. Srivastava
Andrei Stoica
Zahir Tari
Rajeev Tripathi

Prem Uppuluri
Vijay Vaishnavi
Sabrina De Capitani di Vimercati
Tao Wang
Duminda Wijesekera
Tai Xin
Wei Xu
Gi-Chul Yang

Table of Contents

Transaction and Information Dissemination

INTERNET TECHNOLOGY

Query and Retrieval

Protocol and Replica Management

Ontology and Services

SOFTWARE ENGINEERING

Invited Talk – II

Analysis and Modelling

Tools and Techniques

SYSTEMS SECURITY

Keynote Address – III

Intrusion Detection and Access Control

Network and Security

Secured Systems Design

Security Services

WORKSHOP ON DATAMINING, SECURITY & APPLICATION

Taming the Dynamics of Disributed Data

Krithi Ramamritham

IIT, Mumnai, India

Abstract. Data gathered from (wireless) sensor networks and those delivered today via the web reflect rapid and unpredictable changes in the world around us. Clearly, the Quality of Service needs for such delivery are much more stringent than for static data. This talk will examine the nature of dynamics of distributed data, study the suitability of the current infrastructure for disseminating time varying information, and discuss fresh approaches to maintain the temporal coherency of dynamic data. We argue that executing user queries over dynamic data at the edge of the network, e.g., at Data Aggegators, improves scalability and reduce overheads but poses challenges in terms of delivering consistent query results in spite of data dynamics as well as failures in the infrastructure. How these challenges can be met by the judicious design of algorithms for data dissemination, caching, and cooperation forms the crux of the talk.

R.K. Ghosh and H. Mohanty (Eds.): ICDCIT 2004, LNCS 3347, p. 1, 2004.

Data in Your Space

Vijay Kumar

SCE, Computer Networking,
University of Missouri-Kansas City,
5100 Rockhill,
Kansas City, MO 64110, USA
kumarv@umkc.edu

Abstract. We envision a fully connected data space where flow of data between any two points, is continuous. In this paper we discuss the research and development activities for managing this data flow and present our solutions to some of the problems in the areas of mobility, broadcast, web, and security.

1 Introduction

We envision the real world or a part of it as a fully connected and highly dynamic data space where data continuously flows between any two points. The states of the data space are managed by the laws of nature, which we cannot mess around with and the only way to manage our interaction with these states is to be "in sync" with the natural events. The state of "being in sync" is to tame the flow of data. For example, to handle natural events such as earthquake, tornado, flood, etc., we must fetch or acquire and process necessary data on time for making necessary protection arrangements. Thus a perfect synchronization in our interaction with nature can guarantee minimum or no undesirable effects on our lives. Figure 1 illustrates our view of the real world in terms of the fully connected data space.

Our data space is packed with functional entities which continuously exchange information through wired and wireless links to complete the assigned tasks. For example a taxi may communicate with a bus through wireless link or a hot air balloon may communicate with the submarine through wireless link and so on. To achieve the desired synchronization in this highly dynamic set of states one must examine all possible scenarios of data flow. We categorize them into (a) temporal data, (b) temporal and spatial data, and (c) free data [1]. Temporal data represents time-bound events which can be hard, medium or soft real-time. For example traffic event data can fall into any of these categories. Similarly weather data can be time-bound because it must be broadcast under some time constraints. Space and time bound event is related to two parameters consequently the data flow must happen under location and time constraints. Traffic situation is related to a particular location and importance is given to traffic condition in rush hour. Traffic data, therefore, must be broadcast at certain time and from certain location. This gives rise to "Location Dependent Data (LDD)" [1] and its processing must satisfy comparatively more constraints. Finally, the free data represent event which can happen any time and

R.K. Ghosh and H. Mohanty (Eds.): ICDCIT 2004, LNCS 3347, pp. 2–20, 2004.

anywhere. We, however, believe that no event and therefore no data flow is entirely free from temporal or spatial constraints. We may chose to ignore it because the constraints they put may not seriously affect the semantics of the data they generate.

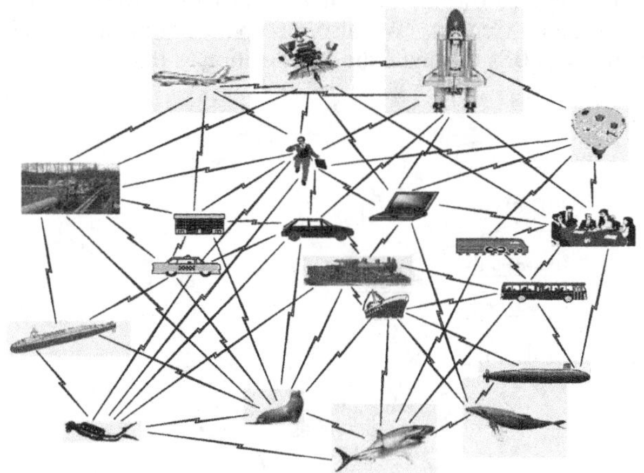

Fig. 1. A fully connected data space

In this paper we deal with data flow through wireless channels which presents many research challenges both from application and system view points.

2 Mobility

The discipline of mobility is an essential component for establishing and maintaining continuous data flow. It is deployed in the data space through a number of gadgets and the most common of them are cell phones and laptops. Telecommunication companies are continuously improving the communication qualities, security, availability and reliability of cell phones and trying to enhance its scope by adding data management capabilities, which is highly desirable. To address the issues of data management on mobile platform we envision an information processing system based on PCS or GSM architecture, which we refer to as the *Mobile Database System* (MDS) [2]. It is essentially a distributed client/server system where clients can move around freely while performing their data processing activities in *connected*, *disconnected* or *intermittent* connected mode. MDS thus can process debit/credit transactions, pay utility bills, make airline reservations, and other transactions without being subject to any geographical constraints. We believe that MDS or a similar system is likely to become an essential gadget of our lives.

2.1 A Reference Architecture of Mobile Database System

Figure 2 illustrates our reference architecture of Mobile Database System (MDS). We have added a number of DBSs (database Servers) to incorporate data processing capability without affecting any aspect of the generic mobile network [3].

A set of general purpose computers (PCs, workstations, etc.) are interconnected through a high-speed wired network, which are categorized into Fixed Hosts (FH) and Base Stations (BS) or mobile support stations (MSS). One or more BSs are connected with a BS Controller or Cell Site Controller (BSC) [Mahi], which coordinates the operation of BSs using its own stored software program when commanded by the MSC (Mobile Switching Center). We also incorporate some additional simple data processing capability in BSs to handle the coordination of transaction processing.

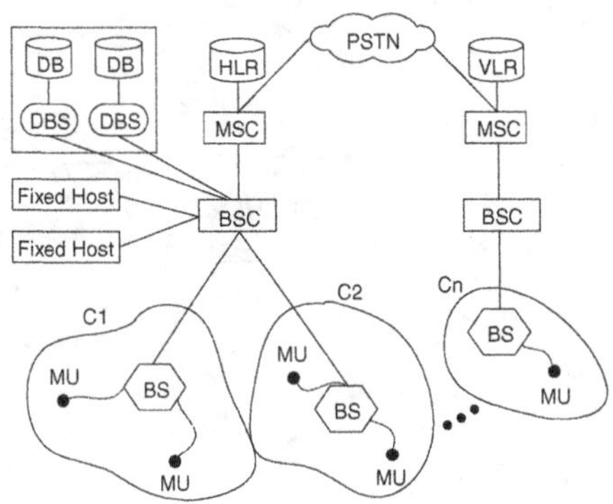

Fig. 2. A reference architecture of Mobile Database System (MDS)

Unrestricted mobility in PCS is supported by wireless link between BS and mobile data processing devices such as PDA (Personal Digital Assistants), laptop, cell phones, etc. We refer to these as Mobile Hosts (MH) or Mobile Units (MU) [3]. A number of MUs communicate with a BS using dedicated wireless channels dedicated to the BS [3] and the power of the BS defines the communication domain, which we refer to as *G*, within which such communication takes place. In reality a high power BS is not used because of a number of factors including the cost rather a number of low power BSs are deployed for managing movement of MUs. Each BS manages wireless communication in a part of *G*, which is referred to as a *cell*. The size of a cell depends upon the power of its BS and also restricted by the limited bandwidth of wireless communication channels. Thus, *G* is defined as $\{C1 + C2 + \ldots + Cn\}$ where *Ci* is the area of a cell *i* (Fig. 2). A MU may be in powered off state or it may be in idle state (doze mode) or it may be actively processing data. It can freely moves from one cell to another in any of its state, however, at any instance of time it exists only in one cell. When the MU crosses a cell boundary, it gets disconnected from its last BS and gets connected with the BS of the cell it enters. During the migration from one cell to another, the *handoff* mechanism makes sure that the boundary is crossed seamlessly and its processing is not affected by such movement.

A DBS provides full database services and it communicates with MUs only through a BS. DBSs can either be installed at BSs or can be a part of FHs or can be independent to BS or FH. It is possible to install DBS at BSs, however, we argue against this approach because BS is a switch and equipping it with database functionality would be unacceptable from mobile communication viewpoint. For these reasons and for the reason of scalability, we created DBSs as separate nodes on the wired network, which could be reached by any BS at anytime.

3 Mobilaction: A Mobile Transaction Model

A transaction mechanism is essential for database processing. In recent years a number of new transaction models such as nested transaction model [30], open nested transaction, sagas [31], etc., have evolved to manage ever changing data processing requirements. These new models, however, are not suitable for MDS because they are unable to deal with the issues of mobility, consequently a new transaction model is required to manage them under the constraints of MDS. The new transaction structure must have the ACID properties and must also be equipped with facilities for handling spatial data flow. Motivated by unique requirements of MDS, we developed a mobile transaction model which we refer to as "*Mobilaction*" [2]. We present here some data characteristics related to mobility before we introduce *Mobilaction.*

LDD (Location Dependent Data) gives rise to Location Dependent Query (LDQ) and Location Aware Query (LAQ) [4, 28]. The answer of a LDQ depends on the geographical origin of the query. For example the answer to a query "*What is the distance of the airport*" is strongly tied to the geographical origin of this query. For example, a person who is traveling by car from Dallas to Kansas City continues to ask "*What is the distance of the airport*" after every few minutes. The system will generate multiple correct answers to this query and each answer will be strongly related with the geographical origin of the query. Thus from these reasoning we conclude that location has to be a basic property of *Mobilaction* and we incorporate it into Mobilaction which is defined as:

An Execution Fragment e_{ij} is a partial order $e_{ij}= \{\sigma_j, \leq_j\}$ where

- $\sigma_j = OS_j \cup \{N_j\}$ where $OS_j = \cup_k O_{jk}$, $O_{jk} \in$ {read, write}, and $N_j \in \{abort_L, commit_L\}$. Here these are location dependent commit and abort.
- For any O_{jk} and O_{jl} where $O_{jk} = R(x)$ and $O_{jl} = W(x)$ for a data object x, then either $O_{jk} \leq_j O_{jl}$ or $O_{jl} \leq_j O_{jk}$
- $\forall O_{jk} \in OS_j, OS_j \leq_j N_j$

A Mobile Transaction T_i is a triple $<F_i, L_i, FLM_i>$ where $F_i = \{e_{i1}, e_{i2}..., e_{in}\}$ is a set of execution fragments, $L_i = \{l_{i1}, l_{i2}, ..., l_{in}\}$ is a set of locations, and $FLM_i = \{flm_{i1}, flm_{i2}, ..., flm_{in}\}$ is a set of fragment location mappings where $\forall_j, flm_{i1}(e_{ij}) = l_{ij}$.

3.1 Mobilaction: Execution and Commitment

A *Mobilaction* may run on multiple nodes which could be located anywhere in the network. Each e_i represents a subset of the total T_i processing. A T_i is requested at a MU, it is fragmented, and are executed at the MU and at a set of DBSs. Note that no fragment of a *Ti* is sent to another MU for execution because it is a personal unit and its use is controlled by its owner who can switch it off or disconnect it from the network at any time. This could force the *Ti* to fail unnecessary. Furthermore, other MUs may not have necessary data to process the fragment generated by another MU, in which case the fragment will end up at a DBS. Also transfer of e_i's to other MUs will incur wireless communication overhead which could be prohibitive.

In MDS, like conventional distributed database systems, a coordinator (CO) is required to manage the commit of T_i [2] and its role can be illustrated with the execution of a T_i. A T_i originates at MU and its BS is identified as the holder of the CO of T_i. The MU fragments *Ti* extracts its e_i, sends T_i - e_i to the CO and begins processing e_i. The MU may move to other cell during the execution of e_i, which must be logged for recovery. At the end of the execution of e_i, the MU updates its cache copy of the database, composes update shipment and sends it to the CO. CO logs the updates from the MU.

Upon receipt of T_i - e_i from MU, the CO splits T_i - e_i into e_j's ($i \neq j$) and sends them to a set of relevant DBSs for execution. Note that the presence of handoff may delay the execution and commit of a T_i. In this situation even a *small* T_i may appear as a *long-running* T_i. Thus, the meaning of *long-running* T_i on MDS could be (a) a *small* T_i (such as debit/credit) may take long time to run because of frequent handoffs and (b) the T_i does access a large number of data items, such as the preparation of bank customer monthly statements, and takes long time to execute in the absence of any handoff. It is, however, meaningless to run statement preparation transactions on MU and long-running transaction in our case will be mostly of (a) type.

It is obvious that a conventional two-phase or three-phase commit protocol [5] would not work satisfactorily in MDS. It will generate excessive overhead, which could not be handled by MDS. We have developed a commit protocol called TCOT [2] (Transaction Commit on Timeout) which (a) uses minimum number of wireless messages, (b) MU and DBS have independent decision making capability, and (c) is non-blocking. In distributed database systems the use of timeout is necessary for developing a "non-blocking" transaction commit protocol [5, 6, 7]. We propose the use of timeout for our commit protocol. We assume that instead of failure the end of timeout period indicates a success. Thus, at the end of the timeout it is *expected* that the receiver has received the message sent by the sender.

TCOT strives to limit the number of messages (especially uplink) needed to commit a T_i. It does so by assuming that all members of a commit set successfully commit their fragments within the defined timeout leading to commit of T_i. Unlike 2PC or 3PC [5, 6, 7], no further communications between the CO and participants take place for keeping track of the progress of fragments. However, the failure situation is immediately communicated to CO to make a final decision about commit.

It is well known that finding the most appropriate value of a timeout is not always easy because it depends on a number of system variables [5]. However, it is usually possible to define a value for timeout, which performs well in all cases. It should be noted that an imprecise value of timeout does not affect the correctness but affects the performance of an algorithm.

4 Data Dissemination Through Wireless Broadcast

Although MDS provided highly desirable transaction management facility to M-commerce, it does not have capability to reach every user in the data space and satisfy their demands for highly consumable information such as airline schedule, stock price quotes, weather information, etc. Users desire to tune some wireless frequencies and retrieve necessary data from the data space. Such facilities can only be developed using data dissemination through wireless channels. In this paper we propose an innovative public data dissemination strategy which is based on a new architecture. We use a hybrid (push and pull based) approach where data is adaptively scheduled to utilize limited bandwidth. We show that the use of data staging helps mobile users to access and stage his data anywhere and at anytime with low latency.

One of the most important problems is the development of a suitable architecture of asymmetric broadcast environment. Few developments in this field such as the Hughes DirectTV [8] and Marimba's Castanet [9] have addressed this issue and we have also considered them in the development of our system. We suggest that any data broadcast architecture should be able to satisfy the following requirements:

a. It should be able to broadcast not only the current data, but also the static data which is used in general by the people in different times of the day.
b. Access latency should be low.
c. The architecture should be energy efficiency.

Two ways to build data distribution system are (a) cellular network and (b) satellite broadcast. System based on cellular technology can be developed at low cost but they would be more area specific and would not be able to reach people globally. System based on satellites broadcast can be used to distribute data to a very large number of users. The low earth object (LEO) satellites can be used for this purpose. The LEO satellites can reach almost everywhere in the earth with a certain number of satellites unfortunately such system would be expensive to build and maintain. Our approach is based on cellular technology.

4.1 A Review of Previous Works

Data dissemination through wireless channels generated noticeable attention and the concept of broadcast disks was proposed and investigated in [10, 11, 12]. This approach created the notion of multiple disks spinning at different speeds on a single broadcast channel to create an effect of a fine grained storage hierarchy. Push and pull based broadcast was proposed in [13]. There has been some work on adaptive broadcast protocols [14] in the mobile computing environment. The goal was to design cooperative strategies between the server and the client to access information where energy expenditure by clients is minimal. Novel techniques have been proposed in [15] to ensure efficient interplay between broadcast, cache management, and disk scheduling [16, 17, 18, 19]. Variance of response time and its minimization has been considered in [11] which also discussed a trade-off in mean and variance of response time. Adaptive and hybrid data delivery in multi channel environment is considered in [21] and [22] considers calculating an optimal cut-off point in deciding the portion which will appear in push based scheduling. The on-demand portion never appears in push broadcast. Several researches [12] have proposed the effective use of caching and pre-fetching as a way to develop efficient broadcast environment. Most papers assume a kind of centralized server with minimum caching only in mobile units. Assumption of a single broadcast channel for push and pull broadcasts imposes serious constraints on the efficiency of data access. The latency time in this case can be as large as a broadcast cycle. Data staging [23] has been proposed as a novel way to cache user specific data to reduce user access latency. The experiments done in this work shows a significant improvement in performance. The topic of data staging has also been investigated in [24, 25, 26].

4.2 The InfoSpace Architecture

We believe that an adaptive and hybrid broadcast based data dissemination system can best address the problems of user access latency and limited bandwidth. We propose a new architecture called "InfoSpace" which uses the concept of *data staging* where data is stored in un-trusted machines, called *surrogates*. Surrogates are connected to the file servers with high speed wired networks and with users with high speed wireless link. The user accesses data either from the broadcast or from the surrogate as directed by the client proxy which resides in mobile units.

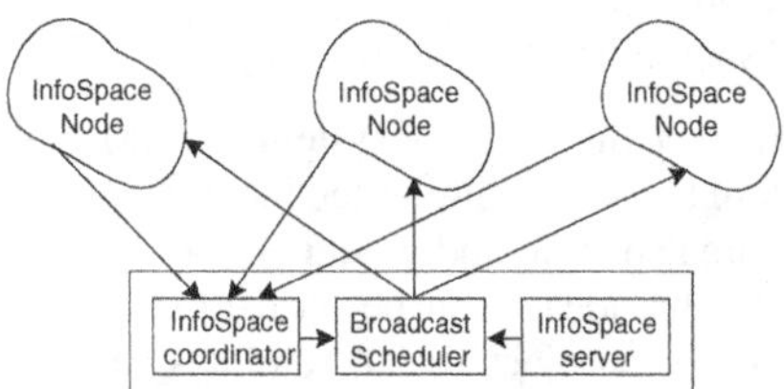

Fig. 3. InfoSpace Architecture

The InfoSpace uses the existing cellular concept for data broadcast. It pushes popular data in the channel and at the same time caches user specific data in file servers (a part of BS) so that they can be accessed individually. The broadcast schedule for pushed data is entirely dynamic and is based on existing popularity level. There is a *popularity threshold*, which identifies which data has to be pushed and which is to be kept for on-demand access. At the same time it also identifies only a certain amount of data to be pushed in the channel. The popularity is calculated at regular intervals based on which the new broadcast schedule is determined. Thus, scheduling is dependent on the user access pattern and as a result at different times during the day, different push broadcast schedule may exist. Figure 1 shows the reference architecture of InfoSpace. The information is composed and stored in the InfoSpace server. The wireless cells are denoted as InfoSpace nodes. We assume that InfoSpace server is connected to all BSs in the respective InfoSpace nodes through high speed networks.

Figure 4 elaborates the architecture of an InfoSpace node and presents the page structure. An InfoSpace node consists of BSs, the mobile units and surrogates. The server contains series of data which are stored in pages along with control information: (a) BT (broadcast type) (b) *PT* (page type), and (c) *T* (time). BT is one bit information with possible values of 0 or 1. Pages which are popular and intended to be pushed into the broadcast channel have their BT bit set to one. The BT bit of the remaining pages has value zero. The scheduler decides which page to push depending on the popularity pattern generated by the InfoSpace coordinator. We show the generation of popularity patterns when we discuss the InfoSpace Coordinator. *PT* can be described as *PT(x,y)*, where *x* bits are used to denote the type of page and *y* bits are used to denote the sequence number of the corresponding type of page. As the size of information generated can always increase or decrease, the value of *y* for a particular *x* varies continuously. But the bit sequence *x*, once assigned to a type of page is kept fixed to avoid inconsistencies at different levels of storage. *T* denotes the time of generation of the page in the InfoSpace server. As the pages are to be cached at different levels, the timestamp is added to the page so that the relevance of the information can be seen at any point of time.

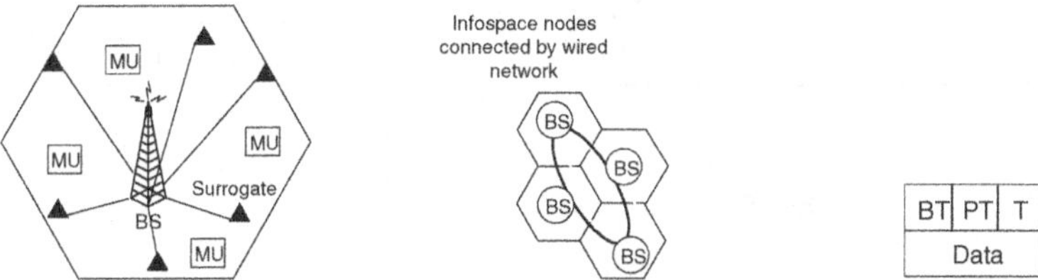

Fig. 4. Data dissemination and page structure

The scheduler develops the broadcast schedule for the pages to be pushed according to the popularity patterns presented to it by the InfoSpace coordinator. The more popular pages get the earlier slots for schedule in the broadcast but each type of pages are kept together to keep the broadcast schedule simple and well structured.

Pages which are intended to be pulled are interleaved with the push schedules to be stored at the file servers. The structure of these pages is exactly the same except that the *BT* bit of the pages are 0. When the BS receives the pages, it only checks the its *BT* bit. If it is 1, then it broadcasts all pages of that type. It doesn't need to check the *BT* bit of every page as all types of a particular page are kept sequentially in the broadcast schedule. All pages are then sent to the file server for caching. When the BS broadcasts the pages, it also prepares a broadcast directory which contains the information of the type and time of the pages to be distributed. This is easy for the BS as it just have to put into the broadcast directory the control information *PT(x,y),* i.e., the type and number of pages, *T*, the last time at which the pages are modified, and *t,* the time of broadcast of the page. It gets the *PT(x,y)* bits and the T bit from the pages which are sent to it by the InfoServer for broadcast. The time at the BS is used to fill the *t* control information in the broadcast directory. The time of each and every BS in different InfoSpace nodes are synchronized for this purpose. This broadcast directory is then interleaved with the pushed pages. We later discuss the organization of the broadcast and the time bounds for getting access to the pages and the broadcast directory.

Figure 5 illustrates file server and page request structures. The pushed pages are kept in one portion and the pulled pages are kept in the other. This can be easily done by checking the *BT* bit of the pages. In one portion, pages containing similar *PT(x)* bits are grouped together. They can be sequentially placed by comparing the y bits of *PT*. Thus, the structure of cache is hierarchical. If the InfoSpace server sends the same page again, then the old page is replaced by the new page from the cache only if the *T* of the pages differs. Otherwise, the page is neglected. If a page's status changes from push to pull or vice versa, then the file server simply changes the *BT* bit of that page. It then shifts the pages to the other category in the file server. If the cache gets filled then the oldest pages can be purged.

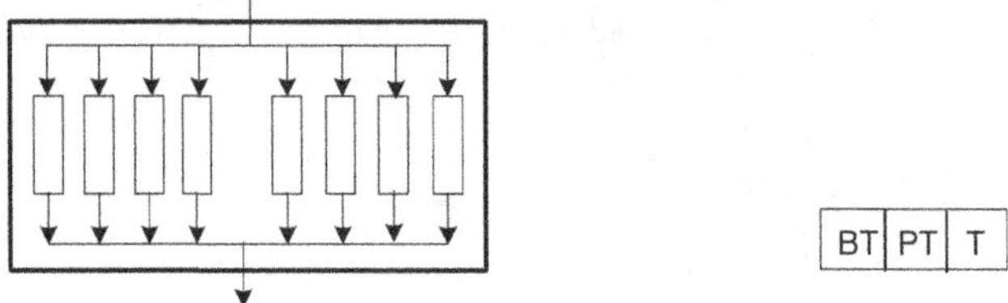

Fig. 5. File server and Page request structures

4.3 Data Staging in InfoSpace

Staging data in a surrogate allows users to extend their limited caching capacity. This is done by borrowing storage space from the surrogate. This process of data staging requires the joint operation of the client proxy of the mobile user, the file server in the BS and the surrogate where data is to be staged. The surrogate is only a single wireless hop away from the mobile unit and connected by wireless technologies such as 802.11. The client proxy continuously monitors the data access operation of the mobile user. It maintains a log file into which it stores the three control information of each page, *BT, PT, and T* for the broadcast pages and the pages which are pulled by the user. In this way it is able to store the information of the user access pattern without using much cache area. At the same time, since it is working internally and doesn't need to log on to the wireless channel continuously, the power consumption of the mobile unit doesn't increase. Based on the information of the log file, the proxy generates a periodic routine which contain the information about what the mobile user is most likely to access at any point of time. The routine contains the control information about the pushed data which is requested and the information about a particular pulled data which has been frequently accessed by the user. The proxy continuously maintains and upgrades this routine.

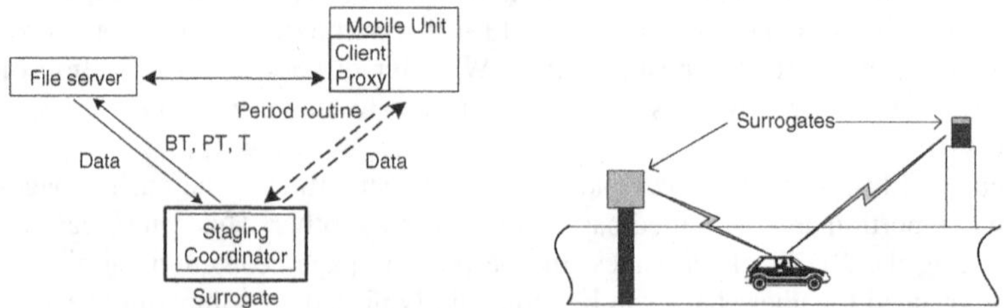

Fig. 6. Data Staging Architecture and Data access from Surrogates

Figure 6 shows the data staging architecture and data access from surrogates. When a mobile user is connected to a nearby surrogate, it registers with the surrogate. A surrogate allows the user to use a certain amount of apace for staging data.

Since the data staged in the machine is public data, we believe that proper handling of data storage in a surrogate can significantly increase the efficiency of data access and thus the overall latency time can be reduced. Figure 6 shows accesses of data from the surrogates by a mobile user.

5 Wireless Web Services

A Web Service (WS) is a programmable application logic accessible using standard internet protocols. It combines the best aspects of component based development and the web and offers functionality that can be easily implemented. Unlike current component technologies which are accessed via proprietary protocols, Web Services are accessed via ubiquitous Web protocols like HTTP using universally-accepted data formats such as XML. In real business terms as Data Warehouse integrated heterogeneous data sources (base databases), Web Services have emerged as a powerful mechanism for integrating disparate IT systems and assets. They work using widely accepted technologies and are governed by commonly adopted standards [29].

5.1 Limitations of Web Services in Wireless and Mobile Environment

The present model of web services has some fundamental limitations which affect their seamless infusion into the wireless and mobile environment. Some of these limitations are related to (a) service discovery, (b) pull based information retrieval, (c) topical Web Services, and (d) limitations of UDDI.

Location based Web Services are an important class of context aware applications. We argue that incorporating location information in a web service can significantly decrease the service discovery time on part of the user. Our approach is to create a framework which is compatible across all platforms. To achieve this, we propose to create a Universal Location domain (ULD). The ULD contains locations which are hierarchically arranged in a structure called the location tree. This idea is motivated by several facts. To provide ubiquitous computing ability, web services should have the compatibility across all types of mobile devices and across all types of platforms. Moreover, Service Providers are not unique across different parts of the world and only the presence of a unique location structure may proliferate the use of location dependent web services.

The location tree is a set of locations arranged in a hierarchical manner. An important property of the locations present in the ULD is *Containment* which helps determining relative position of an object by defining or identifying locations that contains those objects. The subordinate locations are hierarchically related to each other. Thus, Containment property limits the range of availability or operation of a service. We use this important property in location dependent web service discovery.

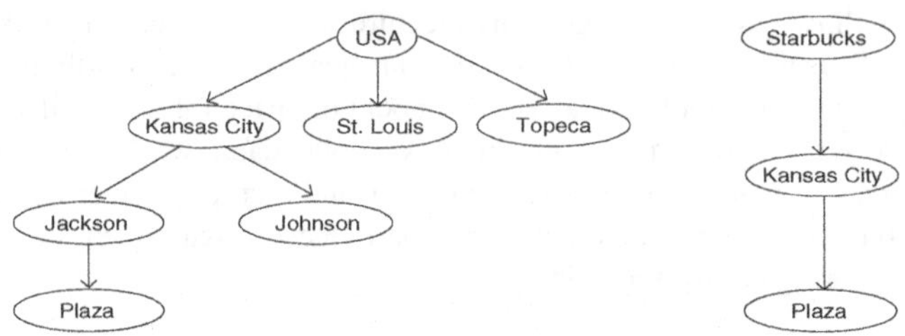

Fig. 7. A part of ULD and Location Structure of the web service

Apart from the ULD, we also define the location of the web service which is provided by the user who intends to access the service. It is the job of the location framework to create a location structure for the service. This location structure is then suitably mapped on the ULD to find the exact location of the web service. We present an example to explain the functionality of the proposed location framework.

A mobile user intends to access the web service of the Star Bucks Coffee Shop and place an order for a home delivery. He initiates the order by placing a query for the availability of his choice of coffee in the Star Bucks Plaza branch of Kansas City. It is the job of the location framework to develop the location structure of the requested web service. The location structure of web service as is illustrated in Fig. 7 is: *Star Bucks → Kansas City → Plaza.* To search and access the required web service, a unique ID for the web service has to be generated. This unique ID is generated by mapping the location structure of the web service with the ULD. The location of the web service in the ULD is: *USA → Kansas City → Jackson → Plaza* (Fig. 7). The Containment property limits the search of the location of the various Star Bucks services which are present only at the subordinate locations of "Plaza ". The number of searched entries for the desired web service is equal to the n where n is the number of subordinate locations near Plaza. Thus, the set of location IDs of the requested web service is: *Star Bucks → USA → Kansas City → Jackson → Plaza →* X_i where i is the number of subordinate locations in "Plaza". It is possible that the Star Bucks coffee shop is not present in all the subordinate locations of the "Plaza". Thus, the number of results will always be greater than or equal to the number of original locations of the web service. The exact number of locations will be found when this calculated IDs will be matched with the entries of the web Service present in the Distributed Service Repository (DSR), a structure which we discuss in our proposed architecture of Web Bazaar in the next section.

5.2 Web Bazaar

The Web Bazaar architecture consists of a Broadcast Server, uplink and downlink Wireless Channels, Distributed Service Repository (DSR) containing Service Marts and the Universal Location Domain. The broadcast server has the central role of service distribution. In this model we propose to broadcast the services instead of the traditional pull based access. We argue that in the future, to make the web services popular among the increasing group of mobile users, efforts should be made not only to publish the services but also to distribute them to the users. This will support both pre-trip planning and on-route information on occasionally found points of interest. Moreover, web service use XML documents the size of which tends to be much larger than traditional text messages. Thus, efforts should be to the minimize number of messages exchanges between a mobile user and the web service provider. Broadcasting web service information may significantly reduce the number of messages required for the process of service discovery. This is our motivation behind the proposition of web service broadcast in Web Bazaar.

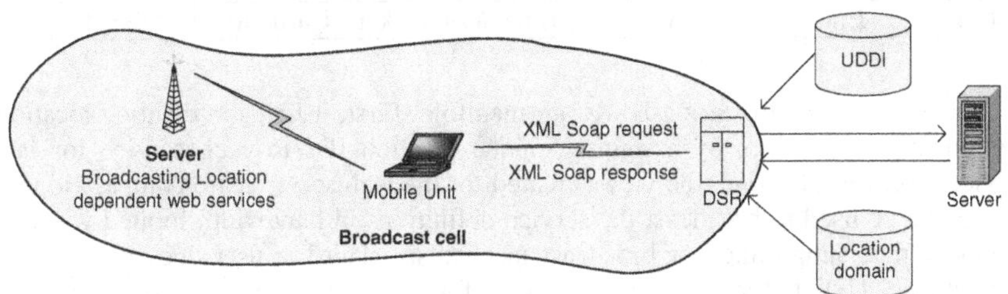

Fig. 8. Web Bazaar: Location dependent Web Service Architecture

Fig. 8 shows the proposed architecture of Web Bazaar. The standards and specifications demand that the structure and role of UDDI should not be changed. Thus, to incorporate location information, we propose the concept of Distributed Service Repositories (DSR). A DSR contains web services entries which are local to the region. Each broadcast region contains a DSR. The DSR incorporates the location information in the web services.

For a particular broadcast region, the web services which cater to the region are extracted from the UDDI. The location ID for the web service is generated by using the Universal Location Domain. For any web service located at particular location, its location structure is generated and mapped with the Universal location domain to get the unique location ID. This means for a single web service, there will be many entries depending on the number of locations at which the service is located. This may increase the size of the DSR, but considering the fact that the DSR contains entries which are local to the broadcast region, the number of entries will be limited. A different view of the web service is then generated. This view contains fewer parameters which makes it suitable for broadcast in bandwidth limited channels. Views are compact documents and contain information about the location dependent web services. The views are broadcasted and are used to initiate the service from a mobile or wireless device.

Within a DSR, the services may be organized by keeping similar web services under one group. For example, the DSR in Kansas City will group the web services related to hotels under one group, grocery stores under another group, and so on. Each specific group is called a Service Mart. This makes the service discovery much easier. Moreover, It helps in creating simple but informative views. For example, if a user in Lenexa intends to use the web service of grocery store in downtown area in Kansas City, he just have to give the location name and type of Service Mart (here, for example, Food Mart) in his request to discover a service. In contrast to the earlier method of searching the UDDI registries and then deciding for a service, our way of service discovery through broadcast of views seems much faster. As evident from table, these views are much simpler than the UDDI entries.

Table 1. Views of two Types of Web services

Mart	Type	Input, Output Parameters	Location
Star Bucks	Food	Coffee, Order Destination, Card No.	Plaza
Theatre	Entertain	Movie, Showtime, # of Tickets, Card No.	Down Town

The advantages of creating DSRs are manifold. First, it helps in creating location dependent web services by assigning unique location IDs to each service for fast service discovery. Second, the views created for the web services are compact so that they could be used to broadcast the service definitions in bandwidth limited wireless channels, thus supporting our broadcast mechanism. Third, a user does not have to contact the UDDI for service discovery for location dependent services. By mentioning the location, the request can bypass the UDDI and contact the corresponding DSR directly. This prevents exhaustive search, allows fewer data download which is suitable for bandwidth limited wireless environment and allows fast access to the service.

There is an important issue which needs to be discussed at this point. There is a large number of web service entries present in the UDDI. Broadcasting all of them through bandwidth limited wireless channels may sound unrealistic at present. At the same time we argue that broadcasting location dependent Web Services present in DSRs which are commonly used in day to day life will certainly make them more popular among the mobile users. Prominent among these services are the Topical Web Services in which the information accessed frequently change when the user is on the move. Important examples are flight bookings, last minute theatre ticket deals, traffic information etc.

5.3 Working of Web Bazaar

The broadcast mechanism consists of a broadcast channel from the broadcast server to the users. It also consists of an uplink channel from the users to the DSR and a downlink channel from the DSR to the user (Fig.3). Each broadcast is preceded by an index which depicts the sequential order of web service broadcast. The index is also interleaved between the broadcast views so that the user does not have to wait for the next broadcast schedule. The structure of the index is helpful to the users in personalization of Web Services which we discuss later. The broadcast includes the compact views which contain WSDL definitions. These definitions are WSDL components. The WSDL components consist of interfaces, bindings, and services.

The service download, request and response of services are managed by a Java based coordinator present in the mobile device. This Java based coordinator is installed in the machine when the user avails the Web Service from the service provider. The Coordinator has the task of listening to the channel, downloading the required service, initiating the request, and receiving the response. The coordinator also has an important task of personalization of the WS.

Personalization of WS means to access and use services only according to a pre-planned schedule fixed by the user. The coordinator downloads the index containing the description of the services to be broadcast. The user checks the index according to his needs and so does not have to bother about the downloading of the services. Based on the service checked and the predetermined schedule from the index, the coordinator estimates the time required for service download. It allows the mobile device to go into doze mode to save power. It becomes active only when the service is about to be broadcasted. The service components are downloaded and the user is notified to start the service request. Thus, only those services needed by the user are downloaded from the channel. This describes the ability of the user to block certain services data and personalize his requirements.

Example

Star Bucks Food	Coffee Type 1, Order, Destination, Card No.	Plaza

↓

Star Bucks Food	Coffee Type 2, Order, Destination, Card No.	Walnut

To initiate a service request, the coordinator creates a SOAP message. The XML document in the message is created according to the downloaded service description which contains the unique location ID (for a location dependent service) and user's ID. Even if the view of WS of the desired location is not present, their structures and properties of XML documents allow changing the view information to access a particular location dependent service.

If the user wants to order coffee of type 2 which is not available in the Plaza branch, he doesn't have to wait for the view of Walnut to be broadcasted. He can simply change the XML information of the views by replacing the *Coffee Type* Information and the *Location* information. It is the job of the ULD to map the location information provided by the user to generate appropriate location IDs which can be used to search the appropriate location dependent service from the DSR.

After XML request is constructed, the coordinator sends this message to the SOAP server present in the DSR through the uplink wireless channel. Since this message is compact, it is the responsibility of the DSR to make it compatible for the Web Server. When all the definitions are added, The SOAP server directs the request to the service provider's web service. If the user requests a service which belongs to another location, the request is transferred to the DSR containing the service description. This identification of location is done by the DSR local to the user.

The web service, after receiving the requests, processes it and creates a response which is also a SOAP message. It is sent to the DSR local to the user. The DSR operates on the response and makes it compact thus making it easier for the DSR to push the response through the downlink channel to the user. The compaction is necessary as the SOAP messages which are several times larger than text messages may overburden the bandwidth limited wireless channels. When the response reaches the user, he is notified about its arrival.

The proposed framework thus provides location dependent web service to the mobile user. Broadcasting web service information signifiicantly reduces the number of messages in the wireless environment. The broadcast XML views are compact and allows efficient service request/response style of messaging. The ULD is used to create appropriate location information for the service entries in DSR and also for service request. The simplified hierarchical structure of the ULD allows smooth addition/deletion of location information when needed.

5.4 Security of Wireless Applications

Wireless systems face greater security risk than wired systems. WWS exposes companies to a massive range of new threats and vulnerabilities. The overall security of a wireless application is only as strong as its weakest link, and in M-commerce, the weakest link is the mobile device. Existing wireless security controls are inadequate to deliver the levels of security that the next wave of WWS will demand. Fig. 9 illustrates the security threats faced by the Wireless Services. We describe the security needs of WWS and then present an idea of our scheme to protect authorized users from serendipitous threats and malicious attacks.

Since the mobile device has a weak radio frequency interface, data transmitted over wireless networks, such as passwords, personal information, security information, etc., can be captured using digital RF scanning equipment. Most wireless protocols do not come with built-in encryption mechanisms. Additional security measures such as secure connections and cryptography are definitely needed, especially for those applications transmitting sensitive data. Insecurity increases over the internet due to additon of large user base and various service providers. As new Application to Application (A2A) integration increases, they create serendipitous threats and new vulnerabilities to the existing Web Service Systems.

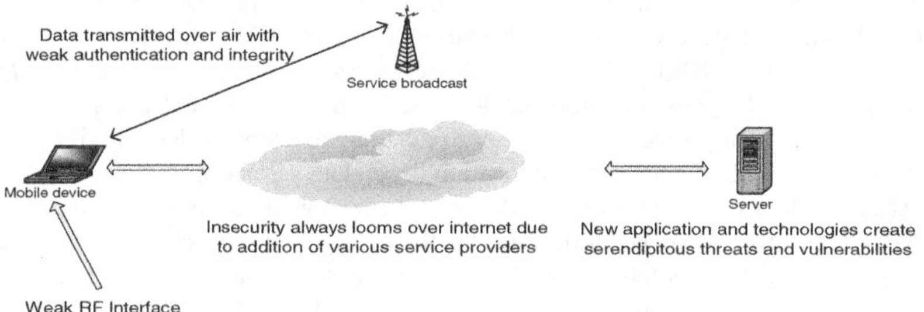

Fig. 9. Insecurity in Wireless Services

5.5 Location Signature Based Security and Authentication

One of the biggest obstacles to the widespread adoption of WWS is winning the trust of mobile users. A single security breach provides a very high profile way of undermining a wireless service. We propose the use of *Symbolic Location Coordinates* identifying the real time location information of a user into existing security mechanisms to improve the efficacy of authentication, authorization, and access controls. We refer to this real time location information which will be unique for a user as *Location Signature (LS)*.

Effective wireless application security depends on the ability to authenticate users and grant access accordingly. Existing authentication and authorization mechanisms fundamentally depend on information known to a user (password or keys), possession of an authentication device (security token or crypto card) or information derived from unique personal characteristics (biometrics). None of this is totally foolproof. Symbolic Location information (building, street, area ID, BS id, etc.) of a mobile device or user adds a fourth and new dimension to wireless application security. It gives extra assurance to users of the wireless applications who want to perform sensitive operations such as financial transactions, access valuable information, or remotely control critical systems. It can supplement or complement existing security mechanisms. The LS can still be used as a security mechanism when other systems have been compromised as it is and will always be unique for a user at any point of time. For highly sensitive wireless applications, a real time LS can be generated so that authorities can trace any malicious activity back to the location of the intruder. Without the incorporation of LS, it will be difficult to trace the origin of malicious activity.

It is almost impossible to replicate a LS because a user cannot exist at two places at the same time and use it elsewhere to gain unauthorized entry. Even if the information is intercepted during communications, an intruder cannot replicate that data from some other place. A LS is continuously generated from location information on real-time basis and is unique to a particular place and time. Such information becomes invalid after a short time interval, which means that the intercepted LS cannot be used to mask unauthorized access especially when it is bound to the wireless protocol messages as checksums or digital signatures. Even if the perpetrator uses other means to masquerade as a legitimate user, the complete set of LS can be used to log the access trail [20].

We propose to develop and incorporate two-way authentication between the wireless client (mobile device) and the Web Server. The Web Server can give access to a wireless client based on the security mechanisms along with the LS. The reverse process - the client receiving Server's LS - ensures a higher lever of security as it will always be a unique mapping between the continuously moving user and the Web Server, especially if this "handshaking" is done periodically. This requires an additional message between the wireless device and the Web Server which is not likely to affect the performance. Location information can provide evidence to absolve innocent users. If illegal activity is conducted from a particular user account by someone who has gained unauthorized access to that account, then the legitimate owners of the account might be able to prove that they could not have been present in the location where the activity originated. The following example gives an idea of the working of WWS based on LS:

Suppose Shyam is on his way back home to Overland Park and wants to buy coffee from Star Bucks. He is tired and in no mood to search the nearest Star Bucks on his way back. He uses his PDA and logs on to the Wireless Broadcast of WWS. He downloads the views of Star Bucks and places the order. He types the necessary information about the type of coffee he wants, the address of order delivery and initiates a query. The mobile device coordinator of Shyam's PDA develops the location information for delivery based on the address. It also develops the location signature and attaches with the query. The LS consists of the mapping among various real time variables like the time, building, street, area ID, mobile device ID, etc. After the LS is developed, it is attached with the query and also stored in a log file corresponding to the time when the signature was generated. The log file is not accessible to the user. This LS is a real time variable (as the values of most of the variables changes every moment) but will always be unique for a particular time. It is also cumulative, i.e., the new signature is a set of old signatures plus the new signature recently added. The Web Server receives the views through the wireless channel and based on the location finds out the service for Star Bucks which is nearest to Shyam's preferred location of Overland Park. It sends back the response and asks Ben to place the order. Shyam enters the necessary information like his credit card number and the address for delivery and completes the order. When the server receives the information, it checks the log file and matches the existing LS set with the newly received LS set. If the user is original and not a malicious one, both the LS set will exactly match except the last entry which is newly generated. The two sets will never match for a malicious user. The Web Server completes the transaction and issues a response. This response will be available to the user only when the received location signature set matches exactly with the signature set present in the mobile device cache.

Thus, location-based authentication can be done transparently to the user and be performed continuously. This means that unlike most other types of authentication information, LS can be used as a common authenticator for all systems the user accesses. This feature makes location-based authentication a good technique to use in conjunction with single sign-on.

6 Conclusions and Future Work

In this paper we discussed issues related to data flow in data space. We developed a Mobile Database System (MDS) to manage M-commerce activities. We proposed a data dissemination system called InfoSpace to provide users their required data through wireless channels. It considers popular data to be broadcasted and less popular data be pulled from the file server. The system works on a cellular based network in which the cells are denoted by InfoSpace nodes. It also contains a file server which caches both the pushed and the pulled data. This file server is accessed by the surrogates through high speed wired network to deliver data to the users when requested. The surrogates are storage machines that are connected to the mobile user through high speed wireless network.

We presented a web service system called Web Bazaar in which a Universal Location Domain is used to develop unique location ID for a service. The unique location ID is subsequently used for fast and efficient service discovery. The wireless broadcast consists of the views of web services. These views are compact XML documents and they can be efficiently used to decrease the message exchange between the mobile user and the web server which is essential in a bandwidth limited wireless environment. Security of wireless applications is a huge concern as the mobile unit has weak radio frequency interface. Moreover, increase of application to application (A2A) integration in web services introduces unexpected security lapses. We developed a user authentication system called location signature. In our future work, we intend to develop the location structure further by introducing a location domain naming system similar to the existing Domain Name Services (DNS) for translating domain names of IP addresses. This will enable simpler and more realistic location identification for location dependent services. The location domain naming system may also be used for the location signature scheme.

References

1. Margaret H. Dunham, and Vijay Kumar, "Location Dependent Data and its Management in Mobile Databases," *Proc. of the Ninth Workshop of Database and Expert Systems Applications DEXA'98*, Vienna, Austria, August 26-28, 1998.
2. Vijay Kumar, Nitin Prabhu, Maggie Dunham, and Yasemin A. Seydim, "TCOT - A Timeout-based Mobile Transaction Commitment Protocol", *Special issue of IEEE Transaction on Computers*, Vol. 51, No. 10, Oct. 2002.
3. Dharma P. Agarwal, Qing-An Zeng: Introduction to Wireless and Mobile Systems, Thomson Brooks/Cole.
4. Margaret Dunham and Vijay Kumar, "Impact of Mobility on Transaction Management," *Int. Workshop on Data Engineering for Wireless and Mobile Access (MobiDE99)*, Seattle, Washington, August 20, 1999.
5. P. A. Bernstein, V. Hadzilacos, and N. Goodman, "Concurrency Control and Recovery in Database Systems". Addision Wesley, 1987.
6. Vijay Kumar and Sang H. Son, "Database Recovery", Kluwer International,
7. Vijay Kumar and Meichun Hsu, "Recovery in Mechanisms in Database Systems", Prentice Hall, 1998.
8. http:// www.direcpc.com, 2001.
9. http://www.marimba.com, 2001.
10. S. Acharya, R Alonso, M Franklin and S. Zdonik. "Broadcasts disks- data management for asymmetric communication environment", *ACM SIGMOD*, May 1995.
11. S. Acharya, M Franklin and S. Zdonik. "Dissemination based data delivery using broadcast disks", *IEEE Personal Communication* (Dec. 95).
12. S. Acharya, M Franklin, and S. Zdonik. "Prefetching from a broadcast disk", *12th International Conference on Data Engineering*, February, 1996.
13. S. Acharya, R Alonso, M Franklin and S. Zdonik. "Balancing push and pull for data broadcast", *ACM SIGMOD*, May 1997.
14. A.Datta. A Celic, J.G.Dim, D.E.Vandermeer and V. Kumar, "Adaptive broadcast protocols to support efficient and energy conserving retrieval from databases in mobile computing environments", *IEEE Data Engineering Conference*, April, 1997.
15. Peter Triantafillou, R. Harpantidou and M. Paterakis. "High Performance Data Broadcasting Systems", *Mobile Networks and Applications*, 7, 2002.
16. S. Su, L. Tassiulas, "Broadcast scheduling for information distribution", *INFOCOM*, 1997.
17. T. Imielinski, S Viswanathan and B.R. Badrinath. "Data on the air- organisation and access", *IEEE Transaction of Data and Knowledge Engineering,* July, 1996.
18. M. Franklin and S. Zdonik, "Data in your Face: Push Technology in Perspective", *ACM SIGMOD*, WA, June 1998.
19. Sohail Hameed and Nitin H. Vaidya. "Efficient algorithms for scheduling data broadcast", *Wireless Networks*, May 1999.
20. Shu Jiang,Nitin H,Vaidya, "Reponse time in Data Broadcast Systems: Mean, Variance and Tradeoff", *Mobile Networks and Applications*, 7, 2002.

21. Chih-Lin Hu and Ming-Syan Chen "Adaptive balance hybrid data delivery for multi channel data broadcast", *ICC*, 2002.
22. Yufei Guo, Sajal K.Das, Critina M. Pinotti. "A new Hybrid Broadcast Scheduling Algorithm for Asymmetric Communication Systems: Push and Pull Data Based on Optimal Cut-Off Point", *MSWIM* 2001, Rome, Italy.
23. Jason Flinn, Shafeeq Sinnamohideen, M. Satyanarayan. "Data Staging on Untrusted Surrogates", *Intel Research*, Pittsburg, Unpublished Report.
24. Garlan D., Siewwiork, D., Smailagic, A., Steenkiste, P. "Project Aura: Towards Distraction free Pervasive Computing", *IEEE Pervasive Computing* 1, 2 (April-June 2002).
25. Yunqing Chen, Jian Yu, and Cong Yu. "Data Staging on NFS", *www.eecs.umich.edu/ ~congy/* December 11, 2002.
26. Demet Aksoy, Michael J. Franklin, Stanley B. Zdonik. "Data Staging for On-Demand Broadcast". *VLDB* 2001.
27. UDDI, www.uddi.org.
28. Yasemin Seydim, Margaret Dunham, and Vijay Kumar, "Location Dependent Query Processing," *2nd ACM Int. Workshop on Data Engineering for Wireless and Mobile Access* (MOBIDE01), Santa Barbara, May 20, 2001.
29. T. Pilioura, A. Tsalgatidou, S. Hadjiefthymiades, "Scenarios of using Web Services in M-Commerce", *ACM SIGecom Exchanges*, Vol. 3, No. 4, January 2003.
30. Eliot Moss. "Nested Transactions: An approach to reliable distributed computing", The MIT Press, 1985.
31. H. Garcia Molina and Ken Salem. "Sagas", ACM SIGMOD, 1987.

Enabling Technologies for Harnessing Information Explosion[1]

Sharma Chakravarthy[2]

Computer Science and Engineering Department
and Information Technology Laboratory,
The University of Texas at Arlington,
Arlington, TX 76019-0015
sharma@cse.uta.edu
http://itlab.uta.edu/sharma

Abstract. The amount of information accessible on the Internet and other repositories is increasing at an alarming rate. Presence and availability of information is quite different from being able to access the right information at the right time. Easy and flexible access to such large repositories of data also poses its own set of problems. Some of the problems faces today are: the ability to access relevant data without information overload, monitor only needed data and receive it in a timely manner, ability to filter data to reduce the amount of information to be analyzed manually, and the ability to classify data into groups that are beneficial.

The focus of this presentation will be on how information explosion, although beneficial in a larger context, baffles the user in terms of the time, energy, and resources spent in searching, browsing, retrieving, monitoring, filtering, and classifying them. We discuss the problem, issues, and various technologies that are needed for harnessing information in a way that provides relevant and useful information in a timely manner (just-in-time) and reduce user involvement as much as possible. One such technology is the "push" technology in contrast to the "pull" technology. WebVigiL is a project at UTA/IT Lab that has explored Internet change monitoring for the above purpose.

In addition to the applicability of the push technology and its uses, we will discuss several other technologies that allow us to harness appropriate information from potentially large repositories that are continuously changing/evolving. Some of the technologies that will be discussed in this talk are: mining, filtering, classification, and monitoring.

In this talk, I will relate the results of some of the projects that are underway at the Information Technology Laboratory at UTA to address the above problem.

---

[1] This work was supported, in part, by the Office of Naval Research, the SPAWAR System Center-San Diego & by the Rome Laboratory (grant F30602-02-2-0134), and by NSF (grant IIS-0123730).

[2] Currently with IBM India Research Laboratory, New Delhi, on Faculty Development Leave from UTA.

R.K. Ghosh and H. Mohanthy (Eds.): ICDCIT 2004, LNCS 3347, p. 21, 2004.

Fair Leader Election by Randomized Voting

Siddhartha Brahma[1], Sandeep Macharla[1],
Sudebkumar Prasant Pal[1], and Sudhir Kumar Singh[2]

[1] Dept. of Computer Science and Enginnering, IIT, Kharagpur, 721302, India
spp@cse.iitkgp.ernet.in
[2] Dept. of Mathematics, IIT, Kharagpur

Abstract. *Leader election* is a fundamental problem in distributed computing where a unique node from a set of nodes declares itself as the leader (a distinguished state). We propose a notion of *fairness* in the leader election problem; a leader election algorithm is said to be *fair* if each node has the same probability of getting elected as leader. We show that existing deterministic algorithms based on comparisons of identifiers fail to achieve fairness. We demonstrate how fairness can be achieved through randomization and propose new leader election algorithms based on randomized voting. We separate the task of fair leader election on unidirectional rings into two subtasks: *attrition* and *solitude detection* following [9]. We show that tight interleaving of these two procedures as in [7], results in fair leader election on asynchronous, anonymous, unidirectional rings using expected $O(n \log n)$ bits of communication, in expected $O(\log n)$ rounds. (Here n is the number of nodes in the ring.) This matches the performance of the optimal algorithm of Abrahamson *et al.* [1]. Similar algorithms are presented for electing a fair leader in other models.

1 Introduction

Leader election is a fundamental problem in distributed computing. Its solution forms a building block for many involved distributed computations. The problem is to designate by consensus, a unique node from the collection of nodes that forms a distributed system [11, 3]. All nodes in the distributed system should agree upon one amongst them as the leader. So, leader election causes a unique node from amongst a collection of nodes, to enter a distinguished final state [7].

Usually the ring topology is considered to be a standard for the design and analysis of leader election algorithms; the symmetry of the ring topology makes the task of leader election non-trivial. A unidirectional ring is a sequence $P_0, P_1, \cdots, P_{n-1}$ of n nodes or processors, where each node sends messages to P_{i+1} and receives messages from P_{i-1}, the subscripts being modulo n. There are several variants of this basic model. Communication between nodes may be synchronous or asynchronous; nodes may have unique identifiers (*asymmetric rings*) or may be indistinguishable (*symmetric or anonymous rings*); nodes may or may not know the size of the ring at the start of the computation. The complexity of

R.K. Ghosh and H. Mohanty (Eds.): ICDCIT 2004, LNCS 3347, pp. 22–31, 2004.

a leader election algorithm is usually measured in terms of the number of messages communicated between the nodes, the total number of bits communicated and the time taken to elect the leader.

There are several deterministic algorithms for leader election in unidirectional rings. Several deterministic algorithms have been developed for finding a leader in an asynchronous, unidirectional, asymmetric ring networks, (see Lelann [11], Peterson [12], Chang and Roberts [3], Hirschberger and Sinclair [8], Burns [10], Dolev [4], Franklin [5]). The problem is simpler for the asymmetric case as compared to that in the symmetric case; the node with the maximum identifier may serve as the leader in the assymetric case.

Angluin [2], established that deterministic algorithms fail to elect a leader if nodes do not have unique identifiers, even if the number of nodes n is known a priori to all the nodes. This limitation was overcome by the use of randomization by Itai and Rodeh [9]. They were also the first to point out the correspondence between leader election and the two tasks - *attrition* and *solitude detection*. Abrahamson *et al.* [1], gave another randomized algorithm for the same problem with the same message complexity as that of Itai and Rodeh, but with an improved bit complexity by tightly interleaving the solutions of the attrition and solitude detection tasks.

Deterministic algorithms in [3, 5, 8] elect the node with the maximum identifier as the leader. This is somewhat *unfair*, as all the nodes do not get a fair chance to become the leader. We define a notion of *fairness*, where all nodes have the same probability of becoming the leader. With this notion of fairness, we develop *fair* randomized algorithms for asynchronous ring networks. Our algorithms have an implicit round structure where nodes are elected to progress to the next round by *randomized voting*. Leader election is achieved by the tight interleaving of solitude detection and attrition procedures.

The motivation for such a notion of fairness is natural and useful in real applications in distributed computing. Managing multiple resources in dynamic environments requires election of resource managing nodes. Fairness as we propose in this paper will help in randomly distributing leadership responsibilities for various resource managing tasks in a uniform manner, thereby balancing loads across the distributed system. Resources may be software services or shared data, possibly managed by semaphores; in a dynamic environment, such resources may be created and destroyed continuously.

The remaining paper is organized as follows. In section 2 we define the notion of fairness in leader election and present our algorithm for fair leader election in asynchronous, anonymous, unidirectional ring networks. In section 3 we extend the above algorithm for variants of the above network model. Finally in section 4, we conclude with a few remarks about future research directions.

2 Fair Leader Election on Rings

We define a leader election protocol to be *fair* if all the nodes have equal probability of getting elected as the leader. If there are c contenders initially, each of them must have probability $1/c$ of being elected leader. Our eader election algorithm proceeds in stages. Suppose the ring is in a certain configuration CF_0 at a particular stage. Let $CF_1, CF_2, \cdots, CF_T$ be the configurations that can result from CF_0 in the next stage. Suppose the probability of occurence of each CF_i , $1 \leq i \leq T$ is $1/T$. If this holds for any intermediate configuration CF_0 of the leader election algorithm, then it is easy to see that the overall algorithm will be fair. In what follows, we achieve fairness by exploiting this fact. Any leader election algorithm should finally accomplish the following two tasks (*i*) eliminate all but one node from contending, and (*ii*) confirm that only one node is contending. As mentioned above, there is a strong relationship between leader election and the two tasks of attrition and solitude detection. The two procedures are defined as follows [7]:

Attrition Procedure: A procedure solves the *attrition problem* if the following holds: when initiated by a set of nodes, it never renders all candidates noncontenders, and it takes all but exactly one of these candidates into a permanent state of noncontention with probabbility 1.

Solitude Detection Procedure: A procedure solves the *solitude detection* problem if teh following hold: when initiated by a set of nodes, it terminates with probability 1, giving a 'yes' answer upon termination when there is exactly one initiator and a 'no' answer when there are more than one initiators. In the latter case, all initiators are set to a 'no' state.

Typically, the attrition procedure does not terminate. Solitude detection is required to break this infinite loop. We approach the problem of attrition using a process of *voting*. As we wish to ensure fairness, the idea of a node randomly casting a vote in favour of another node is natural. So, each node votes randomly for another node; nodes voted for in one round, contend in the next round. This *randomized voting* protocol ensures fairness in the election process. Each node has an infinite FIFO buffer where incoming messages are stored and processed one by one. In the next three subsections, we explain the attrition procedure, the solitude detection procedure and the overall leader election algorithm.

2.1 The Attrition Procedure

Our attrition procedure is based on the idea of one node sending its vote to another node based on a random number generated by itself. The attrition procedure has an implicit round structure. The contender nodes are called *active* and the rest are called *passive*. Let the number of nodes in the ring be n and let the number of active nodes in the beginning be c ($c \leq n$). In each round, an active node generates a random number r and sends its vote to a node which is r hops away. Clearly, r is the number of active nodes between the sender and the receiver, including the receiver. The intermediate passive nodes simply relay votes. The nodes that receive a non-empty set of votes in the current round, survive to become contenders in the next round. Note that the part of the leader elction algorithm that dictates which node will ultimately become the leader is the attrition procedure. Since, voting is based on random numbers and passive nodes only relay votes, all the active nodes have an equal chance of going to the next round. So, all the configurations that are possible in the next round are equally likely in a particular round of the attrition procedure, thereby ensuring fairness in the attrition procedure. This also ensures fairness in leader election. By setting the range of values that r can take, the attrition procedure can be varied. We consider the following two cases :

(i) **Procedure I**
r lies in the interval $[0, A)$, where A is the number of active nodes in the beginning of a particular round.
(i) **Procedure II**
r lies in the interval $[0, K)$, where K is a positive integer constant.

The implicit round structure in the attrition procedure is enforced as follows. Since the network is asynchronous, there must be a way for the nodes to detect the end of a round. Let $\beta_0, \beta_1, \cdots \beta_{n-1}$ be the n nodes in the ring. Let $\alpha_0, \alpha_1, \cdots \alpha_{t-1}$ be the t contenders ($t \geq 2$) in an arbitrary intermediate round j. Every node α_i has a set of potential voters. α_i can detect the end of a round if it has the knowledge that all its potential voters have already, either voted for it or for somebody else. Every node α_i maintains two variables z_{i_1} and z_{i_2} which are initialized to zero in the beginning of each round. z_{i_1} keeps track of the number of votes obtained in a particular round and z_{i_2} maintains the number potential voters for α_i that have already voted in that particular round. Every active node generates a random number and sends a message $< x, y >$ to its neighbor, where x is the random number generated and $y = A$ or $y = K$ for **Procedure I** and **II** respectively. An active node checks whether $x = 0$. If x is zero, then it means the vote has gone to that node. Then, if $y > 1$ the message $< 0, y-1 >$ is forwarded and z_{i_1} and z_{i_2} are incremented, otherwise the message is no longer forwarded. If x is non-zero, then z_{i_2} is incremented and the message $< x - 1, y - 1 >$ is forwarded. It is easy to see that a node can be sure that a round has ended when z_{i_2} is A or K, for **Procedure I** and **II** respectively. Thus, in each round a contender gives its vote and waits until z_{i_2} becomes A or K, whence it checks the value of z_{i_1}. If it is nonzero it remains active in the next round otherwise it becomes passive. If we assume that there is no loss of messages in the network, then the above attrition procedure works correctly in the sense that a node that should have been active in a particular round is surely active and a node that should have become passive in a particular round is never active, as shown in the following lemma.

Lemma 1. *If there is no loss of messages in the ring, every round in the above attrition procedure is completed correctly.*

Proof. Let us assume that the attrition procedure has worked for p rounds correctly, where $p \geq 0$. Let us consider the FIFO buffer corresponding to the active node α_{i+1} for some i. Any message in this buffer comes from the previous active node α_i. Since α_i has completed round p successfully, it will send all the messages of round $p+1$ to α_{i+1} before going into the next round. This implies that in the buffer of α_{i+1} there will be no messages of any other round in between the messages of round p. Since, the node we are considering is arbitrary, this is true for all nodes. It is easy to see that the attrition procedure may not work correctly only when the messages from two rounds overlap in the buffer. Since this does not happen in round $p+1$, it will also be completed correctly. By induction on the number of rounds, all the rounds are completed correctly and the lemma is proved. □

Procedure I

In this case, in the beginning of each round every node is required to know the number of active contenders. The task of discovering the number of active nodes and informing all the active nodes about the number is left to the solitude detection procedure which is interleaved with the attrition procedure in the leader election algorithm and is explained later.

The correctness of the attrition procedure in the sense that all the rounds are completed correctly has been proved in **Lemma** 1. Also, since the votes are sent only to active nodes, in each round there will be at least one node which receives a vote, and hence will remain a contender. Therefore, at all intermediate stages there is at least one contender. Also, the probability that a node is eliminated in round j is $\eta_1 = \left(1 - \frac{1}{t}\right)^t$. Since $1/e > \eta_1 \geq 1/4$ for $t \geq 2$, in each round there at least a non-zero constant probability of a contender getting eliminated and hence the number of contenders decreases to 1 with probability 1.

The attrition procedure goes into an infinite loop when only one contender remains. This loop can broken by a suitable solitude verification algorithm. The complexity analysis of the attrition procedure therefore excludes the last solitude detection round. Consider an arbitrary round numbered j. Let X_j be a random variable denoting the number of contenders in round j. So, $X_1 = c$. Let Y_i, $0 \leq i < t$, be a random variable defined as $Y_i = 1$ if α_i is a contender in round $j+1$ and, 0 otherwise. Then, it is easy to see that $E(Y_i) = 1 - \eta_1$, where $t \geq 2$. So, if $t \geq 2$, $E(X_{j+1}|X_j = t) = E\left(\sum_{i=0}^{t-1} Y_i\right) = \sum_{i=0}^{t-1} E(Y_i) = (1-\eta_1)t$. Therefore, $E(X_{j+1}) = \sum_{t\geq 1} E(X_{j+1}|X_j = t)Pr(X_j = m)$. Since $E(X_{j+1}|X_j = 1) = 1$, we have $E(X_{j+1}) = \sum_{t\geq 2} E(X_{j+1}|X_j = t)Pr(X_j = t) + Pr(X_j = 1) = (1-\eta_1)E(X_j) + \eta_1 Pr(X_j = 1) \leq \frac{3}{4}E(X_j) + \eta_1 Pr(X_j = 1)$ So, after an expected $\log_{4/3}(c)$ rounds of the attrition procedure, the number of contenders will be negligible (constant), and hence will contribute negligibly to the overall complexity. So, in an expected $O(\log n)$ rounds, the number of contenders converges to 1. The message complexity is derived as follows. Let M_j be a random variable representing the number of messages transferred in round j. Let N_i , $(0 \leq i \leq t-1)$, be a random variable denoting the number of messages transferred for the vote of α_i in round j. Let the number of passive nodes between α_i and $\alpha_{i+1(\text{mod } t)}$ be $n_i - 1$. Then, $E(N_i) = \frac{1}{t}\sum_{l=0}^{t-2}\sum_{m=0}^{l} n_{i+l(\text{mod } t)} + n - n_{i+t-1(\text{mod } t)}$. Therefore, $E(M_j|X_j = t) = \sum_{i=0}^{t-1} E(N_i) = \frac{t-1}{2}\sum_{i=0}^{t-1} n_i + \sum_{i=0}^{t-1} n - n_{i+t-1(\text{mod } t)} = \frac{3n(t-1)}{2}$. Therefore, $E(M_j) = \sum_{t\geq 2} E(M_j|X_j = t)Pr(X_j = t) < \frac{3n}{2}\sum_{t\geq 1} t \cdot Pr(X_j = t) = \frac{3n}{2}E(X_j)$ Let M be the random variable denoting the total number of messages required in the attrition procedure. Then, $E(M) = \sum_{j\geq 1} E(M_j) < \frac{3n}{2}\sum_{j\geq 1} E(X_j) \leq$

$\frac{3n}{2}\left(\sum_{j\geq 1} E(X_1)\cdot\left(\frac{3}{4}\right)^j + d\right) \leq \frac{3n}{2}(4c+d)$ where, using the fact that $Pr(X_j = 1) \leq 1$ for all j and $\eta_1 < 1/e$, $d \leq \eta_1 \sum_{j\geq 0}\left(\frac{3}{4}\right)^j < \frac{4}{e}$. Since, each vote can be implemented using $O(\log c)$ bits, this attrition procedure converges in expected $O(\log c)$ rounds using an expected $O(nc\log c)$ bits. The structure of the procedure ensures that it leads to fair leader election. Although the expected number of rounds required is only $O(\log c)$, the expected bit complexity is $O(nc\log c)$, which is far from optimal. Next, we show that the attrition procedure in **Procedure II** has an optimal bit complexity.

Procedure II
There is no need here for the active nodes to know the total number of active nodes in the ring. Since the votes are sent only to active nodes, there will be at least one node which receives a vote in each round, thereby ensuring a contender. Also, the probability that a node is eliminated from contention in a particular round is $\eta_2 = \left(1 - \frac{q+1}{K}\right)^r \left(1 - \frac{q}{K}\right)^{t-r}$ where $K = t\cdot q + r$. Since, there is at least a non-zero constant probability of a contender getting eliminated in each round, the number of contenders decreases to 1 with probability 1.

Let X_j and Y_i be a random variable defined as in Case(i). It is easy to see that $E(Y_i) = 1 - \eta_2$ where $t \geq 2$ and η is as defined above. So, if $t \geq 2$, $E(X_{j+1}|X_j = t) = E\left(\sum_{i=1}^{t} Y_i\right) = \sum_{i=1}^{t} E(Y_i) = (1-\eta_2)t$. Therefore, $E(X_{j+1}) = \sum_{t\geq 1} E(X_{j+1}|X_j = t)Pr(X_j = m)$. Since $E(X_{j+1}|X_j = 1) = 1$, we have $E(X_{j+1}) = \sum_{t\geq 2} E(X_{j+1}|X_j = t)Pr(X_j = m) + Pr(X_j = 1) = (1-\eta_2)E(X_j) + \eta_2 Pr(X_j = 1)$. So, after an expected $\log_{1/1-\eta_2}(c)$ rounds of the attrition procedure, the number of contenders will be negligible (constant), and will contribute negligibly to the overall complexity. The bit complexity for each round of attrition is $O(nK\log K)$. Since we have used randomized voting in each round by each node, each active node has the same chance of surviving the current round. Fairness in electing the leader is therefore assured by such a attrition procedure. Therefore, we have the following lemma.

Lemma 2. Procedure II *reduces the number of contenders from c to a negligible number (a constant) in expected* $O(\log_{1/1-\eta_2})(c)$ *rounds, with a bit complexity of* $O((K\log K)n\log c)$.

2.2 The Solitude Detection Procedure

A solitude detection procedure determines whether there is a lone active node in a ring. Such a node can be declared leader. A suitable solitude detection procedure for the attrition **Procedure I** is as follows. A particular node α_0 initiates the solitude procedure. It initializes a counter F to 0. If it is active it increments the counter by 1, otherwise, it does nothing. The counter is forwarded to the next node. Each active node increments F and forwards it. All passive nodes simply forward the counter F. When the counter returns back to α_0, the value of F is the number of active nodes in the ring. This value of F is then broadcast to all the nodes, whence every node updates its knowledge of the number of the active nodes. If $F = 1$, the only active node declares itself as the leader. This procedure requires $O(n \log c)$ bits of communication and not only achieves solitude detection, but also ensures that all the active nodes know the number of active nodes in the ring.

A solitude detection algorithm suitable for use with **Procedure II** is given in [9]. We reproduce it here for the sake of completeness. All the nodes β_i maintain a counter c_i initialized to zero. The variable $d_i > 0$ of node β_i, where $1 \leq i \leq n$, denotes the distance of the node β_i from its preceding active node. The algorithm maintains the invariant: node β_i has received j bits if and only if $c_i = d_i \bmod 2^{j_i}$. The actual number of nodes in passive state preceding node β_i is d_i. This is calculated as the bits are received. For an active node to conclude that it is the only node surviving, there must be $n-1$ nodes in the relay state preceding this active node. For maintaining the invariant, the active nodes first send 0. Thereafter, all nodes alternately receive and send bits. If node β_i is passive, then it will send the j_i^{th} low order bit of d_i in its j_i^{th} message. The active nodes continue to send 0. Whenever a node k receives its j_k^{th} message, it computes the first j_k bits of d_k and updates the value of c_k. The j_k^{th} message received by node k contains the j_k^{th} bit of $d_k - 1$ because it is sent by the preceding neighbor to node k. In this algorithm each message is of a constant number of bits. $O(n)$ messages are communicated in each step. If there is exactly one active node, the algorithm confirms the survival of this single node in $\log n$ steps. Solitude detection can thus be done using $O(n \log n)$ messages of constant length, resulting in bit complexity $O(n \log n)$.

2.3 The Leader Election Algorithm

In the previous two subsections we have proposed two attrition procedures and solitude detection procedures that can work with them. The structure of the attrition procedure ensures that the leader election algorithm in which they will be used is fair. Since **Procedure I** leads to an algorithm which has high and non-optimal bit complexity, we only describe the leader election algorithm for **Procedure II**. The leader election algorithm is obtained by interleaving the attrition procedure with the solitude detection procedure. There is a trivial way to interleave the two procedures coarsely. In this method the attrition procedure is run until (with very high probability) the number of contenders reduces to one. This is followed by a round of solitude detection. In most cases solitude will be confirmed. In the rare case when solitude is not achieved, the attrition procedure is restarted. These two procedures are repeated until solitude is confirmed. It can be shown by an analysis similar to that given in [6] that even this naive approach achieves an $O(n \log n)$ expected bit complexity.

The above leader election algorithm has a deficiency that it cannot be adapted to work in a ring where the nodes have no knowledge of the ring size or the number of contenders, even if each node has a unique identifier. This deficiency can be overcome by a tighter interleaving as shown in [7]. This new procedure also has added advantage of stopping early if the attrition procedure proceeds more quickly than expected. We discuss the main aspects of the algorithm in [7], adapted to work with our attrition procedure.

The second solitude detection procedure as outlined in section (2.2) essentially tries to maintain gap information between two adjacent active nodes. In a leader election algorithm where attrition and solitude detection are tightly interleaved, the gaps keep on changing from one round to another. This problem is eliminated by the use of restart flags in the messages. In each round, each contender sends a message consisisting of three parts - an attrition part (as described in section (2.1)), a solitude detection part (as described in section (2.2)) and a solitude restart flag initialized to FALSE, to the next contender. If a message arrives at a passive node α_i that was active in the previous round, then all nodes following it upto and including the next active node have gap information that is no longer valid. β_i notifies this by setting the restart flag to TRUE so that the succeeding nodes reinitialize their solitude detection variables. Since β_i was active in the previous round it had received information about the gap between itself and the preceeding active node. It can send the first bit of this unchanged gap information as the solitude detection bit.

Each node maintains the following three variables for solitude detection apart from the variables for the attrition procedure.

1. j_i: count of the number of messages received containing correct gap information.
2. c_i: counter variable containing the value $d_i \bmod 2^{j_i}$.
3. o_i: position of the outgoing solitude detection bit.

All nodes initialize their local variables j_i, c_i and o_i to 0. In each round, an active node generates a random number and sends its vote in the form of a message as mentioned above. Depending on the message an active and a passive node act in the following ways :

Active Node: The attrition part of the message is handled in the way described in section (2.1). If the restart flag is TRUE, it reinitializes its local variables j_i, c_i and o_i to 0 and resets the restart flag to FALSE. Based on the received solitude detection bit, it updates counter variable c_i to maintain $c_i{=}d_i \bmod 2^{j_i}$ and increments j_i and o_i. Now it forwards a message containing the modified attrition part, the solitude detection bit and restart bit set to FALSE to its neighbor.

Passive Node: In each round, a passive node β_i receives messages that it has to forward. If the restart bit in the received message is set, it will reinitialize its local variables j_i, c_i and o_i to 0. Based on the solitude detection bit, it updates its counter variable c_i to maintain $c_i{=}d_i \bmod 2^{j_i}$ and increments j_i and o_i. If the position variable o_i is one, β_i is a node that was active in the previous round, and as reasoned above it sets the restart flag to TRUE. It uses the first bit of the counter c_i as the new solitude detection bit. With the new values for the solitude detection bit and the restart flag and keeping the attrition part unchanged β_i forwards the message to its neighbor.

In our attrition scheme, a node receives more than one message in a particular round. However, a node requires to update its solitude detection variables only once in each round. The solitude detection parts of all subsequent messages are ignored in that round; note that the actual gap distance can only increase and the counter c_i is so maintained that it is a lower bound on this distance. This distance eventually increases to the correct gap distance in $O(\log n)$ rounds.

Following the correctness of our second attrition procedure (see Lemma 2) and the above mentioned interleaving of the attrition procedure and the corresponding solitude detection procedure (adapted from [7] as explained above), we now summarize our main result in the following theorem.

Theorem 1. *Fair leader election in a unidirectional, asynchronous, anonymous ring can be done in expected $O(\log n)$ rounds with $O(n \log n)$ bits of communication where the nodes know the size n of the ring. Fairness here means that each node has the same probability of getting elected as leader.*

3 Extensions to Other Models

Our algorithms above work for an anonymous, asynchronous ring where the number of nodes n is known to every node. Even when n is known only within a factor of less than 2, i.e. $n \in [N, 2N-1]$ and N is known to every node, the solitude detection procedure for **Procedure II** can be modified to work correctly. There can be at most one gap of length N or more between neighboring contenders and if the gap is less than N, non-solitude is confirmed. If a particular node detects a gap greater than N, it can confirm solitude by initiating a single round to check whether the next gap also remains the same. This modified procedure detects solitude when every node has the knowledge of N, where $n \in [N, 2N-1]$.

The leader election algorithm can also be adapted to a situation in which each node has a distinct identifier but no knowledge of the ring size or the number of contenders. This is achieved by a simpler solitude detection procedure. In the new solitude detection procedure, an active node verifies its solitude by confirming that the preceeding active node has the same identifier as itself. Thus solitude can be verified using only $O(nm)$ bits where m is the length of the longest identifier. Our leader election algorithm can be easily be adapted to work with this new solitude detection procedure.

4 Conclusion

In this paper we have proposed a new notion of fairness in the leader election problem. Fairness ensures that each contending node has the same probability of getting elected as leader. We have designed algorithms for fair leader election amongst c contending nodes in an n-node unidirectional, asynchronous and anonymous ring ($c \leq n$) using randomized voting, achieveing optimal $O(n \log n)$ expected communication bit complexity in expected $O(\log n)$ rounds. We assume that the ring size n is known. We also show how to adapt our algorithms for slightly different unidirectional ring models.

It may be worthwhile investigating fair leader election algorithms for other network models such as trees and complete graphs. Reuse of random bits between rounds is also an important research issue since randomness is a precious resource.

References

1. Karl Abrahamson, Andrew Adler, Rachel Gelbart, Lisa Higham, and David Kirkpatrick. The bit complexity of randomized leader election on a ring. *SIAM J. Comput.*, 18(1):12–29, 1989.
2. Dana Angluin. Local and global properties in networks of processors (extended abstract). In *Proceedings of the twelfth annual ACM symposium on Theory of computing*, pages 82–93, 1980.
3. E. Chang and R Roberts. An improved algorithm for decentralized extrema-finding in circularly configurations of processes. *Commun. ACM*, 22(5):281–283, 1979.
4. Danny Dolev, Maria M. Klawe, and Michael Rodeh. An $O(n \log n)$ unidirectional distributed algorithm for extrema finding in a circle. *J. Algorithms*, 3(3):245–260, 1982.
5. Randolph Franklin. On an improved algorithm for decentralized extrema finding in circular configurations of processors. *Commun. ACM*, 25(5):336–337, 1982.
6. Lisa Higham. *Randomized Distributed Computing on Rings.* Phd thesis, University of British Columbia, 1988.
7. Lisa Higham. Simple randomized leader election with extensions. Technical report, University of Calgary, 1988.
8. D. S. Hirschberg and J. B. Sinclair. Decentralized extrema-finding in circular configurations of processors. *Commun. ACM*, 23(11):627–628, 1980.
9. Alon Itai and Michael Rodeh. Symmetry breaking in distributed networks. *Information and Computation*, 88(1):60–87, 1990.
10. J.E.Burns. A formal model for message passing systems. Technical Report TR-91, Indiana University, 1980.
11. G Le Lann. Distributed systems-towards a formal approach. In *Proceedings of the IFIP Congress 77*, pages 155–160. North-Holland, 1977.
12. Gary L. Peterson. An $O(n \log n)$ unidirectional distributed algorithm for the circular extrema problem. *ACM Transactions on Programming Languages and Systems*, 4(4):758–762, 1982.

An Efficient Leader Election Algorithm for Mobile Ad Hoc Networks

Pradeep Parvathipuram[1], Vijay Kumar[1], and Gi-Chul Yang[2],

[1] SICE, Computer Networking, University of Missouri-Kansas City, 5100 Rockhill Kansas City, MO 64110
Pkp39c(kumarv)@umkc.edu

[2] Division of Information Engineering, Mokpo National University, 61 Dorim-ri, Chungkye-myun, Muan-gun, Jeonnam, 534-729 Korea
gcyang@mokpo.ac.kr

Abstract. Nodes communicate under peer-to-peer level in ad-hoc mobile networks. To manage the inter-node communication and data exchange among them a leader node is required. In this paper we present a leader election algorithm for distributed mobile ad hoc networks where inter-node communication is allowed only among the neighboring nodes along with the correctness of the algorithm. The algorithm uses least amount of wireless resources and does not affect the movement of the nodes.

1 Introduction

A mobile ad hoc (dynamic network) consists of a set of peer-to-peer nodes, which communicate with each other through wireless channels. The nodes are free to move around in a geographical area and are loosely bounded by the transmission range of the wireless channels. Since a node is completely free to move around, there is no fixed final topology. A mobile node communicates with a set of nodes, which are within its transmission range. These nodes are said to be the *neighbors* of the communicating node and the mobile nodes present in between the source and the set of neighbors (destination nodes) act as routers as they route packets to destinations from the source. To coordinate the communication among nodes and to manage their data requirements a leader (node) is identified. The identification problem of leader is referred to as "leader election problem".

The leader election problem originally appeared in token ring network for managing the use of tokens [13]. The problem resurfaced again in ad hoc or dynamic networks, however, with added complexity. Since then a number of papers have discussed the nature of algorithms [2, 3, 4, 5] and to our knowledge only few papers [2, 3] have presented such algorithms. One of the main reasons for such lack of work in this area is the complexity involved in finding an efficient solution for a highly dynamic network. Unlike conventional distributed systems, designing a leader election algorithm for mobile ad hoc networks is challenging mainly because (a) the nodes are highly mobile, (b) the mean time failure of these nodes are relatively high compared to static wired network nodes, (c) the transmission range

R.K. Ghosh and H. Mohanthy (Eds.): ICDCIT 2004, LNCS 3347, pp. 32–41, 2004.

and bandwidth of wireless channels are limited, (d) *neighbor* configuration may change randomly, and (e) there is no fixed network topology. For these reasons, an efficient leader election algorithm must do everything, which an algorithm for static networks does, and in addition it must handle the movement of the nodes. Furthermore, the algorithm must guarantee that (a) there should be a leader at the end of the execution of the algorithm and (b) there cannot be more than one leader in a single connected component.

Our aim is to develop an efficient leader election (identification) scheme for this highly dynamic system that (a) incurs minimum messaging cost and time to elect a leader (b) is correct, that is, at any time there cannot be two or more conflicting leaders in the network, and (c) it does not hinder or restrict the geographical movement of nodes. In our approach we do not impose any specific structure for the mobile ad hoc network We assume followings for our algorithm. Consider a system of N mobile nodes, which are managed with the following set of assumptions (a) each mobile node has a unique identifier, (b) all communication links are bi-directional and reliable, and (c) the topology changes are finite.

Our leader election algorithm ensures only one leader for each connected component in a network. When a partition occurs in the network, a new leader is elected in each component and its id is propagated through out the component. We have used ZRP (zone routing protocol) [1] to propagate this information.

2 A Review of Existing Work

The algorithm presented in [2] uses *compulsory* and *non-compulsory* protocols on the movement of the mobile nodes. Non-compulsory protocols do not impose any restriction on the movement of the mobile nodes but the compulsory protocols do. Both types assume that the movement of these mobile nodes is bounded by the three dimensional space S where S is quantized by a regular polyhedron. Neither of the protocols addresses networks partitions. Non-compulsory protocols might not even elect a leader under certain circumstances and the compulsory protocols perform random walk. For this algorithm to run, the mobile nodes need to know the type and dimension of the polyhedron. This was the first algorithm for mobile ad hoc networks and although it has limitations, it does provide some useful information for leader election algorithm. The algorithm assumes that the mobile hosts move in such a way that each host performs a random walk in the specified space S. Because of this assumption, it is proved that the algorithm terminates in times asymptotically linear to the size of the space S, which is measured as its volume divided by the volume of the sphere defined by the range of transmission of the mobile host. A graph theoretic model has been proposed for the ad hoc networks and a mobile host has been viewed as being covered by a sphere with a radius of transmission range.

The algorithm presented in [3] uses the TORA [6] (Temporally Ordered Routing Algorithm) routing protocol for the leader election and imposes a DAG (Directed Acyclic Graph) structure for the network. This algorithm takes care of the partitions in the network as TORA can detect partitions when reversal reaches a node with no downstream links and all its neighbors have the same reflected reference level. We think that imposing a DAG structure is quite an overhead for a particular network as the leader is assumed to be the sink with DAG and each DAG is said to be leader oriented. Each time a change occurs the DAG structure needs to be maintained. There are two algorithms proposed for leader election in this paper. One when there is only one change and after that change the whole network stabilizes before the intervention of a new change, the second one deals with concurrent multiple topology changes, i.e., concurrent changes can take place before the network gets stabilized. So as the topology changes keep increasing, the cost of maintaining the DAG structure also increases. The whole algorithm is based on the routing protocol called TORA and the orientation of the DAG has been changed from destination oriented to leader oriented.

The multicast operation of the AODV (Ad hoc On Demand Distance Vector routing protocol) [4] for ad hoc network performs the leader election only during multicasting. It also ensures that only one of the nodes is elected as a leader when a network gets partitioned and when the components get merged. This algorithm basically deals with the multicast and shows that multicasting can be done in ad hoc network and AODV can unicast, broadcast and multicast. A multicast group leader maintains the multicast group sequence number and these group members agree to act as routers in the multicast tree. In case of partitions, the algorithm ensure that only one multicast leader exist.

In [5], an algorithm has been presented to maintain a rooted spanning tree for dynamic networks. This algorithm does not propose a scheme for leader election but can be viewed as maintaining a leader (root) as it maintains a spanning tree structure for the network. Just as TORA imposes a DAG structure, this algorithm imposes a spanning tree structure. This algorithm does incorporate changes in the network but doesn't deal with network partitions. Moreover, imposing and maintaining a spanning tree structure for a network is quite an overhead in mobile ad hoc networks, as the whole network keeps moving. Basically this paper mainly describes the protocol to maintain the spanning tree in dynamic topology. This scenario can be seen similar to an ad hoc network where in the network changes its topology frequently.

3 Zone Routing Protocol (ZRP)

We use ZRP [1] as the routing protocol for mobile ad hoc networks. It uses both the proactive and reactive type routing protocols. The whole network is divided into zones of radius *r*, and the information of all the nodes present in the zone is recorded in the *zone routing table*. It proactively maintains the route information for all the nodes present in the zone. Each node has a routing table, which consists of the information for all the nodes within radius r (routing zone) for that particular node. If a node of a zone wants to communicate with the nodes of other zones, then it uses *bordercasting* to get the information. It uses IARP (intra zone routing protocol) and IERP (Inter zone routing protocol) for routing. IARP proactively maintains the routing information for all the nodes present in the routing zone and IERP is used if a node in one zone wants to communicate with the nodes in another zone. The border nodes of the routing zone are called *border routers* or the *peripheral* nodes. If a node in one zone wants to communicate with the nodes of another zone, then it propagates the query to the border routers. These border routers look for the nodes inside their routing zone and the process continues until the destination is reached. This way the number of messages to locate the destination is greatly reduced.

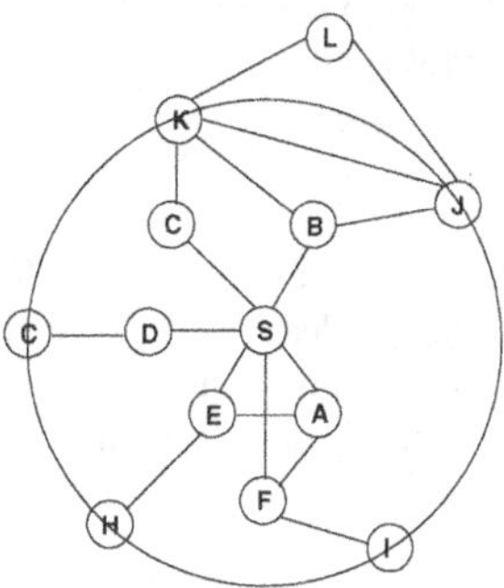

Fig. 1. A routing zone with radius 2

Consider node *S* (figure 1), and let size of the radius be *two hops* (distance metric). Then for node *S* all nodes except for *L* come in its zone and has a route to every node in the zone. To communicate with a node outside the zone, node *S* sends the query to all the border routers in the zone and in turn those border routers check to see whether the node is present in its zone and if not then it keeps bordercasting the query until it finds the destination. Some of the query termination techniques are also been implemented in ZRP if a query that has been looked into a zone before comes again. It achieves multiple paths for a single destination and the shortest one is selected. Note that it reduces the number of messages, as it does not use flooding to propagate the information. This comes in handy when the leader information needs to propagate throughout the network and when a node requires knowing the presence of leader, thus decreasing the communication cost. The objective of reducing the message complexity is obtained by using ZRP.

4 Our Approach

Our approach basically selects the largest identity node as the leader using minimum wireless messages. A mobile ad hoc network can be considered as a static network with frequent link or node failures, which can be thought of as a mobile node of an ad hoc network going out of reach. We use the *diameter* concept to cover all the nodes in the network. A *diameter* is defined as the longest *distance* between any two nodes in the network where the *distance* is defined as the shortest path between the nodes. In figure 2, the diameter of the network is 6, which is the distance between the nodes L and I. The distance metric is measured in number of hops. We assume the network gets stabilized after a single change occurs during leader election process. We further assume that there are only a finite number of changes in the network. The steps of the algorithm can be stated briefly as follows and later we provide the pseudo code for the algorithm.

Consider a network of *N* nodes. Our algorithm may take more than diameter rounds to terminate since the topological changes are considered during the leader election. If, however, the topological changes are not considered, then it takes diameter rounds to elect the leader.

Leader Election

For each round, each node propagates its unique identifier to its neighbors and a maximum identifier is elected as a leader. This maximum identifier is propagated in the subsequent rounds. All the rounds need to be synchronized. idlist (i) identifies identifier list for $node_i$, which consists of all the neighbors for $node_i$. Lid(i) = max(idlist(i))

Termination

At (rounds >= diameter), for each $node_i$

If all identifiers in idlist (i) are the same, then the $node_i$ stops sending the maximum identifier further and elects the maximum identifier in the idlist (i) as the leader. The termination may not be at the end of the diameter rounds, the algorithm gets terminated if for each $node_i$ the elements in idlist (for each node) are the same.

Algorithm:
For each node i in the network, we have the following.
idlist - Identifier list, lid(i) – leader id of node i.
For each round,
Begin
Each node say nodei transmits its unique identifier in the first round and Lid(i) in the subsequent rounds to their neighbors and all these ids will be stored in idlist.
Lid(i) = max (idlist(i));
End
A unique leader is elected in diameter rounds, if there are no topological changes in the network. The algorithm is modified to incorporate topological changes in between the rounds and below is the description of how the algorithm is modified.

Case 1: *If a node has no outgoing links then lid(i) = i;*

Case 2: *If a node leaves between the rounds, then the neighbors would know this.*

Suppose $node_i$ *leaves the network after round r and let its neighbors be j and k.*

Begin
∀neighbors of i (i.e. j, k).
Delete (ilist, idlist(j & k)) *// delete ilist from idlist*
Where ilist contains the group of identifiers that nodei has sent to its neighbors before round r along with i.

The ilist information is also deleted from all the neighbors of j and k if the ilist identifiers have been propagated in the previous rounds. This process continues until all the nodes in the network are covered.

While (round > = diameter), // Termination condition
Begin
∀nodes in the network
say for nodei,
compare all the identifiers present in idlist(i)

If all the identifiers in idlist(i) are equal, $node_i$ stops propagating its maximum identifier and elects the maximum identifier as the leader.

All nodes in the network follow this process and a unique leader is elected in a single connected component.

End //end of while loop
End //end of case2

***Case 3:** If a new node i joins the network in between the rounds say round r then the neighbors will update its idlist.*

Begin
∀Neighbors of i say nodej is the neighbor for nodei.
add (i, idlist(j));

The normal algorithm continues (the ids are propagated), nodes keep exchanging the information till diameter rounds.

while (round > = diameter),
Begin
∀ nodes in the network. Say nodej, and nodej receives an identifier i at diameter round.

If i is greater than the maximum identifier nodej has propagated in the previous round (diameter-1).

Propagate nodei to all the neighbors of j.
Also propagate the nodei information to all the neighbors of neighbors of i until the whole network is covered, if the above condition satisfies.
Else Do not propagate the information.
∀nodes in the network // Termination Condition
say for nodei,
compare all the identifiers present in idlist(i)

If all the identifiers in idlist(i) are equal, nodei stops propagating its maximum identifier and elects the maximum identifier as the leader.

All nodes in the network follow this process and a unique leader is elected in a single connected component.

End //end of the while loop
End //end of case3

So the time taken for the algorithm to elect a leader will be O (diam + Δt) where Δt is the time taken for all the nodes to converge and Δt depends on the topology changes in the network (Δt might be the time taken for few more rounds). The algorithm terminates when all nodes have exactly one identifier as a leader.

The message complexity for the leader election algorithm depends on the network topology and the number of messages propagated as the topology changes. Even for multiple concurrent changes in the network, our algorithm ensures only one leader but the time Δt may increase. Since all the cases are considered in the algorithm, even if multiple topological changes occur the algorithm can still elect a unique leader as different cases are called for different changes in the network at different times.

5 Proof of Correctness

We assume that the leader has been elected and we are permitting only one change to occur after the network gets stabilized. We also assume that the system is synchronized. At each round, messages are sent to all the neighbors. We prove that there is only one leader elected at any time.

Case 1: If a link appears at time *t* causing two components say *C1* and *C2* to merge together and form one component *C*, then we prove that there is only one leader for *C*. Once a leader is elected, we need to make sure that this information is propagated through out the component whose leader has been defeated by the leader of the other component.

Let us consider the case where the leader *l1* of *C1* is greater than the leader *l2* of component *C2*. Let the diameters of *C1* and *C2* be *d1* and *d2* respectively. The information of the leader *l1* should be propagated through *C2*. Also assume that the link appears between the nodes *n1* and *n2* corresponding to *C1* and *C2* making the two components merge. Let *k1* be the maximum shortest distance between the node *n1* and any other node in *C1* and *K2* the maximum shortest distance between the node *n2* and any other node in *C2*.

Lemma 1: *l1* is elected as the leader of *C* in *k2* rounds.

Proof: There can be only one leader in *C* if the propagation of the leader is successful. As we assumed *l1* > *l2*, we now need to propagate the value of *l1* through *C2*. Since *n2* is the node that needs to propagate the information all through *C2*, we can construct a tree with *n2* as the root (Figure 2) and its neighbors as the descendents of n2 and so on until all the nodes are covered in the network. The depth of the tree will be equal to *k2*. So, at the end of *k2* rounds the information is propagated throughout *C2*.

At round *r* = *1*, *n2* knows that *l1* is the leader and it will propagate this information to its neighbors. At *r* = *k2* - *1*, all the nodes that are present at a distance of *k2* - *1* has been informed. At *r* = *k2* - *1*, only the nodes that are at a distance of *k2* do not know about the new leader and when *r* = *k2*, the nodes present at *k2* - *1* rounds propagate to their neighbors thus covering *C2*. So at the end of *k2* rounds, the information about the new leader is propagated. Since we are assuming that there is no change in the network before the network stabilizes after a single change (i.e. during propagating the information) there will be only one leader in the network.

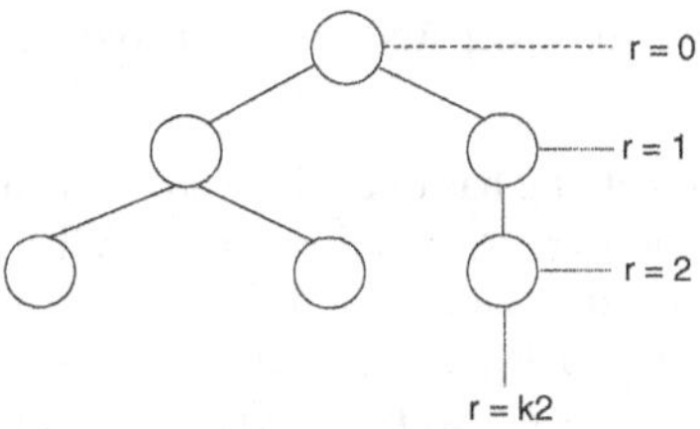

Fig. 2. A node tree with root at n2

Case 2: A link breaks at time *t* due to the mobility of nodes causing a connected component partitioned into two separate components.

Lemma 2: Two separate leaders need to be elected in the two separate components.

Proof: Consider a connected *C*. Let us assume that *(k1, k2)* be the link between the two nodes *k1* and *k2*. When it breaks due to the movement of the node say *k2* causes a partition in the network. To detect the partition, the neighboring nodes of *k2* tries to establish a connection with the leader. The leader should be present in any one of the components. Suppose it is in *C1* with *k1*. *k2* knows that it has been disconnected from the network and elects itself as the leader and propagates the information of the new leader across *C2*.

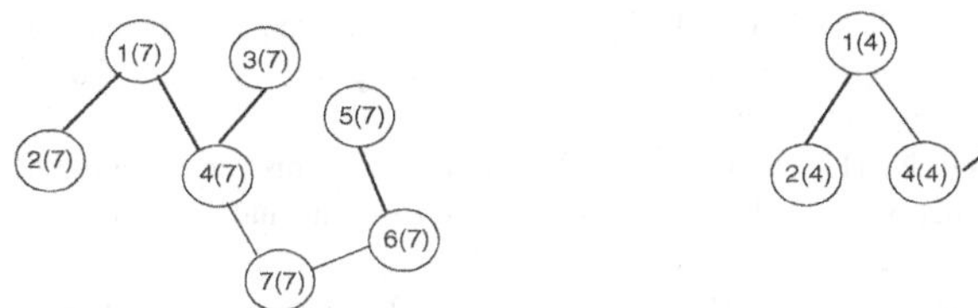

Fig. 3. Before Partition

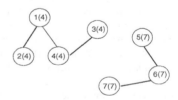

Fig. 4. After Partition

The information is propagated as in the case of lemma 1 and the same argument can be used here to prove that only one leader gets selected for each and every connected component.

Figure 3 represents a network before partition and Figure 4 represents a network after partition. In figure 3, if the link between 4 and 7 is removed by the movement of node7, then the network gets partitioned in to two. Since *node 4* and *node 6* are the neighbors, both these try to establish connection with the leader (*node 7*). *Node 6* reaches *node 7* so it is not disconnected but *node 4* fails reach *node 7*, as it is no more in the network. *Node 4* detects that a partition has occurred and it establishes itself as the leader and this information is propagated throughout the component. After partition (Figure 4) two components are formed with *node 4* as the leader of one component and *node 7* as the leader of the other component.

Case 3: When a single node, say *j*, departs from the network, then for every neighbor *i* of *j*, we have the following:

If *(lid(i) <> uid(j))* then nothing has to be done since *j* is not a leader otherwise the node that has moved is the leader. A situation arises. What to do if the leader itself goes away. A new leader should be elected in the connected component, if *i* is only the neighbor of *j*, then it knows that leader has left and elects itself as the leader since there is no other contender in the network. The argument of lemma 1 can be used to prove that only one leader gets elected in a connected component.

6 Conclusions

We have presented two algorithms (Leader election and Termination) for leader election and discussed their capabilities. We believe that our algorithms are easy to implement as the messages are exchanged only between the neighbors. We have used the concept of time stamping to distinguish the messages so that the most recent information is taken into consideration. All cases are considered in the algorithms and show that only one leader is elected at a particular time.

References

1. Z.J. Haas and M.R. Pearlman, "The Zone Routing Protocol (ZRP) for Ad Hoc Networks," Internet Draft, draft-ietf-manet-zone-zrp-02.txt, June 1999
2. Kostas P Hatzis, George P. Pentaris, Paul G. Spirakis, Vasilis B. Tampakas and Richard B. Tan Fundamental Control Algorithms in Mobile Networks Proc. 11th Annual ACM Symp. on Parallel Algorithms And Architectures.
3. N. Malpani, J. L. Welch. N. H. Vaidya, Leader Election Algorithms for Mobile Ad Hoc Networks, Fourth International Workshop on Discrete Algorithms and Methods for Mobile Computing and Communications, Boston, August 2000.
4. Elizabeth M. Royer and Charles E. Perkins. "Multicast Operation of the Ad-hoc On-Demand Distance Vector Routing Protocol." *Proceedings of MobiCom '99*, Seattle, WA, August 1999, pp. 207-218.
5. Chunhsiang Cheng and Srikanta P.R. Kumar. A loopfree spanning tree protocol in Dynamic topology. Proc. 27th Annual Allerton Conference on Communication, Control and Computing, sep 1989. PP.594-595.
6. Vincent D. Park and M. Scott Corson. A Highly Adaptive Distributed Routing Algorithm for Mobile Wireless Networks. Proc. IEEE INFOCOM, April 7-11, 1997.
7. A. Acharya, B. R. Badrinath, T. Imielinski, Impact of mobility on distributed computations. Operating Systems Review, April 1993.
8. A. Acharya, B. R. Badrinath, T. Imielinski, Structuring distributed algorithms for mobile hosts. In Proc. Of 14th International Conference on distributed computing systems, June 1994.
9. Z.J. Haas and S. Tabrizi, "On Some Challenges and Design Choices in Ad-Hoc Communications,"*IEEE MILCOM'98*, Bedford, MA, October 18-21, 1998.
10. A.Tsirigos and Z.J. Haas, "Multipath Routing in Mobile Ad Hoc Networks or How to Route in the Presence of Topological Changes," IEEE MILCOM'2001, Tysons Corner, VA, October 28-31, 2001.

11. J. Haas and B. Liang, "Ad-Hoc Mobility Management with Randomized Database Groups," *IEEE ICC'99,* Vancouver, BC, Canada, June 6-10, 1999.
12. Z.J. Haas and M.R. Pearlman, "The Performance of Query Control Schemes for the Zone Routing Protocol," *ACM DialM 1999,* Seattle, WA, August 20, 1999.
13. B. Liang and Z.J. Haas, "Virtual Backbone Generation and Maintenance in Ad Hoc Network Mobility Management," *IEEE INFOCOM'2000,* Tel Aviv, Israel, March 26-30, 2000.
14. G. LeLann, "Distributed Systems: Towards a formal approach." In Proc. Information Processing '77, B. Gilchrist (ed.), North-Holland, 1977.
15. Kevin Fall, Kannan Varadhan. NS user manual, "The VINT project". A Collaboration between researches at UC Berkeley, LBL, USC/ISI, and Xerox PARC.

Performance Evaluation of Gigabit Ethernet and SCI in a Linux Cluster

Rajesh Kalmady and Digamber Sonvane

Computer Division, Bhabha Atomic Research Centre,
Trombay, Mumbai-400085, India
{rajesh, sonvane}@barc.ernet.in

Abstract. Clusters are now one of the most preferred architectures for building high performance computing systems. The emergence of high speed commodity microprocessors, network technologies and Open Source operating systems have propelled the cluster concept to an unparalleled high. Even though most clusters nowadays use LAN technologies such as Fast and Gigabit Ethernet as the interconnect, there is a growing breed of new interconnection technologies called SAN (System Area Network) specifically designed for HPC. These new technologies boast characteristics such as high bandwidth, low latency for communications and scalability to large number of nodes that are so essential for most HPC applications. In this paper, we compare the performance of Gigabit Ethernet (LAN), and Scalable Coherent Interface (SAN) on a 128-processor Linux cluster. We present the raw bandwidth and latency figures of the two networks and then discuss the performance of several benchmark programs.

1 Introduction

Parallel computers are considered as a cheaper alternative to conventional supercomputers. It is possible to achieve supercomputing speeds by interconnecting large numbers of commodity microprocessors through an interconnection network. The success of this concept is borne by the fact that the leading computers in the Top500 list are all parallel computers. Parallel computing has successfully replaced the traditional concepts of supercomputing such as vector processing. In the last few years, a new wave of change is sweeping parallel computing itself. This is the rise of the clusters. Once considered as a cheaper alternative to 'conventional' parallel architectures such as MPP, the cluster has now emerged out of the labs of academic or research institutions to become one of the most preferred architectures for high performance computers. The growth of the cluster has been fuelled by the availability of high-speed commodity processors and high bandwidth commodity interconnection networks. Fast Ethernet, which operates at 100 Mbps, has been a traditional favourite for clusters for several years due to its inexpensiveness and widespread availability. But Fast Ethernet is now proving a serious bottleneck for today's fast processors such as the Pentium-4, Xeons and Itaniums, forcing cluster builders to look for higher bandwidth alternatives. The logical step would, of course, be to choose the successor

R.K. Ghosh and H. Mohanthy (Eds.): ICDCIT 2004, LNCS 3347, pp. 50–59, 2004.

to Fast Ethernet, Gigabit Ethernet with a bandwidth of 1 Gbps as the cluster interconnect. But there are several new alternatives to Gigabit Ethernet such as Myrinet, SCI and Quadrics, which are collectively called SAN (for System Area Network). These SANs are specifically designed for building large clusters with hundreds and thousands of nodes with a pretty good bandwidth of the order of several Gbps and a latency of a few microseconds.

Bhabha Atomic Research Centre (BARC) has been working in the field of HPC over the last decade, developing a series of parallel computers using various processors and interconnect technologies ranging from Intel 860 to Pentium-4 and Multibus to Fast Ethernet. Over the last 5 years, several Linux clusters were built ranging from small 8 cpu clusters to 128 processor configurations. These clusters have mostly been built using personal computers with Intel processors such as Pentium-II, III and IV. Fast Ethernet has been the interconnect of choice in most systems we have built. In order to build larger systems with faster processors, a choice has to be made on which networking technology to use. Hence an effort was made to evaluate cluster performance for two interconnect technologies – Gigabit Ethernet and SCI [1].

2 Test Setup and Methodologies

2.1 Test Setup

The setup on which the performance tests were conducted is the latest in the series of parallel computers developed by BARC. This is a 64 node Linux cluster with each node comprising dual Intel Xeon processors @ 2.4 GHz and 2 GB of memory. This 128 cpu cluster has two networks – Fast Ethernet and SCI. Each node runs a copy of Redhat Linux 8.0 operating system. There is a set of file servers from which file systems are NFS mounted on the nodes. The Fast Ethernet network caters mainly to the NFS traffic whereas the SCI interconnect handles the message passing traffic from parallel applications. For these tests, a third network, Gigabit Ethernet was added to the system. Details of Gigabit Ethernet and SCI interconnects are given below.

Gigabit Ethernet. Gigabit Ethernet is the logical progression after Fast Ethernet in the Ethernet family. It uses the same protocols and frame formats as Fast Ethernet but with 10 times the speed. Gigabit Ethernet is available on many physical media such as twisted pair and fiber. Though there is no theoretical scalability figure for Gigabit Ethernet, the largest Gigabit Ethernet switch available today has 576 ports. Moreover, it is not just the port count of a switch that matters but also the switching speed of the switch's fabric. For best results, the fabric switching speed should be 2*(number of ports) Gbps. But in practice, the fabric switching speed of large Gigabit Ethernet switches is less than the above figure, which matters when communication intensive applications are run. Nowadays, most server motherboards have built-in Gigabit Ethernet ports. The main strength of this technology is that it is Ethernet and there is enormous support for Ethernet in hardware and software.

The Gigabit Ethernet setup for our tests consists of a 64 port Gigabit Ethernet switch with a switching speed of 128 Gbps. Each node consists of a PCI Gigabit Ethernet adapter, which is plugged into a 64 bit, 66MHz PCI slot. CAT5E cables are used for the interconnection from node to switch. LAM is the MPI implementation used for the tests on Gigabit Ethernet.

SCI. Scalable Coherent Interface is an interconnect standard (IEEE 1596) for high performance networking which aims to provide high bandwidth, low latency and low cpu overhead for communication operations. An SCI interconnect is defined to be built only from unidirectional point-to-point links between participating nodes. This feature of the SCI links makes it possible to achieve high bandwidths. In contrast to a LAN, the SCI provides hardware based physical distributed shared memory (DSM), thus exhibiting some characteristics of a NUMA machine. Because of this architecture, internode communication translates into simple cpu load and stores into DSM segments which are mapped from remote node memories. Hence there is no need for a protocol stack, which results in low latencies for communication. The SCI standard specifies a bandwidth of 1 GB/s but current implementations achieve a link speed of 667 MB/s. The theoretical maximum number of nodes in a SCI cluster is 64K with current implementations limiting it at around 256. SCI clusters can have many topologies such as ring, switch and torus.

The SCI network for our tests consists of 64 Dolphin [2] D336 2-D cards and associated cables. The 64 nodes are connected in an 8*8 2-D torus. The SCI cards too are inserted in 64 bit, 66 MHz PCI slots in the nodes. We have used Scali's SCAMPI as the MPI implementation on SCI.

2.2 Test Methodology

The test procedure comprises a set of benchmark programs in MPI, which were run on both networks. Each program was run on increasing numbers of processors. GCC was used as the compiler for C programs and Absoft compiler for Fortran programs. The programs are described below

Nwtest. This is a simple MPI application written to measure the bandwidth and latency obtained from a MPI application using the networks. The transfer mode is ping-pong where data is sent and received to and from a remote node. Data is sent in varying packet sizes from 4 bytes to 4 MB. Latencies are measured by sending and receiving a zero byte packet and dividing the round trip time by two. For Gigabit Ethernet, we have also measured the bandwidth for varying MTU sizes from 1500 to 9000 bytes.

High Performance Linpack. High Performance Linpack (HPL)[3] is a well-known benchmark program used for measuring performance of parallel computers. This program solves a system of simultaneous equations using LU decomposition method and involves high amount of computation and communication. We have conducted two kinds of HPL tests – one with a fixed problem size (matrix size) of 40000 and the other with problem sizes varying with the number of processors used such that the amount of memory consumed per processor would remain constant.

NAS Parallel Benchmarks. NAS Parallel Benchmarks [4] is a widely used benchmark suite for parallel computers. There are eight programs in this suite and each program has several classes with increasing problem sizes. We have chosen class C of each problem to run on the system.

3 Results

Here we present the results obtained from our tests. Following is a set of graphs that depict the readings.

3.1 Nwtest

Figure 1 shows the performance of the 'nwtest' program on Gigabit Ethernet and SCI networks. For GbE, this program was run with different MTU settings. The standard MTU for Gigabit Ethernet is 1500 bytes, but many adapter cards and switches support Jumbo frames up to 9000 bytes. The uppermost curve in the graph shows the SCI performance in which the peak bandwidth obtained was about 250 MB/s. For GbE, the peak obtained was around 90 MB/s for 1500 byte MTU (the second curve in the figure). Surprisingly, setting a higher MTU proved detrimental to the performance of the network. This goes against the common perception of jumbo frames and we suspect that TCP stacks and Ethernet drivers are now most optimized to run at an MTU of 1500 bytes. Therefore, going by the raw bandwidth figures, we found that SCI performs at about 3 times the speed of Gigabit Ethernet.

SCI is impressive in latency figures too. The 'nwtest' program was also used to measure the latency of each network, measured as half the round trip time for a zero byte packet. Since latency figures for a network also include the latency for the protocol stack such as IP as the data travels through it, we have also measured this value by running 'nwtest' within two processes in the same node. Table 1 lists these figures.

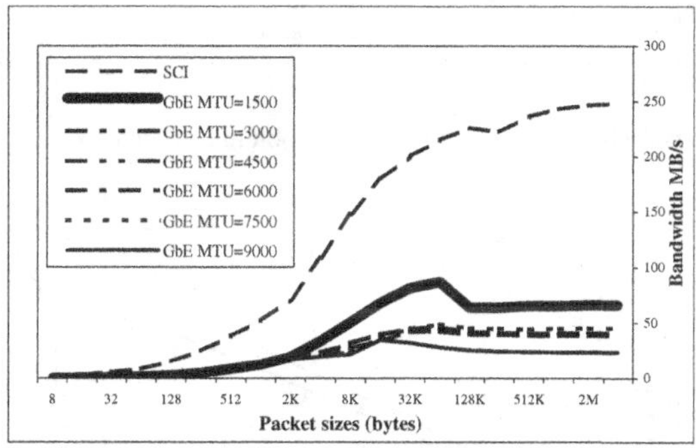

Fig. 1. Curves showing bandwidth figures achieved on Gigabit Ethernet with different MTU sizes (*the lower 6 curves)* and the SCI network (*the topmost curve)*

Table 1. Latency figures in microseconds obtained on Gigabit Ethernet and SCI networks. It can be seen from the figures that the higher latency for Gigabit Ethernet within a node is due to the IP protocol stack in each node that is absent in SCI

Gigabit Ethernet		SCI	
Total latency (μs)	Latency within node (μs)	Total Latency (μs)	Latency within node (μs)
44.93	16.88	5.55	1.61

3.2 High Performance Linpack

The graphs in figures 2 and 3 depict the performance of the HPL benchmark on Gigabit and SCI in two kinds of tests. The first test, with a fixed problem size of 40000x40000, shows us how the performance of the program saturates with increasing number of processors. The other test involved increasing the problem size with increasing numbers of processors such that the memory utilization per node would remain constant. In the first test, the curve should rise almost linearly and then flatten at some point. In the second test, the curve should be linear all the way through because we are scaling up the workload along with the processor count.

Figures 2 and 3 show the graphs for the two tests. The curves are as expected. But the interesting observation that can be made here is that the 1:3 ratio of bandwidths between the two networks does not make significant difference in the HPL ratings.

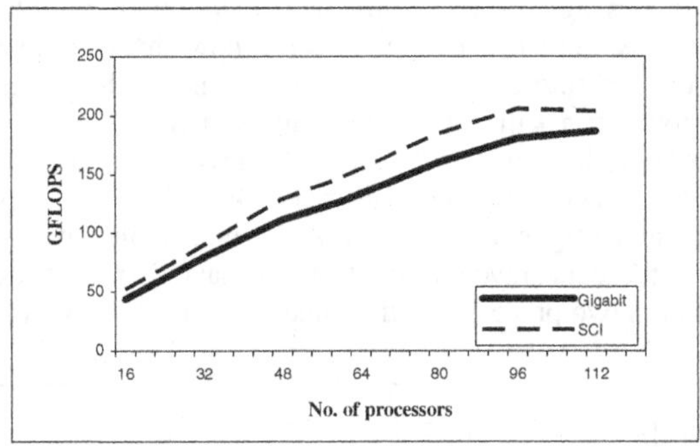

Fig. 2. HPL over Gigabit and SCI for fixed problem size (matrix size), 40000x40000

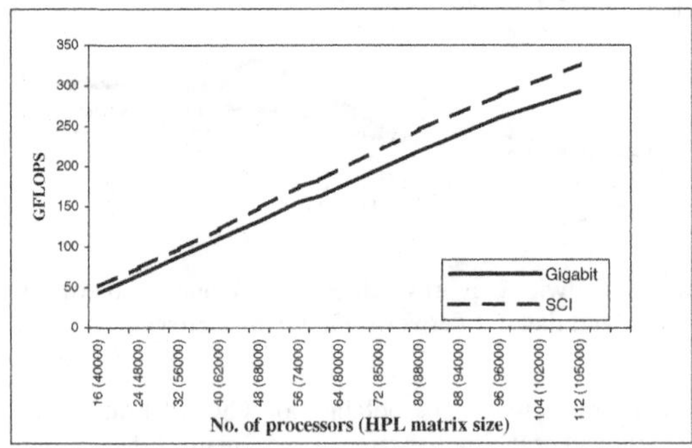

Fig. 3. HPL over Gigabit and SCI for varying problem sizes and fixed memory usage per processor. The sizes of the HPL matrices are taken such that it occupies 800 MB of memory per processor

There is at best a difference of about 15% or about 30 GFLOPS between the two readings. HPL is a program with heavy communication but it also has a massive computation load and the two balance each other very well.

3.3 NAS Parallel Benchmarks

The NAS Parallel benchmark suite consists of eight programs, all related to aerospace applications, each having four classes A, B, C and D out of which class C (large size) was chosen for the system. The parallelism in these programs range from embarrassingly parallel to highly communication intensive [5]. For each program, runs were taken on Gigabit and SCI networks and the results are presented in the following set of graphs. The programs EP, BT, SP, LU and MG are compute intensive with moderate communication and the programs CG and IS are more communication than compute intensive.

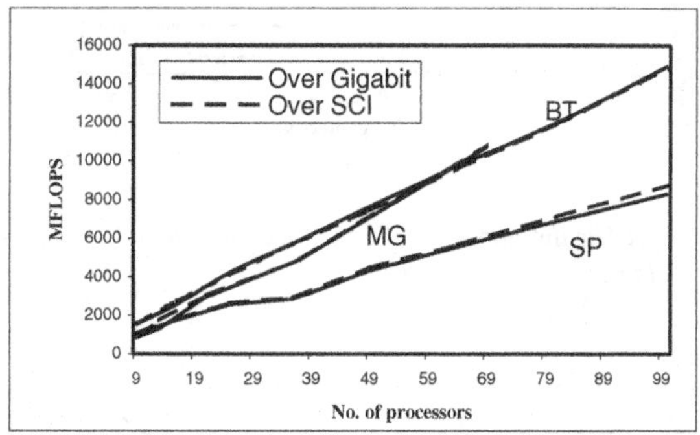

Fig. 4. Performance curves of the BT, SP and MG benchmarks on Gigabit and SCI interconnects

The BT, SP and MG programs are application benchmarks that have large granularity and send fewer messages. This shows up in Figure 4 where the Gigabit and SCI curves for BT, SP and MG overlap each other showing that there is no dependence at all on the type of network used.

The conjugate gradient kernel CG has extensive communication load and this is reflected in Figure 5 where we see that the SCI network outperforms Gigabit Ethernet by as much as 50% at higher number of processors and 25% at lower cpu counts.

EP is a Monte Carlo kernel that generates a large set of random numbers in parallel over number of nodes. This is an embarrassingly parallel program which consists of no communication except for 4 calls to *'MPI_Allreduce'* at the end of the program, which are called only once [6]. Interestingly, for this program, Gigabit Ethernet performed better than SCI for 32 or more processors (Figure 6). On profiling the program, it was found that in SCI, the first collective communication call (for example, *MPI_Allreduce)* takes an enormous amount of time (about 14 seconds in our test setup) though only a scalar data was communicated. Further measurements showed that this was true even for the first point-to-point call between any pair of nodes even though the overheads were less than that for the collective calls. The overheads for collective calls increase with the number of processes involved. This overhead in SCI communication is because of the procedure for setting up communication channels, which involves creation of shared DSM segments between the participating nodes. This is done only during the first communication between a pair of nodes.

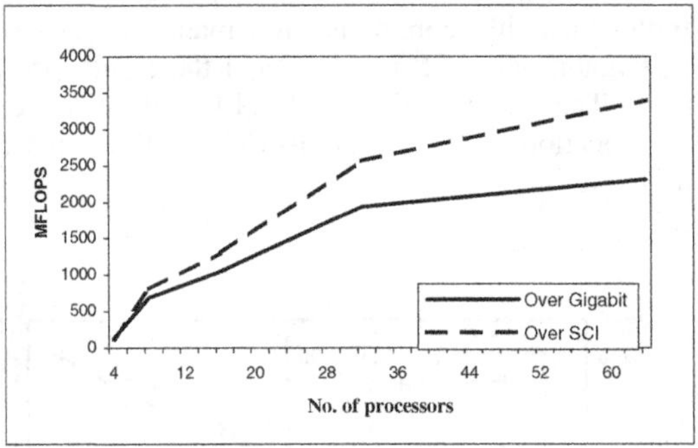

Fig. 5. CG Class C over Gigabit and SCI. The SCI network (*dotted line*) performs better than Gigabit Ethernet (*solid line*)

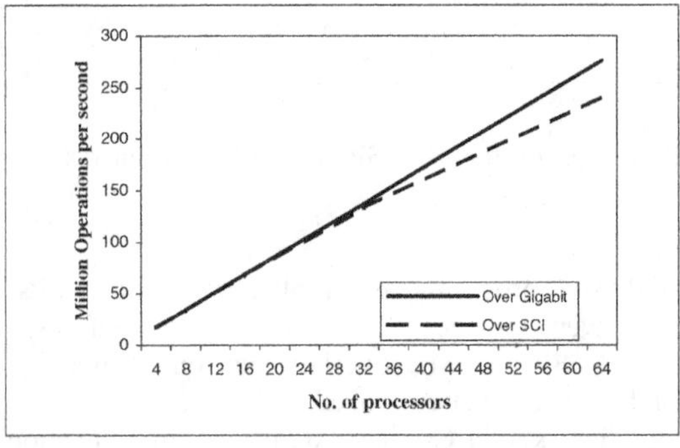

Fig. 6. EP Class C over Gigabit and SCI. Gigabit performs better than SCI due to the heavy setup overhead time in SCI

IS is another communication intensive program in the suite and from the graph in Figure 7, it is evident that SCI outperforms Gigabit Ethernet by about 25 % throughout.

LU is a simulated application that solves systems of linear equations using LU decomposition. The program is sensitive to cache availability and MPI message latencies. Hence it can be observed from the curve in Figure 8 that after 32 processors, the whole problem fits into the cache and there is a super linear increase in speedup. This is more pronounced in SCI where the superior latency figures make a large difference in the readings compared to Gigabit Ethernet.

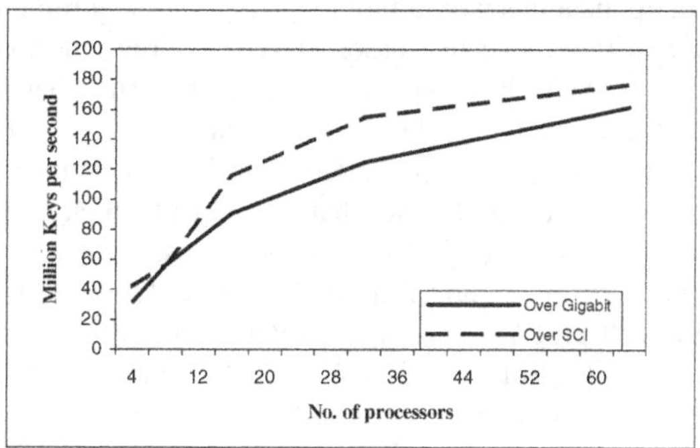

Fig. 7. IS Class C over Gigabit and SCI. SCI beats Gigabit Ethernet here due to the heavy communication pattern in IS

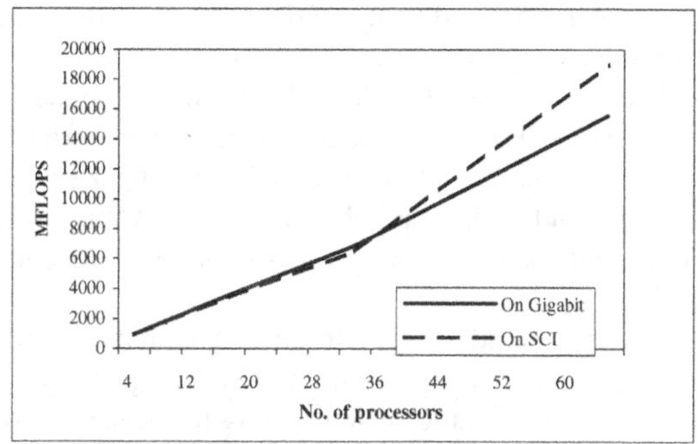

Fig. 8. LU Class C over Gigabit and SCI. LU is a matrix operation application that is both cache and latency sensitive

Summarizing, we find that programs – BT, SP and MG do not show appreciable difference between their performances using SCI and Gigabit Ethernet. This is because the programs do not fully utilize the available bandwidth of the networks. The other two programs CG and IS are communication intensive and SCI outperforms Gigabit by about 25% in IS and 50% in CG. LU performs better on SCI on large number of nodes. EP performs worse in SCI than Gigabit Ethernet because of the high overheads involved in setup of communication channels.

4 Conclusions

The tests and measurements of performance of various programs on Gigabit Ethernet and SCI interconnects shows that at this point of time, it is hard to prefer one network over the other. Going by the raw bandwidth and latency figures of the networks, it would appear that applications would fare much poorer when run on Gigabit Ethernet than on SCI. But in the above test cases, only two programs CG and IS perform significantly well on SCI than on Gigabit Ethernet. In other applications, SCI performs slightly better than Gigabit Ethernet. In the case of HPL, the massive computational load of the application offsets the large amount of communication. Though in all tests, SCI has fared better than Gigabit Ethernet, it makes a significant difference only in communication intensive applications.

A few years back, when Gigabit Ethernet was initially developed, the bandwidths obtainable from a MPI program was of the order of 300-400 Mbps and the latencies about 150 microseconds. But with PCI 64/66 and PCI-X interfaces available, the bandwidths obtained has risen to 700-800 Mbps and latencies of about 45 microseconds are achievable. It is evident from these figures that Ethernet technology is not too far away from the SANs.

The current SCI links operate at 667 MB/s out of which we are able to achieve about 250 MB/s. This arises because of the bottlenecks in PCI 64/66. In the future, we expect to see PCI-X based cards where higher speeds can be achieved. The SCI standard prescribes a peak bandwidth of 1 GB/s and over the next few years the hardware for such speeds may be available.

If the size of the cluster is small, Gigabit Ethernet would be the logical choice for the interconnection network. It is easy to setup, inexpensive, there is plenty of choice in the hardware such as adapters and switches with excellent switching speeds and whole lot of applications and tools available for Ethernet. Conversely, SCI hardware comes mostly from a single source, Dolphin, it is expensive and comparatively more difficult to setup and manage.

When the objective is to build a large cluster of hundreds of nodes, the choice is not very clear. Gigabit Ethernet switches with hundreds of ports are hard to come by. In this case, SCI, which is designed to scale up to 64 K nodes seamlessly, would be a good choice.

Making a choice of interconnection networks for a large cluster is a difficult problem. Benchmarking is a way of estimating the performance of a system or a network but it should not be the only criteria. Characteristics of the applications to be run in a production environment and non-performance issues such as availability of the networking infrastructure, complexity of the setup and ease of use are also factors to be considered.

Acknowledgements

The authors gratefully acknowledge the help received from Pankaj Saksena and Vaibhav Kumar of Computer Division, BARC in setting up the test environments.

References

1. Hermann Hellwagner, "The SCI Standard and Applications of SCI", SCI: Scalable Coherent Interface, Architecture and Software for High Performance Compute Clusters, Springer, 1999.
2. Marius Christian Liaanen, Hugo Kohmann, "Dolphin SCI Adapter Cards", SCI: Scalable Coherent Interface, Architecture and Software for High Performance Compute Clusters, Springer, 1999.
3. A. Petitet, R. C. Whaley, J. Dongarra, A. Cleary, "HPL - A Portable Implementation of the High-Performance Linpack Benchmark for Distributed-Memory Computers", http://www.netlib.org/benchmark/hpl/
4. "The NAS Parallel Benchmarks", http://www.nas.nasa.gov/Software/NPB/
5. Frederick Wong, Richard Martin, Rmezi Arpaci-Dusseau, and David Culler, "Architectural Requirements and Scalability of the NAS Parallel Benchmarks", Proc. of SC99 Conference on High Performance Networking and Computing, Nov. 1999.
6. Ahmad Faraj and Xin Yuan "Communication Characteristics in the NAS Parallel Benchmarks," Fourteenth IASTED International Conference on Parallel and Distributed Computing and Systems (PDCS 2002), pages 729-734, Cambridge, MA, November 4-6, 2002.

Performance Evaluation of a Modified-Cyclic-Banyan Based ATM / IP Switching Fabric

V.S. Tripathi[1] and S.Tiwari[2]

[1] Department of Electronics and Communication Engineering, MMMEC, Gorakhpur, India
vijay_s_t@yahoo.com
[2] Department of Electronics Engineering, MNNIT, Allahabad, India
sudarshan_tiwari114@hotmail.com

Abstract. This paper focuses on designing a large N X N high-performance Fast Packet switch suitable for mixed ATM and IP traffic. It is a Banyan network using cyclic interconnection among switching elements of the same stage. We employ deflection-routing algorithm in each switching element. The proposed routing is as simple as that of the generic Banyan network, and all the switching elements (SE's) have a uniform structure. To design the proposed network and to develop its self-routing property we observe that all the SE's of the Banyan network are arranged in a regular pattern topologically. We, thus, present a growable switch architecture based on the topological properties of Banyan Networks. As a result, we show that the new network has a far better performance than the other networks.

1 Introduction

Fast Packet switches route the packets towards their respective destinations at a high speed of a few Giga Bits per second. They provide low bit-error rates, and are well supported for use on high-speed fiber links. They find their application in Broadband Integrated Services Digital Networks (B-ISDN) and Asynchronous Transfer Mode / Internet Protocol Integrated Networks (A/I Net)[1 – 3]. An ATM/IP fast packet switch is shown in figure 1.

The core of a fast packet switch, which influences both the performance and the cost, is its switching fabric. Banyan network is a popular choice due to its suitability to VLSI implementation and its self-routing capability [7]. The switching fabrics based on Banyan Networks are self-routing, simple and modular but they are blocking type switches.

To treat the problem of blocking, deflection routing is used in high-speed networks, since it gives a good performance and is easy to implement. Deflection routing in Delta networks was proposed by Park, Yoon and Lee for implementation of a Cyclic Banyan Network [8]. It requires complex routing decisions at switching element level, which increases delay.

R.K. Ghosh and H. Mohanthy (Eds.): ICDCIT 2004, LNCS 3347, pp. 60–64, 2004.

We present a high-performance Modified-Cyclic-Banyan (MCB) Network based Fast Packet switch. It is a cyclic-deflection self-routing Banyan network. The proposed network has a far better performance and scalability than other networks.

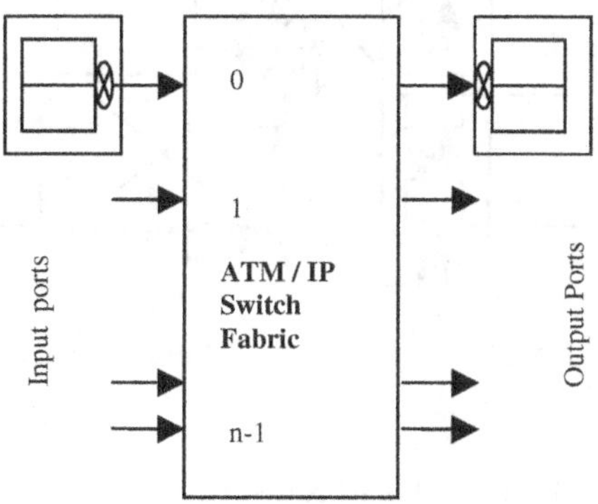

Fig. 1. ATM/IP Switch

2 Architecture of MCB Network Based ATM / IP Switching Fabric

Banyan networks belong to the class of Multistage Interconnection Networks (MINs). They were defined in [5] and are characterized by the property that there is exactly one path from any input to any output. This network consists of Switching Elements (SE) and links. Each SE is a 2 X 2 crossbar switch, which can receive packets at each of its two input ports and send them through each of its two output ports. The SEs are joined in a systematic manner to form stages of SEs. Each SE in stage j is connected to SEs in stages j -1 and j +1 through links. In an N X N Banyan network, there are log_2N stages and each stage has $N/2$ SEs.

2.1 Cyclic Banyan Network

Topological properties of Banyan network were first studied in [8]. Each stage of the Banyan network is composed of a sequence of the cyclic group, realized with SEs.

The cyclic Banyan network can be obtained from the basic Banyan network by the addition of links chaining all SE's of a stage. Park et. al. proposed a destination-tag based routing algorithm for this network. They also illustrate fully adaptive routing control algorithm. This Algorithm is good for Delta network, which has a uniform pattern for links between successive stages. When link pattern is stage-dependant, as in Banyan network, this routing algorithm will take huge amount of time. Moreover, a packet destined to last output port of an n stage Banyan network can not reach there in a short time, if it is somehow de-routed to first SE at the $(n-1)$ th stage.

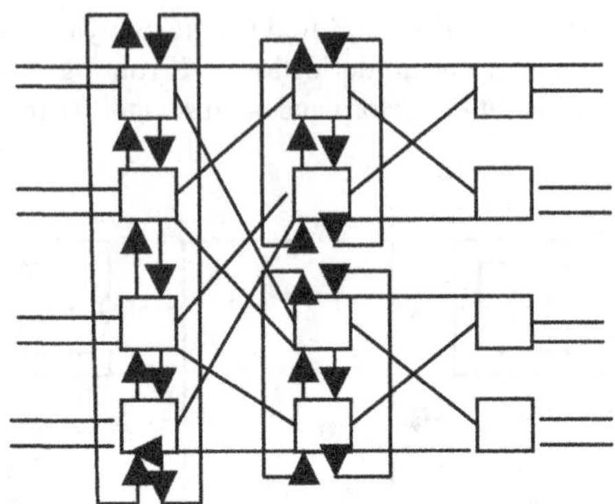

Fig. 2. MCB Network based ATM/IP switching fabric

2.2 Modified Cyclic Banyan (MCB) Network Based ATM / IP Switching Fabric

Modified Cyclic Banyan network based ATM / IP Switching fabric has following properties and advantages: simplicity, self-routing property, modularity, systematic link pattern, reliability and robustness. The MCB network can be obtained from the basic Banyan network by addition of lateral links at all Switching Elements (SE's) of a cyclic group in the stage. Starting from the first (0th) stage, k^{th} stage has 2^k number of cyclic groups within it. The number of switching elements in each cyclic group of kth stage is $(n/2^{k+1})$, where n is number of ports. Implementation of additional links requires augmented SE's, each having lateral-in links and lateral-out links along with the input and output links. SE is thus a 4X4 crossbar switch. Figure 2 shows an example of an 8X8 MCB network.

2.3 Routing Algorithm

When the SE's are grouped in the given way, the routing decision becomes very simple. A blocked packet will try to start from next SEs situated in the same cyclic group. Whenever a path is found, the packet is transmitted otherwise it keeps trying from next SE in a cyclic manner. All SE's have a single algorithm, independent to the stage, so its implementation in VLSI for all SE's is universal and therefore, simple.

3 Performance Evaluation

Following the analytical tool presented in [6] we can assume that:

(i) Loading is balanced. With a balanced load the state of each switching network in stage k should be statistically the same.

(ii) The states of the two buffers within a switching element are statistically independent. We can make some definitions as follows:

$p_0(k,t)$=the probability that the switching element buffer at stage k is empty at the beginning of the tth clock.

$p_1(k,t)=1-p_0(k,t)$

$q(k,t)$=the probability that a packet is ready to enter a switching element buffer at stage k during the tth clock period.

$r(k,t)$=the probability that a packet in a switching element buffer at stage k is able to move (forward) into the next stage during the tth clock period.

The set of equations that models the dynamics of the system is:

$$q(k,t)=8/9\times p_1(k-1,t).p_1(k-1,t).p_1(k-1,t).p_1(k-1,t)+10/13\times p_1(k-1,t).p_1(k-1,t).p_1(k-1,t) p_0(k-1,t) + 9/12\times p_1(k-1,t).p_1(k-1,t).\ p_0(k-1,t).p_0(k-1,t) + 1/2\times p_1(k-1,t).p_1(k-1,t)\ .\ p_1(k-1,t)\ .p_0(k-1,t);\quad k=2, 3, 4.........n. \qquad ....(1)$$

$$r(k,t)=[p_0(k,t)+8/9p_1(k,t)]\times[p_0(k+1,t)+p_1(k+1,t)\ r(k+1,t)],\quad k=1,2,3,......,n-1.$$

$$r(n,t)=[p_0(n,t)+8/9\ .\ p_1(n,t)] \qquad ....(2)$$

$$p_0(k,t+1)=[1-q(k,t)]\ [p_0(k,t)+p_1(k,t)r(k,t)],$$

$$p_1(k,t+1)=1-p_0(k,t+1) \qquad ....(3)$$

If there is an equilibrium solution, these quantities should converge to time-independent values for $q(k), r(k), p_0(k)$ and $p_1(k)$. The two performance measures of most interest - normalized throughput and delay can be calculated after solving these equations iteratively for the equilibrium values.

4 Results and Conclusion

The results of analysis and simulation of a 16X16 MCB network based switch are shown in figures 3 and 4. The graphs clearly depict that the MCB network has very good delay/throughput performance as compared to simple Banyan network. The basic building blocks are small modules, and can be used to construct a large-scale ATM / IP Switching fabric. This modular architecture can provide multicast services

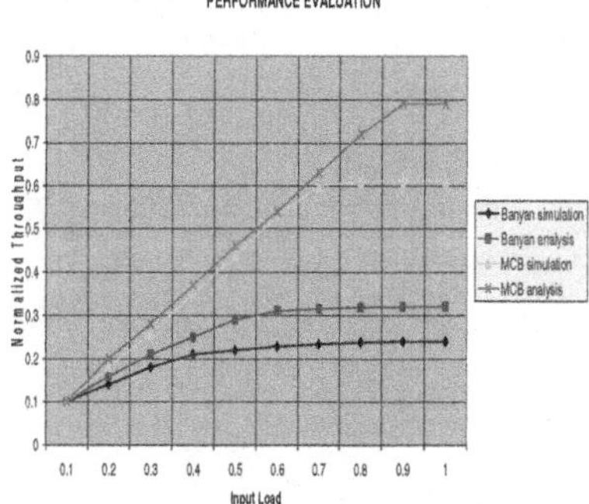

Fig. 3. Normalized Throughput

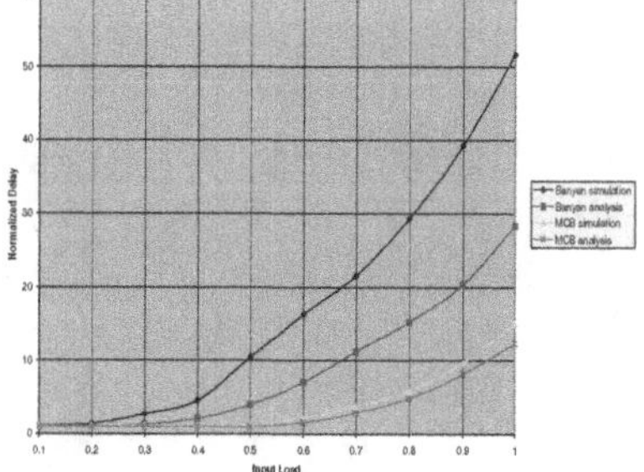

Fig. 4. Normalized Delay

also. Routing is very simple and easy to implement. Physically, it can be realized as an extension of existing Banyan Networks. This flexible and distributed architecture is the key to simplify the operation of the whole switching system. The modularity implies less stringent synchronization requirements, and makes higher speed implementation possible.

References

1. C. Y. Tsui, LC. Kwan, and C. T. Lea, "VLSI Implementation of a switch fabric for Mixed ATM and IP Traffic", Design Automation Conference, 2000. Proceedings of the ASP-DAC 2000. Asia and South Pacific, pp. 5-6, 25-28 Jan. 2000.
2. C. T. Lea, C. Y. Tsui, L. C. Y. Kwan, S. K. M. Chan and A. H. W. Chan, "A/I Net: A network that integrates ATM and IP"; IEEE Network, pp 48-55, January, 1999.
3. J. Schmitt, M. Karsten, R. Steinmetz; "Design and implementation of a flexible, QoS-aware IP/ATM adaptation module", High Performance Switching and Routing, 2000. ATM 2000. Proceedings of the IEEE Conference on, Pages: 267 – 274, 26-29 June 2000.
4. R. Onvural, "Asynchronous Transfer Mode Networks: Performance Issues", Norwood, MA, Artech House, Inc., 1995.
5. G. R. Goke and G. J. Lipovski, "Banyan Networks for partitioning multiprocessor systems", in Proc. 1st Annu. Symp. Compu. Arch., pp.21 -28, 1973.
6. Y. C. Jenq, "Performance analysis of a packet switch based on single-buffered Banyan Network", IEEE Journal on Selected areas in Communication, Vol SAC-1, no. 6, pp.1014-1021, December 1983.
7. S. Cheneemalavagu and M. Malek, " Analysis and simulation of banyan interconnection networks with 2 x 2 , 4 x 4, and 8X 8 switching elements, In proc. Real-Time Syst. Symp. LA, CA, Dec, 1982.
8. J. H. Park, H. Yoon, H. K. Lee, "The cyclic banyan network: a fault tolerant multistage interconnection network with the fully-adaptive self-routing", 7th IEEE Symposium on Parallel and Distributed Processing, Texas, pp 702, October, 1995.
9. H. S. Laskaridis, G. I. Papadimitriou, A. S. Pomportsis; "Reconfigurable ATM switch fabrics using traffic history"; IEEE Communications Letters, Volume: 6 , Issue: 7, Pages:300 – 302 , July 2002.

A Scalable and Robust QoS Architecture for WiFi P2P Networks

Sathish Rajasekhar, Ibrahim Khalil, and Zahir Tari

School of Computer Science and Information Technology,
RMIT University, Melbourne - 3000
(sathish, ibrahimk, zahirt)@cs.rmit.edu.au

Abstract. Peer-to-Peer (P2P) resource sharing between mobile devices in Wireless Fidelity (WiFi) hot-spots environment is a challenging problem. This would require an infrastructure with automated process for registering new mobile devices, as well as authentication and authorisation of existing devices. Further, issues such as maintenance, and updating the state information, as devices join and leave the P2P network; optimising route selection and protection of the existing mobile devices from malicious devices are crucial. To address these issues, we propose a generalised architecture and a dynamic protocol for effective and optimal file transfer between devices. We use quality of service (QoS) capacity-to-hop count ratio, routing algorithm, to find an optimal mobile device for a service request. The goal and contribution of this paper is to provide a scalable, robust and reliable architecture incorporating QoS; effective and optimal communication for P2P networks in a cooperative manner.

1 Introduction

Internet is exponentially exploding and as changes to the electronic technology evolve, P2P will play a pivotal role in enduring information sharing, resource management enabling interoperability and QoS. 80% of data collected on an edge router at France Telecom IP backbone network was P2P traffic [2]. Also on the Sprint IP backbone P2P and unknown traffic type was about 80% [6]. As the processing power and memory of mobile devices such as personal digital assistant (PDA) is increasing, resource sharing between these devices becomes more rampant in the near future and users will start demanding QoS. Unfortunately, current P2P technology does not provide a stable, scalable, reliable and robust architecture addressing QoS issues.

We propose a super-peer based architecture for P2P resource sharing in the core network addressing signalling, reliability, scalability and QoS issues. A super-peer is a static and powerful device, which intelligently and collectively manages the entire operation of file transfer and assists peers in finding optimal QoS path. Most peer devices exhibits different characteristics with respect to their capabilities such as bandwidth, storage, and processing power. These capabilities are exploited by super-peers. Peer devices update their location and state information to super-peers. Each device has the same range to send and receive information. These devices form a connected multi-hop wireless network.

R.K. Ghosh and H. Mohanty (Eds.): ICDCIT 2004, LNCS 3347, pp. 65–74, 2004.

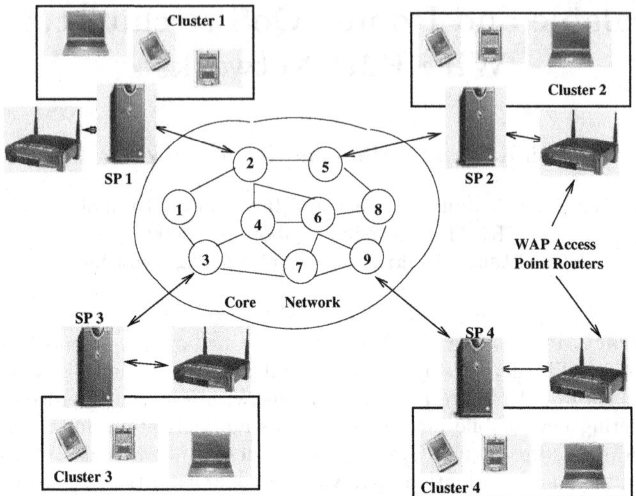

Fig. 1. Mobile Devices in WiFi Hot-spots

For example, let us consider an airport where passengers with hand held devices wants to share resources. Super-peers SP1, SP2, SP3 and SP4 as shown in Figure 1 are connected to the core network through the wireless access point (WAP). If a passenger within SP1 wants to download a file, the passenger's device is sensed by the WAP router. SP1 initiates a file search in the network. If the file is found in devices that belong to SP2 and SP3, an optimal QoS path based on capacity-to-hop count [12] is selected.

Most of the existing work done in P2P systems are to effectively look for data [3][15]. Napster [1], Gnutella [1] and Freenet [1] are P2P technologies developed and have problems such as single point of failure, signalling and scalability issues. A. Klemm et al in [11] propose a protocol called Optimised Routing Independent Overlay Network (ORION). This protocol works on a centralised approach leading to a central point of failure. In [4] the authors define XREP protocol, but repositories on peers cause load burden. None of these existing approaches address scalability, reliability, load sharing and QoS path selection criterion.

Our goal is to provide a generalised scalable, reliable and robust architecture for resource sharing incorporating QoS path selection for P2P systems. We propose a Mobile Authentication and Resource eXchange (MARX) protocol for this purpose. Resource sharing is done using the state information obtained by IDMaps [5]. IDMaps provides the network distances in terms of available bandwidth between two hosts. The available bandwidth information obtained by IDMaps is used by capacity-to-hop count ratio routing [12] algorithm to help super-peers find optimal QoS paths. We also incorporate caching schemes for efficient information retrieval and replicate super-peer database, to encounter single point failure. Our objective is to propose a QoS architecture and investigate such issues. We also show that use of super-peer based QoS architecture helps in authentication and authorisation of devices.

This paper is organised as follows. Section 2 is related work and puts our work in context. The architecture is detailed in section 3. In section 4, the protocol and routing issues are discussed with an example to illustrate capacity-to-hop count routing algorithm. We conclude in section 5 with directions for future work.

2 Related Work

A huge body of work has been done in efficient information retrieval systems such as CAN [13], Chord [15], Pastry [14], and Tapestry [9]. These information retrieval approaches implement distributed hash tables (DHT). A query is associated with a key and the query is routed to a peer holding the key value in DHT to locate information. Napster [1], Gnutella [1], Freenet [1] etc are some of the early P2P approaches. Napster, a centralised scenario, leads to single point failure. In Gnutella, a decentralised model, peers generate redundant signals all over the network. Freenet tries to overcomes these issues to some extent, but do not address QoS issues.

A protocol for dynamic file sharing was proposed by Klemm et al [11], called ORION. This protocol has redundant data at nodes and is prone to single point failure. A cluster based architecture was proposed in [10], where peers are clustered based on content awareness. This defeats the purpose of a mobile environment as peers should be allowed to move freely from one WiFi hot-spot to another. Also, the authors indicate that the quality of the clusters formed is not guaranteed.

Damiani et al in [4] propose a secure and robust reputation mechanism for choosing reliable resources using XREP protocol. They emphasise on two repositories, a resource repository and a servant repository on every peer device. In a WiFi environment, holding two repositories by a mobile device is a daunting task and is not achievable.

Our approach attempts to eliminate the above pitfalls by providing a a scalable, robust, reliable architecture and protocol ensuring QoS path selection amongst peer devices in WiFi hot spots.

3 WiFi P2P File Sharing Architecture: An Overview

Mobile devices are capable of exchanging information using Wireless Fidelity. WiFi defines the wireless technology in the IEEE 802.11 specification including the wireless protocols 802.11a, 802.11b, and 802.11g in a WiFi hot-spot. A WiFi hot-spot is a location in which 802.11 wireless technology exists and is available for use to consumers [8]. We propose to build a generalised architecture with existing technologies. The main components of our proposed architecture are detailed in Figure 2 and discussed below.

Super-Peer: A new wave in P2P systems, providing advancements of having a centralised database in a decentralised environment. They are responsible for

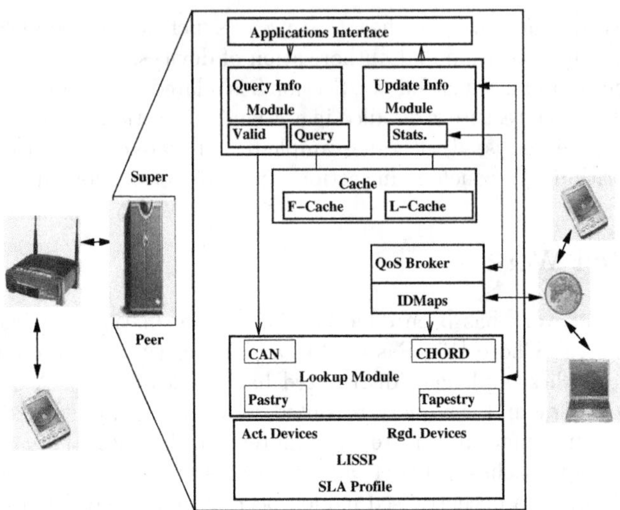

Fig. 2. Internal Architecture Overview

servicing a request from a peer. Super-peers are powerful static devices that helps in selecting optimal QoS paths. Also, super-peers help in registration, authorisation, authentication and accounting of a device.

Query Information Module: The functions are two fold. Module **Valid** checks for peer authorisation. This is done by checking the super-peer database. The module **Query** initiates search to find suitable resources that satisfies the QoS requirements of the generated query.

Update Information Module: The availability of the optimal peer device for file transfer based on the QoS requirements is updated. The module **Stats** updates the cache with the most popular files accessed based on the frequency of down-load.

Caching: A popular file may be accessed more frequently. Instead of searching the same file every time, these files are cached. We classify cache as file cache (F-Cache) and location cache (L-Cache). **F-Cache** stores the most frequently accessed files. **L-Cache** stores the most frequently accessed location. Caching reduces signalling and overhead traffic.

QoS Module: This module consists of QoS interface and IDMaps Interface. **QoS Broker** ensures that the QoS requirements between the service requester and the device that is offering service is met. It establishing a reliable connection in an optimal manner using capacity to hop count ratio routing algorithm [12]. QoS broker thus updates the information regarding the file and its statistics to update info module. Internet Distance Map Service (IDMaps) a global architecture for Internet host distance estimation and distribution [5], provides quickly and efficiently the network distances in terms of metrics such as latency or bandwidth between Internet hosts. Higher level services collect distance information and bandwidth to build a virtual distance map of the Internet and estimate the distance between any pair of IP addresses. For example in Figure 1, a device in SP1 requests for a resource that is found in SP2 and SP3. IDMaps provides the available bandwidth information between SP1 and SP2, and SP1 and SP3 respectively. Based on the information provided, a routing decision is made by the QoS broker using capacity to hop count routing algorithm. Thus IDMaps provides network distance in terms of latency or bandwidth and it is scalable.

Lookup Module: A search for requested resource is carried on using any one of the existing lookup modules such as CAN, Pastry, Chord, Tapestry algorithms.

LISSP: The Local Information Source Super Peer, is a centralised information database. This aids in authentication of a mobile device. The services for any peer device is processed though LISSP. It contains a list of active devices **Act devices** and registered devices **Rgd devices**. Act. devices are devices currently present in the super-peer cluster. Rgd. devices are devices registered in the super-peer but currently not available. **SLA** is the service level agreement between WiFi customers and WiFi service providers. The SLA profile is maintained in the LISSP module.

A device requesting service is called *service receiver*, and that offering the service is called as *service provider*. The LISSP checks the device's profile for authorisation. If the device is registered in the WAP database or the LISSP, then file request query is generated and serviced. The F-Cache and L-Cache is checked for the resource. The update info module informs the service receiver regarding the requested file or its location. Else, the lookup module initiates search for the requested resource. IDMaps gathers available bandwidth of service providers and informs the QoS broker. The broker selects an optimal device based on capacity to hop count ratio algorithm, which is discussed in the routing sub-section. In the next section, we discuss the properties and working of the proposed protocol.

4 Mobile Authentication and Resource eXchange (MARX) Protocol

The proposed dynamic MARX protocol aids in *file discovery, connection setup and maintenance, file transfer and termination of connection*. The protocol takes into consideration the search initiated by the lookup module through IDMaps and selects the optimal peer based on capacity-to-hop count routing algorithm.

4.1 MARX Overview and Assumptions

For example, from Figure 1 a mobile device in super-peer SP1 wants to download a file. The steps involved are summarised as follows:

1. The device is registered and authenticated with a unique address under SP1 or some other super-peer.

2. MAC address of a new device is made known to the local super-peer.
3. The device requests its super-peer (SP1) for a file.
4. The device gets a response from SP1 regarding the file availability; after initiating a search, QoS broker identifies the service provider, which may be within SP1 or a different super-peer.
5. QoS Broker selects the optimal peer based on capacity-to-hop count ratio.
6. The device requests for connection from the identified service provider.
7. The device receives data from the service provider peer.
8. The device disconnects from service provider after file transfer.

Some basic assumptions are made to define our protocol. The communicating peer devices may be in the same or different cluster of the same super-peer or in a different super-peer altogether. The clusters are independent and may be under one super-peer. Sharable information from peer devices are periodically updated to their super-peer LISSP database. A cluster of peer devices connected to the super-peer through a WAP is depicted in Figure 3. The peer devices are sensed through the WAP and its database for authentication as they enter the cluster.

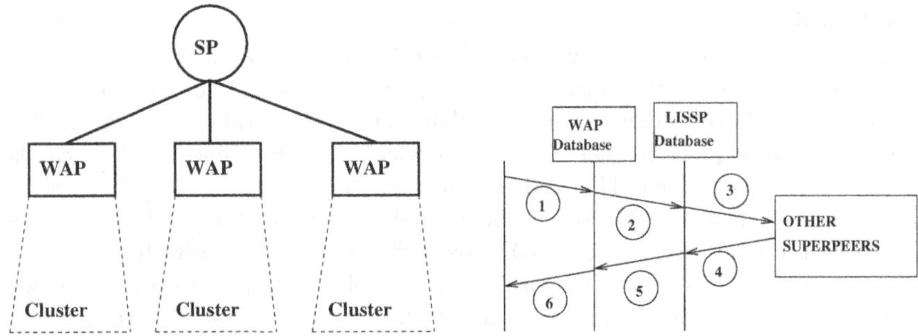

Fig. 3. Logical Overview of Clusters and Super-Peer Connectivity

Fig. 4. Global Device Authentication

During the process of authentication, one of the three possibilities rise. The device information can be found in the clusters WAP or LISSP database of the super-peer; if not found, a search is initiated amongst other super-peers as shown in Figure 4. Steps 1 and 2 of Figure 4 fail to authenticate the peer device and hence the other super-peers are queried for authentication as shown in step 3. The steps 4, 5 and 6 informs the device regarding its authenticity; thirdly, the device may be a new device accessing the WAP. The new device has to register first with a super-peer. Once a query is generated by a device, a search is initiated in the super-peer cache, within the super-peer or a device in different super-peers.

Resource in Cache: Figure 5 illustrates how communication between the device and cache takes place. Once a query is initiated (step 1), the cache is checked for the requested resource (step 2). Steps 3 and 4 confirm that the resource is present in cache. The device (service requester) requests for the file (step 5) and establishes a connection. Step 6 represents file transfer between the cache and the service receiver. Step 7 indicates disconnection.

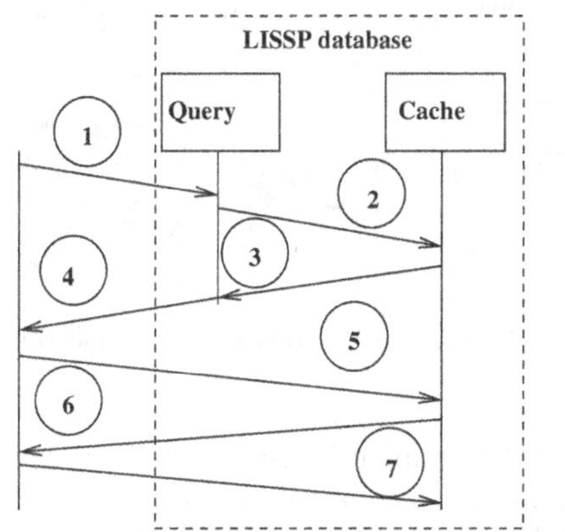

Fig. 5. Cache Access

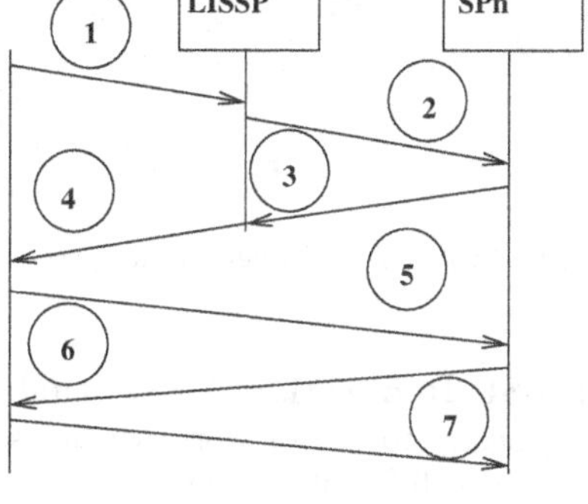

Fig. 6. Cluster Access

Resource Within Cluster: If the cache does not contain the requested file, query is passed on to the lookup module. The lookup module initiates a search within its LISSP database (step 1) and the super-peer (step 2) as shown in Figure 6. If one or more devices within the cluster has the file (step 3), then the QoS broker identifies the optimal peer, based on certain policies, such as distance, load, how long the device was in the cluster and informs the service receiver. Load is defined as the number of devices that are using the services of the device identified. Based on the QoS broker information, update info module informs the service receiver, regarding service provider (step 4). Steps 5, 6 and 7 of Figure 6 represents file transfer request, the file transfer and termination of connection amongst peer devices within a cluster.

Resource in different Super Peer: The service provider at times cannot be found in the same vicinity or in the same super-peer. Also, peers may not respond due to other activities. Hence, a request is issued to other super-peers and networks as shown in Figure 7. The QoS broker gets an updated list of super-peers that are willing to share information through IDMaps. The QoS broker decides the optimal super-peer based on certain parameters such as delay, available bandwidth, and hops in terms of capacity to hop count ratio [12]. The information is then passed on to update info module and data transfer takes place. Step 1 in Figure 7 initiates a query. Step 2 issues a search. Step 3i return multiple hits. The QoS broker selects optimal service provider device and informs the service requester through update info module as in step 4 of Figure 7. Steps 5, 6 and 7 indicate file transfer and its completion.

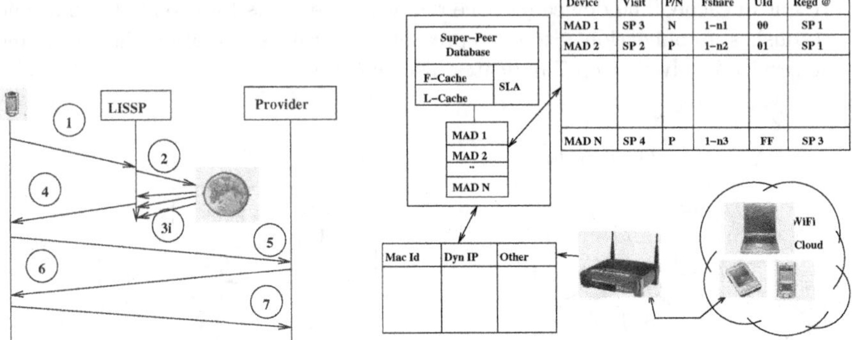

Fig. 7. Access to Different Networks

Fig. 8. LISSP Database and Connectivity

LISSP Replication: LISSP database prohibits unauthorised users from gaining access to the network resources. Figure 8 depicts a LISSP database, SLAs between different clusters and the mobile access devices (MAD). Each MAD holds information in the LISSP database regarding its identity (MAC address), super-peers visited, and list of sharable information. Devices update the LISSP as and when they have new information to share. Also the devices inform LISSP where they were first registered. Any centralised system is prone to single point of failure. Hence we propose replication of the LISSP database in super-peers. Each super-peer node will have its nearest two neighbouring super-peer LISSP databases as backups thus eliminating single point failure.

4.2 Routing

QoS path selection is the process of selecting a path based on QoS requirements such as bandwidth or delay [7]. Our QoS routing algorithm maximises the available path capacity to hop count as described in [12]. The objective of QoS routing is to eliminate the inaccurate state information, the proposed QoS routing can achieve higher efficiency and better optimisation. As we increase the number of hops, the ratio path capacity to hop count is applied. Mathematically,

$$\frac{C_{avl}(P)}{h(P)} \tag{1}$$

The available capacity is denoted as C_{avl}, P a path and $h(P)$ the hop count of a path P. The available capacity to hop count ratio is computed as follows:

$$C_{avl}(P) = min_{l \in P}(b_{avl}(l)) \tag{2}$$

The routing algorithm uses the available capacity to hop count ratio as the criterion for optimality, and its correctness is proved in [12]. This algorithm obtains paths with maximal ratio of available capacity to hop count from the source super-peer node to all the other super-peer nodes. We illustrate QoS

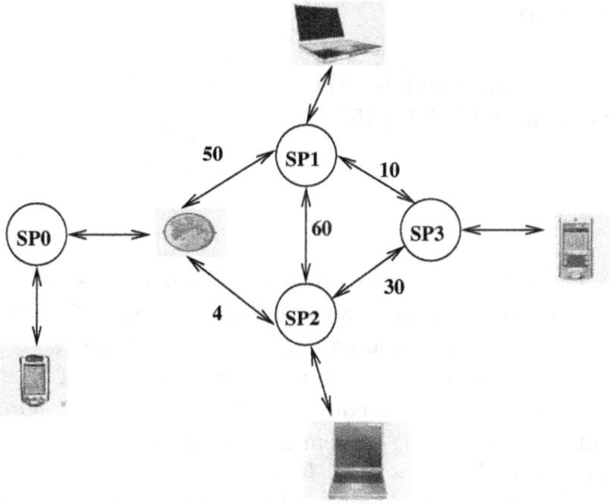

Fig. 9. Routing Illustration using Capacity-to-Hop Ratio Algorithm

path selection using an example as shown in Figure 9. If super-peer $SP0$ wants to route to super-peer $SP3$, the optimal route has to be determined. Initially bandwidth (B) at the super-peer SP0 is set to ∞ and all the other super-peers, SP1, SP2 and SP3 to zero. Predecessor of all super-peers are set to NIL. After the first hop from $SP0$, we have $B[SP1]$=50, $B[SP2]$=4 and $B[SP3]$=0. We also have the hop count $h[SP1] = h[SP2] = h[SP3]$=1. After the second hop from $SP0$, there is no change for $SP1$, while $B[SP2]$=25 and $h[SP2]$=2. The details for $SP3$ are successively updated to $B[SP3]$=5 and $h[SP3]$=2, followed by $B[SP3]$=10 and $h[SP3]$=3. The complexity of the algorithm is similar to that of Bellman-Ford algorithm.

5 Conclusion

In this paper, we have described a scalable, robust, reliable, generalised QoS architecture for P2P systems. We provide an optimal QoS path selection based on capacity-to-hop count ratio routing algorithm for efficient file transfer between devices in a P2P network. We propose a dynamic protocol MARX, to effectively carry out file transfer using customer-provider SLAs. Our super-peer based architecture do not allow unauthorised devices to access the network and protects existing devices from malicious devices. A new device is registered and the whole process is automated without any human intervention.

While we have not carried out simulation on P2P networks to show the effectiveness of our proposed architecture, the QoS path selection algorithm applied in our current approach was validated in IP networks [12]. In our future work, we would like to further simulate/emulate our QoS architecture and QoS path selection algorithms for P2P networks. We envisage a prototype model for validation and verification purposes. Also, we would like to investigate and propose new techniques for load balancing among peer devices in a P2P network.

Acknowledgement

This work is proudly supported by the Australian Research Council (ARC), under discovery Scheme, DP 0346545.

References

1. K. Abeer and M. Hauswirth. "Peer-to-Peer information systems: concepts and models, state-of-the-art, and future systems," Proceedings of ACM SIGSOFT Software Engineering Notes, Vol. 26, Issue 5, pp. 326-327, 2001.
2. N. B. Azzouna and F. Guillemin, "Experimental analysis of the impact of peer-to-peer applications on traffic in commercial IP networks," [Online]. Available: http://perso.rd.francetelecom.fr/guillemin/PDFfiles/paper20.pdf
3. H. Balakrishnan, M. F. Kaashoek, D. Karger, R. Morris and I. Stoica, "Looking Up Data in P2P Systems" Proceedings of Communications of the ACM, Vol. 46, No. 2, pp. 43-48, 2003.
4. E. Damiani, S. De. C. Vimercati, S. Paraboschi, P. Samarati and F. Violante, "A Reputation-Based Approach for choosing Reliable Resources in Peer-to-Peer Networks," Proceedings of ACM Conference on Computer and Communications Security, pp. 207-216, 2002.
5. P. Francis, S. Jamin, C. Jin, D. Raz, Y. Shavitt, L. Zhang, "IDMAPS: A Global Internet Host Distance Estimation Service," *IEEE/ACM Transactions on Networking*, 2001.
6. C. Fraleigh et al, "Packet-Level Traffic Measurements from the Sprint IP Backbone", IEEE Network, 17(6), pp. 6-16, 2003.
7. R. Guerin and A. Orda, "Computing Shortest Paths for Any number of Hops", IEEE/ACM Transactions on Networking, 10(5), pp. 613-620, 2002.
8. C. Hesselmen, H. Eertink, I. Widya and E. Huizer, "A Mobility-aware Broadcasting Infrastructure for a Wireless Internet with Hot-spots," Proceedings of WMASH, pp. 103-112, 2003.
9. K. Hildrum, J. Kubiatowicz, S. Rao and B. Zhao, "Distributed Object Location in a Dynamic Network," In Proceedings of 14th ACM Symp. on Parallel Algorithms and architectures, 2002.
10. I. A. Klampanos and J. M. Jose, "An Architecture for Information Retrieval over Semi-Collaborating Peer-to-Peer Networks," Proceedings of ACM Symposium on Applied Computing, pp. 1078-1083, 2004.
11. A. Klemm, C. Lindemann, and O. P. Waldhorst, "A Special-Purpose Peer-to-Peer File Sharing system for Mobile Ad Hoc Networks." [Online]
12. S. Rajasekhar, B. Lloyd-Smith, and Z. Tari, "QoS Path Routing based on Capacity to Link Ratio in Networks," Proceedings of International Conference on Networks, Parallel and Distributed Processing, and Applications, Japan, pp. 188-142, 2002.
13. S. Ratnaswamy, P. Francis, M. Handley, R. Karp and S. Shenker, "A Scalable content-addressable network," In Proceedings of ACM SIGCOMM, 2001.
14. A. Rowstron and P. Druschel, "Pastry: Scalable, distributed object location and routing for large-scale peer-to-peer systems," In Proceedings of the 18th IFIP/ACM International Conference on Distributed Systems Platforms, 2001.
15. I. Stoica, R. Morris, D. Karger, M. F. Kaashoek and H. Balakrishnan, "Chord: A Scalable Peer-to-Peer Lookup Service for Internet Applications," Proceedings of SIGCOMM, pp. 149-160, 2001.

NEC: Node Energy Based Clustering Protocol for Wireless Sensor Networks with Guaranteed Connectivity*

Shilpa Dhar[1], Krishnendu Roy[2], and Rajgopal Kannan[3]

[1] Department of Computer Science, Louisiana State University, Baton Rouge, LA 70803, USA
sdhar1@lsu.edu

[2] Department of Electrical and Computer Engineering, Louisiana State University, Baton Rouge, LA 70803, USA
kroy1@lsu.edu

[3] Department of Computer Science, Louisiana State University, Baton Rouge, LA 70803, USA
rkannan@csc.lsu.edu

Abstract. Wireless sensor networks are continually being deployed in various application areas which are posing various new challenges. Yet, one problem that still remains central to the operability and applicability of sensor networks is the limited energy of the sensor nodes which directly limits the network lifetime. Various schemes have been proposed to optimize the energy conservation, some of which use network-redundancy to switch off the radios of some nodes. Ensuring minimum connectivity in such a case is the main objective, which the existing papers address inadequately. We propose a scheme of topology control based on the concept of strong and weak nodes. In our protocol clustering is done keeping in mind the lifetime of all the nodes that are awake and not just the lifetime of the cluster-head hence ensuring that minimum connectivity is always guaranteed.

Keywords: Wireless sensor networks, Energy conservation, Strong nodes, Weak nodes, Connectivity.

1 Introduction

Wireless sensor networks are increasingly being used in varied applications. Some of the potential applications of wireless sensor networks are environmental monitoring, smart spaces, military, medical systems, robotic explorations etc. A wireless sensor network usually consists of a large number of sensor nodes that self-configure themselves into a multi-hop network. These nodes are untethered [2]

* This work was supported in part by NSF grant IIS-0329738 and an ITR grant #0312632.

R.K. Ghosh and H. Mohanty (Eds.): ICDCIT 2004, LNCS 3347, pp. 75–84, 2004.

and have to rely on local battery power. Thus the single most important metric that dominates these wireless sensor networks is energy consumption in the nodes as it directly influences the network lifetime. In a densely deployed wireless sensor network node redundancy is used to optimize the energy consumption in the network and increase the operational lifetime of the network.

Previous research shows that the radio in the sensor nodes consumes energy while sending, receiving, overhearing and listening to the medium. The large amount of energy consumed by the nodes while idle listening and overhearing leads to the conclusion that energy consumption can be optimized only if the radio in the sensor nodes is periodically powered off. In a densely deployed large sensor network multiple paths exists between the nodes hence minimum connectivity in the network can still be ensured even if some of the intermediate nodes are selectively powered off [2, 5, 6].

Clustering is one of the most fundamental ways used to design scalable sensor networks. A clustering algorithm arranges the network into subsets of nodes with a cluster-head at the center of each cluster. A regular high level structure is obtained from good clustering [1]. It is easier to design efficient energy conserving protocols for this high level structure than at the level of individual nodes. Localized algorithms can be used in these clusters which reduce the centralized coordination necessary and require that nodes interact with only their neighbors thus reducing the communication costs.

In this paper we propose Node Energy based Conserving Protocol (NEC), a new protocol for clustering in wireless sensor networks which conserves energy as well as ensures minimum connectivity in the network. NEC takes into account the energy of the cluster-head and all the nodes in the cluster which are awake at any time to ensure minimum network connectivity. For the purpose of energy conservation only the cluster-head and the nodes of the cluster which provide reachability to other clusters are powered on. Thus to provide connectivity in the network the cluster-head as well as the nodes in the cluster which provide reachability to other clusters have to be operational for the same amount of time before re-clustering takes place. In NEC the energy of communicating nodes has to be monitored so that minimum network connectivity is ensured.

2 Related Work

For the last few years optimizing energy consumption has been the focus of research in sensor networks. LEACH [3] (Low-Energy Adaptive Clustering Hierarchy), is one such clustering based protocol that uses randomized rotation of cluster-heads to evenly distribute the energy load among the sensors in the network. In order to avoid the energy drainage of cluster-heads, the cluster-head positions are not fixed and are self elected at different time intervals.

We studied the Cluster-based Energy Conservation (CEC) protocol [5] which directly and dynamically measures the network connectivity so that energy can be conserved by identifying the nodes which can be selectively powered off. In CEC cluster formation takes place in a distributed fashion and clusters are interconnected to each other through overlapping nodes. Each cluster has a cluster-head and all the members are within direct radio range of the cluster-head. In CEC initially each node broadcasts a discovery message that contains its node ID, cluster ID and estimated lifetime. Here a node which is a member of more that one cluster is called a gateway. CEC first selects the cluster-head and then the gateway nodes connecting the clusters. A node elects itself as the cluster-head if it has the longest lifetime of all its neighbor, breaking ties by node ID. Gateway selection from multiple gateways is done on the basis of rules like the gateway with the longest lifetime has highest priority.

We observed that if the gateway node between two clusters has a very small lifetime then that node may die and in that scenario the network connectivity is lost till the re-clustering is done again. Figure 1 shows the formation of clusters on the basis of CEC. Now we consider the situation where different node have different lifetimes. Here the wakeup time T_S [5] after which all the nodes in the cluster are powered on again is set to $enlt/2$ where $enlt$ is the estimated lifetime of the cluster-head. Thus the lifetime of the cluster ($LT_{cluster}$) depends on the lifetime of the cluster-head. Hence if the lifetime of any gateway ($LT_{gateway}$) of the cluster is less than the lifetime of that cluster, then there will not be any connectivity in the network for $LT_{cluster} - LT_{gateway}$ amount of time. Our protocol ensures that the connectivity in the network is maintained even in the case of the above stated scenario while consuming minimum energy.

3 Node Energy Based Clustering Protocol (NEC)

In this paper we propose NEC a clustering protocol which ensures minimum connectivity in the network and optimizes energy consumption. In this protocol we propose and define the concept of strong and weak sensor nodes based on their operational lifetime.

First we define the following :

- A cluster is defined as a set of nodes that are mutually reachable in at most two hops. Each cluster has a cluster-head which is directly reachable from all members of the cluster.
- A gateway is defined as a node which is a member of more than one cluster and provides interconnection between the clusters.
- Re-clustering Interval (I) is defined as the time after which re-clustering is initiated in a cluster.
  $I = \alpha \times$ Estimated lifetime of the cluster head, where $0 < \alpha < 1$.
  Both the value of the estimated lifetime of the cluster-head as well as I change with time. Each cluster has its own re-clustering interval.
- Strong and weak nodes : A node is defined as a strong node if its lifetime $\geq I$ when it operates at full power for the entire duration of its lifetime otherwise it is defined as weak node.

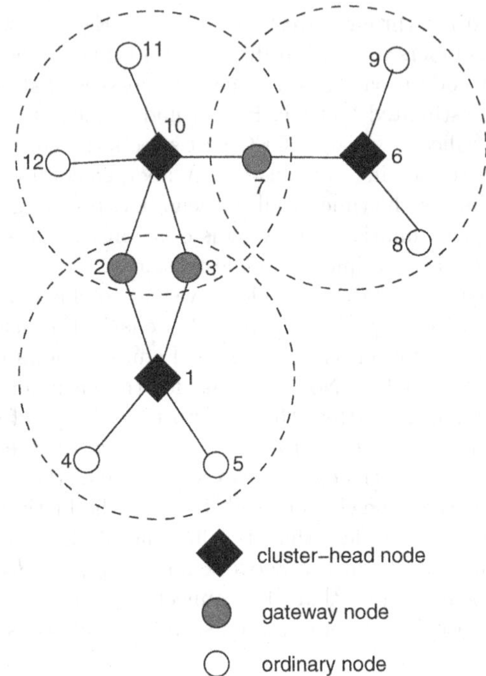

Fig. 1. Example of clustering. The dotted circles show the radio transmission range of the cluster-heads

3.1 Cluster Formation

1. **Potential Cluster-Head Selection**
   Initially each node broadcasts a discovery message which contains its node ID, its Cluster ID, and estimated lifetime [5]. A node elects itself as a potential cluster-head if it has the longest lifetime among all its neighboring nodes (ties are broken by node ID). After a node elects itself as a potential cluster-head it broadcasts this information along with its lifetime to all its neighbors.
2. **Gateway Selection**
   A node which is directly reachable from more than one cluster-head is called a primary gateway. A node which is connected to the cluster- head of another cluster through a member of that cluster is called a secondary gateway.

   When a node receives messages from more than one potential cluster-heads it knows that it is a gateway and then decides whether it is a strong node or a weak node with respect to the potential cluster-heads. The gateway node then passes the information whether it is a strong or a weak node to the potential cluster-heads. A gateway node between two potential cluster-heads can thus be a strong node with respect to one potential cluster-head and weak with respect to the other potential cluster-head. In this case it sends two different messages to the two different potential cluster-heads.

3. **Cluster-Head Selection and Cluster Formation**
   If a potential cluster-head receives the information that all its gateways are strong then it elects itself as the cluster-head and broadcasts this to all its neighbors which set their cluster Id to that of the cluster-head and a cluster is formed. The cluster-head broadcasts the value of I to all the members of the cluster.
   If a potential cluster-head receives the information that one or more of its gateways are weak nodes it elects itself as the cluster- head but while broadcasting this information to its neighbors it reduces the value of α hence reducing the re-clustering interval.
   After the cluster formation except for the cluster-head and the gateways all the other cluster members switch off their radios for the re-clustering interval to minimize the energy consumption.

Figure 2. shows an example of a cluster formation according to NEC. Here node 2 and node 3 are strong gateways since their remaining energy will allow them to survive the usual re-clustering interval (when $\alpha = 0.50$) while node 7 is a weak gateway since its remaining energy will not allow it to survive the re-clustering interval I if $\alpha = 0.50$.

An alternative approach can be once a gateway discovers that it is a weak node with respect to a cluster-head it sends intermediate node search messages containing its cluster ID to all its neighbors at some fraction of its maximum transmission power (minimum transmission power is preferred so that the node can last for a longer time) [7]. If it gets a reply from its neighbors having the same cluster ID it then uses this neighbor as a bridge node between the cluster-head and itself so that it can be operational for a longer duration of time.

4 Simulation of NEC

We simulated the node energy based clustering algorithm (NEC) proposed in this paper. We also ran CEC on the same simulation scenario and compared NEC to the CEC protocol in terms of the impact of node energy level on network connectivity. We also studied the node lifetime as well as the network operational lifetime in the two protocols. We showed that selecting gateways and cluster-heads based on strong/weak nodes as proposed in NEC increased the amount of time the network remains connected compared to CEC. The simulations were performed on a simple topology consisting of eleven nodes. We first ran NEC on this simple topology and initially obtained three clusters with one weak and one strong gateway. For simulation purposes we assumed for both the protocols that a constant amount of energy is expended for transmitting a message as well as for receiving a message. In the definition of re-clustering interval (I) We used a value of $\alpha = 0.50$ for strong gateways and $\alpha = 0.25$ for weak gateways.

From the results of our simulation for the above stated scenario we found that the first node dies at 19 secs in our NEC protocol. As the re-clustering interval for the cluster to which this node belonged to was 23 secs, the network

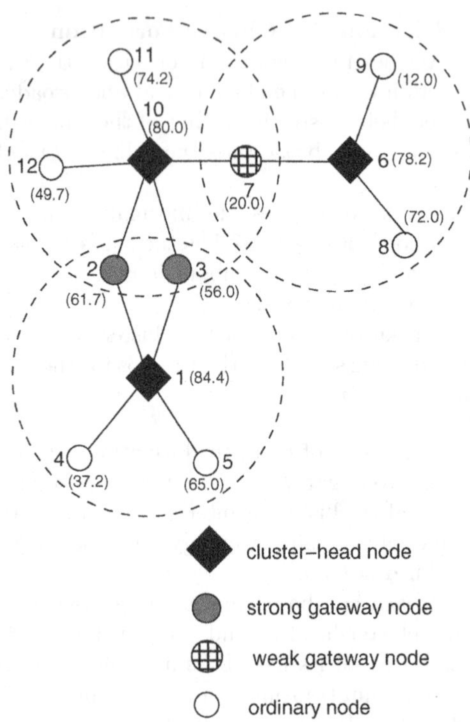

Fig. 2. Example of NEC. The numbers within the parenthesis denote the energy of each node

was partitioned and connectivity was lost for 4 secs in this case. For CEC under the same simulation scenario we found that the network was disconnected for a longer period of time of about 23 secs. Figure 3, which shows the connectivity/disconnectivity of the network, is an illustration of this result. This happens because NEC takes into consideration the effect of the energy level of the gateway node during cluster formation and if the energy level of the gateway node is low, NEC causes the cluster to re-cluster according to a reduced re-clustering interval. Thus in the case of NEC a weak node is not usually selected either as a gateway or a cluster-head during re-clustering and behaves as an ordinary node which is powered off after the cluster formation. Thus the energy of the weak nodes is conserved. NEC thus balances the energy usage of the nodes in the network. Figure 4 plots the number of active nodes in NEC with respect to time. From this figure it is evident that in NEC, for a long period of time the majority of the nodes remain alive.

Thus from the simulations results of NEC we see that when the first node of the network dies the node being a part of the cluster causes a disconnection in the network, But NEC usually causes the cluster to go into re-clustering before the weak gateway node dies or shortly after the weak gateway node dies resulting

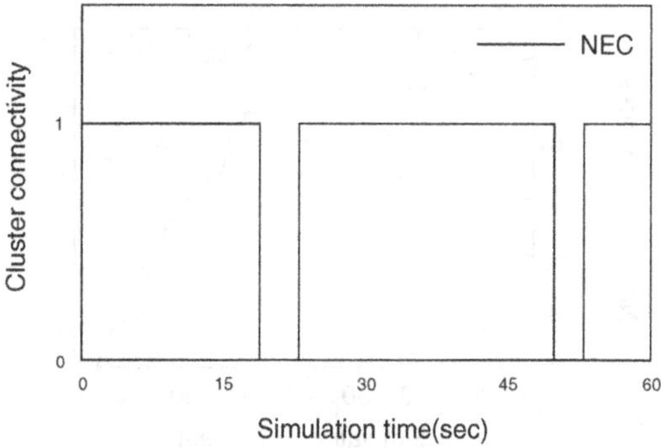

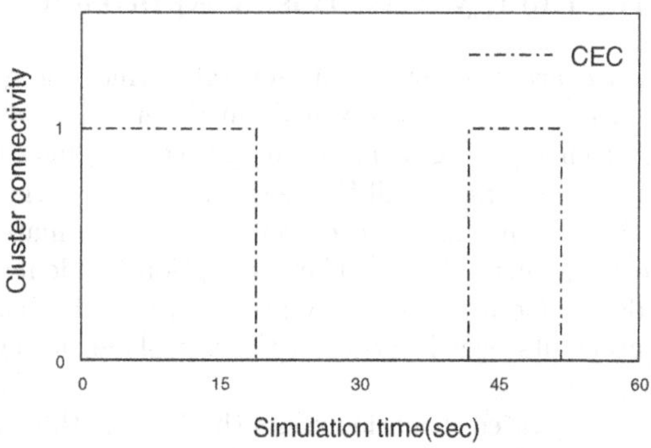

Fig. 3. The status of the network (connected/disconnected) with time in case of NEC (top) and CEC (bottom)

in the network being disconnected for a very small amount of time. But in other protocols like CEC the energy of the gateway is not taken into account and the cluster waits for a long time before re-clustering even after the weak gateway node dies.

We have carried out simulations for a simple topology with a small number of sensor nodes. We expect that for a topology with a large number of densely deployed sensor nodes NEC will also show better performance in terms of energy balancing in the network and increase the network operational lifetime. This is because NEC tries to conserve the energy of the weak nodes and by using them sparingly as compared to the strong nodes. Hence analytically with a lower value of the constant α in the re-clustering interval the first node death in NEC should occur at a later time compared to other protocols.

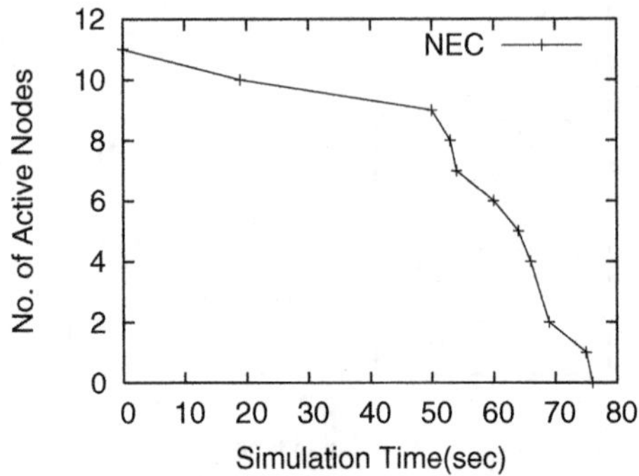

Fig. 4. No. of nodes alive with time in NEC

5 Alternative Energy Tree Based Approach

We can consider a scenario where there are several distinct energy ranges/bands in the network and the energy of every node in the network falls into any one of the given distinct energy ranges. These energy bands/ranges are fixed before the deployment of the sensors and all the sensor nodes know the values of these energy bands so that at any instant each sensor node can map its own energy level to one of the given energy bands. The assumptions made here are that each sensor node can determine its own energy level and also that each sensor node has information about its own location in the x-y plane(through GPS or any other mechanism).

In case of the above stated scenario we can think of another topology control approach that greatly facilitates data aggregation in the sensor network at low energy overhead. The data sensed/collected by the sensors has to be transmitted to the base station. In this case instead of having each node transmitting the data to the base station it is much more desirable in terms of energy and communication overhead to have an approach where a set of sensor sends data to an aggregator and aggregator then performs data aggregation and the aggregated data is then sent to the base station. Optimal data aggregation is known to be an NP complete problem [4]. We assume that the network is graph $G(V, E)$ where V denotes the sensor nodes and E denotes the set of edges where an edge exists between two node if they are within each others radio range. We propose a new topology control approach where a single tree or a number of trees can be constructed such that for any two given tree nodes u and v, u being the parent of v, it is ensured that u has a higher (or equal) energy level than that of v.

Some of the benefits of a tree based topology control approach are as follows:

- Once one or more trees are formed in the network, even after the energy of any node in a tree runs out the probability of the tree being connected is higher, this is because the tree is formed in such a way that the lower energy nodes are at a lower level and there are no high energy nodes at a level below

a low energy node. Hence usually a leaf of the tree will run out of energy before that happens to a internal node which is at a higher energy.
- The tree structure is inherently suitable for data aggregation. Tree nodes of subsequently higher levels can aggregate data they receives from their children and so on.
- Various security measures can be implemented at various levels while aggregating data as one goes higher up the tree.
- If multiple trees are formed only the root nodes can send the final aggregated data in each tree to the base station leading to further conservation in energy.

The following section briefly describes a heuristics to form such an energy tree. We assume that there are n energy bands $(E_1, E_2, \cdots, E_n)$ numbered as 1 to n. Band 1 corresponds to the lowest energy band and band n corresponds to the highest energy band. We also assume that each node knows its own location.

Directed Graph Formation

In the first phase an imaginary weighted directed graph is formed by the sensor nodes by local communication. Each node sends a message to all of its neighbors containing its node ID, energy band number E_i and geographic location. A node ignores the message if it is from a node with lower energy band number. When a node receives a message from a node with a higher or equal energy band number, it store the node ID of that node and also calculates a weight for the edge between that higher or equal energy node and itself. The edge between node i and node j is directed form i to j if j has a higher or equal energy band number than i. The weight w_{ij} for any edge between nodes i and j is calculated as follows,

$$w_{ij} = k \times \; dist_{ij} \; / \; difference_{ij} \text{ where } k \text{ is some constant}$$

$$dist_{ij} = \text{Euclidean distance between } i \text{ and } j$$

$$difference_{ij} = \begin{cases} E_j - E_i, & \text{if } E_j > E_i \\ 1, & \text{if } E_j = E_i \end{cases}$$

i can calculate $dist_{ij}$ as j's location information is contained in the message from j to i.

Tree Formation

In the second step when an underlying weighted directed graph has been created amongst the nodes in the network an algorithm generating a minimal spanning tree in the directed graph is initiated in the network.

Once the tree formation step is complete, the sensor nodes which will become a part of some tree will know who their parents are in the tree and will send any data that it senses or receives from any of its children to that parent.

6 Conclusion

In this paper we have proposed the node energy based clustering protocol (NEC), a protocol which conserves energy as well as ensures minimum connectivity in the network. As opposed to CEC, the primary characteristics of NEC is the use of the concept of strong and weak nodes to decide which nodes should be selected as cluster-heads and gateways. NEC requires that the energy of communicating nodes in the network be taken into consideration to ensure network connectivity at minimum energy expenditure at the nodes. We also showed that selecting gateways and cluster-heads based on strong/weak nodes as proposed in NEC increased the amount of time the sensor network remains connected compared to CEC. NEC does not require geographic location information or any kind of distance or directional estimation between nodes. NEC is completely distributed and does not require knowledge of the global network in order to operate. NEC relies only on local communication between neighbors and hence can dynamically adapt to the changes in the network.

We have presented preliminary simulation results and analysis to show that the NEC conserves energy while ensuring minimum network connectivity compared to other conventional protocols. In NEC if the network is disconnected at all it is so for a much shorter period of time compared to CEC. In order to verify our assumptions about the performance of NEC we are currently extending the network simulator ns-2 to simulate NEC. This will verify our assumptions and give us a more accurate picture of the advantages and disadvantages of using NEC compared to other clustering protocols.

References

1. Chan, H., Perrig, A.: ACE: An Emergent Algorithm for Highly Uniform Cluster Formation, Proceedings of European Workshop on Wireless Sensor Networks 2004, Berlin, Germany (2004) 154–171
2. Estrin, D., Girod, L., Pottie, L., Srivastava, M.: Instrumenting the world with wireless sensor networks, Proceedings of the International Conference on Acoustics, Speech, and Signal Processing (ICASSP), Salt Lake City, Utah, USA (2001)
3. Heinzelman, W.R., Chandrakasan, A., Balakrishnan, H.: Energy-Efficient Communication Protocol for Wireless Microsensor Networks, Proceedings of the 33rd Hawaii International Conference on System sciences, Maui, Hawaii (2000)
4. Krishanamachari, B., Estrin, D., Wicker, S.: The Impact of Data Aggregation in Wireless Sensor Networks, Proceedings of the International Workshop of Distributed Event Based Systems (DEBS), Vienna, Austria (2002)
5. Xu, Y., Bien, S., Mori, Y., Heidemann, J., Estrin, D.: Topology Control Protocols to Conserve Energy in Wireless Ad Hoc Networks, CENS Technical Report UCLA, Number 6 Los Angeles, USA (2003)
6. Ye, W., Heidemann, J., Estrin, D.: An Energy-Efficeint MAC Protocol for Wireless Sensor Networks, Proceedings of the IEEE Infocom, New York, USA (2002) 3–12
7. Zuniga, M., Krishnamachari, B.: Optimal Transmission Radius for Flooding in Large Scale Sensor Networks, Proceeding of 23rd International Conference on Distributed Computing Systems Workshops, Providence, Rhode Island, USA (2003) 697

Energy Efficient Cache Invalidation in a Disconnected Mobile Environment

Narottam Chand, Ramesh Joshi, and Manoj Misra

Electronics and Computer Engineering Department,
Indian Institute of Technology,
Roorkee – 247 667 India
{narotdec, joshifcc, manojfec}@iitr.ernet.in

Abstract. Caching at mobile host is a prominent technique for improving the performance of wireless data dissemination. It can reduce number of uplink requests, server load, query latency and can increase data availability. A cache invalidation strategy ensures that cached data in a host has same value as on the origin server. Due to battery energy constraints of mobile host and unreliable limited bandwidth over the wireless channel, the host may disconnect from the server. Frequent disconnections of a host add many challenges to the cache invalidation process. In this paper, we present a Synchronous Stateful (SS) cache maintenance strategy with the objectives to minimize the overheads for mobile hosts to validate their cache on reconnection, reduce the use of wireless channel and conserve the host energy. Simulation experiments are performed to evaluate the proposed strategy and compare it with Asynchronous Stateful (AS) scheme. Results show that our strategy performs better in terms of reconnection overheads, bandwidth utilization and host energy consumption.

1 Introduction

The prodigious advances in the field of portable hardware and wireless technology have made the mobile computing a reality. Mobile computing suffers from limited and unreliable bandwidth, limited client resources and frequent disconnections of hosts from the network. Users of mobile devices wish to access dynamic data, such as stock quotes, news items, current traffic conditions, weather reports, email and video clips via wireless networks independent of location and time. However, limited battery energy and scarce wireless bandwidth hinder the full realization of ubiquitous data access in mobile computing. Caching at mobile client can relieve bandwidth constraints imposed on wireless and mobile computing. Copies of remote data from server can be kept in the local memory of the mobile client, thus, substantially reducing user requests for retrieval of data from the origin server. This not only reduces the uplink and downlink bandwidth consumption but also the average query latency. Caching frequently accessed data in mobile client can also save energy used to retrieve the repeatedly requested data at client side.

Cache invalidation strategy is used to ensure that the data items cached in a mobile client are consistent with those stored on the server. Frequent disconnections of mo-

R.K. Ghosh and H. Mohanthy (Eds.): ICDCIT 2004, LNCS 3347, pp. 85–95, 2004.

bile client make the task of cache invalidation more complex since the cache maintenance strategy must optimally utilize limited wireless bandwidth and client energy. The client may voluntary switch off to save energy, or a client may be involuntary disconnected due to network failure, processor failure or battery failure.

Recently, we [20] addressed various cache invalidation issues in mobile environment and introduced the concept of Cache Directory (CD) based invalidation. To evaluate the effectiveness of the CD strategy, it was compared with TS [4] and counter based scheme [1], [15], and it has been shown that our strategy performs better in terms of client tuning time, query latency and client energy consumption.

This paper presents a Synchronous Stateful (SS) cache maintenance strategy where cache consistency is maintained by broadcasting update reports. The cache state for each client is maintained at the home MSS in the form of cache vector (CV). Use of cache vectors enables the server to filter out non-cached items from an IR, handle arbitrarily long disconnection and support client mobility. In IR based strategies, even though many clients cache the same updated data item, all of them have to query the server and get the data from the server separately. It wastes a large amount of wireless bandwidth and battery energy. To minimize uplink requests and downlink broadcasts, we use a broadcast strategy, called update report (UR), where all the recently updated or requested items are broadcast immediately after the invalidation report (IR). To further conserve the client energy, the proposed strategy uses selective tuning.

The rest of the paper is organized as follows. Section 2 gives a description of the related work. In section 3, we present our caching strategy. In section 4, we describe simulation experiments for establishing the performance of our methodology. Conclusion is given in section 5.

2 Related Work

Caching in mobile environment is complicated by the fact that the caches need to be kept consistent. A number of broadcast based cache invalidation strategies have been proposed for mobile environments. Barbara and Imielinski [14] provided three cache invalidation schemes, namely Broadcasting Timestamps (TS), Amnesic Terminals (AT) and Signatures (SIG), which use different invalidation reports for a stateless server. Jing et al. [10] proposed a Bit-Sequence (BS) scheme that uses a hierarchical structure of binary bit sequences with an associated set of timestamps to represent clients with different disconnection times. Tan [7] reexamined the BS method and studied different organizations of the invalidation report. These new organizations facilitate clients to selectively tune to the portion of the report that are of interest to them. Hue et al. [12] proposed a scheme to reduce the false invalidation rates based on BS reports. Wu et al. [6] proposed a scheme which modifies the TS or AT algorithms to include cache validity checks after reconnection. Hu and Lee [3] have proposed a family of invalidation algorithms. The essence of these algorithms is that the type of invalidation report to be sent is determined dynamically based on system status such as disconnection frequency and duration as well as update and query pattern. G. Cao in [4], [5] addresses the problem of long query latency with a UIR based approach. In this approach, a small fraction of the essential information (called *updated invalidation report (UIR)*) related to cache invalidation is replicated several times within an IR interval, and hence the client can answer a query without waiting until next IR. However, if there is a cache miss, the client still needs to wait for the data to be delivered. In [1], [15], author addresses various problems associated with the IR based cache invalidation strategies. To improve the query latency and cache hit ratio, clients intelligently prefetch the data that are most likely used in the future. Kahol et al. [2], [9] present an asynchronous stateful (AS) scheme to maintain cache consistency. Each mobile client maintains its own Home Location Cache (HLC) to deal with the problem of disconnections. Yuen et al. [8] proposed a cache invalidation scheme based on absolute validity interval (AVI) for each data item. To solve the problem of large size invalidations reports and duplicate uplink requests, K. Y. Lai et al. [18], [19], proposed two techniques Validation-Invalidation Reports (VIR) and Delayed Request Scheme (DRS). Wang et al. [21] proposed an invalidation strategy called Scalable Asynchronous Cache Consistency Scheme (SACCS), which is hybrid of both stateful and stateless algorithms. Unlike stateful algorithms, SACCS maintains only one flag bit for each data item in MSS and unlike the existing synchronous stateless approaches, it does not require periodic broadcast of IRs. Because of asynchronous nature of SACCS approach, it does not provide any guarantee on waiting time of clients and hence they can rarely switch to power save mode. Authors in [22] describe the cache consistency maintenance for intra- and inter-roaming MHs. Three strategies: homogenous IR, inhomogeneous IR without roaming check and inhomogeneous IR with roaming check are applied to TS and SACCS strategies.

3 The Proposed Cache Invalidation Strategy

In this section, we present our synchronous stateful (SS) caching strategy. The strategy concentrates on reducing the number of uplink requests, downlink broadcasts, overheads due to reconnection after an arbitrarily long disconnection, tuning time and client energy consumption.

3.1 Mobile Caching Model

The environment consists of two distinct sets of entities: *Mobile Hosts (MHs)* and *Fixed Hosts (FHs)*. Some of the FHs called *Mobile Support Stations (MSSs)*, are augmented with a wireless interface in order to communicate with the mobile hosts, which are located within a radio coverage called a cell. Each MSS stores a complete copy of the database and also acts like a database server. Henceforth, we use the terms MSS and server interchangeably. An MH communicates with a server over asymmetric wireless communication link (i.e. the uplink bandwidth is much less than that of downlink). An MH can move within a cell or between cells while retaining its network connection. It either connects to an MSS through a wireless link or disconnects from the MSS by operating in a power save mode [2].

It is assumed that the database is updated only by the server. The servers themselves form a wired distributed system in which a fully replicated database resides.

The database D comprises a set of N data items and each item is identified by unique id. For each item d_i, two time stamps t_i and t_i^r are maintained at the server. t_i is the most recent *timestamp* when d_i got updated and t_i^r, called *latest request time*, represents the most recent time when d_i was last requested.

A client sends an uplink request to the server for the data it needs and the server responds by broadcasting the requested data on the downlink. In order to minimize the number of uplink requests, the client caches a portion of the database in its local memory. We assume that the cache at mobile client is a nonvolatile memory such as hard disk so that after a long disconnection, the content of the cache can still be retrieved. To ensure cache consistency and serve the client requests, server periodically broadcasts update reports (URs). All active mobile hosts while roaming listen to the reports and invalidate/update their cache contents accordingly.

Following assumptions are made:

- Database D is collection of N data items and is replicated at each server. An item is identified by unique identifier d_i ($1 \leq i \leq N$). D_i denotes the actual data of an item d_i. Each item has same size S_{data} (in bits).
- Unique identifier is assigned to each MH. The system has total of M hosts and MH_i ($1 \leq i \leq M$) is a host identifier. Each MH has cache capacity of C items.
- CV (details in Section 3.2) stored in the local disk of server, maintains the state information for a host. An MH informs its server before it stores any data item in its local cache and the server updates the CV accordingly.
- Servers are reliable i.e. they handle the failure with some fault tolerance techniques.

3.2 Using Cache Vectors (CVs) to Maintain State Information

In a stateless strategy when an item updates at the server, its id is broadcast as part of IR irrespective of whether the item has been cached or not. Including a non-cached item as part of IR, makes poor utilization of the available wireless bandwidth and it also increases the client energy consumption since they have to listen to the broadcast channel for longer duration to download the report. To filter out all those recently updated items from an IR which are not cached by any client, we have used a stateful strategy.

To keep the state information, for each MH a binary cache vector (CV) is maintained at the home MSS. The vector has N bits, each bit representing one item. Consider a cell with H hosts (MH_i, $1 \leq i \leq H$) at any given time. For any j, CV_j for MH_j, as maintained on its home MSS, keeps track of what data has been locally cached at MH_j. In general $CV_j = (1\ 0\ 1\ \ldots\ 0)^T$, if $CV_j[k] = 1$, then the host MH_j has cached the item d_k. Using CV, the MSS includes only those recently updated items as part of IR which have been cached by one or more clients. When a host moves to a new cell, the copy of its CV is replicated at the new MSS.

3.3 Broadcast UR to Utilize Bandwidth

To reduce the number of uplink requests and downlink broadcasts, we introduce the concept of update report (UR). A similar technique using L_{bcast} has been described by

G. Cao [1], [4], [5], [15]. Update reports (URs) are broadcast synchronously with period L. The structure of a UR is shown in Fig. 1.

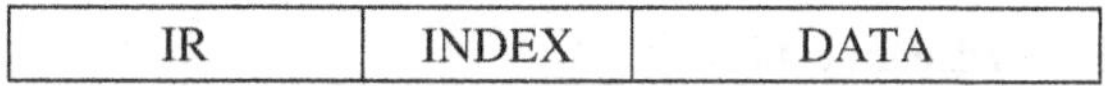

Fig. 1. Structure of a UR

At interval T_i:

$IR_i = \{(d_x, t_x) | (d_x \in D) \wedge (n_x > 0) \wedge (T_i - w.L < t_x \leq T_i)\}$

$INDEX_i = \{d_x | ((T_{i-1} < t_x \leq T_i) \wedge (n_x > 0)) \vee (T_{i-1} < t_i^r \leq T_i)\}$

$DATA_i = \{D_x | d_x \in INDEX_i\}$

Where n_x is number of clients who have cached the item d_x. $INDEX_i$ defines the order in which data appears in $DATA_i$. IR contains the update history of past w broadcast intervals whereas DATA contains actual data value for the items which have been updated during previous interval. In most IR based algorithms [2], [3], [6], [7], [8], [10], [11], [13], [14], [16], [17], updating a data item that has been cached, may generate many uplink requests and downlink broadcasts, and thus make poor utilization of available wireless bandwidth. This is due to the reason that when an item is updated and IR is broadcast, each client who has cached that item will generate an uplink request for the item and the server responds to each request by broadcasting the item. For example, for an item with id d_x which is cached by n_x clients, there will be n_x uplink requests and n_x downlink broadcasts due to update. We address the problem by asking the server to broadcast all the data items which have been recently requested or updated and are cached by one or more clients. So, in comparison to n_x uplinks and downlink broadcasts for an updated item, our strategy makes only single broadcast without any uplink request. Also, during one UR interval, due to cache miss an item may have been requested by many clients, but our scheme broadcasts the item only once. Thus, reducing the number of uplink requests and downlink broadcasts due to recent updates or cache misses, the UR strategy heavily saves on wireless bandwidth.

3.4 Saving Client Energy by Making Synchronous Broadcasts

In asynchronous invalidation methodology, there is no guarantee on how long a client must wait for the next report and hence the clients those are in doze mode may lose some of the reports, thus compromising the cache consistency or further increasing the query latency. We use a synchronous approach where clients may wake up during the UR broadcast time and selectively tune to the channel to save energy. After broadcasting IR, the server broadcasts INDEX followed by actual data DATA. Every client listens to the IR if not disconnected. At the end of IR, a client downloads INDEX and locates the interesting item that will come, and listens to the channel at that time to download the data. This strategy saves energy since the client selectively tunes to the channel and can stay in doze mode most of time.

3.5 Handling Host Disconnection

Since a UR contains information about all the changes occurred during past w.L time, the SS strategy handles the disconnection of hosts less than w.L without any additional overhead. When a host reconnects after a disconnection time longer than w.L, it sends an uplink request with the last received UR time stamp T_l (before disconnection) to the server. On receipt of the request, the server constructs a binary vector DIV called disconnection information vector. DIV is of size C bits and contains the validity information about the cached items by a host. For a host MH_i, the server constructs DIV_i as follows:

1. Scan the cache vector CV_i. If $CV_i[j] = 1$, MH_i has cached the item d_j otherwise not.
2. For an item d_j, cached by MH_i, compare its last update timestamp (t_j) with T_l. If $t_j > T_l$, the item d_j has been updated since MH_i received last UR before disconnection. In case, $t_j > T_l$, then set $DIV_i[k] = 1$, where MH_i has stored the item d_j at kth cache location ($1 \le k \le C$). If $t_j \le T_l$, then set $DIV_i[k] = 0$.

Once the DIV_i has been constructed, the server sends DIV_i to MH_i over the downlink channel. After downloading DIV_i, MH_i finds whether a particular cached item is still valid. If $DIV_i[k] = 1$, then the kth cached item is invalid otherwise it is still valid. After checking for each cached item, the host will send an uplink request for all the invalid items and the server responds by broadcasting the requested items during following UR.

As compared to previous caching strategies [1], [2], which handle disconnection by sending the ids for updated items, our strategy uses only one bit for an item, thus reducing the reconnection overheads tremendously. For our strategy the reconnection overhead is C bits, which is very less as compared to [1], [2]. Because of smaller size of overhead, our strategy is also very much effective in terms of bandwidth utilization, client tuning time and energy consumption.

Following example illustrates the working of the strategy to handle host disconnection:

Example
Consider a database having 10 items with the shown last update timestamp t_i.

d_i	1	2	3	4	5	6	7	8	9	10
t_i	20	16	17	13	5	6	2	9	23	19

Let a host MH_x of cache size $C = 4$, has cached the items with id 1, 2, 4 and 7. Let MH_x got disconnected at time 17 such that it has received the last UR at $T_l = 15$ and wakes up again at time 30.

Then

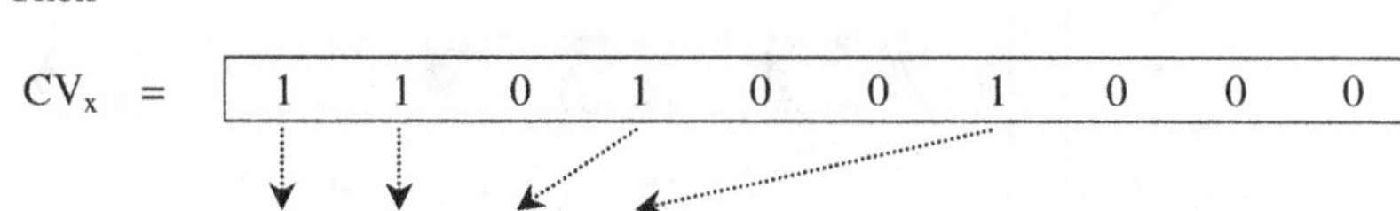

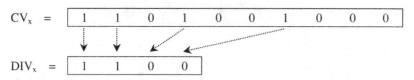

While MH_x receives DIV_x, it is interpreted as: 1st cached item i.e. d_1 is invalid, 2nd cached item i.e. d_2 is invalid whereas d_4 and d_7 are still valid.

The reconnection overhead for our strategy is 4 bits. For [1], [2], the overhead = number of cached items invalidated during disconnection*Item id size (S_{id}). Generally S_{id} = 32 bits, therefore the overhead value = 64 bits.

3.6 Handling Host Mobility

When MH_i moves from old cell to a new cell, it will be registered in the new cell and a copy of CV_i from the home MSS will be replicated at the new MSS. If the old MSS is not the home MSS, it (old MSS) deregisters MH_i by deleting CV_i from its local disk and transfers pending request (if any) of MH_i to the new MSS. MH_i resumes its operation in the new cell and more requests can be directed to the new MSS after the pending data items have been received. While away from the home cell, the changes which occur in the contents of CV_i at current MSS will also be propagated back to the home MSS so that both the copies are consistent.

The above scheme can be easily integrated with Mobile IP (MIP) where home MSS and new MSS also handle the functions of home agent (HA) and foreign agent (FA) respectively.

4 Performance Evaluation

To evaluate the performance of the proposed scheme, we have developed a simulation model as shown in Fig. 2. Table 1 shows the system parameters and their corresponding values. The rational behind the choices is as follows. These values are very similar to the corresponding ones in [1], [2], and represent a realistic asymmetric wireless environment. The simulation model consists of a single server per cell serving multiple clients. The database can only be updated by the server, while the queries are generated by the clients following an exponential distribution. The mean inter-arrival time of queries generated by all clients is T_q. The inter-arrival time of updates at the server is distributed exponentially with a mean of T_u. A client has a probability p_d to enter the disconnection mode only when the outstanding query has been served. A client follows exponential distributed disconnection with mean time T_d. The server periodically broadcasts update reports (URs) every L seconds. The IR part of UR covers a broadcast window of w broadcast intervals.

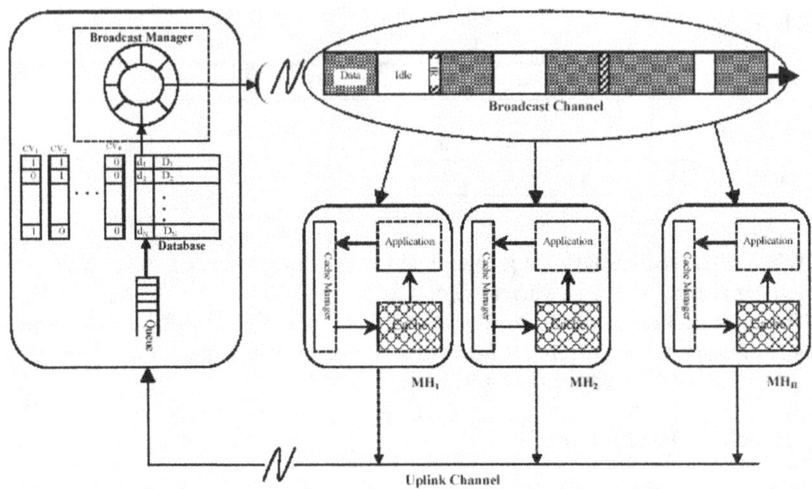

Fig. 2. The simulation model

Table 1. Simulation parameters

Parameter	Value	Parameter	Value
Server database size (N)	1000 items	Broadcast window (w)	10 L
Item size (S_{data})	4096 bits	Mean query generate time (T_q)	2 sec
Client cache size (C)	30 items	Mean update arrival time (T_u)	1 - 10000 sec
Maximum clients per cell (H)	30	Mean disconnection time (T_d)	0-400 sec
Item id size (S_{id})	32 bits	Disconnection probability (p_d)	0.10
Timestamp size (T_{data})	32 bits	Uplink bandwidth (B_{up})	19.2 Kbps
Broadcast interval (L)	20 sec	Downlink bandwidth (B_{down})	100 Kbps

In the experiments, we study the effect of different disconnection times on the overhead. The overhead considered is the additional number of bits transmitted on downlink channel due to items those have become invalid during the period of disconnection. Since our strategy has no overhead due to disconnection time less than 200 sec (w.L), the comparison between AS and SS strategies has been shown for disconnection time longer than 200 sec. Fig. 3 shows that the AS strategy has always higher overhead than SS strategy. As SS strategy uses disconnection information vector (DIV) of size C (number of cached items), the overhead is same at all the disconnection times. In AS strategy, the number of invalid items increases with the increase of disconnection time, thus increasing the reconnection overhead.

To evaluate the effectiveness of SS strategy to bandwidth utilization and conserving client energy, we study the effect of update arrival time over number of uplink requests and tuning time, and compare the results with AS based invalidation strategy. In Fig. 4, the mean number of uplink requests per 100 queries is plotted against the mean update arrival time. At low update arrival time (i.e. high update rate), the number of uplinks is higher because more items are invalidated. The SS scheme performs better than AS scheme, as in SS most of the uplink requests are generated because of cache miss whereas in AS both the cache miss and invalidation cause the uplink requests. As shown in Fig. 5, the SS scheme which uses selective tuning, performs better under all update rates than AS scheme, and thus, conserves the client energy.

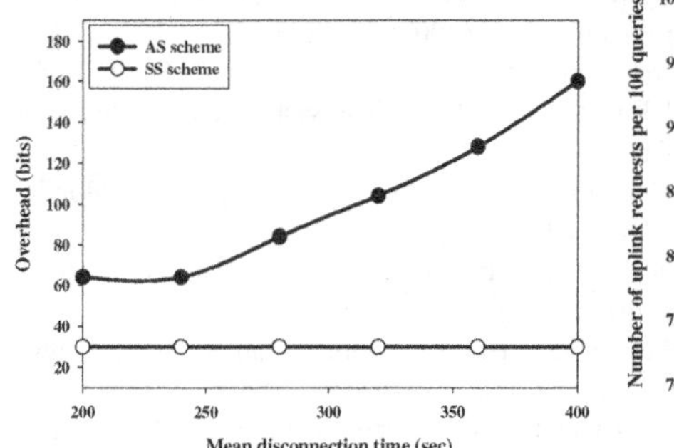

Fig. 3. Overhead as a function of mean disconnection time

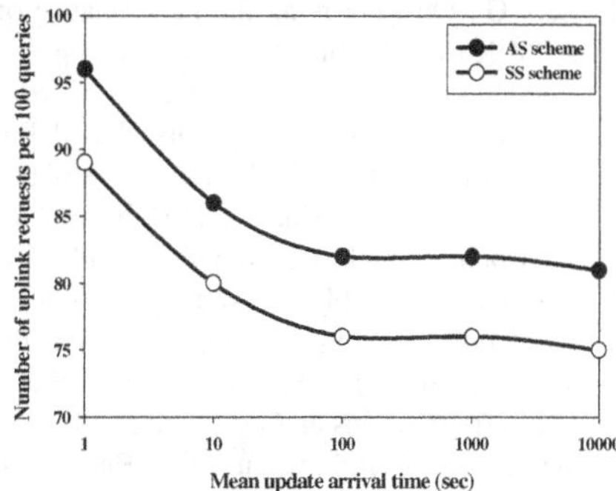

Fig. 4. Uplink requests as a function of mean update arrival time

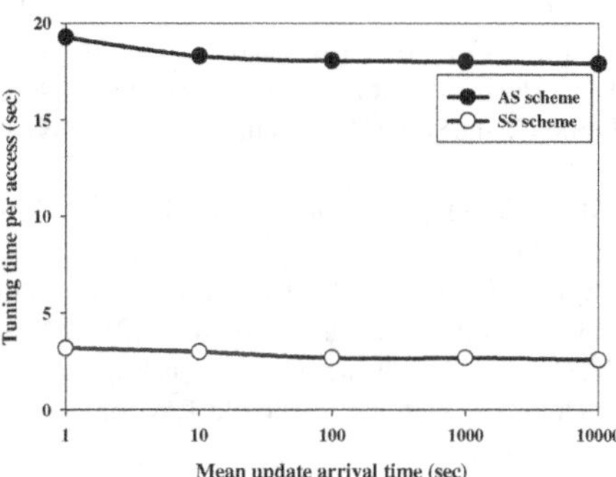

Fig. 5. Tuning time as a function of mean update arrival time

5 Conclusions

The paper presents a Synchronous Stateful (SS) cache invalidation strategy to minimize the overheads for mobile clients to validate their cache on reconnection, reduce the use of wireless channel and conserve the client battery energy. Simulation experiments show that our strategy performs better than Asynchronous Stateful (AS) scheme. Future work will consider the comparison of proposed SS scheme with Scalable Asynchronous Cache Consistency Scheme (SACCS) [21]. To further enhance the performance of SS, use of prefetching in integration with caching is also a consideration during our future research.

References

1. Cao, G.: On Improving the Performance of Cache Invalidation in Mobile Environments. ACM/Kluwer Mobile Network and Applications, 7(4). (2002) 291-303.
2. Kahol, A., Khurana, S., Gupta, S.K.S., Srimani, P.K.: A Strategy to Manage Cache Consistency in a Disconnected Distributed Environment. IEEE Transaction on Parallel and Distributed Systems, 12(7). (2001) 686-700.
3. Hu, Q., Lee, D.K.: Cache Algorithms Based on Adaptive Invalidation Reports for Mobile Environments. Cluster Computing, 1(1). (1998) 39-50.
4. Cao, G.: A Scalable Low-Latency Cache Invalidation Strategy for Mobile Environments. ACM Intl. Conf. on Computing and Networking (Mobicom), (2001) 200-209.
5. Cao, G.: Proactive Power-Aware Cache Management for Mobile Computing Systems. IEEE Transactions on Computers, Vol. 51, No. 6 (2002) 608-621.
6. Wu, K.L., Yu, P.S., Chen, M.S.: Energy-Efficient Mobile Cache Invalidation. Distributed and Parallel Databases, Kluwer Academic Publishers, Vol. 6. (1998) 351-372.
7. Tan, K.L.: Organisation of Invalidation Reports for Energy-Efficient Cache Invalidation in Mobile Environments. Mobile Networks and Applications, 6 (2001) 279-290.
8. Yuen, J.C., Chan, E., Lam, K., Lueng, H.W.: Cache Invalidation Scheme for Mobile Computing Systems with Real-Time Data. SIGMOD, (2000) 34-39.
9. Kahol, A., Khurana, S., Gupta, S., Srimani, P.: An Efficient Cache Maintenance Scheme for Mobile Environment. Int. Conf. on Distributed Computing Systems, (2000) 530-537.
10. Jing, J., Elmagarmid, A., Helal, A., Alonso, R.: Bit-Sequences: An Adaptive Cache Invalidation Method in Mobile Client/Server Environments. Mobile Networks and Applications (1997) 115-127.
11. Yao, J.F., Dunham, M.H.: Caching Management of Mobile DBMS. Journal of Integrated Computer-Aided Engineering, Vol. 8, No. 2 (2001).
12. Hou, W.C., Su, M., Zhang, H., Wang, H.: An Optimal Construction of Invalidation Reports for Mobile Databases. In Proceedings of CIKM, (2001) 458-465.
13. Nam, S.H., Chung, Y., Cho, S.H., Hwang, C.S.: Asynchronous Cache Invalidation Strategy to Support Read-Only Transactions in Mobile Environments. IEICE Trans. Inf. and Syst. Vol. E85-D, No. 2 (2002).
14. Barbara, D., Imielinski, T.: Sleepers and Workaholics: Caching Strategies in Mobile Environments. ACM SIGMOD Conference on Management of Data, (1994) 1-12.
15. Cao, G.: A Scalable Low-Latency Cache Invalidation Strategy for Mobile Environments. IEEE Trans. on Knowledge and Data Engineering, Vol. 15, No. 5 (2003) 1251-1265.
16. Lee, S.K.: Caching and Concurrency Control in a Wireless Mobile Computing Environment. IEICE Trans. Inf. and Syst. Vol. E85-D, No. 8 (2002).
17. Tan, K.L., Cai, J., Ooi, B.C.: An Evaluation of Cache Invalidation Strategies in Wireless Environments. IEEE Trans. on Parallel and Distributed Systems, Vol. 12, No. 8 (2001).
18. Lai, K.Y., Tari, Z., Bertok, P.: Cost Efficient Broadcast Based Cache Invalidation for Mobile Environments. SAC, (2003) 871-877.
19. Lai, K.Y., Tari, Z., Bertok, P.: An Analytical Study of Broadcast Based Cache Invalidation in Mobile Computing Networks. CoopIS/DOA/ODBASE, (2003) 554-572.

20. Chand, N., Joshi, R. C., Misra, M.: An Energy Efficient Cache Invalidation Strategy in Mobile Environment. Proceedings of National Seminar, Advances in Computer Communication Networks (IE – India), (2004), 188-196.
21. Wang, Z., Das, S. K., Che, H., Kumar M.: Scalable Asynchronous Cache Consistency Scheme (SACCS) for Mobile Environments. ICDCS, (2003) 797-802.
22. Wang, Z., Kumar, M., Das, S. K., Shen, H.: Investigation of Cache Maintenance Strategies for Multi-cell Environments. Mobile Data Management (MDM), (2003) 29-44.

An Efficient Data Dissemination Schemes for Location Dependent Information Services

KwangJin Park, MoonBae Song, and Chong-Sun Hwang

Dept. of Computer Science and Engineering, Korea University,
5-1, Anam-dong, Seongbuk-Ku, Seoul 136-701, Korea
{kjpark, mbsong, hwang}@disys.korea.ac.kr

Abstract. Location dependent information services (LDISs) produce answers to queries according to the location of the client issuing the query. In LDIS, techniques such as caching, prefetching and broadcasting are effective approaches to reducing the wireless bandwidth requirement and query response time. However, the client's mobility may lead to inconsistency problems. In this paper, we introduce the broadcast-based LDIS scheme (BBS) for the mobile computing environment. In the BBS, broadcasted data items are sorted sequentially based on their location and the server broadcasts the location dependent data (LDD) along with an index segment. Then, we present a data prefetching scheme and OBC (Object Boundary Circle), in order to reduce the query response time. The performance of the proposed scheme is investigated in relation to various environmental variables, such as the distributions of the data items, the average speed of the clients and the size of the service area.

1 Introduction

In today's increasingly mobile computing world, people wish to be able to access various kinds of services at any time any place. However, the mobile computing environment is characterized by narrow network bandwidth and limited battery power. Furthermore, the changes in locations of the mobile clients can be difficult to handle in an LDIS, particulary in the areas of query processing and cache management [1]. Techniques such as caching, prefetching and broadcasting provide effective means of reducing the wireless bandwidth requirement and can also save the client's battery power consumption.

Location dependent data is a data whose value depends on the location. The answer to a query depends on geographical location where the query originates. Let's consider an example in which a salesman drives a car and has to visit all of his customers. The salesman sends a query, such as, "what are the names and addresses of the markets near to my current location?", using his mobile device. Once the salesman gets the answer from the server, he will visit the other markets by the nearest order, and the markets that visits already is going to except in the visiting list. To handle such a query, the positions of the objects and the clients must be found.

R.K. Ghosh and H. Mohanty (Eds.): ICDCIT 2004, LNCS 3347, pp. 96–105, 2004.

In this paper, we propose the broadcast-based LDIS scheme under a geometric location model. We first introduce the broadcast based location dependent data delivery scheme (BBS). In this scheme, the server periodically broadcasts reports, which contains the IDs of the data items (e.g., building names)and the values of the location coordinates to the clients. The broadcasted data objects are sorted sequentially based on their location before being broadcasted. Then, we introduce the prefetching scheme in LDIS for the mobile computing environment. By using the proposed schemes, the client's access and tuning times are significantly reduced.

The rest of the paper is organized as follows: Section 2 gives the background of the broadcast model and LDIS scheme. Section 3 describes the proposed BBS scheme and prefetching method. The performance evaluation is presented in section 4. Finally, section 5 concludes this paper.

2 Background

With the advent of high speed wireless networks and portable device, data requests based on the location of mobile clients have increased in number. However, there are several challenges to be met in the development of LDISs [1], such as the constraints associated with the mobile environment and the difficulty of taking the user's movement into account. Hence, various techniques have been proposed to overcome these difficulties.

2.1 Broadcast Model

Data broadcasting in a wireless network constitutes an attractive approach in the mobile data environment. However, the wireless broadcast environment is affected by the narrow network bandwidth and the battery power restrictions of the mobile clients. Air indexing is one of techniques that attempts to address this issue, by interleaving indexing information among the broadcast data items. At the same time, the client can reduce its battery power consumption through the use of select tuning [6, 7]. Air indexing techniques can be evaluated in terms of the following factors:

- *Access Time*: The average time elapsed from the moment a client issues a query to the moment when the required data item is received by the client.
- *Tuning Time*: The amount of time spent by a client listening to the channel.

The *Access Time*: consists of two separate components, namely:

- *Probe Wait*: The average duration for getting to the next index segment. If we assume that the distance between two consecutive index segment is L, then the probe wait is $L/2$.
- *Bcast Wait*: The average duration from the moment the index segment is encountered to the moment when the required data item is downloaded.

The *Access Time* is the sum of the *Probe Wait* and *Bcast Wait*. These two factors work against each other [6, 7]. There are several indexing techniques such as the distributed indexing approach [6], the signature approach [9], and the hybrid approach [10].

2.2 LDIS Schemes

In the mobile computing environment, caching data at the client's side is a useful technique for improving the performance. However, the frequently disconnection and mobility of the clients may cause cache inconsistency problems. In [2], authors propose location dependent cache invalidation schemes for mobile environments. In this scheme, they use bits to indicate whether the data item in the specific area has been changed. For instance, if there are eight service areas and the values of the bit vector are 00010011, this means that the data item is valid in 4th, 7th, and 8th only. And they organize each service area as a group in order to reduce the overhead for scope information. In [3], authors proposed a PE (Polygonal Endpoint) and AC (Approximate Circle) schemes. The PE scheme records all the endpoints of the polygon representing the valid scope, while the AC scheme uses an inscribed circle from the polygon to represent the valid scope of the data.

3 Proposed Algorithms

In this section, we present two schemes for LDIS. We first introduce the broadcast-based LDIS scheme (BBS). In this scheme, the server broadcasts reports which contains the IDs of the data objects (e.g., building names) and the values of the location coordinates. The data objects broadcast by the server are sorted based on the locations of the data objects. Then, we present a data prefetching scheme and OBC in order to reduce the client's tuning time.

3.1 BBS (Broadcast Based LDIS) Scheme

An index gives the ability of selective tuning. The drawback of this solution is that the client has to wait and listen for an index segment in order to identify the nearest data object. In the BBS method, the sever broadcast data objects are sorted sequentially according to the location of the data objects. Moreover, based on the distance between the data objects, we assign the difference weight values to each data object, by using the OBC (Object Boundary Circle). Also, the data objects can be sent using different broadcast frequencies, by classifying them into hot and cold groups [4]. For instance, the data objects selected as a hot group will broadcast more frequent than the other groups. We discuss this issue in the section concerning the performance evaluation. In the BBS method, since the data objects broadcasted by the server are sequentially ordered based on their location, it is not necessary for the client to wait for an index segment, if it has already identified the nearest object before the associated index segment has arrived. In this method, the structure of the broadcast affects the distribution of the data objets. For example, as shown in Fig. 1, if the data objects are horizontally distributed, the server broadcasts data objects sequentially, from the leftmost data object to the rightmost data object. A simple sequential broadcast can be generated by linearizing the two dimension coordinates in two different ways: i.e. horizontal broadcasting (HB) or vertical broadcasting (VB). The client uses the following algorithm to identify the nearest object:

Notations:

- S: server data set
- O: broadcast data object, where $O \in S$
- O_c: current broadcast data object (initially O_c regarded as an O_n), where $O_c \in S$
- O_p: previous broadcast data object, where $O_p \in S$
- O_n: nearest data object
- C_l: client's location

Algorithm 1. Client Algorithm Used to Identify the Nearest Object

```
if (current data item is an index segment)
    find k-NN using index segment
else
{   for each object O ∈ S
    {
        do {
            compare dist|O_c − C_l| and dist|O_n − C_l|
            if (O_c is the first broadcast data object
                or dist|O_c − C_l| < dist|O_n − C_l|)
                then O_n = O_c
            else if (dist|O_c − C_l| > dist|O_n − C_l|)
                then O_n = O_p
        } while (getting to the index segment or dist(O_c, C_l) < dist(O_n, C_l))
    }
}
```

Since it does not have the location information of all of the data objects, the client cannot estimate which data will be broadcast next. Hence, even if the server delivers data objects sequentially based on their coordinate values, it is difficult to determine which data object is the nearest to the client. If the client loses the desired data object, it has to wait until the next broadcast period.

In our scheme, the client maintains a queue and determines the size of window w (hereafter referred to as w_q), which indicates the number of data objects that will be left in the queue. The client maintains objects in the queue based on the size of w_q and this queue can be represented as follows:

Notations:

- O_j: an object in the map
- T_o: the timestamp of an object
- T_c: the timestamp of the current broadcasted object

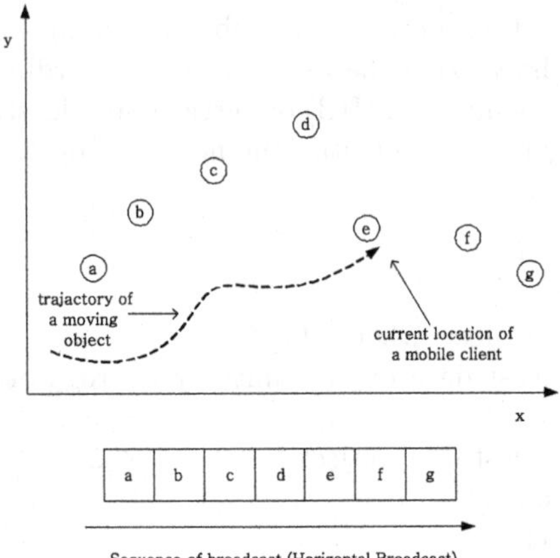

Fig. 1. An example of Horizontal Broadcast

- S: set of objects in the map
- S_q: set of objects in the queue
- w_q: size of the windows in the queue

Then $S_q = \{\langle O_j, T_o\rangle | (O_j \in S) \wedge (T_c - w_q \leq T_o \leq T_c)\}$.

3.2 Prefetching Scheme

The result of the NN query is changed if the client moves. Thus, the client has to tune its broadcast channel every time it moves. Data prefetching has been proposed as a technique for hiding the access latency of data item that defeat caching strategies. In this section, we present a prefetching method for use in LDIS. In this method, the client prefetches the data object for future use. Let w_p be the size of prefetched data objects. The client adjusts the size of w_p according to the speed and size of the cache. Moreover, in order to adjust the value of k based on the k-nearest objects, the proposed scheme simply adjust the size of w_p. Let client's current location be point q and object's location be point p. And we denote the Euclidian distance between the two points p and q by $dist(p, q)$. In the map, we have $dist(p, q) := \sqrt{(p_x - q_x)^2 + (p_y - q_y)^2}$.

Let $P := \{p_{-n} \ldots, p_{-2}, p_{-1}, p_0, p_1, p_2 \ldots, p_n\}$ be a set of n distinct points that represent the data objects, and q represents a query point.

Notations:

- $w, n \geq 0$ and $(w - n) \geq 0$
- target= an object p_0, where $p_0 \neq p_n$ and $\{p_{-n}, p_0, p_n\} \in P$ then $dist(p_0, q) \leq dist(\forall p_{-n}, q)$ or $dist(p_0, q) \leq dist(\forall p_n, q)$
- p_{min} = an object p_{-w}, where $dist(p_{-(w-n)}, q) \leq dist(p_{-w}, q) \leq dist(p_{-(w+n)}, q)$

– p_{max} = an object p_w, where $dist(p_{w-n}, q) \leq dist(p_w, q) \leq dist(p_{w+n}, q)$

A query can be categorized as the nearest or the k-nearest based on the number of returned objects. The number of returned objects depends on the value of w_p. If we regard the value of w_p as n, the number of returned objects is $2n + 1$. Hence, w_p= set of $2n + 1$ points. In order to adjust the value of k of the k-nearest objects, the proposed scheme simply adjusts the size of w_p. The formal description of the algorithm used for prefetching at the client side is as follows:

Algorithm 2. Client Algorithm for Data Prefetching

```
while (a client looking for the nearest object) {
    active mode (listen to the broadcast channel)
    if (desired data comes from the server) {      // use algorithm 1
        then current broadcast data object= p0(target object)
        and prefetch a data object from pmin to pmax
    } else
        wait until the desired data comes from the server
}
doze mode
```

4 Performance Evaluation

In this paper, we evaluate the performance with various kinds of parameters settings such as the client's speed and the distributions of the data objects. Then, we compare the performance of the BBS scheme and the R-Tree index scheme. We assume that the broadcast data objects are static such as restaurants, hospitals, and hotels. We use a system model similar to that in [3, 5]. In this paper, two datasets are used in the experiments (see Fig. 2(a)). The first data set $\mathcal{D}1$ contains data objects randomly distributed in a square Euclidian space. The second data set $\mathcal{D}2$ contains the data objects of hospitals in the Southern California area, which is extracted from the data set at [8]. Table 1 shows the notations and default parameter settings used in the simulation.

4.1 Latency

In this section, we present the Object Boundary Circle (OBC) which represents the distance between the objects as shown in Fig. 2(b). The radius of circle represents a distance between objects. And a circle which has the longest radius is selected as a hot data object such as c and d in Fig. 2(b). The server broadcasts data objects with different frequency such as hot and cold data objects [4].

Effect of the Client's Speed. In this section, we study the effect of the client speed. First, we vary the client's speed from 5 to 50 in $\mathcal{D}1$. When the client's

Table 1. Simulation Parameters

Parameter	Description	Setting
ServiceArea	Service area	1000(km)*1000(km)
GroupServiceArea	% of service area	30-100
NoObj	No. data objects	10-1000
SizeObj	Size of data object	256 bytes - 8192 bytes
BroadBand	Broadcast bandwidth	144kbps
No_Client	No. of clients	0-90
MinSpeed	Minimum moving speed of the client	10
MaxSpeed	Maximum moving speed of the client	90
$size\_W_q$	size of W_q	0-5
$size\_W_p$	size of W_p	0-5
NoPeriod	No. of broadcast period	50-100
Size_max_OBC	Size of *max_OBC*	longer than 900m

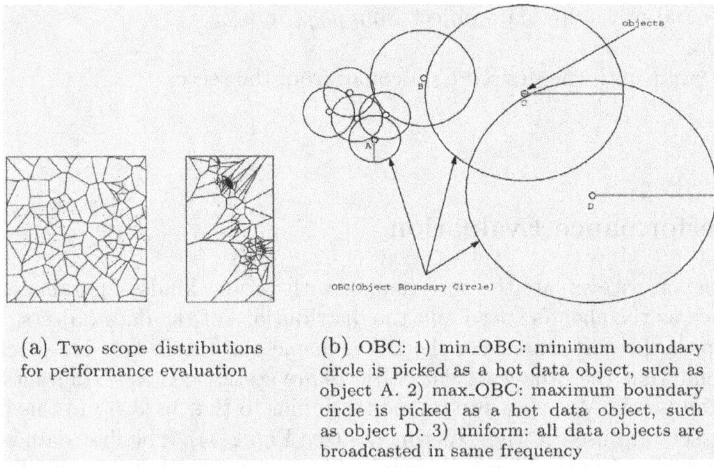

(a) Two scope distributions for performance evaluation

(b) OBC: 1) min_OBC: minimum boundary circle is picked as a hot data object, such as object A. 2) max_OBC: maximum boundary circle is picked as a hot data object, such as object D. 3) uniform: all data objects are broadcasted in same frequency

Fig. 2. Scope distributions and OBC

speed is the lowest, broadcast size of 10% (of the coverage area) is the best. However, as the client's speed increases, its performance is degraded in comparison with that of others since the most of the client's speed exceeds the service coverage area as shown in Fig. 3(a). Second, we study the performance for different parameters such as *min_OBC*, *max_OBC* and uniform (see Fig. 2(b)) in $\mathcal{D}2$. In this experiment, we assume that the clients are uniformly distributed in the map. Fig. 3(b) shows the result as the client speed increases from 5 to 50. And Fig. 3(c) shows the result as the number of clients increased from 15 to 90.

Effect of the Distribution of Data Objects and the Clients' location. In this section, we study the effect of the distributions of the data objects and

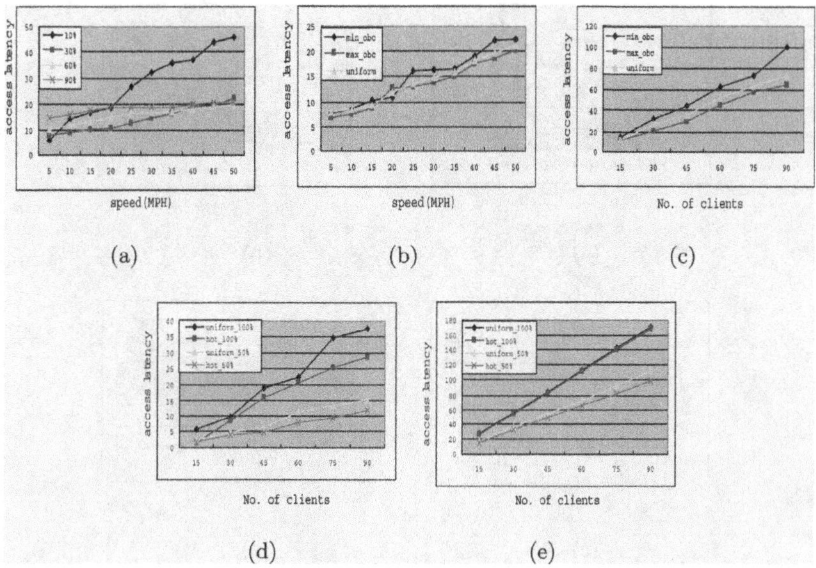

Fig. 3. Access latency

the clients' location. First, we assume that the clients are crowded in a specific region such as downtown. Those data objects which are located in such a region are selected as hot data objects. In this experiment, we evaluate the performance in relation to four different parameters as follows:

- *uniform*_100%: The server broadcasts data objects with the same frequency and the service coverage area is the whole geographic area.
- *hot*_100%: The server broadcasts data objects with different frequencies such as those corresponding to hot and cold data objects and the service coverage area is the whole geographic area.
- *uniform*_50%: The server broadcasts data objects with the same frequency and the service coverage area is set to 50% of the whole geographic area.
- *hot*_50%: The server broadcasts data objects with different frequencies such as those corresponding to hot and cold data objects and the service coverage area is set to 50% of the whole geographic area.

Fig. 3(d) shows the result as the number of client is increased from 15 to 90 in $\mathcal{D}1$. As shown in figure, the *hot*_50% outperform compare to others as the number of client increases. Second, we assume that the clients are uniformly distributed in $\mathcal{D}2$. Fig. 3(e) shows the result as the number of client increases from 15 to 90. As shown in figure, in this case, the broadcast hot data object does not affect the query response time since the clients are uniformly distributed in the map. However, the size of the service area affect the query response time.

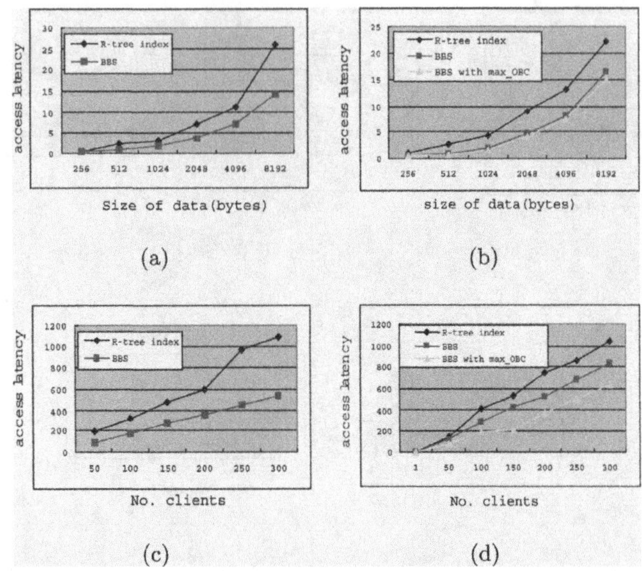

Fig. 4. Compare the Performance of BBS Scheme and R-Tree Index

4.2 Comparison of the Performance of the BBS Scheme and the R-Tree Index

In this section, we compare the BBS scheme with the R-Tree index. First, we vary the size of the data item from 256 bytes to 8192 bytes in $\mathcal{D}1$ and $\mathcal{D}2$. In this experiment, the server broadcast 506 data items periodically to the clients. In $\mathcal{D}2$, we also evaluate BBS with *max_OBC* (see Fig. 2(b)). Since the clients do not need to wait and tune an index segment if they have already identified the nearest object, the BBS shows lower latency compare to the R-Tree index as the data size increases as shown in Fig. 4(a). The BBS with *max_OBC* outperform the R-Tree index and BBS in $\mathcal{D}2$ as shown in Fig. 4(b). Second, we vary the number of clients from 50 to 300. As shown in Fig. 4(c) and Fig. 4(d), the BBS shows lower latency compare to R-Tree index in $\mathcal{D}1$ and the BBS with *max_OBC* shows the lowest latency compared to the R-Tree index and BBS in $\mathcal{D}2$.

5 Conclusion

In this paper, we studied the broadcasting and prefetching schemes for LDIS. For broadcasting in LDIS, we present the BBS and prefetching methods. The BBS method attempts to reduce the access time for the client. Furthermore, the proposed prefetching and OBC can also reduce the query response time and tuning time respectively. We do not change the previous index schemes, such as R-tree index [11] and D-tree index [12]. Rather, we sort the data objects based on their locations and the server broadcasts the data objects sequentially to the mobile clients.

With the proposed schemes, the client can performs the k-NN query processing while it moves without having to tune the broadcast channel, if the desired data items have already been prefetched into the cache. Therefore, the client can reduce its query response time and the battery power consumption. The proposed schemes were investigated in relation to various environmental variables such as the distributions of the data objects, the average speed of the client and the size of the service area. The experimental results show that the proposed BBS scheme significantly reduces the access latency compared to the R-tree index since the client does not always have to wait for an index segment.

In this paper, we are not consider the moving data objects in LDIS. Hence, we are planning to extend this study to the case of a moving object database.

References

[1] Dik Lun Lee, Jianliang Xu, and Baihua Zheng, "Data Management in Location-Dependent Information Services," *IEEE Pervasive Computing*, 1(3), 2002.
[2] Jianliang Xu, Xueyan Tang, and Dik Lun Lee, "Performance Analysis of Location-Dependent Cache Invalidation Schemes for Mobile Environments," *IEEE Trans. Knowledge and Data Eng*, 15(2), 2003.
[3] Baihua Zheng, Jianliang Xu, and Dik L. Lee, "Cache Invalidation and Replacement Strategies for Location-Dependent Data in Mobile Environments," *IEEE Trans. Comp.*, 51(10), 2002.
[4] Swarup Acharya and Michael Franklin, "Broadcast Disks: Data Management for asymmetric communication environments," In *Proc. of SIGMOD*, 1995.
[5] Daniel Barbara, "Sleepers and Workaholics: Cashing Strategies in Mobile Environments," In *Proc. of SIGMOD*, 1994.
[6] T. Imielinski, S. Viswanathan, and B.R.Badrinath, "Data on Air: Organization and Access," *IEEE Trans. Knowledge and Data Eng*, 9(3), 1997.
[7] T. Imielinski, S. Viswanathan, and B.R.Badrinath, "Energy efficient indexing on air," In *Proc. of SIGMOD*, 1994.
[8] Spatial Datasets, `http://dias.cti.gr/~ytheod/research/datasets/spatial.html`.
[9] W.-C. Lee and D. L. Lee, "Using signature techniques for information filtering in wireless and mobile environments," *Distributed and Parallel Databases*, 4(3), 1996.
[10] Q. L. Hu, W.-C. Lee, and D. L. Lee, "A hybrid index technique for power efficient data broadcast," *Distributed and Parallel Databases*, 9(2), 2001.
[11] A. Guttman, "R-trees: A dynamic index structure for spatial searching," In *Proc. of SIGMOD*, 1984.
[12] J. Xu, B. Zheng, W.-C. Lee, and D. L. Lee, "Energy Efficient Index for Querying Location-Dependent Data in Mobile Broadcast Environments," In *Proc. of ICDE*, 2003.

A Publish/Subscribe Based Architecture of an Alert Server to Support Prioritized and Persistent Alerts[1]

Sharma Chakravarthy and Nishant Vontella

Computer Science and Engineering Department and Information Technology Laboratory,
The University of Texas at Arlington, Arlington, TX 76019-0015
sharma@cse.uta.edu

Abstract. This paper discusses the design and development of a publish/subscribe based distributed alert server whose requirements include: priority-based delivery, persistence, recovery, time-to-live and various other features. The approach described in this paper provides a lightweight implementation that is general-purpose and can be used for a number of applications. A new efficient sweeping algorithm is used to make sure alerts are delivered correctly and satisfy several requirements such as priority, sending existing alerts to new subscribers, and regular expression based subscription.

1 Introduction

Enterprise messaging products (or as they are sometimes called, Message Oriented Middleware products or MOM) [4] are becoming an essential component for integrating intra-company operations. They allow separate business components to be combined into a reliable, yet flexible, system. In addition to the traditional MOM vendors, several database vendors and a number of Internet related companies also provide enterprise-messaging products. Message-oriented middleware (MOM) is a client/server infrastructure that increases the interoperability, portability, and flexibility of an application by allowing the application to be distributed over multiple heterogeneous platforms.

This paper discusses the design and implementation of one such messaging system called the Alert Server. Alert Server is a general-purpose alert and acknowledgement message queue and distribution mechanism. It maintains transaction logs for a comprehensive audit trail of alerts, acknowledgements and receipts. At the alerts server, the alerts are logged and queued and if necessary persisted. The Alerts Server determines if there are any subscribers for this alert and if so, forwards it to the destination. An alert producer could be a human operator who "fills in the blanks" of an alert message through a GUI or other means. Alert producers can also be software components that execute "under the hood", invisible to human operators. An alert producer assembles the alert in reaction to some system condition and then sends for distribution. Alert consumers are those applications that are interested in receiving (a

[1] This work was supported, in part, by the Office of Naval Research, the SPAWAR System Center-San Diego & by the Rome Laboratory (grant F30602-02-2-0134), and by NSF (grant IIS-0123730).

R.K. Ghosh and H. Mohanthy (Eds.): ICDCIT 2004, LNCS 3347, pp. 106–116, 2004.

subset of) alerts. This is always accomplished via "registering" or "subscribing" for alerts that contain a particular pattern in the alert destination or topic data element by specifying a filter (in the form of a regular expression) during alert registration. This Server has been designed to handle C/C++ as well as Java clients.

Alert Server Objectives: If our Alert Server provided a union of all the existing features of messaging systems it would be much too complicated for its intended users. It is crucial that the Alert Server includes appropriate functionality needed to implement sophisticated enterprise applications. Our design and implementation of the alert server attempts to minimize the set of concepts a programmer must learn to use enterprise-messaging products. It strives to maximize portability. We start with the concept of alert producers, consumers and distributors that act as servers.

Alert Clients: A client can be either a producer or a consumer or both. The alert producer does not necessarily need to know who the receiver(s) of the message will be. The producer "publishes/sends" the messages to the Alert Server which is responsible for the distribution of messages. Alert Consumers are responsible for processing and responding to the alert (message) by subscribing/registering through the alert server.

Alert Server: Alert Server manages the alert and acknowledges messages, distribution of alerts, and crash recovery. Important goals of an alert server are:

1. Implement a publish/subscribe model. This model has been chosen over the point-to- point model because point-to-point (PTP) models are built around the concept of message queues. Each message is addressed to a specific queue; clients extract messages from the queue(s) established to hold their messages. Clients have to pull the message from the server rather than the server pushing it to the client after processing the messages. Publish and subscribe (Pub/Sub) clients send messages to the alert server. Publishers and subscribers are generally anonymous and may dynamically publish or subscribe to the alert server. The alert server pushes the messages arriving from a node's multiple publishers to its (multiple) subscribers.
2. Insure delivery of alerts before it expires (time-to-live) based on priority.
3. Dynamic delivery of alerts between multiple producers and consumers based on their registration/subscription topics.
4. Persistence of alerts and acknowledges to handle to crash recovery of clients.
5. Maintain the privacy and integrity of the messages.

2 Design of the Alert Server

First, we describe the functionality to be supported by the Alert Server and then describe how the Alert Server has been designed to achieve this functionality. The Alert Server should provide API to send messages from one application to another. The client applications should also be able to register and unregister topics of interest. They should be able to cancel messages and should also be able to send acknowledgements and/or receipts. Besides, the Alert Server should have a delivery logic in order to send, and if necessary persist, messages to different destinations on the basis of their priority. Finally, the alert server should be able to recover from crashes. The next section describes the types of messages handled by the alert server.

Alert: An alert message contains an alert header as well as an optional alert body. All messages support the same set of header fields. Header fields contain values used by both clients and the Alert Server to identify and route messages. Body, on the other hand, can be any Java Object for Java-based clients and an arbitrary string for C/C++ clients. A header of the alert message has the following data elements.

1. Destination: The destination field in the data element is the "topic" and synonymous to, for example, a message "topic" or an email "subject". It is the value in this field the alert consumers register or unregister by specifying a pattern in the registration request. The value of this field must begin with one of 3 prefixes (with colon included and all the letters capitalized) TAG:, PROFILE:, USER:
2. Alert Type: This field in the header identifies the message type. There are basically two types of alerts, alert itself and an acknowledgement for the alert.
3. Duration: Duration data element in the header helps in identifying the messages that have expired. Alerts or acknowledgements will remain active and available for distribution from the Alert Server according to its time-to-live indicator. Once the alert server receives and forwards the message to any registered recipients, it will remain in the Server's queue for the specific duration. The Server deletes the expired messages. Indefinite storage of messages in the queues is handled by setting this data field to zero. These alerts should be explicitly cancelled by the original producer or by any client.
4. Priority: This field in the header helps in priority based delivery of messages. The priority levels are 0-9, where 0 is designated as the lowest and 9 as the highest priority. Messages having the same priority are delivered in the order they arrive.
5. Classification: This part of header information allows application specific classification. Unclassified, Confidential, Secret and Top Secret are used.
6. Persistence: The producer designates messages as persistent, by setting this field in the header. The Alerts Server stores persistent messages so that they are reloaded in case of restart after recovery from a crash.
7. Acknowledge Policy: This field ensures the delivery of messages to the destination. An alert can have one of the three acknowledgement policies attached to it: None, Client Acknowledgement, and Receipt. A client acknowledgement requires the receiving client to generate an acknowledgement alert where as a client receipt is automatically constructed and submitted to the server after the client is notified of an incoming alert. Client receipts are not stored as clients make blocking calls when they send alerts that require receipts.
8. Cancel Policy: This field helps in the cancellation of alerts that persist indefinitely on the server. An alert can be cancelled (i.e., deleted) from the queue on the server by any client if the Cancel Policy field is set to ANY, or only by the producer of the alert if it is set to the ORIGINATOR.

9. Alert ID: Alert ID is a unique integer that is generated by the alert server to identify a particular alert or acknowledgment.
10. Body: The alert body is any JAVA object that can be sent with the message while it is a character string in the case of C/C++ alert producers. The body in the case of acknowledgement is a string "ACK".

Subscription/Registration: As explained above every alert contains a destination header field, the value of which starts with one of the prefixes: For example: TAG: Alert, PROFILE: watch officer, USER: Smith. The TAG: prefix helps alert consumers to subscribe to receive specific alerts by specifying a filtering mechanism that employs regular expression masks. For example: .* specifies all alerts. ABC specifies all alerts where destination contains the string ABC. ^A specifies all alerts where destination begins with A. X$ specifies all alerts where destination ends with X. PROFILE: prefix helps alert consumers to subscribe to any message that belong to a specific profile. The USER: prefix as the name indicates helps in subscribing to a message to a particular user.

When the Alert Server processes an incoming alert, it places the filtering mask that the consumers subscribed upon the pattern contained in the alert's destination. For example, if there is a consumer subscribed to a filter of "TAG:Alert" and an alert with the destination "TAG:AlertXYZ" comes in, then the subscription "TAG:Alert" is matches against the topic or destination "TAG:AlertXYZ" because the regular expression mask of "TAG: alert" placed against the topic "TAG: alertXYZ" matches true ("TAG: alert is a sub string of "TAG:AlertXYZ"). In the case of the other prefixes, the matching is performed by string comparing the subscription filter with the destination in the alert header. Consumer clients have the option to subscribe to multiple topics using separators. Multiple topics with the same prefix are submitted by separating with commas, for example, TAG:a, b, c will produce three subscriptions; TAG:a, TAG:b, and TAG:c. Similarly, multiple topics with multiple prefixes are submitted using a semicolon to separate prefixes, for example, TAG:a, b;USER:a, b will produce four subscriptions, TAG:a, TAG:b, USER:a, USER:b. The next section discusses the alert server architecture. It tries to explain the reasons for different decisions taken for designing the architecture.

3 Alert Server Architecture

Most messaging products support either point-to-point (PTP) or the publish/subscribe approach to messaging. PTP is useful when the message needs to be processed successfully by one consumer. As one of the objective of Alert Server is the delivery of messages to multiple clients, it implements a publish-subscribe model. In a publish/subscribe (pub/sub) product or application, clients address messages to atopic. Publishers and subscribers are generally anonymous and may dynamically publish or subscribe to the content hierarchy. The system takes care of distributing the messages arriving from a topic's multiple publishers to its multiple subscribers.

The Alert Server uses this messaging model as it has to delivery messages to zero, one or many consumers that are anonymous. This timing dependency is relaxed by allowing the producers to create persistent alerts. Persistent alerts can be received even when the subscribers are not active. Thus, persistent alerts provide the durability and reliability provided by the queues and still allows clients to send alerts to many consumers.

Message Consumption: Messages can be consumed in either of the two ways.

- Synchronously: A subscriber or a receiver explicitly fetches the message from the destination by calling a method. The method can block until a message arrives, or it can time out if a message does not arrive within a specified time limit.
- Asynchronously: A subscriber need not wait for the delivery of the message. Whenever the message arrives, the server forwards it to the consumers that have registered for that message. The consumers do not have to wait for the delivery of the message.

Message Delivery Mode: The producers send alerts to the Alert Server in two modes. As already explained the producers can set the delivery mode of the message in the persistent header field.

- The NON-PERSISTENT mode is the lowest-overhead delivery mode because it does not require that the message be logged to stable storage. Alert Server failure can cause a NON-PERSISTENT message to be lost.
- The PERSISTENT mode instructs the Alert Server to take extra care to insure the message is not lost in transit due to its failure. Its logs the alerts and helps in retrieving them during normal start ups as well as in the case of recovery after crashing. The data structures used in the fast retrieval of alerts is explained in the next section.

Logging and Retrieval of Alerts: The persistent mode delivery of the alerts causes them to be stored to a stable storage (disk). The alerts are stored in files depending on their priority. There is a file for each level of priority. Each file contains the following:

1. Index Table: The index table is a data structure stored in the log file for fast retrieval of alerts. Each log file has its own index table to store and retrieve the alerts belonging to its priority. The index table reduces the search time and thus helps in the fast retrieval of alerts. The index table and the alerts are stored in a serialized manner. The table has records that hold the information of the location of the alert in the log. Each record has a log sequence number (LSN), pointer to the position of storage of the alert in the file (fp), size of the alert (size) and a cancel bit. The log sequence number helps in indexing into the table and obtains the record that has information regarding the storage of alert. The record has file pointer that points to the alert in the file and the size of the file.
2. BLSN: BLSN in each file is an integer stored in each log along with the index table. BLSN is set to the ID of the alert that has recently been added to the priority queue. There is a BLSN for each priority queue in its corresponding log.
3. DLSN: DLSN, like BLSN, is also an integer stored in each log for corresponding priority queue. DLSN, unlike BLSN, is set to the ID of the alert that has been recently sent from the priority queue.
4. CANCEL BIT: The cancel bit indicates whether the alert has been cancelled or not.

5. Both DLSN and BLSN help in the retrieval of NON-PERSISTENT alerts in case of crash of the Alert Server. Instead of reading all the non-persistent alerts from the log when the server recovers, only those alerts whose IDs fall between BLSN and DLSN are read from the log and put into the priority queue, thus reducing the number of alerts read from the logs. The serialized log files always contain capacity of the index table at beginning followed by BLSN after 4L bytes. DLSN is at 8L bytes followed by index table with its records at 12L bytes, followed by storage of actual alerts from 20L bytes in each file. An example log file for one of the priority levels is shown in **Fig. 1.**

1. Capacity of the log (0L)
2. BLSN (4L)
3. DLSN (8L)
4. Index Table (12L)

LSN	fp	Size
1	20L	24L
3	45L	27L

Alert with ID 1 Alert with ID 3

Fig. 1. Contents of a log file. LSN is the log sequence number, fp is the file position and size is the size of the object

The alerts, after storing in the log, are sent to the queue for distribution to the consumers who have subscribed to their topics. As acknowledgements are alerts with just the correlation ID set to that of their alert, they are handled as if they are alerts.

3.1 Subscription and Unsubscription for Alerts and Acknowledgement

Consumers that have subscribed for specific alerts or acknowledgements are stored in hash tables. There are three primary hash tables one for each prefix TAG, USER and PROFILE. These hash tables have entries with alert type as key and another secondary hash table as value. The secondary hash table has keys for each topic, pointing to the consumer list as their values. This list contains consumer nodes that hold information regarding different consumers registered with the Alert Server. Each node in the list has unique ID. Apart from this, the list also contains information regarding the number of consumers added and number of consumers deleted. For each consumer added to the list, this attribute of the list increases by one while each deletion decrements the other attribute by one. These attributes help in reducing the sweep time of the priority queue. This is explained later in detail. Every consumer list in the secondary hash table has a unique ID.

All consumers registered for alerts are stored in one hash table while all consumers are registered for ACKs are stored in another secondary hash table. Consumers for a specific topic are store in the same consumer list in the secondary hash table. All consumers for an alert are obtained by using the alert topic as the key in the secondary hash table. Every new consumer registration causes that consumer object to be added to the beginning of its respective list. The primary hash table at the top level is for indexing purpose. This reduces the search time in finding the consumers registered for a specific alert type (ALERT or an ACK). The second level hash table is used for determining the consumers for a specific topic. A hash table has been chosen for the first level over other possibilities of array of lists as it would be easier to add more keys, such as CLIENT RECEIPT if needed in the future. The unsubscription for alerts and acknowledgements by a consumer results in the deletion of that consumer from the consumer list preventing the Alert Server from distributing any messages further.

The data structure with the hash table and consumer lists is shown in **Fig. 2.** The primary hash table contains topics as keys while the secondary hash table distinguishes the consumers registered for alerts and acknowledgements.

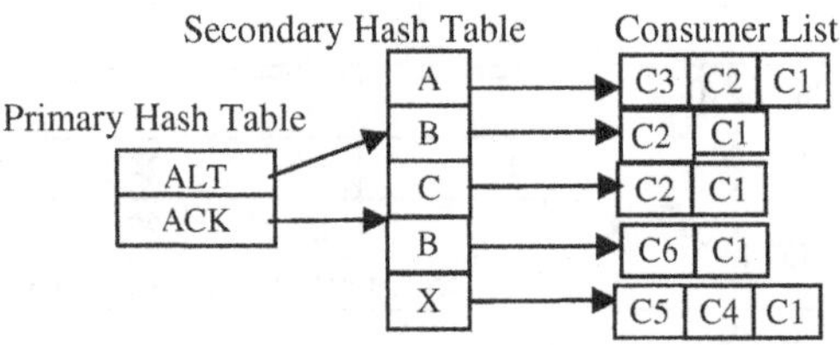

Fig. 2. Hash tables that store the consumers that are registered with alert server for a topic. All consumers registered for an alert are stored in ALT and those registered for an acknowledgement are stored in ACK table. A, B, C are the topics and C1, C2, C3... are the consumers

3.2 Queuing and Distribution of Alerts

The alerts are stored in the logs if needed depending on their delivery mode and later put in the priority queue. There are ten queues one for each priority level. The data structure used for the queues is an array of queues. The alert priority level is used for indexing into the array and getting the queue at that index. Every new alert is always added at the beginning of the queue. Therefore insertion of the alert always takes a constant time. Queuing and distribution of alerts are two independent operations. Therefore they are handled simultaneously using two different threads. The data structures used and the algorithm for sweeping are explained below.

Queuing: Producers publish alerts independently of the distribution of alerts on the Alert Server. Therefore they are queued for delivery by the Alert Server. The queuing of alerts is simple. Whenever a new alert comes in, it is indexed into the queues array using its priority and then put in the beginning of its queue. After putting the alert into the queue, the BLSN of the log file depending on the alert priority level is updated with the id of the alert. Thus the alerts put into the queue are now available for distribution. The queue is swept in order to distribute the alerts. Similarly, when an alert is cancelled, the alert is removed from the queue. The canceling of the alert depends on its cancellation policy. The expired alerts are removed when the queue is swept. The queue array with queues for each priority level are shown below in **Fig. 3**. The priority of alert is used as an index into this array of queues that will reduce the time in searching and adding an alert at its proper position.

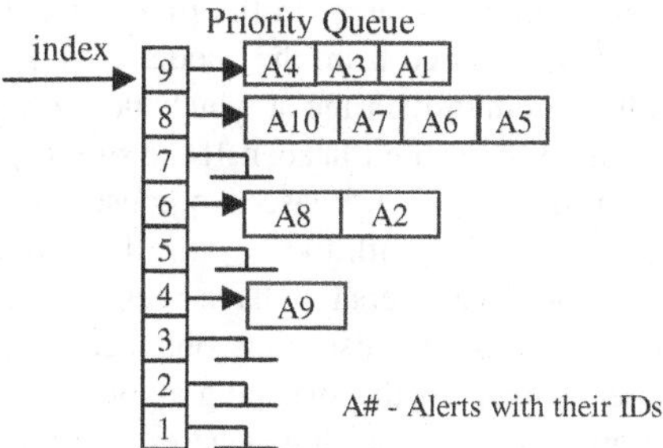

Fig. 3. Priority queue data structure. Each alert is stored in its respective priority level queue. A1, A2… are alerts with their Ids that are stored in this data structure

Distribution: Alerts are distributed to their respective consumers by comparing their topic with the topic in the consumer object that is created and stored in the consumer list data structure when the consumer registers. The priority queues are swept and the alerts are distributed. It is during this sweeping of the priority queue that the expired alerts are purged. Since the goal of distribution is the delivery of alerts on the basis of priority, the higher priority level alerts are delivered before the lower ones. Higher priority numbers indicate higher priority. Alerts of the same priority are delivered on LCFS (last come first served) basis since the new alerts are added at the beginning of the queue. The way in which the queues are swept is discussed next.

Sweeping Algorithm: The algorithm makes use of the information held in the alert and consumer objects. The alert object, apart from the header and body field, contains a hash table that holds mapping between each consumer list and max ID of the consumer in the list that it has been sent. This hash table contains the consumer list id as the key and the highest consumer ID that received the alert as its value. This information is necessary in trying to stop sending the message to consumers that have already received it. This also reduces the time for sweeping the priority queues. As already explained, each consumer object in the consumer list has unique ID in that list and similarly every consumer list also has its ID. Consumer list ID serves as an index to the hash table of the alert message which indicates that the alert has been sent up to this consumer in the list and needs to be sent to all the consumers before this consumer in the list. Since new consumers are always added at the beginning of the list, the consumers are always in decreasing order of their ID. This information is used to prevent from resending the same message to the same consumer more than once. The sweeping algorithm guarantees the delivery of alerts in the order of their priority. The algorithm takes a queue of the highest priority from the priority queue data structure and then traverses the queue to send the alerts to the registered consumers. There are two possibilities of changes to the priority queue and consumer table data structures: either an alert has been added or deleted from the one of the queue resulting in change of state of the priority queue data structure or some consumers might have been added or deleted from the consumer list resulting in a change in consumer table.

The algorithm executes in three phases. In the first phase the alert is checked for expiration. Expired alerts are removed from the queue. This is checked by comparing current system time with the sum of the time at which alert was received on the server and the time-to-live data field in the alert header. If the sum is greater than the system time then it is removed from the queue. Phase two consists of finding the consumer list. Comparing the alert destination with the keys in the consumer hash tables does this. This phase also filters out consumers that have been registered for alerts that may be published in future. The consumer lists thus obtained are used further in phase three. In the absence of consumer list the sweeping algorithm continues with the next alert in the queue and applies the same three phases. During the third phase, hash table in the alert is used to reduce the traversal of the consumer list. This also prevents resending of alerts to the same consumers. The unsubscription of consumers is not of much concern as they are simply deleted from the consumer list and there is no need to worry about the delivery of the alerts to them. During the third phase, the max ID of the consumer the alert had been sent to is obtained from the hash table in the alert by using the consumer list id which serves as a key. If this is zero, it means we have a new alert in the queue and the alert is sent to all the consumers in the list. If the ID of the consumer retrieved is more than zero, then the alert has been sent to some consumers and needs to be sent to the newly added ones.

Algorithm: Sweeping algorithm is shown in **Fig. 4.** Initially, queue Q with the highest priority is sent to the algorithm. Let A_0, A_1, A_2... be the alerts in the queue.

```
SweepingAlgorithm (Q) {
    A_current = A_0
    while (A_current != null) begin
      if (expired (A_current) = false)
        findconsumerlist(A_current)
      else
        Q = Q - A_current
      A_current = A_next
    end of while
findconsumerlist (A_current)
    ST = PT (alerttype [A_current] )
    if (prefix = TAG)
      for each key in ST begin
        if (matches (key, topic [A_current]))
          list = ST [topic [A_current]]
          sendtoOutputQueue (list, A_current)
      end
    else
      list = ST[topic [A_current]]
     sendtoOutputQueue (list, A_current)
sendtoOutputQueue (list, A_current)
    if (list != null)
    consrecv = get (HT[ID[list]] [A_current])
      if (consrecv = 0)
        send to all the consumers between added [list] and
    deleted[list]
        put (HT [A_current], added [list])
      else
        if (added [list] > consrecv) {
          send to all consumers between added [list] and consrecv
        put (HT [A_current], added [list])
```

Fig. 4. Sweeping algorithm that sweeps through the priority queue

Their subscripts indicate their positions. Alerts are added at the beginning of the queue. $A_{current}$ be the current alert that is being distributed in the queue and A_{next} be the alert after the current alert. ST and PT are the secondary and primary hash tables that store the information about the consumers registered. The descriptions of these data structures have been described in earlier sections. HT is another hash table in each alert. This stores the consumer ID that has recently received the alert in that consumer list. All the lists that have the same topic that match the alert topic have an entry in this table. X[Y] indicates an attribute X of an object Y. For example, topic [$A_{current}$]

3.3 Multithreading the Server

The Alert Server uses Java Remote Method Invocation [RMI][3] in its communication interface. RMI calls are blocking therefore these calls need to be handled asynchronously. Client requests are queued. Since each request is independent and there is no guarantee that they will arrive within a certain time there is a queue for each type of request and a different thread handles each different request. Multithreading also helps in making the server scalable.

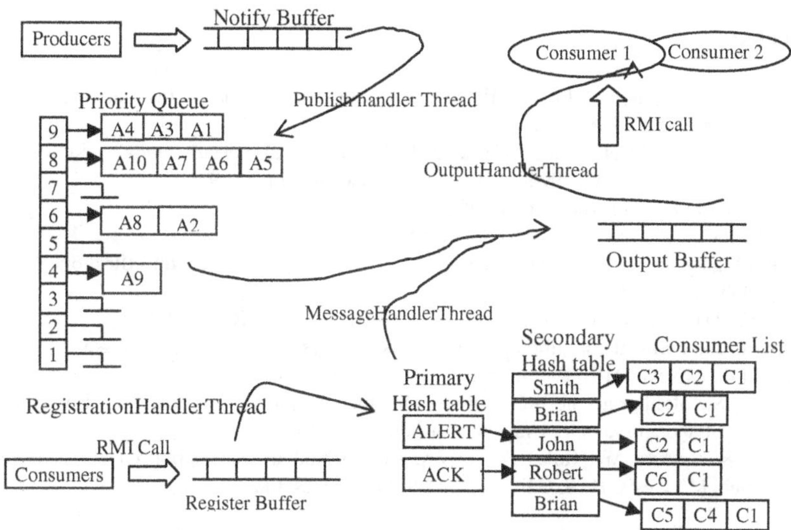

Fig. 5. Alert Server Architecture Overview

The clients put the messages in the queue and continue with their processing. Since each queue has a thread listening on it, the thread is awakened when the queue is not empty. The data structures handled by each thread are shown in **Fig 5.**. There are other threads for handling other requests like canceling an alert, unsubscribing for a topic. The threads shown in **Fig 5.** are the threads that handle registration for a topic, publishing an alert and the delivery of alerts to different consumers. The publish handler listens on the notify buffer that holds the alerts that are published by different clients. It places these alerts in the priority queue data structure on the basis of their priorities. On the other hand, registration thread handles the registration in the registration buffer independent of publishes. This thread constructs consumer nodes that hold consumer information that is used while sending the alert to the respective consumers by the output handler thread and places them in their respective consumer lists in the secondary consumer hash table. The Message handler thread runs sweeping algorithm on the priority queues and places the alert and its consumers in the output queue. The output handler thread picks up these alerts and delivers them to the consumers. This thread makes RMI calls to the clients to deliver the messages.

4 Conclusions

This paper proposes a novel sweeping algorithm for the requirements of the alert server based on the pub/sub paradigm. A number of requirements had to be satisfied for the real-world application that was given to us. The sweeping algorithm is efficient and is amenable to multi-threaded implementation.

References

[1] Rao, B. R. "Making the Most of Middleware." Data Communications International 24, 12 (September 1995): 89-96.

[2] The Common Object Request Broker: Architecture and Specification, Version 2.0. Framingham, MA: OMG, 1996. <URL: http://www.omg.org/> (1996).

[3] The Remote Method Invocation Specification

[4] Vondrak, C., Message-Oriented Middleware. 1997.

[5] Object Management, G., {CORBAServices: Common Object Services Specification v1.0}. 1995: John Wiley \& Sons Inc. NJ.

[6] Schmidt, D.C. and S. Vinoski, The OMG Events Service. C++ Report. 1997.

[7] http://msdn.microsoft.com/library/en-us/cossdk/htm/pgservices_events_20rp.asp?frame=true, COM+ Events Architecture. 2001.

[8] Scarlett, S., Monitoring the Behaviour of Distributed Systems, in Cambrigde University Computer Laboratory. 1996, University of London: London.

[9] Dasari, R., Events And Rules For JAVA: Design And Implemenation Of A Seamless Approach, MS thesis. 1999, University of Florida: Gainesville.

A Nested Transaction Model for LDAP Transactions

Debmalya Biswas and K. Vidyasankar[1]

Dept. of Computer Science, Memorial University of Newfoundland,
St. John's, NL, Canada A1B 3X
{debmalya, vidya}@cs.mun.ca

Abstract. Lightweight Directory Access Protocol (LDAP) directories have recently proliferated with the growth of distributed computing. They are being used in a variety of network based applications to store information about not only people and organizations but also network resources and policies. Given the diversity of its applications and its frequent use in conjunction with transaction aware applications (databases, application servers), there is a great demand for LDAP servers to support transactions. In this paper we focus on LDAP servers using a relational database to store the data. We propose a nested transaction model for implementing LDAP transactions. The proposed model not only simplifies the LDAP to SQ translation but also imposes minimum requirements on the underlying relational database platform. We also present a locking based concurrency control protocol and recovery mechanism for LDAP transactions.

1 Introduction

Lightweight Directory Access Protocol (LDAP) is a standard, extensible client-server protocol for accessing and managing directory information. LDAP has been around for quite some time now. LDAP version 3 was approved as an Internet standard [12] in Dec 1997. During the last few years, LDAP's popularity has grown by leaps and bounds, which explains the large number of LDAP implementations available nowadays from companies like IBM, Oracle, Microsoft, Novell (to name just a few). When well established companies come up with a new product, they try to reuse their already developed products as much as possible. This was perhaps responsible, in part, for starting the trend towards using a relational database for LDAP data storage. Till then, given the hierarchical nature of LDAP data, B-tree packages were the popular choice for storing the LDAP data. Whatever the business strategy might have been, a relational database has some proven advantages in its favor when it comes to data storage (more details in Section 3). From an LDAP perspective, the main concerns regarding the use of a relational database are 1) LDAP to SQ translation complexity and 2) performance issues.

[1] This research is supported in part by the Natural Sciences and Engineering Research Council of Canada Individual Research Grant OGP0003182.

R.K. Ghosh and H. Mohanthy (Eds.): ICDCIT 2004, LNCS 3347, pp. 117–126, 2004.

Also, the frequent use of LDAP in transaction oriented applications has led to a demand for LDAP implementations to support transactions. In this paper, we propose a nested transaction model for LDAP implementations. Our model allows simplification of the LDAP-SQL translation, places minimum requirements on the underlying relational database platform, and allows exploiting the inherent benefits of a nested transaction model to overcome the performance issues.

As such, the model allows loose coupling with the underlying relational database. Any transaction model would not be complete without a concurrency control and recovery mechanism. We present an optimized concurrency control and recovery mechanism which can be used by the LDAP layer irrespective of the mechanisms supported by the underlying relational database. We also show that the mechanisms need not be more complex than that required for a single (flat) transaction model.

The rest of the paper is organized as follows. LDAP concepts are introduced in section 2. Section 3 focuses on LDAP data storage. In section 4 we discuss the current status of LDAP transactions as well as introduce our nested transaction model. In sections 5 and 6, we discuss a concurrency control protocol and recovery mechanism, respectively, for the proposed model. Section 7 concludes the paper.

2 LDAP Concepts and Operations

Readers already familiar with basic LDAP concepts can skip this section. The material in this section is mainly from [9], some taken directly and some expanded. LDAP is a lightweight implementation of the X.500 Directory Access Protocol (DAP), first published in 1990. LDAP runs directly over TCP/IP as compared to X.500 which runs over the OSI networking stack.

As evident from Fig. 1, LDAP data is hierarchical in nature. A brief description about how information is stored in a directory is as follows:

Entries: In a directory, each collection of information about an object is called an entry. This object may be a person, a printer or some other shared resource, a department within a company, or even the company itself. To name it and to identify its location in the directory hierarchy, each entry is assigned a unique distinguished name (DN). The DN of an entry consists of the entry itself, known as the relative distinguished name (RDN), and its parent entries, connected in ascending order, from the entry itself up to the root (top) entry in the tree. Collectively, these entries form a directory information tree (DIT). Fig. 1 represents a portion of a DIT belonging to the educational institute "mun", designated by the entry dc (domain component)=edu, dc=mun. The highlighted DN "uid= debmalya, ou (organizational unit)=computer science, ou=people, dc=mun, dc=edu" is an entry within the DIT.

Attributes: An entry consists of a set of attributes, each describing a unique feature of the entry. An attribute consists of two components, an attribute type and one or, sometimes, more values. Some attributes that the entry "uid=debmalya", might contain are: "dn: uid=debmalya, ou=computer science, ou=people, dc=mun, dc=edu", "objectClass: myPerson", "uid (unique identifier): debmalya", "cn (common name): Debmalya", "sn (surname): Biswas", "givenname: Deb", "dept:

Computer Science", "email: debmalya@cs.mun.ca, debmalyabiswas@hotmail.com (Multivalued attribute)".
Object Classes: An object class is a collection of attributes that is used to define an entry. Some of these attributes are mandatory; others are optional. If, for example, we assign the LDAP-defined object class organizationalPerson to the entry "uid=debmalya ",..we must include common name (cn) and surname (sn) as attributes for the entry. Rules for the object class organizationalPerson also allow us to include the attributes telephoneNumber, uid, and userPassword, but these are not required, they are optional.

Basically, LDAP operations can be grouped into two categories:

Query: search and compare. These operations are used to retrieve information from the directory. The search function allows the user to specify the search criteria, scope and the starting point. The starting point is called the base DN. The scope of the search can be a single entry (base level), the children of an entry (one level), or subtree search.
Update: add, delete, and modify. Users can use these operations to update the contents of the directory. The modify operation allows the user to update/add/delete multiple attributes of an entry simultaneously.

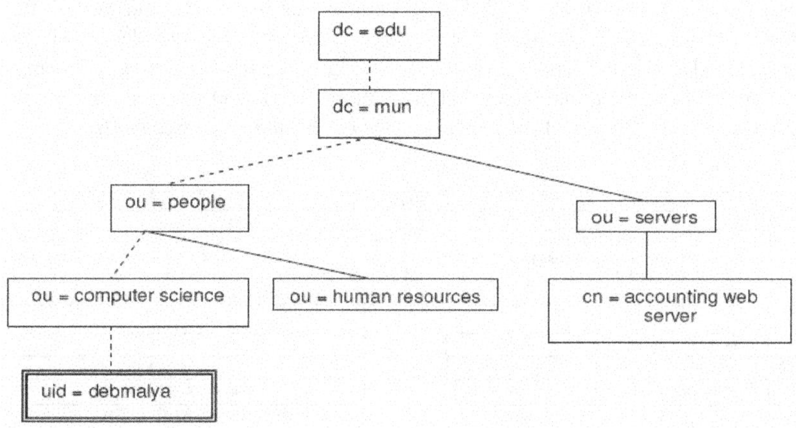

Fig. 1. LDAP Directory Information Tree (DIT)

3 LDAP Data Storage

Considering the hierarchical nature of LDAP data, B-trees or hierarchical databases would seem as ideal options for storing the LDAP data. Recently, however, there has been a trend towards storing the LDAP data in relational databases. [1] discusses an implementation of LDAP that uses DB2 as the data store and query engine to meet the directory service requirements. The main reason behind the trend is that databases provide inherent solutions for most of the problems associated with any data store such as handling large amounts of data, complex search and indexing facilities, and resilience against failures.

Below we outline a scheme, followed in [1], which allows efficient storage of the LDAP data into relational tables. Each LDAP entry is assigned a unique identifier (EID) by the backing store.

Attribute Tables. There is one attribute table per searchable attribute.

Entry Table. The Entry table holds the information about an LDAP entry. This table is used to obtain the EID of the entry and to support base and one level search scope. In order to support one level search, the Entry table contains a field PEID, which is the unique identifier of the parent LDAP entry in the naming hierarchy. For example, the LDAP entry with DN "ou=computer science, ou=people, dc=mun, dc=edu" is the parent of the entry having DN "uid=debmalya, ou=computer science, ou=people, dc=mun, dc=edu".

The purpose of the Descendant table is to support the subtree search feature of LDAP. For each entry that is an ancestor of one or more descendant entries in the hierarchy (that is, an ancestor entry AEID), there is a tuple for each of the descendents, at any level in the hierarchy.

For example, the rows corresponding to the LDAP entry having DN "uid=debmalya, ou=computer science, ou=people, dc=mun, dc=edu" in some of the tables would be as shown in Fig. 2. Fig. 2 assumes that the LDAP entries with RDN "dc=edu", "dc=mun", "ou=people", "ou=computer science" and "uid=debmalya" from Fig. 1 have EIDs 1, 2, 3, 4 and 5 respectively. In Fig. 2, we have shown only the important columns of the relational tables. [1] gives more details and justification regarding the storage model. The rest of the paper is based on the above storage model.

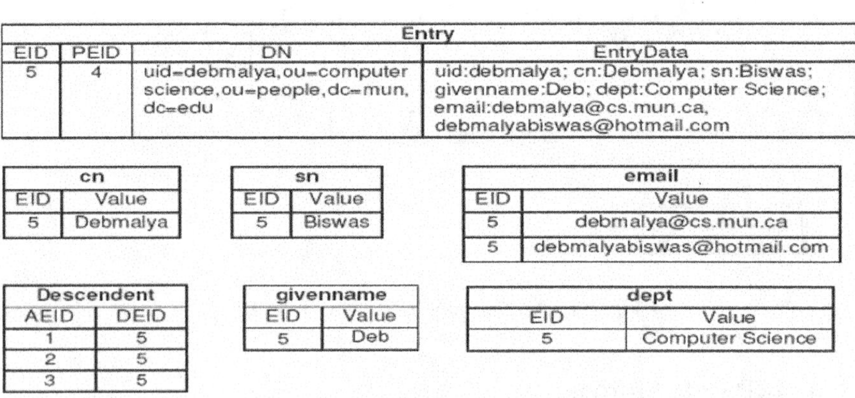

Entry			
EID	PEID	DN	EntryData
5	4	uid=debmalya,ou=computer science,ou=people,dc=mun, dc=edu	uid:debmalya; cn:Debmalya; sn:Biswas; givenname:Deb; dept:Computer Science; email:debmalya@cs.mun.ca, debmalyabiswas@hotmail.com

cn	
EID	Value
5	Debmalya

sn	
EID	Value
5	Biswas

email	
EID	Value
5	debmalya@cs.mun.ca
5	debmalyabiswas@hotmail.com

Descendent	
AEID	DEID
1	5
2	5
3	5

givenname	
EID	Value
5	Deb

dept	
EID	Value
5	Computer Science

Fig. 2. Relational Table representation

4 Nested Transaction Model

[2] is the proposed specification outlining how LDAP can be extended to support transactions. However, [2] considers transactions from an interface point of view and

does not give details regarding how LDAP servers are supposed to implement it internally. Currently, ACID properties in LDAP are restricted to the update operations. The LDAP implementation discussed in [1] maps each query or update operation to a single SQ statement.

In order to understand how we can map LDAP transactions to a nested transaction model, let us start by having a look at an LDAP query operation example.

Example 1. `ldapsearch -LLL -b "dc=edu" "(&(cn=Debmalya)(sn =Biswas))" cn sn email` performs a subtree search at the "dc=edu" level for all entries having cn and sn attributes equal to "Debmalya" and "Biswas respectively. The cn, sn and email attribute values are displayed as output.

Basically, any LDAP query operation can be divided into the following steps:

1. Obtain the EIDs matching the search filter from the attribute tables.
2. Retrieve the EID corresponding to the base DN. The corresponding children EIDs can also be retrieved simultaneously in case of a one-level search. Retrieve the corresponding descendent EIDs from the Descendent table (subtree search).
3. Perform an intersection of the EIDs retrieved in steps 1 and 2 to get the EIDs satisfying both the filter and search scope criteria.
4. Once the relevant EIDs have been obtained, retrieve the data from the Entry table.

As can be observed, steps 1 and 2 can be executed concurrently. However, step 4 can occur only after steps 1, 2 and 3 have completed. Although, Step 3 is not a transaction read/write step, it can be considered as a synchronizing step. For the purpose of allowing some subtransactions to proceed simultaneously and some sequentially, we use the concept of synchronous and asynchronous transaction invocation [7]. If a subtransaction is invoked synchronously, none of its sibling subtransactions can be invoked till the time it finishes. On the other hand, invoking a subtransaction asynchronously allows sibling transactions to execute concurrently.

Now, let us have a look at an LDAP Update operation example:

Example 2. `ldapmodify -f /details`, assuming that the file /details has the following contents: "dn: uid=debmalya, ou=computer science, ou=people, dc=mun, dc=edu; changetype: modify; replace: email; email: debmalya_biswas@yahoo.com; add: title; title: Student; delete: dept". The above operation replaces the contents of "uid=debmalya" entry's email attribute with the value "debmalya_biswas@yahoo .com", adds a title of "Student" and removes the dept attribute.

Similar to query operations, an LDAP Update operation can be divided into the following steps:

1. Retrieve the EID corresponding to the DN of the entry to be modified from the Entry table. For an add (delete) operation, this step might involve accessing the Entry table to check for duplicates (check if the entry to be deleted is a leaf entry).
2. Update the relevant attribute tables and/or Entry table and/or Descendent table.

Although, steps 1 and 2 need to be performed sequentially. Step 2 in itself provides sufficient scope for concurrency as can be seen from Fig 4.

As can be observed from Fig. 3 and 4, since each SQ statement deals with a single relational table, LDAP to SQ translation is considerably simplified. Also, the only expectation from the underlying relational database is that the execution of SQ statements should satisfy ACID properties. From an LDAP point of view, this allows the LDAP layer to consider the SQ statements as atomic operations (similar to the read/write operations of traditional transactions).

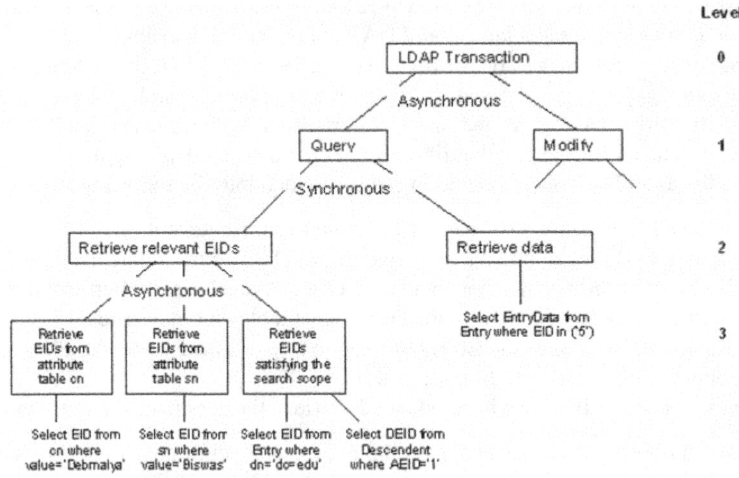

Fig. 3. Nested transaction representation of the Query operation given in Example 1

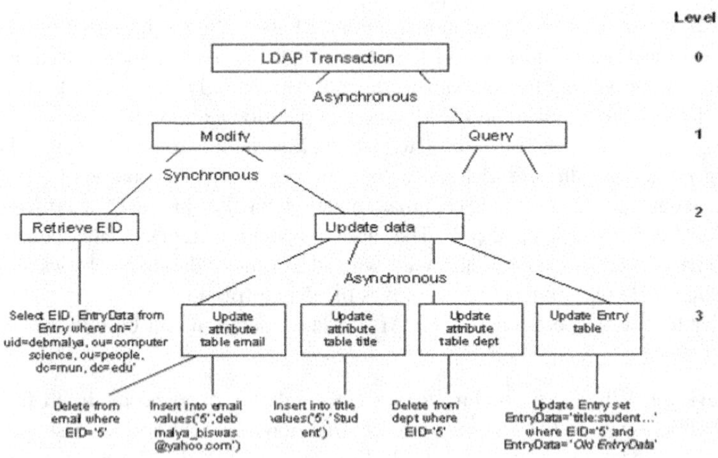

Fig. 4. Nested transaction representation of the modify operation given in Example 2

5 Concurrency Control for the Nested Transaction Model

In this section, we present a concurrency control protocol for the nested transaction model discussed above. Before discussing the rules, we would like to review the locking rules proposed by Moss [3] for nested transactions. Moss's concurrency control protocol for nested transactions is based on the concept of upward inheritance of locks. A transaction can acquire a lock on object O in some mode M. Doing that, it holds the lock in mode M until its termination. Besides holding a lock, a transaction can retain a lock in mode M. When a subtransaction commits, its parent transaction inherits its locks and then retains them. If a transaction holds a lock, it has the right to access the locked object (in the corresponding mode). However, the same is not true for retained locks. A retained lock is only a place holder and indicates that transactions outside the hierarchy of the retainer cannot acquire the lock, but that descendants potentially can. As soon as a transaction becomes a retainer of a lock, it remains a retainer for that lock until it terminates. The actual rules:

1. A transaction may hold a lock in write mode if no other transaction holds the lock and all retainers of the lock are superiors of the requesting transaction.
2. A transaction may hold a lock in read mode if no other transaction holds the lock in write mode and all retainers of the lock are superiors of the requesting transaction.
3. When a transaction aborts, all its locks (held and retained, of all modes) are simply discarded.
4. When a transaction commits, all its locks (held and retained, of all modes) are inherited by its parent (if any). This means that the parent retains each of the locks (in the same mode, as the child held or retained them).

In our case, lock management can be simplified by considering:

1. Locks are held at the table level (Please note that table level locking is not a requirement for our model, as such other more complex mechanisms such as tuple level locking can used to achieve further concurrency. To keep the model simple and easy to understand, table level locking is assumed for the rest of the paper).
2. A subtransaction can read/write relational table data provided any of its superiors holds a lock on the table in the corresponding mode. This is different from a traditional environment, where the subtransaction itself would be required to hold a lock of the appropriate type on the object to access it.

Given the above rules, it is sufficient if the subtransactions at level 1 hold locks. There is no need for subtransactions at any other level to hold locks. This should not be confused with downward inheritance of locks [4], as it is not required for the descendent subtransactions to acquire locks in this case. The subtransactions at level 1 represent the LDAP operations. As such, it is reasonable to assume that level 1 subtransactions know the read/write sets of their children. This enables the subtransactions at level 1 to acquire and hold locks on behalf of their descendent subtransactions. Level 0 transactions would retain the locks held by level 1 subtransactions in the same mode on their commit.

For the correctness proof of the above concurrency control algorithm, please refer to [13].

6 Recovery

Nested transaction recovery has been studied extensively in literature. [8] discusses an undo/redo log based approach while [6] proposes an approach based on compensating operations. Undo/Redo based approaches are widely used for single-level transaction recovery. However, compensation based approaches seem to be more popular for nested transactions because of the nature of subtransaction commits which are relative to their parent/ancestor transaction's commit. In this section, we propose a simple mechanism for recovery which uses the concepts of both undo/redo and compensation.

The motivation for using compensation here can be explained in terms of the model's loose coupling with the underlying relational database platform. Since SQ statements are the only interface with the database, there is no option but to execute a compensating SQ statement if some update operation needs to be undone. Also, since the effects of SQ Update/Insert/Delete statements become permanent upon execution, there is no need for the LDAP recovery algorithm to redo transactions. We associate LDAP recovery with two components: LDAP Recovery Manager (LDAP_RM) and LDAP log (LDAP_log). LDAP_RM is responsible for executing the transaction operations like Begin, Commit/Abort, Read/Write and also acts as the LDAP interface with the database. Although, we use the terms Read/Write as transaction operations, in reality they would be SELECT, UPDATE, INSERT or DELETE SQ statements as shown in Fig. 3 and 4. We also assume that all LDAP_log entries are written to stable storage. LDAP_RM and LDAP_log should not be confused with the Recovery Manager and log maintained by the underlying relational database for its own recovery purposes. As such, we consider recovery from an LDAP, and not a relational database, point of view. The algorithm below outlines the LDAP_RM steps for each of the operations discussed above.

Undo/No-Redo LDAP Recovery algorithm

RM-Begin (Ti, PTi) /* Applies to both transactions and subtransactions. PTi is the identifier of Ti's parent transaction or subtransaction. As such, would be blank if Ti is a top level transaction */
Append [Begin, Ti, PTi] to the LDAP_log; Acknowledge the processing of RM-Begin (Ti,PTi);
RM-SQ-Select (Ti, SQS) /* SQ is the SELECT SQ statement */
Execute the SELECT SQ statement SQ; Return the values read by executing the SQ statement;
RM-SQ-Insert (Ti, SQI) /* SQ is the INSERT SQ statement */
Add Ti to the active list, if it's not already there; /* SQI is the compensating SQ for SQ*/ Append [Ti, SQI] to the LDAP_log; Execute the INSERT SQ statement SQ Acknowledge the processing of RM-SQInsert (Ti, SQ;
RM-SQ-Delete (Ti, SQD) /* SQ is the DELETE SQ statement */
Add Ti to the active list, if it's not already there; /* Get the values required to form the compensating SQ statement */ Execute the Select SQ statement corresponding to SQ; /* SQD is the compensating SQ for SQ */ Append [Ti, SQD] to LDAP_log; Execute the DELETE SQ statement SQ; Acknowledge the processing of RM-SQDelete (Ti, SQ);
RM-SQ-Update (Ti, SQU) /* SQ is the UPDATE SQ statement */
Add Ti to the active list, if it's not already there; /* SQU is the compensating SQ for SQ */ Append [Ti, SQU] to LDAP_log; Execute the Update SQ statement SQ; Acknowledge the processing of RM-SQUpdate (Ti, SQ);

RM-Commit(Ti) /* Top level transaction commit */
Add Ti to the commit list; Acknowledge the commitment of Ti; Delete Ti from the active list;
RM-SubCommit(Ti,PTi) /* Subtransaction commit */
Append [Commit, Ti, PTi] to the LDAP_log; Add Ti to the commit list; Acknowledge the commitment of Ti; Delete Ti from the active list;
RM-Abort(Ti) /* Applies to both transactions and subtransactions */
Construct a list L of the transactions to be aborted including Ti; Start processing the LDAP_log backwards till [Begin, Ti, PTi] is encountered {For each LDAP_log entry [Tj, SQ_], if L contains Tj, do /* _ may be U/I/D */ {Execute the SQ statement SQ_. /* Undo */}}If any transactions in L are in the commit list, remove them from the commit list; Add all transactions in L to the abort list; Acknowledge the abortion of Ti; Delete Ti from the active list;
System Restart
Start with the last entry in the LDAP_log and scan backwards. Repeat the following steps until there are no more LDAP_log entries to examine {For each LDAP_log entry [Ti, SQ_], if Ti does not belong to the Commit list, then execute the SQ statement SQ_; For each LDAP_log entry [Commit, Ti, PTi], if PTi does not belong to the commit list, then remove Ti from the commit list;}For each Ti in the commit list, if Ti is in the active list, remove it from there; Acknowledge the completion of Restart;

Some comments regarding the algorithm are as follows:

The algorithm maintains three lists stored as part of the LDAP_log. The lists active, commit, abort contain the identifiers of the set of transactions that are active, committed or aborted (respectively). Appending [Begin, Ti, PTi] to the LDAP_log is required for the RM-Abort (Ti) procedure. Also, appending LDAP_log entries of the type [Commit, Ti, PTi] is required for the System Restart procedure.
Regarding Step 2 of RM-SQDelete (Ti, SQ), the step is required for creating the compensating SQ statement for the Delete SQ statement. Some examples of compensating statements are as follows:
Original: Insert into title values ('5','Student');
Compensating: Delete from title where EID='5';
Original: Delete from email where EID='5';
Compensating: Insert into email values ('5', 'debmalya@cs.mun.ca'); Insert into email values ('5', 'debmalyabiswas@hotmail.com');
Original: Update Entry set EntryData='title:student'..where EID='5' and EntryData= 'Old EntryData';
Compensating: Update Entry set EntryData='Old EntryData' where EID='5';
Techniques like checkpointing can be used to restrict the number of LDAP_log entries to be examined during restart.

For the correctness proof of the recovery algorithm, please refer to [13].

7 Conclusion and Summary

We started by having a look at LDAP in general and current LDAP implementations. Then we looked at a nested transaction model for implementing LDAP transactions. We have not considered the authentication part of LDAP operations. However, considering the fact that the access control attributes would be stored in attributes tables, authentication can be easily incorporated into the model. We showed how the nested transaction model simplifies LDAP-SQ translation. We then discussed how we can use the semantics of LDAP operations to achieve concurrency comparable to non serializable concurrency control protocols (snapshot isolation provided by Oracle). Since, we use a locking based protocol the possibility of deadlocks cannot be ruled out. However, deadlocks do not require any special consideration here. As such, any of the standard deadlock prevention or elimination methods can be used to overcome them. Finally, we presented a simple recovery algorithm for the proposed model. The algorithm considers recovery from an LDAP perspective and is independent of the recovery mechanism used by the underlying database.

References

[1] B. Shi, E. Stokes, D. Byrne, C. F. Corn, D. Bachmann, and T. Jones. An enterprise directory solution with DB2. http://www.research.ibm.com/journal/sj/392/ shi.html.

[2] Kurt D. Zeilenga. Internet Draft: LDAP Transactions. https://www1.ietf.org/internet-drafts/draft-zeilenga-ldap-txn-06.txt.

[3] Moss, T.E.B. Nested Transactions: An Approach to Reliable Distributed Computing. Ph.D. Thesis, MIT Laboratory for Computer Science, 1981.

[4] Theo Härder, Kurt Rothermel. Concurrency control issues in nested transactions. The VLDB Journal, v.2 n.1, p.39-74, January 1993.

[5] P. A. Bernstein, V. Hadzilacos, and N. Goodman. Concurrency Control and Recovery in Database Systems. Addison-Wesley, 1987.

[6] Lomet D. MLR: a recovery method for multi-level systems. ACM SIGMOD Record 21: 185-194, 1992.

[7] Theo Härder, Kurt Rothermel. Concepts for transaction recovery in nested transactions. In Proceedings of ACM-SIGMOD 1987, pages 239-- 248.

[8] Moss, J.E.B. Log-Based Recovery for Nested Transactions. Proc. 13th VLDB Conference, 1987.

[9] Oracle9i Directory Service Integration and Deployment Guide. http://tahiti. oracle.com/pls/db901/db901.to_pdf?partno=a90153&remark=docindex.

[10] Understanding locking in SQ Server. h ttp://msdn.microsoft.com/library/en-us/acdata/ ac_8_con_7a_7xde.asp.

[11] How Oracle processes SQ statements. http://www.cise.ufl.edu/help/database/oracle-docs/appdev.920/a96590/adg08sql.htm.

[12] Lightweight Directory Access Protocol (v3). http://www.ietf.org/rfc/rfc2251.txt.

[13] Debmalya Biswas, K. Vidyasankar. A nested transaction model for LDAP transactions. Tech. Report, Memorial University of Newfoundland, Canada, 2004.

Team Transaction: A New Transaction Model for Mobile Ad Hoc Networks

Ankur Gupta[1], Nitin Gupta[1], R.K. Ghosh[1], and M.M.Gore[2,*]

[1] Department of Computer Science and Engineering, Indian Institute of Technology, Kanpur-208016, India
rkg@cse.iitk.ac.in

[2] Department of Computer Science and Engineering, Motilal Nehru National Institute of Technology, Allahabad-211004, India
mmgore@ieee.org

Abstract. In this paper, we propose a new transaction model, named as *Team Transaction* for distributed, cooperative computing on mobile ad hoc networks. The proposed model captures the mobility and distributive properties inherently found in a vigorous team activity as in a game of soccer and also has an efficient recovery mechanism to cope up with the failures of mobile nodes.

1 Introduction

A widely accepted architectural model that supports mobile computing consists of two different types of hosts or computing nodes, namely, fixed hosts, and mobile hosts. A fixed host is a computer on the fixed network. It can communicate with a mobile host only through a Mobile Support System (MSS). An MSS is equipped with a wireless interface and services all mobile hosts within its wireless range – a predefined area known as cell. A cellular architecture based mobile computing support systems can not be deployed rapidly. On the other hand *ad hoc* networks are infrastructure-less wireless networks. Hence, an ad hoc network can be easily deployed where an infrastructure is not desired or is infeasible. In such networks, a transaction model needs to be formulated that addresses issues unique to both ad hoc and wireless networks. Conventional transaction models do not perform well in wireless environments [1].

In this paper, we propose a new transaction model for distributed, cooperative computing on mobile ad hoc networks. The proposed model captures the mobility and distributive properties inherently found in a vigorous team activity as in a game of soccer and also has an efficient recovery mechanism to cope with the failures of mobile nodes. We present this new transaction model called *Team Transaction* proposed initially for cellular environments in [2], [3]. A formal description of team transaction model is available in [3], using ACTA [5]

* Partially supported by Ministry of Human Resource Development Government of India sponsored project on Extended Transaction Processing.

R.K. Ghosh and H. Mohanty (Eds.): ICDCIT 2004, LNCS 3347, pp. 127–134, 2004.

formalism. Here we extend these to mobile ad hoc networks. The rest of the paper is organized into 6 sections. Section 2 gives an overview of the model, Section 3 presents the system architecture for the model. Section 4 deals with the recovery aspect. Section 5 provides some applications where the model can be used, and finally, Section 6 presents the conclusions.

2 Team Transaction

A team transaction consists of several mobile nodes working in a cooperative fashion. There are certain objectives that motivated us to think of a new transaction model for the ad hoc mobile computing environment namel, *Transactions should be long-lived, transaction should allow distributed and cooperative computing*, and *transaction should not fail in case one or more nodes die.*

At the top level, a *Team Transaction* consists of three entities namely *Coordinator, Players*, and *Data Access Agent (DAA)*[1]. The coordinator is the captain of the team. It is responsible for coordinating the operations of a team transaction. A player is a sub-transaction spawned by the coordinator and it does the job assigned to it by the coordinator.

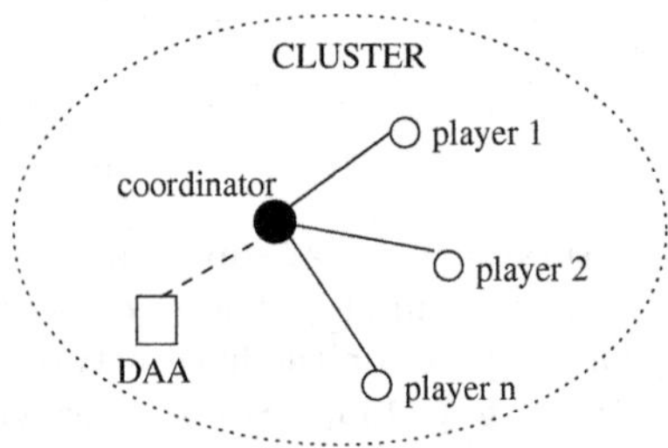

Fig. 1. A Cluster

DAA performs following three tasks:

1. Provides the database access to the coordinator.
2. Creates necessary transaction logs which may be used for the recovery in the event of the current coordinator's death.
3. Delegates job of the current coordinator to another node in case the former crashes.

A node that has been assigned the job of DAA would not normally be responsible for any other work. This will ensure that DAA node conserves its energy for its critical tasks.

The coordinator, all the players and the DAA forms a cluster as indicated by the figure 1.

[1] The notion of DAA also appears in [6].

2.1 Team Transaction Working

Whenever the job at hand requires distributed computing, a node forks a team transaction (*tt*) and becomes the coordinator of the transaction. The node also appoints one of the mobile nodes as the DAA of the *tt*. The coordinator then spawns players and assigns a part of the job to each player node. A player node reports its results periodically to the coordinator. At the time of reporting, the coordinator requests the DAA to make a log entry of the reported results. This is important as the log will help in saving the state of the data objects, which in turn will be helpful in appointing a new coordinator in event of the death of the original coordinator. The players can only report their results to the coordinator who reserves the right to accept or reject the results. No player is allowed to write to the database.

In case a coordinator crashes, the DAA invokes appropriate recovery algorithm to restore the work that was done by the deceased coordinator. It creates a new coordinator and assigns the unfinished job of the old coordinator to the new one.

A coordinator keeps track of its players. In case a player dies, the coordinator simply assigns the job to some other player. Of course, it is possible to restore a player also by logging its work periodically as is done for the recovery from death of the coordinator. But logging players' work puts pressure on the bandwidth, which is generally low in case of a mobile scenario. The players periodically report their result to coordinator and only at that point logging is done. Therefore, when a player dies, only the work that has been done by the player between the time of last report and the time of the crash is lost. One can safely assume that this will not be substantial.

2.2 Generalized Team Transaction

The above transaction model can easily be generalized. If a player determines that its work load is more; or the work that has been assigned to it requires

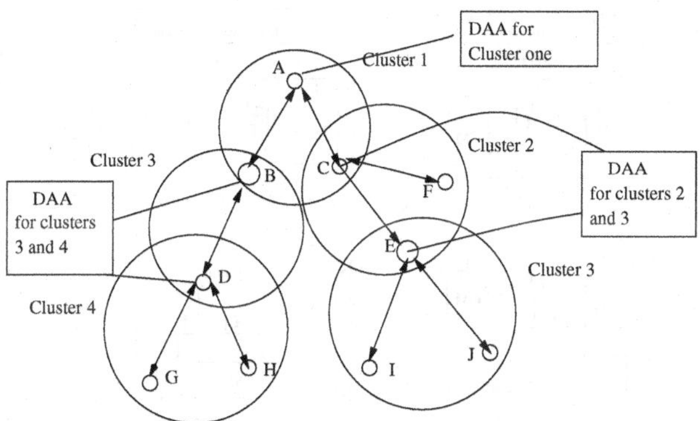

Fig. 2. Generalized Team Transaction

distributed computing, it can redistribute the assigned job by forming a new team transaction. However, the coordinator of the cluster to which the player belongs is not aware of the formation of such sub-clusters. Figure 2 provides a picture of the cluster hierarchy. For the sake of brevity, in the rest of the paper whenever we say team transaction we mean the *generalized team transaction.*

3 System Architecture

An axiomatic analysis of the model, found in [3], provides ample insight into the design of system components of a transaction processing support system to implement team transaction.

The underlying system consists of the modules namely, *Log Manager (LM)*, *Transaction Manager (TM)*, *Recovery Manager (RM)*, *Communication Manager (CM)*, and *Module Interface Manager (MIM)*. Figure 3 illustrates the major system components.

Log Manager: The local logs are maintained on all nodes which include all operations performed by the node so far. In addition, a coordinator maintains the log its own team. The team log includes the work done by the coordinator and all the players. The local logs of the coordinator are periodically flushed on to the stable storage of the DAA which stores the global log for one team or a cluster. The logging at each node is managed by the LM. The LM is accessible through interface provided by MIM. The TM works in close association with the LM as each and every action of TM must be logged.

Transaction manager: It provides the basic primitives for transaction, report, and spawn to the application. The TM must interact with the CM and the LM as some significant events are considered to be complete semantically only after some portion of the log has been transferred. For example, in the case of report, the transfer of log is important. The transaction manager ensures

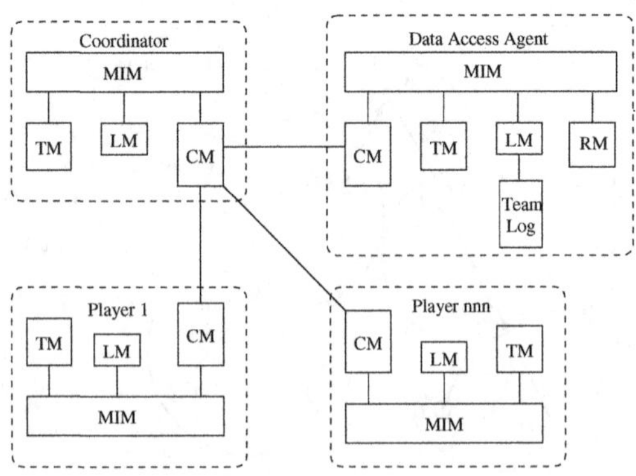

Fig. 3. System architecture

that the significant events like coordinator selection, failure, and others become transparent to the application. The application simply invokes the primitives provided by the TM and is unaware of the underlying data transfers, the selection algorithms for the coordinator and the player in the case of failures. The TM provides a primitive corresponding to each significant event. The application can invoke appropriate primitives to perform the desired task. The invocation of each of these is associated with a log entry.

Recovery Manager: It deals with recovery in case of crashes. It exists at the special nodes called DAA. Since DAA possesses the team logs, DAA takes up the responsibilities to recover a crashed coordinator of the team under it. The recovery algorithm is inspired by ARIES [7] and based on [4]. The RM keeps track of all the coordinators it is serving, and detects the crash, as soon as it occurs. When a crash is detected, the RM first broadcasts a crash message to all the concerned nodes. The log of the crashed node up to the last *Log Flush* received from that node is read from the stable storage and processed.

Communication Manager: The CM is responsible for enabling the nodes to communicate. It does so by sharing the two queues named as *input queue* and *output queue*. The CM spawns two threads – *input thread* and *output thread*. Each thread is tied with the queue named after it. One thread places an arriving packet in the input queue, the other sends the packet at the front of output queue to its destination. The MIM reads the arriving packets in FCFS manner from the input queue. More precisely, the CM provides primitives that are used for data transfer and communication.

Module Interface Manager: In order to run a team transaction, first MIM has to be created at a node which in turn creates other entities. In case the node is to act as a DAA, RM is also created. The MIM also provides the front end for the node where a user can create new applications and launch a query as well as view both incoming and outgoing messages. The front end of a DAA is slightly different. The MIM creates two queues, namely, *input queue* and *output queue*. These queues are used in conjunction with the CM for storing message packets as explained earlier. The MIM starts a main thread called *job allocator* whose main functions are:

1. Start a new application and assign a unique `TTID` to it.
2. Process all incoming packets and direct them to concerned system components for further processing.

In the case of a DAA, the work of main thread differs in the sense that it can not create a transaction or participate as a player to any transaction in a team. In nutshell, the MIM provides a common interface for all system component to talk to each other and cooperate to process a transaction and effect the recovery of a transaction when needed.

4 Recovery Aspect

When the coordinator transaction crashes, the DAA invokes the Team Transaction Recovery (TTR) algorithm to restore the state of the crashed transaction. The TTR algorithm depends on the following.

- Write-ahead Logging (WAL).
- Accept of Report event and Work event is assumed to be complete only when the corresponding log entry has been transferred to the stable cluster log.
- Commit of a player transaction is assumed complete only after log trail has been transferred to stable cluster log with a log entry for `Commit` event.
- There is periodic log transfer from the coordinator to the stable cluster log.
- The player should report to the coordinator at regular intervals.

The TTR algorithm is based on [4] which was inspired by ARIES [7] recovery algorithm. Our recovery algorithm performs the analysis phase and the redo phase similar to [4] to restore the state of database objects. However, we do not undo the effects of incomplete transactions. This is important as our aim is restore the (partial) work that was not written to the database. After recovery, the state of the database objects would be that at the time of crash; and it is not necessary that it should be in a consistent state. A brief outline of the algorithm is presented in next subsection.

4.1 Team Transaction Recovery

The recovery algorithm is as follows:

1. The log is first put through an *analysis phase*. It is scanned and a table is created that gives information about all the player transactions of the crashed coordinator with their statuses.
2. The table created in the first phase is used in the next phase, called *redo phase*, to either reject the work done by the player subtransactions which failed to commit due to abort of kill, or to determine the subtransactions that were still active at the time of crash. In case of committed player transactions, the updates are committed to the database items. The log is scanned backwards updating the database items only by the last modified values.
3. A new coordinator is identified to complete the remaining part of the transaction.
4. The modified database items and the still-to-be-done operation set is assigned to the new coordinator. The new coordinator processes the unfinished transaction job normally.

It is important to note that the state of database objects obtained after stage 2 of the algorithm above may not be the same as the state of the DB objects that would have been reflected by the database at the time of crash of coordinator. This because the change of the state of DB objects made by player transaction is not reflected in database. Only the root coordinator can write to the database. The cluster log helps in obtaining the recent most state of DB objects. Of course, the state may not be a consistent state.

A prototype implementation of the team transaction model including the recovery scheme for above system architecture is not included here due to lack of space. The interested readers may find it in [8].

5 Applications

One of the most important applications where team transactions are particularly useful are in military operations and relief work in disaster-hit areas. In such applications, distributed tasks need to be done in a cooperative fashion. The transaction may last for several days. The notable among some of the other applications where team transactions can be used are in survey operations such as demographic survey depicted by the picture in figure 4, conducted by a company/organization to obtain feedback from consumers/clients on its products.

The demographic survey illustrates how a generalized team transaction can be used to conduct the operation. In a national demographic survey, the complete head-counting procedure can be conducted as follows: at the national level there can be a national coordinator (NC) who will be responsible for collating the data reported by the state level coordinators (SLC). The SLC assigns each district level coordinator (DLC) to collect demographic data of his/her district and report back. The DLC, in turn, may subdivide the task and appoint field persons to report the data for each locality in the district. In such a scenario, the NC and the SLCs can form a team transaction. Similarly, the SLC and the DLCs can form another team transaction. Note that NC is not concerned how the SLC divided the work, and similarly the DLC and the field persons can form its own cluster. The

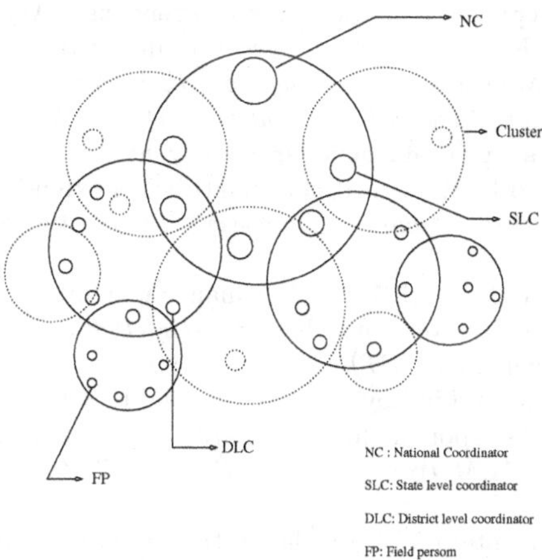

Fig. 4. Demographic Survey example

figure 4 provides the picture of the transaction scenario which may be found to be structurally identical to the organization of team transactions shown in figure 2.

6 Conclusion

The mobile computing paradigm has given rise to several issues unique to wireless networks and mobility of computing devices. In a mobile environment, the long-lived nature of transaction coupled with frequent disconnections and mobility makes the reliability and availability of data key issues to be tackled by a transaction model. In this paper a new transaction model called team transaction has been proposed to address these issues. It is based on the idea of mimicking the team activity as witnessed in a soccer game with the goal of winning the game. The paper also discusses logging and the recovery aspects to deal with crashes and failures which can be particularly bothersome in case of long-lived transactions. It outlines the system architecture implementing the new transaction model. The model, therefore, is specially suitable for ad hoc network application where long-lived nature of the mobile transaction is of critical importance.

References

1. D. Barbara. Mobile computing and databases - a survey. *IEEE Transactions on Knowledge And Data Engineering*, 11(1):108–117, February 1999.
2. M. M. Gore and R. K. Ghosh. Contention-free Team Transaction Management and Recovery on Mobile Networks with Ad Hoc Groupings. In *Proceedings of the 4th International Conference on Information Technology (CIT-01)*, pages 31-36, December 2001.
3. M. M. Gore. *Extendible, Long-lived, Transaction Processing on Distributed and Mobile Environments with Recovery Guarantees.* PhD thesis, Dept of CSE, IIT-Kanpur, INDIA, `http://www.cse.iitk.ac.in/reports/`, April 2002.
4. M. M. Gore and R. K. Ghosh. Recovery in Distributed Extended Long-lived Transaction Models. *Proceedings of Sixth International Conference on Database Systems for Advanced Applications (DASFAA)*, pages 313-320, 1999, `http://citeseer.ist.psu.edu/gore99recovery.html`
5. P. K. Chrysanthis and K. Ramamritham. Synthesis of extended transaction models using acta. *ACM Transactions on Database Systems*, 19(3):450–491, September 1994.
6. M. H. Dunham, A. Helal, and S. Balakrishnan. A mobile transaction model that captures both data and movement behavior. *ACM-Baltzer Journal on Mobile Networks and Applications (MONET)*, 2:149–162, 1997.
7. C. Mohan, D. Haderle, B. Lindsay, H. Pirahesh, and P. Schwarz. ARIES: A transaction recovery method supporting fine-granularity locking and partial rollbacks using write-ahead logging. *ACM Transactions on Database Systems*, 17(1):94–162, March 1992.
8. S. Varshney. Implementation of a collaborative transaction processing system on manet. Master's thesis, Dept of CSE, IIT-Kanpur, May 2002.

An Efficient Protocol for Checkpoint-Based Failure Recovery in Distributed Systems

D. Goswami and S. Sahu

Indian Institute of Technology Guwahati,
North Guwahati - 781039, India

Abstract. Synchronous checkpointing is an attractive approach as it simplifies the process of failure recovery by storing a consistent global checkpoint. Efforts have been made to minimize the number of synchronizing messages and the number of checkpoints in such an approach. Taking the checkpoint without blocking the underlying computation is another important feature of the checkpointing process. In this paper, we present a synchronous checkpointing algorithm which forces a minimum number of nodes to take a checkpoint. Underlying computation needs to be blocked partially and only in rare cases. The algorithm tolerates the failure of an arbitrary number of nodes during the progress. Consistency of the checkpoint is ensured during the checkpointing process and hence no time needs to be spent during recovery.

1 Introduction

There are two main approaches for checkpointing in distributed systems – synchronous and asynchronous. In a synchronous approach, a consistent global snapshot of the system is maintained by going through an exchange of messages among the constituent nodes. Rollback recovery is then straightforward since the nodes can be readily rolled back to the latest global checkpoint. In asynchronous algorithms, each node takes a local checkpoint independent of the other nodes in the system. As a result, it is at the time of the rollback that the consistency of the global snapshot is scrutinized. As opposed to the synchronous approach much effort needs to be expended for rollback since *domino effect* [1] should also be taken care of. A good snapshot collection algorithm should be nonintrusive and efficient. A nonintrusive algorithm does not force the nodes in the system to freeze the computations during snapshot collection. An efficient algorithm keeps the effort required for collecting a snapshot to a minimum. But it is observed that a trade-off in both these issues has to be set since [2] proves that minimality and non-intrusiveness cannot be maintained together.

The global state of a distributed system comprising of processes $\langle p_1, p_2, ..., p_n \rangle$ at an instant t can be defined as the snapshot of events at each p_i at t and the state of the communication channels at t. The events in this context are the send and receive of messages at p_i. For a global state comprising of $\langle C_1^k, C_2^k, ..., C_n^k \rangle$, where C_i^k is the kth local snapshot at p_i, to be consistent, a message m whose receive has been recorded at some C_i^k, then its send must also be recorded at some

R.K. Ghosh and H. Mohanty (Eds.): ICDCIT 2004, LNCS 3347, pp. 135–144, 2004.

C_j^k. A violation of this rule would result in an effect without a cause. However, the reverse condition is acceptable in which the send has been recorded while a receive m is yet to be recorded. Considering the state of the communication channels, such a message can be accounted for as under transit.

In this paper, we propose a synchronous checkpointing-based rollback recovery protocol. A minimum number of nodes are made to checkpoint and non-intrusiveness is dealt with optimality. However, the algorithm does block the underlying computation but the cases which force this to happen are very rare.

1.1 System Model

The system consists of N nodes and communication channels are assumed to be FIFO in nature. Message propagation may take a finite but indefinite amount of time. Reliable message delivery is assumed in the sense that no message loss is assumed under normal circumstances. The nodes are fail-stop in nature. Under the present configuration, there is a pre-designated node called the *initiator*, whose role is central to the working of the algorithm. A number of message types are involved in the system which include the following.

1. *ckpt_init Messages:* The non-initiator nodes send these messages to the initiator on expiry of their checkpoint interval. Messages of this kind contain the information pertaining to the sender node about the communication it has had with other nodes till the time of this message being sent.
2. *ckpt_req Messages:* The initiator sends these messages to the other nodes as a request to take a checkpoint.
3. *ckpt_resp Messages:* These are response messages sent by the participating nodes to inform the initiator of the action taken in response to the *ckpt_req* messages described above.
4. *ckpt_comp Messages:* As the name suggests, these are checkpoint completion messages sent by the initiator to inform the other nodes that the current instance of the algorithm has been successfully completed and the requisite housekeeping operations be done by the receiver.

Any message exchanged as a part of the underlying computation will be denoted as a *computation message*. Each node has logging facility where the incoming messages can be held. The log is emptied at appropriate times as dictated by the checkpointing protocol.

2 A Synchronous Checkpointing Protocol

This section presents a partially blocking synchronous checkpointing algorithm for a given distributed system. Each node has the following data structures.

- **mesg_send[1..N]:** An array of N integers used by each node to record the number of messages it has sent to the other nodes. The jth element of this array at node p_i indicates the number of messages that p_i has sent to p_j since the last checkpoint was taken.

- **mesg_recv[1..N]:** This is the receive counterpart of the *mesg_send* array above. The jth element of this array at node p_i indicates the number of messages that p_i has received from p_j since the last checkpoint was taken.
- **ckpt_num:** An integer to indicate the number of checkpointing instances a node has gone through. A copy of this is appended to every computation message.
- **received:** A boolean field to mark whether the node had received a checkpoint request *ckpt_req* from the initiator. The role of this field is vital in deciding whether an incoming computation message needs to be logged or can be delivered safely.
- **deliver:** A boolean flag, it is used in combination with the *received* flag. Using this flag a node determines whether a computation message received from other nodes can be delivered immediately or not.
- **ckpt_time:** A long integer which keeps the checkpoint time for the node.

The initiator, in addition, has the following:

- **msg_sys_recv[1..N, 1..N]**: An $N \times N$ boolean array. The ith *N-Vector* of the array corresponds to the *recv_mesg* array of process p_i.
- **dep_graph[1..N]**: This is a boolean vector of size N. The initiator constructs this array from the *mesg_recv* arrays it had received in the *ckpt_init* messages from other nodes in the system. For a process p_i if the ith field in the array is set, it indicates that p_i is participating in the checkpointing instance.
- **response[1..N]**: A boolean vector of size N to mark whether *ckpt_resp* message had been received from all the participating nodes.

2.1 The Algorithm

The actions taken by the nodes during the progress of the algorithm are described below.

Initiation: The individual non-initiator nodes on expiry of the checkpoint interval, i.e when the time becomes greater than *ckpt_time*, sends a *ckpt_init* message to the *initiator*. In this message, the node copies the *mesg_recv* and resets the *receive* flag to indicate that the checkpoint request message from the initiator had not been received. Any computation messages which it now receives are not delivered instantly but only after ascertaining certain conditions, as will be discussed subsequently, are fulfilled.

The *initiator* on reception of the *ckpt_init* message from process p_i copies the *mesg_recv* array contained in the message to *msg_sys_recv[i]*. It waits until *ckpt_init* messages from all the nodes are received. Every node will eventually send a *ckpt_init* message. After receiving the *ckpt_init* message from all the nodes, the initiator constructs the *dep_graph* array as explained below.

1. For every node p_i, if *mesg_recv[i]* at the initiator is not zero, *dep_graph[i]* is set.
2. For every i above, if *msg_sys_recv[i][k]* is non-zero *dep_graph[k]* is set.

The *dep_graph* array essentially contains system wide dependency information. Since the initiator is going to take a checkpoint, all nodes from which it had received a message directly should also take a checkpoint as indicated by the first condition above. In addition, the nodes on which the initiator has a causal dependency transitively should also take a checkpoint. This is dictated by the step 2 above. After construction of *dep_graph* the initiator itself takes a checkpoint and sends *ckpt_req* messages to all the other nodes in the system. To these messages it attaches a copy of the *dep_graph* array it had constructed.

Reception of ckpt_req Messages: On reception of *ckpt_req* message at p_i the *dep_graph* array contained in the message is inspected. If *dep_graph[i]* is not zero, this is an indication that p_i must have directly or transitively effected the initiator and is thus a participant in this instance of checkpointing. Accordingly p_i takes a checkpoint and sends a *ckpt_resp* message to the initiator as an indication that appropriate action had been taken by it. If however, *dep_graph[i]* is zero then p_i doesn't take a checkpoint since it is not a participant. In either case the *received* flag is set to 1 to indicate that the *ckpt_req* message had been received from the initiator. Any computation messages arriving now on can be instantly delivered. In addition, any messages which were held in log due to *ckpt_req* message not being received are now delivered and the *deliver* flag is set. p_i on sending a computation message to a process p_k after this attaches the *dep_graph* array it had received from the initiator into the computation message, if this is the first message addressed to p_k. Also, every computation message is appended with the *received* flag to indicate to the recipient whether a checkpoint request message had been received prior to sending this message.

Reception of Computation Messages: During the course of the progress of the algorithm, we strive to achieve maximum non-intrusion. To achieve this, computation messages received during the course of the algorithm are not delivered instantly. If the received flag at node p_i is set then any incoming computation messages can be instantly delivered. Since the delivery of the message will not be violating the consistency of the global checkpoint as the checkpoint must have already been taken or it must have been ascertained that p_i is not participating in the current checkpointing instance, otherwise the receive flag would not have been set. Otherwise, p_i peeks into the message to determine if it contains a *dep_graph* array. If a *dep_graph* array is contained, then this is the first message from the sender after it had taken a checkpoint. p_i then checks *dep_graph[i]*. If it is zero then the initiator had inferred that p_i is not participating and so even after receiving the *ckpt_req* message p_i won't be taking a checkpoint. Thus, there is no danger of the consistency being violated. So, the message can be delivered. Otherwise, if the *dep_graph* array slot corresponding to p_i is set, thep_i will be receiving a *ckpt_req* message (it had not received already). Consequently, the message is not delivered and is held in log. To indicate this condition for further messages the status of *deliver* flag is reset. If however, the *received* flag in the message is not set, then even the sender had not received a *ckpt_req* message and consequently we have no information as to whether or not the delivery of this message will cause a violation of consistency. As a result, this message is not delivered but is held in log. However, in this case the *deliver* flag is not reset, since this is not the first message from the sender as the received flag is not set and the sender had not taken a checkpoint. If the message does not contain a *dep_graph* array, then this is not the first message from the sender and a decision as to whether any messages from this sender may be logged or delivered, had been made when a prior message was received and the status of the *deliver* flag was changed accordingly. As a result, if the *deliver* is set, then the message can be delivered, otherwise the message is held in log.

Housekeeping Operations: The initiator on receiving *ckpt_resp* message from all the nodes p_i for which *dep_graph[i]* is set, sends a *ckpt_comp* message to all nodes as an indication that this instance of checkpointing is successfully completed. The nodes on receiving such a message increment the *ckpt_num* data field. This is necessary to prevent any messages from this instance to interfere with the subsequent instances of checkpointing on account of indefinite message propagation delay.

2.2 Correctness Proof of the Checkpointing Algorithm

We provide a proof to show that the global snapshot obtained at the end of the algorithm is consistent.

Theorem 1. *The proposed checkpointing algorithm constructs a consistent global checkpoint.*

Proof. Assume for contradiction that there exists a message m whose receive has been recorded at a checkpoint C_j^k of a process p_j and whose send from p_i hasn't been recorded at p_i's checkpoint, C_i^k.

Suppose m is the first message from p_i to p_j after taking a checkpoint. The following 4 cases arise.

Case 1: p_i is participating in this checkpointing instance and p_j isn't. Since p_i is participating in this checkpointing instance and this is the first message from p_i to p_j it will be having a copy of the *dep_graph* array. Now a receive of m is recorded only if the *dep_graph* array contains a 1 at ith position. However, this would mean that p_j is also participating. A contradiction.

Case 2: Both p_i and p_j are not participating. An argument similar to above provides the necessary contradiction.

Case 3: p_i is not participating and p_j is participating. The following 4 subcases arise:

Subcase 3.1: p_i had received a *ckpt_req* message from the initiator and p_j had also received it. A receive of a message is recorded, if the message is received and delivered and a checkpoint request is received subsequent to that. As per our assumption, the receive has been recorded which implies that the checkpoint request was received after the delivery of the message. Hence a contradiction.

Subcase 3.2: p_i had received a *ckpt_req* message and p_j hadn't. Since p_i had received the checkpoint request and since this is the first message from p_i to p_j it will be having a copy of the *dep_graph* array. Since the message is delivered and is recorded this is possible if either the *dep_graph* array had a 0 at position p_j which means that p_j isn't participating in the checkpointing instance or if the deliver flag was 1. A contradiction is again reached here.

Subcase 3.3: p_i had not received a *ckpt_req* and p_j had received. An argument similar to Subcase 3.1 provides contradiction since a record of the message is possible only if the checkpoint request is received after the reception of message.

Subcase 3.4: Both p_i and p_j hadn't received a *ckpt_req* message. Since the message receive has been recorded by our assumption. This is possible if deliver was 1. However, since this is the first message, its delivery implies that the received bit at p_j is set. This implies that the *ckpt_req* message had been received. This contradicts our assumption that the both p_i and p_j hadn't received a *ckpt_req* message.

Case 4: Both p_i and p_j are participating. Again 4 subcases arise.

Subcase 4.1: p_i had received a *ckpt_req* message and p_j had also received. A message receive is recorded in a checkpoint only if the checkpoint request is received after the delivery of the message. However by our assumption the message receive has been recorded implying that the *ckpt_req* had been received after the delivery of the message. A contradiction to our above assumption.

Subcase 4.2: p_i had received a *ckpt_req* message and p_j had not. Since p_i had received a *ckpt_req* message and this is the first message from p_i to p_j it will have the *dep_graph* array. Now, since the message receive has been recorded this means that either deliver is 1 or the *dep_graph* had a 0 at position j. A contradiction in both cases.

Subcase 4.3: p_i hadn't received a *ckpt_req* message and p_j had also received. An argument similar to Subcase 3.3 provides the contradiction.

Subcase 4.4: Both p_i and p_j hadn't received a *ckpt_req* message. By our assumption the message receive has been recorded while the message send hasn't been recorded. But since p_i hadn't received a checkpoint request before sending m hence it will be receiving a checkpoint request upon which the message send will be recorded. Hence a contradiction.

Now suppose that m is not the first message from p_i to p_j. Almost similar arguments as above can be provided for all possible cases that arise in this case and have been omitted here for this obvious reason.

2.3 Node Failure During the Progress of the Algorithm

A node may fail during the progress of the algorithm which can hamper the collection of the snapshot. Node failures can occur at two possible instances. Before sending a *ckpt_init* message to the initiator and after sending the *ckpt_init* message but before receiving a *ckpt_req* message.

Node failure before sending a *ckpt_init* message: If a node p_i fails before *ckpt_init* message, the failure of this node is discovered by the initiator since it will not receive a *ckpt_init* message Freon this node. On receiving *ckpt_init* messages from the other nodes except p_i, the initiator waits for an additional period of time. In the present context, a round trip message traversal time to each of the nodes is known apriori to the initiator. The initiator waits for this interval of time before it starts deducing the *dep_graph* array. If a *ckpt_init* message is not received during this interval, the initiator assumes that the node had failed and deduces the *dep_graph* array excluding p_i. If the initiator later receives the *ckpt_init* message from p_i, it is discarded. p_i on recovering from failure checks whether it had sent a *ckpt_init* message after its previous checkpoint. If it had not sent the message then it goes through a recovery phase. If however, the node had sent a *ckpt_init* message and the initiator had mistakenly assumed that p_i failed, it sends a QUERY message to the initiator to know what had been done with its incarnation of the *ckpt_init* message. On receiving the QUERY message the initiator responds by sending a *ckpt_req* message with the status of *dep_graph[i]* in the message appropriately set to indicate that the *ckpt_init* message had in fact been discarded. Since the initiator had excluded p_i in order to direct the other nodes to construct a global snapshot, the checkpoint so constructed will not be including p_i so p_i can rollback safely.

Node failure after sending a *ckpt_init* message but before receiving a *ckpt_req* message: Since immediately after receiving a *ckpt_init* message, the received flag is reset to zero, messages would have had been delivered at p_i if it were not participating in the checkpointing instance by not having affected the initiator causally. Moreover any exchange of messages will not cause a violation of consistency, since p_i had already provided the initiator with its dependency information. In case of failure of p_i after sending the *ckpt_init*, the initiator will receive the message and will send a *ckpt_req* message. However, owing to failure this message is susceptible to be lost in transit. If p_i would not be participating in the checkpointing instance the operations performed are straightforward since even after receiving the *ckpt_req* message p_i will not be taking a checkpoint. The node p_i then waits for a fixed period of time after which it sends a QUERY message to the initiator to inquire of its participation in the instance. The initiator on receiving such a message sends a *ckpt_req* message looking at which p_i concludes that it was not involved in the checkpointing instance and would go through a rollback phase.

Conversely, if p_i is participating in the checkpointing instance, after waiting for a fixed period and receiving a *ckpt_req* message in response to the QUERY message, it takes a checkpoint and increments the checkpoint number *ckpt_num*. It should be noted here that p_i does not to go through a rollback phase in this case. It is worth a mention here that the initiator waits for a QUERY message or a *ckpt_resp* message from p_i, since participation by p_i implies that the initiator won't be sending *ckpt_comp* messages unless it receives *ckpt_resp* message from every participant. The computation can, however, proceed once the *ckpt_req* messages are received by the nodes.

3 Recovery from Node Failure

Unlike the checkpointing algorithm which is controlled mainly by the initiator, we follow a more distributed approach in recovery from node failure. The concept of causal dependency again plays a key role here. In this work, a recovery algorithm is devised in which only a minimum number of nodes are made to rollback and extensive logging of messages on stable storage is not required. The concept of causal dependency is used to arrive at such a minimality. For example suppose a node p_i fails and has to rollback. If no new dependencies have been created from p_i to p_j since p_i's last checkpoint, then there is no need for p_j to rollback in response to p_i's rollback. While presenting the algorithm we assume that the node has ascertained, after an interaction with the initiator, that it indeed needs to rollback.

Each node employs the following additional data structures for recovery from failures.

1. **initiator_id:** An integer of range 1 to N to store the *initiator of a rollback instance.*
2. **rollback_received:** An integer to indicate the *ckpt_num* corresponding to which the latest rollback request was received.
3. **msg_send_inc[1..N]:** An integer array of size N. This array is used to store a copy of the *msg_send* array which is attached in the rollback request.

3.1 Rollback Recovery Algorithm

We now explain in details the working of the proposed rollback algorithm.

Initiation: A node p_i on recovery sends a *rollback_req* message to the nodes to which it had sent a message after its previous checkpoint. In the message it attaches its latest *ckpt_num* and the *msg_send* array along with its own node *id.*

Reception of *rollback_req* message: On receiving a *rollback_req* message a node p_i checks the fields contained in the message. If the *ckpt_num, initiator_id* contained in the message are respectively equal to p_i's own version of these fields viz *rollback_received initiator_id* and *mesg_send_inc* then a rollback request had earlier been received on account of this rollback instance, therefore such a message is discarded. If *ckpt_num* is not the same as *rollback_received,* this implies that this is a new rollback instance being undertaken. Consequently, the node rolls back to the previous checkpoint and copies the data contained in the message to its own respective fields. It also sends a *rollback_req* message to the nodes which have a non-zero entry in its *msg_send* array. In order to prevent more than one node sending the rollback request to the same node p_k as all of them might have sent messages to p_k, it is required that rollback requests are sent to only those nodes which have a zero in the *msg_send* array received in the rollback request p_i had received and a non-zero in the nodes own version of *msg_send.* In addition, it updates its data structures with the respective values contained in the message.

Handling multiple initiations of the rollback recovery algorithm: We allow for the possibility of more than one node initiating the rollback recovery algorithm. The data structures *ckpt_num* and *msg_send* are used to handle this. When a node p_i receives a rollback request, it checks for the *initiator_id* present in the request. If the *initiator_id* is the same as one stored at the node, this suggests that the initiator of the rollback is requesting for another rollback. The possibility of more than one request arriving at a node for the same rollback instance is ruled out by checking the *msg_send* array in the message against its own copy before forwarding the message to the other nodes. In the present case, this is a different instance of the rollback hence p_i inspects its *msg_send* array to see if it had sent any further messages after the last rollback. It goes for a rollback, requesting the other nodes to which new dependencies had been developed.

If the *initiator_id* is different from that stored at the node, it stores the new *initiator_id* and checks for the *msg_send* array (its own version), since if new dependencies had not been created there is no good in forwarding the message to other nodes. If new dependencies had been created p_i rolls back and sends *rollback_req* message to the nodes to which it had sent a message since the last rollback.

4 Comparison with Earlier Work

The worst case message complexity of our approach is $O(n)$. Lai and Yang's [3] synchronous algorithm forces every node in the system to take a checkpoint. This involves extra overhead even for those nodes which have not affected the initiator causally. Approaches for recording a global snapshot in [4] and [5] force the underlying computation to be completely frozen. The approach we have followed, forces computation blocking under very rare circumstances as the computation can proceed once *ckpt_req* message from the initiator is received by the individual nodes. Koo and Toueg's [6] algorithm requires the underlying computation to be suspended. No messages are sent by a node after the initiation of the checkpointing instance. In addition, only direct dependencies are taken into consideration as opposed to transitive dependencies accounted for in this work. Leu and Bhragava [7] proposed an efficient algorithm for checkpointing on static nodes which allows for concurrent instances of the checkpointing being in progress. To surmount the concurrency, the use of the antecedence graph is made which is piggybacked on every computation message which increases the size of computation messages. Also, only one instance of snapshot collection can be under progress. Vekateshan and Juang's optimistic failure recovery algorithm [8] does not require sending dependency information with the messages. However it entails several iterations to roll back to a consistent state. Manetho [9] has a low overhead for failure free operations but the failure recovery procedure is very complicated. We have a developed a simple recovery algorithm, since nodes recovering from failures should be restored to an error-free state at the earliest.

5 Conclusion

We have developed an efficient checkpointing protocol and a rollback algorithm that keeps the underlying computation non-blocked for an optimal period of time. We utilize the concept of causal dependency in order to force only a small number of nodes to checkpoint. Message logging is used in cases where the consistency of the snapshot is endangered, though the events which forces logging are rare. Work in the direction of minimizing the overhead for the initiator, keeping the advantages afforded by our algorithm intact, can be undertaken as a future accomplishment.

References

1. B. Randell, "System stucture for sofware fault tolerance," *IEEE Trans. Software Engg.*, vol. 1, no. 2, pp. 220–232, 1975.
2. G. Cao and M. Singhal, "On the impossiblity of min-process non-blocking checkpointing and an efficient checkpointing algorithm for mobile computin systems," in *Proc. 27th Intl Conf. Parallel Processing*, pp. 37–44, August 1998.
3. T. Lai and T. Yang, "On distributed snapshots," *Information Processing Letters*, pp. 153–158, May 1987.
4. F. Cristian and F. Jahanian, "A time based checkpointing protocol for long lived distributed computations," in *Proc. IEEE Symp. Reliable Distributed Systems*, pp. 12–20, 1991.
5. P. Ramanathan and K. Shin, "Use of common timebase for checkpointing and rollback recovery," *IEEE Trans. Software Engg.*, pp. 571–583, June 1993.
6. R. Koo and S. Toueg, "Checkpointing and rollback-recovery for distributed systems," *IEEE Trans. Software Engg.*, vol. 13, no. 1, pp. 23–31, 1987.
7. P. Leu and B. Bhargava, "Concurrent robust checkpointing and recovery in distributed systems," in *Proc. 4th IEEE Intl. Conf. Data Engg.*, pp. 154–163, February 1988.
8. S. Venkatesan and T. Juang, "Low overhead optimistic crash recovery," in *Proc. 11th Intl. Conf. Distributed Computing Systems.*, pp. 454–461, 1991.
9. E. Elnozahy and W. Zwaenepoel, "MANETHO: Transparent rollback-recovery with low overhead, limited rollback, and fast output commit," *IEEE Trans. Computers*, vol. 41, pp. 526–531, May 1992.

Cybersecurity: Opportunities and Challenges

Pradeep Khosla

Carnegie Mellon University, USA

Abstract. The world is reliant on Information more than ever. This reliance has resulted in a significant impact on our quality of life – more than two thirds of the productivity gains in the US economy are attributable to IT. During the past decade the number of attacks on our infrastructure have grown at an exponential rate. In this talk we will identify the sources of these attacks and offer a vision for the future. We will describe the research agenda being pursued in Carnegie Mellon CyLab and how it contributes to the future vision.

R.K. Ghosh and H. Mohanty (Eds.): ICDCIT 2004, LNCS 3347, p. 145, 2004.

Vulnerabilities and Threats in Distributed Systems

Bharat Bhargava and Leszek Lilien

Department of Computer Sciences and Center for Education
and Research in Information Assurance and Security (CERIAS),
Purdue University, West Lafayette, IN 47907, USA
{bb, llilien}@cs.purdue.edu

Abstract. We discuss research issues and models for vulnerabilities and threats in distributed computing systems. We present four diverse approaches to reducing system vulnerabilities and threats. They are: using fault tolerance and reliability principles for security, enhancing role-based access control with trust ratings, protecting privacy during data dissemination and collaboration, and applying fraud countermeasures for reducing threats.

1 Introduction

Security vulnerabilities dormant in a distributed system can be intentionally exploited or inadvertently triggered. The threats of exploitation or triggering are only potential, and materialize as an attack or an accident. Efficient elimination and masking of vulnerabilities and threats requires cost-based risk analysis.

Vulnerabilities exist in hardware, networks, operating systems, database systems, and applications. New ones are being discovered every day. Information about identified vulnerabilities and threats can be obtained from the well-known security incident databases, or *metabases*, such as ICAT, CERT, vdb, or CVE, from notification systems such as Cassandra [22], or from other sources of information on security incidents.

After discussing vulnerabilities and threats, this paper presents briefly four different ideas or mechanisms for reducing them:

Applying Reliability and Fault Tolerance Principles to Security Research. Many ideas or algorithms from research in reliability and fault tolerance provide useful analogies to research in security. Examples include disabling quorums to deny access, use of checkpointing for intrusion detection, and adaptability to timing, severity, duration, and extent of attacks.

Using Trust in Role-Based Access Control. Trust is needed for access control in open systems. There are problems with identity-based approaches and use of digital credentials. Ongoing research can produce credible trust ratings for a user based on multiple types of evidence, including credentials, observed behavior, recommendations, and reputations. Trust ratings are used to enhance the role-based access control (RBAC) mechanism. We are building a testbed for experiments to validate the process of trust, and study privacy and fraud.

R.K. Ghosh and H. Mohanthy (Eds.): ICDCIT 2004, LNCS 3347, pp. 146–157, 2004.

Privacy-Preserving Data Dissemination. Trust and privacy are closely intertwined in interactions among cooperating entities. Preserving data privacy is essential. Objects can encapsulate privacy policies, owner's preferences, and other metadata along with owner's data. They can include mechanisms such as *apoptosis* that leads to a clean self-destruction whenever this object feels threatened, and *evaporation* that allows gradual and adaptive object distortion and erasure in proportion to perceived misuse.

Fraud Countermeasure Mechanisms. Vulnerabilities can be identified via studies of fraud. Fraud can be detected by identifying patterns of deceiving behavior. We identified three types of fraudulent user behavior, and developed schemes to evaluate threats and detect fraud.

2 Vulnerabilities

Modeling Vulnerabilities. A *vulnerability* can be defined as a flaw or weakness in system security procedures, design, implementation, or internal controls. A vulnerability can be accidentally triggered or intentionally exploited, causing security breaches [27].

Modeling vulnerabilities includes analyzing their features, classifying them and building their taxonomies, and providing formalized models. Many diverse models of vulnerabilities in various environments and under varied assumptions are available in the literature. A detailed analysis of four common computer vulnerabilities in [17] identifies their characteristics, the expected policies violated by their exploitation, and the steps needed for the eradication of such vulnerabilities in future software releases. A vulnerability lifecycle model has been applied in [4] to three case studies, which show how systems remain vulnerable long after security fixes. During its lifetime, vulnerability can be in any of the following six states: birth, discovery, disclosure, correction, publicity, and death.

A model-based analysis technique to identify configuration vulnerabilities in distributed systems [23] involves formal specification of desired security properties, an abstract model of the system that captures its security-related behaviors, and verification techniques to check whether the abstract model satisfies the security properties.

Two kinds of vulnerabilities can be distinguished: operational and information-based. The former include an unexpected broken linkage in a distributed database, and the latter include unauthorized access (secrecy/privacy), unauthorized modification (integrity), traffic analysis (inference problem), and Byzantine input [3].

Vulnerabilities do not have to be exhaustively removed since they only create a potential for attack. Feeling threatened by vulnerabilities all the time is not desirable. Vulnerabilities exist due to not only mistakes or omissions, but can be a side effect of a legitimate system feature, as was the case with the `setuid` UNIX command [14]. Some vulnerabilities exist in systems and cause no harm in its life cycle. Some known ones have to be tolerated due to economic or technological limitations. Removal of others may reduce usability. To require passwords not only for logging in, but also for any significant resource request may make it secure but lowers usability. The system design should not let an adversary know vulnerabilities unknown to the system owner.

Fraud Vulnerabilities. A *fraud* can be defined as a deception deliberately practiced in order to secure unfair or unlawful gain [2]. Disclosing confidential information to unauthorized people or unauthorized selling of customer lists to telemarketers constitutes fraud. This shows an overlap of fraud with privacy breaches.

Fraud can make systems more vulnerable to subsequent fraud. This requires protection mechanisms to avoid future damage.

Fraudsters can be classified into two categories: impersonators and swindlers [13]. An *impersonator* is an illegitimate user who steals resources from victims, for instance by taking over their accounts. A *swindler* is, in contrast, a legitimate user who intentionally benefits from the system or other users by deception. For instance, swindlers obtain legitimate telecommunications accounts and use the services without intention to pay the bills.

Fraud involves abuse of trust [12, 29]. A fraudster strives to present himself as a trustworthy individual and friend. In a clear way, the more trust one places in others the more vulnerable one tends to become.

Vulnerability Research Issues. Vulnerabilities, analogously to faults, enable failures and attacks. They could be characterized as flaws in design, implementation, or deployment. The severity of a flaw and its impact on an application need analysis. Qualitative impact may be expressed as a low/medium/high degree of degradation in terms of performance and availability. Quantitative impact is in terms of economic loss, measurable cascade effects, and time needed to recover. It could include quantification of reoccurrences of failures or attacks.

Procedures and methods are needed for efficient extraction of the characteristics and properties of the known vulnerabilities. This is analogous to understanding how faults occur. Tools that search for known vulnerabilities in the metabases have limitations. Security mechanisms that add or modify entries in the metabases can only follow, not anticipate, the steps of an attacker. Characteristics can be learnt from the behavior of the attacker or using ideas such as honeypots.

A comprehensive taxonomy of vulnerabilities for different application areas need be constructed. Medical systems may have critical privacy vulnerabilities, whereas vulnerabilities in defense systems might destroy or distort resources and capabilities. A good taxonomy will facilitate both prevention and elimination of vulnerabilities. A metabase of vulnerabilities reveals characteristics in flaws for preventing not only identical but also similar vulnerabilities. It also contributes to identification of related vulnerabilities, including dangerous synergistic ones. Characterization of and a model for a set of synergistic vulnerabilities can lead to uncovering gang attack threats or incidents. It should be noted that the characteristics for a set are, in general, more than a simple "sum" of individual characteristics.

Formalisms to represent vulnerabilities and their contexts are needed. The challenge is to investigate how vulnerability in one context propagates to another. Different kinds of vulnerabilities might be emphasized in different contexts.

Quantitative lifecycle models for vulnerabilities should be built after a thorough analysis of vulnerabilities for a given type of application or system, exploiting their unique characteristics. In each lifecycle phase, the cumulative system vulnerability should be determined, and the most dangerous or the most common types of vulnerabilities recognized. Knowledge of the degree of system vulnerability, the duration of the lifecycle phases, and the prominent types of vulnerabilities for a given phase will be helpful in protecting the system against these types of vulnerabilities. The best defensive procedures can be adaptively selected from a predefined set.

The lifecycle models should help solving a few problems. First, they should help avoid vulnerabilities in a deployed system most efficiently by discovering and eliminating them at the design and implementation stages. Second, they should facilitate evaluations and measurements of vulnerabilities in system components and subsystems and of the system as a whole at each lifecycle stage. Third, the models would assist in most efficient discovery of vulnerabilities in a deployed system before they are exploited by an attacker or a failure. They would assist in most efficient elimination or masking of these vulnerabilities, e.g. based on principles analogous to fault-tolerance. Alternatively, an attacker can be kept unaware or uncertain of important system parameters by, for example, non-deterministic or deceptive system behavior, increased component diversity, or multiple lines of defense.

Research should provide methods of assessing the impact of vulnerabilities on security in applications and systems. It should create formal descriptions of the impact of vulnerabilities, and develop quantitative vulnerability impact evaluation methods. Resulting ranking will help in risk analysis. Investigators can identify the fundamental design principles and guidelines for dealing with system vulnerabilities at any system lifecycle stage. Based on these principles and guidelines, the best practices for reducing vulnerabilities at different lifecycle stages should be developed. Finally, interactive or fully automatic tools and infrastructures encouraging or enforcing use of these best practices at each lifecycle stage should be developed.

Research is also needed on vulnerabilities in security mechanisms themselves, and on vulnerabilities due to non-malicious but threat-enabling uses of information [21].

3 Threats

3.1 Models of Threats

We define *threats* against systems as entities that can intentionally exploit or inadvertently trigger specific system vulnerabilities to cause security breaches [16, 27]. An *attack* is an intentional exploitation of vulnerabilities, and an *accident* is an inadvertent triggering of vulnerabilities. Both materialize threats, changing them from potential to actual.

Threats can be classified according to actions and consequences [26]. Actions can be of the following types: observe, destroy, modify, and emulate threats. Consequences include disclose, execute, misrepresent, and repudiate threats, integrity threats. A threat can be tolerated or eliminated based on the degree of risk acceptable to an application. Threat to human life may require complete elimination. Threat to redundant software or hardware can be tolerated briefly.

Threats can be countered by their avoidance (prevention) or tolerance.

Threat Avoidance. The analogy between fault avoidance in the reliability area [24, 5, 21] and threat avoidance should be considered in the system design. Once the system is deployed, the designers cannot change the basic system structures and mechanisms. The threat avoidance methods, petrified in the system, are effective only against less sophisticated attacks. Executors of the most sophisticated attacks have motivation, resources, and the whole system lifetime to discover its vulnerabilities. Such attacks need to be approached from the threat tolerance side [20], and knowledge of fault avoidance in the reliability area can be leveraged.

Understanding different threat sources is necessary for effective threat avoidance. Different human threats, their motivation and potential attack modes are described in [27]. Attacks can be classified as target-of-opportunity attacks, intermediate attacks, or sophisticated attacks [20].

Several research efforts focus on providing guidelines for better designs that prevent threats. A model for secure protocols is proposed in [15]. Formal models for the analysis of authentication protocols are proposed in [25] and in our paper [10]. Security models for statistical databases useful to prevent data disclosures are discussed in [1], and a detailed comparative analysis of the most promising methods for protecting dynamic-online statistical databases is presented there.

Threat Tolerance. Fault-tolerant schemes are neither concerned with each individual failure nor spend all resources in dealing with them. Transient and non-catastrophic errors and failures are ignored if this can benefit the system. In the same way, we need to conduct research on using a form of intrusion tolerance for dealing with lesser security breaches, which are common in daily activities. Applying the fault tolerance approach to security attacks on database systems [3], we can list the following phases: attack avoidance (a.k.a. prevention), attack detection, damage confinement, damage assessment, reconfiguration, repair, fault treatment to prevent a recurrence of similar attacks, and continuation of service.

Fraud Threat Detection for Threat Tolerance. Fraud threats can be viewed as a special category of general security threats, and as the first step in some threat tolerant solutions (majority voting is an example of threat tolerance without threat detection). Fraud detection systems are widely used in telecommunication, online transactions, computer and network security, and insurance. Effective fraud detection uses both fraud rules and pattern analysis. Due to the skewed distribution of fraud occurrences, one challenge in fraud detection is a very high false alarm rate.

3.2 Fraud Threats

Fraud threats can be viewed as a special category of general security threats that should be analyzed considering salient features of fraud [9]. It should be noted that fraud often occurs as a malicious opportunistic reaction, triggered by a careless action. Threat analysis should also consider that fraud escalation seems to be a natural phenomenon. Gang fraud can be especially damaging since gang fraudsters can cooperate in misdirecting suspicion on others.

Individuals or gangs planning fraud thrive in an environment with fuzzy assignment of responsibilities between participating entities, be they human or artificial [9].

Very powerful fraudsters might be able to create environments that facilitate fraud that they plan. Examples include CEO's involved in insider trading.

3.3 Threat Research Issues

Since threats are context-dependent, an analysis of threats already present in the security incident metabases has to start with identifying threats relevant for the context. The analysis needs to find salient features of these threats, as well as indirect associations between threatsalso via their links to related vulnerabilities. Next, a threat taxonomy, specialized for the considered context, should be defined.

Formal models of threats, including their context-dependent aspects, are needed. Qantifying the notion of a threat calls for measures to determine threat levels. Avoiding/tolerating threats via unpredictability or non-determinism should be tried.

The formal qualitative and quantitative modelssuch as a lifecycle threat modelcan provide a solid basis for detecting known and discovering unknown threats, and for establishing threat measures. Since threat analysis is strongly linked to the analysis of vulnerabilities, this should result in identifying characteristic features of related vulnerabilities that link them to specific threats. Similarly, one can investigate the links from threats to vulnerabilities. The results of this reverse link analysis may necessitate correcting our vulnerability analysis models and methods.

Development of quantitative threat models can use analogies to the reliability models. An example is a Markov chain model to compute security measures. Two variables *time* and *effort* can be used to rate different threats or attacks. By investigating the nature and properties of attacks, threats, and vulnerabilities, one can formulate the distribution of their random behavior. The security measure named the Mean Effort To security Failure (METF), which is analogous to the Mean Time To Failure (MTTF) reliability measure, could be used. New security measures can be introduced, starting with an evaluation of the suitability of two measures, namely the Mean Time To Patch and Mean Effort To Patch. They are analogous to the Mean Time To Repair (MTTR) reliability measure, and the METF security measure.

An evaluation a specific threat impact can start with the relevant threat properties, such as direct damage, indirect damage, recovery cost, prevention overhead, and interaction with other threats and defensive mechanisms.

Research must include inventing algorithms, methods, and design guidelines to reduce the number and the severity of threats. Injection of unpredictability or uncertainty may increase system security. As an example, one can enhance data transfer security in a distributed system by sending portions of critical data through different routes. Research is also needed on threats to security mechanisms themselves.

Finally, since threat detection is needed for threat tolerance, it should be studied. This includes investigation of fraud threat detection for fraud threat tolerance.

4 Mechanism to Reduce Vulnerabilities and Threats

4.1 Applying Reliability and Fault Tolerance Principles to Security Research

We have been conducting research in reliable distributed systems for a very long time. We have worked on the development of concepts such as consistency, atomicity, durability, availability, rollback, checkpoints, adaptability, etc. [8, 10].

We perceive that the ideas, concepts, or algorithms known from reliability area can have analogies in the security area. We need to apply the science and engineering of reliability research to the research in security and vice versa [6].

The analogies start with basic notions used in security and reliability. Vulnerability corresponds to a fault, a threat corresponds to an error, and a security breach corresponds to a failure/crash [6, 7].

We perceive an analogy between fault tolerance and threat tolerance. The approaches to handling a threat are: *threat disregarding* (ignores a potential threat), *threat avoidance* (avoids a threat by eliminating it, its cause, or its consequences), and *threat tolerance* (gracefully adapts to threats that have materialized) [27].

The analogy between the notion of time for accidental failures and the notion of expended effort for intentional security breaches can be exploited [18]. The effort-to-breach distribution of security is analogous to time-to-failure distribution of reliability. There are differences between seemingly identical notions in reliability and security areas, such as the notion of system boundariesnarrowe r for reliability and more open for security. Further, reliability analogies are not helpful in some situations, including the instance of intentional breaches arising from intentional malicious faults, and the instance when expenditure of effort is instantaneous. In this case, analogy to time in the area of reliability is meaningless, due to the sequential nature of time. The security function *R(e),* analogous to the reliability function, can be defined to address some quantitative aspects of operational security.

The following examples of solutions illustrate reliability-security analogies. To increase reliability in distributed systems, a quorum of replicas can be formed in the presence of failures. To make systems secure against unauthorized access, one can use the reverse strategy of making it difficult to form quorums. Research on checkpointing can be applied to intrusion detection. The checkpoints ensure that the systems can be brought back to a secure status. To deal with failures, we build systems that are fault tolerant. We must build systems *attack tolerant* to security attacks. We need to deal with common and less severe security violations as we have learned to deal with every-day and relatively benign reliability failures.

4.2 Using Trust in Role-Based Access Control

The traditional, identity-based approaches to access control are inadequate or even inapplicable to open computing, including Internet-based computing [28]. In addition, the common user authorization approach of granting access privileges to users based solely on user's ownership of digital credentials (evidence), presented directly to the system, has its share of problems. First of all, holding credentials does not certify that the user will not carry out harmful actions [12].

Authorization based on both credentials and trust is more credible than one based on credentials alone, since it makes access control adaptable to users' behavior. This is the reason why we included trust in access control mechanisms in open computing. Existing computational trust management models can be classified as authorization-based or reputation-based. Our design integrates them into one framework.

In our model of trust [12], we have incorporated comprehensive aspects of trust in social systems and computer science applications. One challenge was to select carefully all and only useful trust aspects needed for our system design in a way preventing adverse affects on the flexibility or performance.

We developed algorithms for automating evaluation of trust, or inference of trust. They produce trust ratings for a user based on: (a) dynamic, continuously updated system's own view of user's behavior in interactions with the system, (b) system's own evidence records, (c) evidence records obtained from "foreign" reputation servers, and (d) system security policies. It is important to note that in producing the trust ratings the algorithm considers credibility of the evidence provider.

Good trust inference algorithms needs to accommodate multiple types of evidence. They should be adaptive, and able to tolerate uncertainty, incompleteness or inaccuracy of evidence (especially in case of subjective evidence). Before the algorithm is able to infer trust for a specific application, available and acceptable evidence must be identified. Examples of pieces of evidence include credentials, observed user behavior, recommendations, and reputations. The credibility, availability, and volatility of different types of evidences differ, and they are all affected by societal value, privacy concerns, relevant legislation, and other factors.

The capability to use trust ratings for users was applied for enhancing the well-known role-based access control (RBAC) mechanism. Trust management is performed in this system by a *trust-enhanced role-mapping (TERM)* server, which interacts with RBAC and a reputation server in the process of user authorization.

TERM uses two kinds of evidence for producing trust ratings: (a) direct, first-hand experiences reported to TERM by RBAC, and (b) recommendations of users about others users. The TERM server does not accept recommendations at a face value but assigns to them its credibility rating. TERM server interacts with a reputation server, which is a dynamic trust information repository, and evaluates reputationbased on trust informationby using algorithms specified by the TERM server. We have built a testbed prototype system, named Trust Enhanced Role Assignment (TERA), for experiments verifying the system's process of producing trust ratings for its users, and studying trust, privacy, and fraud.

4.3 Privacy-Preserving Data Dissemination

Trust and privacy are closely intertwined. For any collaborationor even any interactiona level of trust must be established. Even just perceived threats to users' privacy by a collaborator may result in substantial lowering of trust. This could result in rejection of collaboration between prospective partners, a loss to all of them. Therefore, protecting and ensuring privacy of sensitive information are necessary components of mechanisms for reducing vulnerabilities and threats.

We briefly sketch our approach [11]. A *guardian* is either the original owner, or a subsequent stakeholder of sensitive data. A guardian may pass private data to another guardian in a data dissemination chain (actually, a cyclic graph). The risk of privacy violations grows with the chain length and milieu fallibility and hostility.

Traditionally, owner's privacy preferences or policies are *not* transmitted due to neglect or failure. If a privacy policy is not included with data, even an honest receiving guardian is unable to honor them. A simple solution is encapsulation of policies and other metadata including owner's privacy preferences with owner's sensitive data and ensuring that owner's metadata are never decoupled from his data.

Suppose that a customer "deposits" his data in a bank. The bank immediately encapsulates data within an atomic private object, which includes private metadata with customer's privacy preferences. Obviously, transmitting complete metadata is inefficient. They are extensive, describing all foreseeable aspects of data privacy that can be needed to address privacy issues under any circumstances. For efficiency reasons, based on the application semantics, only some metadata are carried along.

With atomic self-descriptive objects, there is no way that a sending guardian can transmit to a receiving guardian an incomplete object. This solution solves the problem for friendly environments.

The solution must be extended to embrace hostile and unfamiliar environments. In the first step, the extension will involve an atomic *apoptosis*, that is a clean self-destruction, whenever the object feels threatened. A private object is here a binary-state or atomic entity, which can be either intact or safely destroyed. In the second step, we generalize the notion of apoptosis with the idea of *evaporation*. Object's private data are not destroyed all at once but evaporate gradually, adaptively and in proportion to the object's distrust towards its current milieu.

Perfect passing of objects is not always desirable. When data are captured by spyware embedded in browser extensions, owners want to see them distorted once they leave their computer. Owners are often willing to share their data locally, e.g., with colleagues in their lab, but want to prevent any wider dissemination. This suggests that private objects should be evaporating in proportion to their "distance" from their source. Owners generally trust their original guardians more than subsequent and more distant ones. Unauthorized data disclosures become more probable further away. Different context-dependent proximity metrics can be used.

4.4 Fraud Countermeasure Mechanisms

We have concentrated on swindler detection. The major challenge is to react to a suspicious action or cooperation that may lead to a fraud. Three approaches were considered: (1) detecting an entity's activities that deviate from legitimate patterns; (2) constructing state transition graphs for existing fraud scenarios and detecting frauds similar to the known ones; and (3) discovering an entity's intention based on past behavior. An architecture incorporating all three approaches is proposed in [13].

The deceiving intention prediction (DIP) algorithm is the critical element of the architecture. Its role is discovery of deceiving intention of an entity, based on entity's history and current behavior.

We have identifies three types of deceiving user behavior: (a) *uncovered deceiving intentions,* where swindler's trust ratings are stably low and vary in a small range over time, (b) *trapping intentions,* where a swindler first exhibits intentionally blameless behavior to gain trust, and then commits a fraud, and (c) *illusive intentions,* where a swindler exhibits cycles of blameless behavior followed by intervals of fraudulent actions. We see *cycles* of preparation and entrapment in Case (c), in contrast to Case (b) where one preparation interval precedes one entrapment period.

We have experimentally evaluated the DIP algorithm [13] investigating its performance for different types of user behavior, including the deceiving behaviors defined above. Given a user behavior sequence, DIP calculates for it the value of the *DI-confidence indicator*, which is a real number ranging over [0,1] with the higher values indicating higher chances of an illegitimate behavior.

Our experimental results can be summarized as follows [13]:

- For a swindler with uncovered deceiving intentions: Since the probability of fraud is high, the swindler is put under system supervision most of the time. The final trust values are at 0.1, close to the minimum. The DI-confidence is around 0.9.
- For a swindler with trapping intentions: DIP responds very quickly with a drop in trust ratings when a swindler ends preparation and enters the entrapment phase: increasing DI-confidence from 0.22 to 0.76 takes only a sequence of 6 ratings.
- For a swindler with illusive intentions: DI-confidence increases (trust falls) when the swindler ends the preparation phase of a cycle and starts an entrapment. DI-confidence decreases (trust grows) when the swindler ends the entrapment phase and reenters the preparation phase. Still, DIP is able to catch this smart swindler because her DI-confidence eventually increases to about 0.9. This demonstrates that an effort to hide periods of fraudulent activities with periods of good behavior is less and less effective with each repetition of the preparation-entrapment cycle.

5 Conclusions

Investigation of vulnerabilities and threats and devising countermeasures is an important research area with a high potential for practical impact. Our contributions of four different ideas and mechanisms for reducing system vulnerabilities and threats, presented in the paper, show a few of the possible directions for research.

We are using the presented mechanisms in our experimental testbed for investigation of new solutions for security and privacy in distributed systems. (More information is available at: http://raidlab.cs.purdue.edu//NSFtrust//.html.).

Acknowledgements. We are grateful for contributions made by Ms. Anjali Bhargava (fault tolerance and security) and Ms. Yuhui Zhong (trust in RBAC and fraud). Research is supported in part by NSF grants IIS-0209059 and IIS-0242840.

References

1. N.R. Adam and J.C. Wortmann, "Security-Control Methods for Statistical Databases: A Comparative Study," *ACM Computing Surveys*, Vol. 21, No. 4, Dec. 1989.
2. *The American Heritage Dictionary of the English Language, Fourth Edition,* Houghton Mifflin, 2000.
3. P. Ammann, S. Jajodia, and P. Liu, "A Fault Tolerance Approach to Survivability," in *Computer Security, Dependability, and Assurance: From Needs to Solutions*, IEEE Computer Society Press, Los Alamitos, CA, 1999.
4. W.A. Arbaugh, et al., "Windows of Vulnerability: A Case Study Analysis," *IEEE Computer,* pp. 52-59, Vol. 33 (12), Dec. 2000.
5. A. Avizienis, J.C. Laprie, and B. Randell, "Fundamental Concepts of Dependability," *Research Report N01145*, LAAS-CNRS, Apr. 2001.
6. A. Bhargava and B. Bhargava, "Applying fault-tolerance principles to security research," in *Proc. of IEEE Symposium on Reliable Distributed Systems*, New Orleans, Oct. 2001.
7. B. Bhargava, "Security in Mobile Networks," in *NSF Workshop on Context-Aware Mobile Database Management (CAMM),* Brown University, Jan. 2002.
8. B. Bhargava (ed.), *Concurrency Control and Reliability in Distributed Systems,* Van Nostrand Reinhold, 1987.
9. B. Bhargava, "Vulnerabilities and Fraud in Computing Systems," *Proc. Intl. Conf. IPSI*, Sv. Stefan, Serbia and Montenegro, Oct. 2003.
10. B. Bhargava, S. Kamisetty and S. Madria, "Fault-tolerant authentication and group key management in mobile computing," *Intl. Conf. on Internet Comp.*, Las Vegas, June 2000.
11. B. Bhargava and L. Lilien, "Private and Trusted Collaborations," *Proc. Secure Knowledge Management (SKM 2004): A Workshop*, Amherst, NY, Sep. 2004.
12. B. Bhargava and Y. Zhong, "Authorization Based on Evidence and Trust," *Proc. Intl. Conf. on Data Warehousing and Knowledge Discovery DaWaK-2002,* Aix-en-Provence, France, Sep. 2002.
13. B. Bhargava, Y. Zhong, and Y. Lu, Fraud Formalization and Detection," *Proc. Intl. Conf. on Data Warehousing and Knowledge Discovery DaWaK-2003,* Prague, Czechia, Sep. 2003.
14. M. Dacier, Y. Deswarte, and M. Kaâniche, "Quantitative Assessment of Operational Security: Models and Tools," *Technical Report, LAAS Report 96493*, May 1996.
15. N. Heintze and J.D. Tygar, "A Model for Secure Protocols and Their Compositions," *IEEE Transactions on Software Engineering*, Vol. 22, No. 1, 1996, pp. 16-30.
16. E. Jonsson *et al.*, "On the Functional Relation Between Security and Dependability Impairments," *Proc. 1999 Workshop on New Security Paradigms*, Sep. 1999, pp. 104-111.
17. I. Krsul, E.H. Spafford, and M. Tripunitara, "Computer Vulnerability Analysis," *Technical Report, COAST TR 98-07,* Dept. of Computer Sciences, Purdue University, 1998.
18. B. Littlewood *at al.*, "Towards Operational Measures of Computer Security", *Journal of Computer Security*, Vol. 2, 1993, pp. 211-229.
19. F. Maymir-Ducharme, P.C. Clements, K. Wallnau, and R. W. Krut, "The Unified Information Security Architecture," *Technical Report, CMU/SEI-95-TR-015*, Oct. 1995.
20. N.R. Mead, R.J. Ellison, R.C. Linger, T. Longstaff, and J. McHugh, "Survivable Network Analysis Method," *Tech. Rep. CMU/SEI-2000-TR-013*, Pittsburgh, PA, Sep. 2000.
21. C. Meadows, "Applying the Dependability Paradigm to Computer Security," *Proc. Workshop on New Security Paradigms*, Sep. 1995, pp. 75-81.

22. P.C. Meunier and E.H. Spafford, "Running the free vulnerability notification system Cassandra," *Proc. 14th Annual Computer Security Incident Handling Conference*, Hawaii, Jan. 2002.
23. C. R. Ramakrishnan and R. Sekar, "Model-Based Analysis of Configuration Vulnerabilities," *Proc. Second Intl. Workshop on Verification, Model Checking, and Abstract Interpretation (VMCAI'98)*, Pisa, Italy, 2000.
24. B. Randell, "Dependabilitya–Unifying Concept," in: *Computer Security, Dependability, and Assurance: From Needs to Solutions*, IEEE Computer Society Press, Los Alamitos, CA, 1999.
25. A.D. Rubin and P. Honeyman, "Formal Methods for the Analysis of Authentication Protocols," Tech. Rep. 93-7, Dept. of Electrical Engineering and Computer Science, University of Michigan, Nov. 1993.
26. G. Song *et al.*, "CERIAS Classic Vulnerability Database User Manual," Technical Report 2000-17, CERIAS, Purdue University, West Lafayette, IN, 2000.
27. G. Stoneburner, A. Goguen, and A. Feringa, "Risk Management Guide for Information Technology Systems," *NIST Special Publication 800-30*, Washington, DC, 2001.
28. M. Winslett *et al.*, "Negotiating trust on the web," *IEEE Internet Computing Spec. Issue on Trust Management*, 6(6), Nov. 2002.
29. Y. Zong, Y. Lu, and B. Bhargava, "Dynamic Trust Production Based on Interaction Sequence," Tech. Rep. CSD-TR 03-006, Dept. Comp. Sciences, Purdue Univ., Mar.2003.

A TNATS Approach to Hidden Web Documents

Yih-Ling Hedley, Muhammad Younas, and Anne James

School of Mathematical and Information Sciences, Coventry University,
Priory Street, Coventry CV1 5FB, UK
{y.hedley, m.younas, a.james}@coventry.ac.uk

Abstract. Hidden Web databases maintain a collection of documents, which are dynamically generated using Web page templates in response to user queries. This paper presents a technique, *Text with Neighbouring Adjacent Tag Segments* (*TNATS*), to represent the contents of documents retrieved from an underlying database. TNATS exploits tag structures that surround the textual content of a document. This representation facilitates the process of detecting Web page templates and extraction of query-related information from documents. We compare the performance of TNATS with existing techniques based on tag tree and text only representations. Experimental results demonstrate that TNATS requires less processing time for information extraction than a tag tree representation. It also produces optimum results in terms of detecting Web page templates and extracting query-related information.

1 Introduction

Hidden Web databases [4] maintain a collection of documents such as archives, manuals and news articles. These databases dynamically generate a list of documents in response to users' queries submitted through search interfaces. Such information is beyond the indexing capability of general-purpose search engines (such as Google) in which Web pages are indexed through hyperlinks [1]. The development of specialised subject directories (such as Search.com) provides a channel for information searches from the Hidden Web. As the number of databases proliferates, it has become prohibitive for these services to manually evaluate individual databases in order to answer users' queries.

Current techniques such as database selection [2, 6, 11] or categorisation [7] have facilitated the retrieval of information from databases. In particular, information (such as terms and frequencies) is collected from data sources for their selection or categorisation. However, in the domain of Hidden Web databases, such statistics are often unavailable. Furthermore, it is not feasible to retrieve all documents from an underlying database to gather information about its content. Therefore, a number of research studies [2, 6, 11] automatically generate terms and frequencies from documents through sampling. These approaches extract terms that are irrelevant to queries, since terms contained in Web page templates for descriptive or navigation purposes are also extracted.

R.K. Ghosh and H. Mohanthy (Eds.): ICDCIT 2004, LNCS 3347, pp. 158–167, 2004.

Existing techniques that extract information from dynamically generated Web pages focus on the textual contents of Web pages, or analyse their contents in a tree-like structure. For instance, approximate string matching techniques are applied in [8] to extract information from Web pages, but this approach is limited to textual contents only. By contrast, dynamically generated objects are discovered from Web pages through analysing their contents in tree-like structures [3, 9]. This approach requires Web pages with well-conformed HTML tag trees. Moreover, Web pages are clustered into groups of similarly structured Web pages based on a set of pre-defined page templates, such as exception page templates and result page templates.

This paper extends our previous work in [5], which presents a form of representation that describes the contents of template-generated documents. Our approach exploits the textual contents of a document and information from tags that surround the content – which we refer to as *Text with Neighbouring Adjacent Tag Segments* (*TNATS*). We also describe a mechanism that detects information contained in Web page templates and identifies the sections of documents that are relevant to queries.

Our experiments in [5] has also been extended to assess the effectiveness of the proposed approach in terms of: (i) time required for processing and extracting information from template-generated documents (ii) effectiveness in detecting information contained in Web page templates, and (iii) the accuracy of extracting query-related information. The results show that TNATS requires less processing time for extracting information in comparison to a tag tree representation. Our technique also provides an effective mechanism to detect Web page templates and produces optimum results in the extraction of query-related information.

The remainder of the paper is organised as follows. Section 2 introduces current approaches to acquiring statistics from databases and the associated problems. It also describes existing techniques that extract information from Web pages along with their limitations. Section 3 presents the proposed approach. Experimental results are discussed in section 4. Section 5 concludes the paper.

2 Related Work

A number of research studies discover the information contents of Hidden Web databases through sampled documents, from which statistics (i.e., terms and frequencies) are generated and referred to as Language Models, Textual Models or Centroids [2, 6, 11, 7]. Such statistics are then utilised to facilitate the selection or categorisation of databases. However, these techniques extract terms that are often contained in Web page templates for descriptive or navigation purposes. For instance, a language model generated from the sampled documents of Combined Health Information Database (CHID) consists of terms extracted from Web page templates with high frequencies [2]. These terms (such as 'author' and 'format') are not relevant to the queries but are used to describe the document contents. The use of additional stop-word lists has been considered in [2] to eliminate irrelevant terms, but this technique can be difficult to apply in practice. Textual models generated in [6, 11] contain additional topic terms through sampling Web databases. These models also contain terms extracted from Web page templates.

Current techniques employed to extract information from Web pages analyse page contents through text or tag tree representations. For instance, the technique applied in [8] extracts texts that are different. This approach is limited to finding textual similarities and differences. The technique proposed in [3] discovers objects from dynamically generated Web pages by analysing their contents based on a tag tree representation. However, it requires that Web pages contain well-conformed HTML tag-trees prior to information extraction. Moreover, this technique clusters Web pages into groups of similarly structured Web pages based on a number of pre-defined page templates, such as exception page templates and result page templates.

By contrast, our approach considers texts and information from their neighbouring tags as opposed to analysing document contents based on texts or tree-like structures. In addition, we detect Web page templates used to generate documents. This differs from the approach in [3, 9] that analyses grouped Web pages according to a pre-defined set of templates.

3 Query-Related Information Extraction

This section describes the technique proposed in our previous work [5], which detects information contained in Web page templates from template-generated documents and extracts information relevant to queries. Our approach represents and analyses a document based on its textual content and information from neighbouring tag structures associated with the content. This facilitates the detection of Web page templates. As a result, it improves the accuracy of information extracted from documents. Fig. 1. illustrates the process of extracting query-related information from Hidden Web documents.

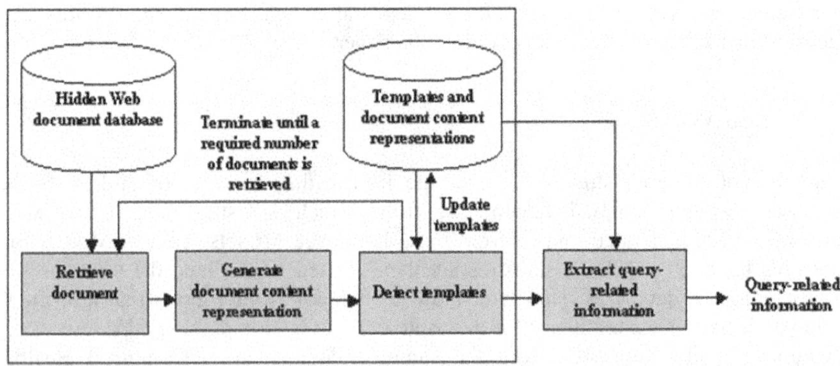

Fig. 1. Extraction query-related information from Hidden Web documents

Our technique retrieves documents through querying a database with randomly selected keywords. Qery keywords can be obtained from frequently used terms or those contained in documents retrieved from the database, as proposed in [2].

Alternatively, a set of terms can also be retrieved from the search interface pages of the database, which provide a source of information that is closely related to the database content.

The content of each document retrieved from the underlying database is represented by a list of text segments and their neighbouring tag segments. Web page templates are then detected through analysing the content representations of documents. We eliminate information contained in Web page templates and extract information that is relevant to queries. The generation of a document content representation, mechanism of template detection and the process of information extraction are detailed in section 3.1, 3.2 and 3.3 respectively.

3.1 Generation of Document Content Representation

This paper presents a form of document content representation, which we refer to as *Text with Neighbouring Adjacent Tag Segments* (*TNATS*). The content representation of a document contains a list of text segments and each with its neighbouring tag segments. That is, each text segment is identified through the textual content and information from its neighbouring tag segments. The neighbouring tag structures of a text segment describe how the text segment is structured within a Web document and how the segment relates to its adjacent text segments.

Prior to the generation of a content representation, the content of a document is first converted into a list of HTML (HyperText Markup Language) tag segments and text segments. Tag segments include paired start tags and end tags (such as <B> and </B>), and single tags (such as <HR>). A text segment is the text that exists between two tag segments.

In the TNATS representation, the neighbouring tag segments of a text segment are defined as the list of tag segments that are located immediately before and after the text segment until another text segment is reached. Assume that a document contains n segments, a text segment, txs, is defined as: $txs = (tx_i, tg\text{-}lst_j, tg\text{-}lst_k)$, where tx_i is the textual content of ith text segment, $1 \le i \le n$. $tg\text{-}lst_j$ represents p tag segments located before tx_i and $tg\text{-}lst_k$ represents q tag segments located after tx_i until another text segment is reached. $tg\text{-}lst_j = (tg_1, \ldots\ tg_p)$, $1 \le j \le p$ and $tg\text{-}lst_k = (tg_1, \ldots\ tg_q)$, $1 \le k \le q$. Given a Hidden Web document, d, with n text segments, the content of d is then represented as: $Content(d) = \{\ txs_1, \ldots\ txs_n\}$ where txs_i represents a text segment, $1 \le i \le n$.

Consider a document retrieved from the CHID database as shown in Fig. 2. Fig. 3 gives a sample of its source code. In this example, text segment, '5. Positive HIV Antibody Test.', can be identified by the text (i.e., '5. Positive HIV Antibody Test.') and its neighbouring tag segments. These include the list of tags located before the text (i.e., </TITLE>, </HEAD>, <BODY>, <HR>, <H3>, <B> and <I>) and the neighbouring tags located after the text (i.e., </I>, </B>, </H3>, <I> and <B>). Thus, this segment is represented as ('5. Positive HIV Antibody Test.', (</TITLE>, </HEAD>, <BODY>, <HR>, <H3>, <B>, <I>), (</I>, </B>, </H3>, <I>, <B>)). The document content representation based on TNATS for the sample code is given in Fig. 4.

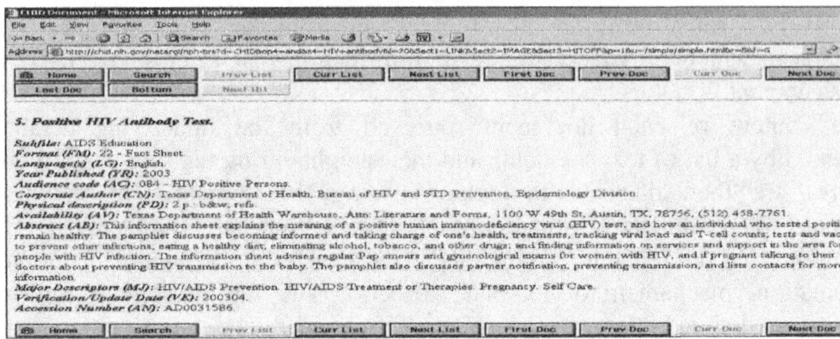

Fig. 2. A template-generated document retrieved from CHID

```
...
<HTML><HEAD><TITLE>CHID Document </TITLE></HEAD>
<BODY>
<HR><H3><B><I> 5. Positive HIV Antibody Test.
</I></B></H3>
<I><B>Subfile: </B></I>
AIDS Education<BR>
...
```

Fig. 3. The source code for the CHID document

```
...
'CHID Document', (<HTML>, <HEAD>, <TITLE>), (</TITLE>,
</HEAD>, <BODY>, <HR>, <H3>, <B>, <I>);
'5. Positive HIV Antibody Test.', (</TITLE>, </HEAD>, <BODY>,
<HR>, <H3>, <B>, <I>), (</I>, </B>, </H3>, <I>, <B>);
'Subfile:', (</I>, </B>, </H3>, <I>, <B>), (</B>, </I>);
'AIDS Education', (</B>, </I>), (<BR>, <I>, <B>);
...
```

Fig. 4. The document content representation of the CHID document based on TNATS

Fig. 5 illustrates the CHID document (given in Fig. 2) in a tree-like structure. Fig. 6 demonstrates the tag tree representation of the document as employed in [3]. For instance, text segment, 'CHID document', is uniquely identified by the path, *HTML[1].HEAD[1].TITLE[1]*, where the numbers in brackets represent the order of the child in the tag tree.

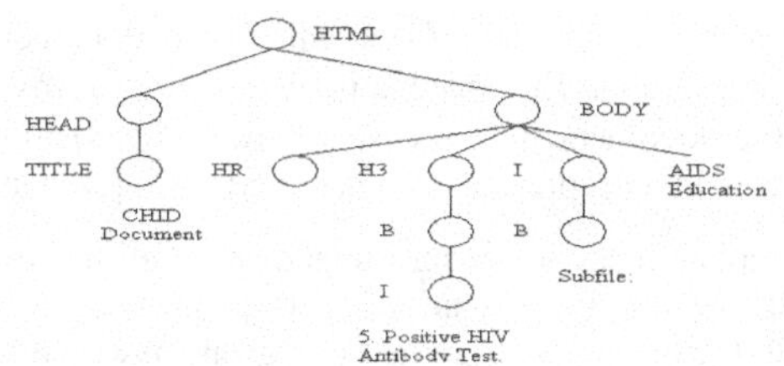

Fig. 5. The tag tree representation of the CHID document

...
'CHID Document', HTML[1]. HEAD[1]. TITLE[1];
'5. Positive HIV Antibody Test.', HTML[1]. BODY[2]. H3[2]. B[1]. I[1];
'Subfile:', HTML[1]. BODY[2]. I[3]. B[1];
'AIDS Education', HTML[1]. BODY[2];
...

Fig. 6. The document content representation of the CHID document based on tag trees

TNATS differs from a tag tree representation in that individual textual contents of a document are identified through information from their neighbouring tag structures. This approach utilises information from tag segments that surround a text segment, thus it is not limited to well-conformed Web pages. Furthermore, it requires less processing time for generating a TNATS document content representation in comparison to a tag tree representation.

3.2 Detection of Web Page Templates

This section describes a template detection mechanism that identifies Web page templates from dynamically generated documents. Documents retrieved from Hidden Web databases are often generated using one or more templates. Such templates are typically employed to describe document contents or to assist users in navigation.

Each document retrieved from a database is represented based on TNATS. Template detection is then carried out as follows:

1. Detect Initial Templates. Detect an initial Web page template through searching for identical patterns (i.e., the matched text segments along with their neighbouring tag segments) from the first two documents retrieved. Identical patterns are eliminated from their document content representations. Both documents are assigned to a group associated with the template. If no repeated patterns are found, the content representations of both documents are stored for future template detection.
2. Detect Subsequent Templates. Detect new templates through comparing each of the subsequently retrieved documents with existing templates generated or the previously stored document content representations. Assign the document to a

group associated with the template from which the document is generated if identical patterns are found. Eliminate any identical patterns from the content representation of the document. In the case where no identical patterns are found in the document, its content representation is stored for future analysis.

The process of template detection is terminated when all retrieved documents are analysed. This results in the identification of one or more templates. For each template, two or more documents are assigned to a group associated with the template from which the documents are generated. Each document contains text segments that are not found in their respective template. These text segments are partially related to their queries. In addition to a set of templates, the content representations of zero or more documents in which no matched patterns are found are stored.

3.3 Extraction of Query-Related Information

Text segments that remain in the documents (as described in section 3.2) are further analysed through the computation of text similarities. That is, the text segments of different documents from the group associated with a particular template are compared in terms of text similarity. This identifies any text segments (with identical tag structures), which are similar in their textual contents.

The textual content of a text segment is represented as a vector of terms with weights. A term weight is obtained from the occurrences of the term in the segment. Cosine similarity [10] given in (1) is computed on the textual contents of two text segments.

$$sim(txs_i, txs_j) = \sum_{k=1}^{t} (tw_{ik} * tw_{jk}) \Big/ \sqrt{\sum_{k=1}^{t} (tw_{ik})^2} * \sqrt{\sum_{k=1}^{t} (tw_{jk})^2} \quad (1)$$

where txs_i and txs_j represent two text segments in a document; tw_{ik} is the weight of term k in txs_i, and tw_{jk} is the weight of term k in txs_j.

The similarity is computed for text segments with identical neighbouring tag segments only. Two segments are considered to be similar if the similarity of their textual contents exceeds a threshold value. The threshold value is determined experimentally. This process results in the extraction of text segments with different tag structures. It also extracts text segments that have identical neighbouring tag structures but are significantly different in their textual content.

4 Experimental Results

A number of experiments (extended from our work in [5]) are conducted on 3 real-world Hidden Web document databases, Help Site, CHID and Wired News, which provide user manuals, healthcare archives and news articles respectively. These databases are summarised in Table 1. For each database, 10 documents are randomly retrieved by querying the database with keywords, which are obtained from its search interface pages and the documents retrieved.

We assess the effectiveness of TNATS in terms of: (i) time required to process documents and extract query-related information, (ii) template detection, and (iii) accuracy of extracting query-related information from documents. The results are then compared with those from tag tree representations (abbreviated as TTR) and text only representations (abbreviated as TX).

Table 1. 3 Hidden Web document databases used in the experiment

Document databases	URL	Content	Templates employed	Document size
Help Site	www.help-site.com	Homogeneous	Multiple templates	Varying sized (4-300 KB)
CHID	www.chid.nih.gov	Homogeneous	Single templates	Similar-sized (4-9 KB)
Wired News	www.wired.com	Heterogeneous	Single templates	Similar-sized (10-35 KB)

First, for each database, we assess the efficiency of information extraction in terms of time required to process 10 documents that are transformed based on TNATS and TTR. Next, the documents retrieved from each database are manually examined to obtain the number of templates used to generate documents. This is then compared with the number that is detected through TNATS, TTR and TX.

Finally, for each database, we compare information extracted from the retrieved documents based on TNATS with that extracted from TTR. In this experiment, a textual content transformed through TTR is represented by a list of tags from the root of the tag tree to the content. For instance, text segment, 'CHID Document', (given in Fig. 2) is represented by the path, *HTML/HEAD/TITLE*.

For each document, the extracted terms are also manually compared with those contained in the original document to determine the accuracy of information extraction. Recall and precision techniques (of information retrieval systems) are adopted in order to measure the accuracy of query-related information extraction [10]. In this paper, the recall is defined as the ratio of the number of relevant terms retrieved over the total number of relevant terms contained in a document. The precision is given by the ratio of the number of relevant terms retrieved over the total number of terms retrieved from a document.

Experimental results in Table 2 show that TNATS requires less processing time for extracting query-related information in comparison to TTR. In particular, considerably less processing time is required when TNATS is applied to larger-sized documents. For instance, 930 ms is obtained for TNATS to process Help Site documents whose sizes are ranged from 4 KB-24KB. By comparison, 3230 ms is required by TTR.

Table 2. Processing time for information extraction from 10 documents retrieved from each database based on TNATS and TTR

Document databases	Processing time in milliseconds (ms)	
	TNATS	TTR
Help Site	930	3230
CHID	330	440
Wired News	870	3290

Table 3 show that TNATS and TTR detect the number of templates more effectively than TR. For instance, a total of 3 templates are found in 10 documents retrieved from the Help Site database. The number of templates is successfully identified by TNATS and TTR, whereas only one template is detected when TR is applied. TNATS and TTR consider tag structures in the generation of a document content representation. By contrast, TR focuses on the textual contents of a document without considering how the contents are structured. As a result, TNATS and TTR effectively identify information contained in Web page templates.

Table 3. The number of templates employed to generate the documents retrieved from each database and the number detected by TNATS, TTR and TR

Document	Number of templates			
databases	Employed	TNATS	TTR	TR
Help Site	3	3	3	1
CHID	1	1	1	1
Wired News	1	1	1	1

Table 4 gives the accuracy of information extraction from the documents represented by TNATS and TTR, in terms of recall and precision. Results show that TNATS and TTR achieve similar performance in recall. In particular, TNATS and TTR both obtain a high recall value, 0.999, for the Wired News documents.

In terms of precision, TNATS performs better than TTR for Help Site and Wired News, whereas TNATS has lower precision for CHID. For instance, the precision attained from the Help Site documents for TNATS and TTR is 0.960 and 0.872, respectively. However, the precision of TNATS for CHID is 0.992, which is lower than the value obtained by TTR. Our observation is that TNATS is more effective when it is applied to the documents that vary in size and structure (such as Help Site documents), whereas the CHID documents are similar in sizes (i.e., 5KB-6KB). Furthermore, TNATS utilises information from the tag structures of the text segments adjacent to a given text segment to detect Web page templates. As a result, some template information may not be successfully detected.

Table 4. Average recall and precision for extracting query-related information from the Help Site, CHID and Wired News documents based on TNATS and TTR

Document	TNATS		TTR	
databases	Recall	Precision	Recall	Precision
Help Site	0.998	0.960	0.998	0.872
CHID	0.920	0.992	0.920	1.000
Wired News	0.999	0.981	0.999	0.810

5 Conclusion

Current techniques generate terms and frequencies from sampled documents to represent the information contents of Hidden Web document databases. These techniques also extract information contained in Web page templates. Consequently, the accuracy of extracting query-related information has been reduced.

In this paper we describes a form of content representation, TNATS, which represents a document content based on the textual content and information from their neighbouring tag structures. We then introduce a mechanism that analyses document contents based on TNATS and detects information contained in Web page templates. The application of TNATS facilitates template detection and information extraction. This is in contrast to those that analyse document contents based on text only or in a tree-like structure. Experimental results demonstrate that TNATS is more efficient in transforming document contents and extracting information. Our technique also attains a high degree of accuracy in terms of recall and precision.

We obtain promising results by applying TNATS in the experiments on three databases that differ in nature. However, experiments on a larger number of Hidden Web documents are required in order to further assess the effectiveness of the proposed technique.

References

1. Bergman, M. K.: The Deep Web: Surfacing Hidden Value. Appeared in The Journal of Electronic Publishing from the University of Michigan (2001).
2. Callan, J., Connell, M.: Query-Based Samp ling of Text Databases. ACM Transactions on Information Systems, Vol. 19, No. 2 (2001) 97-130
3. Caverlee, J., Buttler, D., Liu, L.: Discovering Objects in Dynamically-Generated Web Pages. Technical report, Georgia Institute of Technology (2003)
4. Gravano, L., Ipeirotis, P. G., Sahami, M.: QProber: A System for Automatic Classification of Hidden-Web Databases. ACM Transactions on Information Systems (TOIS), Vol. 21, No. 1 (2003)
5. Hedley, Y.L., Younas, M., James, A. Sanderson M. A Two-Phase Sampling Technique for Information Extraction from Hidden Web Databases. In Proceedings of the 6th ACM CIKM Workshop on Web Information and Data Management (WIDM) (2004)
6. Lin, K.I., Chen, H.: Automatic Information Discovery from the Invisible Web. International Conference on Information Technology: Coding and Computing (2002) 332-337
7. Meng, W., Wang, W., Sun, H., Yu, C.: Concept Hierarchy Based Text Database Categorization. International Journal on Knowledge and Information Systems, Vol. 4, No. 2 (2002) 132-150
8. Rahardjo, B., Yap, R. Automatic Information Extraction from Web Pages. In Proceedings of the 24th Annual International ACM SIGIR Conference (1999) 430-431
9. Ramaswamy, L., Iyengar, A., Liu, L., Douglis, F.: Automatic Detection of Fragments in Dynamically Generated Web Pages. In Proceedings of the 10th International Conference on World Wide Web (2004) 443-453
10. Salton, G., McGill, M.: Introduction to Modern Information Retrieval. McCraw-Hill, New York (1983)
11. Sugiura, A., Etzioni, O.: Query Routing for Web Search Engines: Architecture and Experiments. In Proceedings of the 9th International World Wide Web Conference: The Web: The Next Generation (2000) 417-430

Querying XML Documents from a Relational Database in the Presence of DTDs

Manjeet Rege, Izabell Caraconcea, Shiyong Lu, and Farshad Fotouhi

Department of Computer Science,
Wayne State University,
Detroit MI 48202
{rege, izabell, shiyong, fotouhi}@cs.wayne.edu

Abstract. Many researchers have investigated the problem of storing and querying XML documents using an RDBMS. Two situations are considered in this approach based on whether or not an XML schema is available. In a schema-oblivious relational approach, an XML schema is not available, or it is available but is not used. The advantage of schema-oblivious relational approach is that no XML schema is required, and the fixed generic schema can be used to store XML documents with arbitrary structure. However, since XML schema is not exploited, this approach usually implies a query engine where join operations dominate the query time and performance might suffer significantly. On the other hand, rare work on the problem of schema-based XML-to-SQL query mapping has been published in the literature. In this paper, we present an algorithm to address this problem.

1 Introduction

In the last few years, XML has emerged as a standard for representing and exchanging data. Though, this enables data scalability while easing the tasks of data interchange between business corporations, it also poses a problem of querying the growing number of XML documents efficiently. There have been primarily two approaches to handle this problem. One approach is to develop native XML repositories that support XML data models and query languages directly [1,2]. To achieve this, various XML query languages have been proposed such as XML-QL [3], XQL [4], Lorel [5], XPath [6] and more recently XQuery [7]. The second approach is to *shred* the XML documents and store them into a relational database in order to take advantage of mature and robust technologies that have already been developed for relational databases over the last few decades [8, 9]. The major challenges of the latter approach include: (1) XML data model needs to be mapped into the relational model; (2) XML data needs to be stored into the relational database; (3) Queries posed in XML query languages need to be translated into SQL; (4) The query result set needs to be returned back by converting the data into XML format.

Our contribution in this paper is pertaining to the challenges (3) and (4) stated above. There has already been research conducted on translating XML queries into

R.K. Ghosh and H. Mohanthy (Eds.): ICDCIT 2004, LNCS 3347, pp. 168–177, 2004.

SQL [13, 14, 15]. I. Tatarinov et al. propose storing and querying ordered XML using a relational database system in the absence of an existing DTD Schema for XML documents [10]. In their approach, they propose creating one table viz., the *Edge* table to store the shredded XML document. A key issue is how to map an XML path query into SQL queries and generate XML data from relational databases when DTD schema is available and relational data has been created by mapping XML data in the presence of DTDs. None of the above cited works tackle this problem. Recently, in [16], the problem was addressed when the XML schema is recursive. This problem is different from the one that we have attempted to solve in this work. Our work is based on a simplified DTD that gets generated based on the algorithm presented in [11]. Also, in [16], they create a relational table for each non-leaf DTD node that results in a large number of tables and hence might lead to table joins while querying. We extend on the work presented in [10] for querying XML data stored in a relational database when the XML DTD is available. We present an algorithm to query XML documents stored in a relational database in the presence of DTDs using XML path queries similar to XPath [6].

The rest of the paper is organized as follows. Section 2 gives a brief overview of the schema mapping algorithm [11] and the data mapping XInsert algorithm [12]. Section 3 discusses our proposed algorithm. In Section 4, we present the experimental results. Finally, section 5 concludes with suggestions for future work.

2 An Overview of Schema Mapping and Data Mapping Algorithms

Our algorithm assumes that the schema mapping from DTD to Relational Schema has been accomplished using the DTDMap algorithm presented in [11], and that the XInsert algorithm presented in [12] populates the relational database with XML documents.In this section we will provide the reader with a succinct overview of these algorithms.

One approach for mapping DTDs to relational schema is mapping each node in the DTD to a table. This approach results in many tables in the corresponding relational schema resulting in table joins causing query processing to be inefficient. Alternatively, the authors of the DTDMap algorithm suggest combining every single child node in a DTD, to its parent node, if it appears in its parent at most once. We call this operation *inlining*. A node is said to be *inlinable* if it has exactly one parent node, and its cardinality is not equal to either "*" or "+". An inlinable node is mapped with its parent node into the same table. Hence, we reduce the number of tables and consequently the average number of joins for queries. As an example, given the DTD in Figure 1, *tel*, *fax*, and *website* are inlinable to their common parent *dep*.

DTDMap algorithm takes a DTD as input and produces a relational schema as output. In addition, it outputs mapping functions σ, θ, and δ between XML elements and attributes in the input DTD, and corresponding tables and relational attributes in the output schema. For example,

- σ(e) maps an element type to a corresponding relational table.
  Therefore, σ(univ) = univ, σ(colleges) = univ, etc.
- θ(a) maps an XML attribute to a relational attribute.
  Therefore, θ(uName) = uName, θ(dName) = dName, etc.
- δ(e) maps a leaf element to a relational attribute.
  Therefore, δ(tel) = tel, δ(fax) = fax, etc.

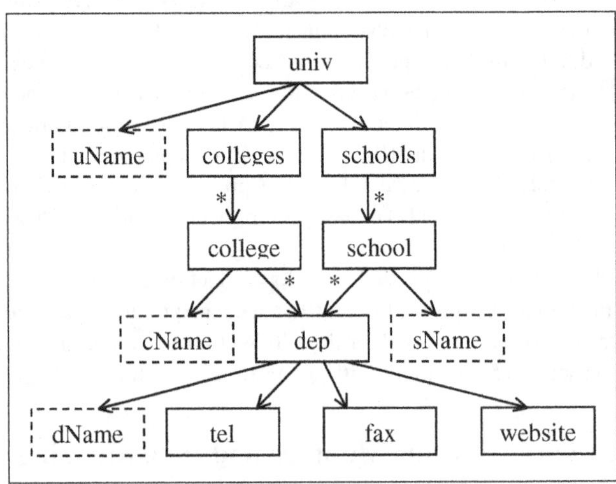

Fig. 1. The DTD graph of univ.dtd

In the above examples, some mappings happened to be identity mappings. This is not always the case in practice; they can be general enough and used to resolve name conflicts. For a more detailed explanation of the schema mapping algorithm, we refer the reader to [11].

The XML document is modeled as an XML element DOM tree in which nodes represent XML elements and edges represent parent-child relationships between elements. The root of the DOM tree is the top-level element, which does not have any incoming edges. The DOMTree for *univ.xml* is shown in Figure 2. The ID next to the nodes is the ID that XInsert assigns (or does not assign) to each node. Elements those are not inlined to some other element get a unique ID for themselves. In univ.xml example, *colleges* is inlined to *univ* while *website* and *tel* are inlined to their respective *dep* nodes.

The XInsert algorithm accepts DOMTree, DTDGraph and Schema mappings σ, θ, δ as input. The algorithm visits every node of the DOMTree and populates the relational database by generating the necessary INSERT SQL statements. As providing intricate details of the algorithm here is not possible due to lack of space, in Figure 3 we directly show the state of the database for *univ.xml* after both algorithms run completely. A complete discussion of XInsert can be found in [12].

3 Proposed Solution

In this section, we will first begin by establishing the notations used, followed by a detailed discussion of the algorithm with the help of our running example *univ.xml*.

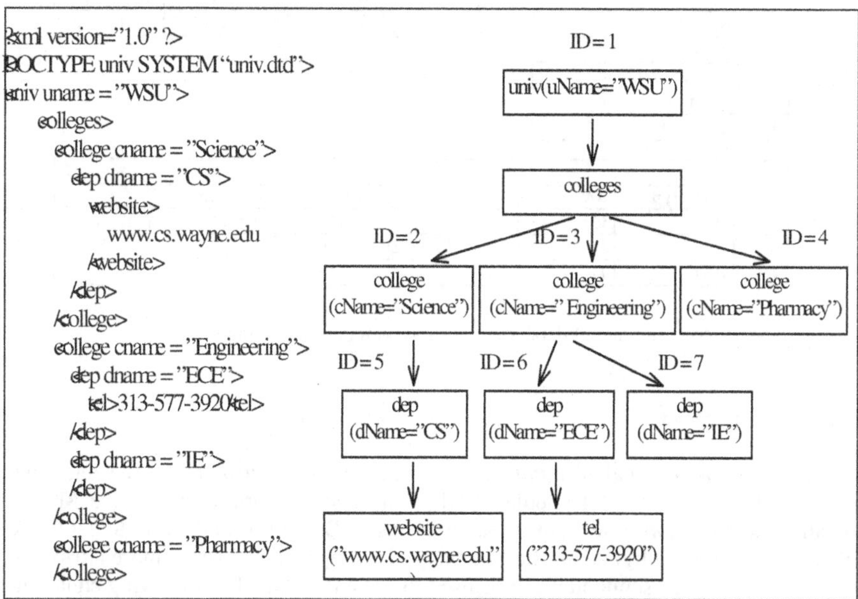

Fig. 2. Sample XML document univ.xml and its DOMTree

3.1 Notations and Functions Used in the Algorithm

- A typical XML Path expression has the following syntax:
  Path :: = /Step1/Step2/./StepN where each step can be defined as follows:
  Step :: = Axis :: Node-test Predicate*
  Predicate :: = '[' PredicateExpr ']'
  The Axis specifies the direction in which the document should be navigated.
  The PredicateExpr specifies the selection criteria for the query.
- For our work we will consider the default 'child' axis, '/' and '//' operators, and we only allow predicate in the last step. Therefore a step considers all child nodes of the context node.
- A Query Element e is characterized by an ID, a name, and its path. These properties were associated to e at the Insert time; e.ID is equal to h.ID if e is an inlinable element and e is inlined to h, otherwise e has a new ID; e.path is the absolute path of the element in the DOMTree.

Univ		
ID	*nodetype*	*uName*
1	univ	WSU

School	
ID	*sName*

College	
ID	*cName*
2	Science
3	Engineering
4	Pharmacy

Edge			
parentID	*childID*	*parentType*	*childType*
1	2	univ	college
1	3	univ	college
1	4	univ	college
2	5	college	dep
3	6	college	dep
3	7	college	dep

Dep					
ID	*nodetype*	*dName*	*tel*	*fax*	*website*
5	dep	CS	null	null	www.cs.wayne.edu
6	dep	ECE	3135773920	null	null
7	dep	IE	null	null	null

Fig. 3. State of database after univ.xml is stored using XInsert

3.2 Our Approach

We introduce a table called *pathtable*(*element*, *ID*, *path*, *attribute*) to the relational schema. This table can get populated when the XInsert algorithm parses the XML document, and it stores the element name, element ID, path from the root to get to the element (absolute path) and attributes (if any). Incase, we have two or more attributes, then a delimiter like semicolon can be used to separate them. The following equations hold among values in *path* column (1) and *ID* column (2):

$$\text{child.path} = \text{parent.path} + \text{"/"} + \text{child.name} \tag{1}$$

$$\text{f.ID} = \text{e.ID} \quad \text{if the f is inlinable to e} \tag{2}$$

The pathtable for *univ.xml* is shown in Figure 4. This table is used extensively by our algorithm to obtain IDs of the elements based on some criteria such as the path, attribute, etc. The basic idea is to first query the pathtable to retrieve all elements satisfying the input path expression. Each element is then processed based on whether it has been inlined and possibly exists as an attribute of a relational table or non-inlined and exists as an independent table in the relational schema.

The algorithm (see Fig. 5) accepts as inputs an XML based Path query, and σ and θ mapping functions that result from the XInsert algorithm. The goal of our algorithm is to let the user query the XML document that has been shredded and stored in the relational database created previously. To achieve this, we convert the original Path query into SQL, query the database, and convert the returned result set into XML, which is then returned back as an output. The resulting XML fragment is the union of all XML subdocuments obtained for all elements satisfying the input query (line 10 of Fig. 5).

pathtable			
element	*ID*	*path*	*attribute*
univ	1	/univ	uName=WSU"
colleges	1	/univ/colleges	null
college	2	/univ/colleges/college	cName=Science"
college	3	/univ/colleges/college	cName=Engineering"
college	4	/univ/colleges/college	cName=Pharmacy"
dep	5	/univ/colleges/college/dep	dName=CS"
dep	6	/univ/colleges/college/dep	dName=ECE"
dep	7	/univ/colleges/college/dep	dName=IE"
website	5	/univ/colleges/college/dep/website	null
tel	6	/univ/colleges/college/dep/tel	null

Fig. 4. *Pathtable* for univ.xml

```
Algorithm
  1. Input: Path query, σ, θ mappings
  2. Output: Result of the query in XML format
  3. begin
  4. sql = null;
  5. resultSet = null;
  6. elemSet = GetQueryElements(query);
  7. for each QElement e in elemSet do
  8.      processElement(e);
  9. end for
  10. return ∪ returnXML(e);
End Algorithm
```

Fig. 5. Main Algorithm

```
Function GetQueryElements (pathQuery q)
    elemSet = empty set;
    sql = GenSQL(q);
    resultSet = database.execute(sql);
    while resultSet.isNotEmpty()
         create new QElement e;
         e.ID = resultSet("id");
         e.name = resultSet("element");
         e.path = resultSet("path");
         add e to elemSet;
    end while
    return elemSet;
End Function
```

Fig. 6. Function GetQueryElements

GetQueryElements function in line 6 of Figure 5 takes the user Path query as a parameter and returns the XML elements to be queried on (see Fig. 6). For instance,

GetQueryElements(/univ/colleges/college/dep) will return all the *dep* elements under /univ/colleges/college.

GenSQL function in line 2 of Figure 6 has been defined to generate a SQL statement in order to query the *pathtable* to get the corresponding query elements. Its parameter is also the input Path query (see Fig. 7).

```
Function GenSQL (pathQuery q)
  1. whereClause = null;
  2. sql = null;
  3. if q has steps of the form  '//'<ElementName> then
  4.        replace '//' by '/%' ;
  5. if q has a Predicate in the Last Step then
  6.        whereClause = "path like " + simpleQuery +
              + " and attribute like " + predCond;
  7. else
  8.        whereClause = "path like " + q;
  9. end if
  10. sql = "select element, id, path from pathtable " +
              + whereClause;
  11. return sql;
End Function
```

Fig. 7. Function GenSQL

The line 3 of the above subroutine deals with paths having empty steps // where the node and all its descendants will be returned. For example, a Path query "e1//e2" yields the SQL statement

```
"select element, id, path from pathtable
 where path like '/e1/%e2'"
```

which will extract e2 but also e3 with e3.path = "/e1/e3/e2".

In lines 5-9, we construct the where clause for each of the following cases:

- Line 6 constructs a where clause for path queries that have an attribute predicate in the last step, i.e. values of attributes as selection criteria are used to retrieve the XML elements. We call *simpleQuery* the query without predicate, in other words simpleQuery = Step1/Step2//StepN.

For example, /univ/colleges/college[@cName="Science"] will return the college element that has attribute cName with value "Science" and has a path of /univ/colleges/college from the root of the XML document to its location. Here "cName=Science" is the *predCond*. The pathtable is queried to get the IDs of all query elements that not only have the path specified in the query but also satisfy the attribute condition. A SQL statement for the above Path query would be:

```
"select element, id, path from pathtable
 where path like '/univ/colleges/college'
 AND attribute like'cName=Science'"
```

- Line 8 constructs a where clause for path queries that do not have attribute predicate in the last step. For example, /univ/colleges/college/dep will return all the dep elements having this path from the root to their location in the XML document. The corresponding translated SQL is:

```
"select element, id, path from pathtable
where path like '/univ/colleges/college/dep'"
```

The next step in our algorithm is to get the content of the query elements from the relational database (line 8 of Fig. 5). In order to do that, each element is tested for inlinability to an ancestor by a recursive function processElement (see Fig. 8).

```
Function processElement(QElement e)
  returnXML(e) = "<" + e.name + ">";
  if e <> σ(e) then    /* e is inlined */
       returnXML(e) = processInlinedElement(e);
  else   /* e is not inlined, so e has its own table
       returnXML(e) = processNonInlinedElement(e);
  end if
  childrenSet = e.getChildren();
  if childrenSet.isNotEmpty() then
       for each child c in childrenSet do
            returnXML(e) = returnXML(e) + processElement(c);
       end for
  end if
  returnXML(e) = returnXML(e) + "</" + e.name + ">";
  return returnXML(e);
End Function
```

Fig. 8. Function processElement

After establishing whether the element was inlined or not during the XInsert operation, the corresponding method is called: processInlinedElement or processNonInlinedElement. If the element has children in the DOMTree, the XML subtree rooted at each child element will be added to the final result recursively. Due to space limitations, instead of providing the complete function algorithm, we present a brief description of the following two functions

- Function *processInlinedElement (QElement e)*. This function first checks if the query element is a relational attribute of a table of a different element. In such a case, the function simply queries the required column and constructs an XML fragment to return. On the other hand, there could be an element that is inlined to some other element but does not contain any PCDATA (*dummy* elements). When such an element happens to be a query element, then the function returns the empty string;
- Function *processNonInlinedElement (QElement e)*. This function retrieves the content of a leaf element, stored in a PCDATA column of its table. If the non-inlined element has children, they will be processed one by one by the processElement function.

Both functions make use of the element ID. The ID and the path uniquely identify the query element. The difference consists in the name of the column that is being queried.

4 Experimental Results

We ran our experiments on a Windows XP machine with a 2.4 GHz Pentium processor and 256MB of RAM. The algorithm was implemented in Java and the XML data was stored and queried using the Oracle9i database system. Three different pairs (DTD, XML document conforming to the DTD) were considered as input. For each document we formulated a complete set of queries and computed the average time to get the answer to a simple query, as well as to a query with predicate in the last step. Table 1 illustrates the performance of our algorithm.

Table 1. Algorithm performance

XML Document	Number of elements	Number of attributes	Max depth	Average time (sec)	
				Simple Query	Query with predicate
ubid.xml	342	0	5	4.7	-
sigmod.xml	1580	1	6	154.7	2.7
reed.xml	5716	0	4	453.1	-

The answer time is function of the number of elements that satisfy the query, which in turn depends on the size of the query. A simple path query of size 1 will have only one step and will retrieve the whole document under the root element. This is the most expensive case, since all elements have to be processed. A simple path query of size equal to the depth of the DOMTree will extract only the content of the leaf nodes. Therefore, we expect this to be the fastest answer for queries without predicates. For a query of intermediate size, we included in our experiments both possibilities: the last step node is or is not leaf. For example, given the Sigmod Records DTD, there are three possible path queries of size 3: "/sigmodrecord/issue/articles", "/sigmodrecord/issue/volume", "/sigmodrecord/issue/number"; *volume* and *number* are leaf nodes.

The performance will improve in case the input path query has a predicate in the last step. As the predicate translates in a selection criterion, the cardinality of the set returned by GetQueryElements function (see Fig. 6) becomes, in most situations, smaller. For example, if there exists an attribute *id,* which uniquely identifies an element *e*, GetQueryElements ("//e.[@id = 'value'] ") will output at most one element and the answer to that query will be the XML fragment rooted at *e*. Of course, the time complexity still depends on the depth of the last step element in the DOMTree.

5 Conclusions and Future Work

We presented an algorithm to query XML documents that are stored in a relational database using the algorithms presented in [11, 12]. We achieve this by converting the original path query into SQL queries. The SQL queries are then used to query the relational database. The query results are then tagged and converted into the XML format and returned back to the user. An algorithm to query XML from a relational database using a schema less approach has been discussed in [10]. However, our work falls in the schema-aware category. Our contribution has been to query inlined XML documents from a relational database in the presence of DTDs.

As future work, apart from looking into the optimization issues pertaining to our algorithm we would like to extend our algorithm to work with XQuery and XPath queries. We also plan to integrate this work to build a larger XML-RDBMS query system.

References

1. Tamino XML Server. Software AG. http://www.softwareag.com/tamino
2. eXtensible Information Server (XIS). eXcelon Corporation. http://www.exln.com
3. Deutsch, A., Fernandez, M., Florescu, D., Levy, A., Suciu, D.: XML-QL: A Query Language for XML (August 1998)
4. Robie, J., Lapp, J., Schach., D.: XML Query Language (XQL) (1998) http://w3.org/TandS/QL/QL98/pp
5. Goldman, R., McHugh, J., Widom, J.: From Semistructured Data to XML: Migrating the Lore Data Model and Query Languages (1999).
6. World Wide Web Consortium: XML Path Language (XPath), Version 1.0, W3C Recommendation (Nov 1999)
7. Chamberlin, D., Florescu, D., Robie, J., Simeon, J., Stefanascu, M.: XQuery: A Query Language for XML (February 2001) http://www.w3.org/TR/xquery
8. Florescu, D., Kossmann, D.: Storing and Querying XML Data using an RDMBS. IEEE Data Engineering Bulletin, Vol. 22930 (1999) 27-34
9. Varlamis, I., Vazirgiannis, M.: Bridging XML-Schema and Relational Databases: A System for Generating and Manipulating Relational Databases using Valid XML Documents. In the proceedings of ACM Symposium on Document Engineering, Atlanta USA (Nov. 2001)
10. Tatarinov, I., Viglas, S., Beyer, K., Shanmugasundaram, J., Sheikta, E., Zhang, C.: Storing and Querying Ordered XML using a Relational Database System. ACM SIGMOD 2002, June 4-6, Madison, Wisconsin, USA (2002)
11. Lu, S., Sun, Y., Atay, M., Fotouhi, F.: A New Inlining Algorithm for Mapping XML DTDs to Relational Schemas. In Proc. of the First International Workshop on XML Schema and Data Management, in conjunction with the 22nd ACM International Conference on Conceptual Modeling (ER'2003). Lecture Notes in Computer Science, Vol. 2814, Chicago, Illinois, USA (2003) 366--377
12. Atay, M., Sun, Y., Liu, D., Lu, S., Fotouhi, F.: Mapping XML Data to Relational Data: a DOM-Based Approach. In Proc. of the 8th IASTED International Conference on Internet and Multimedia Systems and Applications (IMSA'2004). Kauai, Hawaii, USA (August 2004)
13. Manolescu, I., Florescu, D., Kossmann, D.: Answering XML Queries over Heterogeneous Data Sources. In VLDB (2001)
14. Shanmugasundaram, J., Kiernan, J., Shekita, E. J., Fan, C., Funderburk, J.: Querying XML Views of Relational Data. In VLDB (2001)
15. Shanmugasundaram, J., Shekita, E., Kiernan, J., Krishnamurthy, R., Viglas, S., Naughton, J., Tatarinov, I: A General Technique for Querying XML Documents using a RDBMS. SIGMOD Record, 30(3) (2001)
16. Krishnamurthy, R., Chakravarthy, V., Kaushik, R., Naughton, J.: Recursive XML Schemas, Recursive XML Queries, and Relational Storage: XML-to-SQL Query Translation. In ICDE (2004)

SAQI: Semantics Aware Query Interface

M.K. MadhuMohan, Sujatha R. Upadhyaya*, and P. Sreenivasa Kumar

AIDB Lab
Department of Computer Science and Engineering,
Indian Institute of Technology Madras - India
{madmohan, sujatha, psk}@cs.iitm.ernet.in

Abstract. In this paper we present a conceptual framework and the implementation details of a semantic web tool named SAQI (Semantic Aware Query Interface) that enables querying across structurally disparate XML documents that use the vocabulary from a shared ontology. Through this tool we provide an interface for querying the web pages of a group of participants with common interest who have agreed to use the common base ontology for publishing their data. Our interface guides a naive user in his querying process. It helps him to formulate his queries and retrieve semantically correct information from the web pages of this user group.

Keywords: Semantic Web, querying the web, ontologies.

1 Introduction

Often we find many web pages floated on World Wide Web by different establishments, with a particular domain as their focus. Anyone interested in finding information relevant to him in the domain, is expected to perform a search and browse through each of these pages to gather relevant information. A web search tool which can understand the semantics behind the vocabulary it encounters in a web page and semantically interpret the terms in this web document could prove to be extremely useful. Such a tool would also demonstrate the enormous advantages offered by the semantic web over the current web. Semantic web is proposed to be built on a foundation of ontologies. Semantic web efforts consist of building ontologies, deploying them on the web and developing applications that are ontology aware. The first two steps require enormous effort on standardization. We simplify this problem by assuming the existence of a small group of organizations that has reached a consensus on an ontology. This paper presents a search tool that is ontology aware and demonstrates the methodology for this group to migrate to the semantic web.

Our system provides a common gateway to query information provided by a group of participating establishments who are at liberty to publish the information in the form of their choice. Our application SAQI (Semantics Aware Query Interface) does not require that the web pages adhere to some strict structure or

* Supported by Infosys Technologies Limited.

R.K. Ghosh and H. Mohanty (Eds.): ICDCIT 2004, LNCS 3347, pp. 178–193, 2004.

meta data representation. Our system assumes that web sites of the participating establishments are built on a XML base and use vocabulary specified in the ontology that has been agreed upon [1]. We intend to solve the problem of semantic interoperability and present a methodology for smooth migration to semantic web by making use of the presently available languages and tools for querying XML [2]. In this process, we attempt to establish the limits of semantic interoperability, as deciphered from an ontology that is represented in a tree model.

Since all members of the group follow one ontology, we do not consider the issues relating to ontology integration. We do assume an open world assumption, that the information is never complete. New organizations are allowed to join the group provided, they use the shared ontology. All web pages that uses the vocabulary from an ontology qualify as valid target documents for a search using SAQI.

2 Motivation

Here we have tried to focus our research on a methodology that will facilitate a smooth migration from the current Web to semantic web by making use of existing web technologies. The task of building standard Ontologies and sharing them among a group of users can be looked upon as the starting point of the intended migration to the semantic web. It would be easier for small groups to come to consensus on an ontology than trying to establish standard ontologies that are globally accepted. In this context we may consider groups of users like manufactures of specific products like computers, cameras, cellular phones, who reach their audience through World Wide Web, by publishing complete detail about their products. Educational Institutions also reach prospective students through World Wide Web. In such environments it is easier to establish the concepts and relations among them and agree upon their use.

While XML documents are finding their place on the WWW, it would be difficult to call the evolving XML query systems as user friendly. In support of our pursuit for finding a method for smooth migration to semantic web, we build a query interface between a naive user and XML query engines. The query interface provides the same functionality of a Web Search tool in the semantic web. The XML query engine is expected to handle the web sites based on XML documents which in turn use the vocabulary from the shared ontology. The query interface uses the inference rules provided by the ontology to achieve the semantic interoperability. Thus prospective students interested in enrolling for programs offered by a group of participating academic institutions can use the interface provided by SAQI to retrieve semantically relevant information provided by these institutions without having to browse through the individual web pages of each institution.

3 Overview

We assume that a group of organizations have found a common ontology suitable for representing information about themselves. We call this a Base ontology. One method of deployment would be to let the organizations populate the ontology by adding their own individuals for the concepts defined in the ontology. One can use a suitable ontology editor, preferably Protege [3], to add individuals to the ontology. SAQI provides a module called 'OntoXML' to convert the OWL file to an XML file populated with instances under the *Class*/concept tags. This *Class* hierarchy tree which is in the form of a XML document itself can provide full information about that particular organization and act as a base for the organization's web site. This method of ontology deployment requires minimal effort. On the other hand this gives little scope for extending the ontology.

Alternatively, the organizations can be allowed to extend the base ontology without violating any existing concepts. The organization is allowed to define new concepts based on the existing concepts and introduce a new term to refer to an existing concept. This offers greater flexibility at the cost of an additional effort to understand and modify ontologies suitably. Once the modified ontology is ready, one can use the OntoXML Module of SAQI as mentioned above and initiate participation in this system. The two methods discussed, provide a single document that has to be queried by SAQI to extract information from a particular web site. However, one can also directly float any number of XML documents that conform to the specified Base ontology to present the information. Again, one can choose to extend the base ontology either by instantiation or by creating new concepts.

The current version of SAQI supports the first method of ontology deployment where the ontology itself is not extended. However the web sites are expected to be based on a set of XML documents conforming to the ontology rather than a single XML document. SAQI when presented with a base ontology, converts it in to a user friendly directory like interface through which a naive user can easily present his query. The user's query is semantically enriched based on inference rules from the ontology and formatted to an XML query syntax. An XML query engine performs the query operation using this query string over the set of XML documents that represents the web sites adhering to this ontology and returns all the semantically relevant results to the user.

4 Background and Related Work

There have been efforts in the past to initiate participation into semantic web [4] [5] [6] [7]. Structuring data on the web and so laying a foundation for interoperable web sites of the future has been the very purpose of all these efforts. OntoBroker, the system discussed In [6] uses ontologies to derive DTDs, which are later used for accessing documents and Mangrove, the system presented in [4], uses an annotation tool for creating semantic data, where as our application creates an annotated XML document, the ontology equivalent XML tree, which is used as a base for querying. Our system provides much stronger inference mechanism, supporting all aspects of ontology representation discussed in OWL Lite [8]. The earlier systems like OntoBroker capture hierarchy among concepts and do not dwell much on other inferencing efforts. None of the above approaches provide a ontology supported interface that guides the user in querying. We take a different approach for initiating participation into semantic web by providing a common interface for semantically inter-operable web sites. What makes our system unique is the integration of the current web technologies to facilitate a smooth migration to semantic web and demonstrate a intelligent web search system in a manner not yet attempted before.

5 System Architecture

SAQI uses ontologies written in OWL [8] [9] [10] and created using Protege [3]. In this document we describe the system functionalities with the an example academic ontology developed by us using Protege. Ontology refers to a shared and common understanding of a domain. The Base Ontology contains the complete description of concepts and relationships in the domain. Ontology uses *Classes* to represent concepts. A *Class* defines a group of individuals that belong together because they share some properties. The Figure 1 shows the architecture of SAQI.

The Semantic Extractor has two sub modules called OntoXML and Inference module. This module preprocesses the Base Ontology to create the output documents as shown in the Figure 1. Internally, the OntoXML module converts the the base ontology written in OWL into an equivalent XML document that represents the the ontology in a tree structure. This tree structure, called "Ontology Equivalent XML Tree" is used by the Inference module to create the OntoIndex. This in turn is used by SAQI to perform reasoning over an ontology. In a sense it is an attempt to come up with a completely decidable set from given assertions.

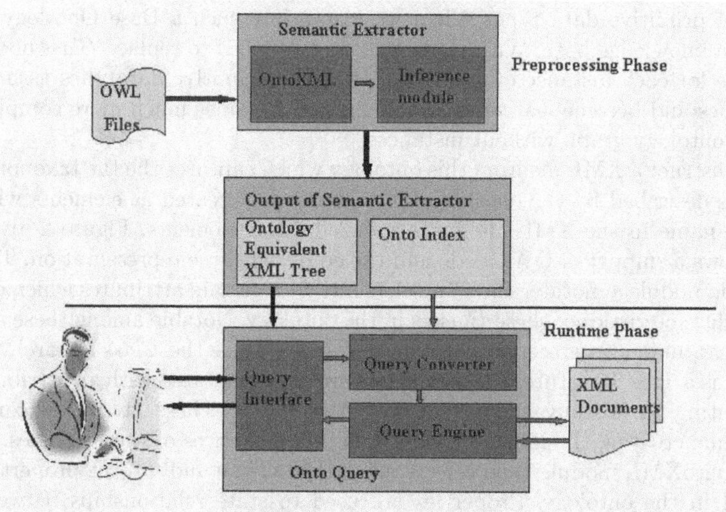

Fig. 1. System Architecture

The OntoQuery module operates at runtime and has three modules within. The 'Query Interface' that serves an interface between the user and the system provides a GUI that guides the user in querying through the ontology. It provides a directory like structure, which is actually created from the "Ontology Equivalent XML Tree" that was generated by the OntoXML module. The "Query Converter" uses the inferred results stored in the OntoIndex data structure which are nothing but the synonyms for the vocabulary defined by the ontology and a set of identifiers for instances based on the *Class* name. The index is stored in XML query language syntax for ease of use later. The user's query is re written using OntoIndex and passed it on to a XML Query Engine. The prototype uses "Galax XQuery Engine" [11]. The Galax Query Engine performs the query over the target XML documents that are tagged with the vocabulary from the ontology.

6 Semantic Extractor

As seen in the Figure 1 the Semantic Extractor with its two components the OntoXML and the and the Inference module are the major actors in the Preprocessing phase.

6.1 OntoXML

This module accepts an ontology in the form of an OWL file. ontology uses a Graph model. When we perceive the ontology as a graph, the *Class*es will be nodes in the graph. Object properties become edges which lead from *Class* nodes to another *Class* node. *dataTypeProperty* leads to some other nodes which are *Class*es of primitive data types.When we instantiate such a Base Ontology it becomes a knowledge base. With these instances we need to replace *Class* nodes by a node for each instance of the *Class*. Here the primitive datatypes assume some values and become leaf nodes. Such a graph becomes much more complex than the ontology graph without instances.

We construct a XML file from this ontology which captures the the taxonomy of *Class*es described by the ontology. The *Class*es are created as elements with the same name in the XML file and are called *Class* elements. Figure 2 given above shows a snippet of OWL code and the equivalent tree representation. The OntoXML module annotates the *Class* elements with certain attributes which depict the characteristics of these *Class*es in the ontology. Notable among these are disjointness, union, intersection with other *Class*es. Once the *Class* hierarchy is captured as a Tree Structure, *Class* elements are also annotated with an attribute for indicating their equivalence with any other *Class*. These attributes come handy while creating the index for identifying the instances of these *Class*es.

The OntoXML module then selects all the dataType and Object properties described in the ontology. Properties are used to state relationships between individuals or from individuals to data values. The properties have a *Domain* and *Range Class* specified in the ontology. A *Domain* of a *Property* limits the

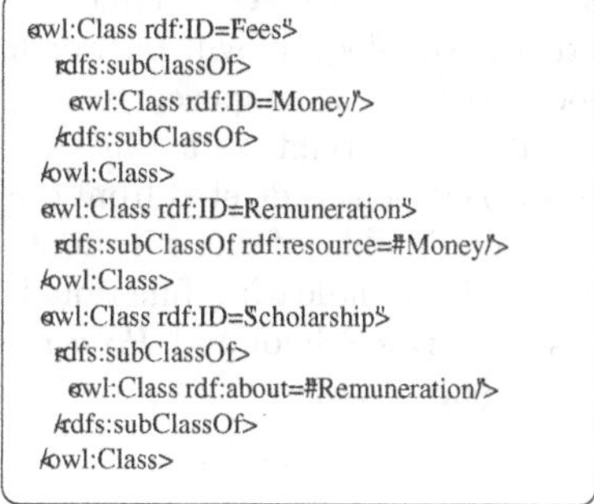

Owl Code

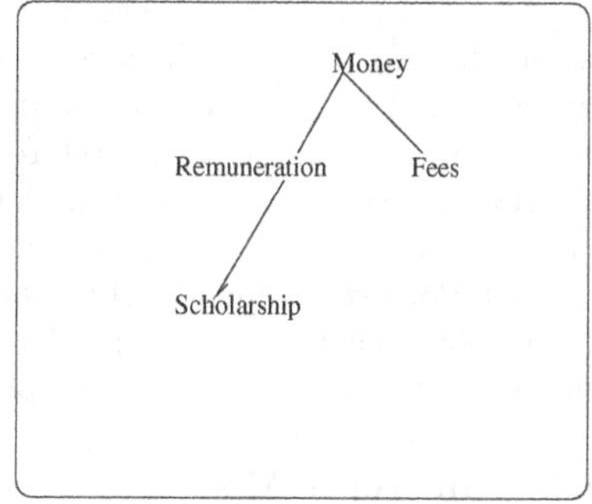

Tree Representation

Fig. 2. Class Hierarchy Captured as Tree

individuals to which the *Property* can be applied . Similarly the *Range* of a *Property* limits the individuals that the *Property* may have as its value.

These properties are inserted as child elements of the *Class* elements that correspond to the *Domain* of the properties in the Tree structure. Henceforth we shall refer to these elements as *Domain Class* elements and *Property* elements respectively. The *Class* name indicating the *Range* of each of the *Property* are added as an attribute to the *Property* elements for easy reference. If a *Property* has multiple *Domains* it is inserted as a child element under each of its *Domain Class* elements. The special characteristics of the *Property* such as being functional, symmetric, transitive etc are also indicated as attributes to the *Property* element.

The OntoXML then captures the synonyms of *Property* names by searching for the *owl:equivalentProperty* tag from the ontology. The equivalent *Property* are indicated under the respective *Property* elements as child elements of a tag "equivalent". The *Property* elements from the *Domain Class* elements are percolated down to all its child elements which correspond to some *Classes* in the ontology to capture their inheritance characteristic. In the case of *ObjectProperty* elements the *dataTypeProperty* elements from its *Range Class* are also added as child elements to *ObjectProperty* element.

To summarize the "Ontology Equivalent XML Tree" stores the *Classes* as elements, the properties under the *Classes* as their sub elements. Property Characteristics and *Range* are added as attributes to the Property elements. Figure 3 illustrates this with some *Classes*, *ObjectProperty* and *dataTypeProperty* described in OWL and corresponding output of OntoXML Module. The OntoXML captures all the restrictions associated with a *Class*. The restrictions are added as child elements to the *Class* elements. These restrictions provide many inferences which are used to construct the OntoIndex. Like in the case of properties the restrictions are also percolated down to all sub *Class* elements.

The XML file created acts as the input to the Query Interface module. To avoid forming queries which do not conform to the ontology it will be worth while to adjust the tree depending on the local restrictions imposed on the *Class*es by the ontology. Therefore if the cardinality constraint on a *Class* restricts a *Property* not to occur under it, the *Property* element is deleted from the child elements of the *Class* element. Similarly the cardinality of one will imply a child *Property* element to be functional. The attribute indicating functionality is reset accordingly. Figure 4 illustrates this for *Class* School and *Property* offersPrograms which is an appropriate example of such a case.

6.2 Inference Module

An ontology populated with instances becomes a knowledge base. Normally reasoners make inferences from the knowledge base using pre defined rules. We assume that in an XML file that follows an ontology, the instances of a *Class* will appear as text nodes under a tag bearing their parent *Class* name. Therefore to achieve the aim of semantic interoperability the query system has to infer from the instances it encounters in any XML document as to which *Class* they are of. Listed below are few of the rules and some of the inferences that can be made from the ontology based on these rules.

Sub Class. *Class*es are organized in a specialization hierarchy using *subClassOf* construct in OWL. In Figure 3, for instance the *Class* "PostGraduateProgram" is a sub *Class* of "Program". If "M Tech Computer Science" is an instance of *Class* "PostGraduateProgram", it can be inferred to be an instance of "Program" as well.

```
<owl:Class rdf:ID="PostGraduateProgram">
  <rdfs:subClassOf rdf:resource="#Programs"/>
 </owl:Class>
<owl:ObjectProperty rdf:ID="haveCoreCourses">
  <rdfs:range rdf:resource="#Course"/>
  <rdfs:domain rdf:resource="#Programs"/>
</owl:ObjectProperty>
<owl:DatatypeProperty rdf:ID="hasCredit">
  <rdfs:domain rdf:resource="#Course"/>
  <rdfs:range rdf:resource="http://www.w3.org/2001/XMLSchema#int"/>
</owl:DatatypeProperty>
<owl:ObjectProperty rdf:ID="fees">
  <rdfs:domain>
   <owl:Class>
    <owl:unionOf rdf:parseType="Collection">
     <owl:Class rdf:about="#Programs"/>
     <owl:Class rdf:about="#Facility"/>
    </owl:unionOf>
   </owl:Class>
  </rdfs:domain>
  <rdfs:range rdf:resource="#Fees"/>
 </owl:ObjectProperty>
<owl:DatatypeProperty rdf:ID="value">
  <rdfs:domain rdf:resource="#Money"/>
  <rdfs:range rdf:resource="http://www.w3.org/2001/XMLSchema#float"/>
  <owl:equivalentProperty>
   <owl:DatatypeProperty rdf:about="#amount"/>
  </owl:equivalentProperty>
 </owl:DatatypeProperty>
```

owl code snippet

```
<PostGraduateProgram type="Class">
  <haveCoreCourses type="objectProperty" range="Course">
    <hasCredit type="dataProperty" range="int"/>
  </haveCoreCourses>
  <fees type="objectProperty" range="Fees">
    <value type="dataProperty" range="float">
      <equivalent dataProperty="amount"/>
    </value>
  </fees>
</PostGraduateProgram>
```

Tree representation in XML

Fig. 3. Property Representation in Class Tree

```
<owl:Class rdf:ID="School">
  <rdfs:subClassOf>
    <owl:Restriction>
      <owl:cardinality>
      >0</owl:cardinality>
      <owl:onProperty>
        <owl:ObjectProperty rdf:about="#OffersPrograms"/>
      </owl:onProperty>
    </owl:Restriction>
  </rdfs:subClassOf>
  <rdfs:subClassOf rdf:resource="#AcademicInstitution"/>
</owl:Class>
<owl:Class rdf:ID="College">
  <rdfs:subClassOf rdf:resource="#AcademicInstitution"/>
</owl:Class>
<owl:ObjectProperty rdf:ID="OffersPrograms">
  <rdfs:range rdf:resource="#Programs"/>
  <rdfs:domain rdf:resource="#AcademicInstitution"/>
</owl:ObjectProperty>
<owl:SymmetricProperty rdf:ID="coOperatesWith">
  <rdf:type rdf:resource="http:/#FunctionalProperty"/>
  <rdf:type rdf:resource="http://#ObjectProperty"/>
  <rdfs:range rdf:resource="#AcademicInstitution"/>
  <rdfs:domain rdf:resource="#AcademicInstitution"/>
</owl:SymmetricProperty>
```

OWL Code Fragment

```
<AcademicInstitution type="Class">
 <College type="Class">
   <OffersPrograms type="objectProperty" range="Programs"
    functionalType="false" domain="AcademicInstitution"
    Hierarchy="inherited"/>
   <coOperatesWith type="objectProperty" range="AcademicInstitution"
    functionalType="true" symmetricProperty="true"
    domain="AcademicInstitution"/>
 </College>

 <School type="Class">
  <coOperatesWith type="objectProperty" range="AcademicInstitution"
   functionalType="true" symmetricProperty="true"
   domain="AcademicInstitution"/>
  <restriction property="OffersPrograms" restrictionType="cardinality"
  occurence="0"/>
 </School>

 <OffersPrograms type="objectProperty" range="Programs"
  functionalType="false" domain="AcademicInstitution"/>
 <coOperatesWith type="objectProperty" range="AcademicInstitution"
 functionalType="true" symmetricProperty="true"
 domain="AcademicInstitution"/>
</AcademicInstitution>
```

Equivalent Optimised tree representation

Fig. 4. Optimization Based on Local Restrictions

Domain. If a *Property* relates an individual to another individual and the *Property* has a *Class* as one of its *Domains*, then the individual must belong to the *Class*. From the owl code snippet in the same figure, we can observe that *Domain* of *ObjectProperty* "haveCoreCourses" is "Programs". If we encounter in the course of a search a statement in a target XML file like

<A>X<haveCoreCourses>...</haveCoreCourses></A>

we can infer that X is a instance of "Program" although A is not explicitly written as "Programs".

Range. If a *Property* relates an individual to another individual, and the *Property* has a *Class* as its *Range*, then the other individual must belong to the *Range Class*. In the same example *Range* of *ObjectProperty* "haveCoreCourses" is "Courses". From this we can infer "Advanced DataBases" to be an instance of "Course" *Class* when we encounter XML code of type

<A>X
<haveCoreCourses>Advanced DataBases</haveCoreCourses>
</A>

Equivalent Classes. Two *Class*es may be stated to be equivalent. Equality can be used to create synonymous *Class*es. If *Class*es A and B are equivalent, an instance of *Class* A will always be an instance of *Class* B.

AllValuesFrom Restriction. The restriction allValuesFrom is stated on a *Property* with respect to a *Class*. It means that this *Property* on this particular *Class* has a local Range restriction associated with it. From the figure 5 we see that core courses for "MastersProgram" are from the *Class* "PostGraduateCourses". Therefore from a XML code of form

```
<owl:Class rdf:ID=MastersProgram">
  <rdfs:subClassOf rdf:resource=#PostGraduateProgram"/>
  <rdfs:subClassOf>
    <owl:Restriction>
      <owl:allValuesFrom rdf:resource=#PostGraduateCourse"/>
      <owl:onProperty>
        <owl:ObjectProperty rdf:about=#haveCoreCourses"/>
      </owl:onProperty>
    </owl:Restriction>
  </rdfs:subClassOf>
</owl:Class>
```

AllValuesFrom Restriction

```
<owl:Class rdf:ID=MastersStudent">
  <rdfs:subClassOf rdf:resource=#PostGraduateStudent"/>
  <owl:equivalentClass>
    <owl:Restriction>
      <owl:onProperty>
        <owl:ObjectProperty rdf:about=#appliedForProgram"/>
      </owl:onProperty>
      <owl:someValuesFrom rdf:resource=#MastersProgram"/>
    </owl:Restriction>
  </owl:equivalentClass>
</owl:Class>
```

SomeValuesFrom Restriction

Fig. 5. AllValuesFrom

<MastersProgram>X
<haveCoreCourses>Semantic Web</haveCoreCourses>
</MastersProgram>

we infer that "Semantic Web" is an instance of "PostGraduateCourse". However such an inference can not be drawn from the "someValuesFrom" restriction. We can only say that instances of *Class* "MastersStudent" will have at least one instance from the *Class* "MastersProgram" against the *Property* "appliedForProgram".

Same Individuals. Two individuals may be stated to be the same. OWL construct *<owl:sameAs>* depicts synonymity between any two individuals. These constructs may be used to create a number of different names that refer to the same individual. If X is an instance of *Class* "A" and X is "sameAs" Y we can infer that Y is also an instance of *Class* "A".

We use these inference rules to pre process the "Ontology equivalent XML Tree" constructed by the OntoXML module and generate OntoIndex, a Thesaurus of vocabulary used in the ontology and a quick index to identify instances based on *Class* names . Thus from the Base Ontology all the information required for the inferences except for the "Same Individuals" case are available. We also make use of the equivalent properties which were discovered and stored in the tree.

The data structure used for the OntoIndex is a hash table, and uses the *Class/property* name as the key and all the synonyms for it duly separated by the character '|'. The hash table is stored in a file and loaded at run time . Figure 6 shows the hash table populated with the synonyms for the *Class*es/*Propert*ies seen in earlier examples. The data to the left of = is the key and to the right the corresponding synonym. Properties which are functional can occur as an attribute to the *Class* element in the target XML document since they take a single instance as their value. The application takes care of this aspect while rewriting the query. In case of same instances, if the information is available as part of the ontology they are also added to the hash table.

7 OntoQuery Module

This module with its subparts Query Interface and Query Converter come into play at run time.

```
PostGraduateCourse  = PostGraduateCourse
                      |MastersProgram/haveCoreCourses
Course              = Course|(Programs|PostGraduateProgram|MastersProgram)/haveCoreCourses
PostGraduateStudent = PostGraduateStudent|MastersStudent
MastersStudent      = MastersStudent
AcademicInstitution = AcademicInstitution|College|School|
                      (AcademicInstitution|College|School)/coOperatesWith
School              = School
College             = College
Programs            = Programs|PostGraduateProgram|MastersProgram
                      |(AcademicInstitution|College|School)/OffersPrograms
PostGraduateProgram = PostGraduateProgram|MastersProgram
MastersProgram      = MastersProgram
Money               = Money|Fees|Remuneration|Scholarship
                      |(Programs|PostGraduateProgram|MastersProgram)/fees
Fees                = Fees|(Programs|PostGraduateProgram|MastersProgram)/fees
                      |Facility/fees
Remuneration        = Remuneration|Scholarship
value               = value|amount
amount              = amount|value
```

Fig. 6. OntoIndex

7.1 Query Interface

The query interface uses the "Ontology equivalent XML Tree" created and stored as XML file by the OntoXML module. In general SAQI supports two types of queries. In the first case we want to retrieve all instances of a particular *Class* say all Academic Institutions. We could also make the query more specific by retrieving the instances that are targeted using a *Class/ObjectProperty* construct such as instances of Programs specified by **AcademicInstitution / offersPrograms**. In the second case we may specify a condition such as name of an instance against the *ObjectProperty* or a value against a *dataTypeProperty* such as **Programs /fees /amount = "100"**.

In the query interface the user is guided to form the query using the tree view generated from the ontology equivalent XML document. Once the user selects a node,it is translated to a query string which at most can be of form *Class/object Property/dataTypeProperty*. The user can specify the query criteria by using boolean operators and string values in a text box. The query interface diagram shows a screen snap shot of SAQI in execution. Some additional optimization apart from those done by the OntoXML module are also performed. For example if a *Class* has a local restriction "hasValue" on a *ObjectProperty* it may be wiser to prevent a naive user from entering values against this property which do not exist in any document with out violating the ontology. In such cases the property is not displayed at all under the concerned class.

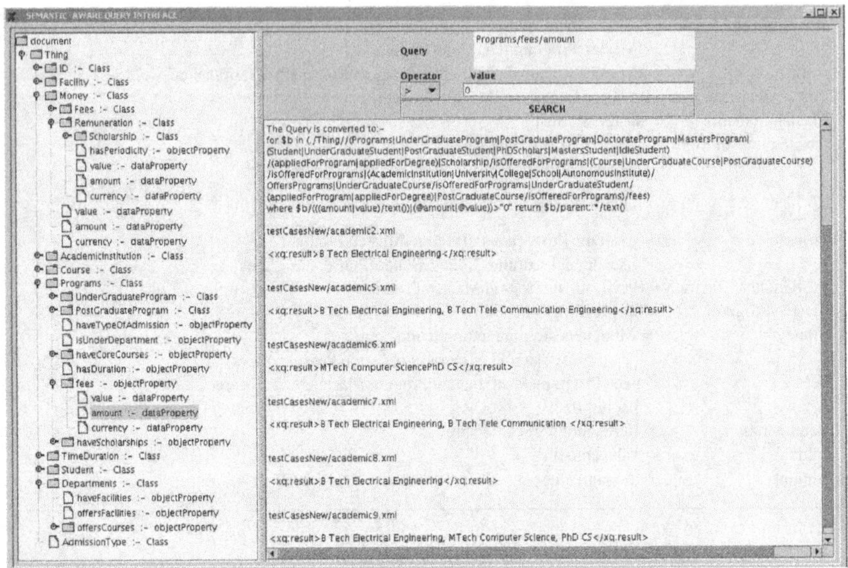

Fig. 7. Query Interface

7.2 Query Converter

The Query Converter needs to do a **"Semantics enriched rewriting"** [12]. This rewriting needs to be done using a sufficiently expressive XML query language so that intended inference mechanism is easily built in to the query where necessary. The query converter uses the OntoIndex created and stored by the Inference module. The query string formed by the user using Query Interface is first tokenized. Each token forms a string which is replaced by the synonym for the string from the OntoIndex. For a user generated query of the form **Course/hasCredit** the tokeniser creates two strings "Course" and "hasCredit". The converted query consists of each of these strings replaced by its synonym and rewritten as a XQuery Statement. Therefore the query **PostGraduateCourse/hasCredit='4'** is rewritten as following XQuery statement

for $b in ./root//(PostGraduateCourse|(Programs|
PostGraduateProgram|MastersProgram)
/haveCoreCourses)/hasCredit
where $b/text()='4'
return $b

Unlike any other search engines or XML query engine, such a rewritten query which has been semantically enriched automatically can retrieve both the following sets of XML data. This would not have been possible without semantic enrichment.

<PostGraduateCourse>ADB<hasCredit>4</hasCredit>
</PostGraduateCoursesCourse> and <PostGraduateProgram>
MCA<haveCoreCourses> CO<hasCredit>4</hasCredit>
</haveCoreCourses></PostGraduateProgram>

Although in this example it may appear that a XQuery string such as "//hasCredit" rather than the elaborate string as shown above can also easily retrieve this result, such a query conversion may also end up retrieving invalid results (may retrieve undergraduate courses as well). The query conversion mechanism of SAQI guarantees semantically valid results based on the ontology and it is one of the most significant advantage offered by SAQI. If the property "hasCredit" is functional then it can occur as an attribute in a target XML document. This can happen only for the property which is the last token in a query string. In that case query is rewritten as

for $b in ./root//(Course|(Programs|PostGraduateProgram|MastersProgram)/haveCoreCourses)
where $b/hasCredit/text()='4' or $b/@hasCredit='4'
return $b

Similarly a query of form **Programs/fees/value='100'** is written as

for $b in ./root//(Programs|PostGraduateProgram|MastersProgram|(AcademicInstitution| College|School)/OffersPrograms)/fees/(value|amount)
where $b/text()='100'
return $b

In case the query involves an *ObjectProperty* and *ObjectProperty* has some characteristics like transitive, symmetric, inverse functional or functional the query has to be handled differently. For example to evaluate a query such as **"find all academic Institutions that coOperate with IIT Madras"**, the user would have have formed the query string **AcademicInstitution/coOperates With =IIT Madras**. Since the property "coOperatesWith" is symmetric both the following XML code fragments should satisfy the query.

<AcademicInstitution> IIT Mumbai
<coOperatesWith> IIT Madras</coOperatesWith>
</AcademicInstitution> and

<AcademicInstitution> IIT Madras
<coOperatesWith> IIT Delhi</coOperatesWith>
</AcademicInstitution>

Such a query can be expressed as

for $b in ./root//(AcademicInstitution|College|School)/coOperatesWith
where $b/text()='IIT Madras'
return $b/parent::/text() union*
for $a in ./root//AcademicInstitution|College|School
where $a/text()='IIT Madras'
return $a/coOperatesWith /text()

If the same property "coOperatesWith" was transitive rather than symmetric we need to find the transitive closure of all the binary relations involving the *ObjectProperty* "coOperatesWith". This can only be established after the query engine evaluates the entire set of target XML documents. SAQI has the capability to handle queries involving such properties as well.

Inferring two individuals to be same also need to be done more often while querying. This inference can be made either because of a OWL "SameAs" construct or relations involving inverse functional properties. There again the target set of XML documents may have to be searched twice. In some situations we may need to handle real time systems or XML documents whose contents vary dynamically. In all such cases we may be able to avoid multiple passes over the target set of XML documents by treating them as streaming XML data [13].

All the examples illustrated so far are nearly equivalent to replacing a broad term by union of narrow terms or a super *Class* element name by union of *subClass* element names, using the knowledge the application extracts from the ontology. It is also possible to replace a *subClass* by super *Class*. From the "someValuesFrom" example illustrated in Figure 5, we can say that if an instance X of class "PostGraduateStudent" has a *Property element* "appliedForProgram" and the *Property* element in turn points to an instance under class "MastersProgram", then the instance X is an instance of Class "MastersStudent". This is true only because of the equivalent class statement used in this OWL code snippet. This inference rule can be represented in the form of following XQuery string.

```
let $c :=./root//MastersProgram/text()
for $a in ./root//PostGraduateStudent
let $b :=$a/appliedForProgram/text()
where $b=$c
return $a/text()
```

Thus an instance of the super *Class* has satisfied the necessary and sufficient condition for the *subClass* and therefore is retrieved as an in instance of *subClass*.

If we replace the "someValuesFrom" by a "allValuesFrom" restriction, all we need to do is re write the above query string in the following format.

```
let $c := ./root//MastersProgram/text()
for $a in ./root//PostGraduateStudent
let $b := $a/appliedForProgram/text()
where every $d in $b satisfies $d=$c
return $a/text()
```

Restrictions of type "hasValue" can be evaluated using simple equality expressions. SAQI can handle these as well. Similarly using the count() function provided by XQuery, we can reproduce scenarios where cardinality restriction have been specified locally for a class.

7.3 Query Engine

The rewritten query is passed on to the Query engine, in this case Galax, which evaluates the query and returns the results. While deploying SAQI as a real time system, it may be worth while to store these results for an finite time duration especially for queries involving special properties such as transitive if the target set of XML documents are likely to be static over a long time.

8 Performance

SAQI is a key concept demonstrator and a stepping stone toward semantic web. The implementation has been done using existing technologies to aid in a smoother migration to our vision of semantic web. We have made a deliberate effort to identify grey areas and plan for a more dynamic and versatile future version as discussed in subsequent sections.

8.1 Implementation

The Ontologies used to test SAQI were developed using the OWL Plug in, which is a comprehensive OWL Editor based on the Protege ontology development platform. The application uses the Java API for XML Processing (JAXP) to parse the OWL file and transform it to XML documents. The required information is extracted by searching for particular OWL keywords in the ontology. The application also uses XPath queries with the help of XPath packages [14] available in J2SE 1.4 whenever it makes it easier to select a set of nodes. Since the source document is a Protege OWL-Plug in created OWL file, the application follows the syntax used by the Plug in as the base OWL constructs in order to extract the semantics from the ontology. For the querying part the application relies on the Java APIs provided by the Galax XQuery engine.

We have created an ontology to represent the domain describing the Academic Institutions and an extended version of Camera ontology [15]. We tested the application using structurally dissimilar XML documents conforming to these ontologies. SAQI was able to retrieve semantically equivalent results from this diverse set of target XML documents for a variety of queries. Some details of SAQI is available at "http://aidb.cs.iitm.ernet.in/projects.html".

8.2 Limitations

The performance of SAQI is largely dependent on how best an ontology written in OWL, that inherently follows a graph structure can be successfully represented by a tree. When we try to create an equivalent tree representation of the base ontology we are forced to make a conscious decision to leave out certain paths in the graph. Other wise the query interface or the query conversion becomes far too complex even for the query engine to handle after conversion. The Query Interface of SAQI does not allow you to follow an *ObjectProperty* edge and reach another *Class* node. We can not specify a query of the form *Class/ObjectProperty/ Class/dataType Property*. We can only specify the name of an instance against an *ObjectProperty* as illustrated earlier. We also restrict ourselves to a maximum of two object properties to occur consecutively while using the inference rules in Query conversion. To amplify this point further consider the example below *for $b in ./root//(Programs|PostGraduateProgram|MastersProgram| (AcademicInstitution|College|School)/OffersPrograms) /fees/(value—amount) where $b/text()='100' return $b"*

The two Object properties that occur consecutively are **"OffersPrograms"** and **"fees"**. We do not replace the string

(AcademicInstitution|College|School) with
(AcademicInstitution|College|School)/coOperatesWith

by again looking up the OntoIndex though such a path is very much legal when we construct a graph of the ontology populated with instances. We impose this restriction to simplify the process of query conversion and interface building without inconveniencing a naive user. It would be pertinent to point out that such a restriction is unlikely to affect the retrieval of correct results from a valid set of XML documents if these documents are created as per the methodology suggested in the earlier section.

Although it appears that the querying options available to the user is limited, the interface can be easily modified to allow users to specify conjunctions and disjunctions. This involves modifying the query interface and building these into the query conversion module.

8.3 Future Work

The current version of SAQI supports ontologies conforming to OWL Lite specification. While advancing to an OWL DL complaint version some additional issues are likely to come up. For example an *ObjectProperty* can have multiple *Class*es as its Range. In such a case we can not infer apriori that an instance associated with this property is of a particular *Class*. We have to reason out from a set of *Class*es which form the Range of the property and identify the particular *Class* of which the instance is a member. Issues like multiple inheritance will also need some changes to construction of the tree from ontology.

In the future versions of SAQI it is proposed to validate target XML documents and the instances that are returned as results against the ontology or constraints specified for their parent *Class*. We intend to extend SAQI to a Web Search Portal which permits query formulation based on natural language.

9 Conclusion

This paper discusses the implementation details of an application named SAQI, a tool for querying the semantic web. It is developed with a motivation for providing an interface for querying web pages that share common ontology. Internally, the Semantics Extractor module creates an XML document that well represents an ontology. This document is then used for building the OntoIndex, a datastructure that stores the mapping rules. User poses queries through an ontology guided Query Interface. The so formed queries are rewritten using information captured in the OntoIndex and Ontology Equivalent XML Tree. The rewritten query is then passed on to a Galax Query Engine, which retrieves semantically relevant information that match the query from XML documents. The present version supports querying ontologies written in OWL Lite. We intend to extend this to support OWL DL in future.

References

1. Hendler, J., Parsia, B.: XML and Semantic Web. XML Journal (2002)
2. Abiteboul, S., Buneman, P., Suciu, D.: Data on the Web -From Relations to Semistructured Data and XML. Morgan Kaufmann (2000)
3. http://protege.stanford.edu: Protege:an ontology editor. (2004)
4. McDowell, L., Etzioni, O., Gribble, S.D., Halevy, A., Henry Levy, W.P., Verma, D., Vlasseva, S.: Mangrove: Enticing Ordinary People onto the Semantic Web via Instant Gratification. In Fensel, D., Sycara, K., Mylopoulos, J., eds.: International Semantic Web Conference. Number 2870 in Lecture Notes in Computer science, Sanibel Island, Florida, USA, Springer-Verlog (2003) 754–770
5. J. Hefflin, J.A. Hendler, S.: A prototype language for the semantic web. Electronic Transactions on Artificial Intelligence **5** (2001)
6. Erdmann, M., Studer, R.: How to structure and access XML Documents with ontologies. Data and Knowledge Engineering (2000)
7. Decker, S., Erdmann, M., Fensel, D., Studer, R.: OntoBroker: Ontology Based access to distributed and semistructured information. In: Eighth Working Conference on Database Semantics. (1999) 351–369
8. Smith, M.K., Welty, C., McGuinness, D.H., eds.: OWL Web Ontology Language Guide. W3C Proposed Recommendation (2003)
9. Bechhofer, S., Harmelen, F.V., Hendler, J., Horrocks, I., Guinness, B.L.M., Patel-Scheider, P.F., Stein, L.A.: OWL Web Ontology Language Reference. (2003)
10. Costello, R.L.: Using OWL to avoid Synatactic Rigor Mortis. http://xfront.com/avoiding-syntactic-rigor-mortis/ (2003)
11. Fernandez, M.F., Siméon, J., Choi, B., Marian, A., Sur, G.: Implementing XQuery 1.0: The Galax Experience. In: VLDB 2003:29th International Conference on Very Large Data Bases, Berlin, Germany, Morgan Kaufmann Publishers (2003) pp. 1077–1080
12. Erdmann, M., Decker, S.: Ontology aware XML Queries. In: Technical report 410, University of Kalsruhe, Institute AIFB. (2001)
13. Peng, F., Chawathe, S.S.: XPath Queries on Streaming Data. In: ACM SIGMOD, San Diego, CA (2003)
14. http://www.w3.org/TR/xpath: XML Path Language. W3C Recommendation (1999)
15. http:protege.stanford.edu/plugins/owl/owl-library/: (Owl ontology library)

Hybrid-Chord: A Peer-to-Peer System Based on Chord

Paola Flocchini, Amiya Nayak, and Ming Xie

School of Information Technology and Engineering,
University of Ottawa,
800 King Edward Avenue,
Ottawa, ON K1N 6N5, Canada
{flocchin, anayak, mxie}@site.uottawa.ca

Abstract. In this paper, we present a new model for a peer-to-peer system based on Chord, called *Hybrid-Chord*, to improve the routing performance and data availability of Chord. Our main focus is on reducing the number of hops that is needed to locate a data item. Through simulations, we demonstrate the improvement of the routing performance and fault tolerance capabilities of the proposed system and compare that with the original Chord system. The hybrid system can reduce the number of lookup hops significantly by up to 50% compared to Chord, is robust and handles node failures better than Chord, can always find the desired data with high probability and has better data availability than Chord. Above all, the hybrid system has same complexity as Chord.

1 Introduction

Peer-to-peer systems can share the computing resources and services by directly communicating within a widely distributed network such as the Internet. Thus, it is important that these systems are scalable and can efficiently locate, in as few hops as possible, the node that stores the desired data in a large system. In other words, reducing the hop count is extremely important from the cost and performance point of view. Furthermore, nodes must be able to join and leave the system frequently without affecting the robustness or the efficiency of the system, and the load must be balanced across the available nodes.

Earlier P2P systems employ a single index server (Napster[10]) or flooding-based mechanism (Gnutella[8] and Freenet[9]) to search desired data, which are not suitable for large systems. Most latest P2P systems, including Chord[1], Content-Addressable Networks (CAN)[2], D2B[4], Tapestry[5], Pastry[6] etc., use distributed hash tables(DHT) to support scalability, load balancing and fault tolerance. All these systems employ a distributed hash table that maps names/keys to values and that is used as a supporting lookup service. DHTs manage the distribution of data among the dynamic network, and allow nodes to contact any participating node in the network to find any stored resource by keys.

In P2P systems, the number of lookups for desired data is significantly high which means that locating data efficiently can save huge network communication

R.K. Ghosh and H. Mohanty (Eds.): ICDCIT 2004, LNCS 3347, pp. 194–203, 2004.

resource. On the other hand, with the development of computer technology, local storage expense becomes negligible. Thus, it is worth consuming some extra storage to obtain efficient routing performance.

In this paper, we present a new model for a peer-to-peer system based on Chord, called *Hybrid-Chord*, to improve the routing performance and data availability of Chord. Our main focus is on reducing the number of hops that is needed to locate a data item. Through simulations, we demonstrate the improvement of the routing performance and fault tolerance capabilities of the proposed system and compare that with the original Chord system. The hybrid system can reduce the number of lookup hops significantly by up to 50% compared to Chord, is robust and handles node failures better than Chord, can always find the desired data with high probability and has better data availability than Chord.

2 Hybrid-Chord System

Chord[1] is a peer-to-peer lookup protocol known for its simplicity, provable correctness and performance. Unlike Chord which uses one ring with a successor list of size $\Omega(\log n)$, where n is the number of nodes, we propose a peer-to-peer syetem, called *Hybrid-Chord* or simply *Hybrid* system, which has the following two key features: multiple chord rings overlayed one top of the other and multiple successor list of constant size. The multiple chord rings system and the successor list system could be employed independently as a peer-to-peer model. More details on the hybrid system can be found in [11].

2.1 Multiple Chord Rings

We overlay k Chord rings one top of the other to generate a virtual network to speedup data lookup and make the system more robust. The idea is based on the fact that, if several Chord rings are overlayed, one could choose, at each step of the lookup, the best Chord ring to achieve better routing performance. Each node has k identifiers and every identifier logically corresponds to a location in one Chord. Each data item has a unique key and is mapped into the same location on different virtual Chord rings. In other words, there are k identifiers for a node, and the node is located in k logical Chord rings with different location. Since in each Chord, every data item owns only one key and is located at the same location on different Chord rings, then there are k replicas of each data item distributed in k different nodes that are in charge of its location on different Chord rings in the overlay network. We will often refer this as $k-$*Chord* model.

Figure 1 shows a k-Chord model for $k = 2$. In the figure, every node has two identifiers (Id_1, Id_2), where Id_1 is the identifier in the first Chord ring and Id_2 is the identifier in the second Chord ring. For example, node 1 on the first Chord ring has identifier 3 on the second Chord ring. Through these identifier pairs, two virtual Chord rings are organized. On the other hand, each data item has two replicas which are distributed in these two logical Chord rings. For example, if a data item has key 5, then this data item is stored in nodes with identifier

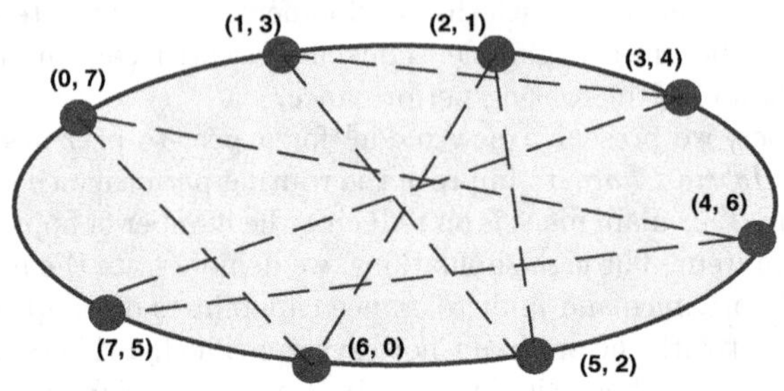

Fig. 1. 2-Chord topology

pair (7, 5) and (5, 2), which means that if any identifier of a node's k identifiers matches a data item's key, this node will have a replica of that data item.

Since each data item has k replicas that are distributed in k Chord rings, a lookup request will try to find the numerically closest one to satisfy the query. At each hop during a lookup, the local routing information is used to select the current closest one to route the request. Thus, a search may switch from one Chord to another to speedup routing by choosing the closest replica of the desired data item at each step.

In overlaying k Chord rings, one of the fundamental problems is how to choose the k identifiers of each node. Assuming the size of identifier name space is N, the nodes' identifier name space can be expressed as $\mathbb{R} = (r_0, r_1, \ldots, r_{N-1})$, and we consider the name space of the first Chord ring to be $\mathbb{R}^0 = (0, 1, 2, \ldots, N-1)$. Thus, we can view all the possible nodes' identifiers on the other Chord rings as a permutation of $\mathbb{R}^0$. A well-chosen permutation which could make routing more efficient is desirable. Various permutations are possible, namely reverse permutation, shift permutation, random permutation, and modular permutation. We will consider random permutation in which we rearrange the name space randomly to generate the new name space for another Chord ring.

2.2 Multiple Successor Lists of Constant Length

Chord[1] uses a successor list of variable length to increase system robustness, and CFS[3] uses it for data replication. In the hybrid system we propose, each node maintains a successor list of size d, where d is a constant, containing the node's first d successors. Effectively, the total number of successor lists is equal to the number of overlayed rings. The successor list contributes a lot for efficient routing, failure recovery and data replication.

3 Data Lookup and Routing in Hybrid-Chord

In the hybrid system, each node maintains a k dimensional finger table and a successor list of size d. During a lookup, each intermediate node resolves the query and checks if the destination is located within the range of its position and its last successor in the successor list on each Chord ring. If the destination is located within one of those ranges, it finds the desired node and jumps directly to that node; if not, it applies the greedy strategy to forward the query. The greedy algorithm scans the k-dimensional finger table, finds the k predecessors of the destination on the k Chord rings, and then chooses the node that is numerically closest to the destination as the next hop node.

The k-Chord model reduces the distance between the source and the destination node sharply to within the first few hops, which also helps compressing the node density between the current location and the destination. In other words, the nodes located within the distance of the last few hops have shorter intervals between each other, because if the distance is long enough, the lookup of the k-Chord model may try to switch to another Chord ring that has stored a replica much closer with high probability.

Although the k-Chord model may not locate the destination accurately within the remaining distance through small hops, immediate successors as a part of the routing table solves this problem by offering only one hop to locate the destination directly if the destination is located within the range of successors. The hybrid system achieves better performance than multiple Chords or multiple successor lists alone. It is also helpful for fault tolerance and re-routing in the event of failures.

4 Scalability

Since each node in the hybrid system needs to maintain a k-dimensional finger table and a successor list of size d on each Chord ring, the joining/leaving cost is $O(k(log^2n + d))$. With k and d being constant (e.g., $k = 4$ and $d = 20$), the total joining/leaving cost is $O(log^2n)$ which is the same in Chord.

When a new node joins the network, it can start from any node already in the system. Through the start node, the joining node can recursively call the *join*() function (same as in Chord) to find its immediate successor or to create a new network if it is the first node to join the system. The newly joined node will construct the connection to its predecessor and successor on each Chord ring, and create the finger table and the successor list for each Chord ring. Its successor on each Chord ring sends back the data associated with the keys that belong to the new node. To guarantee the correct lookup process, every node runs the *stabilize*() function (same as in Chord) periodically to refresh its k-dimensional finger table, and ensures that the successor list and successor pointers on each Chord ring are up to date with the evolution of the network. When a node leaves, it transfers the data to corresponding successors on each Chord ring before it departs; it also notifies its predecessor and successor on each Chord ring to adjust their pointers. The successor lists of the related nodes are refreshed periodically.

5 Fault Tolerance

5.1 Data Replication

The successor list mechanism helps data replication and places replicas in a way that nodes can easily find them. We adopt the same replication scheme as CFS in our model. The replicas of a data item are stored on r immediate successor nodes of the target node that is responsible for the keys associated with the data to increase data availability. Naturally, the number of replicas is smaller than the length of the successor list $r \leq d$. The target node keeps track of its r successors and propagates data to new replicas automatically when it detects that successors come and go.

Thus, in the hybrid system, replicas of a data item are stored in the same location on k different Chords associate with its key and the d successors. The priority of lookup for a data item is routed first to the numerical closest destination, if the target node failed, it re-routes to that node's successor directly. If all d successor nodes fail, it abandons this Chord ring, and re-routes to the numerical closest Chords within the left valid Chords and does the same lookup mechanism until it finds the desired data or all the nodes storing the replicas of the data fail.

5.2 Failures and Recovery

In the event of random failures which affect the routing procedure on the intermediate nodes along the lookup path, the strategy is to bypass the failed nodes and choose the numerically closest *alive* node to the destination as the next hop node from the k-dimensional finger table and the k successor lists.

Each node periodically checks every entry in its finger table and successor lists: if there is a failure, it tries to find the failed node's alive successor for substitution. As time passes, the scheme will correct finger table entries and successor list entries pointing to the failed node.

6 Experimental Results

We simulated the *Hybrid-Chord* system in C^{++} programming language. In the experiments, the size of circle name space is $N = 10^6$. The number of nodes n is varied from 100 to 18,000 or appropriately as needed. The n nodes are hashed by their randomly generated IDs and distributed uniformly along the Chord ring. In each simulation run, we choose 200 pairs of valid source nodes and desired keys randomly. The simulation is repeated 100 times in each case to get average value for the length of the lookup path (in hops).

6.1 Lookup Performance

We studied: (i) the effect of the number of multiple Chords (k) for a particular permutation of name space (we have chosen random permutation in this paper), (ii) the effect of the length of the successor list on the lookup performance.

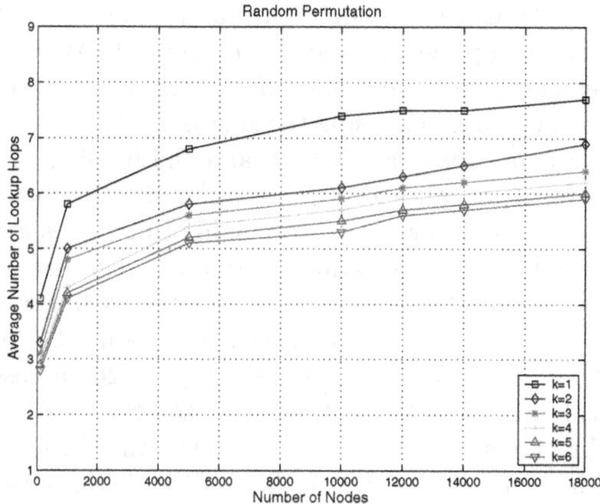

Fig. 2. Lookup Hops for Random Permutation

Figure 2 shows the lookup performance when we vary k from 1 to 6. A performance improvement up to 30% is achievable depending on the value of k. As we can observe, most switches happen within the first three hops of each lookup. When $k = 2$, the average improvement is about 1.1 to 1.4 hops compared to Chord ($k = 1$) for each lookup. When $k > 2$, the average improvement is only about 0.5 hop with increase in k.

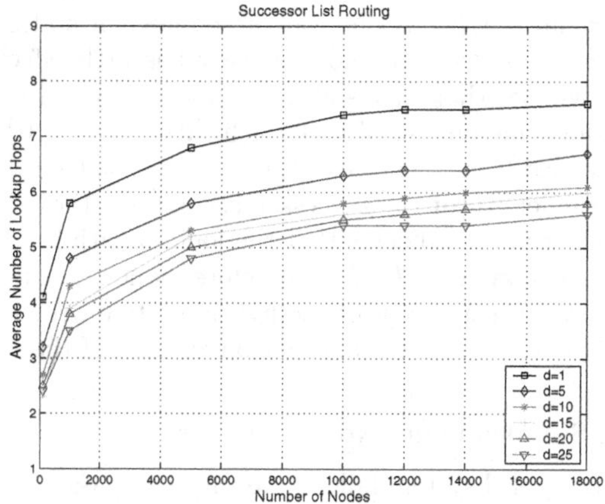

Fig. 3. Lookup Hops in Successor List of Different Sizes

In Figure 3, the length of the successor list (d) is varied from 1 to 25. The n nodes are hashed by their random generated IDs and distributed uniformly on the Chord ring. We can see from Figure 3 that we can achieve significant improvement in the lookup performance for d up to 10. When $d > 20$, the performance improvement becomes considerably insignificant. One simple example can show the rationale behind choosing the successor list size = 20. Assume that the size of the ring name space is 100,000, and the number of nodes is 10,000. Through hashing function, all 10,000 nodes can be distributed uniformly on the ring, which means the interval of two neighboring nodes is about 10. Thus, $10 \sim 15$ successors of a node can almost cover the distance about $100 \sim 150$ possible nodes close to it. The distances of the node's finger nodes are about $2^0, 2^1, ..., 2^i, ..., 2^{\log N}$; when $i = 7$, the distance is about 128 long (when $i = 8$, the distance of $2^8 = 256$ will request at least $\frac{256}{10} \approx 26$ successors under ideal case), and $i < 4$ will be covered by the first successor. So $(7-3) = 4$ hops distance may be covered by the successor list with the length of $10 \sim 15$. However, in real system, each hop can at least reduce half of the distance to the destination, so in most of the lookups, the last $2 \sim 5$ hops can be merged into one hop by successor routing list in the simulation. Basically, the reduction in lookup hop is achieved regardless of the size of the name space since bigger space means one successor will cover longer distance.

Overall, an improvement in the range of 26 - 40% is possible depending on d and n. With $k = 2$, we get a lookup performance improvement in the range 30 - 50%. Similarly for $d = 20$, the improvement is in the range 38 - 53% which is very significant. Therefore, $k = 2, d = 20$ seems to be a good combination for the hybrid system.

6.2 Effect of Distribution Density

In Chord [1], the nodes are distributed uniformly along the Chord ring; hence, the lookup performance depends only on the number of nodes in the network, which means that if n is fixed, the node density has little effect on the routing performance. We will see that this is also true for the hybrid system.

In our simulation, the number of nodes is fixed (i.e., $n = 10^4$), the size of the name space N is varied from 20000 to 10^7, the number of Chord rings k is varied from 1 to 4 and the length of the successor list is fixed (i.e., $d = 20$) as shown in Table 1. The experiment indicates that the lookup path length increases very little with N for each value of k. We, therefore, conclude that under uniform node distribution, the routing cost of the hybrid system depends mostly on the number of nodes (n) in the system and not on the size of the name space (N).

6.3 Effect of Simultaneous Node Failures

After a node in the hybrid system fails, some time will pass before the remaining nodes react to the failure, by correcting their finger tables and successor pointers and by copying replicas to maintain the replication. The hybrid system is able to perform lookups correctly and efficiently before this recovery process starts, even in the event of massive failure.

To test that, 1000 data items were inserted into a 1000-node system, each data item having 6 replicas. For $k = 2$, $d = 20$, a fraction p (varied from 10%

Table 1. Effect of Distribution Density on the Hybrid System ($d = 20$)

N	$k = 1$	$k = 2$	$k = 3$	$k = 4$
20000	5.26	4.34	4.06	3.87
50000	5.31	4.33	4.03	3.99
100000	5.38	4.49	4.11	3.91
1000000	5.41	4.58	4.25	4.01
10000000	5.48	4.70	4.31	4.10

to 50%) of all nodes were randomly chosen as failure nodes. After that, we performed 10000 random lookups. For each lookup, we recorded if the lookup was a success and if it was, we calculated the lookup path length. We then derive statistics of the lookup success rate and the average lookup path length (only for the successful lookups).

Table 2 shows the lookup failed rate when the failure fraction p varies from 10% to 50%, and the number of the successors r that store the data replicas. The size of the successor list $d = 20$ in both systems. The result shows that our hybrid system can always find the desired data with high probability, and has a similar data availability as Chord. Table 3 shows the average lookup path length when failures occur. The result indicates that the our hybrid system has better lookup performance when failures occur. Based on the above observations, we can claim that our hybrid system outperforms the Chord in handling node failures.

Table 2. Hybrid and Chord Lookup Failure Rate

p(fraction of failure)	10%	20%	30%	40%	50%
Chord ($k = 1, r = 6, d = 20$)	0	0	0.002	0.010	0.016
Hybrid ($k = 2, r = 3, d = 20$)	0	0	0	0.009	0.014

Chord considers that if the successor list has length $d = \Omega(\log n)$, both the success rate and the performance of Chord lookups will not be affected even by massive simultaneous failures. Furthermore, it has been shown that, if the successor list of length $d = \Omega(\log n)$ and every node fails with independent probability 1/2, the system can find the closest living desired node and the expected lookup time is $O(\log n)$. However, with the evolution of the network, a node cannot know the exact number of nodes existing in the network at a certain time. More practically, in our model we use a reasonable constant number ($d = 20$) as the length of the successor list. Assuming the independent failure probability of a node is 1/2, the full failure for a successor list is $(\frac{1}{2})^{20}$ which is very small. It means that the data items are always available with high probability.

The correctness of lookup scheme relies on the fact that each node knows its successor. Failure nodes will result in incorrect successor pointers, and incorrect successor will lead to incorrect lookup. To increase robustness, in the same way

Table 3. Hybrid and Chord Lookup Path Length for Failures

p(fraction of failure)	0%	10%	20%	30%	40%	50%
Chord ($k = 1, r = 6, d = 20$)	5.8	6.0	6.2	6.5	6.8	7.2
Hybrid ($k = 2, r = 3, d = 20$)	3.1	3.5	4.1	4.8	5.6	6.6

as Chord, each node maintains a successor list of size d, containing the node's first d successors. If a node's immediate successor does not respond, the node can substitute the second entry in its successor list. All d successors would have to simultaneously fail in order to disrupt the Chord ring, an event that can be made very improbable with modest values of d. Assuming each node fails independently with probability p, the probability that all d successors fail simultaneously only p^d. Increasing the size d of successor list can strengthen system robustness.

7 Conclusions

Many recent P2P systems such as Pastry[6], Tapestry[5], Koorde[13], CAN[2] try to increase base(prefix-based routing schemes) or degree to improve routing performance. *Hybrid-Chord* system has efficient routing performance and good balance of the routing performance and the storage overhead.

DKS[12] also applies multiple Chord rings to improve routing performance, which is totally different from our *Hybrid-Chord* system. In DKS, a specified key is stored in one certain node. At the beginning of the search, the search space is equal to the whole identifier space. At each step of the search, the current search space is divided into k equal parts. Each part is under the responsibility of a well chosen node. This partitioning of the search space is repeated until the k equal parts containing each only one element. This procedure can be viewed as searching on multiple Chord rings, and each ring owns $\frac{1}{k}$ part of the former ring. In *Hybrid-Chord* system, k replicas of a key are stored in k nodes which distributed on k different logical Chord rings. Its performance improvement is based on data redundancy and well-chosen name space permutation, while DKS's performance improvement is based on increasing logarithm base.

Hybrid-Chord system combines a multiple chord system and a successor list system to improve the routing performance and system robust. The simulation (see Table 4) shows that the hybrid system can reduce the lookup hops to $\frac{1}{4}\log n$, which is half of the Chord system. Actually, if we apply reverse permutation, *Hybrid-Chord* can achieve significantly improvement with only one extra Chord ring.

Table 4. Comparison of Hybrid-Chord with Chord

	$n = 1000$	$n = 5000$	$n = 10000$	$n = 15000$	$n = 18000$
Chord	5.8	6.8	7.4	7.5	7.7
Hybrid ($k = 4, d = 20$)	2.5	3.4	3.9	4.1	4.2

References

1. I. Stoica, R. Morris, D. Karger, M. Frans Kaashoek, and H. Balakrishnan, "Chord: A Scalable Peer-to-peer Lookup Service for Internet Applications," *ACM SIGCOMM*, pp. 149-160, 2001.
2. S. Ratnasamy, P. Francis, M. Handley, R. Karp, S. Shenker, "A Scalable Content-Addressable Network," *Proceedings of ACM SIGCOMM*, pp. 161-172, 2001.
3. F. Dabek, M. Frans Kaashoek, D. Karger, R. Morris, and I. Stoica, "Wide-Area Cooperative Storage with CFS," *Proceedings of the 18th ACM Symposium on Operating Systems Principles (SOSP)*, 2001.
4. P. Fraigniaud, P. Gauron, "The Content Addressable Network D2B", Technical Report LRI1349, University Paris-Sud, 2003.
5. B. Y. Zhao, J. D. Kubiatowicz, and A. D. Joseph, "Tapestry: An Infrastructure for Fault-tolerant Wide-area Location and Routing", U. C. Berkeley Technical Report UCB//CSD-01-1141, 2000.
6. A. Rowstron and P. Druschel, "Pastry: Scalable, Distributed Object Location and Routing for Large-Scale Peer-to-Peer Systems", Middleware'2001, Lecture Notes in Computer Science Vol. 2218, pp. 329-350, 2001.
7. J. Kubiatowicz, D. Bindel, Y. Chen, S. Czerwinski, P. Eaton, D. Geels, R. Gummadi, S. Rhea, H. Weatherspoon, W. Weimer, C. Wells, B. Zhao, "OceanStore: An Architecture for Global-Scale Persistent Storage," *In Proceedings of the Ninth international Conference on Architectural Support for Programming Languages and Operating Systems (ASPLOS)*, 2000.
8. M. Ripeanu, I. Foster, and A. Iamnitchi. "Mapping the Gnutella Network: Properties of Large-Scale Peer-to-Peer Systems and Implications for System Design," *IEEE Internet Computing Journal*, Vol.6, 2002.
9. I. Clarke, O. Sandberg, B. Wiley, T.W. Hong, "Freenet: A Distributed Anonymous Information Storage and Retrieval System," *In Proc. of the ICSI Workshop on Design Issues in Anonymity and Unobservability*, Berkeley, CA, 2000.
10. Napster, http://www.napster.com/.
11. M. Xie, "A Decentralized Redundant Peer-to-Peer System Based on Chord: Routing, Scalability, Robustness", Masters Thesis, University of Ottawa, 2003.
12. Luc Onana Alima, Sameh El-Ansary, Per Brand, and Seif Haridi,"DKS(N, k, f): A Family of Low Communication, Scalable and Fault-Tolerant Infrastructures for P2P Ap- plications," *In The 3rd International workshop on Global and Peer-To-Peer Computing on large scale distributed systems* - CCGRID2003, 2003.
13. Frans Kaashoek, David R. Karger, "Koorde: A Simple Degree-optimal Hash Table," *In 2nd International Workshop on Peer-to-Peer Systems (IPTPS '03)*, pp.98-107, 2003.

A Generic and Flexible Model for Replica Consistency Management

Corina Ferdean and Mesaac Makpangou

INRIA Rocquencourt, France, BP 105, 78153 Le Chesnay Cedex

Abstract. This paper presents a flexible consistency model, aggregating a parameterized representation common for all the models along the spectrum delimited by strong consistency and eventual consistency. A specific model, required by a particular *Data Object*, is derived from this representation by selecting and combining the proper consistency parameters values.

1 Introduction

The basic unit of replication and of consistency management, that we consider, is the *Data Object*. A *Data Object* is basically a passive entity encapsulating any data -representing the object's state- and the operations for consulting and manipulating that data -representing the object's access interface-.

The problem we address consists in accommodating the suitable consistency model for a particular Data Object, when it is replicated, with its replicas being accessed concurrently. The base hypothesis that we consider are the variety of Data Objects and the heterogeneity, which happens in most cases, for the services provided by the same Data Object. Although the existence of a spectrum of models delimited by strong consistency and eventual consistency has already been identified [9], existing approaches remain too rigid with respect to the consistency level they capture along this spectrum. For example, bounding discrepancy observed when reading data and relaxing total ordering of concurrent updates could be both required by the same Data Object. However, at our knowledge, there is no existing consistency framework which support this combination. Also, not all update operation calls should be associated the same propagation policy. Neither this particular flexibility feature is met throughout the state of art on the consistency models.

2 Our Model Description

In order to meet various application needs, we define our model in two successive steps. They provide, respectively, the model's genericity and flexibility features. The first step consists in identifying the different concerns of the consistency aspect. We attach to each concern one or several parameters. The second step consists in providing one or several options for each parameter.

R.K. Ghosh and H. Mohanty (Eds.): ICDCIT 2004, LNCS 3347, pp. 204–209, 2004.

```
gid, gid1, gid2 identifying groups of accesses
consistency_concern = liveness | safety
liveness = visibility | observed_state_quality
safety = pre-scheduling | scheduling

consistency _model = {consistency constraint}
consistency constraint = visibility constraint | observed_state_quality constraint |
pre-scheduling constraint | scheduling constraint
visibility constraint = ([gid;] transfer_instant)
observed_state_quality constraint = ([gid;] tolerated_divergence)
pre-scheduling constraint = ([gid;] execution_mode)>
scheduling constraint = ([gid1, gid2;] scheduling_relation)
```

Fig. 1. Generic constraints on consistency concerns

2.1 Consistency Granularity

We define an *access* as an operation invocation, issued at a particular replica. We define a *group_of_accesses* as a collection of accesses, related by some common attribute(s) (e.g. the operation identifier, the caller identifier, the replica identifier). We define a special group named *interface_group*, which contains all the calls to all operations. According to its type, a consistency option can be associated to a *group of accesses* (by default this is the *interface_group*) or to a pair of two *groups of accesses.*

2.2 Generic Consistency Constraints

We classify the consistency concerns hierarchically on two levels. On the first level, we distinguish between *liveness* and *safety* concerns (Fig. 1) . A liveness constraint enforces the progression of replicas towards an equivalent state. It states that all operations issued at a replica should be transferred sooner or later to all the peers. A safety constraint enforces replicas convergence by correct scheduling of the global set of operations, issued at different replicas and which have to be applied all over. Scheduling aims to stabilize updates, by finding their position within the global history. This is done with respect to conflicting and/or non-commutative updates issued concurrently at peers. On the second level, we refine a *liveness concern* into a *visibility* and an *observed state quality concern*, and a *safety concern* into a *pre-scheduling concern* and a *scheduling concern.* A *visibility constraint* targets the progression of peers towards the final state, by enforcing the spreading of locally issued updates. An *observed state quality constraint* targets the progression of the local replica towards a particularly advanced state (in particular, the final state), by requiring relevant remote updates to be pulled locally.

A *visibility concern* is parametrized by the *transfer instant.* It specifies when the spreading of local updates should be proceeded. An *observed state quality concern* is attached the *tolerated divergence* parameter. It specifies if a discrep-

```
transfer_instant = “immediate” | lazy
lazy = sync_lazy | async_lazy
sync_lazy = absolute_clock_time | relative_clock_time | <“periodical”, frequency> |
getTransferInstant()
absolute_clock_time = [0-12]”-”[00-31]”T”[0-23]”:”[0-59]
relative_clock_time = [0-12] months | [0-31] days | [0-23] hours | [0-59] min
frequency = {relative_clock_time}

async_lazy = <“async_push”, propagation_conds>
propagation_conds = checkPropagationConds() | gid1

tolerated_divergence = “no_divergence” | bounded_divergence | “un-
bounded_divergence”
bounded_divergence = {metric-based_option | dependency-based_option}
metric-based_option = <divergence_metric, threshold>
divergence_metric = “staleness” | “distanceToIdeal” | “maxTentative”
threshold = [-][0-9]+
dependency-based_option = user_session_option | op_dependency-based_option
user_session_option = {“RYW” | “WW” | “WFR” | “RR” }
op_dependency-based_option = <gid2 [, areSemDependent()]>

execution_mode = “pessimistic” | “optimistic”

scheduling_relation = user-centric_relation | order_relation | getSchedRelation()
user-centric_relation = “alternative” |“atomic” | <“conflicting”, resolution_action>
order_relation = “commutative” | “total_order” | “real-time_order” | “global_order” |
“causal_order” | “fifo_order” | <“predecessor”, whoIsPredecessor>
whoIsPredecessor = “first” | “second” | getPredSucc()
resolution_action = <“exclusive ” “any” | “first” | “second” | “both”> | <“merge”,
resolveConflicts()> | getResoAction()

by default: weight = 1, gid = 0, gid1 = 0, gid2 = 0, transfer_instant = “im-
mediate”, tolerated_divergence = “unbounded_divergence”, execution_mode = “pes-
simistic”, scheduling_relation = “commutative”
```

Fig. 2. Available options for concerns parameters

ancy between the local replica and the real object state is allowed. If this is the case, the parameter's specification also includes a quantification of the discrepancy which can be tolerated.

A *pre-scheduling concern* is configured with the parameter *execution_mode*. This parameter concerns updates which may generate conflicts or which are not commutative with other updates.

A *scheduling concern* is tuned in with a *scheduling relation* parameter. This parameter makes the distinction between the situations when concurrent updates can be processed independently or not, due to potential conflicts or non-commutativity, for example. If a member of the pair, to which a scheduling relation is attached, is not specified, it is automatically substituted by the *interface_group*.

A group of accesses represents the granule for a *visibility constraint*, an *observed state quality constraint* and *a pre-scheduling constraint. A pair of groups of accesses* represents the granule for a *scheduling constraint.*

2.3 Consistency Parameters Options

Visibility Options. The options available for the *transfer instant* parameter are: *immediate* and *lazy* (Fig. 2). The *lazy* option is further refined to include synchronous and asynchronous propagation events. The former events associates the moment of transfer to concrete time references that can be specified statically and fixed or computed dynamically by means of a function getTransferInstant(). This function may perform the option computation, based on the object state and/or on different accesses characteristics. A time reference is defined as an *absolute clock time* or a *relative clock time.* The former represents a concrete point in time, while the latter represents a reference relative to a given point in time (e.g. an invocation issuance time). The most common lazy option is *periodical.* The periodicity relies on the transfers *frequency*, defined in terms of *relative clock times* between successive transfers. The function getTransferInstant() allows the frequency value to be adjusted dynamically. The latter events corresponds to the option "async_push", where the moment of transfer is decided based on certain conditions *propagation_conds.* These concern the local copy state (as checked by the function checkPropagationConds() or the transfer of other updates gid_1 (so as to propagate the updates from the current group gid at the same time as updates from gid_1).

Observed State Quality Options. The parameter *tolerated_divergence* provides one of the following alternative options: *no divergence, bounded divergence* and *unbounded divergence* (Fig. 2). The former option claims for an always up-to-date replica state, while the latter admits an isolated replica, with an arbitrary stale state. A *bounded divergence* option is further specialized only into a *metric-based option* and a *dependency-based option.* They characterize the particularly advanced state, whom the current operation needs to observe. Precisely, they determine if and what remote updates should be integrated within the local replica state before the current operation, as it needs to observe their effects. A *metric-based option* specifies couples, containing a *divergence metric* and a *threshold* to be satisfied on the metric before the access could proceed. The divergence metrics we support for now are: *staleness, distanceToIdeal, maxTentative.* They are similar to the staleness, numerical error and order error metrics of TACT [9]. There are two types of *dependency-based_options*: *user_session_option* and *op_dependency-based_option.* The option *user_session_option* includes the session guarantees of Bayou [8]: *RYW* (Read Your Writes), *WW* (Monotonic Writes), *WFR* (Writes Follow Reads), *RR* (Monotonic Reads). An option *op_dependency-based_option* specifies the group with semantical dependencies for the accesses from the current group. The actual dependencies are computed using a boolean function areSemDependent(). It takes as arguments a pair of accesses and checks the conditions for the first access to be semantically dependent to the second one.

Pre-scheduling Options. The parameter *execution_mode* provides two alternative options: *pessimistic* and *optimistic* (Fig. 2). The former option defers the application of updates until their final position within the history is decided. The latter option allows updates to be applied tentatively before being scheduled.

Scheduling Options. The concrete scheduling relations between a pair of groups of accesses can be specified once-forever or determined at run-time by using the function getSchedRelation() (Fig. 2). A *scheduling_relation* can be specialized into a *user-centric_relation* and an *order_relation*. We consider two types of *user-centric_relations*: *alternative*, *atomic* and *conflicting*. They relate two accesses which provide a non-deterministic execution choice (i.e. by executing one of them), which require "all or nothing" execution (i.e. by executing either both or none of them), respectively which may generate conflicts. Two updates are said to be conflicting, if they are incompatible with respect to the user-expected results. This means that at least one of the two updates can't satisfy the user request at all or return results which mismatch the user-intention, because of the other update. The former situation happens usually due to a pre-condition failure or to the violation of an object invariant. In this case, the pertinent resolution action is to *reject* one of the two updates. The latter situation claims for combining the updates or transforming one of them so as to provide the user-intended results. This functionality is provided by the function resolveConflicts() within the *merge* option of the *resolution_action* parameter.

An *ordering relation* provides the following options: *commutative*, *total_order*, *real-time_order*, *global_order*, *causal_order fifo_order*, and *predecessor*. The latter option can also be configured with a function getPredSucc(), specifying among the two updates which one should precede the other, and if the precedence should happen consecutively or it doesn't matter.

3 Conclusion

In this paper we described a generic and flexible consistency model aimed to accommodate the needs of various Data Objects. The features of genericity and flexibility are obtained by designing the model in two successive steps. Firstly, we provide a parameterized description of the consistency aspect, by decomposing it into several concerns, and attaching to each concern one or several parameters. Secondly, we identify for each parameter different possible options, to be specified statically or computed at run-time. A specific model is derived from this representation by selecting and combining the proper consistency parameters values.

References

1. R. Alonso, D. Barbara, and H. Garcia-Molina. Data caching issues in an information retrieval system. TODS, 15(3):359– 384, 1990.

2. Douglas B. Terry, Marvin M. Theimer, Karin Petersen, Alan J. Demers, Mike J. Spreitzer and Carl H. Hauser, Managing Update Conflicts in Bayou, a Weakly Connected Replicated Storage System, Computer Science Laboratory, Xerox Palo Alto Research Center Palo Alto, California 94304 U.S.A., SOSP 1995.
3. R. Ladin, B. Liskov, and L. Shrira. Lazy replication: exploiting the semantics of distributed services. In Proceedings of the 9th ACM symposium on Principles of Distributed Computing, pages 43–57, Quebec City, CA, August 1990.
4. A.M. Kermarrec, A. Rowstron, M. Shapiro, and P. Druschel. The IceCube approach to the reconciliation of divergent replicas. In Proc. of Twentieth ACM Symposium on Principles of Distributed Computing PODC, Newport, RI USA, August 2001.
5. S. Krishnamurthy, W. H. Sanders, and M. Cukier, An Adaptive Framework for Tunable Consistency and Timeliness Using Replication, Proc. of the 2002 International Conference on Dependable Systems and Networks (DSN-2002).
6. Yasushi Saito and Marc Shapiro, Optimistic Replication. Microsoft Research Technical Report MSR-TR-2003-60, October 2003.
7. Sai Susarla and John Carter, Khazana: A Flexible Wide Area Data Store, {sai, retrac}@cs.utah.edu UUCS-03-020 School of Computing University of Utah Salt Lake City, UT 84112 USA, 2003.
8. D. B. Terry, A. J. Demers, K. Petersen, M. J. Spreitzer, M. M. Theimer and B. B. Welch. Session guarantees for weakly consistent replicated data. Proceedings Third International Conference on Parallel and Distributed Information Systems, Austin, Texas, September 1994, pages 140-149.
9. Yu, H. And Vahdat, A. Design and evaluation of a continuous consistency model for replicated services. In 4th Symp. on Op. Sys. Design and Implemen. (OSDI) (San Diego, CA, USA, Oct. 2000), pp. 305 318.

An Efficient Distributed Scheme for Source Routing Protocol in Communication Networks

Vijayalakshmi Hadimani[1] and R.C. Hansdah[2]

[1] Center for Development of Telematics, Bangalore - 560052, India
vijaya_h@cdotb.ernet.in

[2] Department of Computer Science and Automation, Indian Institute of Science, Bangalore - 560012, India
hansdah@csa.iisc.ernet.in

Abstract. In this paper, we propose an efficient source routing algorithm for unicast flows, which addresses the scalability problem associated with the basic source routing technique. Simulation results indicate that the proposed algorithm indeed helps in reducing the message overhead considerably, and at the same time it gives comparable performance in terms of resource utilization across a wide range of workloads.

1 Introduction

QoS routing algorithms denote a class of routing algorithms that base path selection decisions on a set of requirements or constraints, in addition to the destination. QoS requirements are generally expressed in terms of bandwidth constraint, end-to-end delay, total cost, delay jitter, packet loss probability etc.

QoS routing performance is sensitive to the accuracy of information used, the network topology, and the network traffic characteristics. Source routing[1, 3], distributed routing[5, 7] and Hierarchical routing[8] are the three basic techniques used to compute the path satisfying QoS constraints. Flooding is another approach for QoS routing. A few variants of this technique have been proposed [4, 6]. However, all these techniques have both advantages and disadvantages [2].

The performance of a QoS routing algorithm is characterized by scalability, resource utilization, connection setup time and flexibility. In this paper, we address the scalability issue by dividing the network into smaller partitions. Only the border nodes(defined in a later section) stores the link-state information of the links within the partition. Therefore, the data stored at each node is significantly reduced. We improve the resource utilization by diverting the traffic to the path which has the maximum residual bandwidth. The broadcast of link-state messages is limited to the border nodes within the same partition, which reduces the message overhead significantly.

Our approach can also be used for supporting multiple metric, and thereby, providing flexibility. We present the algorithm for the widest path constrained by the bandwidth, though it can be used for other QoS attributes also. We use the call blocking ratio and the message overhead as the performance metrics to compare the different algorithms.

R.K. Ghosh and H. Mohanty (Eds.): ICDCIT 2004, LNCS 3347, pp. 210–216, 2004.

2 Problem Statement

The network is modelled as a directed graph $G = (V, E)$, where V denotes the set of nodes, E denotes the set of edges(links). Any two nodes in the network are directly connected by at most one link $e = (u, v) \in E$, which connects the two nodes u and v, where $u, v \in V$. The links are assumed to be symmetric and are associated with various metrics such as cost $C(e)$, available bandwidth $B(e)$ and delay $D(e)$. These metrics may take any non-negative real value.

We define a path from a node v_0 to a node v_k as $P(v_0, v_k) = v_0, v_1, v_2, .., v_k$, where $e_i = (v_{i-1}, v_i)$ such that $e_i \in E$ for $0 < i \leq k$.

For a given source node s and a destination node d, there can be more than one distinct paths. Let PS_{sd} denote the set of all these paths from source node s and a destination node d and let $PS_{sd} = \{P_1(s,d), P_2(s,d), ...P_n(s,d)\}$, where $P_i(s,d)$ is a distinct path from node s to node d. Available bandwidth of a path $P_i(s,d)$ is defined as:

$$Bandwidth(P_i(s,d)) = \min_{\forall e \in P_i(s,d)} (B(e))$$

Unicast Routing Problem: For a given source node s, a destination node d and a constraint B for bandwidth, the unicast QoS routing problem for the widest path is to find a path $P_k(s,d)$, $1 \leq k \leq n$ such that $Bandwidth(P_k(s,d))$ is maximum and $Bandwidth(P_k(s,d)) \geq B$.

3 The Distributed Source Routing Algorithm

The basic goal in the proposed algorithm is to address the scalability issue associated with the source routing and the sequential search involved in the existing algorithms.

We partition the network into disjoint sets of nodes. A partition can be connected to one or more other partitions by the inter-partition links. Two partitions can be connected by zero, one or more links. A node in a partition stores the information about the nodes in each partition and the inter-connectivity among the partitions in the network. The border nodes, in addition, store the link-state information of the links in the partition. It is to be noted that a node does not store the internal details of other partitions. An example network is shown in Figure 1 where the network is divided into four partitions.

3.1 Definitions

Partition: A set of nodes or routers. Each node in the network belongs to a partition and the partitions do not intersect.

Border Node: A node in a partition is a border node if it is attached to at least one link that is connected to a node in another partition.

Border Link: A link that connects two border nodes such that each border node belongs to different partitions.

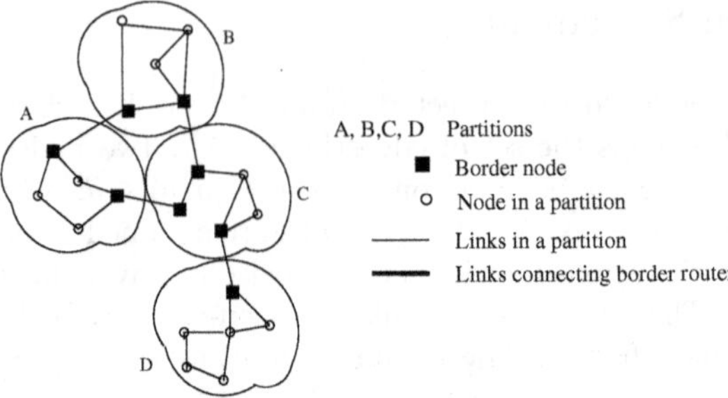

Fig. 1. A sample network with partitions

Reduced Network Topology: This represents the basic connectivity of the entire network hiding the internal details but sufficient enough to know the reachability between partitions. The partitions are represented as nodes in this graph. The border link(s) between any two partitions is represented as a link between these nodes.

3.2 The Algorithm

The aim behind partitioning the network is to reduce the number of link update messages. Each node stores the precomputed sets of border routers to each partition to which query message has to be sent while finding the QoS path. These sets do not change dynamically and is independent of the state of the network. However, changes in these sets may appear due to joining of a border node to the network or when a border node leaves the network, in which case, the topology information stored at each of the nodes need to be updated. The entire routing happens in three steps.

Step I: A connection request arriving at a node, specifies the destination node and a set of QoS constraints. The source node sends a control probe *PATH_QUERY* to all the border nodes that have to participate in the path selection.
Step II: In response to the query message, the border nodes send *PATH_INFO* message. A *PATH_INFO* message contains: the QoS metric of the best path to the other border nodes in the partition satisfying the QoS constraint and, the QoS metric of the border links. If the destination node is present in the partition, the QoS metric of the best path to the destination node is included in the *PATH_INFO* message. Since the source node, if not a border node, does not have the link-state information of the links in the partition, the border nodes return the QoS metric of the best path to the source node in the *PATH_INFO* message.
Step III: The source node waits till all the responses are received limited by a *TIMEOUT*. As the source node receives the $PATH\_INFO$ message, it builds the reduced graph G_R comprising of the border nodes in the network and the destination node. The reduced graph is defined as

$G_R = \{V_R, E_R, LS_R|$ *where* V_R *is the set of nodes in the reduced graph,* E_R *is the set of links, and* LS_R *is the link state matrix of the reduced graph*$\}$

Using the reduced graph, the source node computes the best path to the destination node.

The set of border nodes to reach a partition is precomputed and needs to be re-computed only if a border node is deleted from the network or a new border node is added. Therefore, we can assume that this set is static at all nodes. The complexity of the algorithm is thus, the sum of complexity of computations of the best path within the various partitions and of computing the feasible path using the reduced graph at the source node.

4 Simulation Experiments

In this section, we have compared the performance of our algorithm (Distributed source(ds) routing) with the following algorithms: Minimum-hop algorithm(mh), Prune algorithm(prune), Widest-shortest path(wsp), Shortest-widest path(swp), and Bounded Flooding(fld). All the above algorithms follow source routing except the bounded flooding algorithm. We have adopted the call blocking ratio and message overhead as the performance metrics.

4.1 Simulation Parameters

Simulations are carried for the expanded ANSNET topology given in Figure 2 [9, 4]. All links are bidirectional with a capacity of 12 units. We assume connections arrive following an exponential distribution. The mean holding time is considered to be exponentially distributed with a mean of 200 units. The bandwidth requirement of a request is uniformly distributed between 1 and 5 units. We study two traffic patterns: balanced and unbalanced traffic. For unbalanced traffic, five pairs in this topology are considered as hot spot pairs with a probability of 0.8. For simulations, we divided the network into four partitions.

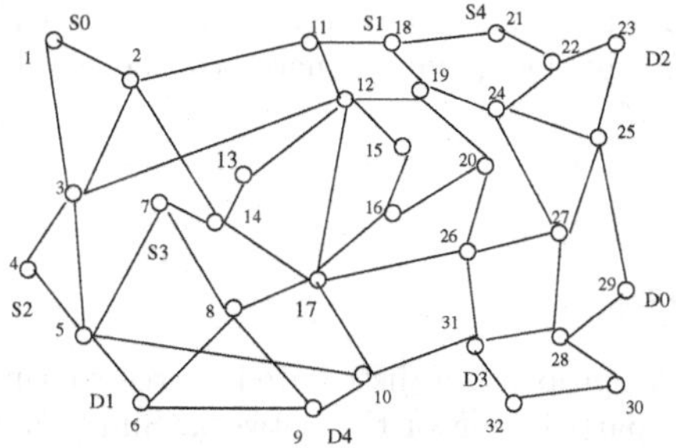

Fig. 2. Expanded ANSNET topology

(a)

(b)

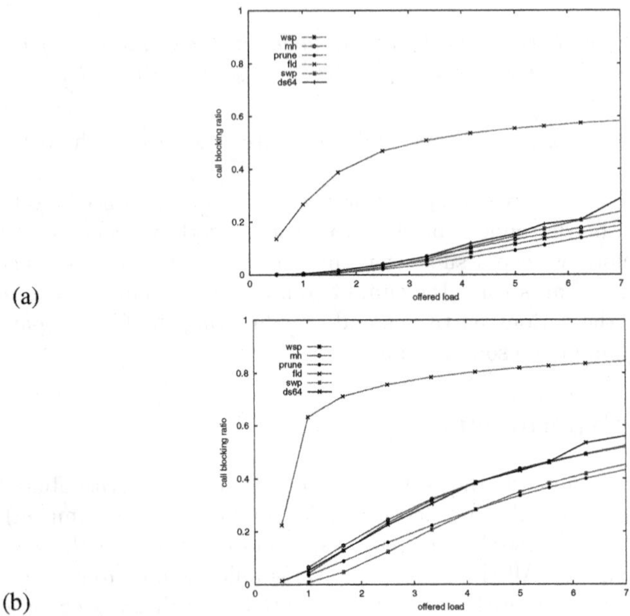

Fig. 3. Call blocking ratio as a function of load offered, $B \in [1, 5]$ and update interval = 64 units of time: (a) evenly distributed traffic, (b) unevenly distributed traffic

4.2 Simulation Results

The performance of the algorithms with link state update interval of 64 units is shown in figure 3. The graphs indicate that the performance of our algorithm is comparable with that of other algorithms for both balanced and unbalanced traffic. Figure 4 shows the call establishment overhead or the message overhead for the algorithms under consideration. It is clear from the graphs that our algorithm shows a tremendous improvement in reducing the message overhead. This is because the link-state advertisement is now restricted to the border nodes within a partition. However, the number of *PATH_QUERY* messages increases with the load, which increases the total number of routing messages.

5 Conclusions

In this paper, we have proposed a distributed source routing algorithm for unicast flows, based on partitioning of the network. Simulation studies show that the proposed algorithm reduces the message overhead considerably while maintaining the routing performance for both balanced and unbalanced traffic load.

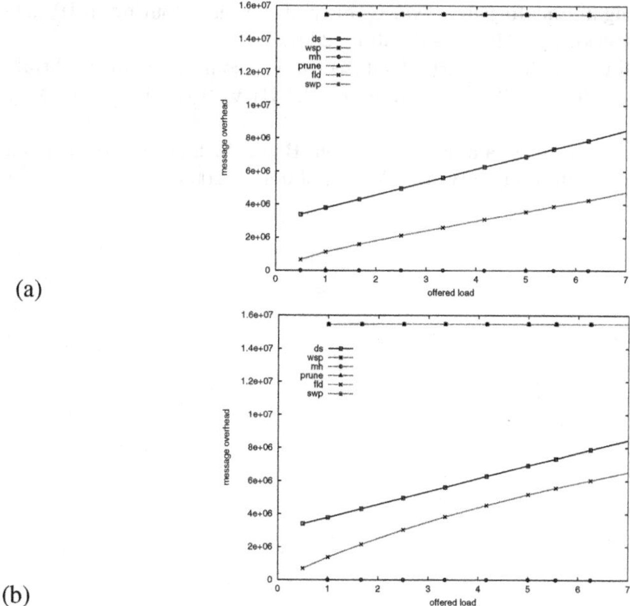

Fig. 4. Call Establishment overhead or the message overhead as a function of load offered, $B \in [1, 5]$ and update interval = 64 units of time: (a) evenly distributed traffic, (b) unevenly distributed traffic

Another key point to note about is that the proposed algorithm gives good performance even at higher link-state update interval and at higher load. Future work includes investigating the algorithm taking more than one QoS constraint parameters or QoS optimization parameters into account such as end-to-end delay, cost etc.

References

1. Z. Wang, J. Crowcroft. Quality-of-Service Routing For Supporting Multimedia Applications. IEEE Journal of Selected Areas in Communications, September 1996
2. S. Chen and K Nahrstedt. An overview of quality-of- service routing for the next generation high-speed networks: Problems and solutions. IEEE Network Magazine, December 1998.
3. R. Guerin, A. Orda, and D. Williams. QoS Routing Mechanisms and OSPF Extensions. IETF Internet Draft, January 1998.
4. S. Chen, K. Nahrstedt. Distributed Quality-of-Service Routing in High-Speed networks based on Selective Probing. In Proc. of IEEE Local Computer Networks, August 1998.
5. D. S. Reeves, H. F Salama. A Distributed Algorithm for Delay-Constrained Unicast Routing. IEEE Transactions on Networking, April 2000.

6. D. Ghosh, V. Sarangan and Raj Acharya. Quality-of- Service Routing in IP networks. IEEE Transactions on Multimedia, June 2001.
7. Samphel Norden, Jonathan Turner http://citeseer.nj.nec.com/InterDomain.html.
8. ATM forum, private Network Network Interface(PNNI) v1.0 specifications, May 1996.
9. Yi Yang, Lei Zhang, J. K. Muppala, S. T. Chanson. Bandwidth Delay Constrained Routing Algorithms. Computer Networks, Vol 42, January 2003.

The Roles of Ontology and Metadata Registry for Interoperable Databases

Jeong-Oog Lee, Myeong-Cheol Ko, Woojin Paik, Heung Seok Jeon, Junghwan Kim, Hyun-Kyu Kang, and Jinsoo Kim

Dept. of Computer Science, Konkuk University,
322 Danwol-dong, Chungju-si, Chungcheongbuk-do, 380-701, Korea
{ljo, cheol, wjpaik, hsjeon, jhkim, hkkang, jinsoo}@kku.ac.kr

Abstract. In order to make multiple autonomous databases to interoperate effectively, semantic heterogeneities have to be detected and resolved. Another difficulty is that users can be allowed to handle information easily from different heterogeneous databases that refer to the same real-world entity. To solve these problems, in this paper, I present an information integration system for interoperable databases using metadata registry and ontology. A metadata registry is a place to keep facts about characteristics of data that are necessary for data sharing and exchange in a specific domain. An ontology defines concepts and relations among concepts. The purpose of the proposed architecture is to define an information integration model, which combines characteristics of both standard specification of metadata registry and functionality of ontology for the concepts and relations.

1 Introduction

Many databases have been built or are being built to provide quality information services. Their search functions are still insufficient, however, due to their heterogeneity. It makes it difficult to enjoy a total integrated search. In order to give users integrated access to those environments, we need an effective and efficient mechanism for enabling knowledge to be shared and exchanged. Exchange of knowledge, to be effective, must take place in an environment where it can be ensured that an information source interprets the information in exactly the same way as intended by the other sources. The information must also be easy to locate and retrieve. This is only possible where the meaning and method of representation of the information are known and agreed upon by the information sources.

In this paper, using metadata registries, ontology, and agent technology, I suggest an information integration system which frees users from the tremendous tasks of acquiring domain knowledge and schema information of each database and allows new databases to join in the system easily.

A metadata registry(MDR) is a place to keep facts about characteristics of data that are necessary for data sharing and exchange in a specific domain[1].

R.K. Ghosh and H. Mohanty (Eds.): ICDCIT 2004, LNCS 3347, pp. 217–226, 2004.

An ontology defines concepts and relations among concepts[2]. Through conceptualization of data elements in MDRs and management of relations, ontology can be used to resolve schema heterogeneity among concepts of data elements. Data heterogeneity which is due to the differences of representation such as format, size, unit, and etc. among data elements can be resolved by constructing knowledge base. In order to provide semantic mappings between data elements using ontology and knowledge base, the system needs autonomous and intelligent agents which act independently when new databases are added to the system.

The rest of this paper is organized as follows. In section 2, I discuss about considerations for information sharing and address semantic heterogeneity. The roles of ontology and metadata registry are described in section 3. In section 4, I suggest an information integration system for interoperable databases using metadata registries and ontology. Also I explain agent architecture for the system. In section 5, I explain the evaluation of the proposed system comparing with other systems. Finally, section 6 offers conclusions.

2 Information Sharing Among Interoperable Databases

2.1 Considerations for Information Sharing

In open and dynamic environments such as the Web, numerous information sources exist and new information sources can be created autonomously and continuously without formal control. In order to give a multidatabase system adaptability in those environments, we need a mechanism for enabling information to be shared and exchanged. Sharing of information, to be efficient and effective, must take account of several considerations;

1. The meaning of the information in each component database must be represented in a unified way (*semantic representation*)
2. A multidatabase system must interpret the meaning of the information in each component database (*semantic interpretation*)
3. A multidatabase system must integrate the information in all the component databases (*information integration*)
4. An efficient and effective access mechanism must be provided to retrieve desired information from the integrated information (*information access*)

2.2 Schema and Data Heterogeneity

Making it possible for two or more databases to interoperate effectively has many unresolved problems. The most basic and fundamental problem is heterogeneity[3][4][5]. It can be categorized into platform heterogeneity and semantic heterogeneity.

The platform heterogeneity consists of hardware, data model, DBMS heterogeneities and so forth. Network communication protocols and standards such as SQL standards, OLE, ODBC, ODMG, and CORBA help to overcome these kinds of heterogeneities. Another aspect of platform heterogeneity is concurrency heterogeneity, which concerns the different kinds of concurrency control supported by individual databases[3].

While there is a significant amount of researches discussing platform heterogeneity, work on semantic heterogeneity is insufficient. Semantic heterogeneity includes differences in the way the real world is modeled in the databases, particularly in the schemas of the databases.

Since a database is defined by its schema and data, semantic heterogeneity can be classified into schema heterogeneity and data heterogeneity. Schema heterogeneity mainly results from the use of different structures for the same information and the use of different names for the same structures. Data heterogeneity is due to the inconsistent data in the absence of schema heterogeneity[6][7].

3 A Model for Interoperability Using Ontology and Metadata Registry

3.1 Overview of the Model

It needs abstraction phase to make objects in real world to be available sources in computer world. As in figure 1, objects in real world can be abstracted by concepts. And interaction among objects can be described by some kinds of relations. An ontology keeps these abstracted concepts of objects and relation information, which provides a mechanism for extracting concepts in user's queries. Though a concept must be unique in discourse of universe, objects which represent the concept may be vary.

A metadata registry manages standard representations of these various objects. Standard representation means that it defines various data in a domain of interest using representative representations. As in figure 1, representations of some standardized data elements can be mapped to a concept in ontology. What must be considered in this structure is the heterogeneity between data elements in MDRs. In my approach, intelligent agents resolve heterogeneity according to the kinds of data heterogeneity using knowledge base.

3.2 Ontology

An ontology is an explicit specification of a conceptualization[8]. When the knowledge of a domain is represented in a declarative formalism, the set of objects that can be represented is called the universe of discourse. This set of objects, and the describable relationships among them, are reflected in the representational vocabulary with which a knowledge-based program represents knowledge. Ontologies can be applied for inter-operability among systems, communications between human being and systems, increasing system's reusability and so forth. There are several endeavors within the industrial and academic communities that address the problem of implementing ontologies, such as TOP, WordNet, Ontolingua, Cyc, Frame Ontology, PANGLOSS, MikroKosmos, SENSUS,

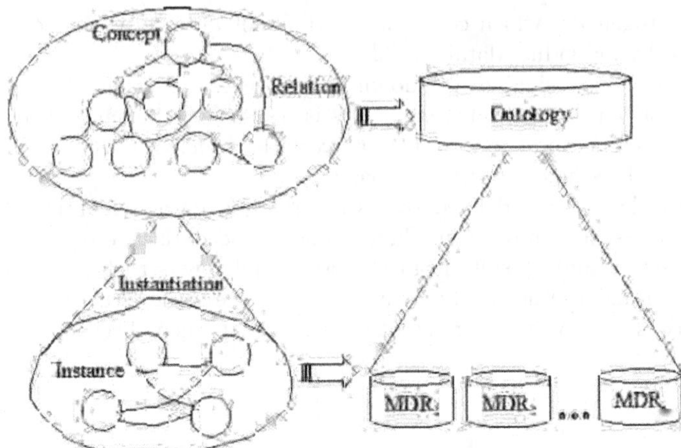

Fig. 1. Overview of the information integration model using ontology and MDRs

EngMath, PhysSys, TOVE, and CHEMICALS[9][10]. In my approach ontology has a role of semantic network which is for extracting concepts from user's queries and integrating information of data elements in MDRs.

3.3 Metadata Registry

In ISO/IEC 11179, metadata refers to descriptions of other data. Metadata is data, so metadata may be stored in a database. A database of metadata that supports the functionality of registration is a metadata registry[1]. ISO 11179 - Metadata registries, specifies basic aspects of the kind and quality of metadata necessary to describe other data, and it specifies the management and administration of that metadata in a metadata registry. It applies to the formulation of data representations, meanings, and relationships between them to be shared among people and machines, independent of the organization that produces the data. One of the important classes of metadata is data element. Data elements are the fundamental unit of data an organization creates, manages, and disseminates. A data element is composed of two parts: data element concept and representation. Data element concept is the conceptual part of a data element, described independently of any particular representation. Representation includes a value domain, data type, units of measure, and representation class. A data element is produced when a representation is associated with a data element concept. In my approach, a MDR has role of as follows.

- provides standard information to integrate component databases
- manages mapping information between data elements and component database schemas

3.4 The Roles of Ontology and Metadata Registry

Let's assume that A and B are sites which manage information about components which can be applied to various platforms such as COM, EJB, JavaBean, CORBA, VCL, and CLX. Both site A and B which provide the information of components to the users who need them, or other sites, have their own metadata registry in which component databases related to each site refer to data elements. Figure 2 shows an example of association of ontology and metadata registries. Site A uses 'Name' for component name, while site B uses 'Component Name' for the same information. The terms 'Name' and 'Component Name' have a IS-A relation. Agents decide whether 'Name' and 'Component Name' are semantically related or not, using concepts and relations in ontology. In a similar way, cost of component is represented as 'Cost' in site A and as 'Price' in site B, and 'Cost' and 'Price' have a IS-A relation.

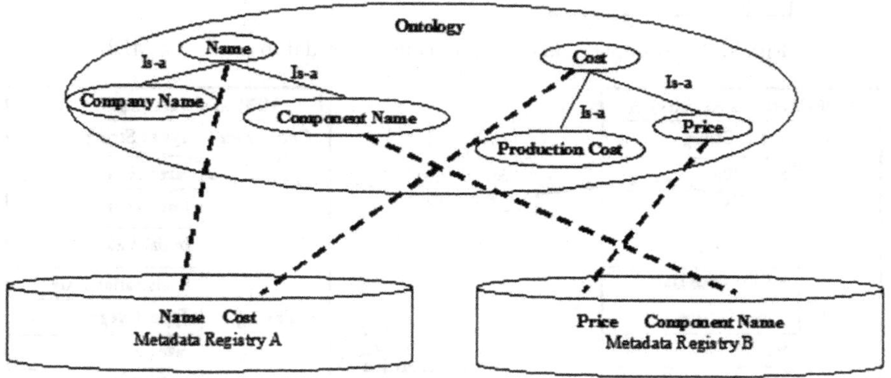

Fig. 2. An example of association of ontology and metadata registries

Each data representation in a MDR can be identified by examining data element and its attributes as in figure 3. New user who attempts to register his database to site A can construct his own database according to the data elements in the MDR provided by site A. In the case of schema information of conventional databases, they can be mapped to data elements in the MDR by agents.

When two or more MDRs involve in the system, there are some problems of information integration. In figure 4, the size of data element 'Name' is 200 in MDR A, while the size of 'Component Name' which is semantically equivalent to 'Name' of MDR A is 1024. Also, in 'Cost' and 'Price', data heterogeneity of monetary units can be identified. For solving these differences of representations of data elements, mutual transformation between types, sizes, and units is needed.

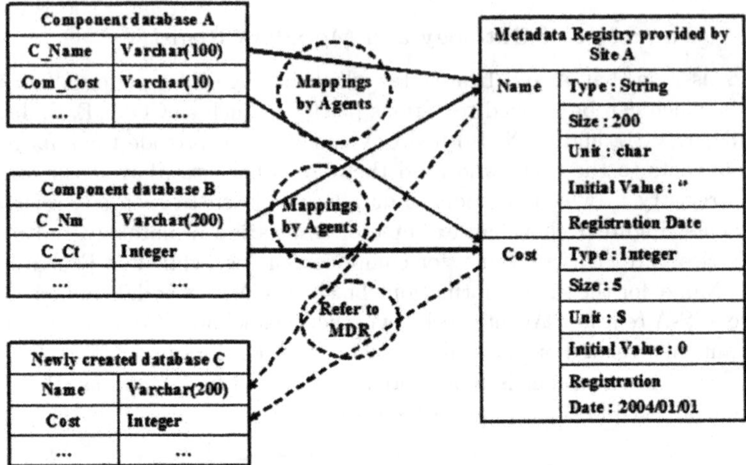

Fig. 3. An example of mappings of component databases and a MDR

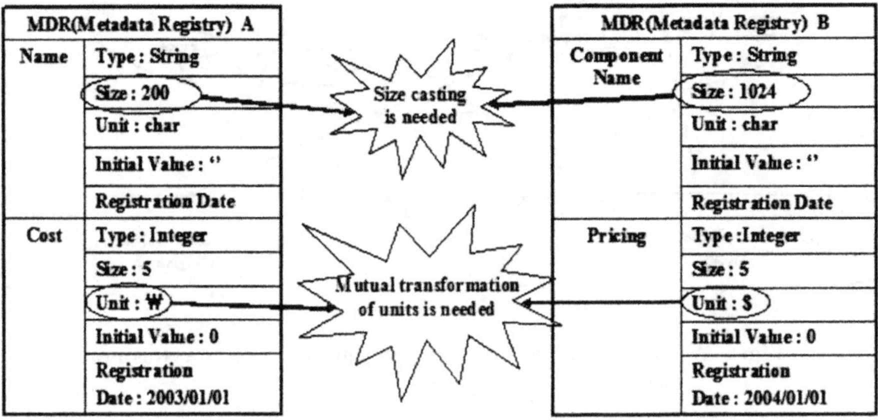

Fig. 4. The differences of representations of data elements in different MDRs

4 Information Integration System for Interoperable Databases

I have constructed an information integration system for interoperable databases using ontology and metadata registries. Basis of information integration has been established by constructing semantic network using ontology and by using information sharability and standardization of metadata registries. The main components of the system are ontology, metadata registry, structure mapping agent, value mapping agent, broker agent, and so forth, as in figure 5. For independability of the system components, agents with intelligent are needed[11].

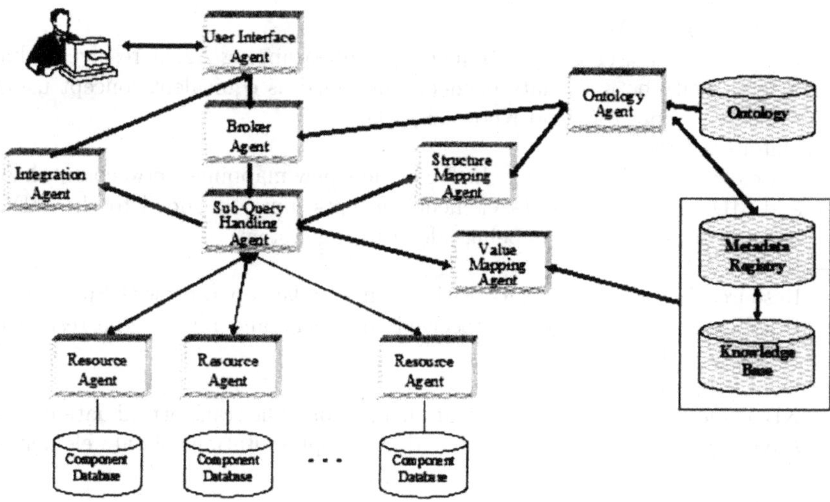

Fig. 5. An architecture of the proposed information integration system for interoperable databases

The descriptions of main system components and agents are as follows.

- Ontology
  Ontology defines concepts and relations among concepts and has a role of semantic network which is for extracting concepts from user's queries and integrating information of data elements in MDRs.
- Metadata Registry(MDR)
  Metadata Registry provides standard information to integrate component databases and manages mapping information between data elements and component database schemas.
- User Interface Agent
  User Interface Agent parses user's query, extracts concepts in the query using concepts and relations in ontology, requests query processing, and displays the processed results to the user.
- Broker Agent
  With assistance of Ontology Agent, Broker Agent identifies information sources where all the concepts extracted by User Interface Agent exist.
- Sub-Query Handling Agent
  Sub-Query Handling Agent re-formulates the original user's query into multiple sub-queries for each component database schema according to the information provided from Structure Mapping Agent and Value Mapping Agent and sends the sub-queries to the component databases.
- Structure Mapping Agent
  Structure Mapping Agent generates mappings between concepts in original query and schema of identified information sources.

- Value Mapping Agent
  In the process of creating sub-queries, Value Mapping Agent resolves value heterogeneity between data elements identified as equivalent concept using Metadata Repository and Knowledge Base.
- Ontology Agent
  Ontology Agent is an agent which conducts new mappings between ontology and MDR, when new data element concepts must be added to the MDR because of new databases being added to the system.
- Resource Agent
  Resource Agent manages information source and co-operates with Sub-Query Handling Agent. It executes received sub-query and returns the result to Sub-Query Handling Agent.
- Knowledge Base(KB)
  KB defines the rules of transformation and stores the transformed data for resolving data heterogeneity originated from representations of data elements.

5 Evaluation

Many approaches for resolving semantic heterogeneity and integrating information in multidatabase systems have been developed with the various technical improvements. Early researches focused on procedures to merge individual heterogeneous databases schema into a single global schema[12][13]. A global schema multidatabase supports a single, integrated global view to the user and provides simple and effective paradigm. However, creating and maintaining the global schema is difficult. Also, a small change to a local schema may require huge changes to the global schema. As the proposed approach in this paper needs not build a global schema, it is easy to construct an information integration system.

In several researches such as SIMS[14], HERMES[15], InfoSleuth[16], and etc., new approaches have been developed for integrating of information using new technological developments such as agent technology, domain ontologies, intelligent mediator, and high-level query languages, in dynamic and open environments. These approaches were designed to support flexibility and openness. However, a common assumption of these dynamic approaches is that the users know domain knowledge for integrating information, which might be a burden to the users. The proposed approach provides common domain knowledge using ontology as knowledge base, so that each information source can be merged into the system without needing to know specific domain knowledge of other sources.

A metadata registry has procedures for creating, registering, and authenticating standard data elements. And it can manage data consistently with referring registered data elements. However, as in the aspect of common use, it has limitations for representing relations among data elements. Ontology-based information integration systems can create semantic networks for representing various relations among terms. However, as in the aspect of representation ability in data level, they can not provide standard data representations as in a metadata registry. In my approach, for effective information integration, I have combined advantages of both ontology-based and MDR-based approach. That is, ontology undertakes responsibility for identifying semantic relations among data elements and metadata registry provides standard representations of data elements.

The proposed system combined the advantages of both kinds of systems adopts the aspect of system extensibility using standardability of metadata registry and constructs semantic network which represents relations among terms(or concepts) using domain-independent ontology. It does not have overheads of adding new databases or deleting exiting databases and is independent of the operation environment. Also, it gives users an efficient method for performing general semantic queries.

6 Conclusions

Seen from a semantic perspective, the process of database design proceeds from the real world to the data. The designer develops his own conceptualization of the real world and turns his conceptualization into a database design. This has led designers to develop different, often incompatible, schemas for the same information. Therefore, users needing to combine information from several heterogeneous databases are faced with the problem of locating and integrating relevant information.

This paper has suggested an information integration system which merges the characteristics of the MDR-based information integration systems and the ontology-based information integration systems. When a user who does not have domain knowledge issues a query in a semantic query language using his/her own concepts, ontology provides semantic network for analyzing concepts in the query and mapping these concepts to the data elements in a metadata registry. A metadata registry plays an important role in resolving semantic heterogeneity and integrating component databases through management of standard data elements.

References

1. ISO/IEC, "ISO/IEC FDIS 11179 : Information technology-Specification and standardization of data elements", 1999.
2. Mike Uschold and Michael Gruninger,"Ontologies: Principles, Methods and Applications", Knowledge Engineering Review, 1996.
3. R. Hull, "Managing semantic heterogeneity in databases: a theoretical prospective", Proc. 16th ACM SIGACT-SIGMOD-SIGART symposium on Principles of database systems, pp. 51-61, 1997.
4. C. Batini, M. Lenzerini, and S.B. Navathe, "A comparative analysis of methodologies for database schema integration", ACM Computing Surveys, 18(4), 1986.
5. A. M. Ouksel, A. P. Sheth, "Semantic Interoperability in Global Information Systems: A Brief Introduction to the Research Area and the Special Section". SIGMOD Record, 28(1), pp. 5-12, 1999.
6. G. A. Miller, R. Beckwith, C. Fellbaum, D.Gross, and K. Miller, "Five Papers on WordNet", CSL Reort 43, Cognitive Systems Laboratory, Priceton Univ., 1990.

7. M. Garcia-Solaco, F. Saltor, and M. Castellanos, "Semantic Heterogeneity in Multidatabase Systems", in Object-Oriented Multidatabase Systems: A Solution for Advanced Applications, ed. O. A. Bukhres, A. K. Elmagarmid, pp. 129-202, Prentice Hall Inc., 1996.
8. Thomas R.Gruber, "Toward Principles for the Design of Ontologies Used for Knowledge Sharing", International Journal of Human-Computer Studies, 1995.
9. Maurizio Panti, Luca Spalazzi, Alberto Giretti, "A Case-Based Approach to Information Integration" , Proceedings of the 26th VLDB conference, 2000.
10. J. Hammer, H. H. Garcia-Molina, K. Ireland, Y. Papakonstantinou, J. Ullman, J. Widom, "Information translation, mediation, and mosaic-based browsing in the tsimmis system", In Proceedings of the ACM SIGMOD International Conference on Management of Data, 1995.
11. Joseph P. Bigus, Jennifer Bigus, 'Constructing Intelligent agents with Java', Wiley Computer Publishing, 1998.
12. R. Ahmed, P. De Smedt, W. Du, W. Kent, M. A. Ketabchi, W. A. Litwin, A. Rafli, and M. C. Shan, "The Pegasus heterogenous multidatabase system", IEEE Computer, 1991.
13. C. Collet, M. Huhns, W. Shen "Resource Integration Using a Large Knowledge Base in Carnot", IEEE Computer, 1991.
14. C. A. Knoblock et al., "Modeling Web Sources for Information Integration", In Proceedings of 11th Nat'l Conference on Artificial Intelligence, 1998.
15. S. Adali, K. S. Candan, Y. Papakonstantinou, and V. S. Subrahmanian, "Query caching and optimization in distributed mediator systems", In Proceedings of the ACM SIGMOD International Conference on Management of Data, 1996.
16. Marian Nodine, Jerry Fowler, Brad Perry, "An Overview of Active Information Gathering in InfoSleuth", InfoSlueth Group, 1998.

DHL: Semantically Rich Dynamic and Active Hyperlinks

Gi-Chul Yang[1] and Sanjay K. Madria[2]

[1] Division of Information Engineering, Mokpo National University, Korea
[2] Dept. of Computer Science, University of Missouri-Rolla, USA
gcyang@mokpo.ac.kr, madrias@umr.edu

Abstract. A novel hyperlink that can access more than one Web site dynamically by using semantic information attached on the link and each Web site is introduced in this paper. The (semantic) descriptions of Web sites are represented by conceptual graphs and stored in a database. When a link is clicked, the matching between the link and the sites is performed by a dynamic hyperlink processor, which in turn performs a query to the database through a technique of conceptual graph matching. It is definitely better than full-text search and easier to implement.

1 Introduction

Presently, hyperlinks in Web sites are static and passive. The static hyperlink has only one pre-designated URL as a destination and the passive hyperlink can faces the problem of broken link. Hence, a user can access only one Web site with one hyperlink and has no provision to access any other related Web site in case of the designated Web site is down. Hence, the dynamic and active hyperlink is preferred in many situations. Presenting more than one Web site would be advantageous in some cases. For example, consider the hyperlink (i.e., research group) in the sentence "There are many **research groups** for semantic Web in America". It would be preferable if the hyperlink has multiple URLs for its destinations. Dynamic hyperlink can retrieve multiple Web sites.

Moreover Web sites are ephemeral, like living things. Many new Web sites are born and many existing Web sites cease to exist every day. Hence, the hyperlink should be active in order to keep it functioning. Active hyperlink can retrieve the relevant Web sites even though the Web sites previously connected are down. Hence, we propose the dynamic and active hyperlinks to be used in the Web pages to increase the usability of the Internet. A unique way of implementing the dynamic and active hyperlink is introduced in this paper. The implemented *dynamic and active hyperlink* called **DHL**(**D**ynamic and active **H**yper**L**ink). DHL uses semantic information in order to retrieve the designated URLs. The semantic information is in the description and is represented by conceptual graphs. Each Web site that participates in the retrieval process has it's own semantic description and the DHL has corresponding conceptual graph attached in each DHL works as a query. Then a conceptual graph matching is performed between the query graph and the conceptual graphs in semantic descriptions to retrieve the destination Web sites.

R.K. Ghosh and H. Mohanthy (Eds.): ICDCIT 2004, LNCS 3347, pp. 227–236, 2004.

The component, which performs this match, is called ***DHL-Processor*** (DHLP). The DHLP has the capability of exact matching as well as partial Matching. Partial matching includes both syntactic and semantic partial matching. The range of partial matching can be set when the DHLP is created.

The basic idea of DHLP is described in the next section and the architecture of DHLP is presented in section3. In section 4, the matching process of DHLP is presented with an example and an application of DHL in Web Warehouse is introduced in section 5. The paper is concluded in section 6.

2 Overview of the Dynamic and Active Hyperlink

Dynamic and active HyperLink (DHL) performs a semantic search for the World Wide Web (WWW). The essential component of DHL is **DHL-Processor** (DHLP). The DHLP can retrieve semantically matched descriptions among the many descriptions of the WWW sites. In order to use DHLP, each Web site should have Semantic Description (SD) attached to it. This SD can be represented in any language that can describe semantics of the document, and in our case Conceptual Graph (CG) is used. Since, CG can describe semantics efficiently and it is easy to read by human and machine. Also, the metadata represented in RDF (Resource Description Framework) statements can be interpreted into CGs automatically [5]. The World Wide Web Consortium (W3C) has introduced RDF [4,6] and it is widely used for Semantic Web construction. The need of Semantic Web is more and more emphasized [2,3,14] in order to manage the huge amount of information efficiently by using the content semantics.

The relationship between DHL and destination Web sites is shown in Figure 1. Any DHL in a Web site (i.e., DHL1 & DHL2 in Figure 1) has an attached conceptual graph behind it instead of a destination URL. This conceptual graph is used as a query. It is then matched with SDs in other Web sites by DHLP. As the DHLP finds its matched SD, the corresponding URL(s) is (are) retrieved. Retrieved URLs are listed in the pop-up window. The user will then be able to see the preferred Web site by clicking the URL.

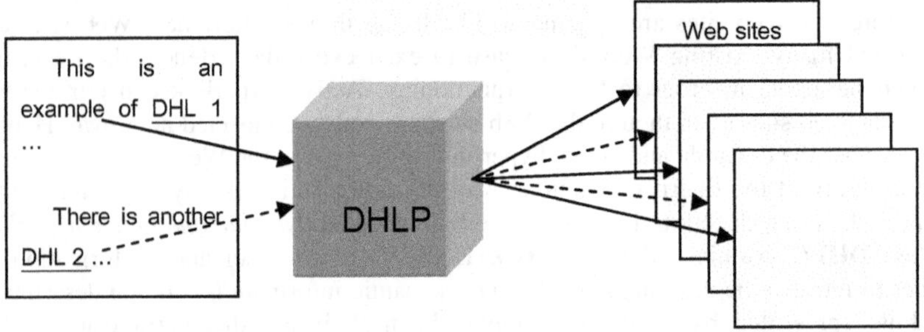

Fig. 1. Relationship between DHL and destination Web sites

The number of Web sites to be retrieved is not fixed, but the implementers of the DHLs can control the range of the search. The details of this process are explained in section 4. There is a Semantic Index Table (SIT) which holds (SD, URL) pairs. The URL attached to each SD is the address of the Web site that contains the document explained in the corresponding SD. Hence, the SIT work as a bridge between SDs and actual Web sites. Therefore, users can search the semantically relevant Web sites easily through SIT by using DHLP.

3 DHL-Processor

Dynamic and active HyperLink (DHL) - Processor (DHLP) is a kind of semantic search engine. When the user clicks a DHL the DHLP is triggered automatically and the semantic search begins. The DHP is organized as shown is Figure 2.

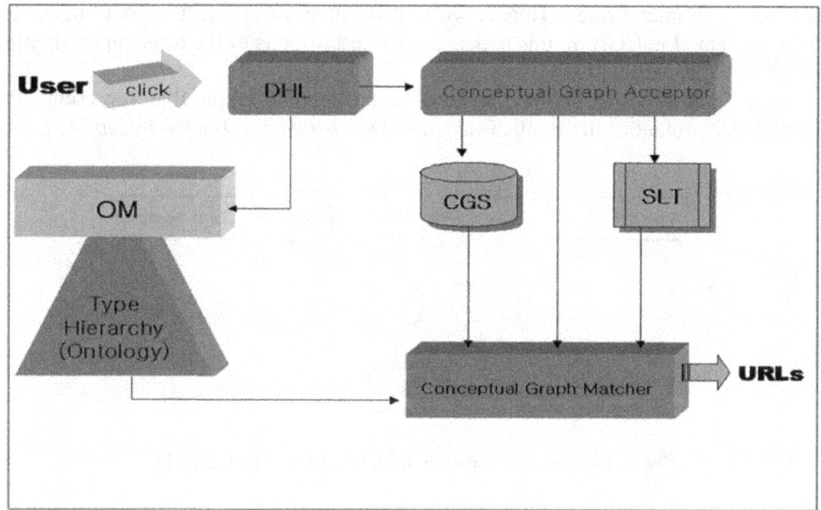

Fig. 2. Architecture of DHLP

The DHLP consists of five components. The five components are Conceptual Graph Acceptor (CGA), Conceptual Graph Storage (CGS), Semantic Index Table (SIT), type hierarchy(ontology), and conceptual graph matcher. The CGA accepts the conceptual graph attached in the pressed DHL. Incoming Conceptual Graphs (CG) are stored in CGS with id number and corresponding URL attached in front of each CG. In addition, it creates the indices and stores them in a table called Semantic Index Table (SIT), thus maintaining semantic indexing information. Ontology Manager (OM) is used to create and maintain the ontology (type hierarchy). Different representation forms of CG with a brief introduction are shown in section 3.1. The CGS is explained with an example in section 3.2 and SIT is described in section 3.3.

3.1 Representations of Conceptual Graph

As we mentioned in section 2, conceptual graph is used to represent the Semantic Description (SD) of each Web site. Conceptual Graph (CG) is one of a good formal language for representing the meanings of natural language sentences [10,12,13] and the RDF sentences can be interpreted to CGs automatically[5]. Hence, it is a good idea to use CGs for SD. A CG is a finite connected bipartite graph. There are two kinds of nodes; concept nodes (displayed as a box in graph notation) which represent entities, attributes, states, and events, and relation nodes (displayed as a circle in graph notation) which represent the relationship among concept nodes.

A CG can be represented in three different forms. There is a graphic notation called the *display form* (DF), a more compact notation called the *linear form* (LF) as well as a concrete syntax called the *conceptual graph interchange form* (CGIF), which has a simplified syntax and a restricted character set designed for compact storage and efficient parsing. Both DF and LF are designed for communication with humans or between humans and machines. For communication between machines, the CGIF has a simpler syntax. Hence, we will develop an efficient search engine for SD's represented in CGIF in this paper. Below descriptions of the three representation forms are adapted from [12].

Figure 3 shows the display form of a conceptual graph that represents the prepositional content of the English sentence *John is going to Boston by bus* [12].

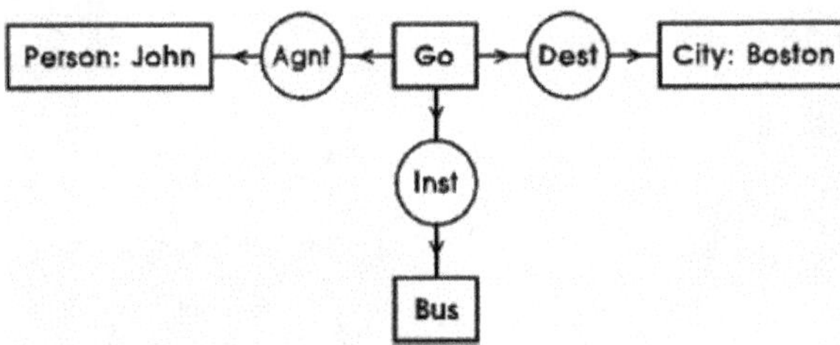

Fig. 3. CG Display Form for John is going to Boston by bus

In DF, concepts are represented by rectangles: [Go], [Person: John], [City: Boston], and [Bus]. Circles or ovals represent conceptual relations: (Agnt) relates [Go] to the agent John, (Dest) relates [Go] to the destination Boston, and (Inst) relates [Go] to the instrument bus. The linear form for CGs is intended as a more compact notation than DF, but with good human readability. Following is the LF for Figure 3:

```
[Go]-
        (Agnt)->[Person: John]
        (Dest)->[City: Boston]
        (Inst)->[Bus].
```

In this form, the concepts are represented by square brackets instead of boxes, and the conceptual relations are represented by parentheses instead of circles. A hyphen at the end of a line indicates that the relations attached to the concept are continued on subsequent lines. Following is the CGIF for Figure 3:

[Go *x] (Agnt ?x [Person: John]) (Dest ?x [City: Boston]) (Inst ?x [Bus])
or (Agnt [Go] [Person: John]) (Dest [Go] [City: Boston]) (Inst [Go] [Bus])

The developed **DHL-Processor** (DHLP) is intended for use of CGIF. CGIF can be translated into different logical languages such as *Knowledge Interchange Format* (KIF). Hence, it is better to have a system for CGIF instead of DF or LF.

3.2 Conceptual Graph Storage

Conceptual Graph Storage (CGS) is a simple storage that holds CGs. Here are four CGs, which represents semantics of the corresponding natural language sentences, to be used to show the structure of CGS. The CGs are:

a) John reads a book.

In CGIF: (AGNT [READ][PERSON:John])(OBJ [READ][BOOK])

b) Tom reads an interesting book.

In CGIF: (AGNT [READ][PERSON:Tom])(OBJ [READ][BOOK])
(ATTR [READ][INTERESTING])

c) Nancy gives a book to John.

In CGIF : (AGNT [GIVE][PERSON:Nancy])(OBJ [GIVE][Book:@1])
(RCPT [GIVE][PERSON:John])

d) John reads a book fast.

In CGIF : (AGNT [READ][PERSON:John])(OBJ [READ][BooK])
(MANR [READ][FAST])

If above four sentences (CGs) are given to CGS, the structure of CGS would be

G1: (AGNT [READ][PERSON:John])(OBJ [READ][BooK])
G2: (AGNT [READ][PERSON:Tom])(OBJ [READ][BooK])
(ATTR READ)[INTERESTING])
G3: (AGNT [GIVE][PERSON:Nancy])(OBJ [GIVE][Book:@1])
(RCPT [GIVE][PERSON:John])
G4: (AGNT [READ][PERSON:John])(OBJ [READ][BooK])
(MANR [RAD][FAST])

As we can see above, CGS just stores the incoming CGS with a unique graph id (called G-id) attached in front of each CG. Each G-id is connected to the corresponding URLs of the Web sites. CGS is not enough to provide an efficient retrieval system. An efficient indexing mechanism is necessary for a sophisticated retrieval approach. Section 3.3 will present an efficient indexing mechanism.

3.3 Semantic Index Table

As we know, Conceptual Graph Interchange Format (CGIF) is organized with parenthesis and each parenthesis contains one conceptual relation. Hence, the relation name could be a table name for indexing in a database. When the first sentence is coming into CGS, the unique graph id called G-id attached to the coming graph and stored in CGS. The structure of the index storage named **Semantic Index Table** (SIT) will be

AGNT := (1 [READ][PERSON:John]2)
OBJ := (1 [RAD][BOOK]2)

Now we have two lists, named AGNT and OBJ, in the SIT with one element (e.g.,(1 [READ][PERSON:John] 2) in the list AGNT) in each list. Since, the first graph has two relations AGNT and OBJ. So, two Lists are created in an empty SIT. Now the list named with AGNT contains one item, (1 [READ][PERSON:John] 2), in it. Similarly, the second list, named OBJ, has one item: (1 [READ][BOOK] 2). The first number in each item is the graph id (called G-id) and the number after the concept indicates the length of the graph (i.e., the number of relations in a graph). The length can be used to speed up the exact matches by discarding graphs, which are different in length.

The list has been used as a data structure for the SIT, since it is simple and easy to explain the basic concept of the SIT. Actual implementation should be done via a more efficient data structure. We suggest extendable hashing for fast retrieval and a commercial database for practical systems with large number of CGs. We used a database for the developed System. The corresponding database tables are shown at the end of this section. After the second sentence is accepted, the SIT becomes

AGNT := (1 [READ][PERSON:John] 2) (2 [READ][PERSON:Tom] 3)
OBJ := (1 [READ][BOOK] 2) (2 [READ][BOOK] 3)
ATTR := (2 [READ][INTERESTIN] 3).

As the second graph is coming in, a new list named ATTR has been created in SIT since there was no relation named in the first graph. The final SIT contains following after the four graphs are stored.

AGNT := (1 [READ][PERSON:John] 2) (2 [READ][PERSON:Tom] 3)
(3 [GIVE][PERSON:Nancy] 3) (4 [READ][PERSON:John] 3)
OBJ := (1 [READ][BOOK] 2) (2 [READ][BOOK] 3)
(3 [GIVE][Book:@1] 3) (4 [READ][BOOK] 3)
ATTR :=(2 [READ][INTERESTING] 3)
RCPT :=(3 [GIVE][PERSON:Jhon] 3)
MANR :=(4 [READ][FAST] 3)

We explained SIT by using a data structure list, however, as we mentioned earlier SIT can be a table in a relational DBMS. Followings are the tables for relations used in the incoming CGs.

AGNT

G-id	*Concepts*	*LENGTH*
1	[READ][PERSON:John]	2
2	[READ][PERSON:Tom]	3
3	[GIVE][PERSON:Nancy]	3
4	[READ][PERSON:John]	3

OBJ

G-id	Concepts	LENGTH
1	[READ][BOOK]	2
2	[READ][BOOK]	3
3	[GIVE][Book:@1]	3
4	[READ][BOOK]	3

ATTR

G-id	Concepts	LENGTH
2	[READ][INTERESTING]	3

MANR

G-id	Concepts	LENGTH
4	[READ][FAST]	3

RCPT

G-id	Concepts	LENGTH
3	[GIVE][PERSON:John]	3

SIT can be created and updated automatically depending on the incoming CGs.

4 Matching Process of DHLP

In this section, we show how the destination URLs can be retrieved. The basic access mechanism is matching, in which a query representation is matched to representations of semantic description in each Web site. There are different conceptual graph matching algorithms [7,9,11]. The DHLP use the similar conceptual graph matching algorithm as in [11].

A query match can be performed through the SIT. For example, a query "John reads a book." Is translated into the following conceptual graph:

[READ] – (AGNT)->[PERSON:JOHN]
(OBJ)-> [BOOK]

which is represented in CGIF as

(AGNT [TEAD][PERSON:JOHN])(OBJ [READ][BOOK])

This query graph is separated into (relation concept) pairs. There are two pairs in this case. The first step is to take the last pair from the query CG and search the SIT. In this case, take the pair (OBJ [READ][BOOK]) and look at the OBJ table. The system will find (1 [READ][BOOK] 2)(2 [READ][BOOK] 3)(4 [READ][BOOK] 3). Here we got three G-ids; 1, 2 and 4. The next pair is (AGNT [READ][PERSON: JOHN]; the search, in the AGNT table will find (1 [READ][PERSON: JOHN] 2) and (4 [READ][PERSON: JOHN] 3). Each time any new elements are found then the G-ids of those elements (i.e., 1 and 4 in this case) are intersected with the G-ids of old elements (i.e., 1,2 and 4 in this case). Hence, G-id '1' and '4' are the G-ids left so far. This process is performed until we have no more pairs in the query graph. The Remaining G-ids are the result graph ids for the matching.

Partial matching is possible. In the case of partial matching, both syntactic and semantic differences can be covered. For instance, we can get an answer with both queries "John reads a book" and "Tom reads a book fast" by using partial match with the current SIT. In the case of semantic partial match, a concept type hierarchy (i.e., ontology) is utilized. The type hierarchy can be built by using Ontology Manager (OM) that is implemented in DHLP. We can add new concept in the type hierarchy through the OM. The newly added concept will be the sub-concept of the current concept. Also the user can change the current concept by clicking any concept that appeared in OM. In this way the user can "look around" the ontology.

"Tom reads a book." and "A man reads a book." are matched by semantic partial matching, since 'man' is a super type of 'Tom' in the concept type hierarchy. On the other side, "Tom reads a book in Edinburgh." and "Tom reads a book." can be matched by syntactic partial matching. In each case of partial matching, DHLP allows the user to select the Degree of Matching (DoM) and Degree of Inheritance(DoI) for retrieval of relevant information where exact information is absent in the database. The DoM and DoI show the closeness between a query graph and the matched graph(s) form a different point of view. The DoM is calculated as

DoM = number of matched relation(s) / number of relation(s) in a query graph.

The DoM is crucial to retrieve the necessary information in a certain case. For example, let us assume that the CGS contains "Tom reads an interesting book yesterday." and a user wants to match that with "Tom reads an interesting book." If DoM is not allowed or a user request 100% of DoM, then DHLP will not be able to return any match, even though the CGS contains the relevant information (i.e., "Tom reads an interesting book yesterday"). DHLP, however, will return a graph for "ToM reads an interesting book yesterday", for the query with 80% of DoM. DoI indicates the inheritance path length in the type hierarchy. Path length of the immediate predecessor of a concept is +1, and the immediate successor concept's path length is –1. Therefore, the positive integers can be used for generalization and the negative integers can be used for specialization.

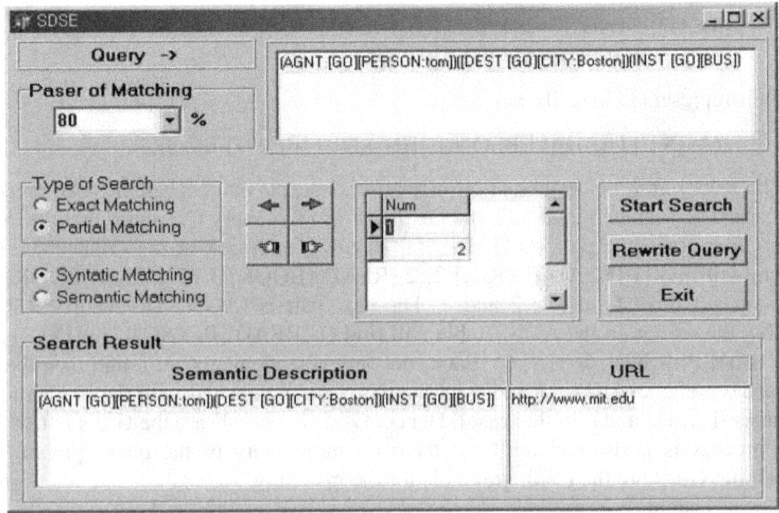

Fig. 4. Interface of the Semantic Description Search Engine

For example, if a user wants to consider generalized graph matching (i.e., find the graph more general than the query graph), then the user can specify the value of DoI by using a positive integer (e.g., +3). In the case of the generalized graph matching, DHLP allows the user to determine how many levels of the type hierarchy should be searched for each concept in the query graph. Thus, the number indicates the levels in the type hierarchy (e.g., +3 means three levels up). The implementer of DHLP can predefine the DoI and DoM of the each DHL for the range of the retrieved Web sites. This feature of DHLP offers great flexibility to the user and provides efficiency to the system.

Figure 4, shows the interface of the semantic description search engine that is using same matching technique with DHLP.

5 Application of Semantically Rich Dynamic Links in Web Warehouse

As most users obtain WWW information using a combination of search engines and browsers, these two types of retrieval mechanisms do not necessarily address all of a user's information needs. The search engines do not incorporate effective query mechanisms to address user needs, as they are purely resource locators with no capability to reliably suggest the contents of the websites they return in response to a query. Furthermore, the task of information retrieval still burdens the user, who has to manually sift through 'potential' sites to discover the relevant information. The presence of mirror sites makes the task of finding the document of user interest even more tedious [1].

WHOWEDA (**W**are**H**ouse **Of** **We**b **Da**ta) [1] is a project that deals with the design and implementation of a web warehouse that materializes and manages useful information from the Web to support strategic decision-making. WHOWEDA is a meta-data repository of useful, relevant web information, available for querying and analysis. As relevant information becomes available on the WWW, it is coupled from various sources, translated into a common web data model (Web Information Coupling Model), and integrated with existing data in the repository. At the warehouse, queries can be answered and web data analysis can be performed quickly and efficiently since the information is directly available. Accessing data at the warehouse does not incur costs that may be associated with accessing data from the information sources scattered at different geographical locations. In a web warehouse, data is available even when the WWW sources are inaccessible.

In the current form of the query graph in web warehouse context, if the query is not able to match constraints on hyperlinks (i.e., sports) on the query web page then it does not process the query. Using the concepts discussed in this paper, the query graph can be modified by adding DHL which uses the semantic information attached to the links as discussed earlier. When the query is executed the semantic information are compared with the conceptual graphs of the web site, and it can return the multiple web sites in a single run of the query. Thus, it can retrieve much more results as it also returns partial matches.

6 Conclusions

A new type of hyperlink (Dynamic and Active HyperLink) called DHL has been introduced in this Article. The DHL work through a DHL-Processor (DHLP), which has the capability of syntactic and semantic partial matching. The semantic description of the Web sites is represented in conceptual graphs. Unlike current hyperlinks, DHL can show multiple destination Web sites. Internet users cannot receive any help with current hyperlinks if the pre-defined designated Web sites are down. However, we can retrieve relevant Web sites with DHL even in case of some of the possible destination Web sites were down. The properties of DHL can increase the usability of the Internet considerably. The DHLP is reliable and can handle a large number of graphs easily since it uses a commercial DBMS. Also, the DHLP can be used as basic conceptual graph retrieval engine for many different applications such web warehouse discussed in the paper.

References

[1] Bhowmick, S., Madria, S. and W. K. NG, Wed Data Management: A Warehouse Approach, Springer-verlag, pp. 1-459, 2003

[2] Berners-Lee, T. Semantic Web Road map. http://www.w3.org/DesignIssues /Semantic. html

[3] Berners-Lee, T., D. Conoly, R. Swick. Senmantic Web. http://www.w3.org/1999/04/ WebData.html

[4] Brickley, D. & Guha, R. Resource Description Framework (RDF) Schema Specification, W3C (World-Wide Web Consortium). At http//www.w3.org/TR/ 1999/ PR-rdf-schema-19990303, 1999.

[5] Corby, O., R. Dieng, and C. Hebert. A Conceptual Graph Model for W3C Resource Description Framework, Proceedings of the ICCS'00, Darmstadt, LNAI1867, 2000.

[6] Lassila, O. & Swick, R. Resource Description Framework (RDF) Model and Syntax. W3C (World-Wide Web Consortium). At http//www.w3.org/TR/1999/REC-rdf-syntax-19990222

[7] Mayaeng, H., et al. Conceptual graph matching: a flexible algorithm and experiments, Journal of experimental and theoretical artificial intelligence, Vol 4, 1992.

[9] Poole, J., J.A. Campbell. A novel algorithm for matching conceptual and related graphs, Conceptual structures : applications, implementation and theory, Eds. G. Ellis et al., New York, (LNAI 954). 1995.

[10] Sowa, J. Conceptual Structure: Information Processing in Mind and Machine, Addison Wesley, Massachusetts, 1994.

[11] Yang, G-C., Y. Choi, & J. Oh. CGMA : A novel conceptual graph matching algorithm, Conceptual structures : theory and implementation, Eds. H.D. Pfeiffer, T.E. Nagle, New York, (LNAI 754), 1993.

[12] http://www.bestweb.net/~sowa/cg/cgdpans.htm#Header_21.

[13] http://www.bestweb.net/%7Esowa/cg/cgdpans.htm

[14] http://www.cs.umd.edu/projects/plus/SHOE/search/

User-Class Based Service Acceptance Policy Using Cluster Analysis

Hea-Sook Park[1], Yan-Ha[1], Soon-Mi Lee[1],
Young-Whan Park[2], and Doo-Kwon Baik[3]

[1] Dept. of Computer & Information Technology, Kyungin Womens's College, 548-4 Gyesan-dong, Gyeyang-gu, Incheon 407-740 Korea
{edpsphs, white, leesm}@kic.ac.kr
[2] Dept. of Computer Science, Hansung University, Seoul, Korea
yhpark@hansung.ac.kr
[3] Dept. of Computer Science Technology, Korea University, Seoul, Korea
baik@software.korea.ac.kr

Abstract. This paper suggests a new policy for consolidating a company's profits by segregating the clients using the contents service and allocating the media server's resources distinctively by clusters using the cluster analysis method of CRM, which is mainly applied to marketing. For the realization of a new service policy, this paper analyzes the level of contribution vis-à-vis the clients' service and profits through the cluster analysis of clients' data applying the K-Means Method. Clients were grouped into 4 clusters according to the contribution level in terms of profits. In addition, to evaluate the efficiency of CRFS within the Client/Server environment, the acceptance rate per class was determined. The results of the experiment showed that the application of CRFS led to the growth of the acceptance rate of clients belonging to the cluster as well as the significant increase in the profits of the company.

1 Introduction

1.1 Background

Given the recent development of the network/Internet technology, the scale of the multimedia contents service market (entertainment, education, etc) has expanded considerably. Obstacles such as service rejection, cutoffs, unstable connection, frequent buffering have been resolved through effective admission control, resource allocation methods, and development of H/W and Internet technology. As a result, the number of clients utilizing multimedia contents services has increased, and the market scale has expanded, thereby resulting in a fiercer competition between corporations.

Currently, it is necessary to develop highly profitable contents and system management methods that will ensure more stable profits to improve competitiveness between corporations. In particular, corporations need to increase the number of ways of utilizing the current system resources to sustain the clients'

R.K. Ghosh and H. Mohanty (Eds.): ICDCIT 2004, LNCS 3347, pp. 237–242, 2004.

satisfaction, pleasure, and usefulness as well as the corporations' demands, thus leading to profits. This is because considerable expenses are necessary in setting up and maintaining a system for the contents service business. This paper aims to provide a CRM basis for contents service through client segmentation based on a corporation's profitability. This is because existing service policies provide all clients with the same connection opportunities, offering service with the same quality after connection.

The rest of this paper is organized as follows: Part 2 covers the existing differentiated service control policies and differentiated resource allocation methods from the market's viewpoint as well as the exact definition and various methods of CRM, Part 3 presents the structure of CRFS, Part 4 covers the experiment and analysis of results by applying the corporation's client data for CRFS efficiency evaluation, Part 5 presents the conclusion.

2 Related Studies

This paper is related to the differentiated service control policy and to the fields of authorization control and CRM.

2.1 Research on a Differentiated Control Model

[1] suggested that it is impossible to maintain a stable service quality and a usage state that will guarantee the transfer band in terms of business, because the current Internet technology is generally provided in its "best effort" format.

Although service models such as Diffserv and Intserv have been suggested to resolve such problems, their application has been found to be difficult. The next-generation Internet will require the accommodation of a new business model alongside the existing features as well as techniques for controlling the clients' service demands. In particular, utilizing the network resources effectively for multimedia contents services is a very important issue, hence the need to divide the class of service according to the different service characteristics (data, sound, audio, and video/broadcast services). This approach manages resource and QoS allocation optimally so that the total utility of the system is maximized through the atonements process, in which operation markets for each resource is done separately.

2.2 CRM (Client Relationship Management)

CRM is a strategy for increasing a corporation's profits by providing better service to the clients and efficiently managing interactions with clients to provide the corporation's top clients with a more effective, personalized service and allocate resources effectively [2]. As a matter of fact, manufacturers, medical service providers, and telecommunications providers are already applying CRM to business management to avoid losing clients and increase profitability.

Client segmentation [3], [4], [5] refers to the process of classifying the many clients into similar groups of consumers. Classifying the clients according to gender, age, profession, etc., is also considered a segmentation operation. Segmentation enables viewing the entire database in a single picture, thus allowing the corporation to treat clients differently according to class and to pursue marketing that is suitable to each class. Most of the segmentation methods use decision tree, cluster analysis, and neural network.

3 CRFS (Client Request Filtering System)

3.1 Architecture of CRFS

The proposed CRFS operates the contribution value of the visiting clients in terms of profitability within the web server. It is split into two major areas: yielding the relevant class and allocating media server resources according to class. Unlike the admission control that operates on the media server, CRFS is designed to operate within the web server for convenience. CRFS is composed of the Client Segmentation Manager, Client Request Filter, Resource Monitoring Manager, Client Information Manager, and Service Provider. Fig. 1 shows the architecture of CRFS.

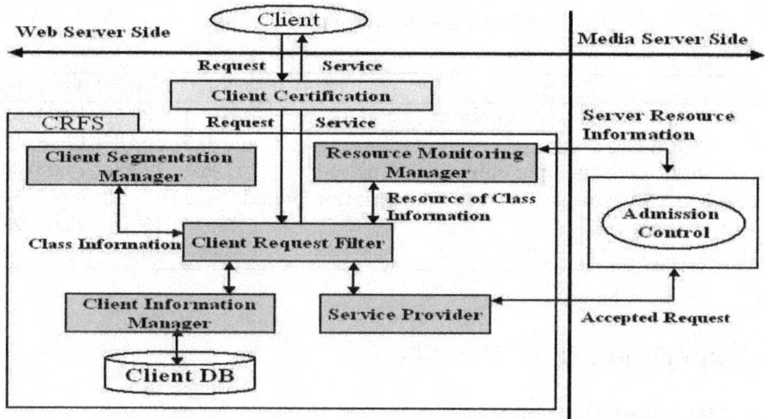

Fig. 1. Architecture of CRFS

The Client Segmentation Manager executes segmentation periodically using the data saved to the client's database. It applies the data of the client's service frequency during the analysis period, period of service usage, expenses, etc.. The number and type of class as well as the percentage of clients per class are yielded as the result of segmentation. Such data are transferred to the Resource Monitoring Manager through the Client Request Filter. The Client Information Manager yields the service requesting for the client's contribution value as requested by the Client Request Filter. The average service time during the website visit, average service time during the signup period, and percentage of client revenues from the total revenues are used to yield the contribution value. The Resource Monitoring Manager monitors the media server resource status and transfers the necessary information related to the request made by the Client Request Filter.

3.2 Client Segmentation

The Client Segmentation Manager analyzes the client's data saved to the database by applying the K-Means Method for the purpose of segmentation [6], [7], [8]. The client's general characteristics (name, gender, residence), service characteristics (service type, date of subscription, interest fields), and service use pattern (total number of visits to the website, service type, service use time, total payment, average service use time, service payment per website visit) are analyzed.

The Resource Monitoring Manager allots the media server resources according to class using the segmentation results. Here, the resource becomes the number of streams allowed by the media server, thus, it is allocated according to the percentage per class within the total profit. The Client Information Manager calculates the contribution value to determine which class does the client who requested for the service belongs. In this paper, the method of references [9], [10] was applied to calculate the contribution value.

Table 1. Segmentation of Clients

Class	First	Second	Third	Fourth
Total number of visits to the website	338.4	228.5	105.4	52.5
Service use days	320.5	202.3	120.8	170.5
Average service use time per subscription period	196.8	120.3	74.0	38.7
Average service payment (USD) per subscription period	281.25	177.83	89.47	54.16
Number of clients (%)	9.8	15.3	46.5	28.4
Profits rate (%)	48.7	30.8	15.5	5.0

4 Experiment and Results

4.1 Design of Experiment

To verify the capabilities of CRFS as suggested in this paper, a comparative evaluation was performed on the acceptance rate per class before and after applying CRFS within the Client/Server environment. The experiment aimed to increase the corporation's profits through an increase in the higher class acceptance.

The subject of this paper is a contents service corporation called iteaching (www.iteaching.co.kr). This corporation provides educational contents and generates annual revenues of USD1.2 million and has about 50,000 clients. A total of 6,000 clients' records in 2003 were used in the analysis. To analyze the data, the segmentation analysis tool, SAS's Enterprise Miner 4.0, was used. Out of the yearly clients' data, the subscription period, total number of visits to the website, service type, service use time, payments, average service time, and average service payment were analyzed for segmentation.

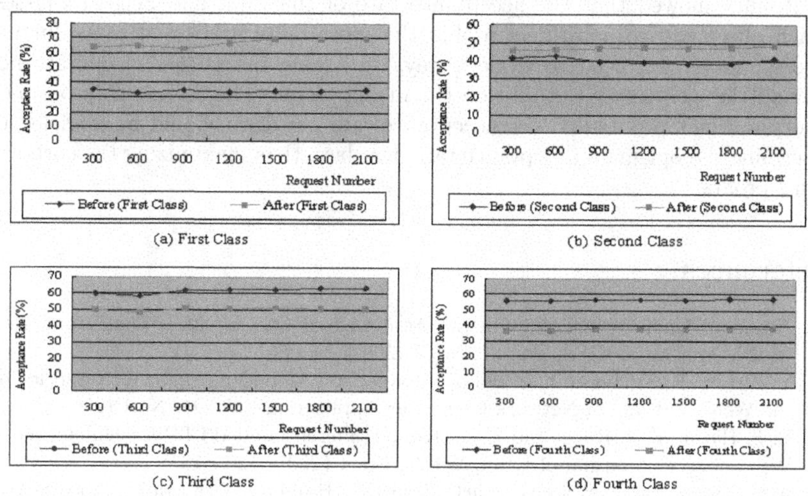

Fig. 2. Acceptance Rate Before and After Applying CRFS

4.2 Acceptance Rate Evaluation by Class Before and After Applying CRFS

Fig. 2 shows the results of the experiment. The acceptance rate per class (First, Second, Third, Fourth Classes) before and after applying CRFS was derived within the Client/Server environment. The results of the analysis revealed several findings. Fig. 2(a) presents the comparison of the acceptance rate of clients belonging to First Class before and after applying CRFS. On the other hand, Fig. 2(b) shows the comparison of the acceptance rate of clients belonging to Second Class before and after applying CRFS. Fig. 2(c) represents the comparison of the acceptance rate of clients in Third Class before and after applying CRFS. Since Third Class has the highest number of clients, the acceptance rate before the CRFS application was 61.54%, decreasing to 50.46% after the CRFS application. Finally, Fig. 2(d) shows the comparison of the acceptance rate of clients in Fourth Class before and after applying CRFS.

5 Conclusion

This paper proposed the system for controlling clients' service requests using the CRM policy of multimedia contents service through client segmentation, based on a corporation's profitability. Thus, clients with higher profitability will have more chances of accessing media server resources. In addition, experiment was conducted to evaluate the performance of the algorithm. The experiment evaluated the acceptance rate per class before and after applying the CRFS.

Results showed that the acceptance rate of the First and Second Classes, which affect the corporation's profits the most, improved greatly. As further studies, there is a need to explore ways to enable the CRFS to operate not only on the web server but also on the media server. The relationship between a corporation's profits and the acceptance rate per class should be modeled to determine the optimum acceptance rate per class, thus maximizing the corporation's profits.

References

1. Jun-kyun Choi, "Technology of the Assurance of QoS for Next Generation Network", Journal of KISS, Vol. 21, No. 8 (2003) 51 - 66
2. Y. J. Lee, E. S. Hyun, T. Y. Kim, "Connection Management for QoS Service on the Web", Journal of Network Computer Applications, Vol.25. No.1 (2002)
3. E. S. Hyun, Y. J. Rhee, and T. Y. Kim, "Differentiated-HTTP for Differentiated Web Ser-vice", Journal of KISS, Vol.28, No. 1 (2001) 126 - 135
4. Alex Berson, Stephen Smith, Kurt Thearing, "Building Data Mining Applications for CRM", McGraw-Hill, 4 - 14, ISBN 0-07-134444-6
5. W. Kamakula, "A Least Squares Procedure for Benefit Segmentation with Conjoint Experi-ments", Journal of Marketng Research (1998) 157 - 167
6. Kye-sun An, Se-Jin Go, Jun Jiong, Phill-Kue, Rhee, "Generator of Dynamic User Profiles Based on Web Usage Mining", Journal of Korea Information Processing Society, Vol.9-B, No.4 (2002) 389 - 398
7. M. Wedel, W. Kamakula, "Market Segmentation: Conceptual and Methodological Founda-tion", Kluwer Academic Publisher (2000)
8. Tae Hyup Roh, Ingoo Han, "Customer Relationship Management Under the Environment of Internet Business", Telecommunications Review, Vol.12, No.1 (2002) 50 - 60
9. Sang-Hee Rou, Su-Kyung Baik, "Market Segmentation of the Clients for CRM of Health Service", Journal of Health Care Marketing, Vol.3 (2002) 22 - 34
10. Hea-Sook Park, Yan-Ha, Soon-Mi Lee, "A User Class-based Service Filtering Policy for QoS Assurance", Journal of KISS: Computing Practices, Vol. 10, No. 4 (2004) 293 - 298

Tools and Techniques for Multi-site Software Development

Satish Chandra

IBM India Research Lab, New Delhi, India
satishchandra@in.ibm.com

Abstract. Business reasons are increasingly causing software development projects to be distributed across the globe. However, software development tools and techniques in use today largely ignore the needs of distributed software development. At IBM India Research Lab, we have been looking at global software development practices to understand problem areas and propose solutions that could be of help. In the first part of this talk, I will chalk out a broad agenda for research in software engineering in aid of multi-site software development. The areas that we will consider are requirements management, application knowledge management, project dashboarding, and software quality assurance. I will touch upon various research efforts at IBM Research and elsewhere in these areas.

In the second part of the talk, I will describe our recent work in multi-site requirements management. Among the many challenges that arise in multi-site development, precise communication and management of requirements appears to be of immense importance. This particular challenge arises in the need for collaboration between the analysts and the systems engineers in mapping business requirements to system requirements, for communication between systems engineers and testers to create test cases for requirements, for coordination between the customer, analyst, developers and testers during requirement changes, and so on. Remoteness and time-zone differences strain each part of this scenario, leading to excessive re-work, delays and cost escalations. We are building a tool for multi-site requirements management. The salient features of this tool include views into the requirements and traceability information, synchronous as well as asynchronous communication facilities integrated in the views to enable in context communication; assisted change management; search on persisted communication and change logs; and visual clues to provide a heightened sense of awareness, indicating which stakeholders are online, which artifacts have pending notifications, current discussions etc.

This talk is based on joint work with Bikram Sengupta and Vibha S. Sinha of IBM India Research Lab.

R.K. Ghosh and H. Mohanty (Eds.): ICDCIT 2004, LNCS 3347, p. 243, 2004.

Specifying a Mobile Computing Infrastructure and Services

Satyajit Acharya[1,*,**], Chris George[2], and Hrushikesha Mohanty[1]

[1] Department of CIS, University of Hyderabad, Hyderabad - 500046, India
satyajit2k3@yahoo.com, hmcs@uohyd.ernet.in
[2] UNU/IIST, P.O. Box. 3058, Macao SAR, China
cwg@iist.unu.edu

Abstract. We present a model of a mobile computing application environment and its formal specification using the RAISE specification language. Special care is taken to specify the location based operations that are typical of mobile computing. In the process of specifying the mobile environment, we give precise semantics to different services identified with Mobichart notations, an extension to Objectcharts and Statecharts to make them suitable for graphical specification of mobile computing environment and applications. Thus we show the usability of both graphical and formal specification methods in development of mobile computing applications. We also discuss different techniques applied to detect faults and gain confidence in the correctness of the specification using consistency and confidence conditions, prototyping and testing.

Keywords: Mobile Computing, Specification, Mobicharts, Testing, RSL

1 Introduction

Mobile computing (henceforth MC) is a new paradigm characterized by the ability of computers to change location while still able to communicate with one another. Because of movement, frequent disconnections, power limitations, bandwidth restrictions, and limited local resources; MC represents a major point of departure from the traditional distributed computing paradigm and existing methods for distributed computing, including client/server computing, are not suitable to handle the typical issues (or challenges) raised by the MC environment [1, 2]. The challenges raised by the (independent) mobility of devices and applications in MC environment requires a rethinking of the classical distributed systems design techniques and these techniques need to be extended taking into

* Part of this work was carried out while the author was a visiting fellow at United Nations University, International Institute for Software Technology (UNU/IIST), Macao SAR, China.

** The author is supported by the CSIR SRF Fellowship under the grant number 9/414(587)/2k3/EMR-I.

R.K. Ghosh and H. Mohanty (Eds.): ICDCIT 2004, LNCS 3347, pp. 244–254, 2004.

account these new challenges. Design of an application has to be sensitized so that it copes up to these challenges and generic solutions should be available (with the infrastructure as *services*) to the developer for developing applications that can have seamless execution and consistent behavior.

In [3], we investigated the application of statecharts [4, 5] and objectcharts [6] to MC environments to find the insufficiency of these formalisms to expressively model MC applications. We extended the Objectchart notation to make it suitable for specifying typical features of MC environment and named it as Mobicharts [3, 7]. The Mobichart notation is capable of modelling generic services (called Mobichart services) like specifying object location, migration, hoarding, cloning, and disconnected operations. Its graphical specification style is intuitive for designers to comprehensively view the behavior of MC applications. But the notation, being graphical, does not provide precise semantics. Also, since execution of applications using the Mobichart services depends on the environment and its infrastructure, specifying these services in detail using Mobichart becomes cumbersome. That is why we have resorted to formal methods for expressing these services in detail. Having precise semantics of the Mobichart services is useful to reason about their validity, correctness and other characteristics. Once validated, application designers can make use of these services in building applications. Since specifying the environment is useful to understand its role in the execution of applications, in this paper, we present a model of an MC environment and its formal specification using the RAISE Specification Language (RSL)[8], a formal, modular, and typed specification language suitable for development of large and complex software systems.

In order to avoid errors in a later stages of system development, it is important to identify and specify the consistency conditions (henceforth CCs) during the initial stages. We discuss the importance of CCs and how these CCs help in finding logical errors in the specification. To gain confidence on the correctness of specification, we adopted techniques like manual inspection of the confidence conditions generated by an automatic tool provided by RSL [9] and testing the executable specification of a prototype by using test cases. Due to limitation of space, we only give a skeletal structure of the specification and discuss the observations made during testing. Readers may refer to [10] (available at [11]) for the detailed specification and discussions on testing methods.

In Section 2, after a brief on the entities involved in an MC environment and the characteristics of applications in this environment, a model of the environment and its RSL specification is given. A brief summary of the Mobichart notation with an example is presented in Section 3. Here, some remarks on the overall RSL specification of the environment and the Mobichart services are also provided. Section 4 describes different techniques we used to gain confidence on the correctness of the specification. The paper concludes with Section 5.

2 Modelling MC Environment

The class diagram that depicts the structure of an MC environment is given in Fig. 1. The environment includes Mobile Support Stations (MSSs) and Mobile Hosts (MHs). Each MSS is responsible for managing a number of MHs in a geographic location called a *cell.* A set of MHs may be present in an MSS's cell. Such an association is given by the link 'Has residing MHs'. In a system, each MSS acts as the Base MSS for a number of MHs and each MH has one MSS as its Base MSS. This is represented in the diagram as a link 'Has MHs as Base'. An MSS is responsible for the authentication information for all the MHs for which it acts as the Base MSS.

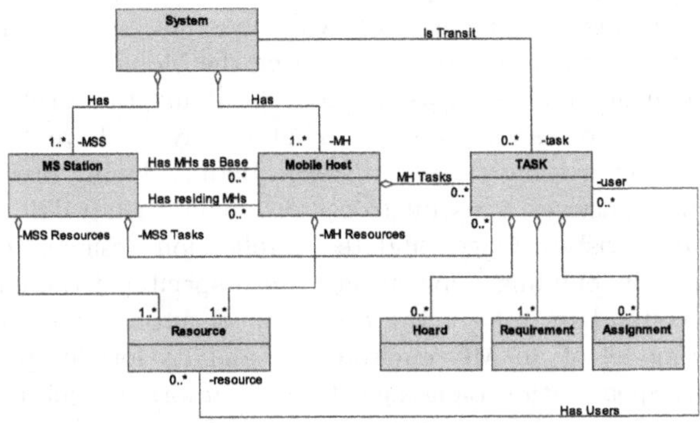

Fig. 1. Class Diagram for MC Environment Specifications

Class **System** consists of all the MHs and MSSs in the system. The system is modelled as a record type `System` given below. The subtype `Sys` is defined with the auxiliary function `consistent` to ensure the well-formedness of the system by specifying certain consistency conditions.

type
  System ::
    msss : M.MSSs ↔ change_mss
    mhs : H.Mhs ↔ change_mh
    task : TS.TASKs ↔ change_task
    res : RS.Resource ↔ change_res,
  Sys = {| s : System • consistent(s) |}

Here, *msss*, *mhs* and *task* represent all the MSSs, MHs and tasks present in the system. Some of these tasks may be running in the MSSs and some others in the MHs. Also, some of them may be in the 'Transit' state [3, 7] and hence do not belong to any MH nor to any MSS but are present in the network (being routed to its destination during migration). This is represented in Fig. 1 as a link between **TASK** and **System.** *res* represents all resources present in the system, i.e. the collection of every resource located at different devices

(MSSs and MHs) in the system. The Class **Mobile Host** consists of a number of tasks and resources. The attributes of the class represents different components of an MH, as given below. Here, *device* represents the device identifier for an MH and *baseMSSid* represents the MSS that acts as the Base station for the MH. *is_active* represents the state of an MH. When *active*, an MH is running some tasks. When the MH does not have any task to run, it goes to 'doze' mode ('`is_active`' is *false*) to save its battery. The fields *tasks* and *resources* represent the set of running tasks and the set of resources *present* in an MH, respectively.

type
  MHost ::
    device : Dev_id
    self : MH_id
    baseMSSid : MSS_id
    is_active : **Bool** $\leftrightarrow$ changeStatus
    location : MH_loc $\leftrightarrow$ changeLoc
    tasks : TSK.TASKs $\leftrightarrow$ changeTasks
    resources : R.Resource $\leftrightarrow$ changeRes

The field *location* gives the current physical (geographic) location of an MH. It is of variant type `MH_loc` i.e. `MH_loc` == `nilL` | `mhloc(l : Location)`. An MH can either be connected to an MSS or it is disconnected. When connected, an MH belongs to the cell for which the MSS is responsible and its location is determined (or inherited) from the `location` value of the MSS. When disconnected, the location of an MH can not be determined and hence its *location* is `nilL`. Items `location` and `device` serve as the values for the container handle variables of the Mobichart notation [3, 7].

Class **TASK** is the aggregation of classes **Hoard**, **Requirement** and **Assignment**. Class **Hoard** represents the items to be hoarded by a task and the locations from where these items have to be hoarded. A task may require different kinds of resources to do its computation and this is modelled by the class **Requirement**. Also, a task may have been assigned a number of resources (possibly from different devices/locations) and this is represented by **Assignment**.

type
  Task_info ::
    taskReqment : RB.RBag $\leftrightarrow$ changeReqments
    assigned : ASIGN.R_assign $\leftrightarrow$ changeAssigned
    hoardList : HL.Hoard $\leftrightarrow$ changeHrdList
    is_transit : **Bool** $\leftrightarrow$ changeStatus
    is_active : **Bool** $\leftrightarrow$ changeActive

Class **Resource** represents a resource in the system and is specified below.

type
R_info ::
kind : R_kind ↔ changeKind
resVal : R_val ↔ changeVal
loc : R_loc ↔ changeLoc
users : T_id-**set** ↔ change_users
is_hoarded : **Bool** ↔ hoardStatus

Here, *kind* represents the kind of a resource. A resource can be of different kinds viz. R_kind == prn | cpu | mem | db | buf | var | file. *resVal* stores the state information of a resource, e.g. files, variables, databases and buffers may have values which can be updated. *loc* represents the resource location (an MH or an MSS). Each resource may have some tasks as its *users*. If the resource is not sharable, then at most one task can use it, else, a set of tasks can share the resource. Since a resource can be shared by a number of tasks and a task can use multiple resources, we have shown in Fig. 1, the many-many link between **TASK** and **Resource**.

3 Formal Specification of Mobichart Services

Mobicharts have extended Objectcharts with the following additions [7, 10]:

Container (Handle): Each state of a task is associated with its operating environment called its *container*. It is used to represent the (location and device) ambients of a task. Containers in Mobicharts enable us to model the physical location of a task by the variable `Loc` and the device containing the task by `Device id`. Thus, *containers* in Mobicharts enable us to model the states of a task at a particular location.

Transit State: A special state designated as *transit* (drawn in dotted lines), is inserted between every two states, between which a task can be disconnected. In this state, a task belongs neither to any MH nor any MSS, but it is being routed on the network to its destination during migration.

Inheritance: When a task joins a new container, all variables qualified with the keyword *inherit* in the task are automatically updated with values of corresponding variables in the container. There is a requirement on a system that there is a collection of inheritable variables that must be defined for all devices and only such variables can be qualified by *inherit*.

Apart from these extensions, different services like migration, cloning, hoarding, sharing have been identified as essential services that are required by the tasks to adapt to typical environmental situations [3]. We take the migration service as an example and explain its descriptive semantics.

Task migration across different hosts and/or MSSs may take place to perform some action in the environment. This requires that a task must be able to save its state prior to migration, and resurrect as a new task with a predetermined state at a new location. The migration behavior of a mobile task

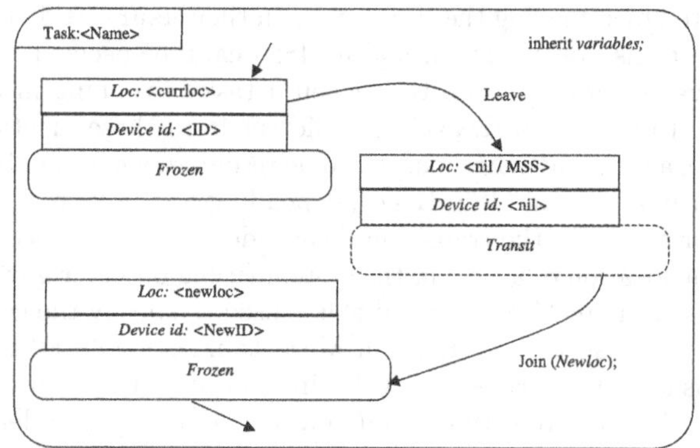

Fig. 2. Migration Behavior of a Mobile Task

is depicted in Fig. 2. In 'Active' state, a task in a device does its computations using local resources from the device and/or remote resources from the network. Before a task migrates, the resources that are used by it are released and the task is 'Frozen' by saving its state. Then it is transmitted to the destination by taking the transition 'Leave'. During migration, a task is in 'Transit' state which represents a task in transition from its source device to a destination device. During this transition, it may be necessary to route a task through different MSSs in the network. When a task is being moved from one device to another, the *Loc* variable in its *container* handle is <nil>. And, when a task is at an intermediate MSS (enroute to its destination) of the fixed network, the *Loc* variable assumes the identity of this MSS. When a task arrives at its destination, the transition 'Join(Newloc)' is taken. Upon joining the new location, a task goes to 'Frozen' state and updates the variables in the container by inheriting the corresponding values from the new device. As shown in the figure, the container after migration has been changed to (*Loc:*<newloc>, *Device id:*<NewID>). Apart from automatic inheritance of the values of container variables, values of other user defined variables qualified with the keyword 'inherit' are inherited by their corresponding values from the new device. After the end of migration, a frozen task can be reactivated at its new location and the required resources may be acquired from the new device.

Service related activities are modelled in terms of events and actions that can be pictorially shown in a Mobichart. With respect to a service, Mobichart shows events, corresponding states and their transitions. For example, consider the transition 'Leave' in Fig. 2. If a task is running in an MSS, this transition causes the task to go from the 'Frozen' state to the 'Transit' state. In 'Transit' state, a task does not hold or use any resources from the host device. So, before a task goes to 'Transit' state, all resources assigned to the task from the MSS are released from the task's assignment and the corresponding resources at the

MSS are updated by removing the task entries in their `users` field. These actions (related to the transition 'Leave' from an MSS) can be specified by a function (e.g. `taskLeaveMSS` below). Note that when a task is running in an MH, the actions related to transition 'Leave' are different from those mentioned above. This is because, a task may have hoarded some resources when running in an MH but not when running in an MSS. Hence, depending on the current location of a task (an MH or an MSS), the transition 'Leave' does its actions accordingly. So, we first find the location of a task in the system (using observer `getTaskLoc`). If the task is present in an MH, `taskLeaveMH` is used to specify the corresponding actions and if the task is present in an MSS, `taskLeaveMSS` is used. When a task (in 'Transit' state) arrives at its destination after the migration, it joins the device by using the transition 'Join(Newloc)'. Here, `Newloc` determines the destination of the task (either an MH or an MSS).

taskleave : T_id × Sys $\stackrel{\sim}{\to}$ Sys
taskleave(t, sys) ≡
  let tskLoc = getTaskLoc(t, sys) **in**
    case tskLoc **of**
      mh_loc(mh) → taskLeaveMH(t, mh, sys),
      mss_loc(ms) → taskLeaveMSS(t, ms, sys)
    end /* CASE */
  end /* let */
pre t ∈ task(sys) ∧ ∼ TS.is_in_transit(t, task(sys)),

We give few remarks about the overall specification for the MC environment and the Mobichart services. A total of 13 modules were written. These modules contained a total of 210 functions (97 generators, 68 observers and 45 functions representing the CCs). The total size of the specification was approx. 3200 lines (including comments, around 20%). For specifying the Mobichart services, we used 16 functions to represent different states (6 functions) and transitions (10 functions) between these states. The CCs found at various levels of the specification helped us to detect some potential conceptual errors.

4 Ensuring the Correctness of Specification

There are various ways by which one can gain confidence on the correctness of specifications viz. validation, verification and formal proof. It is also possible to use formal methods without formal proof, and such use of formal method is sometimes called "lightweight" [8]. We adopted this approach and used various techniques (like specification inspection, prototyping and testing) to increase the confidence in the specification as explained below.

4.1 Consistency Conditions

Consistency refers to situations where specification of a system contains no internal (logical) contradictions. There is a useful slogan, "*No Loss, No Confusion*", related to consistency. CCs try to ensure that there is neither any loss of information (*No Loss*) nor any confusion between various components in a system during its operation *No Confusion.* The effects of loss of information may not be immediately apparent, but they may have devastating effects on the system in the long run. Also, when such an inconsistency is detected later, it may be difficult to find its cause. *No Confusion* means that a system does not do any operation that leads to disparity in information at different parts of the system.

While designing a system, a designer can view it from two perspectives. First, each operation on a system changes the state of the system (*Change Perspective*). A designer tries to make sure that such changes comply with the requirements of the system (provided by the use cases). Second, almost every system has a set of properties (called invariants or CCs) that should not change during the system's lifetime (*Invariants Perspective*). So, every operation on the system should preserve these invariants. Using these two perspectives together helps a designer to identify and deal with problems during design. An operation may give the results expected from it, but, apart from that, the operation may also have some side effects on the system that violates its invariants. The CCs help a designer to find and avoid such side effects.

While specifying the mobile environment, we found 45 different CCs at various levels of the specification. Out of these, 12 CCs were found at the system level. These CCs are to be satisfied (maintained) prior to, during, and subsequent to the actions of Mobichart services. We think of a mobile task as a composition of a set of Mobichart services that conforms to the system level CCs. A task is well behaved if the Mobichart actions taken by the task preserve the consistency of the system. An example of a CC is that every MH in the system must have an MSS in the system as its base, and that MSS must record the MH as belonging to it (which is modelled as the MH's identifier being in the set `mhsAsBASEMSS` for that MSS). Readers will find all the CCs specified in the full report [10].

```
baseCons : System → Bool
baseCons(sys) ≡
    (∀ h : MH_id • h ∈ mhs(sys) ⇒
        (∃ m : MSS_id • m ∈ msss(sys) ∧
            H.HS.baseMSSid(mhs(sys)(h)) = m)) ∧
                h ∈ M.MS.mhsAsBASEMSS(msss(sys)(m)),
```

4.2 Inspecting Confidence Conditions

Confidence conditions are conditions that should generally be true if an RSL module is not to be inconsistent, but that cannot in general be determined as true by a tool. The types of conditions that are generated by the confidence condition generator tool are given in [9]. While writing the specification, confidence conditions helped us to find errors, particularly when a function was applied without considering its preconditions. We inspected the generated (a total of 859) confidence conditions and believe them all to hold. Note that consistency conditions that are expressed as subtype conditions give rise to confidence conditions on the results of functions generating values in the subtypes, and this helps to identify the functions that need careful inspection.

Consistency conditions can (optionally) be translated, so the testing we describe below gave us further assurance that they are in fact satisfied.

4.3 Prototyping and Testing

To generate and run the test cases, we prototyped the system specification by doing a simplified refinement of all the abstract types in it. We then used the RSL to SML translator provided by the RAISE tools [9] to run some test cases. We used the bottom-up testing strategy by first testing each lower level module in the specification and then testing the higher level modules. At least one test case was used to test each function in a module (function coverage). Some examples of test cases used to test the behavior of the function `taskleave` (page 250) are:

test_case
 [test1] init(); consistent(s), /*Result: true*/
  /*Testing `**taskleave**′ of Mobichart*/
 [test2] init(); consistent(taskleave(t1, s)), /*Result: true*/

The test case `[test1]` is used to ensure that initialization of the prototype of the system does not violate any CCs. After ensuring the consistency of initial state of the system, we use test case `[test2]` to call `taskleave` and ensure that the resulting state of the system is consistent. When this function is used, the task `t1` (initially present in an MSS `m1` in the protoype) is removed from MSS `m1` and goes to transit state.

Table 1. Faults found during Testing using 309 test cases. 'New CCs added' indicates the number of new CCs found necessary during testing. 'CCs Changed' gives the number of constraints changed in different CCs. Similarly, 'Functions Changed' indicates the number of functions (other than CCs) where we had to add new statements

Type of Change Made	No. of Changes
Typographic	8
New CCs Added	4
CCs Changed	5
Sequence of Function Calls	1
Functions Changed	10
TOTAL =	**28**

We used a total of 309 test cases on different modules and found 28 errors in the specification. Out of these errors, 8 were typographic (typo) errors and 20 were conceptual/logical errors. A typo is a discrepancy between author's intention and specification. Other errors (conceptual/logical) represent an inadequate or mistaken understanding of the problem. These are potentially more damaging than typos because they are less likely to be discovered during development. Table 1 summarizes the categories of changes made at different levels of specification to fix the errors during testing. Most of these errors were found because of the CCs. Results of some test cases did not give a consistent system. It implies that, if the CCs had not been taken into account, these conceptual errors would have gone unnoticed. It is also interesting to observe here that out of 20 conceptual errors, almost half of them are related to changes in the CCs. Detecting these types of faults in the specification is more useful, since they generally go unnoticed and the effects of such faults can be catastrophic during later stages of system development.

5 Conclusion

There have been efforts to specify this new computing paradigm in formal methods [12, 13, 14]. In this paper we have presented a model of a MC environment and discussed the behavior of applications in this environment. We also discussed the formal specification of the environment and the Mobichart notation and its services to support execution of applications in this environment. In the process of developing the specification, we thereby provide semantics to the Mobichart services. The importance of finding and specifying CCs in a specification is discussed. Different methods were used to gain confidence on the correctness of the specification, like confidence conditions, and specification-based testing using test cases. Some observations on the faults found during testing and their causes have been reported.

This work is a step towards the main objective of developing automated tools to support the process of application development in MC environment using Mobicharts and the semantics of the Mobichart services provided by the specification. We believe that the specification will help in generating such an automated supporting tool for the MC application developers. We also believe that the identified precondition for each operation would help in formulating some exception handlers during the development of such tools.

References

1. B.R.Badrinath et al. Impact of Mobility on Distributed Computation. *ACM SIGOS Operating System Review*, 27(2):15–20, February 1993.
2. G.H.Formen et al. The Challenges of Mobile Computing. *IEEE Computer*, 27(4):38–47, 1994.
3. S.Acharya, H.Mohanty, and R.K.Shyamasundar. MOBICHART: A Notation to Specify Mobile Computing Applications. In *Proc. of the 30th Hawaii International Conference on System Sciences (HICSS'03)*. IEEE, January 2003.
4. David Harel. Statecharts: A Visual Formalism for Complex Systems. *Science of Computer Programming*, 8:231–274, 1987.
5. David Harel and Amnon Naamad. The STATEMATE Semantics of Statechart. *ACM Trans. on Software Engg. & Method.*, 5(4):293–333, October 1996.
6. D.Coleman et al. Introducing Objectchart or How to Use Statecharts in Object-Oriented Design. *IEEE Trans. on Software Engg.*, 18(1):9–18, January 1992.

7. H.Mohanty, S.Acharya, R.K.Ghosh, and R.K.Shyamasundar. Mobichart for Modeling Mobile Computing Tasks. In *Convergent Technologies for the Asia-Pacific*, pages 193–197. IEEE TENCON, Bangalore, India, Oct. 14-17 2003.
8. Chris George. Introduction to RAISE. Technical Report 249, UNU/IIST, P.O. Box 3058, Macau, March 2002.
9. Chris George. RAISE Tools User Guide. Technical Report 227, UNU/IIST, P.O. Box 3058, Macau, February 2001.
10. Satyajit Acharya and Chris George. Specifying a Mobile Computing Application Environment using RSL. Technical Report 300, UNU/IIST, P.O. Box 3058, Macau, May 2004.
11. http://www.iist.unu.edu. UNU/IIST, P.O. Box 3058, Macau SAR, China.
12. L.Cardelli et al. Mobile Ambients. In *Foundation of Software Science & Computational Structures*, LNCS 1378, pages 140–155. Springer, 1998.
13. G.C.Roman et al. Mobile UNITY: Reasoning and Specification in Mobile Computing. *ACM Trans. on Software Engg. & Method.*, 6(3):250–282, July 1997.
14. Luca Cardelli. Abstractions for Mobile Computation. In *Security Issues for Distributed & Mobile Objects*, LNCS 1603, pages 51–99. Springer-Verlag, 1999.

Generating a Prototype from a UML Model of System Requirements

Xiaoshan Li[1], Zhiming Liu[2], Jifeng He[2], and Quan Long[2,3]

[1] Faculty of Science and Technology, University of Macau, Macao, China
xsl@umac.mo

[2] International Institute for Software Technology, United Nations University, Macao, China
{lzm, hjf, longquan}@iist.unu.edu

[3] Department of Informatics, School of Mathematical Sciences, Peking University, China

Abstract. We present a method for automatically generating a prototype from a UML model of system requirements that consists of a use-case model and a conceptual class model. The method is based on a formalization of UML in which a use case is formally specified by a pair of pre and post conditions in the context of a conceptual class model. To generate a prototype, we translate the pre and post conditions of a use case into a sequence of executable atomic actions. These actions are to create or delete an object, update an object, establish or remove a link between two objects with respect to an association. Such a prototype can be used to validate requirements and check system invariants. An automated prototype generator is developed in Java, and a simple library system is used as an example to illustrate the feasibility of the method.

Keywords: *Prototype, Requirements analysis, Formal Specification, Code Generation.*

1 Introduction

Early acquired requirements are difficult to validate without testing. Prototyping is efficient and effective to expose errors in the early stages of requirements analysis and design. The general purposes of building a prototype include [14, 2, 13, 15]

- to ensure that the designers and implementors understand requirements directly,
- to help to demonstrate to the customers for validating the requirements,
- to cope with changing requirements better,
- to be used for test planning.

This paper presents a method for automatically generating a prototype from a *model of system requirements* so that the extra development cost of prototyping can be avoided. A model of requirements consists of a *use-case model* (UCM) and a *conceptual class model* (CCM).

A UCM consists of a use case diagram and textual descriptions of use cases. However, a use case diagram provides only static information about use cases. The dynamic

R.K. Ghosh and H. Mohanty (Eds.): ICDCIT 2004, LNCS 3347, pp. 255–265, 2004.

semantic aspects are described in the textual descriptions as sequences of interactions between actors and the system. Therefore, formalizing and prototyping the requirements of a system should focus on the textual descriptions.

A CCM for an application is a class diagram consisting of *classes* (also called *concepts*), and *associations* between classes. A class represents a set of *conceptual objects* and an association determines how the objects in the associated classes are related (or *linked*). For example, we have two concepts **Publication** and **Copy** in a library system. They are associated so that a copy *is copy of* a publication. In addition to associations between concepts, a concept may have some *properties* represented by *attributes*, e.g., **User** has an attribute *uid*.

The correctness of a requirements model is validated in general by simulations with a prototype of the system. However, a prototype is usually a simplified version of the system with a smaller set of functionalities, but with design and implementation details [7, 15]. The framework presented in this paper supports the generation of prototypes for validating requirements without the need of going into the design. It also supports a fuller scale of prototyping, especially for these object database management functions. We believe this is more cost effective as it is only added as part of the requirements analysis, and its automation can even reduce the cost by making the requirements analysis more efficient and effective.

Outline of the Method. The method is based on a formalization of UML in which a use case is formally specified by a pair of pre and post conditions in the context of a conceptual class model. To generate a prototype, we translate the pre and post conditions of a use case into a sequence of executable atomic actions, as well as non side-effect queries [12, 13]. These actions are to create or delete an object, update an object, and build or remove a link between two objects with respect to an association. Such a prototype can be used to validate requirements and check system invariants which can be embedded into pre and post conditions. An automated prototype generator is developed in Java, and a simple library system is used as an example to illustrate the feasibility of the method.

Based on the formal semantics of a UCM and a CCM, a prototype is generated as follows: first generate a *system entity object database* (SEOD) from the semantics of the CCM, and then a system prototype interface which displays the buttons for the names of the use cases in the UCM (this can be generated from the use-case diagrams), and finally a use-case handler for each use case in the UCM that handles the execution of specification of the use case. A use case handler maps the executable parts of each use case in the UCM into a sequence of atomic actions on the SEOD. The framework architecture of generating prototype is shown in Figure 1.

The rest of this paper is organized as follows. Section 2 describes the formalization of UML models of requirements by using a simple library system as a case study. Section 3 focuses on the method to generate prototype from a UCM and a CCM. An automated prototype generator is designed to achieve this transformation. Consequently, the library prototype is generated automatically from the tool in Java in section 4. Finally, Section 5 discusses some problems and future work.

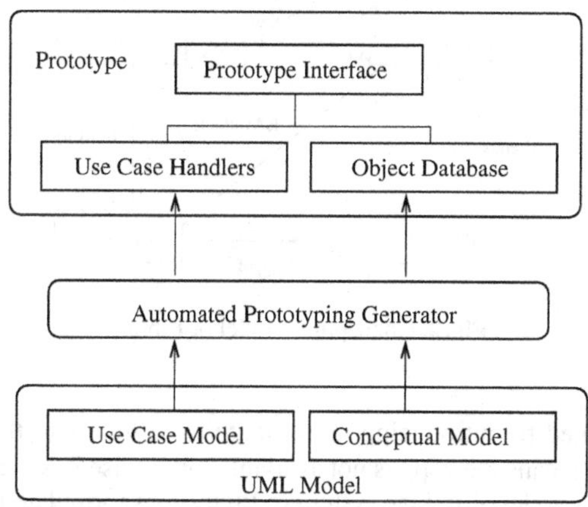

Fig. 1. Architecture of generating prototype

2 Formal Requirement Model of a Library System

We use a library system to describe how we can formally specify CCM and UCM in the formal theory of Hoare and He in [4]. Due to the limitation of pages, for more details about the formal semantics of UML and formal specification of the library case study, please refer to [8, 10].

A Library System. The system provides the services for the librarians of a library. Librarians maintain a catalogue of publications which are available for lending to users. There may be many copies of the same publication. Publications and copies may be added to and removed from the library. Registered users can borrow the available copies in the library. When a copy has been borrowed by a user, it is on loan and is not available for lending to other users. When a copy is returned, it should be available to all users again after deleting the corresponding lending loan.

From above informal description of system requirements, the following use cases can be identified in the system. Librarian maintains the library, such as add and remove publication, copy, and user. And a librarian lends a copy to a user. A user returns a copy.

After analyzing the system, a CCM of the library can be created and it is shown in Figure 2 for realizing the system use cases **AddUser, AddCopy, AddPublication, RemoveUser, RemoveCopy, RemovePublication, LendCopy,** and **ReturnCopy**.

A system state is an object diagram which is the instance or snapshot of system's CCM at a time. A use case is a system operation which can transfer from a pre-state to a post-state. We assume that each class **C** defines a type, also denoted by **C**, of elements similar to records, and allow the construction of a type from the direct product of two types, and the power set $\mathbb{P}(\mathrm{T})$ of a type **T**. For each class **C** and association **A** in CCM, we use global variables C and A to express the current exiting objects of class **C** and links of association **A**.

For simplification, we omit the many-to-many association $IsLendableto$ by assuming any user is allowed to borrow any publication. And association $IsAvailable$ in

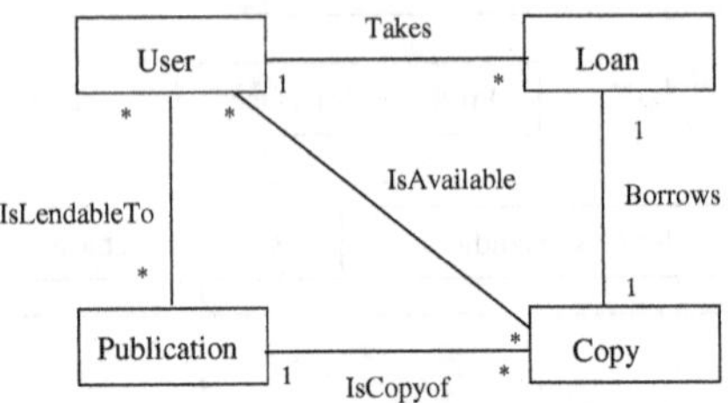

Fig. 2. Conceptual Model of Library

CCM is implemented by introducing an attribute $available$ into the class **Copy**, i.e. $availabe = false$ means the copy is not available; otherwise it is available to any user.

The conceptual model of library system in Figure 2 is formulated as follows:

$$\begin{aligned}
\mathbf{CName} &= \{\mathbf{User}, \mathbf{Loan}, \mathbf{Copy}, \mathbf{Publication}\};\\
\mathbf{attr(User)} &= \{< uid : \mathbf{String} >\};\\
\mathbf{attr(Loan)} &= \{< lid : \mathbf{String} >\};\\
\mathbf{attr(Copy)} &= \{< cid : \mathbf{String} >, < available : \mathbf{B} >\};\\
\mathbf{attr(Publication)} &= \{< pid : \mathbf{String} >, < author : \mathbf{String} >\};\\
\mathbf{AVar} = \{&Takes : \mathbb{P}(\mathbf{User} \times \mathbf{Loan}), Borrows : \mathbb{P}(\mathbf{Loan} \times \mathbf{Copy}),\\
&IsCopyof : \mathbb{P}(\mathbf{Copy} \times \mathbf{Publication})\};\\
\mathbf{CVar} = \{&User : \mathbb{P}(\mathbf{User}), Copy : \mathbb{P}(\mathbf{Copy}), Loan : \mathbb{P}(\mathbf{Loan}),\\
&Publication : \mathbb{P}(\mathbf{Publication})\}
\end{aligned}$$

Therefore, variables in $CVar$ and $AVar$ should be defined as global variables in the prototype system. We also assume initial conditions for these variables before the system carries out any use cases. For above CCM of library system, we have

$$\begin{aligned}
&\mathbb{P}\mathbf{User}\ User = \varnothing;\ \mathbb{P}\mathbf{Copy}\ Copy = \varnothing;\ \mathbb{P}\mathbf{Loan}\ Loan = \varnothing;\\
&\mathbb{P}\mathbf{Publication}\ Publication = \varnothing;\ \mathbb{P}\mathbf{IsCopyof}\ IsCopyof = \varnothing;\\
&\mathbb{P}\mathbf{Takes}\ Takes = \varnothing;\ \mathbb{P}\mathbf{Borrows}\ Borrows = \varnothing
\end{aligned}$$

Use Cases. Informal identifying and describing use cases is important for establishing the CCM [6]. However, formal specification of use cases depends on specification of CCM. We propose a *canonical form* for the specification of a UCM by introducing a *use-case handler* (UCH) for each use case[1]. This class encapsulates the classes and associations of the CCM, and it declares each *system operation* [6, 9] of the use case as a method in the form

$$\begin{aligned}
op \overset{def}{=}\ &\mathbf{pvar}\ x :\ \mathbf{T}_1;\ \mathbf{rvar}\ y : \mathbf{T}_2\\
&\mathbf{Pre} :\ p\\
&\mathbf{Post} :\ R
\end{aligned}$$

where **pvar** and **rvar** declare the value parameter(s) and the result parameter(s). This method was also used by B. Meyer [11], called *design by contract.*

At any time during the execution, this class will only have a single instance. Some methods in the UCH class of the library system are specified as follows.

[1] This is suggested by the *facade controller pattern.*

Use Case AddCopy. Use case $AddCopy$ adds a new copy of a publication to the library after its corresponding publication has already been created. If there is not the corresponding publication of the new copy, we should first call use case $AddPublication$ to create the publication, and then carry out $AddCopy$. The use case $AddCopy$ is therefore defined as follows:

$$\begin{array}{l} AddCopy \stackrel{def}{=} \textbf{pvar}\ c : \textbf{Copy}, p : \textbf{Publication}; \\ \textbf{Pre}\ :\ c \notin Copy \wedge p \in Publication \\ \textbf{Post} :\ Copy' = Copy \cup \{c\} \wedge c.available' = true \\ \qquad \wedge\ IsCopyof' = IsCopyof \cup \{< c, p >\} \end{array}$$

Use Case LendCopy. This use case is about how the library lends a copy of a publication to a user. Obviously, a user u and a copy c are participants in this action, and a loan ℓ should be created for user u and copy c. The three preconditions say that c and u are known by the system, and c is available ; and the post conditions assert that a new loan is created to record the loan of c and u, and that c becomes unavailable shown in figure 2. This use case can be formally specified as

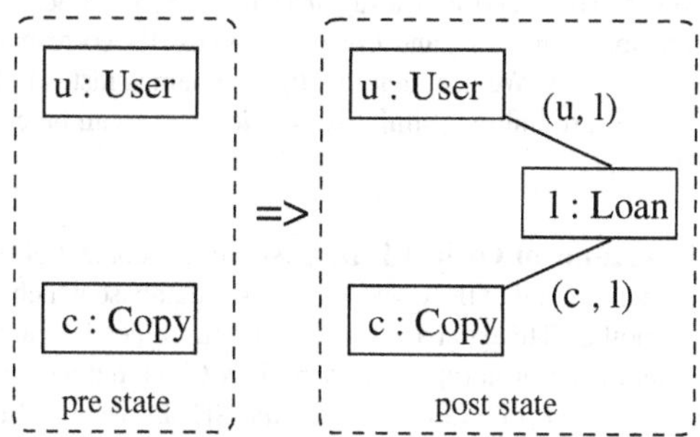

Fig. 3. Pre and Post Object Diagrams of $LendCopy$ Use Case

$$\begin{array}{l} LendCopy \stackrel{def}{=} \textbf{pvar}\ c : \textbf{Copy}, u : \textbf{User}; \\ \textbf{Pre}\ : c \in Copy \wedge u \in User \wedge c.available = true \\ \textbf{Post} : \exists \ell : \textbf{Loan} \bullet \ell \notin Loan \wedge Loan' = Loan \cup \{\ell\} \wedge c.available' = false \\ \qquad \wedge Borrows' = Borrows \cup \{< \ell, c >\} \wedge Takes' = Takes \cup \{< u, \ell >\} \end{array}$$

3 Generating an Executable Prototype

Prototyping of requirements analysis should demonstrate the important functional effects of use cases in terms of atomic state changes rather than the detailed algorithms for internal object interactions. State changes are mainly about creating new objects or links, removing old objects or links, or modifying object attributes. Therefore, the prototype concentrates on the atomic actions on the SEOD which are about creating an object or a link, removing an object or a link, and getting and setting an attribute of an object. A complex functional algorithm on attributes which makes a complex equation satisfaction in post conditions of use cases may not be executable in abstract analysis model, and they will be left for further refinement. However, the prototyping can give the corresponding warning information on the non-executable parts.

As shown by the architecture in Figure 1, the prototype can be generated by a prototype generator. The prototype interface can be generated easily from the names of use cases from the given UCM. The main problem is to generate the SEOD from the given CCM, and to generate the UCH (i.e. its methods) for each use case.

Generating the Entity Object Database. The conceptual model identifies the object entities as well as the associations among them. It corresponds to the declaration part in the program of the prototype. It is used for constructing of the SEOD of the system prototype.

For each class **C** in the CCM, a corresponding class **C** can be defined in the Java program of the prototype. We introduce a special attribute id for each class so that each object can have a unique name for reference since the object name is implicitly as a reference in a Java program. When creating an new object, the object is given a unique identity name id. We use a global variable C for each class **C** to record the set of current existing objects of class **C**, and it is initialized in the prototype declaration part. For simplification, we only record an object's identity name in such a set variable in the prototype implementation.

The attributes of classes in the CCM can be directly coded into the Java notation by syntax translation. An association can be coded as an array of a pair of object names. For example, suppose c and ℓ are objects of corresponding $Copy$ and $Loan$, we can use the corresponding object identity names cid and lid for the objects. We use identity attribute names instead of the object and link identities (references) which are unique. Similarly, $< cid, lid >$ can be considered as the link identity name for $Borrows$.

Defining the Atomic Actions of Object Database. In the context of the CCM that derives the SEOD, the use cases correspond to the operations on the database which transfer the database from one stable state to another. The database state is a UML object diagram.

In the implementation of the prototype, for each class **C** we define auxiliary system methods $C.find()$, $C.add()$, $C.delete()$ and $C.get()$ on the SEOD, where C is variable with type $\mathbb{P}(\mathbf{C})$ defined in the previous paragraph. For example, suppose c is an object of class **Copy**, $Copy.find(c)$ will return a boolean value to check whether c exists in current system state or not, i.e. to return the truth value of the condition $c \in Copy$; $Copy.add(c)$ will add c to the set $Copy$; $Copy.delete(c)$ will remove c from $Copy$; and $Copy.get(cid)$ will get the object reference with name cid.

A use case can be realized by a sequence of atomic actions on the SEOD of two categories: object level actions and attribute level actions. Object level actions include *AddObject (creating an object)*, *RemoveObject(deleting an object)* , *AddLink (creating a link)* , and *RemoveLink(deleting a link)*. In Java programming, $AddObject(c : \mathbf{C})$ can be implemented by creating a new object c of class **C**, and then adding it into the class variable C, i.e. **new** $\mathbf{C}(c)$ or $C.add(c)$. Similarly, *RemoveObject(c:* **C***)* is to delete an existing object c from C, i.e. $destroy(c)$ or $C.delete(c)$). Meanwhile sometimes finding actions are needed, which are *FindObject* and *FindLink* by calling methods $C.find()$ and $A.find()$, where $C \in \mathbf{CVar}$ and $A \in \mathbf{AVar}$.

The attribute level atomic actions are basic reading and writing an object attribute in the database, i.e. class methods: $aget$ and $aset$ for each attribute a of a class. For example, there are two corresponding methods $availableget()$ and $availableset(v)$ for the attribute $availble$ of **Copy**.

Checking a Precondition. The precondition of a use case describes execution constraints, i.e. before executing the use case to modify the SEOD, the constraints are checked on current system state. This checking is static operation on the database. It does not change system state, i.e. without side effects like evaluating expressions of Object Constraint Language (OCL) [16].

The task of checking a precondition is to read the relevant information from SEOD, and then evaluate the condition. If the value is $false$, the prototype will stop the use case and output a corresponding warning information. Otherwise, it will continue executing the use case.

The precondition of a use case can be interpreted as a boolean expression in a Java program. The corresponding actions are finding objects and links, $FindObject()$ and $FindLink()$, as well as reading the object attributes in the database $attributeget()$.

Concretely, if $c \in C$ appears in precondition, it means to check whether object c exists in the current database by calling method $C.find(c)$. An attribute reading can be directly coded as Java get method.

Checking a Postcondition. Each use case describes a sequence of interactions between the actors of the use case and the system, and will be realized as sequences of interactions among objects which are described in sequence diagrams in the design stage. The pre and post conditions of a use case describe the result of the execution of its uses in terms of its pre and post states without any details of the interactions among system objects in the design interaction diagrams. Prototyping is to find the executable parts of a use case specification and translate them into atomic actions on the SEOD. These atomic actions include *attributeset, AddObject, AddLink, RemoveObject*, and *RemoveLink.*

Obviously, each use case generally involves only a few objects. It is not difficult to find out the participating objects and links from the pre and post conditions of the use case. From the precondition, the participating objects and links in the pre state can be identified and put into the sets $preobject$ and $prelink$ of objects. Similarly, two set variables $postobject$ and $postlink$ of objects are used for the postcondition. Of course, a tool can also be designed to generate the sets of objects and links automatically by parsing the pre and post conditions. Another informal way is that we can directly obtain the four sets from the use case state transition diagram like Figure 3.

The four sets contain the information about the change of the SEOD from the pre state to post state. From the four sets, we know that if the use case is successfully executed as required, it will create all the new objects in $createobject$ and all the new links in $createlink$ which only appear in the post state but do not appear in the pre state, and delete all the old objects from $deleteobject$ and all the old links from $deletelink$ which only appear in the pre state but do not appear in the post state. These four sets of objects and links to be created and deleted can be calculated by the following formulas.

$$createobject = postobject - preobject;\ deleteobject = preobject - postobject;$$
$$createlink = postlink - prelink;\ deletelink = prelink - postlink.$$

For example, according to the specification of use case $LendCopy$, its precondition relates two existing objects, a user u and a copy c, and its postcondition requires to create a new object, loan ℓ, and two links, $< u, \ell >$ and $< \ell, c >$ (see Figure 3). We thus get the following four sets:

$$preobject = \{u, c\};\ postobject = \{u, c, \ell\};$$
$$prelink = \varnothing;\ postlink = \{< u, \ell >, < \ell, c >\}$$

And then the set of objects and the set of links to be created:

$$createobject = \{\ell\};\ deleteobject = \varnothing;$$
$$createlink = \{< u, \ell >, < \ell, c >\};\ deletelink = \varnothing$$

So the corresponding Java source code of use case $LendCopy$ method can be generated something like as follows.

```
public void LendCopy(String cid, String uid){
if (User.find(uid) == false)
{System.out.println("Cannot find object" + uid)};
else u = User.get(uid);
if (Copy.find(cid) == false)
 System.out.println("Cannot find object" + cid);
else {c = Copy.get(cid);
  if (c.available_get() == false)
   System.out.println( cid + "is not available");
  else {ℓ = new Loan(lid);
  Loan.add(lid);
  Takes.add(< uid, lid >);
  Borrows.add(< lid, cid >);
  c.availableset(false); }
  }}
```

To summarize, a prototype of a use case demonstrates the sequence of atomic actions on the SEOD. The first step is to check the precondition on *preobject* and *prelink*, i.e. any object and link in the two sets should exist in the SEOD; otherwise, the use case will preform alternative exception scenarios. Also, the precondition should be checked to ensure that the objects and links to be created in *createobject* and *createlink* should not exist in the database in the pre state. And then some actions are performed to transfer system from pre state to post state. That is , the prototype should first create all objects in *createobject*, second create the links in *createlink*, and then delete the links from *deletelink*, and finally delete the objects from *deleteobject*. For example, in the use case *LendCopy*, a loan ℓ should be created, i.e. $\ell \in createobject$. There is a corresponding predicate in the post condition: $Loan' = Loan \cup \{\ell\}$. Supposing that the four sets have already defined, the algorithm can be simply described as the following 8-step sequence of actions.

1. **check** whether all objects of *preobject* set exist in pre-state;
2. **check** whether all links of *prelink* set exist in pre-state;
3. **check** whether all objects of *createobject* set do not exist in pre-state ;
4. **check** whether all links of *createlink* set do not exist in pre-state
5. **create** all objects of *createobject* set in post-state;
6. **create** all links of *createlink* set in post-state;
7. **delete** all links of *deletelink* set in post-state;
8. **delete** all objects of *deleteobject* set in post-state.

Some complex predicate in the postcondition describes the complex algorithm of use case on several attributes from different objects. They may not be executable in the early requirements analysis stage, and need to be refined to be executable in the later. It is acceptable for a prototype to ignore the non-executable parts. However, prototype can print out the corresponding information to explain the post state should make the predicate holds. For example, $ob.x' = f(ob_1.a, ob_2.b)$ appears in a post condition where a, b and x are attributes of objects ob_1, ob_2 and ob. It can be coded in Java programming as an action $ob.xset(f(ob_1.aget(), ob_2.bget()))$ by calling the corresponding attribute *get* and *set* methods.

4 Prototyping Library System

Based on the method described in the previous section, a tool is developed to generate prototype automatically in Java programming language shown in Figure 4. The tool is developed by using

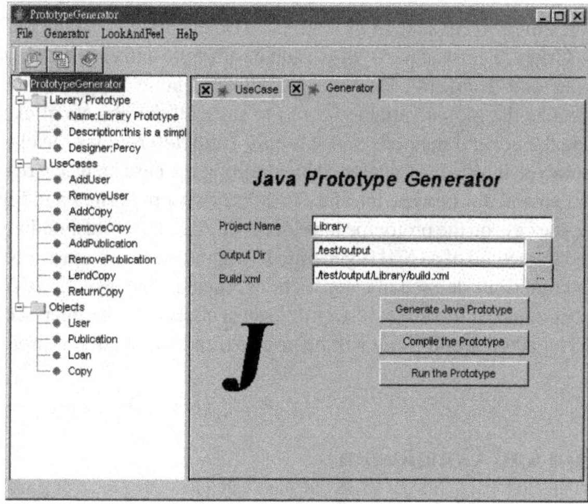

Fig. 4. Interface of prototype generator tool

Applet Viewer: testGridlayout.class
Applet

AddUser	AddPublication	AddCopy	RemoveCopy
RemovePublication	RemoveUser	LendCopy	ReturnCopy

Applet started.

Fig. 5. Prototype interface of library system

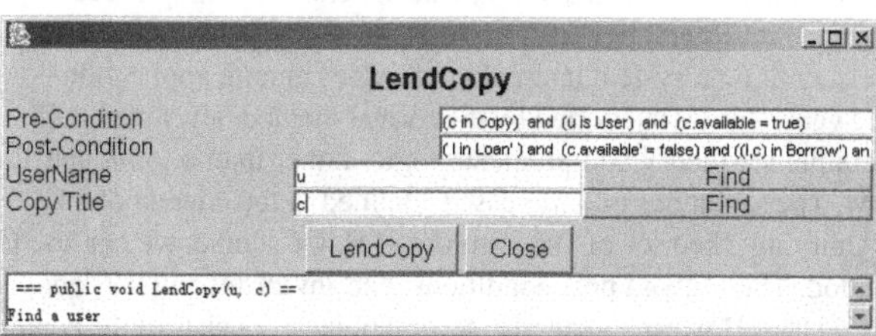

Fig. 6. Prototyping LendCopy use case

Java and XML by reading information of use case diagram and conceptual class diagram from XML files which are generated by MagicDraw or Rational Rose CASE tools, as well as inputting the information of the pre and post object and link sets for each use case manually.

A prototype has three parts as defined by the architecture shown in Figure 1: the SEOD generated after inputting the CCM, the system prototype interface that shows the buttons for execute all the system use cases, and a UCH which defines system methods for all use cases.

The SEOD stores the current state of system, i.e. a object diagram of the CCM. We need for each class, such as **Copy**, a class name"*Copy*", and its attribute names *cid* and *available* as well as their types 'String' and 'Boolean'. The tool will define a class **Copy** in SEOD, and generate class *CopyDB* (realize the global variable *Copy*) to store all the objects of class **Copy** in the system, and provide the general methods $find()$, $add()$ and $delete()$ for the class $Copy()$.

The system prototype interface is generated by inputting use case names or reading from XML files of UCM. The generated prototype interface of library system is shown in Figure 5.

If the name of a use case on the prototype interface is clicked, the corresponding UCH of the use case will be invoked. A method of a UCH is generated by inputting the use case information defined in the pre and post conditions defined in early sections, such as *preobject*, *postobject*, *prelink* and *postlink*. For example, if the use case *LendCopy* is clicked on the interface in Figure 5, the corresponding UCH method *LendCopy* will be invoked, and its function is prototyped as shown in Figure 6.

5 Discussion and Conclusion

Based on the formalization of a UML model requirements [8, 10], a method of prototyping is proposed. A prototype contains three main parts as shown in Figure 1: SEOD generated from the UML conceptual class model, a system prototype interface generated from names of the use cases in the use-cased model, and a UCH generated from each use case in the UCM. The key idea is to map the formal specification of a use case defined on the CCM in pre and post conditions to a sequence of executable atomic actions on the SEOD. The source code of prototype can be generated automatically by tool support. An automated generator has been developed and will be improved for adapting the complex composed use case with an interaction event flow, including and extension cases [1]. We can introduce a sub-interface with some buttons for system interactions in the complex use case which can be decomposed into basic use cases by $<< include >>$ and $<< extend >>$ relationships [13].

The method can be used to generate evolutionary system prototypes [15] step by step following the iterative and incremental RUP [5]. And it can also be used to generate rapid throw-away prototypes. Meanwhile, the prototype system can also be modified to generate different styles corresponding to customers, system analysts and designers. For example, customers are generally interested in system level interaction and explorative dialog prototypes; and system designers usually pay more attention on system internal interactions among application domain objects.

The prototype generation is supported by the formal method developed in [8, 10]. That model is based on the simple set theory and predicate logic, rather than a particular formal language, such as Z or VDM. The semantics of a use case is defined in the context of a CCM as a *design* in Hoare and He's Unifying Theories of Programming [4]. Of course, we can use OCL in [16] for the proposed method. The pre and post conditions, and invariants in OCL are generally used to define methods in a class. However, generally several objects consists of the context of a use case. It is not easy to specify a use case in OCL by using association navigation way under one object context. Therefore, we chose the simple predicate logic in [4] that is easier to understand than other formalisms such as the description declarative language in OCL and the one used in other work on formalizing UML (see the webpage of the precise UML consortium at www.pum.org).

A prototype generated from a formal model of requirements can support the practical use of the underlying formal theory. For example, we can use such a prototype to check system invariants, such as multiplicity constraints, that describe the static conditions that should always hold on any stable state of the system database. This is done in a similarly way by coding the invariants into the pre and post conditions. Prototyping in this way can also be used for checking the consistency between a CCM and a UCM because the precondition will be evaluated to $false$ if the CCM is not consistent with a use case in the UCM. Prototypes of two UML models of requirements can be compared to check whether one model is a refinement of another and this allows software engineers to use the formal method without the need to worry about the "formalities".

One advantage of the prototype generator is that people can use the tool just by deriving the four sets from a use case textual description like in Figure 3, without knowing formal specification or writing out formal pre and post conditions of use cases.

Future work will focus on improving the method and its automated prototype generator tool with some AI techniques to handle non-deterministic and algorithmic non-executable specifications into executable ones, as well as combining design models (class diagrams, sequence diagrams, state diagrams, and activity diagrams) by referring to work and tools of D. Harel's Play-Engine [3]. The method can also be extended by combining scenario descriptions (activity diagram) of use cases in [13].

Acknowledgement: The first author would like to thank his master student, Percy Loi for implementing the prototype generator tool.

References

1. A. Cockburn. *Writing Effective Use Cases.* Pearson Education, 2001.
2. D. Collins. *Designing Object-Oriented User Interfaces.* Benjamin/Cummings, 1995.
3. D. Harel and R. Marelly. *Come, Let's Play, Scenario-Based Programming Using LSCs and the Play-Engine.* Springer-Verlag, 2003.
4. C.A.R. Hoare and J. He. *Unifying theories of programming.* Prentice-Hall, 1998.
5. I. Jacobson, G. Booch, and J. Rumbaugh. *The Unified Software Development Process.* Addison-Wesley, 1999.
6. C. Larman. *Applying UML and Patterns.* Prentice-Hall International, 2001.
7. R.C. Lee. *UML and C++: a practical guide to object-oriented development, 2nd.* Prentice Hall, 2001.
8. X. Li, Z. Liu, and J. He. Formal and use-case driven requirement analysis in UML. In *COMPSAC01*, pages 215–224, Illinois, USA, October 2001. IEEE Computer Society.
9. Z. Liu. Object-oriented software development in UML. Technical Report UNU/IIST Report No. 228, UNU/IIST, P.O. Box 3058, Macau, SAR, P.R. China, March 2001.
10. Z. Liu, X. Li, and J. He. Using transition systems to unify uml models. In *ICFEM2002, in LNCS 2495*, Shanghai, China. Springer-Verlag.
11. B. Meyer. *Object-oriented Software Construction (2nd Edition).* Prentice Hall PTR, 1997.
12. R. Mitchell and J. McKim. *Design by Conctract by Example.* Addison-Wesley, 2002.
13. Reinhold Plosch. *Contracts, Scenarios and Prototypes: An Integrated Approach to High Quality Software.* Springer-verlag, 2004.
14. M.F. Smith. *Software Prototyping: Adoption, Pratice and Management.* McGraw-Hill, 1991.
15. I. Sommerville. *Software Engineering (6th Edition).* Addison-Wesley, 2000.
16. J. Warmer and A. Kleppe. *The Object Constraint Language: precise modeling with UML.* Addison-Wesley, 1999.

A Type System for an Aspect Oriented Programming Language

M. Devi Prasad and Banshi Dhar Chaudhary

MNNIT, Allahabad – 211004, Uttar Pradesh, India
dprasadm@acm.org, bdc@mnnit.ac.in

Abstract. We present a type system for pointcut designators (pcds) and advice forms of an aspect oriented programming langauge. The type system classifies pcds as *static*, *dynamic* and *implausible* based on the static type information of the join points selected by the pcds. Typing the pcds assists in statically restricting the applicability of around advice to procedure call and procedure execution join points. This enables better reasoning about the behavior of around advice.

1 Introduction

In this paper we develop a type system for an Aspect Oriented Programming (AOP) language. The procedure core of this language consists of integer and boolean data types, and recursive procedures. Aspect oriented features of this language support expressive pointcut designators, before, after and around advice. The type system presented here statically types *pointcut designators* (pcds) as *static*, *non-static* and *implausible*, depending upon the kinds of join points they select. It types before and after advice to *void* since they are always executed for effect rather than for value. The type system of this language restricts pcd of an around advice to match only procedure call and procedure execution join points. This enables controlled evolution of new behavior in a type safe manner.

In the following discussion, we assume that the reader is familiar with the abstraction principles of AOP languages. There are some excellent sources widely available, and we refer the reader to [1, 2].

Rest of this paper is organized as follows: Section 2 presents the formal, concrete syntax of the language. Section 3 shows the syntax domains used in type judgements. Section 4 details typing rules for pcds, and section 5 types advice definitions. Section 6 treats *proceed* expression and in section 7 we conclude.

2 Formal Syntax of the Language

The concrete syntax of the language resembles list forms of Scheme language. In Fig. 1, integers and booleans are expressed values, while *void* is the typical *Unit* type [3]. The production rules for procedure declaration, statements and arithmetic, logical and relational expressions are given in [4].

R.K. Ghosh and H. Mohanty (Eds.): ICDCIT 2004, LNCS 3347, pp. 266–272, 2004.

Program	::= (**program** ProcAdv$^+$)
ProcAdv	::= ProceDecl | AdviceDecl
Formals	::= (Type$_{exp}$ *id*)*
Body	::= (Localvar? Stmt*)
Localvar	::= (**auto** (Type$_{exp}$ *id const*)$^+$)
Expr	::= *id* | *const* | (*id* Expr*) | (**proceed** Expr*) | ...
AdviceDecl	::= (**before** (Formals) Pcd Body) | (**after** (Formals) Pcd Body)
	| (**around** Type (Formals) Pcd Body)
Pcd	::= (**call** *id*) | (**execution** *id*) | (**advice-execution**)
	| (**within** *id*) | (**cflow** Pcd) | (**cflowbelow** Pcd)
	| (**args** *id*$^+$) | (**and** Pcd Pcd) | (**or** Pcd Pcd) | (**not** Pcd)
Type	::= **int** | **bool** | **void**
Type$_{exp}$	::= **int** | **bool**

Fig. 1. Concrete syntax of the language

3 Syntax Domains

Figure 2 presents the syntax domains employed in typing judgements of different syntactic phrases in the language.

$fe \in F$	$= (id : \tau)^*$	*formal parameter types*
$pe \in P$	$= id \rightarrow (\tau_{ret} \times F)$	*procedure environment*
$\rho \in E$	$= \tau_{ret} \times F \times (id \rightarrow \tau)$	*type env of advice body*
$o \in AO$	= before | after | around	
$\alpha \in Advice$	$= AO \times \tau_{ret} \times F$	
$\wp \in Pcd_{type}$	$= JP_{type} \times Args_{type}$	
$\kappa \in JP_{type}$	= call_jp[*id*] | exec_jp[*id*]	*static join points*
	| aexec_jp | dynamic_jp	*dynamic join points*
	| nonsat_jp	*impossible ones*
$R \in Args_{type}$	$= \{id_i : \tau_i^{i \in 1 \ldots n}\}$	*record of* args *bindings*
τ	= int | bool	*expressed values*
τ_{ret}	= int | bool | void	*expressed values and* Unit *type*

Fig. 2. Static semantics model

$Args_{type}$ represents record type [3, 5]. The notation used here is identical to the one found in [3].

4 Typing the PCDs

Figure 3 presents typing rules for pcds. A pcd expression is part of advice declaration. It is typed using two environments: P – the procedure environment, and F – the formal parameters in advice declaration.

There are two rules for *(**call** pname)* pcd. The T–CALL–PCD rule verifies that *pname* exists in P and types it to PCD_{type} value. This value is a pair whose first component is a call join point, and the second an empty record indicating no bindings. The second rule, T−CALL−NONSAT is applicable when procedure *pname* does not exist in P. This yields a *nonsat_jp*. Typing an ***(execution** pname)* pcd yields similar judgements [4]. As evident from these rules, *call* and *execution* pcds always offer concrete, static type information about their intended join point *shadows* [6].

$$\boxed{P, F \vdash Pcd : Pcd_{type}}$$

T-CALL-PCD

$$\frac{pname \in dom(P)}{P, F \vdash (\textbf{call}\ pname) : (call\_jp[pname],\ \{\})}$$

T-CALL-NONSAT

$$\frac{pname \notin dom(P)}{P, F \vdash (\textbf{call}\ pname) : (nonsat\_jp, \{\})}$$

T-ADVEXEC-PCD

$$P, F \vdash (\textbf{advice-execution}) : (aexec\_jp,\ \{\})$$

T-ARGS-PCD

$$\frac{for\ each\ i \quad F \vdash id_i : \tau_i}{P, F \vdash (\textbf{args}\ id_1, \ldots, id_n) : (dynamic\_jp,\ \{id_i : \tau_i\ ^{i \in 1 \ldots n}\})}$$

T-CFLOW-PCD

$$\frac{P, F \vdash pcd : (-,\ \{x_i : \tau_i\ ^{i \in 1 \ldots n}\})}{P, F \vdash (\textbf{cflow}\ pcd)\ : (dynamic\_jp,\ \{x_i : \tau_i\ ^{i \in 1 \ldots n}\})}$$

T-AND-PCD

$$\frac{P, F \vdash pcd_1 : \wp_1 \qquad P, F \vdash pcd_2 : \wp_2 \qquad AndPcds(\wp_1, \wp_2) : \wp_{res}}{P, F \vdash (\textbf{and}\ pcd_1\ pcd_2)\ : \wp_{res}}$$

Fig. 3. Typing Rules for PCDs

Rule T−ARGS−PCD verifies that each identifier used in the pcd is bound in the environment of formal parameters and creates a record of these bindings. Since there could be more than one procedure call or execution join point that matches the type signature indicated in args pcd, it is not possible to statically type it to *one concrete* join point. Therefore, it is typed to a PCD_{type} value with the first component being a *dynamic* join point and the second component being a record of bindings.

A ***(cflow** pcd)* is used to pick up join points that occur in the call graph of some other join point. This may in general include too many join points with varying (incompatible) signatures. Therefore, the T−CFLOW−PCD rule types it to a *dynamic_jp* while still retaining the bindings created by the inner pcd.

Rule T–AND–PCD first types operand pcds of **and** operator and combines them using an auxiliary function named *AndPcds*. Figure 4 shows the formal definition of *AndPcds*. It defines two separate operators for composing join point components and parameter-type bindings contributed by operand pcds. The $\otimes_{jp}$ operator deals with join point components while the $\otimes_{bind}$ handles bindings.

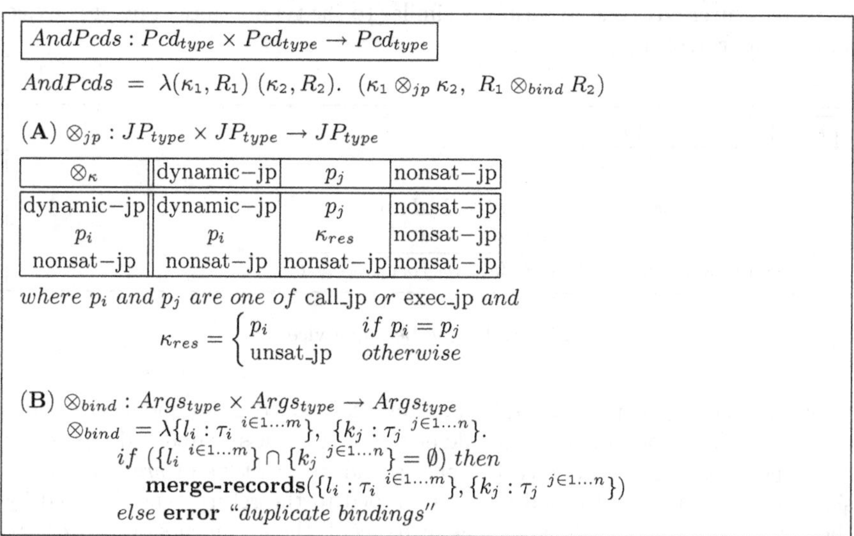

$AndPcds : Pcd_{type} \times Pcd_{type} \rightarrow Pcd_{type}$

$AndPcds = \lambda(\kappa_1, R_1)\ (\kappa_2, R_2).\ (\kappa_1 \otimes_{jp} \kappa_2,\ R_1 \otimes_{bind} R_2)$

(A) $\otimes_{jp} : JP_{type} \times JP_{type} \rightarrow JP_{type}$

$\otimes_\kappa$	dynamic–jp	p_j	nonsat–jp
dynamic–jp	dynamic–jp	p_j	nonsat–jp
p_i	p_i	κ_{res}	nonsat–jp
nonsat–jp	nonsat–jp	nonsat–jp	nonsat–jp

where p_i *and* p_j *are one of* call_jp *or* exec_jp *and*

$$\kappa_{res} = \begin{cases} p_i & if\ p_i = p_j \\ \text{unsat\_jp} & otherwise \end{cases}$$

(B) $\otimes_{bind} : Args_{type} \times Args_{type} \rightarrow Args_{type}$

$\otimes_{bind} = \lambda\{l_i : \tau_i\ ^{i \in 1 \ldots m}\},\ \{k_j : \tau_j\ ^{j \in 1 \ldots n}\}.$

$if\ (\{l_i\ ^{i \in 1 \ldots m}\} \cap \{k_j\ ^{j \in 1 \ldots n}\} = \emptyset)\ then$

merge-records$(\{l_i : \tau_i\ ^{i \in 1 \ldots m}\}, \{k_j : \tau_j\ ^{j \in 1 \ldots n}\})$

else **error** *"duplicate bindings"*

Fig. 4. The *AndPcds* operator

Stage (A) computes join point conjunction while stage (B) determines new set of bindings. The latter step verifies that record labels in both pcds are distinct. It does so by verifying that the intersection of labels from both records is empty. This enforces unique bindings for formal parameters. We presume a function *merge–records* that combines the fields of argument records resulting in a composite record.

The typing rules for *(**or** pcd pcd)* and *(**not** pcd)* are shown in [4].

5 Advice Definition

As seen from the syntax of the langauge, advice forms can declare formal parameters to access the run-time context available at a join point. However, both before and after advice do not declare a return type. They are executed at required join points for their side effect rather than for value. For this reason, we type the body of a before and after advice to *void*.

Figure 5 presents typing judgements for before advice. In T–BEFORE, the formal parameters are first typed in an empty environment. This yields an environment F that binds identifiers with their types. Next, P and F are used to judge the well-typedness of the pcd associated with the advice. Finally, the advice body is typed using P and a new environment consisting of the return type of the advice (*void*), F, and an empty component representing environment of local variables. If an advice body declares **auto** variables, the empty environment component is updated within the advice body with the identifier-type bindings of local variables.

Typing after advice is structurally similar to the typing rules of before advice and is elaborated in [4].

$$\boxed{P \vdash \mathit{AdviceDecl} : \mathit{Advice}}$$

T-BEFORE

$$\frac{\varnothing \vdash \mathit{Formals} : F \qquad P, F \vdash \mathit{Pcd} : \wp \qquad P, (\mathit{void}, F, \varnothing) \vdash \mathit{Body} : \mathit{void}}{P \vdash (\textbf{before}\ (\mathit{Formals})\ \mathit{Pcd}\ \mathit{Body}) : (\mathit{before},\ \mathit{void},\ F)}$$

Fig. 5. Typing before advice

Around advice requires careful attention. First, since an around advice is declared to return typed value, we should ensure that the associated pcd represents a join point with the same return type. Second, return type of *proceed* expression within around advice body must be typed to the return type declared by the advice. Third, in our language, as in AspectJ, the arguments of *proceed* are matched with the formal parameters of the advice and not with the join point selected by the associated pcd.

Figure 6 presents typing judgements for around advice. We show how around advice is typed at a procedure call join point. The other variation involving procedure execution join point is similar in structure and is detailed in [4].

$$\boxed{P \vdash \mathit{AdviceDecl} : \mathit{Advice}}$$

T-AROUND1

$$\frac{\varnothing \vdash \mathit{Formals} : F \qquad P, F \vdash \mathit{Pcd} : (\mathit{call\_jp}[\mathit{pname}], -) \qquad P \vdash \mathit{pname} : (\tau_{ret}, -) \qquad P, (\tau_{ret}, F, \varnothing) \vdash \mathit{Body} : \tau_{ret}}{P \vdash (\textbf{around}\ \tau_{ret}\ (\mathit{Formals})\ \mathit{Pcd}\ \mathit{Body}) : (\mathit{around},\ \tau_{ret},\ F)}$$

Fig. 6. Typing around advice

T−AROUND1 first types formals in an empty environment and carries the resulting bindings F to type the pcd. When the form of pcd type represents a call join point, it ensures that the return type of the procedure (representing the join point) is same as declared in the advice. Finally, it expects advice body be typed to τ_{ret} to establish the well-typedness of the advice definition.

6 Proceed Expression

Figure 7 presents the typing rules for *proceed* expression inside an around advice body. In our formulation, E represents an environment used to type procedure and advice bodies. In rule T–PROCEED, it contains the return type of the (around) advice, types of formals declared in the advice and the types of local variables.

The T–PROCEED rule first extracts τ_{ret} – the return type of the advice, and fe – the formal parameter environment, from E. It ignores the local variable environment component. Next, it uses fe to retrieve the formal parameters-type bindings declared in the advice. A check ensures that n, the number of actual arguments matches m, the number of formal parameters. Then it verifies that the type of each argument matches corresponding formal parameter.

$\boxed{P, E \vdash Expr : \tau_{ret}}$

T-PROCEED

$$\frac{E = (\tau_{ret},\ fe,\ -) \qquad fe = (id_1 : \tau_1, \ldots, id_m : \tau_m) \qquad n = m \qquad P, E \vdash exp_1 : \tau_1 \quad \ldots \quad P, E \vdash exp_n : \tau_m}{P, E \vdash \textbf{proceed}\ (exp_1, \ldots, exp_n) : \tau_{ret}}$$

Fig. 7. Typing *proceed* expression

7 Conclusion

The major contribution of this paper is a type system that uses static properties of join points selected by pcds to type the pcds. It exploits pcd type to statically type the advice forms. It types before and after advice to *void*, and types around advice only at procedure call and execution join points. This ensures type safe evolution of program behavior.

References

1. Special issue on aspect-oriented programming: In Communications of the ACM, **44**(10), October 2001.
2. Kiczales, G., Hilsdale, E., Hugunin, J., Kersten, M., Palm, J., and Griswold, W.: Getting started with AspectJ. In Communications of the ACM, **44**(10):59–73, October 2001.
3. Benjamin C. Pierce: Types and Programming Languages. MIT Press, Cambridge, MA, 2002.

4. Devi Prasad, M., and Banshi Dhar Chaudhari: Type System and Advicve Composition Semantics of an AOP Language. Technical report. Computer Science and Engineering Department, MNNIT, Allahabad. January 2004.
5. Cardelli, L.: Type Systems, Chapter 97. CRC Handbook of Computer Science and Engineering. CRC Press, Second edition.
6. Hilsdale, E., and Hugunin,J.: Advice Weaving in AspectJ. In Third International Conference on Aspect-Oriented Software Development, April 2004.

Secure Requirements Elicitation Through Triggered Message Sequence Charts

Arnab Ray[1], Bikram Sengupta[2], and Rance Cleaveland[3]

[1] Department of Computer Science SUNY at Stony Brook,
Stony Brook, NY 11794-4400, USA
arnabray@cs.sunysb.edu
[2] IBM India Research Labaratory,
Block-1, Indian Institute of Technology, Hauz Khas,
New Delhi-110016, India
bsengupt@in.ibm.com
[3] Department of Computer Science SUNY at Stony Brook,
Stony Brook, NY 11794-4400, USA
rance@cs.sunysb.edu

Abstract. This paper argues for performing information-flow-based security analysis in the first phase of the software development life cycle itself ie in the requirements elicitation phase. Message Sequence Charts (MSC)s have been widely accepted as a formal scenario-based visual notation for writing down requirements. In this paper, we discuss a method for checking if a TMSC (Triggered Message Sequence Chart), a recently propsed enhancement to classical MSCs, satisifes one of the most important information flow properties namely non-interference.

1 Introduction

With our increased reliance on computer systems in all aspects of life, protecting the confidentiality of information being manipulated has become an increasingly important research problem To be confident that a system is secure with respect to confidentiality, it should be rigorously analyzed as a whole to check if it enforces good confidentiality practices. The aim of the analysis should be to demonstrate that the information controlled by a confidentiality policy cannot leak out to a location where that policy is being violated. These policies which govern the movement of information through the system are called *information flow policies*.

Information flow is traditionally checked through run-time monitoring of systems [4], or by static analysis of the source-code [2] [3]. But these are post-implementation approaches—finding spurious information flow at this stage may result in the entire system being sent back to the drawing board for possible redesign and reimplementation. Model-based approaches for information-flow analysis that check for information leaks at the design phase [7], [5] developed out of the need to isolate security bugs as early as possible in the development life-cycle with the broader aim of reducing the cost that would otherwise be incurred implementing an insecurely designed system.

What should be noted however is that models are not the earliest artifacts in the software development process. Before models are constructed by the design team, the

R.K. Ghosh and H. Mohanty (Eds.): ICDCIT 2004, LNCS 3347, pp. 273–282, 2004.

client or customer typically provides requirements which encapsulate her demands from the final system. Traditionally these requirements have been textually represented in a natural language like English. But in modern software engineering, requirements are expressed in precise formalisms like Message Sequence Charts (MSC) [6] which are now accepted as standard notation for systems by the International Telecommunications Union (ITU).

In practice, the software design phase consists of an iterative process with developer's designs being refined by client's requirements and vise versa. A system which is developed based on "sensitive-information leaky" requirements is bound to be insecure no matter how well designed the ultimate system is. An implementation that meets these faulty requirements will be doomed to be information-unsafe. The solution to such a problem would not be found in better implementations or in better models but in more secure requirements. Thus any software engineering solution for secure information-flow that does not analyze requirement elicitation formalisms will always be incomplete. In this paper, we endeavor to provide methods to formally analyze information flow violations on requirements expressed in terms of a recently proposed variant of MSCs called Triggered Message Sequence Chart (TMSC)s [11] which enrich scenarios with the notions of conditional and partial behavior so as to facilitate early stage requirements modeling.

The paper is organized as follows. Section 2 provides the background for the concepts introduced, Section 3 illustrates an example of information-flow analysis on TMSCs while Section 4 shows how TMSCs may be characterized as ready sets. Section 5 illustrates the formal way of doing non-interference analysis on TMSCs and Sections 6 and 7 introduce TMSC expressions and investigates whether application of TMSC operators preserve NI. The last section concludes the paper.

2 Background

A *process* is a tuple $\langle S, A, \rightarrow, s_I \rangle$ where: S is a set of *states*; A is a *action set* consisting of named-actions and the internal transition τ; $\longrightarrow \subseteq S \times A \times S$ is the *transition relation*, and $s_I \in S$ is the *start state*.

A set X of actions is a ready set of a state p in process P ie $Ready(p) = X$ if the state p offers X to the environment. In figure 1 we see an example of a process with the ready set of state 1: $Ready(1) = \{\{a, b\}\}$.

Non-interference (NI) is an information flow property which states that if there are two privilege levels for all the actions of a process –HI and LO it is impossible for an observer who can observe only LO events to deduce any information about HI events. Alternatively this can be interpreted as: for any system trace (sequence of visible actions) consisting of HI(H) and LO(L) events there is a second trace consisting of the same subsequence of LO events as the first trace but with no HI events. Since both these traces are legal traces of the system, an observer (who can look at only LO actions) would not know whether the first trace occurred or the second. Hence he would obtain no information about the HI events from his observation.

If P be a process with its action set partitioned into two sets L and H (corresponding to low and high privilege actions respectively) and tr be a trace then P/tr denotes the process state after executing trace tr and $traces(P)$ denote all the traces of P. Then:

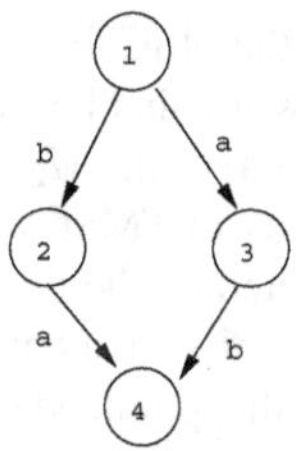

Fig. 1. Process and Ready Set

$ReadySets(P/tr)$= $\{Ready(p) \mid$ for all traces tr from s_I to $p\}$
$ReadySets_L(P)$ denotes $ReadySets(P)$ restricted to the L alphabet.

In [8] a formulation for NI is given as:

$\forall tr \in traces(P).ReadySets_L(S/tr) = ReadySets_L(S/tr \uparrow L))$
$tr \uparrow L$ projects tr down to the event set L ie purges out all the H actions.

[5] provides several characterizations for NI using a process model and ready sets of which we consider one above.

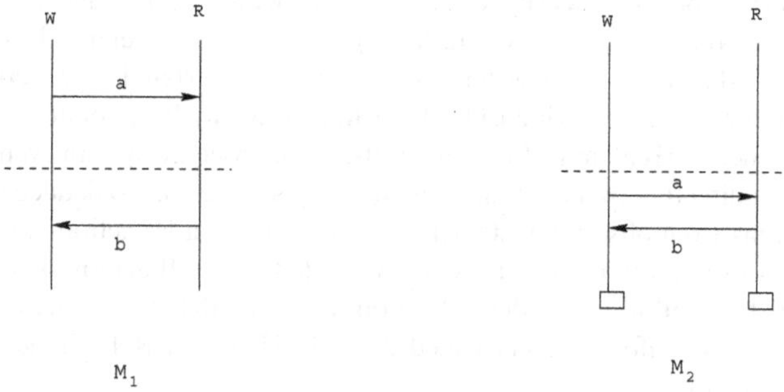

Fig. 2. Two TMSCs M_1 and M_2

Triggered Message Sequence Charts. Triggered Message Sequence Charts (TMSC)s [11], like MSCs [1] describe system scenarios in terms of the atomic actions (message sends and receives and local actions) that each parallel instance may engage in. However unlike traditional MSCs each TMSC instance's action sequences are partitioned into two subsequences: a *trigger* and an *action.* A TMSC scenario stipulates that in any system execution, if the sequence of events performed by an instance constitutes the trigger, then the subsequent behavior of the instance must include the sequence of events that constitute its action. In an implementation, an instance is not *required* to display the behavior performed by the trigger, but if it does so, its subsequent behavior is limited by the action.

Graphically we denote TMSCs as shown in Figure 2. The partitioning of the sequences of events into the trigger and action sequences is indicated by the horizontal line running through the instances of the MSC. For each instance, the sequence of events above the line constitute the trigger while that below constitutes the action.

In Figure 2 we have two TMSCs M_1 and M_2. Each TMSC has 2 instances called W and R respectively. Another novelty of TMSCs, in comparison with MSCs, is that a scenario may be partial. This is depicted by the presence/absence of a bar at the foot of an instance in a TMSC. The presence of such a bar, as in TMSC M_2, indicates that the instance has to terminate on reaching that point, whereas the absence, as in M_1, indicates that there are no constraints on the subsequent behavior of the instance. As such, the scenario is partial, and may be extended later on.

M_1 trigger consists of a message from W to R labeled by a and its action consists of a message from R to W labeled by b. M_2 has an empty trigger followed by the same exchange of messages present in M_1.

3 Information Flow in TMSCs

The information-flow we shall be concerned with in this paper is *Non-interference* or NI for short. We defined non-interference in terms of processes in the previous section. Over here we lift that definition to TMSCs and use it to define the concept of information-safety on requirements.

Let us associate one of 2 security levels (HI or LO) with each message in a TMSC. The intuition behind NI is as follows. Actions having a LO security level may be observed by anyone but not HI actions. For a system to have the non-interference property, it should be impossible for a user observing LO actions to deduce anything about the occurrence or non-occurrence of HI actions. In other words, for an insecure system even though the attacker cannot directly observe HI actions, she may still be able to deduce information about HI actions from observing LO actions only. Thus if a HI action is preceded (or followed) by a LO action, it should also be possible for the HI action to occur without being preceded (or followed) by the LO action. If that be the case, then even if the LO action is observed no information is leaked about the HI action as the HI action can also occur without the LO action.

In Figure 2, let a be a HI action and b be a LO action. In M_1 , a triggers b. However, this does not mean that b cannot occur without the occurrence of a. It just means that if a happens then b has to happen. Hence if any observer observes b she cannot deduce that a definitely happened as b may follow or may not follow a. Hence NI holds for M_1. However M_2 has an empty trigger which means it is always true. This implies that the action *always* has to happen and since the action imposes a total ordering on a and b, an observer who observes b (the LO action) will know for sure that a (the HI action) happened. Information will thus flow in a spurious fashion from HI to LO which means that M_2 does not satisfy NI and consequently is "unsafe".

This example shows the necessity of checking information-flow properties like NI on requirements. As is evident, despite the fact that M_1 and M_2 are requirements very similar to the other one exhibits information-leak while the other does not. This motivates us to look at formal ways of analyzing TMSCs for NI. In Section 2 we saw how NI can be formulated in terms of ready sets on processes. Using that fact, if we may provide a ready set characterization of TMCSs we can obtain a method for checking if a TMSC satisfies the property of NI.

4 From TMSCs to Ready Sets

We will now show how individual TMSCs may be equipped with a ready-set semantics, which makes information-flow analysis on requirements expressed as TMSCs, feasible in practice. The basic idea is that triggers are handled via non-determinism: a TMSC is essentially treated as a non-deterministic choice of all behaviors violating the trigger together with those in which the trigger is satisfied and progresses made on performing the action; and if the action does not terminate the behavior of the instance (i.e. the scenario is partial), then the subsequent allowed behavior is again given by the non-deterministic choice of all possible behaviors.

The formal semantics of single TMSCs is described in detail in [11]. This definition translates a TMSC to an *acceptance tree*. In the TMSC setting, the main difference between the acceptance set semantics of [11] and the ready set semantics we show here, is that the former needs to satisfy a closure property called *saturation*, which simplified the definition of the refinement relation needed in [11], but which is not relevant in the information-flow context. Otherwise, the technical development needed for both the acceptance set and ready set semantics is exactly the same and we will not repeat the account in [11] in its entirety here. Rather, we will present only the relevant definitions for the ready set semantics here, and the interested reader is referred to [11] for details.

In the following, we consider 3 kinds of events: $\mathsf{out}(I_i, I_j, m)$ corresponds to I_i sending m to I_j. I_j will receive m by performing $\mathsf{in}(I_i, I_j, m)$. Also, if I_j is waiting to receive m from I_i but m is yet to be sent, then this will be indicated by the *potential event* $\mathsf{wait}(\mathsf{in}(I_i, I_j, m))$. We will denote by $\mathbb{I}$, $\mathbb{E}$ and $\mathbb{R}$, the set of all instances, all send and receive events, and all receive events respectively.

We assume all events in $\mathbb{E}$ to have a security level associated with them, where the security level has the domain $\{HI, LO\}$. We define the function $sec\_level : \mathbb{E} \longrightarrow \{HI, LO\}$ which maps every event to a security level.

We first define how to associate a ready set with an instance I_i in a TMSC M. The ready set construction differs from the traditional one for LTSs given previously in that it is given relative to a set of "enabled inputs". An instance can only emit an input event if another instance has emitted the corresponding output; otherwise, this input event is not enabled. To capture this behavior, we introduce an additional parameter, $eR \subseteq \mathbb{R}$, into the ready-set definition. An input event in eR is deemed enabled; otherwise, it is defined to be disabled. We also need the following operation on languages. Let $L \subseteq A^*$ and $w \in A^*$. Then the *next set*, $next(L, w) \subseteq A$, of L after w is given by: $next(L, w) = \{a \in A \mid \exists w' \in L.\ w \cdot a \preceq w'\}$. Finally, we define the *nondeterminism set* of $E \subseteq \mathbb{E}$ and enabled inputs $eR \subseteq \mathbb{R}$ as follows.

$$\begin{aligned} ND(E, eR) = (&\{\{e\} \mid e \in E \wedge (e \in \mathbb{R} \Rightarrow e \in eR)\} \\ &\cup \{\{\mathsf{wait}(r)\} \mid r \in ((E \cap \mathbb{R}) - eR)\}) \end{aligned}$$

$ND(E, eR)$ represents the ready set of a system that can nondeterministically decide to perform any event in E that is *enabled*, where any output or local event, and any input in eR, is enabled, or wait for any input event in E that is not yet enabled.

Definition 1. *Let* $I_i \in \mathcal{I}$, $w \in \mathbb{E}^*$ *and* $eR \subseteq \mathbb{R}_{\{I_i\}}$. *Then* $ReadySets(I_i, M, w, eR)$ *is defined as follows.*

$$ReadySets(I_i, M, w, eR) = \begin{cases} \emptyset & \text{if } w \notin L_M(I_i) \\ ND(\mathit{next}(L_M(I_i), w), eR) & \text{otherwise} \end{cases}$$

We will first explain some of the notation used above. The *language*, $L_M(I_i)$, of an instance I_i records the possible sequences of events the instance might generate as it executes. Intuitively, if a sequence does not "satisfy" the trigger of I_i, then it will be admitted as a sequence. Otherwise, it will be constrained to "satisfy" the action. $ReadySets(I_i, M, w, eR)$ is the ready set of instance I_i in TMSC M after w. The first clause above handles the case when I_i is incapable of performing w, while the second one computes the ready set based on events that are possible "next" after w, together with any potential receive events that are not enabled.

We assume that any such instance, whose behavior is not explicitly described in M, has empty trigger and action in M and must terminate.

Definition 2. *Let* $I_i \in \mathbb{I} - \mathcal{I}$. *Then* $ReadySet(I_i, M, w, eR)$ *is defined as follows.*

$$ReadySet(I_i, M, w, eR) = \begin{cases} \{\{\mathsf{end}(I_i)\}\} & \text{if } w = \epsilon \\ \{\emptyset\} & \text{if } w = \mathsf{end}(I_i) \\ \emptyset & \text{otherwise} \end{cases}$$

Thus, any instance $I_i \in \mathbb{I} - \mathcal{I}$ can only perform the event $\mathsf{end}(I_i)$ in M, after which it terminates.

Interpreting TMSCs. We now define the ready set $ReadySets(M, w)$ as follows.

Definition 3. *The ready set* $ReadySets(M, w)$, *of* M *after* $w \in \mathbb{E}^*$ *is defined as:*

$$ReadySets(M, w) = \begin{cases} \emptyset & \text{if } w \text{ is not well-balanced} \\ \bowtie_{I_i \in \mathbb{I}} ReadySets(I_i, M, w\lfloor I_i, e\mathcal{R}(w)) & \text{otherwise} \end{cases}$$

We call w well-balanced if every receive event is preceded by a corresponding send. The projection, $w\lfloor I_i$ returns I_i's contribution in w, i.e. the longest subsequence of w containing only events in which I_i is active. Also, the receive event $\mathsf{in}(I_i, I_j, m)$ is called *enabled* by w if $|w|_{\mathsf{out}(I_i,I_j,m)} > |w|_{\mathsf{in}(I_i,I_j,m)}$. We use $e\mathcal{R}(w)$ to stand for all receive events enabled by w. Finally, the $\bowtie$ operator takes the pairwise union of a set of ready sets. Intuitively, we first compute the local ready set of each instance I_i after the execution $w\lfloor I_i$, and then combine the local states across all the instances in all possible ways, to generate the global system configurations.

5 Example of Readyset Analysis of TMSCs

In section 2, we showed how to characterize TMSCs in terms of ready sets. In order to show non-interference, we need to show that for all traces tr of a TMSC M, $ReadySets_L(M/tr) = ReadySets_L(M/tr \uparrow L))$ where L or LO is obtained from applying the function sec_level on its set of actions.

To illustrate our approach, we take the two TMSCs M_1 and M_2 we had in our initial example where a is a HI action and b is a LO action.

As mentioned before, a TMSC can be looked upon as a non-deterministic choice of all behaviors violating the trigger together with those in which the trigger is satisfied and progress is made on performing the trigger. As a result, for M_1 if the trigger is not satisfied (ie a is not sent from W to R) there are a myriad number of things it can do, some of them being:the sending out and reception of b alone, termination of W at the very beginning, termination of R at the very beginning, the sending out of an event while the receiver is still waiting for it. In other words, for a conditional scenario like M_1 there are many ways in which it may be satisfied.

Revisiting our previous example from the stand-point of the readyset characterization of NI we can see that we get the same result we obtained from intuition. That is in M_2 if the trace considered is $w = out(W, R, a).in(R, W, a).out(R, W, b)$ then readyset of M_2 after the perfomance of this trace projected on the set of low actions ie $RD_L(M_2/w) = \{\{in(W, R, b)\}\}$ is not equal to $RD_L(M_2/w \uparrow L) = \{\emptyset\}$ ie the set containing the empty trace.

However for the same trace in M_1, $RD_L(M_1/w) = \{\{out(R, W, b), in(W, R, b)\}\}$. Since M_1 is a partial scenario, after the performance of $out(R, W, b)$ the actions it can perform (projected on the low alphabet) may be to either receive the emitted b at W or for R to emit another b. For $RD_L(M_1/w \uparrow L)$ the trigger is not satisfied and the projection of the ready set onto the low alphabet will be $\{\{out(R, W, b), in(W, R, b)\}\}$ ie $RD_L(M_1/w) = RD_L(M_1/w \uparrow L)$.

These results tie in with the intuition that a system with more redundancy is likely to be more secure with respect to a behavior obfuscation property like non-interference. A partial scenario like M_1 having more non-determinism than a complete scenario like M_2 has a greater likelihood of being secure.

This leads to an important lesson for requirements and software engineers working together to design a system: while going from partial specifications to more refined ones, it should be remembered that the behaviors which are thrown out during the refinement process may be important in keeping the system's behavior obfuscated from an attacker. Hence, for systems in which security is a concern, there is a need to check for information leaks at every stage of the specification and system refinement process.

6 TMSC Expressions

So far we have been working with single TMSCs that serve as the basic building blocks for structured requirements specifications. An algebra of operators is used to generate larger specifications out of sub-specifications. The resulting terms, which are referred to as *TMSC expressions*, have the following syntax:

$$
\begin{array}{llll}
S ::= & M & & \text{(single TMSC)} \\
| & X & & \text{(variable)} \\
| & S \parallel S & & \text{(parallel composition)} \\
| & S \mp S & & \text{(delayed choice)} \\
| & S; S & & \text{(sequential composition)} \\
| & recX.S & & \text{(recursive operator)} \\
| & S \oplus S & & \text{(internal choice)} \\
| & S \wedge S & & \text{(logical and)}
\end{array}
$$

The TMSC language offers a selection of "behavioral" and "logical" operators (as opposed to purely behavioral constructs typically used in MSC specifications) to facilitate a structured approach to *requirements management* whereby composite requirements are generated by interweaving prescriptive and constraint-based requirements. $\parallel$, $\mp$,; and $recX$ falls into the behavioral category, $\wedge$ is a logical construct, while $\oplus$ falls into both categories. The $\parallel$ operator runs two TMSC expressions in parallel. $S_1 \mp S_2$ represents the "deterministic choice" between S_1 and S_2 while $S_1 \oplus S_2$ represents the nondeterministic choice: a successful refinement can choose either. In this respect $\oplus$ has overtones of logical disjunction. $S_1; S_2$ denotes the *asynchronous* sequential composition [6] of S_1 and S_2. The recursive operator, *rec* allows us to model infinite behavior of processes, where a new execution cycle starts whenever there is a reference within S, to the variable used in the recursive definition (say X). Finally, $S_1 \wedge S_2$ represents the logical conjunction of S_1 and S_2, i.e. it specifies a system that needs to satisfy the requirements expressed by both S_1 and S_2. (A detailed account of the use of the TMSC framework in requirements modeling can be found in [9])

The formal semantics of TMSC expressions is given in [10] by translating them to acceptance trees. Specifically, the TMSC operators are interpreted in terms of acceptance trees, i.e. they take the acceptance trees of the sub-expressions as parameters, and generate the acceptance tree of the larger expression. The ready set semantics of TMSC expressions is defined in an analogous manner, the only difference being we use ready sets in place of acceptance sets, and do not use the saturation operator as in [10]. For more details about the approach, the reader is referred to [10].

7 TMSC Expressions and NI

Now an interesting question is whether NI is preserved by the application of these standard operators. Or in other words if M_1 and M_2 are TMSCs that satisfy NI is it mandatory for M_1 op M_2 also satisfy NI.

The answer to this question is that With the exception of $\oplus$ none of the TMSC operators preserve NI. This means that while building up more complex TMSCs from simpler TMSCs the user has to check NI at each stage of composition as there is no guarantee that just because the components are safe the total system will be safe. Due to shortage of space we demonstrate how $\oplus$ preserves NI and how $\wedge$ does not. Counter-examples of the other operators can be constructed similarly and we plan to provide them in an expanded version of this paper.

Internal Choice. The $\oplus$ operator offers non-deterministic choice. Given two TMSC specifications S_1 and S_2, and a sequence of events w, let $RD(S_1/w)$ and $RD(S_2/w)$ be the ready sets of S_1 and S_2 after a trace w then $RD[S_1 \oplus S_2/w] = RD(S_1/w) \cup RD(S_2/w)$ as shown in [10]. If A is a readyset then $A \uparrow L$ denotes the A projected on the low actions.

As a result,

$$\begin{aligned} RD_L(S_1 \oplus S_2/w) &= (RD(S_1/w) \cup RD(S_2/w)) \uparrow L \\ &= RD_L(S_1/w) \cup RD_L(S_2/w) \\ &= RD_L(S_1/w \uparrow L) \cup RD_L(S_2/w \uparrow L) \text{ [Assuming } S_1 \text{ and } S_2 \text{ satisfy NI]} \\ &= (RD(S_1/w \uparrow L) \cup RD(S_2/w \uparrow L)) \uparrow L \\ &= RD_L(S_1 \oplus S_2/w \uparrow L) \end{aligned}$$

This shows that that internal choice operator preserves NI.

Logical And. In Figure 3 we have 2 TMSCs S_1 and S_2 and their "logical and" $S = S_1 \wedge S_2$ and each $l_i \in L$ and each $h_i \in H$. Again due to shortage of space we do not provide a formal definition for construction of the logical and of the two processes . The intuition is that at each state of the process S_1 we calculate its ready set and logically "and" it with the ready set of the corresponding state in S_2. For example in the state A for S_1 the ready set is $\{\{l_2, h_1\}\}$ while for S_2 it is $\{\{l_2\}\}$ and so state A in S has its ready set as: $\{\{l_2, h_1\}\} \wedge \{\{l_2\}\} = \emptyset$ ie state A in S has no outgoing transitions.

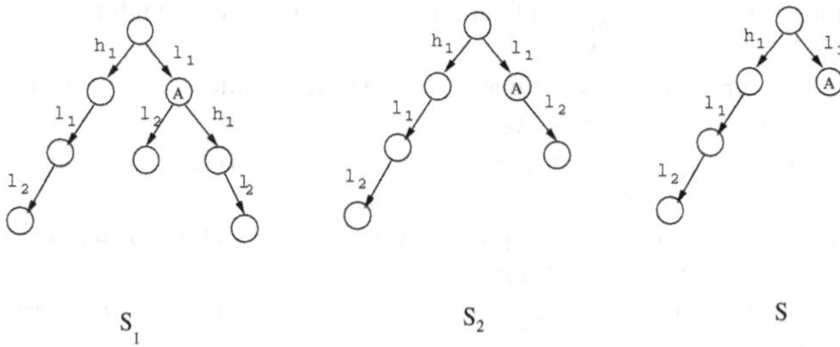

Fig. 3. Two TMSCs S_1 and S_2 and their "logical and" TMSC S

Both S_1 and S_2 satisfy NI because it is evident that by observing l_1 and l_2 we cannot deduce any information about the occurrence or non-occurrence of h_1. However their "logical and" S does not satisfy NI as an observer may observe the occurrence of l_1 and l_2 in sequence and deduce the occurrence of h_1.

The same result may be obtained formally from the ready set characterization of NI. We see that if we consider the trace $w = h_1 l_1$ then $RD_L(S/w) = \{\{l_2\}\}$ while $RD_L(S/w \uparrow L) = \phi$ and hence $RD_L(S/w)$ is not equal to $RD_L(S/w \uparrow L)$.

8 Conclusion and Future Work

This paper provides a way in which information-flow analysis can be done on specifications expressed as TMSCs. As we can see that with a ready-set based analysis of non-interference already in place, all that is needed are means to convert specification input formalisms to their respective ready-set characterizations. We have done this for TMSCs in this paper but there are several widely-used formal/informal/semi-formal notations that may be treated similarly. The analysis presented also makes a case for providing a rigorous formal semantics to a modeling/specification language because once one does that, it becomes easier to provide a translation to a form amenable to information flow analysis. With so many system description languages that still have an informal/semi-formal semantics, there is now an added incentive (ie the power to automatedly analyze information flow) to provide them with a formal semantics.

This paper also provides us an important intuition about the application of security analysis at each phase of requirements construction. As we construct more and more refined specifications by the application of operators, we have to keep note of the fact that by potentially removing traces (ie performing refinement) at each stage we may be introducing information leaks due to the removal of redundancy [In the previous section we saw how the $\wedge$ operator removed a trace that led to the violation of NI in S]. This makes it imperative to do NI analysis at each phase of requirements construction.

References

1. Message sequence charts (MSC). *ITU-TS Recommendation Z.120*, 1996.
2. D.E.Denning and P.J.Denning. Certification of programs for secure information flow. *Comm of the ACM*, 20(7):504–513, 1977.
3. D.Wagner. Static analysis and computer security:new techinques for software assurance. *PhD thesis, University of California, Berkeley*, 2000.
4. J.S. Fenton. Information protection systems. *Ph.D thesis, University of Cambridge, England*, 1973.
5. P.Ryan. Mathematical models of computer security–tutorial lectures. *Foundations of Security Analysis and Design*, 2171:1–62, 2001.
6. M.A. Reniers. Message sequence chart: Syntax and semantics. *PhD Thesis, Eindhoven University of Technology*, 1998.
7. R.Focardi, R.Gorrieri, and F.Martinelli. Information flow analysis in a discrete-time process algebra. *IEEE Computer Security Foundations Workshop*, pages 170–184, 2000.
8. Peter Ryan. A csp formulation of non-interference and unwinding. *Presented at CSFW 1990 and published in Cipher*, Winter 1990/91.
9. B. Sengupta and R. Cleaveland. Refinement-based requirements modeling using triggered message sequence charts. *IEEE International Requirements Engineering Conference*, 2003.
10. Bikram Sengupta. Triggered message sequence charts. *Ph.D Thesis, State University of New York, Stony Brook*, 2003.
11. Bikram Sengupta and Rance Cleaveland. Triggered message sequence charts. *Proceedings of ACM SIGSOFT Foundations of Software Engineering*, pages 167–176, 2002.

Framework for Safe Reuse of Software Binaries*

Ramakrishnan Venkitaraman and Gopal Gupta

Applied Logic, Programming-Languages and Systems (ALPS) Laboratory,
Department of Computer Science,
The University of Texas at Dallas

Abstract. In this paper we consider reusability of software component binaries. Reuse of code at the binary level is important because usually only the machine code for system components is available; vendors do not want to share their source code for proprietary reasons. We develop necessary and sufficient conditions for ensuring that software binaries are reusable and relate them to the coding standards that have been developed in the industry to ensure binary code reusability. These coding standards, in essence, discourage the (i) use of hard-coded pointers, and (ii) writing of non-reentrant code. Checking that binary code satisfies these standards/conditions, however, is undecidable, in general. We thus develop static analysis based methods for checking if a software binary satisfies these conditions. This static analysis rests on the abstract interpretation framework. We illustrate our approach by showing how we statically analyze the presence of hard coded pointer variables in assembly code obtained from binaries of digital signal processing applications. The analyzer we have developed takes the binary to be checked for reuse as input, disassembles it, builds the flow graph, and statically analyzes the flow graph to check for the presence of code that will hinder its reuse.

1 Introduction

Software components have received considerable attention in recent years. The dream is to develop a virtual marketplace of commercial-off-the-shelf (COTS) software components developed by third party vendors. To assemble new applications, developers merely choose the right components and glue them together, perhaps with small amount of additional code (*glue code*). Software components thus promote software reuse (plug-and-play) which helps reduce software development time, development cost, and the time-to-market for new software based systems.

Most third party vendors are unwilling to provide the source code of the component due to proprietary reasons. Thus, in most cases, only binary code is available. Distributing software in binary form means that integration of the software with other applications does not require recompilation but only linking

* Authors have been partially supported by grants from the National Science Foundation, the Department of Education, and the Environmental Protection Agency.

R.K. Ghosh and H. Mohanty (Eds.): ICDCIT 2004, LNCS 3347, pp. 283–293, 2004.

with the application. That is, application developers will use the API provided to call the functions available in the component, the application code will then have to be linked to the software components' binary prior to being loaded in the main memory for execution.

However, the problem that arises then is ensuring that the software component is written in such a way that it does not hinder reuse of its binary. For example, the execution of component binary should not alter the application's binary code. In this paper we are interested in analyzing the necessary and sufficient conditions under which a component binary can be reused.[1] We are also interested in detecting automatically if a binary satisfies these conditions.

Our work is motivated by practical concerns for software reuse in the digital signal processing (DSP) industry [4]. Texas Instruments (TI), world's leading manufacturer of DSP hardware, is interested in developing a marketplace for DSP software COTS component. However, most of the DSP code from vendors is available as a binary for DSP processors in the TI TMS320 family. DSP software developers tend to use low level optimizations to make their software very efficient. One has to ensure that these low level optimization do not interfere with reusability. Researchers at Texas Instruments have developed "general programming rules" as part of their *Express DSP Algorithm Interoperability Standard* (XDAIS) [21] that defines a set of requirements for DSP code (for TI TMS320 family of DSP processors). If DSP software developers follow this code, then it will be possible for system integrators to quickly assemble production quality DSP systems from one or more subsystems. The programming rules essentially lay down the restrictions that, if not followed, will result in code incompatibility during reuse (e.g., one rule restricts the usage of hard coded pointers in the program).

In this paper we analyze necessary and sufficient conditions for software binary code reusability. We relate these conditions to the TI's XDAIS standard. The necessary and sufficient conditions are derived from the fact that linking and loading of binaries is done under certain assumptions. The binaries must not execute any instruction that will violate these assumptions.

Further, we are interested in developing automatic tools that will detect if a program is not compliant with these conditions. However, the compliance checking is undecidable in general (this constitutes the reason why TI has found it hard to develop tool for checking compliance of a program code with XDAIS standard [4]). We propose to use static analysis to perform this compliance check. However, static analysis of the program code is complicated by the fact that the source code of the program is not available—vendors generally just ship their binaries that can be linked with other codes. Thus, to check for compliance assembly code has to be analyzed. It should be noted that static analysis of assembly code is quite hard, as no type information is available. Thus, for exam-

[1] Note that software reusability is a very broad term [11], however, for our work we are primarily interested in reuse of software binary code. In the rest of the paper, the term software reuse should be taken to mean software binary code reuse.

ple, distinguishing a pointer variable from a data value becomes quite difficult. Also, most compilers take instruction level parallelism and instruction pipelining provided by modern processors into account while generating code. This further exacerbates the automatic static analysis of assembly code. Our static analysis framework is based on abstract interpretation. Thus, assembly code is abstractly interpreted (taking instruction level parallelism and pipelining into account) to infer program properties. A *backward analysis* is used since in most cases data type of a memory location has to be inferred by how the value it stores is used. Once a point of use is determined, the analysis proceeds backwards to check for the desired property.

We illustrate our approach by considering how we statically analyze the presence of *hard-coded pointers* (rule 3 of the TI XDAIS [21] standard), i.e., how we check whether a pointer variable has been assigned a constant value by the programmer. We give details of the tool that we have built for this purpose. Other rules can be checked in a similar manner. Note that our goal in this project has been to produce an analyzer that can be used to check for compliance of large commercial quality program codes. Thus, all (nasty) features of C that may impact the analysis have been considered (most DSP code is written in C). For example, in hard-codedness analysis, we have to consider cases where pointers are implicitly obtained via array declarations, pointers with double or more levels of indirections (e.g., int **p), pointers to statically allocated global data area, etc. Our work makes the following contributions:

- Necessary and sufficient conditions are developed for checking if a software binary code is reusable.
- A static analysis based framework is proposed for checking if these reusability conditions are satisfied. We show that software binaries can be successfully analyzed via abstract interpretation based techniques, even in the presence of instruction level parallelism and pipelining.
- The static analysis based framework is used to develop a practical system for compliance checking for one of the conditions (hard codedness of pointers).

We assume that the reader is familiar with abstract interpretation; tutorial introduction can be found in chapter 1 of [1].

2 Reuse of Software Binaries

Third party code is generally made available by supplying a software binary that is linked with the applications that makes use of it. Vendors are generally reluctant to share their source code due to proprietary reasons. If software component binaries are to be reused, then one must ensure that these binaries do not include code that will compromise the reusability of the code. Reusability can be compromised, for example, if the code contains hard-coded pointers, or if the code is self-modifying or modifies other binaries that are linked to it.

Note that it is important to make a distinction between *usability* vs *reusability* of a software system. Certain, programming idioms, if used, may appear to compromise the reusability of the software system, however, on closer analysis they relate to issue of usability. For example, if a binary code makes array references that are out of bound, then this may appear as violating binary code reusability (the references may be to addresses outside the binary's code or data area). Indeed, reusability is compromised if out of bound array references are made unintentionally. However, if out-of-bound array references are present unintentionally, then this means that the program still has software bugs that have not been removed. Thus, the software is not even usable, let alone reusable. In this paper we are not interested in issues of software usability.

Once binary code is given, it goes through two more steps prior to execution: (i) *linking* this binary with other binaries (done by a linker); and, (ii) the final *loading* of the resultant executable in the main memory by the loader after address relocation. A linker primarily performs the task of symbol resolution (determining relative offsets for labels), while a loader adds the proper offsets to addresses so that the program can be loaded in the area of the virtual memory allocated by the OS. Linking and loading operations are performed under certain assumptions. Reusability is compromised if the execution of this binary code results in these assumptions being violated.

A linker obviously assumes that the offset of a label will not change later. That is, given an instruction in a binary B_1 involving a label, e.g., `jump L1`, where `L1` is a label defined in another binary B_2 that is being linked to B_1, then the offset for `L1` should not change after linking. That is, the code starting from location `L1` will not be relocated somewhere else after the linking phase is over. Similarly, a loader assumes that an executable can be loaded anywhere in the virtual memory. Thus, to ensure reusability of binary code the following two conditions must hold:

- **C1** The binary code should not change during execution in a way that link-time symbol resolution will become invalid.
- **C2** The binary code should not be written in a way that it needs to be located starting from some fixed location in the virtual memory.

We assume that no additional information is given w.r.t. conditions under which a software component binary is to be used, apart from a specification of the API.

Theorem: Conditions **C1** and **C2** are necessary for binary code reusability.

Proof: The proof by contradiction is straightforward and is omitted.

These conditions are also sufficient, because they cover all the assumptions made during linking and loading. Note, however, that the necessary conditions above are hard to characterize and even harder to detect. Thus, in practice we broaden these conditions and consider more general conditions that are easier to characterize and detect. A broader condition that captures **C1** is that the binary code should be re-entrant. Similarly, for **C2** it is sufficient to check that there are no hard coded memory addresses in the program. Thus, checking for reusability can be reduced to checking for the following conditions: (i) **C3:** that the binary code is re-entrant; (ii) and, **C4:** the binary code does not contain any hard-wired memory addresses. Note that code re-entrance is a very useful way of characterizing conditions for reusability, because very often the same component binary may be executed by multiple threads or processes. Code re-entrance implies that such concurrent execution can take place safely.

Theorem : If conditions **C3** and **C4** hold, then the binary code is reusable (i.e., **C3** and **C4** are sufficient).

Proof: We will show that if **C1** (resp. **C2**) does not hold then **C3** (resp. **C4**) does not hold either. If **C1** does not hold, then the symbol mapping for address labels determined at link-time does not hold at execution time. This implies that the symbol mapping was altered at execution time, i.e., the binary code got altered during execution, which in turn implies that the code is non re-entrant. Similarly, if **C2** does not hold, then there must be some address in the binary code that is used during the execution that is fixed. Thus, **C4** does not hold. □

Note that while **C1** implies **C3** and **C2** implies **C4**, the implication does not necessarily hold in the other direction. Thus, the code may not be re-entrant yet may be reusable, as long as the modifications made to the binary at run-time are such that the symbol mapping is not altered and only one thread uses the binary code at any given time. Likewise, hard wired addresses may be present, yet the code may still be loaded any where as long as the specific hard-wired addresses are known and they do not interfere with the area where the code is loaded. Thus, **C3** and **C4** are sufficient conditions, but not necessary conditions.

Finally, note that the application must be re-entrant as a whole. Checking for re-entrancy of a component binary may not be enough, because some other component binary may modify it during execution. Thus, each component binary when checked in isolation appears to be re-entrant, but when put together, it is not re-entrant.

2.1 The XDAIS Programming Standard

The coding standard rules, published by TI for software vendors of its DSP chips, that fall under the category of "general programming rules" [21] are the following:

1. All programs must follow the runtime conventions imposed by TI's implementation of the C programming language.
2. All programs must be reentrant within a preemptive environment including time sliced preemption.
3. All data references must be fully relocatable (subject to alignment requirements). That is, there must be no "hard coded" data memory locations.
4. The code must be fully relocatable. That is, there can be no hard coded program memory locations.
5. Programs must characterize their ROM-ability; i.e., state whether they are ROM-able or not. ROM-ability means that if part of the executable is placed in the DSP ROM, it would still function; this restricts the way global data can be accessed (data cannot be placed in ROM) [21].

6. Programs must never directly access any peripheral device. This includes but is not limited to on-chip DMA's, timers, I/O devices, and cache control registers.

Rule 1 is not really a programming rule, since it requires compliance with TI's definition of C. However, rules 2 through 5 are manifestations of conditions **C3** and **C4** above. Thus, Rules 2 and 5 correspond to condition **C3** while Rules 3, 4 and 6 correspond to condition **C4**. In light of these conditions, and examining the entire instruction set of TI's TMS320 family of DSP processors, one can show that indeed the XDAIS standard is sufficient for ensuring that binary code that is compliant with it is reusable.

There are a number of advantages to DSP software vendors writing programs that comply with the published standards [21]. Compliance to standards (i) allows system integrators to easily migrate between TI DSP subsystems; (ii) enable host tools to simplify a system integrators tasks, including configuration, performance modeling, standard conformance, and debugging; (iii) subsystems from multiple software vendors can be integrated into a single system; (iv) programs are framework-agnostic, that is, they are reusable: the same program can be efficiently used in virtually any application or framework; and, (v) programs can be deployed in purely static as well as dynamic run-time environments (due to code relocatability).

2.2 Automatic Reusability Analysis

Next, we are interested in developing tools that automatically detect if a binary code is reusable. This entails automatically determining if any of the 5 programming rules above are not complied with. Detecting if rules 3, 4 or 6 are violated involves checking that there are no hard-coded references in the code. Checking for rules 2 and 5 involves ensuring that no writes are made to the code area during execution. Checking for hard codedness or checking that no writes are made to a specific memory area is undecidable [12] in general. Thus, one has to resort to approximating this automated checking. A standard method is to use static analysis [2]. Static analysis however is complicated by the fact that only binary code is available. All the type information is lost in the binary code, thus even determining if a value is an address or data is not quite that easy. In the rest of the paper we consider the problem of detecting hard-codedness and develop an abstract interpretation based framework for detecting hard-coded references. A similar analysis can be developed to check for code re-entrance (that is, for checking that no writes are made to the code area; we do not discuss this any further due to lack of space.)

3 Analysis of Hard-Coded Pointers

We illustrate our static analysis based approach to compliance checking by showing how we check compliance for rule #3, which states that there should be no hard-coded data memory locations. A data memory locations is hard coded in

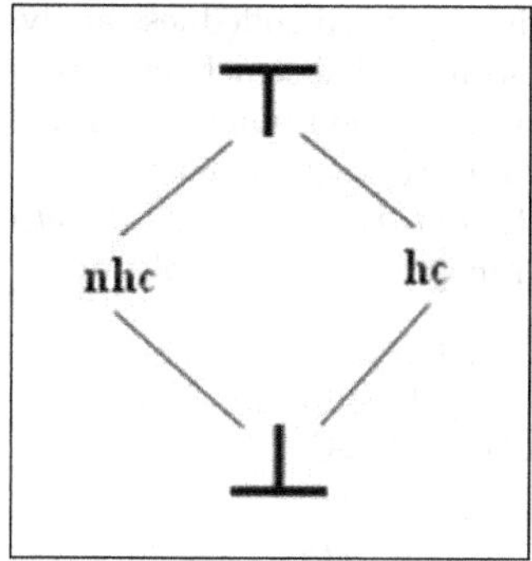

Fig. 1. Lattice Abstraction

the assembly code if a constant is moved into a register R_i, and R_i is then used as a base register in a later instruction. The constant value may of course be transferred to another register R_j directly or indirectly, and then R_j used later in dereferencing. Since most of the TI's DSP code is written in C, data memory locations can be hard coded either in assembly code embedded in a C program, or by using pointers provided in the C language[18]. Note also that the problem of detecting dereferencing of hard-coded pointers subsumes the problem of detecting dereferencing of NULL pointers. This is because a NULL pointer is a pointer that has been assigned a special constant (usually 0x0). Thus our analysis will also detect NULL pointer dereferences. Similarly, hard-codedness analysis subsumes analysis for checking if un-initialized pointer variables are dereferenced. This is because hard-codedness analysis attempts to check if a pointer dereference is reachable from a point of initialization; and thus will detect any pointers that are dereferenced but not initialized. Thus, our hard-codedness analysis performs two of the checks proposed by the UNO project [15] at the assembly level. The UNO project claims that NULL pointers, un-initialized pointers, and array out of bounds reference are three most common run-time programming errors.

3.1 Abstract Interpretation Based Static Program Analysis

Static program analysis (or static analysis for brevity) is defined as any analysis of a program carried out without completely executing the program. Clearly, the problem of detecting hard coded references is undecidable in general. So we employ static analysis for detection of hard codedness (from this point on, we'll call the analysis *hard-codedness analysis*). The hard-codedness analysis analyzes each pointer variable and determines if the pointer is definitely hard-coded (HC), definitely not hard-coded (NHC), or that its hard-codedness status cannot be deduced. The *abstract domain* [7] is quite simple and consists of four values: $\bot$, $\top$, HC and NHC. In the abstract interpretation framework [7], a *collecting semantics* is used which consists of the abstract environments that might be associated with a program point (an arc in the flow-graph). An environment maps a pointer variable to an address in the set $\mathcal{A}$, where $\mathcal{A}$ is the set of all

memory addresses (note that for hard codedness analysis we are only interested in pointer variables). Following the abstract interpretation approach, we define the abstraction and the concretization functions, α and γ, respectively, as maps between concrete and abstract contexts as follows:
α : *Contexts* $\rightarrow$ *Abstract_Contexts*, where *Abstract_Contexts* consists of abstract environments which map pointer variables to values in $\mathcal{A}_\alpha$.

$$\begin{aligned}\alpha(C) &= \bot,\ C = \{\};\\ &= nhc,\ C \subseteq \mathcal{A}_{nhc};\\ &= hc,\ C \subseteq \mathcal{A}_{hc};\\ &= \top \ \ otherwise;\end{aligned}$$

$$\begin{aligned}\gamma : Abstract\_Contexts &\rightarrow Contexts\\ \gamma(S) &= \{\},\ S = \bot,;\\ &= \mathcal{A}_{hc},\ S = hc;\\ &= \mathcal{A}_{nhc},\ S = nhc;\\ &= \mathcal{A},\ otherwise\end{aligned}$$

We next have to abstract the operators involving pointer arithmetic. (Table 1).

Table 1. Pointer Arithmetic

+/-	hc	nhc	$\bot$	$\top$
hc	hc	nhc	$\bot$	$\top$
nhc	nhc	nhc	nhc	nhc
$\bot$	$\bot$	nhc	$\bot$	$\bot$
$\top$	$\top$	nhc	$\bot$	$\top$

Once the abstract operators are defined, we can compute the abstract semantics of the program by computing the fix-point. Finally, we have to show that our analysis is sound. The soundness of the analysis follows if we can show that α and γ are mutually consistent and that *Abstract_Contexts* form a lattice. Detailed description about our abstract interpretation framework and soundness proof can be found in [18].

3.2 The Analysis Algorithm

As discussed earlier, the analyzer has access only to the object (binary) code which is to be checked for compliance with the standard. The analyzer disassembles the object code and to obtain the corresponding *assembly language code.* The disassembly is performed using *TI Code Composer Studio* [21]. The disassembled code is provided as input to the static analyzer which produces a result which indicates whether the code is compliant with the rule. Figure 2 shows the various steps involved in the analyzer we have developed. It should be noted that there are advantages as well as disadvantages of performing static analysis at the assembly level. Detailed descriptions with examples can be found in [18].

The analyzer functions in two phases. In the first phase, it scans through the flow-graph and detects all the register dereferencing that correspond to the dereferencing of pointer variables in the source code. We call such a set a (potentially) *unsafe* set. The unsafe sets represent the abstract contexts discussed earlier. In the second phase the unsafe sets are iteratively refined, until a fix-point is reached. During phase 2, unsafe sets from multiple paths are merged to reduce execution time. Merging results in information loss. But, merging information does not make the analyzer give incorrect results as the integrity of the individual unsafe sets is preserved. The analyzer can handle complex programming constructs including loops, arrays, global variables, functions, multi-level pointers, parallelism, and pipelining. The analyzer was run over a suite of test code obtained from TI. Detailed description of the analysis algorithm and the performance results are reported in [18].

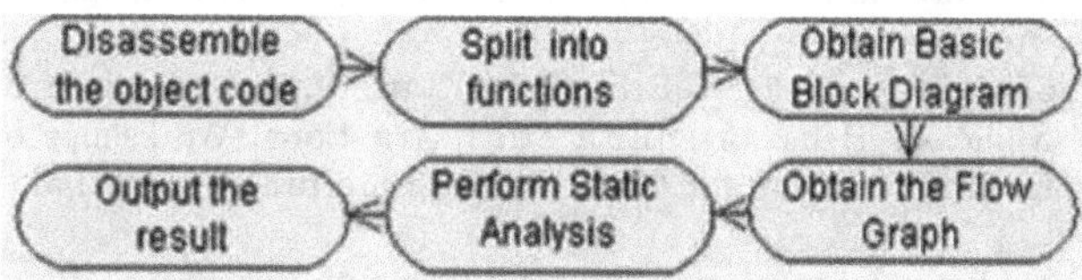

Fig. 2. Activity Diagram

4 Related Work

Static analysis has been recognized as an important technology for software quality assurance [17, 19], however, the limited efforts described in the literature primarily analyze the source code [8, 5, 6, 19, 15, 17]; none of them deal with code reusability. Those that analyze assembly code are only interested in security properties [3, 8] and not in reusability. Thus, to the best of our knowledge there is no existing work that statically analyzes assembly code to check for software reusability.

5 Conclusions and Future Work

In this paper, we developed and analyzed necessary and sufficient conditions for binary code reusability. We showed that absence of hard-coded memory addresses and code re-entrance are sufficient conditions to ensure binary code reusability. However, automatically checking that these conditions hold for a binary code is undecidable in general. We proposed static analysis as a technique for approximating this check. We illustrate the approach by developing a static analyzer for analysis of hard-coded pointers, and develop an abstract interpretation based static analysis framework for this purpose. Our results show that static analysis based approaches are viable in industrial settings for checking for coding standards compliance. Code compliance checking is critical for code reuse and COTS compatibility in applications. A complete analyzer has been developed for pointer hard-codedness analysis and shown to run successfully on code samples taken from Texas Instruments' DSP code suite. The prototype system is currently being refined to provide more accurate results in presence of global pointers and mutually recursive functions. We are also extending the system to handle rules 2, 4 through 6 [21] laid out by TI. The analysis needed for these rules is similar to that for hard-codedness and we are quite confident that a abstract interpretation based static analysis framework is sufficient.

References

1. S. Abramsky and C. Hankin Abstract Interpretation of Declarative Languages, Ellis Horwood, 1987.
2. Alfred V.Aho, Ravi Sethi and Jeffrey D.Ullman Compilers: Principles, Techniques, and Tools. Addison-Wesley, 1988.
3. J. Bergeron, M. Debbabi, M.M. Erhioui, B. Ktari. Static Analysis of Binary Code to Isolate Malicious Behaviors. IEEE 8th International Workshops on Enabling Technologies: Infrastructure for Collaborative Enterprises, 1999. Palo Alto, California
4. S. Blonstein (Texas Instruments). Personal Communication.
5. Hao Chen, Jonathan S. Shapiro. Exploring Static Checking for Software Assurance. SRL Technical Report SRL-2003-06.
6. B.V. Chess. Improving computer security using extending static checking. IEEE Symposium on Security and Privacy, 2002.
7. P. Cousot, R. Cousot. Abstract Interpretation: A Unified Lattice Model for Static Analysis of Programs by Construction of Approximation of Fixpoints. Fourth Annual ACM Symp. on Principles of Programming Languages. 1977. pp. 238-252.
8. Mihai Christodorescu and Somesh Jha. Static Analysis of Executables to Detect Malicious Patterns. 12th USENIX Security Symposium, August 2003.
9. Saumya Debray, Robert Muth, Matthew Weippert Alias analysis of executable code. POPL'98.
10. M. Fernandez and R. Espasa. Speculative alias analysis for executable code. International Conference on Parallel Architectures and Compilation Techniques. 2002.
11. W. Frake, C. Terry. Software Reuse: Metrics and Models. In *ACM Computing Surveys* 28(2):1996.
12. M. R. Garey and D. S. Johnson. Computers and Intractability. W. H. Freeman and Company. New York. 1979.
13. Bill Gates. The Future of Programming in a World of Web Services (keynote address). 17th Annual ACM Conference on Object-Oriented Programming, Systems, Languages and Application Seattle, Washington Friday, November 8, 2002
14. Nevin Heintze, Oiivier Tardieu. Demand-Driven Pointer Analysis Conference on Programming Language Design and Implementation 2001
15. Gerard J. Holzmann. Static Source Code Checking for User-defined Properties. Conference on Integrated Design and Process Technology, IDPT-2002.
16. W. Landi and B. G. Ryder, A Safe Approximate Algorithm for Interprocedural Pointer Aliasing. Proc. SIGPLAN PLDI '92. pp. 235–248.
17. Horst Licheter and Gerhard Riedinger Improving software quality by static program analysis Proc. of SPI 97 software process improvement, Barcelona, 1997

18. R. Venkitaraman and G. Gupta, Static Program Analysis of Embedded Executable Assembly Code. Compilers, Architecture, and Synthesis for Embedded Systems (ACM CASES), September 2004 pp. 157-166.
19. David A. Wagner. Static analysis and computer security: New techniques for Software Assurance. University of California at Berkley Phd Dissertation. Dec. 2000.
20. W. E. Weihl. Interprocedural data flow analysis in the presence of pointers, procedure variables, and label variables. Proc. ACM POPL. Jan. 1980. pp. 83–94.
21. Texas Instruments Code Composer Studio and XDAIS/TMS320 Algorithmic Standards Literature (No: SPRU509C, No: SPRU301C, No: SPRU352D, No: SPRU189F).

Supporting Partial Component Matching

Padmanabhan Krishnan* and Lei Wang

Centre for Software Assurance,
Faculty of Information Technology,
Bond University,
Gold Coast, Queensland 4229,
Australia
{pkrishna, lwang}@staff.bond.edu.au

Abstract. In this paper we define a formal framework for describing components and gaps or holes (where components can be plugged in). This is based on the theory of interface automata. The main focus is to define a component partially satisfying the requirements of a hole. A partial plug-in of a hole will result in other holes. The definition of a partial plug-in does not result in a unique set of holes, i.e., the resulting holes can have different properties. We define an software engineering process which uses the formal framework to complete the component selection and insertion process. The process is defined in terms of the possible interactions between a component vendor and a customer seeking a component.

1 Motivation

Software components have been proposed as the main technology to address the problem of complexity. The principal thesis is that components, by enabling reuse permit one to rely on subsystems developed by external vendors to simplify the customer's design and implementation. This reduces the effort required to develop the entire system. That is by using pre-packaged code, building complex systems can be simplified. Users of components must be able to identify components that suit their needs. This is the problem of component retrieval.

To enable components to be plugged in, frameworks which specify standardized interfaces have been proposed. For example, the Enterprise JavaBeans™ (EJB) framework is aimed at distributed systems and provides support for services such as transactions and persistent objects. The customer can then use tools which perform syntactic checks using the interface signatures.

However, before one can use such components in a meaningful way, it is important to understand the functionality provided. Some of this information is captured by the API of the component and its associated documentation. But this is not adequate for the application specific aspects of components. However, the technique to construct a particular application given a set of beans is not obvious. For both EJBs and JBs the emphasis is only on the signature. Hence a 'type correct' use of the components will not result in compilation errors but could result in unexpected or unwanted behaviours.

* Corresponding Author.

R.K. Ghosh and H. Mohanty (Eds.): ICDCIT 2004, LNCS 3347, pp. 294–303, 2004.

The idea of contracts [Pah01], i.e., the obligations of the provider and the user of the components has been proposed to facilitate smooth integration of components. These contracts usually capture multiparty agreements. There have been various suggestions for specifying contracts — pre and post conditions being the most common. Pre and post conditions are useful in describing the internal features of a component at a high level of abstraction. Semantically components can be described using interfaces [dH01b].

However the key issues that remain include the ability to use the services provided by the component to suit the needs of the application. The selection problem for formally defined components has been addressed via specification matching [ZW97, BG97]. As noted by various practitioners (e.g., `http://www.cbdiforum.com`), having a specification for the component is necessary but not enough. Without a specification, it is not possible to choose a component. However, if the specification is too detailed, it may not match the situation in which it might be relevant. This has been recognised as the retrieval and adaptation problem [ZW97].

Pahl [Pah01] introduces the concept of components to UML. This is achieved by extending packages with the notion of interfaces to capture some semantic information. The main emphasis in the paper is on developing a framework for reasoning about component composition and contracts. This is based on the notion of a connector between the provider and the consumer. The paper also defines suitable notions of refinement and implementation. This is done using the π-calculus [MPW92].

ISpec [Jon00] provides a mixed approach to the specification of interfaces. Specifications in ISpec can range from completely formal to completely informal. All specifications are in general a multi-party contract for services. These can be at one of six levels. The IDL level is mainly syntactic and describes the signature of the interface. The summary level describes the effect of the operations while the model level describes the various abstract classes representing the parties to the contract. The action level describes the effect (presented in the summary level) in an algorithmic style to describe behaviour. One can also use pre and post conditions or a complete formal specification.

Most of the theories for component selection assume that a single component to suit the requirements can be found. However that is rarely the case and in most situations some gluing code has to be written. This can also be viewed as a-posteriori integration without modifying the component code [MO02]. That is the pre or post condition need not match precisely. It can be leave certain conditions to be satisfied by other components. This allows the incremental addition of components to fill the various holes. The use of multiple components to fill different holes needs care. If two components make different assumptions about the flow of data and control they are defined to be mismatched [GAO95].

Greenfield and Short propose the idea of a software factory [GS03]. This is based on the observation that approximately two thirds of a system will consist of pre-built components. A third of the system will contain application specific software and even that will be related to the customisation of components to suit the particular application. This process is called development by assembly.

While the theories above describe the semantics of interfaces and combining them, they do not describe the process for selecting components that can meet the requirements. The interaction between the possible vendors of the components and the consumer of the components is not specified. As we will show there are various possible outcomes when considering partial plug-ins. Hence a suitable software engineering process is necessary to ensure that both vendors and customers are satisfied. The PORE technique [NM99] proposes an iterative technique to ensure compliance between the customer's needs and the services provided by the component. Agent based techniques [WF03] where co-operation between expert agents to solve the component selection problem can also be used to describe a process. Voas [Voa99] advocates the role of the end user to certify components. Here there is an implicit process followed by both the end user and the component creator. In another approach a knowledge based technique for off the shelf components [CC02] is integrated with the requirements process. In many cases this is not suitable as the potential use of components may be known only after detailed design.

In this paper we show how holes in partially assembled systems can be modelled. This includes partial filling of the holes which can then generate other holes. A model based on interface automata and its associated algebraic properties [dH01b, dH01a] is presented. We also show how this presents a number of practical problems, which is then solved by a collaborative process for component selection. The paper is organised as follows. In the rest of this section we present an overview of our notion of pre-assembly, components and filling in gaps with components. In the next section we present the formal details of interface automata [dH01a] and a modified notion of composition that is useful for partial plugins. In Section 3 we develop the process which uses the formal details.

As is typical we assume that both a component and pluggable hole has the notion of input and output ports (see Figure 1 where inputs are shown as circles and outputs as lines). A pre-assembly is an incomplete system which has some existing subsystems along with various holes (see Figure 2). We prefer the term pre-assembly to frameworks as the term frameworks has a variety of meanings.

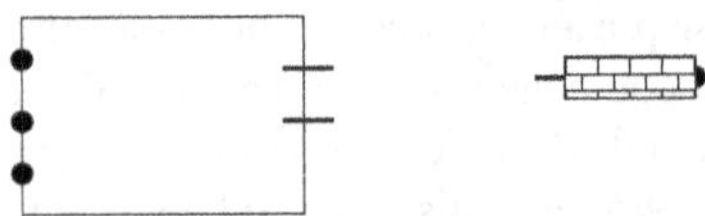

Fig. 1. Hole and Component

The various holes could be interlinked; i.e., the behaviour of one hole can affect another. In general a component's input port can be linked with an output port in a pluggable hole. In this case the link is no longer available. We also allow a synchronous interpretation where a hole and a component can share inputs or outputs. When they are combined these inputs and outputs continue to be remain as inputs or outputs. Figure 3 shows three cases of a partial plugin. Assume that the hole has three inputs and two outputs. In the first case the component consumes one input and generates an output which synchronise with one output and input respectively. Hence they are no longer available in the new preassembly. In the second and third cases the inputs and outputs remain. The benefit of this is shown in the third case where the same input can be reused by two different components.

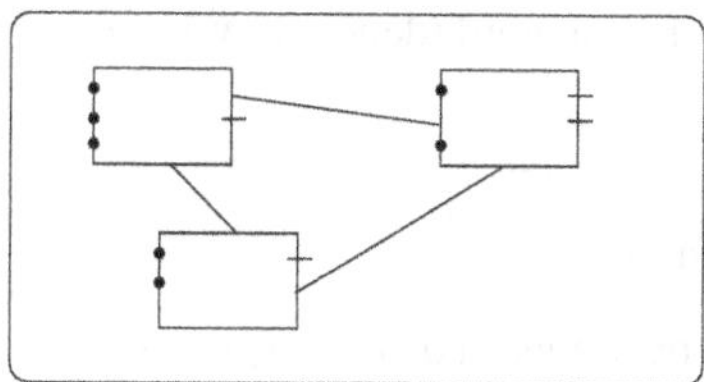

Fig. 2. Preassembly

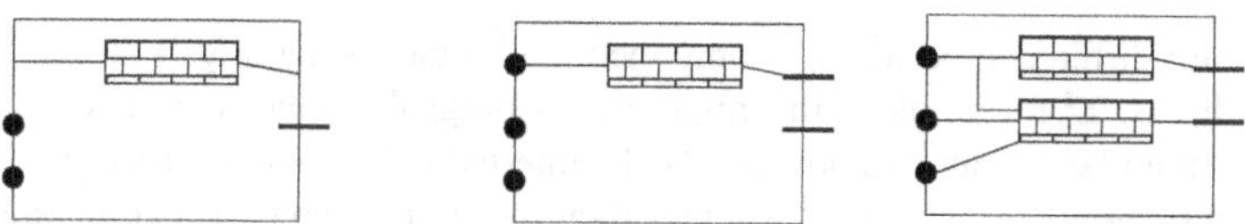

Fig. 3. Partial Plugin: Three Examples

This is related to the semantics of PIN [ISW02] and allows both synchronous and asynchronous composition. If a component only partially satisfies the resulting hole can be viewed as a hole into which another component can be plugged in or can be viewed as a place holder for a connector. In our general model, especially without a specific architecture, the separation between a hole an a place holder for a connector is artificial. Hence we do not formally distinguish a connector and a hole. The definition of holes, components and partial composition is formalised in the next section.

2 Formal Model

As for interface automata, the structure of the automata used to describe the expected behaviour of holes or gaps and components is given in the following definition.

2.1 Behaviour

Definition 1. A finite automaton representing a gap or a component is defined as $\mathcal{A} = (Q, \Sigma, \longrightarrow, q^s)$ where

- Q is a finite set of states with q^s the start state.
- the alphabet Σ is partitioned into three sets Σ^I (the input actions), Σ^O (the output actions) and Σ^τ (the internal actions). As a notational convenience $\Sigma^V = \Sigma^I \cup \Sigma^O$ will denote the set of visible actions.
- $\longrightarrow \subseteq Q \times \Sigma \times Q$ is the transition relation to describe behaviour.

The above definition is standard except for the notion of acceptance. For the purposes of this work, all words that have a run are accepted. That is, there is no accepting state. As the internal actions are not relevant for the behaviour described at the interface, only the strings over the input and output actions are relevant. The language over the visible actions associated with an automaton $\mathcal{A}$ is indicated by $\mathcal{L}^\tau(\mathcal{A})$. The erasing of internal actions and the associated language that is accepted is defined below.

Definition 2. The restriction of a word (denoted by $\uparrow$) to an alphabet Σ is defined as:

$$\varepsilon \uparrow \Sigma = \varepsilon$$
$$aw \uparrow \Sigma = \begin{cases} a(w \uparrow \Sigma) & \text{if } a \in \Sigma \\ w \uparrow \Sigma & \text{otherwise} \end{cases}$$

A run of an automaton over a word $a_0 a_1 \cdots a_n$ is a sequence of states $q_0, q_1 \ldots q_{n+1}$ such that $q_0 = q^s$ and $q_i \xrightarrow{a_i} q_{i+1}$ for every i between 0 and n.

A word w belongs to $\mathcal{L}^\tau(\mathcal{A})$ iff there is a word w' such that there is a run of $\mathcal{A}$ over w' and $w = w' \uparrow \Sigma^V$

The main difference between a component and a gap is that a gap has no internal actions. That is, Σ^τ for a hole is the empty set. A pluggable hole should describe only the input output behaviour and not specify the internal behaviour or structure.

Two automata (irrespective of whether they represent a hole or a component) can be composed if the set of internal actions of one component is disjoint with the actions of the other component. An input for one automata can be the same as the output of another. The linking of the input with the output results in the action being an internal action. Unlike interface automata, input and output actions can be shared (they continue to remain as input our output actions). This adopts a synchronous notion to the actions. This is useful as inputs or outputs when used by one component do not become unavailable to other components. It allows for an input or an output action to be used as many times as necessary. It is only when an input is combined with an output the action becomes an internal action and hence is no longer available.

Definition 3. Formally, the composition of two automata $\mathcal{A}_1 = (Q_1, \Sigma_1, \longrightarrow_1, q_1^s)$ and $\mathcal{A}_2 = (Q_2, \Sigma_2, \longrightarrow_2, q_2^s)$ (written as $\mathcal{A}_1 \otimes \mathcal{A}_2$) is an automaton $\mathcal{A} = (Q, \Sigma, \longrightarrow, q^s)$ where

- $\Sigma_1^\tau \cap \Sigma_2 = \emptyset$ and $\Sigma_2^\tau \cap \Sigma_1 = \emptyset$.
- $Q = Q_1 \times Q_2$
- $\Sigma = \Sigma_1 \cup \Sigma_2$ such that
  $\Sigma^I = (\Sigma_1^I - \Sigma_2^O) \cup (\Sigma_2^I - \Sigma_1^O)$
  $\Sigma^O = (\Sigma_1^O - \Sigma_2^I) \cup (\Sigma_2^O - \Sigma_1^I)$
  $\Sigma^\tau = (\Sigma_1^\tau \cup \Sigma_2^\tau \cup (\Sigma_2^I \cap \Sigma_1^O) \cup (\Sigma_2^O \cap \Sigma_1^I)$
- $(q_1, q_2) \xrightarrow{a} (q_1', q_2')$ iff
  If $a \in \Sigma_1 \cap \Sigma_2$, $q_1 \xrightarrow{a}_1 q_1'$ and $q_2 \xrightarrow{a}_2 q_2'$
  If $a \in \Sigma_1 - \Sigma_2$, $q_1 \xrightarrow{a}_1 q_1'$ and $q_2 = q_2'$ and
  If $a \in \Sigma_2 - \Sigma_1$, $q_2 \xrightarrow{a}_2 q_2'$ and $q_1 = q_1'$
- $q^s = (q_1^s, q_2^s)$

The input actions of the composite automaton include all the original inputs except those that have been combined with an output. Similarly the output actions includes all original outputs except for those that have been combined with an input. These combined actions are added to the set of internal actions. The transition relation requires synchronisation on common actions and asynchronous behaviour on any action that belongs to only one automaton. This definition is similar to the behaviour of asynchronous automata [DR95] and it permits different parts of the system to either evolve asynchronously or co-operate via synchronisation (i.e., reuse the input or output actions).

The partial matching of a component to a hole can now be defined. This is the process of fitting a component which may not exactly match a given hole. The result of such a partial plug is holes which satisfy a modified specification. The end result should be that the new holes combined with the component automata should yield the original behaviour.

The requirement can be defined as follows.

Definition 4. Let $\mathcal{A}_H$ be the original hole or gap and $\mathcal{A}_C$ the candidate component. If plugging in the component into the hole results in the new holes $\mathcal{A}_{H_1} \cdots \mathcal{A}_{H_n}$, then $\mathcal{L}^\tau(\mathcal{A}_H) = \mathcal{L}^\tau(\mathcal{A}_C \otimes \mathcal{A}_{H_1} \otimes \cdots \otimes \mathcal{A}_{H_n})$.

2.2 Partial Assembly

There are various possibilities while filling a hole with a component. There are four main cases to consider. The initial focus is on the alphabet of the interface. In Section 2.3 the behavioural issues for one particular case will be discussed. Due to space limitations the behavioural aspects of the new holes will be discussed only for this specific case.

Assume that Σ_C^I and Σ_C^O are the input and output actions the component that is under consideration. Also assume that Σ_H^I and Σ_H^O are the input and output actions associated with the exist hole.

If $\Sigma_H^I \subseteq \Sigma_C^I$ the component may accept more inputs than the original gap. These extra inputs are valid when considering refinement but from a pragmatic point they could cause difficulty. For instance, these extra inputs could influence the flow of control.

Hence a new hole whose output is the set $\Sigma_C^I - \Sigma_H^I$ is required. The extra inputs accepted (or perhaps required) by the component are not generated by the environment of the original gap. Hence the new gap must be able to generate them from the original set of inputs viz., Σ_H^I. When the new gap is combined with the component the extra inputs will become internal actions.

If $\Sigma_C^I \subseteq \Sigma_H^I$, there are two principal choices for the new hole's input actions. The first is to exploit the synchronous composition and assume that the entire input set is available. The second choice is to restrict the input to only those not used by the component, viz., $\Sigma_H^I - \Sigma_C^I$.

It is possible to consider other cases where the new hole's input language is expanded and another hole which can generate these inputs (there by creating a number of internal actions). This is acceptable as the final set of visible actions remains the same.

If $\Sigma_H^O \subseteq \Sigma_C^O$ the component generates more outputs. This may not be acceptable and a new hole is created whose task will be convert the extra outputs to the original outputs. The input alphabet of the new hole should contain at least $\Sigma_C^O - \Sigma_H^O$ which will make then internal actions after composition. Any action in the Σ_H^I can also belong to the set of input actions. That way, the new hole may be able to communicate (via synchronisation) with the component. The output actions will be Σ_H^O.

If $\Sigma_C^O \subseteq \Sigma_H^O$ two main options are available. The new hole can be permitted to generate all actions in Σ_H^O or it can be restricted to the actions in $\Sigma_H^O - \Sigma_C^O$.

2.3 Analysis of a Particular Case

A particular situation based on the above general conditions is discussed below. The other situations are similar. Using this case we show that the resulting hole after a partial plug-in of a component is not unique.

We consider the case $\Sigma_C^I \subseteq \Sigma_H^I$ and $\Sigma_C^O \subseteq \Sigma_H^O$ to show the existence of various possibilities. It is clear from the above discussion that there are a number of choices for the input/output alphabets of the new hole. Assume that the resulting hole's input and output alphabet is Σ_H^I and Σ_H^O respectively. That is the resulting hole can still use some of the original inputs (that is used by the component) to generate the outputs. This is possible because of the synchronous composition.

Towards understanding the behaviour of the new hole, consider the case when $\mathcal{L}^\tau(\mathcal{A}_C) \subseteq \mathcal{L}^\tau(\mathcal{A}_H)$. If the behaviour associated with the new hole is the same as the $\mathcal{L}^\tau(\mathcal{A}_H)$, the problem is not really solved. Ideally, we need to identify the smallest automaton that characterises the new hole. However, that is not always possible or is not practical [SEM03]. In general we can have a variety of resulting automata that when composed with the component can generate the same language.

Recall that it is also possible that the resulting hole's input and output alphabet can be $\Sigma_H^I - \Sigma_C^I$ and $\Sigma_H^O - \Sigma_C^O$ respectively. In this case the resulting hole can use only those inputs and generate outputs that are not used by the components. Any combination of the above is also possible. That is, the input can be Σ_H^I while the output can be $\Sigma_H^O - \Sigma_C^O$.

Some of these choices may be inappropriate for the new hole. This is shown by the following trivial example. If the behaviour of the original hole is given by the set $\{abc, acb\}$ and the behaviour of the component is $\{ab\}$ no automaton with c as the sole alphabet (which is the difference between the two sets) can satisfy the required result. The alphabet a needs to be part of the alphabet.

Furthermore the synthesis of such implementable automata is in many cases either undecidable or NP-complete [SEM03]. Hence in order to use the theory of interface automata and partial component matching effectively a more user driven process is necessary. In summary, it is not possible to automatically generate the best alphabet and behaviour of the resulting hole.

3 Practical Considerations

As there are various options resulting from a partial plug-in, and not all possibilities can be automatically computed, the notion of a collaboration based component selection is used. One can use a trader to effect this collaboration [ITV04]. Leung and Leung [LL03] propose a domain specific model which does not rely solely on the customer's intuition or detailed evaluation of the component. It is in the vendor's interest to assist in the process of component selection.

The collaboration model (component retrieving protocol) is described informally by the following steps:

1. A component purchaser builds pre-assemblies (in our case described using interface automata) and then starts the component selection process. For each hole in the pre-assembly the following procedure is followed.

2. If a vendor has a complete component assembly (that is, fills the hole completely), it is the best choice.
3. If a vendor only has a partial component, the vendor computes the partial plug-in and returns the new pre-assembly to the purchaser. Here the expertise of the vendor in selecting the properties of the remaining hole is utilised. We assume that the vendor can help to complete the assembly based on their own knowledge of components. The vendor could also advertise the various operations possible on components and allow the customer to select not only the component but also how it partially fits into the hole.
4. If the vendor is unsure about the situation, the interface specification of the component can be shipped to the customer and the customer can decide on the properties of the resulting holes. As the interface specification is only a finite automaton, it is cheaper to send than the component itself. It also solves the problem of sending a component before it is purchased.
5. If more information about interface requirements is required, the vendor and customer can exchange this information. Such information is not described by the theory of interfaces and plug-ins. Other issues as the general architecture of the system can be used.

This process will enable the customer to identify and purchase the appropriate components to complete the assembly of the system. The steps involved in the purchase and completing the assembly are not covered by the above process but can be generated from the interface automata specifications.

Our model is very similar to the DESS (software Development process for real-time Embedded Software Systems) model `http://www.dess-itea.org/`. Although the focus of the DESS approach is real-time or embedded systems the process is similar. We have made the DESS process more concrete by making the role of the interface automata explicit. By shipping only the automata, the customer and the vendor need not release code or other design documents. However, the vendor and customer have to construct suitable interface automata for the task. The vendor and the customer can share the task of identifying the resulting holes. For example, if the customer is prepared to write the software to fill the hole completely, no interface automata specification is necessary. Otherwise the hole can be completed by an iterative process.

We conclude the paper by specifying the tools used in the above process. An abstraction tool which can take a code fragment or a system design and generate an interface automaton is necessary. This can also be template driven where the requirements are specified by completing existing templates. These templates can be designed to hide sensitive information which the customer does not want to release. If necessary the architecture of the intended system can be also be released separately. Extra infrastructure to locate potential vendors is essential. Here agent based technology is useful. The vendor needs a repository of components and some techniques for component matching and plug-in. An interface automata description for the set of available components needs to be publicly available. This will aid the agents in locating potential vendors. An experience repository will also be useful. A particular run of the system is shown in the sequence diagram in Figure 4. Here `p` and `q` indicate pre-assemblies while the various `h`s are holes. Two potential vendors, `v1` and `v2`, are identified by the agent. The vendors return options (hole that they can fill, along with the result of filling the hole) to the customer. The customer chooses from the suggestion made by the second agent and receives a new pre-assembly. The customer re-contacts the first agent with a modified pre-assembly.

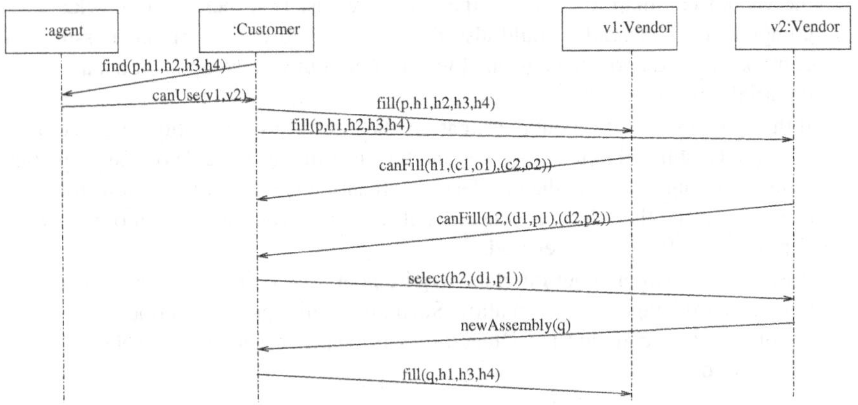

Fig. 4. Sequence Diagram

In summary, we have proposed a framework based on interface automata for partial assembly using components and perhaps custom software. We have identified a few practical problems which prevent complete automation. To overcome this, a collaboration model along with the architecture of a solution has been described. Although we have focused on the use of components to implement a system, a similar approach can also be used at the design phase. That is, designs described using interface automata can be traded. A formal evaluation of the model based on a number of case studies is necessary.

References

[BG97] D. Batory and B. Geraci. Composition validation and subjectivity in GenVoca generators. *IEEE Transactions on Software Engineering*, 23(2):67–82, February 1997.

[CC02] L. Chung and K. Cooper. A knowledge-based cots-aware requirements engineering approach. In *Proceedings of the Software Engineering and Knowledge Engineering Conference*, pages 175–182, Ischia, Italy, 2002.

[dH01a] L. de Alfaro and T. A. Henzinger. Interface automata. In *Proceedings of the Ninth Annual Symposium on Foundations of Software Engineering (FSE)*, pages 109–120. ACM Press, 2001.

[dH01b] L. de Alfaro and T. A. Henzinger. Interface theories for component-based design. In *Proceedings of the First International Workshop on Embedded Software (EMSOFT)*, LNCS 2211, pages 148–165. Springer-Verlag, 2001.

[DR95] V. Diekert and G. Rozenberg. *The Book of Traces*. World Scientific, 1995.

[GAO95] D. Garlan, R. Allen, and J. Ockerbloom. Architectural mismatch: Why reuse is so hard. *IEEE Software*, pages 17–26, November 1995.

[GS03] J. Greenfield and K. Short. Software factories assembling applications with patterns, models, frameworks and tools. In *Proceedings of OOPSLA*, pages 16–27. ACM, 2003.

[ISW02] J. Ivers, N. Sinha, and K. Wallnau. A basis for composition language CL. Technical Report CMU/SEI-2002-TN-026, Software Engineering Institute, 2002.

[ITV04] L. Iribarne, J. M. Troya, and A. Vallecillo. A trading service for cots components. *The Computer Journal*, 47(3):342–357, May 2004.

[Jon00] H. B. M. Jonkers. ISpec: Towards Practical and Sound Interface Specifications. In W. Grieskamp, T. Santen, and B. Stoddart, editors, *Integrated Formal Methods (IFM)*, LNCS 1945, pages 116–135. Springer Verlag, 2000.

[LL03] H. K.N. Leung and K. R.P.H. Leung. Domain-based cots-product selection method. In *Component-Based Software Quality*, LNCS 2693, pages 40–63, 2003.

[MO02] M. Mezini and K. Ostermann. Integrating independent components with on-demand remodularization. In *Proceedings of the 17th ACM SIGPLAN conference on Object-oriented programming, systems, languages, and applications*, pages 52–67. ACM Press, 2002.

[MPW92] R. Milner, J. Parrow, and D. Walker. A Calculus of Mobile Processes I/II. *Information and Computation*, 100(1):1–77, Sept 1992.

[NM99] C. Ncube and N. A. Maiden. PORE: Procurement-Oriented Requirements Engineering Method for the Component Based Systems Engineering Development Paradigm. In *Proceedings of International Workshop on Component Based Software Engineering*, 1999.

[Pah01] C. Pahl. Components, Contracts and Connectors for the Unified Modelling Language UML. In J. Oliveira and P. Zave, editors, *FME–Formal Methods for Increasing Software Productivity*, volume LNCS 2021, pages 259–277, Heidelberg, Germany, 2001. Springer Verlag.

[SEM03] A. Stefanescu, J. Esparza, and A. Muscholl. Synthesis of distributed algorithms using asynchronous automata. In *Proc. of CONCUR'03*, LNCS 2761, pages 27–41, 2003.

[Voa99] J. Voas. User participation based software certification. In *The 5th European Symposium on Validation and Verification of Knowledge Based System*, pages 267–276, 1999.

[WF03] T. Wanyama and B. H. Far. Agent-based commercial off-the-shelf software components evaluation method. In *The First International Conference on Agent Based Technologies and Systems (ATS2003)*, pages 133–141, 2003.

[ZW97] A. M. Zaremski and J. M. Wing. Specification Matching of Software Components. *ACM Transactions on Software Engineering Methodology*, 6(4):333–369, October 1997.

A Novel Approach for Dynamic Slicing of Distributed Object-Oriented Programs

Durga Prasad Mohapatra, Rajib Mall, and Rajeev Kumar

Department of Computer Science and Engineering,
Indian Institute of Technology Kharagpur,
Kharagpur, WB 721 302, India
{durga, rajib, rkumar}@cse.iitkgp.ernet.in

Abstract. Program slicing has many applications such as program debugging, testing and maintenance. We propose a new dynamic slicing technique for distributed object-oriented programs. We introduce the notion of *Distributed Program Dependence Graph* (DPDG). Our dynamic slicing technique uses DPDG as the intermediate program representation and is based on marking and unmarking the edges in the DPDG as and when the dependencies arise and cease during run-time. Our approach eliminates the use of trace files and is more efficient than the existing algorithms.

1 Introduction

The concept of a program slice was introduced by Weiser [1]. A static slice consists of those parts of a program that affect the value of a variable selected at some program point of interest. The variable along with the program point of interest is known as a *slicing criterion.* More formally, a slicing criterion $< s, V >$ specifies a location (statement s) and a set of variables (V). A dynamic slice contains only those statements that actually affect the value of a variable at a program point for a given execution [2, 3]. Therefore, dynamic slices are usually smaller than static slices and have been found to be useful in debugging, testing and maintenance etc. [4, 5, 6].

To slice an object-oriented program, features such as classes, dynamic binding, encapsulation, inheritance, message passing and polymorphism need to be considered carefully. Due to the introduction of inheritance and dynamic binding in OOPs, the process of tracing dependencies becomes more complex than that in a procedural program. Larson and Harrold were the first to consider these aspects in their work [7]. To address these O-O features, they extended the system dependence graph (SDG) proposed by Horowitz et al. [8].

Many of the real life OOPs are concurrent which run on different machines connected to a network. It is usually accepted that understanding and debugging of concurrent OOPs are harder compared to those of sequential programs. The non-deterministic nature of concurrent programs, the lack of global states, unsynchronized interactions among processes, multiple threads of control and a dynamically varying number of processes are some reasons for this difficulty. Slicing techniques promise to come in handy at this point. Although researchers have extended the concept of program slicing to static

R.K. Ghosh and H. Mohanty (Eds.): ICDCIT 2004, LNCS 3347, pp. 304–309, 2004.

slicing of distributed programs, the dynamic slicing of distributed OOPs is still being missing until now.

We propose a new dynamic slicing algorithm for computing slices of distributed C++ programs. Only the concurrency and communication issues in C++ are of concern, many sequential O-O features are not discussed in this paper. Larson and Harrold have discussed about the representation of O-O features in their work [7]. So, these representations can be easily incorporated into our technique to handle the O-O features. We have named our algorithm *edge-marking dynamic slicing* (EMDS) algorithm.

The rest of the paper is organized as follows. In section 2, we discuss about the intermediate program representation. In section 3, we briefly present our edge-marking dynamic slicing (EMDS) algorithm. In section 4, we compare our algorithm with related algorithms. Section 5 concludes the paper.

2 Graphical Representation of Distributed Programs

A distributed program P = $(P_1, P_2, \ldots, P_n)$ is a collection of concurrent sub-programs P_i such that each of the P_i's communicate through reception and transmission of messages. We assume asynchronous send and synchronous receive message passing mechanism in our algorithm. The language constructs for message passing are *msgsnd* and *msgrcv* statements, for sending and receiving messages respectively.

The intermediate representation for a concurrent OOP on a single machine is constructed statically as in [9]. But for distributed programs, we can have data dependency due to shared variables updated by statements executed in some process on some remote machine. Also communication dependency can exist between processes running on different machines. A *msgrcv()* call executed on one machine, might have a pairing *msgsnd()* on some remote machine. To incorporate this paradigm, we introduce a logical(dummy) node in the DPDG. We call this logical node as a C-node. Now, we define the C-node and the intermediate representation for distributed OOPs used by our proposed algorithm.

Definition 1. *C-Node.* Let G_D be a DPDG. Let x be a *send* node and y be the *receive* node. A C-Node represents a logical connection of a node y of a DPDG with a node x of a remote DPDG. The node x is the pairing *send* for a *receive* call at node y, and y is communication dependent on x.

Definition 2. *Distributed Program Dependence Graph (DPDG).* Let P = $(P_1, \ldots, P_n)$ be a distributed program, and P_i be a sub-program of P. The distributed program dependence graph (DPDG) G_D of the sub-program P_i is a directed graph (N_D, E_D) where each node $n \in N_D$ represents a statement in P_i. For $x, y \in N_D$, (y,x) $\in E_D$ *iff* one of the following holds:

- y is *control dependent* on x. Such an edge is called a *control dependence edge.*
- y is *data dependent* on x. Such an edge is called a *data dependence edge.*
- y is *fork dependent* on x. Such an edge is called a *fork dependence edge.*
- y is *communication dependent* on x. Such an edge is called a *communication dependence edge.*

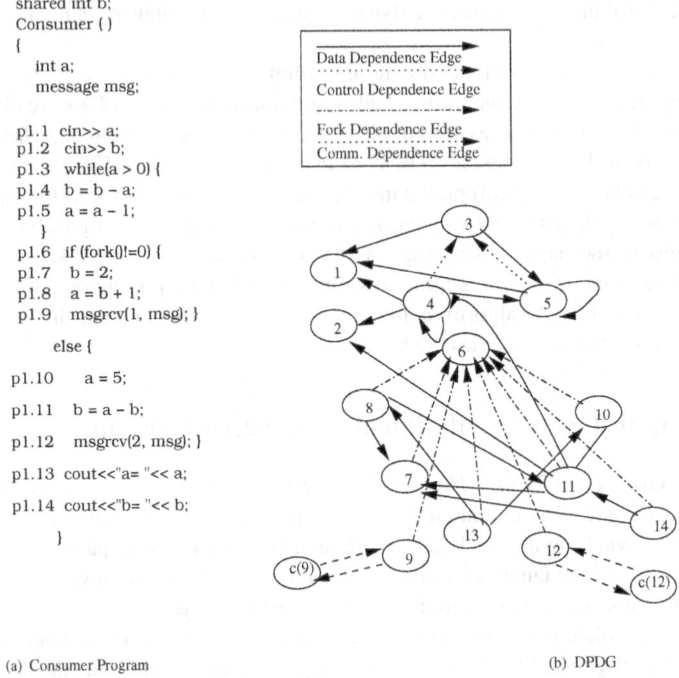
shared int b;
Consumer ( )
{
int a;
message msg;
p1.1 cin>> a;
p1.2 cin>> b;
p1.3 while(a > 0) {
p1.4 b = b – a;
p1.5 a = a – 1;
}
p1.6 if (fork()!=0) {
p1.7 b = 2;
p1.8 a = b + 1;
p1.9 msgrcv(1, msg); }
else {
p1.10 a = 5;
p1.11 b = a – b;
p1.12 msgrcv(2, msg); }
p1.13 cout<<"a= "<< a;
p1.14 cout<<"b= "<< b;
}
Data Dependence Edge
Control Dependence Edge
Fork Dependence Edge
Comm. Dependence Edge
1
2
3
4
5
6
7
8
9
10
11
12
13
14
c(9)
c(12)

(a) Consumer Program (b) DPDG

Fig. 1. The Consumer Program and its DPDG

```
shared int b;
First_producer ( )
{
   int c;
   message msg;

p2.1  cin>> c;
p2.2  cout<<"b= "<< b;
p2.3  c = c + 1;
p2.4  b = b – c;
p2.5  if (fork()!=0) {
p2.6    c = 1;
p2.7    b = b + c;
p2.8    msgsnd(1, msg); }
      else {
p2.9    b = 5;
p2.10   c = b + 1; }
p2.11 cout<<"c= "<< c;
p2.12 cout<<"b= "<< b;
}
```

(a) First_ Producer

```
shared int b;
second_producer ( )
{
   int d;
   message msg;

p3.1  d = 0;
p3.2  cout<<"b= "<< b;
p3.3  d = d – 1;
p3.4  b = b + d;
p3.5  if (fork()!=0) {
p3.6    b = 0;
p3.7    d = d – b;
p3.8    cout<<"d="<<d; }
      else {
p3.9    b = d + 1;
p3.10   msgsnd(2, msg) }
p3.11 cout<<"d= "<< d;
p3.12 cout<<"b= "<< b;
}
```

(b) Second_Producer

Fig. 2. The First_Producer and Second_Producer Programs

For every *receive* node $x$in the sub-program P_i, a dummy node C(x) is taken, and a dummy communication edge (x, C(x)) is added.

Let us consider the distributed C++ program in Figs. 1(a), 2(a) and 2(b) which represent the Consumer, First_Producer and Second_Producer programs respectively. The DPDG of the Consumer program is shown in Fig. 1(b). The DPDGs for the other producer-programs can be constructed similarly.

3 EMDS Algorithm for Distributed Object-Oriented Programs

Before execution of a distributed OOP $P = (P_1, \ldots, P_n)$, the DPDG of each of the subprogram P_i is constructed statically. During execution of the sub-program P_i, we mark an edge of the DPDG when its associated dependence exists, and unmark when its associated dependence ceases to exist. Since in this case we need to consider processes that cross machine boundaries, we have some additional tasks to perform. These tasks include:

- The most recent information of shared variables is to be kept as a part of the distributed shared memory so that it is available to all the programs.
- The addition of C-nodes in the DPDG. They take care of any communication dependency that might exist at run-time between communicating processes on different machines.

During execution of the sub-program P_i, let *Dynamic_Slice (p, u, var)* with respect to the slicing criterion $< p, u, var >$ denotes the dynamic slice with respect to the most recent execution of node *u* in process *p*. Let $(u, x_1), \ldots, (u, x_k)$ be all the *marked* outgoing dependence edges of *u* in the updated DPDG. Then, the dynamic slice with respect to the present execution of node *u*, for the variable *var* is given by:

Dynamic_Slice(p, u, var)=$\{p(u, x_1), \ldots, p(u, x_k)\} \cup Dynamic\_Slice(p, x_1, var) \cup \ldots \cup Dynamic\_Slice(p, x_k, var)$.

Let *var_1*, *var_2*, ..., *var_k* be all the variables used or defined at statement *u* in process *p*. Then, we define dynamic slice of the whole statement *u* as:

dyn_slice(p, u) = $Dynamic\_Slice(p, u, var\_1) \cup Dynamic\_Slice(p, u, var\_2) \cup \ldots \cup Dynamic\_Slice(p, u, var\_k)$.

Our slicing algorithm operates in three stages. In the first stage, the DPDG of each subprogram P_i is constructed statically. The stage 2 of the algorithm executes at run-time and is responsible for maintaining the DPDG as the execution proceeds. The maintenance of the DPDG involves marking and unmarking the different dependencies, as they arise and cease. Stage 3 is responsible for computing the dynamic slices. Once a slicing criterion is specified, the dynamic slicing algorithm computes the dynamic slice with respect to any given slicing criterion by looking up the corresponding *Dynamic_Slice* computed during run time.

Working of the EMDS Algorithm: We illustrate the working of the algorithm with the help of an example. We have shown in Fig. 4, how the above algorithm computes the dynamic slices for a given slicing criterion. For a typical program execution, let the process IDs be 9179 and 9184 respectively representing the if-part and else-part for the *Consumer* program given in Fig. 1(a). Also, let the process IDs be 7639 and 7790 respectively representing the if-part and else-part for the *First_Producer* program given in Fig. 2(a) and that be 7890 and 7566 respectively representing the if-part and else-part for the *Second_Producer* program given in Fig. 2(b).

We are interested to compute the dynamic slice for slicing criterion $< 9184, 14, b >$ with input $a = 1$ and $b = 1$. We have marked all outgoing dependent edges at node 14 as shown in Fig. 3. Due to the use of shared variables the dependency of node 14 in process 9184 can be on nodes executed in other processes running on remote machines. The updated DPDGs for processes 7639 and 7566 can be constructed similarly. The computed dynamic slice is {(9184,P1.6), (7566,P3.1), (7566,P3.3), (7566,P3.5), (7639,P2.4), (7639,P2.5), (7639,P2.6)}.

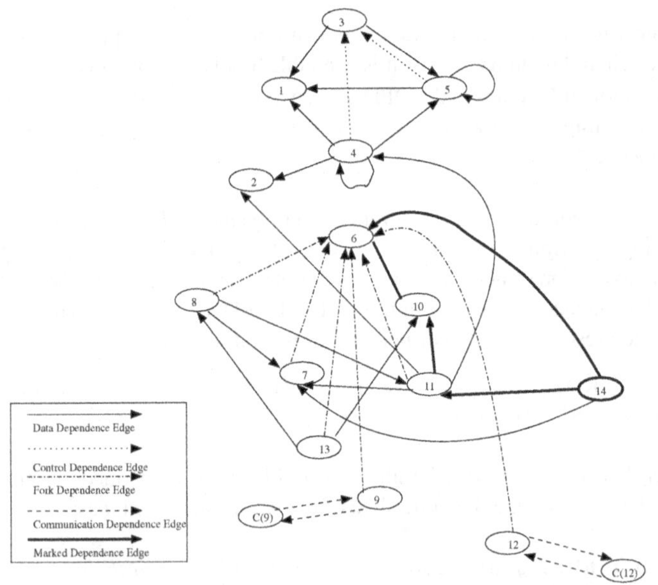

Fig. 3. Updated DPDG showing marked edges at node 14 for process ID 9184

4 Comparison with Related Work

Zhao computed the static slice of a concurrent object-oriented program based on the *multi-threaded dependence graph* (MDG) [10]. In his approach, slices are computed by solving a node reachability problem in the graph. He has not addressed the dynamic aspects and communication dependency among several machines.

Chen and Xu developed a new algorithm to compute static slices of concurrent Java programs [9]. To compute the slices, they have used *concurrent control flow graph* (CCFG) and *concurrent program dependence graph* (CPDG) as the intermediate representations. Since they have performed static analysis to compute the slices, so the resulting slices are not precise. But, we have performed dynamic analysis to compute the slices. So, the slices computed by our algorithm are precise.

5 Conclusions

In this paper, we have proposed a new algorithm for computing dynamic slices of distributed object-oriented programs. We have named this algorithm *edge-marking dynamic slicing* (EMDS) algorithm. It is based on marking and unmarking the edges of the DPDG as and when the dependences arise and cease at run-time. Our algorithm does not require trace file to store the execution history which takes more space. In this work, we have implemented and tested our proposed technique with a piece of C++ code, however, the technique is generic enough. We are currently working to dynamically slice concurrent Java programs running in a distributed environment.

References

1. Weiser, M.: Programmers use slices when debugging. Communications of the ACM **25** (1982) 446–452
2. B.Korel, J.Laski: Dynamic program slicing. Information Processing Letters **29** (1988) 155–163
3. Zhao, J.: Dynamic slicing of object-oriented programs. Technical report, Information Processing Society of Japan (1998)
4. Mall, R.: Fundamentals of Software Engineering. Prentice Hall, India (2nd Edition, 2003)
5. Goswami, D., Mall, R.: An efficient method for computing dynamic program slices. Information Processing Letters **81** (2002) 111–117
6. Mund, G.B., Mall, R., Sarkar, S.: An efficient dynamic program slicing technique. Information and Software Technology **44** (2002) 123–132
7. Larson, L.D., Harrold, M.J.: Slicing object-oriented software. In: Proceedings of the 18th International Conference on Software Engineering, German (1996)
8. Horwitz, S., Reps, T., Binkley, D.: Interprocedural slicing using dependence graphs. ACM Transactions on Programming Languages and Systems **12** (1990) 26–61
9. Chen, Z., Xu, B.: Slicing concurrent java programs. ACM SIGPLAN Notices **36** (2001) 41–47
10. Zhao, J.: Slicing concurrent java programs. In: Proceedings of the 7th IEEE International Workshop on Program Comprehension. (1999)

Pattern Semantic Link: A Reusable Pattern Representation in MDA Context

Jianfei Yin, Heqing Guo, Xinyi Peng, and Manshan Lin

College of Computer Science and Engineering,
South China University of Technology, Guangzhou 510641, China
{yjfhome, ghqhome, pengxinyi, lmshill}@hotmail.com
http://www.scut.edu.cn

Abstract. Currently most of pattern-related specifications represent design patterns limited at specific implementation forms on one abstract level and restrict to reuse patterns across different abstract levels, such as Platform-Independent Models (PIMs) and Platform-Specific Models (PSMs). This paper proposes a novel pattern representation named Pattern Semantic Link (PSL), which provides a centralized and abstract representation for a pattern. Borrowing ideals from the Intentional Programming (IP), the core PSL concepts are capturing the knowledge about relationships between participants of a pattern by instances of the UML Association derived classes, capturing key intentions of the pattern by constraints in the Object Constraint Language (OCL) and rendering the reference implementations for the pattern based on its PSL definition. Through the meta-model inheritance and marking approach, transforming a model with PSLs to its platform-specific counterpart and reusing patterns across PIMs and PSMs can be achieved.

1 Introduction

Design patterns provide a way to reuse the experimental knowledge of expert designers so that a community can benefit and not continually reinvent the wheel. Currently there is considerable work done regarding pattern specifications [1, 2, 3], pattern-based model refactorings [4] and tool supports [5, 6]. Most of them represent patterns limited at specific implementation forms on one abstract level, for instance, class and member structures for implementing a pattern on a platform-independent level. It is hard to reuse these pattern representations in platform-specific environments for the following reasons:

a) The implementation forms for patterns mainly capture specific instances of pattern deployment, rather than the essential pattern itself, thus the spirit of the pattern is often lost in the superfluous details of the specific instances described [7].
b) There are always patterns of platform-specific versions, such as CORBA patterns, J2EE patterns , etc.

R.K. Ghosh and H. Mohanty (Eds.): ICDCIT 2004, LNCS 3347, pp. 310–317, 2004.

c) Little consideration is taken to facilitate transforming those pattern representations to platform-specific counterparts without loss of the semantics of patterns.

In this paper, we propose a novel design pattern representation named Pattern Semantic Link (PSL), which provides a centralized and abstract representation for a pattern. It can support transforming and reusing patterns across PIMs and PSMs in the Model-Driven Architecture (MDA) context. Borrowing ideals from the Intentional Programming (IP) [8], the core PSL concepts are capturing the knowledge about relationships between participants of a pattern by instances of the UML Association subclasses, capturing core intentions of the pattern by constraints in the Object Constraint Language (OCL) and rendering the reference implementations for the pattern by using the UML Action Semantics on the PSL definition. Based on the meta-model inheritance and marking approach, we can transform a model with PSLs to its platform-specific counterpart and reuse patterns in the platform-specific context.

Section 2 overviews the PSL concepts. Section 3 describes the definition of PSLs for a pattern. Section 4 describes an algorithm for rendering a reference implementation for a pattern. Section 5 describes transforming a model with PSLs and reusing patterns. We conclude in Sect. 6.

2 PSL Concepts

In this paper, a Pattern Semantic Link (PSL) serves a pattern application and captures the knowledge about the abstract relationships between model elements participating in a pattern. A PSL is represented by an instance of a particular meta-model element, which is called the PSL meta-class. We extend the UML meta-model with PSL concepts (hereinafter, "the extended UML meta-model") and use the UML Association derived classes as PSL meta-classes based on following reasons:

a) An instance of a UML Association derived class can capture the abstract relationships between participants of a pattern. The abstract relationships are independent of various implementation forms of a pattern.
b) The visual notations (e.g., lines or boxes) of the UML Association derived classes provide concise and centralized representations for patterns. The centralized representations facilitate the patterns detection and navigation.
c) If we can use the information held by a UML association to derive uninteresting operations [9], why not use a PSL to derive the parts of a pattern implementation such as attributes, methods, classes, etc.

Figure 1(a) shows an extended UML meta-model segment. For each pattern, there is a PSL meta-class to capture the relationship semantics between participants of the pattern. Figure 1(b) shows an example of generating an Iterator pattern implementation by meta-programming on the *Iterator* meta-class (shown in Fig. 1(a)).

In next section, we will further present the PSL concepts through an example of defining PSLs for the Abstract Factory pattern.

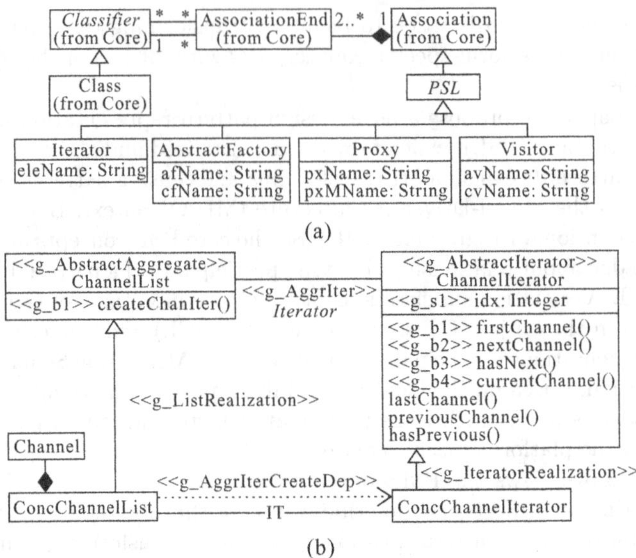

Fig. 1. (a) An extended UML meta-model segment. (b) An Iterator pattern implementation [1] generated by meta-programming on the *Iterator* meta-class. The generative parts are marked with *g_xxx*. The Iterator PSL is the line marked with *IT*

3 Definition of Abstract Factory PSLs

This section focuses on defining PSLs for the Abstract Factory pattern which provides an interface for creating families of related or dependent objects without specifying their concrete classes [10]. Figure 2(a) shows the paradigm of the Abstract Factory pattern. The definition of Abstract Factory PSLs mainly covers the use mode, data structure and static semantic aspects. Through the definition process, we discover the pattern's two key intentions, which are more detailed than those in [10].

We design the use mode of Abstract Factory PSLs as follows: a modeler does not need to draw the constructs inside the rounded rectangle (shown in Fig. 2(a)), the input and output lines across the rounded rectangle and the lines from the *Client* class to the *AbstractProductA/B* interfaces. The modeler only needs to draw Abstract Factory PSLs from the *Client* class to the concrete product classes and configure them (shown in Fig. 2(b)).

In Fig. 1(a), the *AbstractFactory* meta-class shows the most concise data structure of Abstract Factory PSLs:

a) *afName: String.* It is the name of an abstract factory interface. Without it, a *Client* object cannot access the services of the concrete factory objects.
b) *cfName: String.* It is the name of a concrete factory class. A concrete product class must be managed by a concrete factory class. It captures an intention of

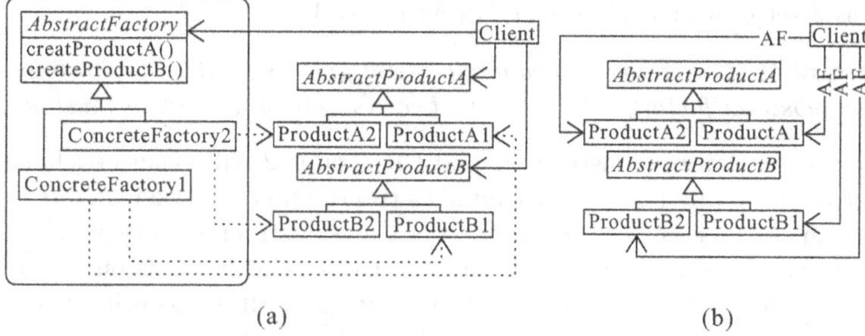

Fig. 2. (a) The paradigm of the Abstract Factory pattern [10]. (b)An abstract representation of Fig. 2(a) by using Abstract Factory PSLs. The lines marked with *AF* are visual notations of the PSLs

the pattern, which is named product family: a concrete factory class stands for a product family.

According to above definition, an Abstract Factory PSL stores a 4-tuple $< clientRole, afName, cfName, productRole >$ based on which we can define the static semantics of Abstract Factory PSLs by building OCL constraints corresponding to the intentions of the Abstract Factory pattern. For reasons of space, we list only two key intentions as follows:

Constraint 1. *All the concrete product classes managed by a concrete factory class must implement different abstract product interfaces.*

When there are two or more concrete product classes implementing the same abstract product interface, the corresponding concrete factory object can't decide to create objects of which concrete product class. With Constraint 1, we can avoid this problem. For the performance of the constraint execution, the evaluation policy of Constraint 1 is after drawing a PSL and setting its attributes (*afName* and *cfName*). The OCL codes are given as follows:

```
context AbstractFactory inv eachProdHasDiffInt:
let sEnds: Set(AssociationEnd)=getNavigableEnds() in
 sEnds->size=1 and let sEnd: AssociationEnd=
 sEnds->any(true), sCls: Classifier=sEnd.participant in
  sCls.isAbstract=false and allInstances->
  select(cfName=self.cfName)->forAll(a| a<>self implies
   let aEnds: Set(AssociationEnd)=a.getNavigableEnds() in
    aEnds->size=1 and let aEnd: AssociationEnd=aEnds->any(true) in
     aEnd<>sEnd and let aCls: Classifier=aEnd.participant in
      aCls.isAbstract=false and not aCls.conformsTo(sCls)
```

Most of above codes can be understood without further explanations. The *getNavigableEnds* method gets the *AssociationEnd* instances whose *isNavigable* attribute values are *true*.

Let K as a set of abstract product interfaces, we have:

Constraint 2. *Given any two concrete factory classes both of which implement the same abstract factory interface, the two Ks managed by them must be equal.*

The satisfaction of Constraint 1 and Constraint 2 will ensure exchangeable product families: any two product families (represented by two concrete factory classes) can replace each other under the same abstract factory interface and the same set of abstract product interfaces. Constraint 2 builds on top of Constraint1, so the evaluation policy of Constraint 2 is after executing Constraint 1. For reasons of space and comprehensibility, the OCL codes for Constraint 2 are not presented here and can be easily written by consulting [11].

By using the definition of PSLs for a pattern, we can render various optional implementations for the pattern and let a modeler further configure the PSLs. The next section describes a rendering algorithm for the Abstract Factory pattern.

4 Rendering a Reference Implementation for Abstract Factory Pattern

Based on a PSL definition, we can meta-program different reference implementations for the pattern to support selecting the most effective implementation form in a particular context. Given Fig. 2(b), we can render a modeler with Fig. 2(a), which is one of implementations for the pattern. For each Abstract Factory PSL p, based on the 4-tuple $< clientRole, afName, cfName, productRole >$ of p, the rendering algorithm is given as follows:

1. Check the validity of p, for example, $p.afName$ and $p.cfName$ cannot be empty. If it is ok, go next else go to 5.
2. Create an abstract factory interface *af*, abstract methods and an association between the *Client* class and *af*. Mark each created model element with a new stereotype whose name is "g_"+*elementRoleName*.
3. Create a concrete factory class *cf*, a generalization between *cf* and *af*, a dependency between *cf* and a concrete product class, an association between the *Client* class and an abstract product interface. Mark each created element as those in 2.
4. Hide p from the modeler.
5. Go next p.

The complexity of the algorithm is $O(N)$, N is the number of the Abstract Factory PSLs. Note that above algorithm description does not cover all details, for example, checks if an element to be created already exists. In 2, the *elementRoleName* denotes the role name of a participant in the pattern. Using a surface language [12] for the UML Action Semantics, the main procedure for above algorithm is given as follows:

```
AbstractFactory::standImpl
actions: AbstractFactory.allInstances->
select(afName<>'' and cfName<>'')->
forAll(a|a.createAF; a.createAFMethod;
       a.createCF; a.createCFDep;
       a.createClientProdIntAs; a.hide)
```

The action definition of each *createXXX* method is obvious and omitted from here. More information about UML Action Semantics can be found in [13]. Working on the rendered implementations for patterns, a modeler can further configure the PSLs in a PIM, and transform the PIM to a PSM through the approaches introduced in next section.

5 Transforming and Reusing a Model with PSLs

For reusing patterns across PIMs and PSMs, we need to transform a model with PSLs to its platform-specific counterpart by the vertical transformation [14] and refine the platform-specific counterpart in the platform-specific context.

To facilitate above processes, we derive platform-specific meta-models from the extended UML meta-model and add them with platform-specific information, such as application protocols, deployments, etc. Because of using the meta-model inheritance to derive platform-specific meta-models, the abstract syntaxes and static semantics of the platform-independent meta-model are reserved, for example, Constraint 1/2 in Sect.3 are still hold in any platform-specific subclass of the *AbstractFactory* meta-class. Figure 3 shows a sample of meta-model inheritance.

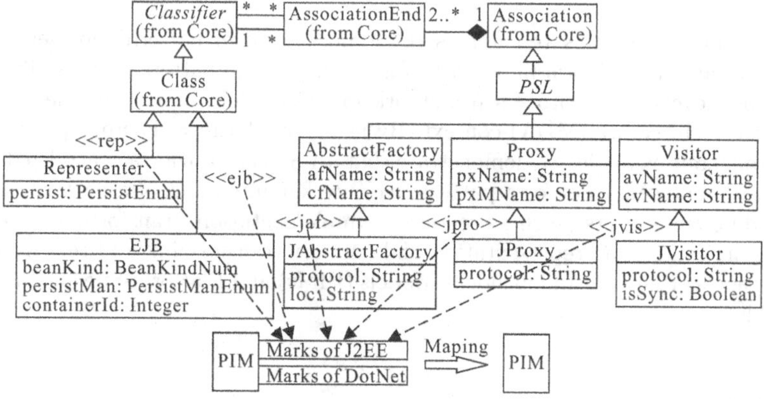

Fig. 3. A simplified meta-model segment for J2EE platform and its transformation

Based on the transformation using patterns and marks [15], we design the transformation process as follows: (briefly shown in Fig. 3)

a) First, a set of marks (stereotypes) is extracted from the platform-specific meta-model, and the compositions of the marks are well defined to ensure the right configuration semantics for the platform;
b) Then, a modeler imports those marks into the modelling environment and marks a PIM to guide the transformation engine to generate a PSM.

By combing the meta-model inheritance and marking approach, we simplify the model transformation interface like this:
T(src: Meta-modelA, marks: Set(Stereotype), dst: Meta-modelB), which can be effectively implemented by the transformation engines (e.g., GReAT [16]).

After transforming a PIM to a PSM, a modeler will need to refine the PSM with platform-specific information based on which the platform-specific PSLs can be used to store the implementation knowledge for the corresponding patterns. A code generator can then use that knowledge to generate codes. For example, we can define the following rule to configure the *JAbstractFactory* meta-object, which is a platform-specific counterpart of an *AbstractFactory* meta-object:

```
If   two EJB meta-objects e1 and e2 are connected by
     a JAbstractFactory meta-object jaf and
     e1.containerId=e2.containerId
Then Jaf.protocol='local'  -- use the EJBLocalHome factory
     interface to create EJB objects.
Else Jaf.protocol='remote' -- use the EJBHome factory
     interface to create EJB objects.
```

6 Conclusions

The main goal of this research is to propose a novel pattern representation named Pattern Semantic Link (PSL) for reusing design patterns across different abstract levels and a process framework for its implementation in the Model-Driven Architecture (MDA) context. By using the Abstract Factory pattern as a throughout example, we demonstrate that a PSL can provide a centralized and abstract representation for a pattern, capture key intentions of a pattern, separate different aspects (such as rendering, implementation, transformation, etc.) from the centralized representation and support transforming and reusing patterns across Platform-Independent Models (PIMs) and Platform-Specific Models (PSMs).

References

1. Dae-Kyoo Kim, Robert France, Sudipto Ghosh, et al.: A UML-Based Metamodeling Language to Specify Design Patterns. In: Proc. Workshop on Software Model Engineering (WiSME) with UML 2003. To be published. (2003)

2. D. Mapelsden, J. Hosking, J. Grundy: Design Pattern Modelling and Instantiation using DPML. In: Proc. 14th. International Conference on Tools Pacific: Objects for internet, mobile and embedded applications. Australian Computer Society, Darlinghurst, Australia, Australia (2002) 3–11
3. Aline Lúcia Baroni, Yann-Gaël Guéhéneuc, Hervé Albin-Amiot: Design Patterns Formalization. Technical Report 03/03/INFO. Computer Science Department, École des Mines de Nantes. (2003)
4. Robert France, Sudipto Ghosh, Eunjee Song, et al: A Metamodeling Approach to Pattern-Based Model Refactoring. IEEE Software, Vol. 20, No. 5. IEEE Computer Society Press, Los Alamitos, CA (2003) 52–58
5. G. Florijn, M. Meijers, P. van Winsen: Tool support for object-oriented patterns. In: Proc. 11th. European conference on Object Oriented programming. Lecture Notes in Computer Science, Vol. 1241. Springer-Verlag, Berlin Heidelberg New York (1997) 472–495
6. M. Schütze, J. P. Riegel, G. Zimmermann: PSiGene - A Pattern-Based Component Generator for Building Simulation. Theory and Practice of Object Systems (TAPOS), Vol. 5, No. 2. Wiley Publishing, Indianapolis, Indiana (1999) 83–95
7. Anthony Lauder, Stuart Kent: Precise Visual Specification of Design Patterns. In Proc. 12th. European Conference on Object Oriented Programming. Lecture Notes in Computer Science, Vol. 1241. Springer-Verlag, Berlin Heidelberg New York (1998) 114–134
8. C. Simonyi: The Death of Computer Languages, the Birth of Intentional Programming. Technical Report MSR-TR-95-52. Microsoft Research, Redmond WA. (1995)
9. DS Frankel: Model Driven Architecture: Applying MDA to Enterprise Computing. Wiley Publishing, Indianapolis, Indiana (2003)
10. E. Gamma, R. Helm, R. Johnson, J. Vlissides: Design Patterns: Elements of Reusable Object-Oriented Software. Addison Wesley, Reading, MA (1995)
11. Boldsoft, et al.: UML 2.0 OCL 2nd revised submission. OMG Document ad/2003-01-07. (2003)
12. Gerson Sunye, Alain Le Guennec, Jean-Marc Jezequel: Using UML Action Semantics for model execution and transformation. Information Systems, Vol. 27, No. 6. Elsevier Science, Oxford, UK (2002) 445-457
13. The Action Semantics Consortium: Action semantics for the uml. OMG Document ad/2001-03-01. (2001)
14. Jeff Gray, Jing Zhang, Yuehua Lin, et al.: Model-Driven Program Transformation of a Large Avionics Framework. In: Proc. Generative Programming and Component Engineering (GPCE 2004). Lecture Notes in Computer Science, Vol. 3286. Springer-Verlag, Berlin Heidelberg New York (2004)
15. Joaquin Miller, Jishnu Mukerji: MDA Guide Version 1.0.1. OMG Document omg/2003-06-01. (2003)
16. Agrawal A., Karsai G. and Ledeczi A.: An End-to-End Domain-Driven Software Development Framework. In: Proc. 18th. Annual ACM SIGPLAN Conference on Object-Oriented Programming, Systems, Languages, and Applications (OOPSLA). ACM Press, New York (2003) 8–15

Compatibility Test and Adapter Generation for Interfaces of Software Components

Johannes Maria Zaha, Marco Geisenberger, and Martin Groth

Chair of Business Informatics and Systems Engineering,
Business Faculty, University of Augsburg,
Universitätsstraße 16, 86159 Augsburg, Germany
johannes.maria.zaha@wiwi.uni-augsburg.de,
marcogeisenberger@web.de, martin.groth@t-online.de,

Abstract. Compositional reuse of software components requires standardized specification techniques if applications are created by combining third party components. Adequate techniques need to be used in order to specify not only technical but also business related aspects of software components. The different specification aspects of software components are summarized in a multi-layer specification framework with formal specification techniques defined for each level of abstraction. The use of formal specification techniques is a prerequisite for compatibility tests on component specifications. Compatibility tests are necessary for the identification of required components, which are traded on component markets. The focus of this paper is to present an algorithm for compatibility test on interface level, where Interface Definition Language (IDL) has been used as formal specification language. In order to test characteristics where e.g. the order of parameter values or the order of consisting data types within a complex data type are not identical with the specification, adapters are generated for mapping the component interfaces.

Keywords: Compatibility test, software reuse, adapter generation, IDL, software component.

Business Components and Software Contracts

The idea of developing application systems from prefabricated software components has been traced at least since the publication of McIllroy in 1968 [1]. Since then different techniques for reusing software artefacts, like code and design scavenging [2] or generative techniques [3], have been developed. Compositional reuse of software instead is a technique to combine the advantages of both standard software and individually programmed software by a plug-and-play-like reuse of black-box-components which are traded on component markets. To achieve this goal, developers and users must be enabled to express the characteristics of a software component in a standardized way. Therefore a specification framework for business components, which are components that offer a certain set of services of a given business domain, has been proposed [4]. This specification framework (cp. Fig. 1) considers technical aspects as well as business related aspects of software.

R.K. Ghosh and H. Mohanty (Eds.): ICDCIT 2004, LNCS 3347, pp. 318–328, 2004.

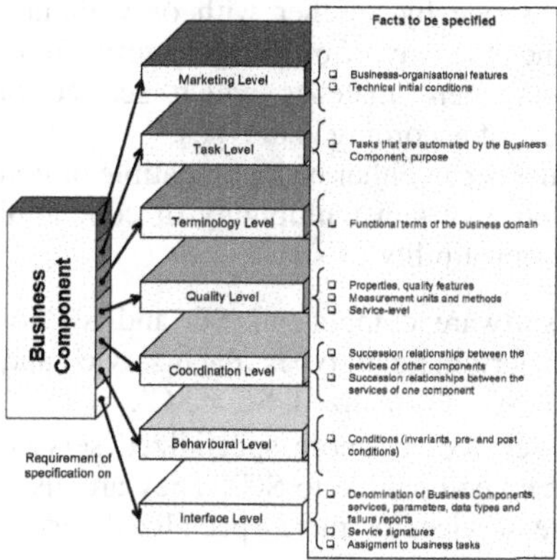

Fig. 1. Software contract levels and facts to be specified (cp. [4])

In this framework standardized techniques for the specification of business components of the different levels of abstraction have been chosen, like the Interface Definition Language (IDL) [5] on Interface Level, the Object Constraint Language (OCL) [6] on Behavioural Level or the Restructured Business Language [7] on Task Level. With this specification framework it is possible to enter into a contract on a piece of software in a standardized way. The concept of software contracts was introduced by Meyer [8] with his programming language Eiffel. This idea of programming by contract was later on extended to the concept design by contract [9].

The design phase should end with a detailed specification of the components and by using standardized specification techniques. With this concept it is possible to decrease the effort to build application systems by reusing existing components. In order to automatically find required components, it is necessary to use algorithms for an automated compatibility test on all of the layers of the specification framework mentioned above. In this paper an algorithm for compatibility test on interface level, where IDL has been chosen as formal specification language, is introduced and described.

Compatibility of Interfaces

To test compatibility of software components by deriving information of their interfaces, Zaremski and Wing introduced a type system for functions and modules [10]. This approach was extended for differing signatures [11] and pre- and post-conditions [12]. Other work extends these approaches for protocols needed for interaction between components [13] and introduces the generation of component adapters [14]. Respecting all work done in this area none of the approaches mentioned provides an algorithm for testing compatibility of specifications or for generating respective adapters. In addition to the presentation of a compatibility algorithm an adapter concept is provided, namely for those parts of the IDL, used in [4].

Compatibility of two components is defined as the equality of two software components, whereas other requirements, like if two software components can work together concerning the interfaces, can be tested by a few modifications of the presented algorithm. Software components are compatible, if it is possible to exchange the components one by another with or without using a corresponding adapter. An adapter defines the way of exchanging software components. It specifies which service of a component matches which service of another component, depending on the matching of according data types.

Two software components can either be incompatible or compatible. Compatibility implies a certain type and a certain multiplicity of compatibility. Referring to [10] three different kinds of compatibility exist:

- Exact compatible software components SC and SC’ offer the same services depending on the underlying data types. Each service and data type of SC needs an exact matching in SC’. Formalized: SC = SC’.
- If SC offers more services or more specialized services and data types than SC’, SC is specialized compatible to SC’. They are also specialized compatible if SC requires more services or more specialized services and data types than SC’. Formalized: SC < SC’.
- Generalized compatibility is the opposite of specialized compatibility. SC is generalized compatible to SC’, if SC’ is specialized compatible to SC. Formalized: SC > SC’.

A software component specifies its services and data types by using parts of the OMG IDL [4]. The required and provided interfaces are defined by the interface declaration of IDL and are integrated in a module. To define the compatibility of components it is necessary to define the compatibility of the OMG IDL declaration used in order to specify a software component. The IDL-declarations used according to [4] are modules, interfaces, operations, data types and exceptions. Thereby a component is defined with the maximum of two interfaces, a provided interface which is mandatory and a required interface which is optional, which are integrated in a module. Two software components are exact compatible if the provided interfaces are exact compatible and - if both need a required interface – the required interfaces are exact compatible as well. A module is specialized compatible to another, if either both interfaces are specialized compatible or if one is specialized compatible and the required interface is exact compatible or not existent. In all other cases the software components are incompatible. The adapter of two modules is represented by a compatibility prefix followed by the adapter for the provided and required interface:

<module-adapter> ::=
“{“ <compatibility_prefix>",“ <interface_adapter> [“,“<interface_adapter >] “}“

Two interfaces are exact compatible if they have the same number of declarations and if each declaration can be mapped exact compatible to a declaration of the other. The different types of declarations used are type declarations, exception declarations and operation declarations of IDL. If one interface has more declarations and all of them can either be mapped exact or specialized compatible to a declaration of the other interface, the first interface is specialized compatible to the second.

<interface adapter> ::=
“«“<compatibility_prefix>“,“ <operation_set_adapter>“,“ <exception_set_adapter> “,“
<data_type_set_adapter> “»“

Two sets of declarations which are of the same type are exact compatible, if they have the same number of declarations and each declaration in one set can be mapped exact compatible to an declaration in the other set. In case one set has more declarations and all declarations of the other set can be mapped to an exact or a specialized compatible declaration of the first set, the first set is specialized compatible to the other. If both have the same number of declarations and at least one declaration mapping is specialized compatible and the rest of the mappings are either specialized or exact compatible, the two sets are specialized compatible. The adapters of the three different kinds of declaration are built in the following way.

<operation_set_adapter> ::=<operation_adapter>(“,“ <operation_adapter>)*

<exception_set_adapter> ::= “”
<data_type_set_adapter> ::= <datatype_adapter> (“,“ <datatype_adapter>)*

Two operations are exact compatible to each other, when their sets of parameters and exceptions and their return types are exact compatible. Specialized compatibility can be caused by specialized return types and compatible sets of parameters and exceptions. The compatibility of these two sets is defined in the same way, as the compatibility of sets of declarations. Each operation mapping is represented in the following way.

<operation_adapter> ::=
“[”<compatibility_prefix>”,” <operation_mapping> (“,“<parameter_mapping>)+“]”
<operation_mapping> ::= “(“ identifier, identifier ”)”
<parameter_mapping> ::= “(“ parameter_declaration, parameter_ declaration “)”

Type declarations can either be a type definition or a structure. The compatibility of two type definitions corresponds to the compatibility of their type specification. Two structures are exact compatible, if their number of members is the same and each member of the first structure is exact compatible to a member of the second structure. They are specialized compatible if the first structure has more members and these members can be mapped either exact or specialized compatible to the members of the second structure. Members of structures can either be other structures or simple types. The compatibility of simple types is defined in a compatibility matrix as shown in table 1.

The mapping of two data types is represented by the following adapter:
<compatibility_prefix> ::= “=” | “<” | “>”
< data_type_mapping> ::= “(“ data_type_identifier, data_type_identifier “)”
<member_mapping> ::= “(“ declarator, declarator ”)”
<data_type_adapter> ::=
“[”<compatibility_prefix> “,“ < data_type_mapping> (“,”<member_mapping>)+ “]”

Table 1. Data type definition matrix

	short	long	long long	float	double	long double	unsigned short	unsigned long	unsigned long long	char	string	boolean	void
short	=	<	<	<	<	<	>	!=	!=	!=	!=	!=	!=
long	>	=	<	<	<	<	>	>	!=	!=	!=	!=	!=
long long	>	>	=	<	<	<	>	>	>	!=	!=	!=	!=
float	>	>	>	=	<	<	>	>	>	!=	!=	!=	!=
double	>	>	>	>	=	<	>	>	>	!=	!=	!=	!=
long double	>	>	>	>	>	=	>	>	>	!=	!=	!=	!=
unsigned short	<	<	<	<	<	<	=	<	<	!=	!=	!=	!=
unsigned long	!=	<	<	<	<	<	>	=	<	!=	!=	!=	!=
unsigned long long	!=	!=	<	<	<	<	>	>	=	!=	!=	!=	!=
char	!=	!=	!=	!=	!=	!=	!=	!=	!=	=	!=	!=	!=
string	!=	!=	!=	!=	!=	!=	!=	!=	!=	!=	=	!=	!=
boolean	!=	!=	!=	!=	!=	!=	!=	!=	!=	!=	!=	=	!=
void	!=	!=	!=	!=	!=	!=	!=	!=	!=	!=	!=	!=	=

The Compatibility Algorithm

As explained in the chapter before, the compatibility of software components can be identified by a combination of tests which compare the number of declarations on the different levels of the used parts of IDL declarations (module, interfaces, types, operations, exceptions) and through an unequivocal mapping of these declarations. To reduce complexity the *compatibility algorithm* is separated into subalgorithms, which can be refined. To reduce the average runtime of the *compatibility algorithm* the subalgorithms are combined in the following way. Subalgorithms with a short runtime are executed as soon as possible in order to reduce runtime. In addition, all subalgorithms are using the results of former executed subalgorithms.

Subalgorithms with a short runtime are number tests which test compatibility on the number of declarations. These subalgorithms are called pretests in the following and can lead to a *global restriction* or have effect on an existing one. If the postulated restriction conflicts with an eventually existing global restriction, the compatibility algorithm terminates and the two components are incompatible. The *global restriction* makes it possible to reduce runtime of all following subalgorithms. More complex subalgorithms are the mapping algorithms which also include pretests.

The *compatibility algorithm* can either be started with or without a *global restriction*. A restriction, regardless if global or local, excludes specialized, generalized or both compatibilities. As shown in figure 2 (representing like all other

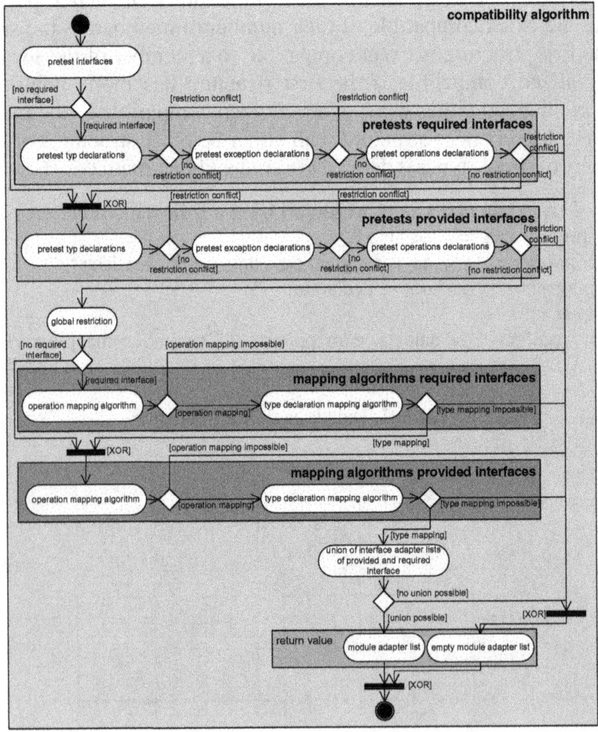

Fig. 2. Compatibility algorithm

diagrams a UML activity diagram [6]), the *compatibility algorithm* begins with the pretest interface. First, a pretest checks, if both modules include the required interface. If both modules contain the required interface, the compatibility algorithm includes the pretests and the mapping algorithm for the required interface. The pretests of the interfaces are the pretest of the type declarations, the pretest of the exception declarations and the pretest of the operation declarations. If the *compatibility algorithm* passes the pretests the operation mapping algorithm starts. If it is possible to map the operations, the *type declaration mapping algorithm* is executed. This algorithm maps the data types which haven't been matched by the *operation mapping algorithm.* If it is additionally possible to map these type declarations, an interface adapter list with at least one item is created. In case of no conflicting compatibility prefixes between provided and required interface adapters, the *union of interface adapter list* leads to a module adapter list and the *compatibility algorithm* terminates. If any subalgorithm fails, the *compatibility algorithm* terminates with an *empty module adapter list.*

In the following the *operation mapping algorithm* (cp. Fig. 3) and its subalgorithms are described. This algorithm maps the operations of the two interfaces. Due to this the operations have to be tested on compatibility by the *operation compatibility algorithm.* The result of each test is saved in an operation adapter list in the cells of the *operation matrix* (cp. Tab.2). The rows represent the operations of the first interface and the columns the operations of the second. The compatibility of operations depends on the compatibility of the types of the return values and the input parameters. Due to the fact that an interface may contain self defined types such as typedefs and structures, the compatibility of these types are saved in a *data type matrix* (cp. Tab. 2) in a data type adapter. Analogue to the *operation matrix*, the rows contain the type declarations of the first interface and the columns the type declarations of the second interface. These two matrices, the global restriction and the matrix defining the compatibility of the simple data types, are the base for the following subalgorithms.

Table 2. Data type and operation matrix

data type matrix	struct 1	...	struct n
struct 1			
...			
struct n			

operation matrix	op 1'	...	op m'
op 1			
...			
op m			

First, *operation matrix* and *data type matrix* are initialized by the *operation mapping algorithm*, shown in figure 3. After this setup phase the algorithm tries to get a mapping for each operation of the two interfaces. Therefore, the *operation compatibility algorithm* tries to get an operation adapter for two operations.

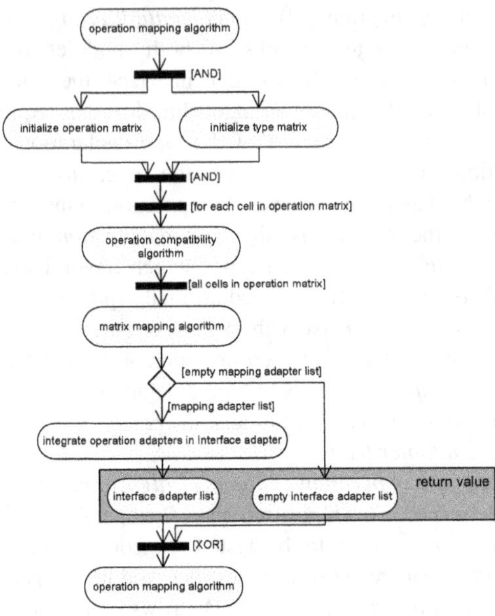

Fig. 3. Operation mapping algorithm

After getting an operation adapter for all operations of the two interfaces, the operations can be mapped to each other by the *matrix mapping algorithm.* According to the mapping adapter list, the operations have to be integrated in an interface adapter. For each mapping adapter, a separate interface adapter is generated.

The *operation compatibility algorithm* (cp. Fig. 4) – a subalgorithm of the *operation mapping algorithm* – tests the compatibility of two operations. This algorithm includes pretests which compare the number of exceptions and parameters and may result in a local restriction, in case there is no global restriction. If there is no conflict between the global and local restriction the algorithm continues. Otherwise no mapping for these two operations is existent and the algorithm terminates with an empty operation adapter list. After the pretests the two return types of the operations are tested on compatibility by the *data type compatibility test.* If it is possible to find an adapter for the return types of the operations, the input parameters of the operations have to be mapped. In case, the return types are incompatible, the algorithm terminates. The parameters of the two operations are likewise mapped by the *matrix mapping algorithm.* The result of this algorithm is a mapping for the sets of parameters of two operations. The *matrix mapping algorithm* may get more solutions for a mapping. These mapping adapter lists have to be integrated into the operation mapping adapter list. After that for each solution an adapter is saved in an operation adapter list. This list, containing all possible mappings of the operations, is saved in the *operation matrix.* The number of operation adapters equals the multiplicity of compatibility of the two operations.

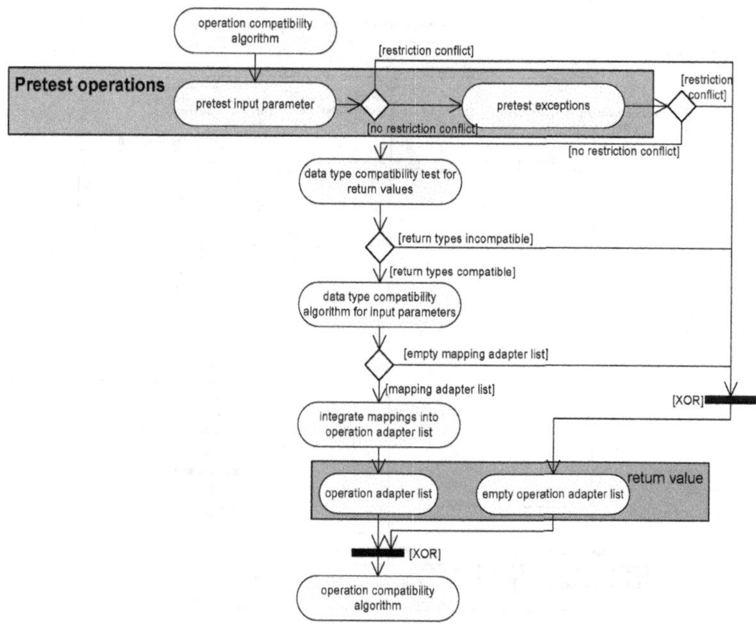

Fig. 4. Operation compatibility algorithm

As mentioned above it is necessary to test data types on compatibility, e.g. the return types and the parameter types of two operations and furthermore the types of the members of structures. This test is performed by the *data type compatibility test* (cp. Fig. 5). The input parameters of the test are two data types and - if necessary - a compatibility restriction. The compatibility of two types depends on their type definition. The types are either defined in the interface, e.g. type declaration (structure) or already defined by the specification of OMG IDL. The compatibility of types of OMG IDL is defined in the *data type definition matrix* for simple data types, as shown in table 1.

Three cases of testing data types are possible: If the two types belong to the simple types, the compatibility can be simply looked up in the *data type definition matrix* and this compatibility is copied into an adapter list. If one type belongs to the group of type declarations in one interface and the other to the group of the simple types, the two types are incompatible. In this case, an empty adapter list will be returned. In case both types are structures, the compatibility of the consisting types is looked up in the *data type definition matrix*. If the compatibility of these two types already exists in the *data type definition matrix*, the list will be returned. Otherwise, a pretest, which compares the number of attributes, is performed. In case of conflicts between the input restriction and the resulting restriction, the two types are incompatible. Otherwise, the *data type mapping algorithm* is invoked with the two lists of data types of the two structures and the according restriction. In case the *data type mapping algorithm* returns solutions for the mapping, the solutions must be integrated into the data type compatibility adapters and saved in the *data type definition matrix*. If the mapping isn't possible, an empty data type adapter list is saved.

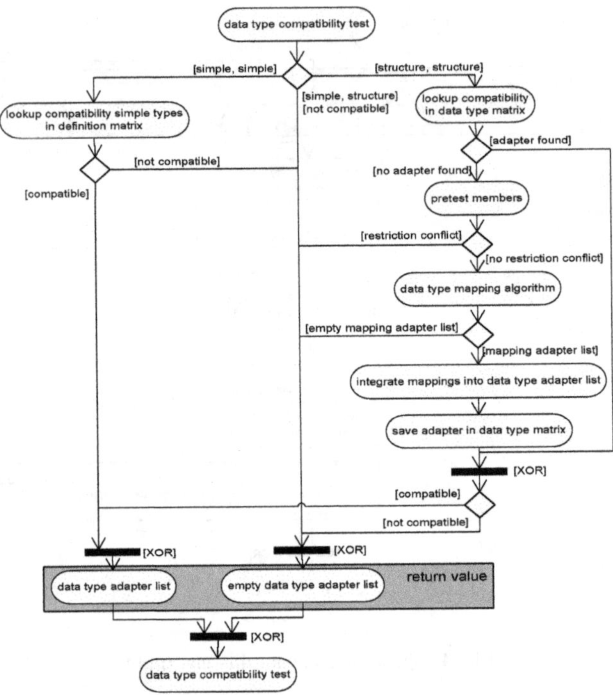

Fig. 5. Data type compatibility test

If the two data types are incompatible, an empty adapter list is returned, or, if the two data types are compatible, a data type adapter list, including all adapters, will be returned.

The input parameters of the *data type mapping algorithm* (cp. Fig 6) are two sets of data types and a restriction. The two sets of data types are either the types of parameters of two operations or the types of two structures. Like the *operation matrix*, a temporary matrix is initialized to map the types of the two sets. The rows represent the types of the first set while the columns represent the types of second set. Afterwards, for each cell, the *data type compatibility* test with the corresponding types is invoked, in order to get the compatibility of the two types. After that the types have to be mapped unequivocally by the *matrix mapping algorithm*. If it is possible to map the types, the mapping information of the rows and columns are returned in a mapping adapter list.

Task of the *matrix mapping algorithm* is to map each row to a column. In case a row-column-mapping was possible, the row and the column must be excluded from the following search for mappings. The mapping must be conforming to the restriction. If no restriction is given and a row-column-mapping is specialized compatible the following mappings may not include a generalized compatibility. Furthermore, it might be possible to map the rows and columns in different ways. To find all possible mappings, a kind of backtracking is needed within the algorithm. That's the reason, why a multiplicity of compatibility is defined. The result of possible row-column-mappings is returned within a mapping adapter list.

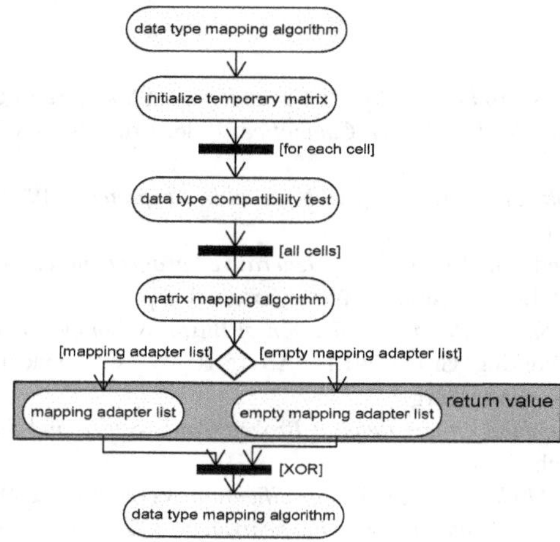

Fig. 6. Data type mapping algorithm

After the *operation mapping algorithm* the *type declaration mapping algorithm* maps the data types which haven't been matched by the *operation mapping algorithm*. This algorithm reduces the *data type matrix* to the types, which don't occur in the operations of the two interfaces. In each cell, a data type adapter is saved, returned by the *data type compatibility test*. After all data type adapters are saved, the *matrix mapping algorithm* maps these data types to each other. By the information of the mapping adapter list of the *matrix mapping algorithm*, the data type adapters are integrated into the interface adapter list.

Conclusion and Outlook

The depicted algorithm tests equivalence of interface specifications and generates simple adapters. Thereby only those artefacts of the Interface Definition Language IDL were considered, that are used in the Memorandum on Standardized Specification of Business Components [4]. The algorithm has been implemented and was integrated in a specification tool, which allows suppliers and buyers to describe their demands. Therewith the users can search for software components that fit their demands concerning the signatures of business components.

Currently an automated test on suitability of a certain component with the according generation of adapters is only possible on Interface Level. The next tasks in our research are to expand the automated testability by moving up the levels towards the business related aspects. In doing so, the semantic aspects of software will come to the force. However the long-term objective must be an integrated test on all specification levels to achieve the goal of combining the advantages of individually programmed software and standard software with Commercial of the shelf (COTS)-software components.

Remarks. An example for the algorithm is available and can be retrieved by sending an e-mail to johannes.maria.zaha@wiwi.uni-augsburg.de.

References

1. McIlroy, M.D. *Mass Produced Software Components*. in *Software Engineering: Report on a Conference by the NATO Science Committee*. 1986. Brussels: NATO Scientific Affairs Devision.
2. Sametinger, J., *Software engineering with reusable components*. 1997; Berlin, New York: Springer. xvi, 272 p
3. Czarnecki, K. and U. Eisenecker, *Generative programming: methods, tools, and applications*. 2000, Boston: Addison Wesley. xxvi, 832 p.
4. Turowski, K., ed. *Standardized Specification of Business Components*. 2002, Gesellschaft für Informatik, Working Group WI-kobAS (5.10.3) - Component Oriented Business Application Systems: Augsburg.
5. OMG, ed. *The Common Object Request Broker: Architecture and Specification: Version 2.5*. 2001, Framingham.
6. OMG, ed. *Unified Modeling Language Specification: Version 1.4*. 2001, Needham.
7. Ortner, E. *Methodenneutraler Fachentwurf: Zu den Grundlagen einer anwendungsorientierten Informatik*. 1997, Stuttgart.
8. Meyer, B., *Object-Oriented Software Construction*. 1988, Englewood Cliffs.
9. Meyer, B., *Applying "Design by Contract"*. IEEE Computer, 1992. **25**(10): p. 40-51.
10. Zaremski, A. M.; Wing, J. M., *Signature Matching: A Key to Reuse*. Proceedings of SIGSOFT '93, 1993.
11. Zaremski, A. M.; Wing, J. M., *Signature Matching: a Tool for using Software Libraries*. ACM Transactions on Software Engineering and Methodology (TOSEM), 1995
12. Zaremski, A. M.; Wing, J. M., *Specification Matching of Software Components*. Proceedings of 3rd ACM SIGSOFT Symposium on the Foundations of Software Engineering, 1995.
13. Nierstrasz, O., *Regular Types for Active Objects*. Proceedings of the eighth annual conference on Object-oriented programming systems, languages, and applications, 1993.
14. Yellin, D. M., Strom, R. E., *Protocol Specifications and Component Adapters*. ACM Transactions on Programming Languages and Systems (TOPLAS), 1997.

A Modern Graphic Flowchart Layout Tool

Sukhamay Kundu

Computer Science Dept, Louisiana State University,
Baton Rouge, LA 70803, USA
kundu@bit.csc.lsu.edu

Abstract. We describe the design of a flowchart layout tool for C-programs, which may contain break, continue, and return statements. We exploit the nesting relationship among the blocks to determine the positions of blocks and sub-blocks, which in turn determine the placement of connecting lines between the blocks. A special labeling technique is used to avoid the crossing of lines.

1 Introduction

A graphical display of a program's flowchart is helpful in understanding the program logic for beginning programmers. Flowcharts have many important uses, including static analyses (definition-use relationship of variables [1] and unreachable code segments [1, 2]), test-data generation and test-converge measures [2], computation of program slice [3, 4], and code optimization [1]. An important consideration in a flowchart-display is the clarity of showing the program blocks and their nesting structure. For large programs, it is also important to be able to form "summary display" by avoiding the details within selected blocks and to be able to expand those blocks when needed. We accomplish these using the nesting-tree of program blocks as the basis for creating the flowchart layout. The blocks with hidden details can be selected on the basis of their nesting levels, size (number of nodes in the block), nesting depth within the block, presence or absence of certain structures within them, etc. We avoid crossing among the connecting lines between nodes of a flowchart by using a special node-labeling scheme for the unstructured constructs involving break, continue, and return. Programs involving these constructs, but without goto's, maybe called *semi-structured*. The JAVAVIS tool [5] shows UML class diagrams (for object oriented programs) but not the flowchart. Our layouts are superior in many ways to those given by the commercial packages //www.fatesoft.com and //www.aisee.com. Flowchart layout is a special case of more general problem of graph drawing [6].

Fig. 1(i) shows the layout of a semi-structured flowchart; its input data, which is shown in Fig. 1(ii), is easily obtained by a simple preprocessing of the *C*-program text. Nodes and blocks with a deeper nesting-level are indicated by a darker shading; one can turn off the shading, if desired. The label 10/11 for the break-node 10 of the while-do loop shows that the original control (going to node 9 and indicated by a dotted line) is now modified going to node 11. In our flowchart layout tool, we first create an output file which describes the display in the "pic" language in UNIX. The actual display is then created by processing this file by the pic-utility in UNIX.

2 Construction of Layout

For our purpose, a *block* is a segment of a code which has single input point and a single output point when we disregard the unstructured control flows due to the

R.K. Ghosh and H. Mohanty (Eds.): ICDCIT 2004, LNCS 3347, pp. 329–335, 2004.

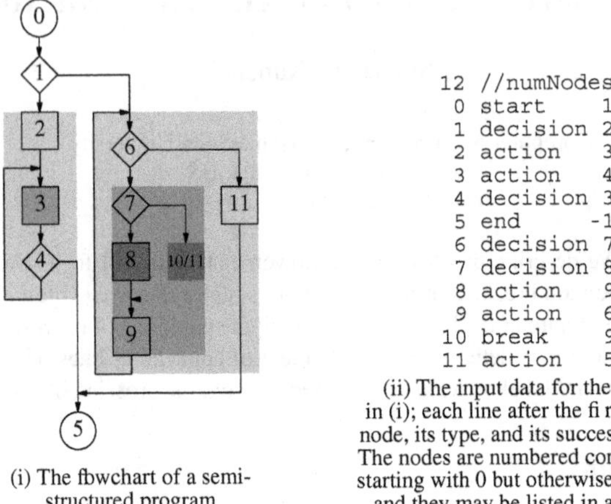


```
12 //numNodes
 0 start     1
 1 decision 2  6
 2 action    3
 3 action    4
 4 decision 3  5
 5 end      -1
 6 decision 7 11
 7 decision 8 10
 8 action    9
 9 action    6
10 break     9
11 action    5
```

(i) The fbwchart of a semi-structured program

(ii) The input data for the display in (i); each line after the fi rst shows a node, its type, and its successor nodes. The nodes are numbered consecutively starting with 0 but otherwise arbitrarily and they may be listed in any order

Fig. 1. An example layout

break, continue, and intermediate returns (other than that at the end of a function). The four basic block types are if-then-else (if-then being a special case), while-do loop (for-loop being a special case), do-while loop, and sequence.

2.1 Notion of Box

We view the layout as a hierarchy of boxes with horizontal and vertical sides. Each box has an entry point on its top side and an exit point on its bottom side; the box is connected to the outside world by a vertical line to and from there points, respectively. The box $B(x)$ associated with a node x in the fbwchart contains x and extends just far enough on all sides to contain all its subboxes, including the connecting lines among them so that for each node $y \in B(x)$, y is reachable from x within $B(x)$ itself and $B(y) \subseteq B(x)$. The box corresponding to the end-node consists of only itself. $B(x)$ but does not contain nodes outside the innermost loop-body containing x, if any. The notion of a box should not be confused with a single entry and single exit block; a block is either contained in a box or disjoint from a box. We build the boxes in a bottom-up and inside-out fashion starting from the end-node.

Fig. 2(i) shows the box for an action node x, which includes x and the box B2 corresponding to the unique next node of x. Fig. 2(ii) shows the box for a white-do loop-test node, where B1 is the box for the loop-body and B2 is the box for the destination node of the false-branch at the loop-test node. There are few exceptions where B2 is not present (or equivalently, it is an empty box); for example, the while-do loop is the else-part of an if-then-else statement or it is the last block of another loop-body. Note that if the height of B2 is larger than the height of B1 plus the vertical separation between a box and an horizontal line, then exit-point(B2) = exit-point(B) and the vertical line (without the arrowhead) joining exit-point(B2) to exit-point(B) is not present. The box for a do-while loop-test node is similar to that of a while-do loop-test node. Fig. 2(iii) shows the box for an if-then-else test node, where B1 is the box for the then-part, B2 is the box for the else-part, and B3 is the box for the node that follows both then and else parts. B3 is empty when the if-then-else statement is the last block in a loop-body; B2 is empty for an if-then statement. We do not use rectilinear-shape boxes to optimize the layout space by packing the boxes horizontally or vertically as indicated in Fig. 2(iv) to avoid loss of visibility of the program blocks in a complex situation. A similar remark applies to Fig. 2(ii).

The vertical line segment to B2 in Fig. 2(i) do not always have the arrow-head; this would be the case, for example, if B2 is the box for an while-do loop because that would create two arrowheads on the line from B1 to the loop-test node in B2. Similar remark holds for the vertical lines to subboxes in Figs. 2(ii)-(iii). For each box B, we maintain the following parameters.

- (P1) width(B) and height(B),
- (P2) topDist(B) = the horizontal distance of the entry-point of B from its west-side and bottomDist(B) = the horizontal distance of the exit-point of B from its west-side, and
- (P3) needArrow(B) = yes, if the vertical entry line to B needs an arrowhead.

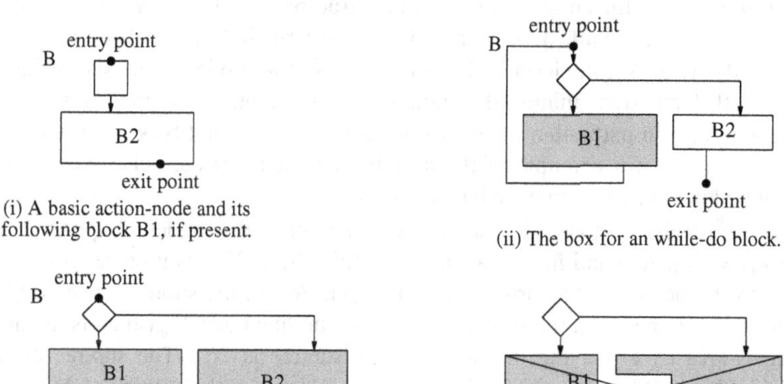

(i) A basic action-node and its following block B1, if present.

(ii) The box for an while-do block.

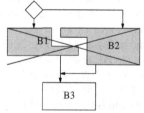

(iii) The box for an if-then-else, which includes the following block B3, if any.

(iv) The use of general rectilinear shapes is avoided to maintain the visibility of blocks.

Fig. 2. The box-structure for sequence, while-do loop, and if-then-else

2.2 Computation of Box-Parameters

For each case in Figs. 2(i)-(iii) and the do-while loop which is not shown there, we can compute the parameters (P1)-(P3) for a box B in terms of those for its component boxes; we can also determine the relative positions of the components within B. We show below the formulas for computing width(B), topDist(B), and bottomDist(B) for Fig. 2(iii), where we let topDist(B3) = bottomDist(B3) = width(B3) =

0 if B3 is not present. Let δ = bottomDist(B1) – topDist(B3) and HS = the unit vertical separation between two boxes.

(4.1) width(B) = max {width(B1) + HS + width(B2), δ + width(B3)}, if $\delta \geq 0$
= max {$-\delta$ + width(B1) + HS + width(B2), width(B3)}, otherwise.

(4.2) topDist(B) = topDist(B1), if $\delta \geq 0$ and
= $-\delta$ + topDist(B1), otherwise.

(4.8) bottomDist(B) = δ + bottomDist(B3), if $\delta \geq 0$ and
= bottomDist(B3), otherwise.

2.3 Computation of Blocks

We determine the blocks from the depth-fi rst tree [7] of the fbwchart digraph, together with its back-arcs and cross-arcs, given in the form shown in Fig. 1(ii) and regarding the break, continue, and return statements as ordinary actions. Fig. 3(i) shows the depth-fi rst tree for the input in Fig. 1(ii). A decision node N_j is a while-do loop-test node if there is a back-arc to N_j itself but to an ancestor of N_j prior to taking false-branch(N_j). The while-do loop-body consists of the nodes in the subtree of the depth-fi rst tree at the child N_k of N_j, where true-branch(N_j) = (N_j, N_k). A decision node N_j is a do-while loop-test node if true-branch(N_j) is a back-arc to an ancestor node N_i of N_j; the loop-body then consists of all nodes in the subtree at N_i of the depth-fi rst tree minus the nodes in the subtree at the end of the false-branch(N_j). In particular, the do-while loop-body may not be known when we backtrack from N_j (for example, if the loop-body contains if-then-else statements), but it will be known by the time we backtrack from N_i.

All other decision nodes N_j are if-then or if-then-else nodes. Suppose true-branch(N_j) = (N_j, N_k) and false-branch(N_j) = (N_j, N_n). N_j has no else-part if and only if false-branch(N_j) is a forward arc to a node N_m in the subtree of the depth-fi rst tree at N_k. Otherwise, the subtree at N_k has a unique node N_m which is the head of all cross-arcs ($\geq$ 1) leaving the nodes in the subtree at N_n. The subtree at N_m gives the nodes in B3 in Fig. 2(iii), the subtree at N_k minus the subtree at N_m gives the nodes in B1, and the subtree at N_n gives the nodes in B2. For N_j = 1 in Fig. 3(i), we have N_k = 2, N_n = 6, and N_m = 5; this gives B1 = {2, 3, 4}, B2 = {6, 7, 8, 9, 10, 11}, and B3 = {5}. Likewise, for N_j = 7, N_k = 8, N_n = 10, and N_m = 9; this gives B1 = {8} and B2 = {10}, and B3 = {9}.

2.4 Nesting-Tree

The *nesting-tree*, which is an ordered tree, shows the nesting structure of the blocks by regarding the break, continue, and return statements as ordinary actions. Fig. 3(ii) shows the nesting-tree for the fbwchart in Fig. 1(i). It has two types of nodes: the fi rst type of nodes are the action nodes, it-test nodes (shown as circles with an inscribed diamond shape), while-do loop-test nodes (shown as double circles), and do-while loop-test nodes (shown as bold circles); the second type of nodes are the place holder nodes for then- and else-parts of an if-test and the root node; they are shown as shaded nodes without labels. For an if-then statement, the second child of the if-test node has no children; the do-while loop-test node also has no

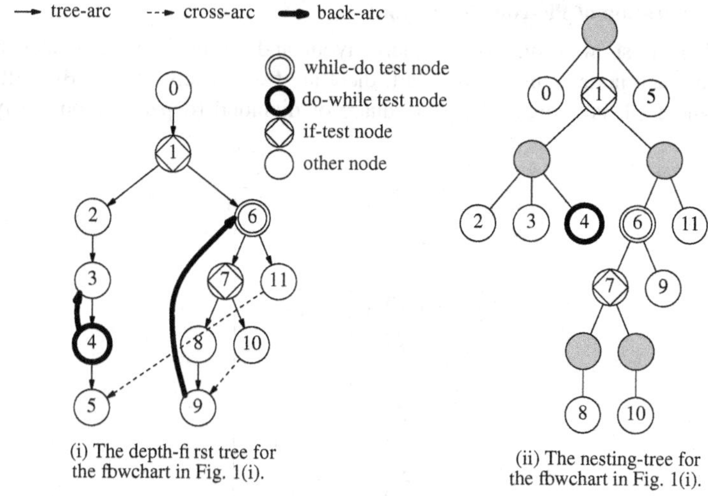

(i) The depth-first tree for the flowchart in Fig. 1(i).

(ii) The nesting-tree for the flowchart in Fig. 1(i).

Fig. 3. The depth-first tree and nesting-tree for the flowcharts in Fig. 1(i)

children. The while-do loop-test node may have an arbitrary number (≥ 1) of children, which correspond to the blocks in the loop-body. The children of a node correspond to a sequence of single input single output blocks, with one exception. The blocks in a do-while loop-body appear as left brothers preceding the loop-test node; the starting block of the body is given by the node which is head of the back-arc (in the depth-first tree) from the loop-test node. See Fig. 3(ii). (We do not make these brother nodes the children of the do-while loop-test node to allow the construction of the nesting-tree with a minimal change to the depth-first tree of the flowchart as we traverse the latter, although this could be done; recall that the do-while loop body may not be completely known if it contains if-then-else nodes at the time we process the back-arc.) The children of the root show the sequential blocks in the program.

Construction of the nesting-tree is straightforward from the results of the depth-first processing. Since the number of links in the flowchart digraph ≤ twice the number of nodes, we get the following theorem.

Theorem 1. The generation of nesting-tree takes $O(N)$ time where N = #(nodes in the flowchart).

Note that the layout in Fig. 1(i) cannot be obtained in a depth-first fashion from the flowchart digraph in Fig. 3(i). For example, the vertical spacing between nodes 4 and 5 cannot be determined until the whole digraph is processed. Likewise, the horizontal space between nodes 2 and 6 cannot be determined at the time of visiting node 6, but only after we know the body of the while-do loop. The creation of a summary display to hide the details within a block means for the most part ignoring the subtree of a node corresponding to that block, with a slightly different processing for do-while loops because of the particular way it is represented in nesting-tree.

2.5 Generation of Pic-code for Layout

Figs. 4(i)-(ii) show a simple flowchart layout and its pic-code generated by our tool. For each node *k* in the flowchart, there are two objects Nk and Bk in the pic-code, where Nk is a small circle or square or diamond (depending on the type of

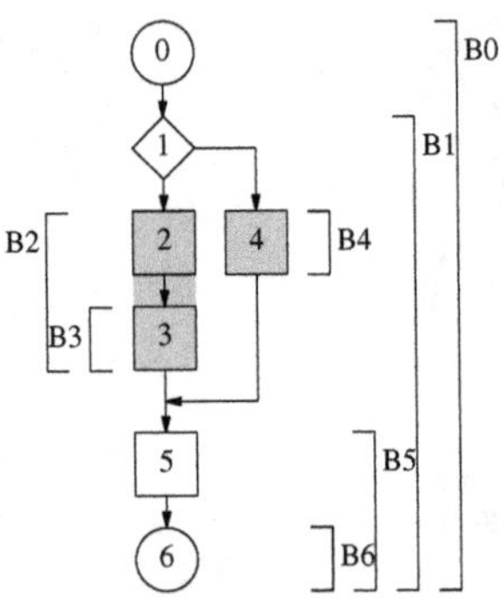

(i) A simple flowchart; the boxes are identified in the order B6, B5, B3, B2, B4, B1, and B0.

```
hu=0.10; vu=0.10; bw=2*hu; bh=2*vu; hs=4*hu; vs=3*vu; f=0.1 #fill-factor
boxwid=bw; boxht=bh; ellipsewid=bw; ellipseht=bh
arrowht=vu/2; arrowwid=arrowht/2
w=5; h=18
B0: box wid w*hu ht h*vu at (0,0) invis filled f*0
N0: ellipse "0" with .n at B0.nw+(1*hu,0)
w = 1+4; h=15
B1: box wid w*hu ht h*vu with .nw at N0.n-(1*hu,vs) invis filled f*(0+0)
N1: box "1" with .n at B1.nw+(1*hu,0) invis
line from N1.n to N1.e to N1.s to N1.w to N1.n
w=1+1; h=5
B2: box wid w*hu ht h*vu with .nw at N1.n-(1*hu,vs) invis filled f*(1+0)
N2: box "2" with .n at B2.nw+(1*hu,0)
w = 1+1; h=2
B3: box wid w*hu ht h*vu with .nw at N2.n-(1*hu,vs) invis filled f*(1+0)
N3: box "3" with .n at B3.nw+(1*hu,0)
line -> from N2.s to B3.nw+(1*hu,0)
line -> from N1.s to B2.nw+(1*hu,0)
w=1+1; h=2
B4: box wid w*hu ht h*vu with .nw at B2.ne+(hu,0) invis filled f*(1+0)
N4: box "4" with .n at B4.nw+(1*hu,0)
line -> from N1.e to (N4.x,N1.e.y) to N4.n
x=B2.sw.x+1*hu; y=B2.sw.y; y2=y-vu
L: line from (x,y) to (x,y2)
line -> from B4.sw+(1*hu,0) to (B4.sw.x+1*hu,y2) to (x,y2)
w=1+1; h=5
B5: box wid w*hu ht h*vu with .nw at L.s-(1*hu,vu) invis filled f*(0+0)
line -> from L.s to L.s-(0,vu)
N5: box "5" with .n at B5.nw+(1*hu,0)
w = 1+1; h=2
B6: box wid w*hu ht h*vu with .nw at N5.n-(1*hu,vs) invis filled f*(0+0)
N6: ellipse "6" with .n at B6.nw+(1*hu,0)
line -> from N5.s to B6.nw+(1*hu,0)
line -> from N0.s to B1.nw+(1*hu,0)
```

(ii) The groupings of pic-code for the various boxes in (i).

Fig. 4. Illustration of the pic-code generated by our tool

node k) for the display of node k itself and Bk is an auxiliary box associated with node k (as described in Section 2.1) for controlling the positioning of the nodes within that box. As we process node k in the nesting-tree in the bottom-up fashion, the block of lines of pic-code indicated in Fig. 4(ii) on the leftside margin starting with the line "`Nk: box ...`" is created by piecing together the pic-code segments generated previously for subtrees at node k. Although the specifi cation of Nk itself refers to Bk, the pic-code "`Bk: box wid ...`" is generated only when we create the block of pic-code for the parent box of Bk. The first three lines in Fig. 4(ii) is the same for all fbwcharts; here, hu = horizontal spacing unit and vu = vertical spacing units. These lines of pic-code are created last along with the next two lines; in particular, B0 is always placed at position (0,0). The pic-code for N6 is determined here first. Our layout-tool generates the pic-code that is simple and directly related to the structure of the display, and is not optimized as such. This is done to simplify the debugging of our tool and to allow easy manual modification for changing the display if such a need should arise. An extreme example of non-optimization of the pic-code can be seen in parts like "`f*(0+0)`", which could be simplifi ed to "`0`". Other examples are the computations of box-width (w) and box-height (h), based on formulas in Section 2.2, before the pic-code line for each Bk.

3 Conclusion

We have described a simple and efficient technique for producing an elegant layout of the flowchart of a semi-structured C-programs, including the choice of hiding the detials within selected blocks. We assume there are no goto's in the C-program because of the diffi culties in defining a suitable notion of a block which is meaningful in terms of program logic (block hierarchy) and hence the layout. Our approach applies equally well to programs in other block-structured languages.

References

1. Aho, A. and Ullman, J.D., *Principles of Compiler Design,* Addison-Wesley Publ. Co., Mass., 1977.
2. Beizer, B. *Softwar etesting techniques,* Van Nostrand Reinhold Comp., 1983.
3. Weiser, M., Program slicing, *IEEE Trans. Soft. Engg,* 10(1984), pp. 352-357.
4. Horwitz, S., Reps, T., and Binkley, D., Interprocedural slicing using dependence graphs, "*ACM Transactions on Programming Languages and Systems 12(1990), pp. 26-60.*
5. Rainer , O. and Thomas, S., JAVAVIS: automatic program visualization with object and sequence diagrams using the Java Debug Interface (S. Diehl, ed.) in *Software Visualization,* LNCS #2269, pp. 176-190, 2002.
6. Battista, G.Di., Eades, P., Tamassia, R., and Tollis, I.G., *Graph drawing*, Precntice Halls, 1999.
7. Coreman, T. H., Leiserson, C. E., Rivest, R. L., and Stein, C., *Introduction to algorithms,* The MIT Press, 2001.

A Flexible Authorization Framework for E-Commerce*

Sushil Jajodia and Duminda Wijesekera

Center for Secure Information Systems, George Mason University,
Fairfax, VA 22030-4444, USA
{jajodia, dwijesek}@gmu.edu

Abstract. Past generations of access control models fail to meet the needs of many applications such as business-to-business (B2B) applications and auctions. This paper describes several access control models that have been recently proposed to address these emerging needs including models that are policy-neutral and flexible in that they permit enforcement of multiple policies on the same server, and models that incorporate richer semantics for access control, such as provisions and obligations.

1 Introduction

Traditionally, access control plays an integral part in overall system security. Over the years, many different access control models, such as discretionary, mandatory, and role based access control models have been proposed. Discretionary access control is based on having subjects, objects, and operations as primitives and policies that specify which subject get to execute what operations on desired objects. Mandatory access control is based on having clearance levels for subjects and classification labels for objects as primitives and policies that grant accesses to subjects whose clearance levels dominate those of the objects. Role based access control has not only subjects and objects but an additional concept, called *role*, that is assigned a set of permissions. Subjects obtain these permissions indirectly by playing appropriate roles. These models have been used in the commercial and military domains, and implemented in operating systems, database management systems, and object systems.

Advances in application areas bring new dimensions to access control models. The needs to support multiple access control policies in one security domain, Internet-based transactions, and cooperating coalitions, have brought new challenges to access control. This paper gives an overview of some of the new access control models that have been proposed in response.

We begin in section 2 by describing the motivation for access control models that are policy-neutral and flexible, followed by the Flexible Authorization

* This work was partially supported by the National Science Foundation under grants CCR-0113515 and IIS-0242237.

R.K. Ghosh and H. Mohanty (Eds.): ICDCIT 2004, LNCS 3347, pp. 336–345, 2004.

Framework (FAF) of Jajodia et al. [JSSS01]. Section 3 discusses the concept of *provisional authorizations* that was introduced to meet the needs of providing conditional authorizations in the area of Internet commerce. Section 4 addresses another problem faced in applications such as the electronic banking area where an access permission in return requires the grantee to fulfill some external obligations, for example promise to pay back loans. Finally, Section 5 concludes the paper.

2 Need for Flexible Access Control Models

Many access control models proposed over the years [DM89] have been developed with a number of pre-defined policies in mind, and thereby have introduced a sense of inflexibility. Two alternatives accommodate more than one access control model simultaneously. The first is to have more than one access control mechanism running at the same time, one for each policy. The second is to make access control an application responsibility. The first alternative calls for every application to be closely bound to its access control module, which decreases their portability. The second alternative requires all applications to enforce a consistent access control. Additionally, the responsibility of enforcing access control is vested in applications that may not impose the same rigorous standards of verification and testing imposed on system code.

Consequently, both alternatives are undesirable. This can be seen by considering a number of access control policies that have been in use over the years [CFS94]. A popular policy is the *closed world* policy, where accesses that cannot be derived from those explicitly authorized are prohibited. A rarely used alternative is the *open world* policy, where accesses that are not explicitly denied are permitted. Some policies include explicit prohibitions in terms of negative authorizations. This, coupled with generalizations, specializations of these policies to structures such as subject and object hierarchies [Bru92] yield numerous combinations. Hence, custom creation of policy enforcement mechanisms or passing of these complications to applications is practically infeasible.

One of the solutions for this problem has been to develop flexible authorization models [JSS97, JSSS01], where the flexibility comes from having an access control model that does not depend on any policies or meta policies, but is capable of imposing any of them specifiable in their syntax. One of the main advantages of this approach is that access control can now reside within the system, yet it is able to impose application specific policies. Given that there is a need for flexible access control models, the following requirements would be desirable:

Expressibility: It must be possible to model existing policies, such as *denials take precedence*, and be able to model policies of emerging applications, such as provisions and obligations (to be discussed shortly).

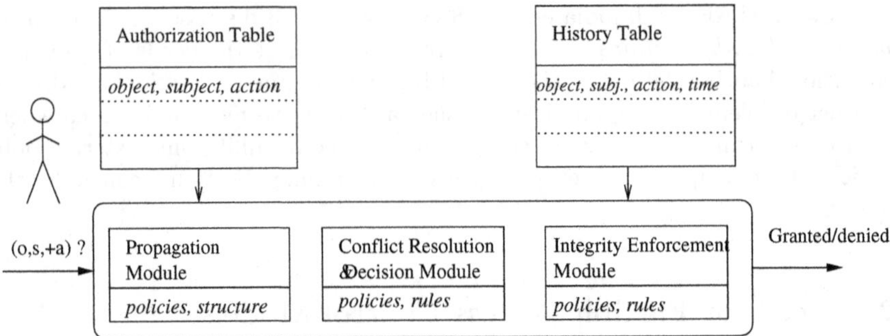

Fig. 1. FAF System Architecture

Decoupling Policies from Mechanisms: The primary need for flexibility is to obtain policy-independent frameworks. Hence, policies expressible in such frameworks must be enforceable using generic enforcement mechanisms.

Conflict Resolution: Having a flexible framework may lead to conflicting policies and, consequently, the framework must be able to facilitate their resolution.

Efficiency: Due to the high frequency of requests coming to access control systems, their processing must be fast. Thus, efficient and simple mechanisms to allow or deny access requests are crucial.

Next we describe one such flexible framework for access control and show how it meets these requirements.

2.1 FAF - A Flexible Authorization Framework

The Flexible Authorization Framework (FAF) [JSSS01] is a logic-based framework to specify authorizations as rules in a stratified rule base. The FAF architecture has four modules as shown in Figure 1.

The *propagation module* contains basic structures such as authorization subjects and object hierarchies (for example, directory structures), and a finite set of rules is used to derive authorizations stemming from structural properties, referred to as *propagation policies.* Propagation policies specify how access permissions are to be propagated through subject and object hierarchies, and FAF allows the system security officer (SSO) to write them. This freedom may result in over specification, implying that the system may allow and deny the same access request simultaneously. Therefore, the *conflict resolution module* implements *conflict resolution policies* to eliminate such inconsistencies, and these policies are specifiable by the SSO. By applying decision policies, which is again a set of rules written by the SSO, a decision will be made either to grant or deny every authorization request. This stage has a meta-policy denying all permissions that cannot be specifically derived using the given set of rules. The last stage consists of checking for integrity constraints, where all authorizations that violate integrity constraints will be denied. This component lives outside the scope of the rule base and is an external module used by FAF. FAF rules are written using a number of predicates, such as `cando`, `do`, and `dercando`. Their semantics are as follows:

1. A ternary predicate `cando(o,s,a)`, representing grantable or deniable requests (depending on the sign associated with the action), where o, s, and a are object, subject, and a signed action term, respectively.
2. A ternary predicate `dercando(o,s,a)`, with the same arguments as `cando`. The predicate `dercando` represents authorizations derived by the system using logical rules of inference (modus ponens plus rules for stratified negation [ABW88]).
3. A ternary predicate `do`, with the same arguments as `cando`, representing the access control decisions made by FAF.
4. A 5-ary predicate `done(o, s, r, a, t)`, meaning subject `s` with role `r` active has executed action `a` on object `o` at time `t`.
5. Two 4-ary predicate symbols $\texttt{over}_{\mathsf{AO}}$ and $\texttt{over}_{\mathsf{AS}}$. $\texttt{over}_{\mathsf{AO}}$ takes as arguments two object terms, a subject term and a signed action term. $\texttt{over}_{\mathsf{AS}}$ takes as arguments a subject term, an object term, another subject term, and a signed action term. They are needed in the definition of some of the overriding policies.
6. A propositional symbol `error` indicating violation of an integrity constraint. It is a rule with an `error` head that must not have a body that is satisfiable.

An example policy governing the electronic trading is given by the following FAF rules:

$$
\begin{aligned}
\texttt{cando}(item, s, +buy) &\leftarrow \texttt{in}(item, Goods, ASH),\\
&\qquad \texttt{in}(s, Buyers, ASH).\\
\texttt{cando}(item, s, +sell) &\leftarrow \texttt{in}(item, Goods, ASH),\\
&\qquad \texttt{in}(s, Sellers, ASH).\\
\texttt{dercando}(item, s, +a) &\leftarrow \texttt{cando}(item, s, +a).\\
\texttt{do}(item, s, +a) &\leftarrow \texttt{dercando}(item, s, +a)\\
\texttt{do}(item, s, -a) &\leftarrow \neg\texttt{do}(item, s, +a).\\
\texttt{error} &\leftarrow \texttt{do}(item, s, +buy), \texttt{do}(item, s, +sell).
\end{aligned}
$$

The predicate `in`(x,y,"hierarchy name") is used to specify properties of subject and object hierarchies AOH and ASH, respectively. In this example, ASH consist of two directories, `Buyers` and `Sellers`. The object hierarchy AOH has one class, `Goods`. Rules whose heads are $\texttt{dercando}(o, s, a)$ literals are derivations of authorizations. Thus, the first two rules state that a subject `s` is allowed to buy or sell if it is in the appropriate directory. The next rule is a derivation. The third rule resolves any potential conflicts and the fourth rule ensures the completeness of access control decisions. The latter two have $\texttt{do}(o, s, a)$ heads. Therefore, in this short example, all derived positive permissions are allowed, and all actions for which positive permissions cannot be derived are denied. The last rule state the *integrity* requirement that no subject is allowed to buy and sell the same item.

Logically, FAF policies are stratified logic programs. They can express many policies such as the closed, open, denials-take-precedence, and Chinese Wall policy [JSSS01]. In addition, to capture the evolving nature of policies and, consequently, their impact on access control, FAF has been enhanced to add and remove rules [JSSS01], and to revoke already granted accesses [WJPPH03]. It has been further expanded to find ways in which constraints specified by important classes of application-level policies such those used in role-based policies [AS00] can be resolved inside the FAF rule enforcement engine [WJ03].

3 Adding Provisions to FAF

Traditional access control uses the model that *a user makes an access request of a system in some context, and the system either authorizes the access request or denies it.* However, today's rapidly expanding environments, such as electronic commerce, make such models that authorize or deny a request overly simplistic and not accommodating. In practice, it is not unusual that decisions regarding accesses depend on specific actions to be performed before the decision is taken and on the guarantee that certain other actions will be taken after the access. Because the two sets of actions are conceptually different and require different management techniques, we distinguish the first and second sets of actions as *provisions* and *obligations*, respectively.

As an example of provisional authorizations, consider purchase of goods for credit over the Internet. A customer can purchase an item online subject to the provision that she enters her credit card, is credit worthy, and agrees to pay the lending institution back. Here, the access decision is based on three provisions:

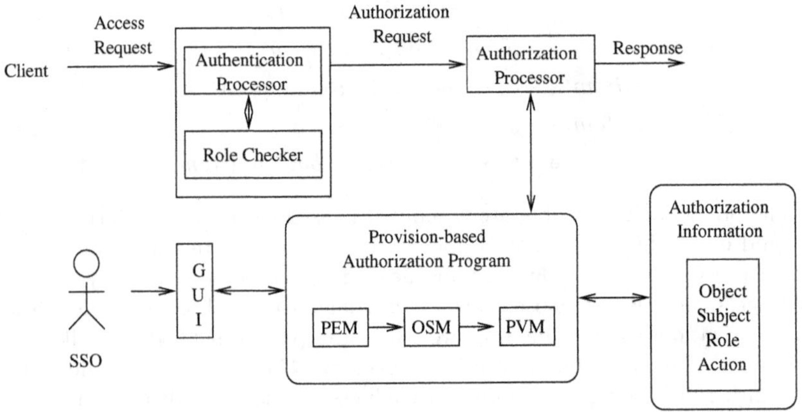

Fig. 2. Provision-Based Authorization Architecture

entering the credit card, finding the purchaser to be credit worthy, and signing the purchase agreement. To capture such applications, *provisional* authorization models have been proposed [JKS01, KH00].

Figure 2 shows the architecture of the provisional authorization system proposed in [JKS01]. When users submit an authorization request, the system invokes its authentication and role-checking modules that verify if the user is who she claims to be and whether she is allowed to assume requested roles. Then, the access request is passed on to the provision evaluation module to find the *weakest* conditions under which the requested access can be honored. Then, the weakest condition under which the access may be granted is passed to an *order specification* module that yields a set of ordering constraints on the actions involved. For instance, the ordering constraints may require that the name and address be filled in before the social security number. Then, the ordering constraints are handed off to a *provision verification module* to check if any conditions were previously fulfilled by the requester and, if so, simplifies the condition (and ordering constraints) and waits for reduced conditions to be fulfilled by the requester before final authorization. Formally referred to as $\mathsf{pASL}_{\mathcal{L}}$, the syntax is enhanced to be of the following form (where $Head \leftarrow Body$ is a FAF rule and ϕ is a predicate external to FAF):

$$\phi : Head \leftarrow Body.$$

The following set of rules models a $\mathsf{pASL}_{\mathcal{L}}$ specification for provisional accesses for an online store:

```
register(s,customer): cando(item,s,+buy) ←
                          in(contract, Contracts).
upGrade(s,prefCust):  dercando(item,s,+buy) ←
                          cando(item, s, +buy).
payFees(s,$100):      do(item,s,+buy) ←
                          cando(item, s, +buy).
payFees(s,$80):       do(item,s,+buy) ←
                          dercando(item,s,+buy).
```

The first two rules allow a customer to purchase by registering and further allows the customer to upgrade her registration to a *preferred customer.* Next two rules state that the purchase price of an item is $100 for a non-preferred cutomer and $80 for a preferred customer. Thus, a customer has the choice of remaining in the non-preferred category and paying $100 or registering as a preferred customer and paying $80 per item. Further, suppose there is a one-time cost of $10 to register as a non-preferred customer and to pay a $20 fee for upgrading. Then it is preferable to buy as a non-preferred customer for a one-time-only purchase, but to become a preferred customer for multiple purchases. This is so because the cost of the one-time purchase is $80 after paying a one-time fee of $30, as opposed to paying $100 after paying a registration fee of $10. $\mathsf{pASL}_{\mathcal{L}}$ provides this computation for its customers. Provisional authorizations have been used in XML documents by Kudo et al. [KH00].

4 Adding Obligations to FAF

As mentioned earlier, provisions alone are insufficient for current e-commerce applications. As an example, consider a loan application and management (payment collection etc.) system. It allows users to initiate a loan application process if they are already registered in the system. If they are not already registered, they are given an opportunity to register with the system by supplying the necessary information and, if this step is successful, they are given permission to proceed with the loan application process. This kind of access can be modeled by having provisions.

Continuing with the example, if a loan application is approved and the applicant accesses funds, then it is the applicant is required to pay back the loan on a regular basis. Thus the access to funds is approved conditional to the customer bearing some obligations. To be able to ensure that the customer pays back the loan as agreed, the system needs to be able to monitor such obligations and take appropriate actions if the obligations are not met. In this work, we model obligations as actions that must be fulfilled after the access control decision is made[BJWW02b, BJWW02a]. Furthermore, if obligations are not fulfilled, the system must be able to take compensatory actions. For these purposes, we introduce compensatory actions.

Extending FAF to incorporate provisions and obligations require another syntactic extension. We represent po by two disjoint sets of predicate symbols **P** and **O** that are also disjoint from the set of predicate symbols **Q** allowed in the policy rule specification language. The sets of variable and constant symbols **V** and **C** admitted in the predicates are the same used in the policy rules. The predicate symbols in **P** and **O** may be of any nonnegative arity.

An atom is either one of the symbols $\top$, $\bot$, or a predicate $P_i(t_1, \ldots, t_k)$ with $P_i \in \mathbf{P}$ or $O_i(t_1, \ldots, t_k)$ with $O_i \in \mathbf{O}$ and each t_i is either a constant from **C** or a variable from **V**. When not clear from the context we distinguish these atoms from those in the policy, by calling them *PO*-atoms. Then, a *PO*-formula is either a *PO*-atom, a disjunction of *PO*-formulas, or a conjunction of *PO*-formulas. A *PO*-atom is ground if it is variable-free, and a *PO*-formula is *ground* if each of the atoms in the formula is ground. An interpretation I of a *PO*-formula is a mapping from each ground atom to the constant **True** or **False**, with the atoms $\top$ and $\bot$ mapping to the constants **True** and **False**, respectively. The satisfaction of a *PO*-formula is defined inductively on the structure of the formula, as usual, considering ground atoms as a basis, and the conjunction and disjunction operators that appear in the formula. Later we give a detailed syntax for specification of obligations, here simply given as a predicate.

For each policy rule R_i in R there is an associated *PO*-formula, denoted by ϕ_{R_i}, representing the po for that rule. We also impose the intuitive constraint that each variable appearing in ϕ_{R_i} must appear in the body of R_i. Note that since these predicates are not part of the policy rule specification (the datalog program), they do not appear in its model M_R. An abstract FAF specification with provisions and obligations are shown in Figure 3.

Rule		PO-formula
(R_1)	$Q_1(x) \leftarrow Q_2(x,y), Q_3(y)$	$O_1(s,x,y)$
(R_2)	$Q_2(a,b) \leftarrow$	$P_1(b)$
(R_3)	$Q_3(b) \leftarrow$	$\top$
(R_4)	$Q_1(y) \leftarrow Q_4(z,y,c)$	$P_2(y,a) \wedge P_3(a) \wedge O_2(y,c)$
(R_5)	$Q_4(c,a,c) \leftarrow$	$\top$

Fig. 3. A set of rules with po

Continuing with the loan example, compensating actions could range from decreasing the trustworthiness of the user, replacing unfulfilled obligations with (perhaps more costly) alternatives, and/or taking punitive actions such as informing relevant authorities of the default or terminating the policy in-force. In order to replace obligations with more stringent ones, the user needs to be informed of changes in contractual obligations. Similarly, for obligations fulfilled as promised, it may be appropriate that a (positive) compensating action such as acknowledging payment of monthly payment, and perhaps rewarding the user's good deeds by upgrading her trustworthiness. Before explaining how we can associate these actions with obligations, we introduce minor extensions to the syntax of obligation expressions.

As syntactic sugar, we allow [`for` $x = 1$ `to` n $O(x)$] to be an obligation when $O(x)$ is an obligation definition with a free integer variable x and n is an integer. In addition, we specify [`If` p `then` O] to be a conditional obligation provided that p is a predicate formed by Boolean combinations of predicates, and O is an obligation. The semantics of [`If` p `then` O] is given by the evaluation of the condition p: if it evaluates to true, then obligation O must be fulfilled, otherwise not. The truth of p is evaluated using classical truth tables.

In order to specify the actions associated with fulfillment and defaulting we attach to an obligation expression a *fulfillment action specification* and a *defaulting action specification*, respectively. The reason for attaching the action specification to a possibly complex obligation expression rather than to each atomic obligation is easily explained by an example. Suppose a policy decision was taken upon satisfaction of a VPOS containing a set of provisions and two obligations, the first requiring a payment by January 1, 2003 and the second a payment by February 1, 2003. Defaulting, and in particular, fulfilling actions will most likely be different for the single obligations and for the global one (the conjunction of them). For example, a reward may be given to the user if all the obligations were honored, while none is given for each single one. We propose the following syntax to associate fulfillment and defaulting clauses to obligations:

OBL ::= [OBL Name
    Definition: *obligationExpression*
    FUL: *ActionList*
    DEF: $\langle$*obligationExpression*, *ActionList*$\rangle$
    ]
ActionList ::= [Action List: $\{A_1, \ldots, A_n\}$]

In order to specify consequences of accepting an obligation and consequently monitoring its fulfillment by the system, we introduce the notion of *action*. Actions are activities performed by the system in order to manage policy rules and to monitor obligations. Common actions are those involving sending information to users or to other system components.

We represent actions by special predicates having any number of parameters. Sending actions are specified by the predicate `send` with at least three, but possibly more parameters. The first parameter is the action name, the second parameter is the recipient's identity and the third is the time at which the action is to be executed. Obligations and action terms may contain both variables and constants (of the appropriate type) as parameters. An example of sending action is `send(loanCancelNotice, system, Jim Lee, 2003-Jan-14:07:30, loan451)`, specifying that the system should send a message `loanCancelNotice` at `7:30` on `2003-Jan-14` to the customer `Jim Lee` to inform that his loan identified by `loan451` was cancelled. The `receive` predicate becomes true as the effect of action `send`. Hence, in the example, the action `send(loanCancelNotice, system, Jim Lee, 2003-Jan-14:07:30, loan451)` will make true the predicate `receive(loanCancelNotice, system, Jim Lee, 2003-Jan-14:07:30, loan451)`. This semantic interpretation implies that actions take effect immediately - i.e., action propagation takes no time. We refer the reader to [BJWW02b, BJWW02a] for detailed examples.

5 Conclusion

In recent years, researchers and developers have devoted a great deal of energy on topics such as firewalls, incorporation of encryption on communication protocols, and intrusion detection systems. However, there is a growing realization that while these are critical to building secure systems, they do not provide all the answers and, consequently, the focus is shifting toward host and application security. We need to accelerate our research and work with vendors to develop the practical uses of our solutions.

References

[ABW88] K.R. Apt, H. Blair, and A. Walker. Towards a theory of declarative knowledge. In J. Minker, editor, *Foundations of Deductive Databases and Logic Programming*. Morgan Kaufmann, San Mateo, 1988.

[AS00] G.-J. Ahn and R. Sandhu. Role-based authorization constraints specification. *ACM Transactions on Information and Systems Security*, 3(4):207–226, November 2000.

[BJWW02a] C. Bettini, S. Jajodia, X. S. Wang, and D. Wijesekera. Obligation monitoring in policy management. In *Proc. 3rd International Workshop on Policies for Distributed Systems and Networks (POLICY 2002)*, pages 2–12, June 2002.

[BJWW02b] C. Bettini, S. Jajodia, X. S. Wang, and D. Wijesekera. Provisions and obligations in policy rule management and security applications. In *Proc. 28th International Conference on Very Large Data Bases*, pages 502–513, August 2002.

[Bru92] H. Bruggemann. Rights in an object-oriented environment. In C. Landwehr and S. Jajodia, editors, *Database Security V: Status and Prospects*, pages 99–115. North-Holland, Amsterdam, 1992.

[CFS94] S. Castano, M. Fugini, and P. Samarati. *Database Security.* Addison-Wesley, Wokingham, 1994.

[DM89] J. Dobson and J McDermid. A framework for expressing models of security policy. In *Proceedings of IEEE Symposium on Security and Privacy*, pages 229–239, May 1989.

[JKS01] S. Jajodia, M. Kudo, and V. S. Subrahmanian. Provisional authorizations. In Anup Ghosh, editor, *E-Commerce Security and Privacy*, pages 133–159. Kluwer Academic Press, Boston, 2001.

[JSS97] S. Jajodia, P. Samarati, and V.S. Subrahmanian. A logical language for expressing authorizations. In *Proceedings of IEEE Symposium on Security and Privacy*, pages 31–42, Oakland, CA, May 1997.

[JSSS01] S. Jajodia, P. Samarati, M. L. Sapino, and V. S. Subrahmanian. Flexible support for multiple access control policies. *ACM Transactions on Database Systems*, 26(2):214–260, December 2001.

[KH00] M. Kudo and S. Hada. Xml document security based on provisional authorizations. In *Proceedings of the 7th ACM Conference on Computer and Communications Security*, pages 87–96, November 2000.

[WJ03] D. Wijesekera and S. Jajodia. Obtaining constraint-compliant authorization lists within the flexible authorization framework. Submitted for publication, February 2003.

[WJPPH03] D. Wijesekera, S. Jajodia, F. Parisi-Presicce, and A. Hagstrom. Removing permissions in the flexible authorization framework. *ACM Transactions on Database Systems*, 2003.

Efficient Algorithms for Intrusion Detection

Niranjan K. Boora[1], Chiranjib Bhattacharyya[2], and K. Gopinath[2]

[1] Dept. of Electrical Engineering,
[2] Dept. of Computer Science & Automation,
Indian Institute of Science, Bangalore, India

Abstract. Detecting *user to root* attacks is an important intrusion detection task. This paper uses a mix of spectrum kernels and probabilistic suffix trees as a possible solution for detecting such intrusions efficiently. Experimental results on two real world datasets show that the proposed approach outperforms the state of the art Fisher kernel based methods in terms of speed with no loss of accuracy.

1 Introduction

Intrusion[1] can be defined as an attempt to either (i) access unauthorized information, or (ii) manipulate information, or (iii) render a system unreliable or unusable. Such intrusions can be further categorized into Denial of Service, User to Root Attacks, Remote to User Attacks, and Probing[2]. In this paper, we address the problem of detecting User to Root attacks. This attack happens when an unauthorized user gets root privileges. To detect such attacks, it maybe useful to study system audit data. System audit data can be, for example, an ordered sequence of system calls, also known as system call traces, made by a privileged program accessible only by the root. The underlying assumption in studying audit data to detect user to root attacks is that privileged programs would behave differently when the system is compromised. The intrusion detection problem can be posed as that of deciding whether a given system call trace is due to normal mode of operation or that of a compromised system.

Given historical data, one can use various pattern recognition techniques to design classifiers to solve such problems. In the context of this paper, such classifiers will be called Intrusion detection systems (IDS) ([3, 4]). Designing such IDS for system audit data can be posed as the problem of classifying sequences, which has a rich literature. Most methods for sequence classification are based on fitting probabilistic models, like Markov Chains, Hidden Markov models (HMMs) etc, to model the class-conditional densities, and then the likelihood is used to compute the class label of a given system trace. However such methods do not yield good discriminators for intrusion detection datasets. Recently [5] (see references therein for other approaches) proposed to use support vector machines(SVMs) along with HMMs to classify system call traces. This proposal uses a scheme suggested by [6] for classifying protein sequences. This method is accurate but extremely slow in deciding the class of a given system trace.

R.K. Ghosh and H. Mohanty (Eds.): ICDCIT 2004, LNCS 3347, pp. 346–352, 2004.

The main contribution of the paper is to examine two methods, namely Spectrum Kernels with SVMs [7] and Probabilistic Suffix Trees (PSTs)[8] proposed in the context of computational biology. These schemes do not attempt to model the class conditional densities very accurately yet they have good discriminative power; they are also fast. Our experiments on two real world datasets show that a hybrid of these two approaches is faster and more accurate.

The paper is organized as follows. In the next section, we discuss Fisher kernels. In Section 3, we discuss Spectrum kernels. In Section 4, PSTs and the hybrid method is outlined. In Section 5, we discuss experimental results.

2 Fisher Kernels

2.1 Hidden Markov Models

Hidden Markov Model (HMM) ([9, 10, 11]) is a generative model to handle variable length strings, i.e., the traces of system calls. HMM is characterized by the transition, emission, and initial probabilities. Let $\mathcal{V} = \{v_1, v_2, \ldots, v_M\}$ be the set of distinct system calls and $S = \{s_1, s_2, \ldots, s_N\}$ be the set of states. The Hidden Markov Model is represented as $\lambda = \{A, B, \pi\}$, where $A = \{a_{ij}\}$, $B = \{b_j(k)\}$, and $\pi = \{\pi_i\}$. Let a trace be represented as $O = \{O_1, \ldots, O_T\}$.

$$P(X(t+1) = s_j | X(t) = s_i) = a_{ij}$$
$$P(O(t) = v_k | X(t) = s_j) = b_j(k)$$
$$P(X(1) = s_i) = \pi_i$$

where $X(t) = s_i$ represents that the model is in state s_i at time t and $O(t) = v_l$ represents, at time t the system call observed is v_l. HMM is a powerful probabilistic model and is well suited to fit the variable length system call traces. Using Baum-Welch algorithm, one can efficiently learn HMMs from a given set of sequences.

2.2 Support Vector Machines

The data for 2 class classification problem is often specified by a dataset $D = \{(x_i, y_i) | x_i \in R^n, y_i \in \{1, -1\}\ i = \{1, 2, \ldots, l\}\}$ which consist of observation vectors x_i, and their class labels y_i. Given D, the learning problem is to find a decision function which will predict y given a novel observation x.

Support Vector Machines (SVMs) ([12]) solves the learning problem by posing it as the following convex quadratic optimization problem:

$$\begin{array}{ll} \max_{\mu_i} & \sum_{i=1}^{l} \mu_i - \frac{1}{2} \sum_{i,j=1}^{l} \mu_i \mu_j y_i y_j K(x_i, x_j) \\ \text{subject to} & 0 \leq \mu_i \leq C, \forall i \\ & \sum_{i=1}^{l} \mu_i y_i = 0 \end{array} \tag{1}$$

The function $K : R^n \times R^n \to R$ is called the kernel function and should be positive definite[12]. Let $\{\mu_i^*\}$ be the optimal values for the problem (1). The decision function is constructed from $\{\mu_i^*\}$ as follows $f(x) = sign(\sum_{x_i \in S} \mu_i^* y_i K(x_i, x) +$

b^*) where $S = \{x_i : 0 < \mu_i^* < C\}$ is the set of support vectors. This powerful classification tool is applicable only to real valued data. However this methodology can still be used if a kernel function can be defined over any two pair of sequences. Recently some progress in this direction has been made in the area of computational biology [13, 7, 14] which can be applied for designing IDS.

2.3 Fisher Score

The Fisher score is a vector of parameter derivatives of log-likelihood of a probabilistic model. The *Fisher score* is given by

$$U_X = \nabla_\Theta \log P(X|\lambda) \tag{2}$$

If we consider the probabilistic model to be HMM (λ), the parameters or sufficient statistics Θ becomes the set of transition and emission probabilities and each component of U_O is a derivative of the log-likelihood probability of the sequence O, given the parameters of the HMM. The vector U can be used to represent each sequence O by a vector. Using this vectorial representation, various kernels can be defined, e.g. $K(O^i, O^j) = U(O^i)^T U(O^j)$.

The components of this vector associated with the emission probabilities can be computed as [13] $U_{kj} = \frac{E_j(k)}{b_j(k)} - \sum_{m=1}^{M} E_j(m)$, where $E_j(k)$ is the number of times symbol k is observed in state j. Likewise, for transition probabilities, the components are calculated as $V_{ij} = \frac{T_{ij}}{a_{ij}} - \sum_{k=1}^{N} T_{ik}$ where T_{ij} is the number of times transition to state j is taken from state i.

3 Spectrum Kernel

Spectrum kernel is a kernel function [7] defined on the input space $\mathcal{O}$ of all finite length sequences of characters from an alphabet $\mathcal{A}$ of size $|\mathcal{A}|$. Given a number $k \geq 1$, the k-spectrum of a sequence is the set of all k-length (contiguous) subsequences that it contains. The k-spectrum kernel is given as $K_k(O^i, O^j) = \Phi_k(O^i)^T \Phi_k(O^j)$ The feature map is defined from $\mathcal{O}$ to $R^{|\mathcal{A}|^k}$ as $\Phi_k(O^i) = (\Phi_a(O^i))_{a \in A^k}$ where $\Phi_a(O^i)$=number of times a occurs in O^i and $\mathcal{A}^k$ is the set of all possible sequences of length k of an alphabet of size $|\mathcal{A}|$. In this paper, the normalized kernel K_k is used

$$K_k^{Norm}(O^i, O^j) = \frac{K_k(O^i, O^j)}{\sqrt{K_k(O^i, O^i)}\sqrt{K_k(O^j, O^j)}}. \tag{3}$$

For computing the kernel values, one needs to build a suffix tree for the collection of k-length subsequences of O^i and O^j, obtained by moving a k-length sliding window across each of O^i and O^j. At each depth-k leaf node of the suffix tree, store two counts, one representing the number of times k-length subsequence of O^i end at the leaf and the other count represents k-length subsequence of O^j end at the same leaf. Once the suffix tree is constructed, the kernel values are obtained by traversing the suffix tree and computing the sum of the products of the counts stored at the depth-k leaf nodes.

4 Probabilistic Suffix Trees

A PST is an n-ary tree whose root node gives the probability of each symbol of the alphabet while the nodes at subsequent levels give next-symbol probabilities conditioned on a combination of one or more symbols having been seen earlier. The probabilities are estimated by relative frequency-counts of symbol occurrences in the training sequences. The tree depth is kept to a minimum by excluding nodes that do not provide stochastic information not already given by existing nodes. Each edge in the tree is represented by a symbol of the alphabet. No two edges emanate from any node having the same symbol, which bounds the degree by the alphabet size. Each node is assigned a string which can be generated by traversing up the tree from that node to the root. Thus PSTs are characterized by the parameter L, the maximal length of a possible string in the PST; in other words, the memory length of the PST. For a more detailed review on PSTs see [14].

4.1 SVM with Spectrum Kernel and PST

We propose a hybrid method which is faster than both Spectrum kernel and PSTs. As a first step, we train SVM with Spectrum Kernel to obtain the support vectors. To test a new trace O (to check whether it is normal or abnormal), n kernel values are to be computed, if there are n support vectors. The computation of each kernel value, $K(O, O^i)$, where O^i is the ith support vector, proceeds by first constructing a suffix tree, then traversing the tree to evaluate the kernel value. The time required in building the suffix tree dominates the prediction time for each sequence. It would be thus interesting to explore the idea of building 2 PSTs rather than n suffix trees and use these 2 PSTs to make predictions. The underlying intuition is that the support vectors have enough discriminatory information which could be efficiently represented by suffix trees. Two PSTs are trained on the support vectors. A normal PST model is trained using support vectors that are from normal class and an abnormal PST model is trained using support vectors that are from the other class. The classification of test traces is carried out by calculating the log-likelihood with respect to the two models and deciding accordingly.

5 Experimental Results

A good IDS should be able to classify all intrusions correctly. This is characterized by Hit Rate (HR) defined as probability of IDS correctly classifying a trace that belongs to the abnormal class. It can be measured on a test set by c_a/l_a where l_a is the number of abnormal traces in the test set and c_a is the number of such traces correctly classified. Having a high HR means having a low false negative error. Another requirement of a IDS is it should have a low False Alarm (FA) rate, defined as the probability of misclassifying a normal trace. It is measured on a test data by m_n/l_n where l_n is the total number of normal traces

Table 1. *SVM with Spectrum kernel and PST* results as spectrum kernel length SKL is varied from 5 to 30 in steps of 5

	MIT	UNM
HR 1	SKL={10,15,20,25}	All values of $SKLs$
FA 0	All values of $SKLs$	All values of $SKLs$
t	0.5 -1 milliseconds	0.3 - 1 milliseconds

Table 2. Anomaly detection using HMM + Fisher score + SVM. The testing times are reported for all values of hidden states (HS) from 5 to 30 in steps of 5. The row corresponding to FA, under MIT or UNM column with the pattern x: y means FA achieved for *HS* equal to x. *HS* varies from 5 to 35 in steps of 5

	MIT	UNM
HR 1	{5,10,15,20,25,35}	{10,15,20,25,30,35}
HR 0.998004	30	5
FA 0	{10,20,25,30}	-
FA	5: 0.003698, 15: 0.009615 35: 0.002219	{5,10,15,20,30}: 0.000465 {25,30}: 0.002327
t	8 -140 milliseconds	9 -135 milliseconds to

Table 3. PST results as L varied from 5 to 30 in steps of 5

	MIT	UNM
HR 0.998004	{5,10,15}	All values of L
HR 1	{20,25,30}	-
FA	For all L, 0.002959	For all L, 0.002792
t	$0.5 - 2$ milliseconds	$0.3 - 3$ milliseconds

while m_n is the total number of such traces which are misclassified. A good IDS should be able to quickly decide the class of a trace. We propose to measure this by the average time t taken to classify a trace over all the traces in a test set.

For our experiments, we have chosen two system call datasets, namely the MIT Live lpr and the UNM Live lpr that are publicly available [15]. In the experiments, 0.5 fraction of dataset (0.5 fraction of normal traces and 0.5 fraction of abnormal traces) was randomly selected for training and the remaining fraction was used as a test set.

The experimental results for SVM with spectrum kernel and PST in terms of the three parameters HR, FA, t are presented in Table 1. For comparison, experimental results are also given for HMM + Fisher score + SVM in Table 2 and PSTs in Table 3. The parameter C (see equation 1) in SVMlight software is set to 100 throughout this work. All the experiments have been done on a computer system powered by a Intel 2.4GHz processor with 1GB RAM. The code for Spectrum kernel and PST have been written in C language. SVMlight software [16] has been used for support vector machines and GHMM software [17] for HMM modeling.

The parameter L associated with PST was varied from 5 to 30 in steps of 5. The best choice was $L = 10$ and $SKL = 10$. In this case, $HR = 1, FA = 0$. As the tables show, one can obtain the same accuracy for other methods, but the hybrid of Spectrum kernel and PST has far smaller value of t. This demonstrates that the proposed method is quicker than the other state of the art methods.

6 Conclusions

A hybrid of spectrum kernel and probabilistic suffix trees outperforms state of the art Fisher kernel methods. The accuracy of the proposed classifier is same as that of the Fisher kernel. The utility of probabilistic suffix trees and spectrum kernels as possible solutions to intrusion detection tasks is also demonstrated.

References

1. J. P. Anderson, "Computer security threat monitoring and surveillance," tech. rep., James P Anderson Co., Fort Washington, Pennsylvania, April 1980.
2. K. Kendall, "A database of computer attacks for the evalutation of intrusion detection," Master's thesis, MIT, June 1999.
3. S. Axelsson, "Intrusion detection systems: A survey and taxonomy," tech. rep., Department of Computer Engineering, Chalmers University of Technology, 2000.
4. A. Sundaram, "An introduction to intrusion detection," *ACM Crossroads Student Magazine*, 1996.
5. J. Baras and M. Rabi, "Intrusion detection with support vector machines and generative models," tech. rep., Institute for Systems Research, University of Maryland, 2002.
6. T. Jaakkola and D. Haussler, "Using the Fisher kernel methods to detect remote protein homologies," in *Proceedings of the Seventh International Conference on Intelligent Systems for Molecular Biology*, pp. 149–58, 1999.
7. C. Leslie, E. Eskin, and W. Stafford, "The spectrum kernel: A string kernel for SVM protein classification," in *Proceedings of the Pacific Symposium on Biocomputing*, pp. 564–575, Jan 2002.
8. D. Ron, Y. Singer, and N. Tishby, "The power of amnesia: learning probabilistic automata with variable memory length," *Machine Learning*, vol. 25(2-3), pp. 117–149, 1996.
9. L. R. Rabiner, "A tutorial on hidden Markov models and selected applications in speech recognition," *Proceedings of the IEEE*, vol. 77, no. 2, pp. 257–286, 1989.
10. L. R. Rabiner and B. H. Juang, "An introduction to hidden Markov models," *IEEE ASSP Magazine*, pp. 4–15, January 1986.
11. R. Duggad and U. B. Desai, "A tutorial on hidden Markov models," tech. rep., Electrical Department, Indian Institute of Technology, Bombay, 1996.
12. C. J. C. Burges, "A tutorial on support vector machine for pattern recognition," in *Data Mining and Knowledge Discovery*, vol. 2, pp. 121–167, 1998.
13. P. Pavlidis, T. S. Furey, M. Liberto, D. Haussler, and W. N. Grundy, "Promoter region-based classification of genes," in *Proceedings of the Pacific Symposium on Biocomputing*, pp. 151–163, January 2001.

14. G. Bejerano and G. Yona, "Variations on probabilistic suffix trees: statistical modeling and prediction of protein families," *Bioinformatics*, vol. 17, no. 1, pp. 23–43, 2001.
15. UNM, Department of Computer Science, "Computer immune systems homepage," http://www.cs.unm.edu/immsec/systemcalls.htm.
16. T. Joachims, "Making large-scale SVM learning practical," *Advances in Kernel Methods - Support Vector Learning, B. Sch+lkopf and C. Burges and A. Smola (ed.)*, 1999.
17. M. P. I. f. M. G. Algorithmics group, "General hidden Markov model library (ghmm)," http://sourceforge.net/projects/ghmm/.

Proxi-Annotated Control Flow Graphs: Deterministic Context-Sensitive Monitoring for Intrusion Detection

Samik Basu[1] and Prem Uppuluri[2]

[1] Dept. of Computer Science,
Iowa State University Ames IA 50011-1040
sbasu@cs.iastate.edu

[2] Dept. of Computer Science and Electrical Engineering,
University of Missouri Kansas City MO 64110
uppulurip@umkc.edu

Abstract. Model or specification based intrusion detection systems have been effective in detecting known and unknown host based attacks with few false alarms [12, 15]. In this approach, a model of program behavior is developed either manually, by using a high level specification language, or automatically, by static or dynamic analysis of the program. The actual program execution is then monitored using the modeled behavior; deviations from the modeled behavior are flagged as attacks. In this paper we discuss a novel model generated using static analysis of executables (binary code). Our key contribution is a model which is precise and runtime efficient. Specifically, we extend the efficient control flow graph (CFG) based program behavioral model, with context sensitive information, thus, providing the precision afforded by the more expensive push down systems (PDS). Executables are instrumented with operations on auxiliary variables, referred to as *proxi* variables. These annotated variables allow the resulting context sensitive control flow graphs obtained by statically analyzing the executables to be deterministic at runtime. We prove that the resultant model, called *proxi-annotated controlflow graph*, is as precise as previous approaches which use context sensitive push-down models and in-fact, enhances the runtime efficiency of such models. We show the flexibility of our technique to handle different variations of recursion in a program efficiently. This results in better treatment of monitoring programs where the recursion depth is not pre-determined.

1 Introduction

Intrusion detection systems (IDS) have shown promise in detecting a large number of host based attacks [4, 12, 15]. They can be categorized into (a) misuse based systems [4, 13], which detect previously known attacks by monitoring the system behavior, (b) anomaly based systems [9, 2, 11] in which machine learning or expert systems learn a system's behavior and attacks are detected as deviations of actual program behavior from learnt behavior, and, (c) specification/model based systems [7, 12] in which the *intended* program behavior is modeled and attacks are detected as deviations from this behavior. Out of these approaches, misuse based approaches cannot detect unknown

R.K. Ghosh and H. Mohanty (Eds.): ICDCIT 2004, LNCS 3347, pp. 353–362, 2004.

attacks as they depend on a rule base of known attacks. On the other hand, while, anomaly based approaches can detect unknown attacks, they may result in large number of false alarms, since legitimate but previously not-learnt behavior can be flagged as an attack. Specification based approaches seek to combine the advantages of both by modeling program behavior. However, traditional specification based approaches [14, 12], in which a domain expert specifies legitimate program behavior using a high level specification language, are not scalable: manual specifications are tedious to write for large programs [8]. Moreover, just as any manually written software can have semantic errors, so can specifications. To counter the problems due to manually written specifications, recent research efforts [16, 8] have focused on automatically developing program behavioral models (PBMs) through static analysis of programs.

From a practical perspective, since the source codes of programs are not always available, such research efforts have focused on developing PBMs by analyzing the executables. These models are typically represented in terms of the system calls executed by the programs [8, 16]. The key requirements of such models are *precision* and *runtime efficiency*. The former requires that the models capture as much context information about the programs as possible in order to prevent false alarms. Moreover, without context information, models represent a superset of the corresponding programs' behavior. Consequently, attacks which exploit the gap between the modeled superset and the actual program behavior (called *impossible path* attacks) escape detection. In addition, the model should be efficient at runtime to be able to detect attacks before they can cause damage to the system. In this paper, we present such a program behavioral model.

Driving Problem. PBMs can be classified based on their precision in capturing program behavior. Control flow graphs (CFG) or finite state machines (FSM) represent the simplest form of such models. While being efficient [1], they are imprecise: CFG/FSM's accept strings in regular languages while programs with procedure calls/returns fall in the class of context-free languages. Hence, they allow the impossible path attacks [16].

To increase precision, push-down system (PDS) have been considered. In such a model, the *context information* of each call, i.e., the return location is recorded explicitly in a pre-defined stack. However here, the precision comes at the cost of poor runtime efficiency [16, 8]. Inefficiency is due to the presence of conditional control paths in the programs; it is not possible to judge statically which of the many paths a program will take and as such the conditional controls in a program are treated as non-deterministic branch points in the program.

To get both precision and efficiency, [8] proposed the Dyke model which removes non-determinism in PDSs. Specifically, [8] instruments the executables by flanking each call site with two distinct *null system calls*. Program behavior is then modeled as a CFG in terms of the system/procedure calls made by the program – the CFGs now include the null system calls. At runtime, execution of a null call precisely identifies the call site, thus determinizing the monitoring mechanism. Intuitively, a Dyke model can be viewed as a PDS with additional calls at each call site.

While the Dyke model is precise, in the worst case if the program path is of size h (size measured in terms of number of system calls made), it requires execution of an additional $2 * h$ number of system calls. Since, interception of system calls in the kernel (the best case) causes about 20% [7] overhead over the actual execution time of the system call, increasing their number in a program will increase this overhead. Moreover, being a variation of the PDS model, Dyke model requires pre-defining the size of a stack to record null call information. In the event of recursion, the stack may overflow resulting in the loss of context information leading to imprecise monitoring.

Our Solution. In this paper, we present a novel model for capturing program behavior in terms of system and procedure calls. The central theme of our approach is to add precision to simplicity. Specifically, we use CFGs to represent programs. To add context to CFGs as well as determinism (and hence efficiency), we instrument the executables with updates to a set of variables called *proxi* variables. We call such a model, *proxi-annotated control flow graph* (PCFG). We prove that a PCFG is as precise as a PDS model and is equivalent to a Dyke model. We claim that, PCFGs make more efficient use of stacks (runtime memory usage) than PDS/Dyke models by using an array of proxi variables. In particular, except for certain types of recursion, these arrays degenerate to simple variables.

Organization. In Section 2, we present a detailed study of existing modeling mechanisms: CFG (Section 2.1), PDS (Section 2.2) and Dyke (Section 2.3). PCFG model is introduced in Section 3 followed by its comparative study with Dyke model (Section 4), with specific emphasis on stack usage by the two models.

2 Background and Related Work

2.1 Control-Flow Graphs

A control flow graph captures the behavior of a procedure. In the context of host-based intrusion detection systems, a control flow graph is typically represented by a set of states, and transition relations between pairs of states labeled by system calls and procedure calls [16]. It has a start state corresponding to the the entry point of the procedure. It can have multiple exit states due to the presence of multiple return statements in the procedure.

Definition 1. *A control flow graph (CFG) for a procedure p is a tuple $CFG_p = (S, s_0, S_E, \longrightarrow, \mathcal{L})$ where S is the set of states, $s_0 \in S$ is the start state of p, $S_E \subseteq S$ is the set of its exit states, $\longrightarrow$ is the set of labeled transitions $\subseteq S \times \mathcal{L} \cup \{\epsilon\} \times S$ and $\mathcal{L}$ ranges over set of system calls and procedure invocations.* □

Figure 1(a) shows CFGs for a program with a *main*, *line* and *end* procedures. The procedure *line* can be invoked from two different call sites, one each in *main* and *end*. Note that the CFGs for individual procedures do not represent the inter-procedural control flow of the program; the reason being transitions from caller to the callee and vice versa are not explicitly present in the CFGs. A naive approach to overcome this problem is to in-line all the called procedures; a call transition is replaced by the CFG of the corresponding called procedure. Typically, such in-lining mechanism results in large global CFG leading to significant increase in space usage. Further, in-lined CFG fails to represent behaviors of recursive programs.

Another technique, which is employed often, is to connect the local CFGs by introducing new transitions (a) from the caller state (with outgoing call transition) to the start

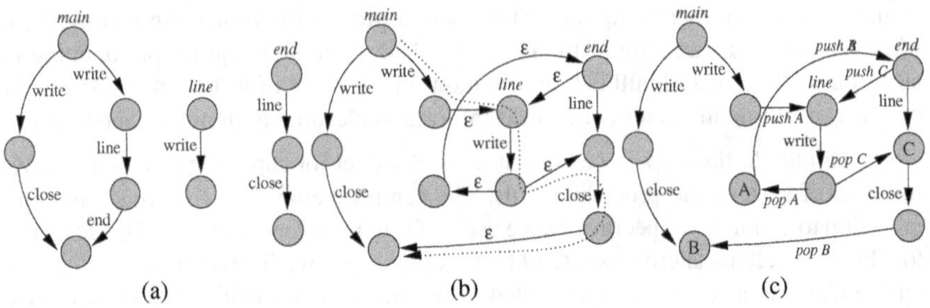

Fig. 1. (a) Local CFG, (b) global CFG with inter procedural transitions and (c) *push* and *pop* operations for PDS model [10]

state of the called procedure and (b) from the exit states of a procedure to all the states which has a incoming transition labeled by call to the procedure under consideration. This technique overcomes the problem of in-lining; size of the global CFG is on the order of the sum of sizes of local CFGs. Figure 1(b) presents global CFG constructed by introducing inter-procedural ϵ-transitions and discarding call-transitions from the call site to the return locations in the local CFGs in Figure 1(a).

Context Insensitivity in CFG. In a global CFG model, impossible paths can occur since it does not keep track of the location to which a program control should return once a procedure exits, i.e., *context* information of a call is lost. Such context insensitivity incorrectly classifies paths with unmatched calls and returns as valid execution sequence in the program. An example of such an impossible path in the global CFG is illustrated using *dotted* lines in Figure 1(b). Call from *main* to *line* is followed eventually by a return from *line* to *end* without any intermediate returns to *main* and calls to *end*. CFG model fails to classify the transition from exit state of *line* to return location at *end* as incorrect and hence erroneous program behavior goes un-noticed. Observe that, an impossible path results from one/more *bad* edges from the callees exit state to the return location of one of its potential callers.

A malicious user, manipulating the executing program, can use impossible paths in the model as an exploit which cannot be detected by the model [10].

2.2 Context Sensitive Model: Push-Down Systems

Push-down systems [3, 5, 6] (PDS) are deployed to detect impossible paths in a program model. A PDS captures, in addition to the intra-procedural control structure, the correct call-return pattern (context) of the program under normal circumstances. This is achieved by explicitly keeping track of the execution stack of the program whose behavior is being modeled by the PDS. Unlike CFG transition, which is between a pair of states, a PDS transition represents the change in the execution stack of the program. Specifically, given a top-of-stack, a PDS transition relation shows the possible ways the stack changes once the statement at the current top-of-stack is executed.

Definition 2. *A push-down system for a procedure p is a tuple $PDS_p = (S, s_0, S_E, \hookrightarrow, \mathcal{L})$ where S is the set of states in p (also referred to as stack symbol set), $s_0 \in S$ is the start state, $S_E \subseteq S$ is the set of exit states, $\hookrightarrow$ is the labeled push-down transition relation $\subseteq S \times \mathcal{L} \cup \{\epsilon\} \times S^*$ and $\mathcal{L}$ is the set of system calls and procedure calls.* □

A PDS transition can be classified as follows (s is the current top-of-stack):

- $s \overset{\epsilon}{\hookrightarrow} \{\}$: $s \in S_E$ is the exit state of a procedure (*pop-transition*).
- $s \overset{\texttt{callp}}{\hookrightarrow} \{t, r\}$: $s \in S \wedge \overline{S_E}$ is call site of a procedure p. The top-of-stack, s, is replaced by start state t of p and the return location r in the caller (*push-transition*).
- $s \overset{a}{\hookrightarrow} \{t\}$: $s \in S \wedge \overline{S_E}$ is the top-of-stackand t is the new top-of-stack.

[10] proposed a technique for run-time monitoring using PDS. Whenever the monitored program makes a jump from one procedure to another via a call, the return location in the caller is pushed in a stack (we will refer to this as *monitor-stack*). On the other hand, if the monitored program exits a procedure and goes to a state in another procedure, the execution is deemed correct only when the destination state is present in the top of the monitor-stack. In the event the transition is allowed, the top of monitor-stack is popped out. Going back to the example in Figure 1(c), every inter-procedural transition is labeled by the operation on the monitor stack (`push(A)`, `pop(A)` etc).

Non-determinism in PDS Monitoring. PDS representation of static models suffers from the major drawback of space and time complexity, specifically, owing to the presence of non-determinism. It can be shown [16] that for a given input string of system calls, both the time and space complexity for monitoring via PDS representation technique is cubic to its size. As an illustration, see the example program in Figure 2(a) (do not consider the statements at Lines 4a, 5a, 8a and 9a). The system/function calls that are monitored are shown in bold fonts. The corresponding PDS representation is presented in Figure 2(b-I). Observe that as the valuation of conditional expression at Line 4 is not evaluated in static models, the PDS representation includes a non-deterministic inter-procedural transition: *pushA/pushB* due to the presence of function invocations at Lines 5 and 9.

2.3 Dyke Model and Stack-Determinism

Recently, [8] proposed Dyke model representation based on code instrumentation to counter the problem of non-deterministic stack operations in monitoring. The central theme of this technique is to instrument the code with *null* system calls at appropriate call sites in order to determinize the stack operations in the PDS. These null calls are executed at runtime. Whenever a call is made in the program, the appropriate null call determinizes the call transitions in the model. The resultant model is equivalent to Stack-Deterministic PDS (sDPDS). The distinguishing feature of sDPDS is that, unlike PDS, there exists exactly one transition in the model corresponding to a call to a procedure in the monitored sequence. The instrumentation of code, proposed by [8], to achieve this is shown in Figure 2(a) at Lines 4a, 5a, 8a and 9a. Each call is flanked by distinct "pre" and "post" calls to identify which branch of the conditional block is being executed by the monitored program. In this model, a Dyke stack is maintained which records the

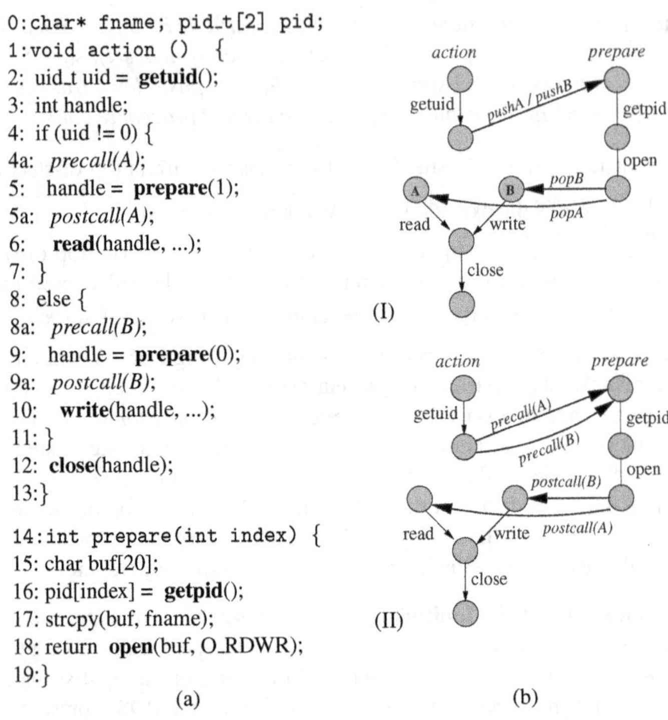
0:char* fname; pid_t[2] pid;
1:void action () {
2: uid_t uid = getuid();
3: int handle;
4: if (uid != 0) {
4a: precall(A);
5: handle = prepare(1);
5a: postcall(A);
6: read(handle, ...);
7: }
8: else {
8a: precall(B);
9: handle = prepare(0);
9a: postcall(B);
10: write(handle, ...);
11: }
12: close(handle);
13:}
14:int prepare(int index) {
15: char buf[20];
16: pid[index] = getpid();
17: strcpy(buf, fname);
18: return open(buf, O_RDWR);
19:}
(a)
action
prepare
getuid
pushA / pushB
getpid
open
A
B
popB
popA
read
write
close
(I)
action
prepare
getuid
precall(A)
precall(B)
getpid
open
postcall(B)
postcall(A)
read
write
close
(II)
(b)

Fig. 2. (a) Source-code (b-I) Non-deterministic PDS (b-II) Dyke Model [8]

pre-calls that are invoked with the last pre-call being at the top-of-stack. Valid or feasible inter-procedural paths are the ones that have matching pre and post null calls. The Dyke model is shown in Figure 2(b-II).

Disadvantages of Dyke Model. There are two key issues when using the Dyke model for monitoring: (a) overhead in monitoring and (b) Dyke stack size. The usage of two extra (null) calls (pre-/post-calls) per procedure-call site adds to monitoring overhead. Since, system call interception incurs ~20% overhead [7], doubling the number of intercepted system calls can raise overhead by two-fold. Secondly, note that, the defining factor for runtime memory usage is the size of the stack used by the Dyke model. The stack usage depends on the type of procedure calls: standard vs. recursive. In standard, the maximum depth of the stack can be determined statically and the Dyke stack size is set to that value. However, for recursion, the depth depends on the program's runtime behavior. If the recursion depth is such that it overflows the Dyke stack, then the model fails to correctly identify the inter-procedural feasible paths and as such the monitoring mechanism becomes vulnerable to impossible path attacks.

3 Proxi-Annotated Control Flow Graphs

In this section, we propose a new technique based on CFG representation which determinizes stack operations without incurring overheads due to null calls. In addition, our approach performs better in terms of memory usage when handling recursion compared to the Dyke model. The central tenet of our technique is that by appropriately updating and checking valuations of auxiliary integer variables introduced at each call site we can detect impossible paths and resolve stack non-determinism efficiently. The auxiliary variables are referred to as *PROcedure conteXt Indicator* (Proxi) and the corresponding CFG as *proxi-annotated CFG*.

Definition 3 (Proxi-Annotated CFG). *A proxi-annotated CFG of a procedure p is a tuple* $PCFG_p = (S, s_0, S_E, \longrightarrow, \mathcal{L}, \mathcal{V})$, *where* $CFG_p = (S, s_0, S_E, \longrightarrow, \mathcal{L})$ *and* $\mathcal{V}$ *is the set of proxi variable arrays where* $|\mathcal{V}|$ *= number of possible return locations of p.* □

Notations. We introduce here the notational convenience used in the rest of the paper. Array names in $\mathcal{V}$ for PCFG$_q$ are denoted by v_s^q and are associated with the called procedure q and the return location/state s of the callee. The maximum index of the array v_s^q holding a non-zero value is denoted by I_s^q. The pre-specified size of a proxi variable array is denoted by N_s^q.

Realizing PCFG Monitoring. The monitoring mechanism via PCFG proceeds by updating the proxi variables in the following fashion:

1. *Initialization.* All proxi variables are initialized to zero, i.e, $\forall v_s^q.\forall i < N_s^q.v_s^q[i] = 0$. Furthermore, each I_s^q is set to zero.
2. *Call to procedure: incrementing proxi variables.* As eluded before, elements in array v_s^q records a call to procedure q with the return location s in the caller.
   (a) If there exists a non-zero $v_r^q[I_r^q]$ less than $v_s^q[I_s^q]$ with $r \neq s$, then $I_s^q = I_s^q + 1$. $v_s^q[I_s^q]$ is incremented by one and all non-zero $v_r^q[I_r^q]$ where $r \neq s$ are also incremented by one.
   (b) Else, $v_s^q[I_s^q]$ are incremented by one and all non-zero $v_r^q[I_r^q]$ where $r \neq s$ are incremented by one.
3. *Return from a procedure: decrementing proxi variables.* If a procedure q returns, the correct return location s in the caller is determined by the array v_s^q. The conditions to be satisfied on return are that the valuation of $v_s^q[I_s^q]$ (a) is greater than zero and (b) is minimum among all non-zero $v_r^q[I_r^q]$.
   $v_s^q[I_s^q]$ is decremented by one. If $v_s^q[I_s^q]$==0 and $I_s^q \neq 0$ then decrement I_s^q by one.

All other proxi variables associated with q, i.e., $v_r^q[I_r^q]$ are decremented by one.

Observation. The updates to the proxi variables ensure that the element of the proxi variable array corresponding the last call in the execution sequence is always less than the proxi variable elements for any prior calls.

Theorem 1. *A sequence of steps, in terms of procedure calls, is feasible in a PDS model iff it is also feasible in a PCFG.*

Calls to procedure q with return locations r and s

↓ Stack operation	PDS	Proxi variable values			
	push(s)	$v_s^q[0]$=1	$v_r^q[0]$=0	I_s^q=0	I_r^q=0
	push(r)	$v_s^q[0]$=2	$v_r^q[0]$=1	I_s^q=0	I_r^q=0
	push(s)	$v_s^q[0]$=2,$v_s^q[1]$=1	$v_r^q[0]$=2	I_s^q=1	I_r^q=0
	push(s)	$v_s^q[0]$=2,$v_s^q[1]$=2	$v_r^q[0]$=3	I_s^q=1	I_r^q=0
	pop(s)	$v_s^q[0]$=2,$v_s^q[1]$=1	$v_r^q[0]$=2	I_s^q=1	I_r^q=0
	pop(s)	$v_s^q[0]$=2,$v_s^q[1]$=0	$v_r^q[0]$=1	I_s^q=0	I_r^q=0

Fig. 3. Updates to proxi variables with sample operation sequence to monitor stack

Proof: The proof proceeds by showing that proxi variables correctly record the monitor stack of a PDS model. Recall that a call to procedure q with return location s results in *push*-ing s to the top of the monitor stack of PDS model (see Section 2.2).

Assume that a procedure q can be invoked multiple times with two different return locations s and r. Let q be a new call, seen with the return location s. Following PDS monitoring mechanism, s is pushed to the top-of-stackdue to the new call to q.

Case I: s is already present in the stack and the top-of-stack is r, i.e. in the execution sequence there are at least two prior calls to q with two different return locations. This implies that $v_r^q[I_r^q]$ is less than $v_s^q[I_s^q]$. The corresponding updates to the proxi variable $v_s^q[I_s^q]$ follows the rule 2(a) (see above). In other words, I_s^q is incremented and $v_s^q[I_s^q]$ is incremented by one. Also $v_r^q[I_r^q]$ is incremented by one. As such, $v_s^q[I_s^q]$==1 and $v_s^q[I_s^q] < v_r^q[I_r^q]$. The return location for the new call to q is correctly identified as s.

Case II: s is present in the top of the stack. This implies the new call to q is a recursive call with the same return location. The updates to the proxi variables follow the rule 2(b) (see above). This ensures that number of recursions to q with same return location s is equal to the valuation of $v_s^q[I_s^q]$. □

Figure 3 shows a sample session of execution monitoring using PDS model and PCFG. The sequence of operations on monitor stack are presented along with the corresponding changes in the proxi variables in PCFG.

Theorem 2. *A PCFG is equivalent to Dyke model.*

Proof: Theorem 1 states that PCFG only allows feasible inter-procedural sequences as per the PDS model. Here we give the proof sketch showing that PCFG also resolves non-determinism in PDS model monitoring.

Recall that a Dyke model instrumentation involves inserting distinct pre-/post-calls at each call site. This ensures determinism in stack operations as each call site is distinguished by its pre-call. A Dyke stack records the pre-call and a path is deemed feasible if each return leads to post-call matching with the last pre-call at the top of Dyke stack.

In identical fashion, PCFG inserts updates to the proxi variables at each call site. In other words, a pre-call of a Dyke model is replaced by incrementing operations of proxi variables and the post-call is replaced by assertions that must be satisfied followed by decrementing the proxi variables. The variables are distinguished by the return locations

Call to q with return state s

Dyke Model	Proxi-annotated CFG
precall(s)	`if` $\exists$`r.`v^q_r`[`I^q_r`]!=0 &&` v^q_r`[`I^q_r`] <` v^q_s`[`I^q_s`] then` I^q_s`++;` v^q_s`[`I^q_s`]++;` $\forall v^q_r$`[`I^q_r`]>0 && r!=s` v^q_r`[`I^q_r`]++;`

postcall(s)	`assert(`v^q_s`[`I^q_s`]> 0);`
	$\forall$`r!=s.if` v^q_r`[`I^q_r`]!=0 then assert(`v^q_s`[`I^q_s`]` $<$ v^q_r`[`I^q_r`]);`
	$\forall$`r!=s.if` v^q_r`[`I^q_r`]` $>$ `0)` v^q_r`[`I^q_r`]--;`
	v^q_s`[`I^q_s`]--;`
	`if` v^q_s`[`I^q_s`]==0 &&` I^q_s`!=0 then` I^q_s`--;`

Fig. 4. Code Instrumentation

of the called procedure. As such, all procedure calls (i.e. stack operations in the context of Dyke model) are determinized in PCFG with respect to their return locations. □

Figure 4 presents the instrumentations for PCFG corresponding to pre- and post-calls in Dyke model. Feasible path in PCFG must satisfy all the assertions corresponding to the post-call.

4 Discussion

There are two important distinguishing aspects of our technique that can make it potentially more efficient than the existing (PDS/Dyke) stack-based techniques.

First, we replace null calls in Dyke model with updates to variables. Note that the number of arrays of proxi variables $|\mathcal{V}|$ is equal to the number of pre-calls introduced by the Dyke model. This will reduce runtime overhead caused by monitoring extra null calls at each call site. The operations on the proxi variables (see Figure 4) can be executed in time linear to the number of proxi variables by clever arrangement of proxi variables in an ascending order.

Secondly, observe that, the bound on recursion depth of the execution sequence that can be correctly monitored is equal to the pre-defined size of the Dyke stack. In PCFG, the recursion bound depends on the *kind* of recursion. Specifically we identify two kinds: *uni-valent* and *multi-valent*. Uni-valent recursion corresponds to the case where the same procedure is invoked with the same return location recursively. In this situation, the proxi variable element corresponding to the concerned procedure is simply incremented (Rule 2(b) for proxi variable incrementation) with each recursion as opposed to Dyke model where pre-calls are pushed in the stack. The bound on recursion depth, therefore, is determined by the integer domain of the proxi variable element.

Multi-valent recursion occurs when there are at least two alternating recursive calls to the same procedure with two different return locations. For example, let q be called with return location s followed by a recursive call to q with r as return location (with no intermediate returns from q). We say that the *depth of alternation*, in this example, is 1. Note that, for a subsequent new call to q with return location s (new alternation depth becomes 2) leads to incrementation of the index I_s^q. As such, the maximum depth of alternation in an execution sequence that can be monitored correctly is determined by the ranges (e.g. N_s^q, N_r^q etc.) of the proxi variable array.

In summary, unlike PDS/Dyke models, PCFG model monitors recursion in two different dimensions. The domain of individual elements in a proxi variable array determines the maximum depth of the uni-valent recursion while the range/size of the array limits the depth of alternation in multi-valent recursion. Such separation of uni- and multi-valent recursive patterns adds to the flexibility and efficiency of monitoring. For example, if it is statically determined that multi-valent recursions are not possible in an execution sequence, then the array sizes of proxi variables are set to 1.

References

1. A.V. Aho. *Handbook of Theoretical Computer Science Vol A*. Elsevier Science Publishers B.V., 1990.
2. D. Anderson, T. Lunt, H. Javitz, A. Tamaru, and A. Valdes. Next-generation intrusion detection expert system: A summary. Technical Report SRI-CSL-95-07, SRI International, 1995.
3. A. Bouajjani, J. Esparza, and O. Maler. Reachability analysis of pushdown automata: Application to model checking. In *CONCURR*, 1997.
4. S. Eckmann, G. Vigna, and R. Kemmerer. Statl. Technical report, UCSB, 2000-19.
5. J. Esparza, D. Hansel, P. Rossmanith, and S. Schwoon. Efficient algorithms for model checking pushdown systems. In *CAV*, pages 232–247. Springer-Verlag, 2000.
6. J. Esparza and S. Schwoon. A bdd-based model checker for recursive programs. In *Computer-Aided Verification (CAV)*, pages 324–336. Springer-Verlag, 2001.
7. T. Bowen et al. Building survivable systems: An integrated approach based on intrusion detection and confinement. In *Darpa Information Security Symposium*, 2000.
8. H. Feng, J. Griffin, Y. Huang, S. Jha, W. Lee, and B. Miller. Formalizing sensitivity in static analysis for intrusion detection. In *IEEE Symposium on Security and Privacey*, May 2004.
9. S. Forrest, R. Henning, J. Reed, and R. Simonian. A neural network approach towards intrussion detection. In *National Computer Security Conference*, 1990.
10. J. T. Griffin, S. Jha, and B. P. Miller. Detecting manipulated remote call streams. In *Usenix Security Symposium*, August 2002.
11. K. Ilgun. A real-time intrusion detection system for unix. In *IEEE Symposium on Security and Privacy*, 1993.
12. C. Ko. *Execution Monitoring of Security-Critical Programs in a Distributed System: A Specification-Based Approach*. PhD thesis, University of California, Davis, December 1996.
13. J. Pouzol and M. Ducasse. From declarative signature to misuse intrusion detection systems. In *RAID*, 2001.
14. R. Sekar and P. Uppuluri. Synthesizing fast intrusion prevention/detection systems from high-level specifications. In *USENIX Security Symposium*, 99.
15. P. Uppuluri and R. Sekar. Experiences with specification-based intrusion detection. In *RAID*, 01.
16. D. Wagner and D. Dean. Intrusion detection via static analysis. In *IEEE Symposium on Security and Privacy*, May 2001.

Using Schemas to Simplify Access Control for XML Documents*

Indrakshi Ray and Marianna Muller

Computer Science Department,
Colorado State University,
Fort Collins, CO 80523-1873
{iray,muller}@cs.colostate.edu

Abstract. Organizations are increasingly using the the eXtensible Markup Language (XML) for document representation and exchange on the Web. To protect an XML document from unauthorized access, authorizations are specified on the XML document itself or on the Document Type Definition (DTD) that defines the type of the XML document. Each XML document or DTD is associated with an XML Access Sheet (XAS) that specifies the authorizations. The DTD not being an XML document complicates the specification and enforcement of authorization policies. To overcome the above mentioned problem, XML Schemas need to be used instead of DTDs. In this paper, we show how XAS DTDs can be specified using XML Schemas and propose an access control architecture that can process XAS authorizations. Enforcement of access control allows users to view only those parts of the documents that they are authorized to view. These parts may not conform to the schema of the original document and hence may not be valid. Towards this end we propose a schema loosening algorithm that generates a schema that will be satisfied by documents satisfying the access control requirements.

1 Introduction

Organizations are increasingly using the world wide web to disseminate and distribute information. Most of this information is specified in XML which is emerging as the de-facto standard language for document representation and exchange over the Web. In order to be processed an XML document must be well-formed (obeys the syntax of XML) and valid (conforms to a proper Document Type Definition (DTD) that defines the particular type of XML document). The information distributed by organizations via the web have different levels of sensitivity: some of this information must be distributed internally, some must be shared with other organizations, and others must be disseminated for public use. Protecting information with different levels of sensitivity is non-trivial. To address this problem, researchers [1, 2, 3, 4, 5, 6, 7, 8, 9] have proposed models and mechanisms for controlling access to XML documents.

To protect XML documents, authorization policies may be specified on the XML document or on the associated DTD. If an authorization policy is specified on the DTD,

* This work was funded by AFOSR under Award No. FA9550-04-1-0102.

R.K. Ghosh and H. Mohanty (Eds.): ICDCIT 2004, LNCS 3347, pp. 363–368, 2004.

the policy applies to all XML documents conforming to the DTD. Such authorization policies are specified in a document known as XML Access Sheet (XAS). XAS is an XML document and must be well-formed and valid.

DTDs not being XML documents do not satisfy the well-formedness and validity requirements of XML. As pointed out by Zhang et al. [9], using DTDs to validate XML documents causes a number of problems in the specification and enforcement of authorization policies. First, the authorization policies for XML documents and DTDs cannot be specified in an uniform manner because the structure of the documents differ. Second, an XML parser is not sufficient for interpreting the authorizations on a given XML document. Third, the use of DTD limits interoperability.

In this paper, we propose the use of XML Schemas, instead of DTDs, for validating XML documents. This simplifies the specification and enforcement of authorization policies. We show how authorization templates can be specified in the form of XML Schemas. We propose an access control system that can process any authorization specified as an XAS that conforms to some XML schema. Enforcing access control on an XML document often results in a pruned document; the pruned document contains only those information that the user is authorized to see. This pruned document may not conform to the schema of the original document. We propose an algorithm by which the original schema can be transformed to a loosened schema. This loosened schema will be satisfied by all the documents generated from the original XML document that satisfy the access control requirements.

The rest of the paper is organized as follows. Section 2 shows how XML schemas can be used to specify authorization templates. Section 3 presents an access control system that can process different kinds of authorizations associated with the documents. Section 4 concludes the paper with some pointers to future directions.

2 Specifying Authorization Templates Using Schemas

Our approach allows for the specification of different kinds of authorization models. We show how authorization policies adapted from the model proposed by Damiani et al. [6] can be expressed using a schema. Each authorization is of the form *(subject, object, action, sign, type)*, where subject is the entity to whom the authorization is granted or denied, object is either a uniform resource identifier (URI) of the resource or is of the form URI:PE, where PE is a path expression on the tree of document URI, action is the operation being authorized or forbidden, sign is either '+' (denoting allow access) or '-' (denoting forbid access), type is one of {LHD, RDH, L, R, LD, RD, LS, RS} depending on the kind of authorization. Figure 1 shows an authorization template for such a model can be specified as an XML schema.

3 Access Control System

In this section we present an access control system for authorizing XML documents. This architecture is adapted from that proposed in [6]. Since we use XAS Schemas instead of DTD, our architecture is not confined to intra-organizational applications.

```
<?xml version="1.0" encoding="UTF-8"?>
<xs:schema xmlns:xs="http://www.w3.org/2001/XMLSchema">

<xs:simpleType name="stringtype">
 <xs:restriction base="xs:string"/>
</xs:simpleType>

<xs:simpleType name="signvaluetype">
 <xs:restriction base="xs:string">
  <xs:pattern value="+|-"/>
 </xs:restriction>
</xs:simpleType>

<xs:simpleType name="typevaluetype">
 <xs:restriction base="xs:string">
  <xs:enumeration value="LDH"/>
  <xs:enumeration value="RDH"/>
  <xs:enumeration value="L"/>
  <xs:enumeration value="R"/>
  <xs:enumeration value="LD"/>
  <xs:enumeration value="RD"/>
  <xs:enumeration value="LS"/>
  <xs:enumeration value="RS"/>
 </xs:restriction>
</xs:simpleType>

<xs:complexType name="actiontype">
 <cs:attribute name="value" type="stringtype" fixed="read" use="required"/>
</xs:complexType>

<xs:complexType name="signtype">
 <cs:attribute name="value" type="signvaluetype" use="required"/>
</xs:complexType>

<xs:complexType name="typetype">
 <cs:attribute name="value" type="typevaluetype" use="required"/>
</xs:complexType>

<xs:complexType name="authorizationtype">
 <xs:sequence>
  <xs:element name="subject" type="stringtype"/>
  <xs:element name="object" type="stringtype"/>
  <xs:element name="action" type="actiontype"/>
  <xs:element name="sign" type="signtype"/>
  <xs:element name="type" type="typetype"/>
 </xs:sequence>
</xs:complexType>

<xs:complexType name="set_of_authorizations_type">
 <xs:element name="authorization" type="authorizationtype" minOccurs="1"
   maxOccurs="unbounded"/>
 <xs:attribute name="about" type="stringtype" use="required"/>
</xs:complexType>

<xs:element name="set_of_authorizations" type="set_of_authorizations_type"/>

</xs:schema>
```

Fig. 1. XAS Syntax Specified as a Schema

Figure 2 shows the architecture of such a system. The following reasons motivate the need for implementing such a system on the server side. First, this prevents the client (user) from viewing or processing information that he is not allowed to see or process. Second, this obviates the need for the client browser to provide XML support for translating XML documents to HTML.

This architecture is based on the fact that an XML document is internally represented as an object-oriented document graph according to the Document Object Model (DOM) Level 1 specification. DOM provides an object-oriented Application Programming Interface (API) for HTML and XML documents.

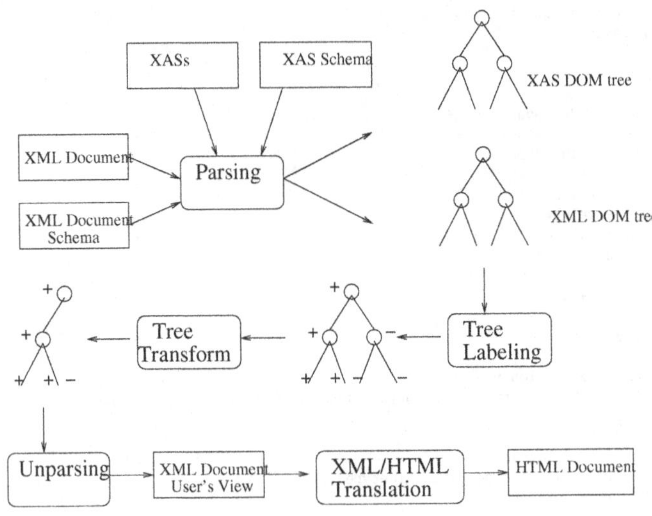

Fig. 2. Architecture of the Access Control System

The following steps are performed by the access control system after receiving a request to access an XML document. The input to the process is the document being requested, the XML Schema against which the document must be validated, the XAS for the document and the Schema, the XAS Schema against which the XAS is validated, and the identity of the requester.

Parsing: The goal of this step is to generate DOM trees for XML and XAS documents. First, the syntax of the XML document is checked with respect to the XML Schema. If the syntax is correct, the XML document is compiled. The compilation results in generating the object-oriented document graph according to the DOM format. The same process is followed for the XAS documents. The output of this step are XML DOM tree and XAS DOM tree(s).

Tree Labeling: The goal of this step is to label the nodes of the XML DOM tree that indicates whether the requester has or does not have access to the node. We follow other researchers and label a node with '+' indicating that the requester has access, a node with '-' indicating that the requester does not have access. The XAS DOM tree(s) are consulted to determine the access the requester has on the different nodes of the XML document. Note that, in determining the access the entire XAS DOM tree need not be consulted. We can prune the parts of the tree that are not related to the access request. The output of this step is a labeled XML DOM tree.

Tree Transformation: The goal of this step is to generate an XML DOM tree that represents the information the requester is permitted to view. The step proceeds as follows. The label of the tree is consulted and the tree is pruned using a preorder traversal. The output is the pruned XML DOM tree. Note that this document may not satisfy the validity requirements of the original XML schema. For this reason, the XML Schema is transformed into a loosened XML Schema that this new document will satisfy. The generation of loosened schema is defined by algorithm 3. We propose generating the loosened schema off-line and not while the access request is getting processed.

Unparsing: The goal of this step is to convert the pruned XML DOM tree into a text version. The step involves a translation process. The output is a text form of the pruned XML document.

Translation: The goal of this step is to translate the XML document such that users having browsers without XML capability can view the document. This step is a translation of the XML Document to an HTML document that can be viewed by the user.

Algorithm: Schema Loosening Algorithm
Input: (i) **A** = $\{a_1, a_2, \ldots, a_n\}$ - the set of access rights obtained from the XASs of the XML Document and the XML Schema for the document. Each element a_i in the set **A** is of the form $(sub_i, obj_i, act_i, sign_i, type_i)$ (ii) obj – the XML Document
Output: XML Schema S'- the loosened schema that specifies the type of all pruned XML documents that satisfy the access control requirements.

Procedure: Loosen Schema(**A**, obj)
begin
  $S = schema(uri(obj))$ /* get schema associated with XML Document */
  $T = CreateTree(S)$ /* function creates tree T from schema S */
  for each a_i in **A** **do**
    if $sign_i ==$ '–'
      $S_i = schema(pe(obj_i))$ /* get sub schema associated with obj_i */
      $T_i = CreateTree(S_i)$ /* function creates tree T_i from schema S_i */
      $N = \{n | n \in T \wedge n \in T_i\}$ /* set of nodes identified by obj_i
      for each $n \in N$ **do**
        if n.Attribute().use == "required"
          n.Attribute().use = "optional"
        if n.minOccurs == "1"
          n.minOccurs = "0"
  $S' = CreateSchema(T)$ /* Create schema with the updated nodes of tree T */
  return S'
end

In this algorithm, we first generate the schema for the XML document and get the corresponding tree. We look at each negative authorization from the set of authorizations. We identify the object pertaining to this authorization and get the tree corresponding to the object. In this tree, we mark all the required attributes and elements as optional. Repeating this process for all the negative authorizations, we get all the set of attributes and elements of the tree that are optional. Generating the schema from the modified tree gives us the loosened schema.

4 Conclusion

In this paper we propose an access control system that is suitable for XML documents that are validated using XML schemas instead of DTDs. We show how to specify authorization templates in the form of XML schemas, and provide an architecture of an access control system that can process the authorizations specified on XML documents and schemas. Enforcement of access control results in pruning of the document such that the users have the authorization to view this pruned document. The pruned document may not conform to the schema of the original document and hence may not be valid. Towards this end we propose a schema loosening algorithm that generates a schema that will be satisfied by documents satisfying the access control requirements. In future, we plan to investigate how to reduce the time taken for evaluating the authorizations specified on XML documents.

References

1. E. Bertino, S. Castano, and E. Ferrari. On Specifying Security Policies for Web Documents with an XML-based Language. In *Proceedings of the First ACM Symposium on Access Control Models and Technologies*, pages 57–65, May 2001.
2. E. Bertino, S. Castano, and E. Ferrari. Securing XML Documents with Author-χ. *IEEE Internet Computing*, 5:21–151, June 2001.
3. E. Bertino, S. Castano, E. Ferrari, and M. Mesiti. Specifying and Enforcing Access Control Policies for XML Document Sources. *World Wide Web Journal*, 3(3):139–151, May 2001.
4. E. Bertino and E. Ferrari. Secure and Selective Dissemination of XML Documents. *ACM Transactions on Information and System Security*, 5(3):290–331, August 2002.
5. E. Damiani, S. Paraboschi, and P. Samarati. A Fine-Grained Access Control System for XML Documents. *ACM Transactions on Information and System Security*, 5(2):169–202, May 2002.
6. E. Damiani, S. Vimercati, S. Paraboschi, and P. Samarati. Design and Implementation of Access Control Processor for XML Documents. In *Proceedings of the Ninth International World Wide Web Conference*, May 2000.
7. A. Gabillon and E. Bruno. Regulating Access to XML Documents. In *Proceedings of the Fifteenth IFIP WG 11.3 Working Conference on Data and Applications Security*, Niagara On the Lake, Canada, July 2001.
8. J. P. Yoon. Bitmap-based High-speed Access Control for XML Documents. In *Proceedings of the Seventeenth IFIP WG 11.3 Working Conference on Data and Applications Security*, Estes Park, CO, August 2003.
9. X. Zhang, J. Park, and R. Sandhu. Schema Based XML Security: RBAC Approach. In *Proceedings of the Seventeenth IFIP WG 11.3 Working Conference on Data and Applications Security*, Estes Park, CO, August 2003.

Automatic Enforcement of Access Control Policies Among Dynamic Coalitions[1]

Vijayalakshmi Atluri and Janice Warner

MSIS Department and CIMIC, Rutgers University, USA
{atluri, janice}@rutgers.edu

Abstract. The need to securely share information on an ad-hoc basis between collaborating entities is increasingly becoming important. We propose a *coalition based access control model* (CBAC), comprised of three layers: coalition, role and user-object layers. Our model enables translation of coalition level policies to implementation level access control in a manner similar to that of the layers of the TCP/IP protocol. We present a *coalition policy translation protocol* that allows the implementation level access control details to be piggy-backed as the access control policy percolates to the coalition level, and similarly, as the coalition level policy trickles down to the implementation level. Under our approach, a user's request to access an object belonging to another coalition entity is automatically translated by employing an approach that considers attributes associated with user credentials and objects. Our approach ensures that the individual access control policies of each coalition entity as well as the agreed-upon coalition policies for sharing are enforced.

1 Introduction

There is an increasing need by applications to access shared resources among different autonomous entities for the purposes of achieving a common objective. This is widespread in environments such as military, emergencies, government agency collaborations, and virtual enterprises. Such sharing is accomplished by forming *coalitions* (or alliances or collaborations). In most cases, these coalitions are *dynamic* in nature. They are formed in an ad-hoc manner and members may leave and new members may join. For example, in a natural disaster, a dynamic coalition of government agencies (e.g., FEMA, local police and fire departments), non-government organizations (e.g., Red Cross) and private organizations (e.g., Doctors without Borders, suppliers of emergency provisions) may be formed and need access to information from one another about victims, supplies, and logistics, etc. [PTD02a]. Similarly, domestic or international governmental coalitions may be put in place to share information between different agencies. For example, in a homeland security setting, a coalition between agencies may be created for the purpose of conducting comprehensive data mining. In the commercial world, companies often team up and form virtual enterprises to benefit from complementary skills and expertise.

[1] This work is supported in part by the National Science Foundation under grant IIS-0306838.

R.K. Ghosh and H. Mohanty (Eds.): ICDCIT 2004, LNCS 3347, pp. 369–378, 2004.

In these scenarios, the coalition members normally have internal access control policies in place. Secure sharing of data requires that the members be able to exercise fine-grained access control over the shared resources governed by their own security policies. Typically, when entities agree to share their information resources, the access control policies are agreed upon at the coalition level. These agreements are not at the implementation level, in the sense that they do not specify which specific users can access the data object. For example, an agreement between agencies A and B is not an access control policy stating "a user Alice of agency A can access the "immigration" file of agency B." Therefore, enforcing these *coalition-level security policies* requires transforming them to implementation level. A trivial solution would be to form teams (workgroups) of employees at the corresponding levels of both agencies. However, such a straightforward solution is not viable or scalable, may result in delays and is not practical in case of dynamic coalitions.

Current approaches to facilitate sharing include three basic mechanisms: (i) Users from one coalition entity are explicitly given permission to access resources from another coalition entity. This approach is administratively time consuming and requires explicit revocation after the coalition is disbanded or when a user is no longer affiliated with the coalition entity. (ii) A single access id is provided to all of the users of the coalition entity. While this simplifies administration, fine-grained access control is not possible. (iii) The resources are copied to the coalition entity that requires access to them. Updates are difficult and and this case may result in uncontrolled sharing. Moreover, all three approaches are not suitable for dynamic, ad-hoc coalitions and are only feasible among entities that have long-term partnerships.

We propose a *coalition-based access control model* comprising of multiple layers - coalition, role and user-object layer. Our model enables translation of coalition level policies to implementation level access control in a manner similar to that of the TCP/IP protocol. We envision that such a framework will enable the implementation level details to be piggy-backed as the access control policy percolates to the coalition level, and similarly, as the coalition level policies trickles down to the implementation level. Our approach is based on the following three principles:

1. *The Existing Access Control Mechanisms Within Each Entity Should Remain Intact.* It would be naïve to expect that coalition members could and would change their internal access control systems. Therefore, middleware systems between the coalition partners are needed to negotiate and translate access.
2. *A Common Access Control Model Will Best Facilitate Automation of Policy Decisions.* Because Role Based Access Control (RBAC) is policy neutral and has been shown to be able to model a variety of access control mechanisms including discretionary and mandatory access control [JSSS01, OSM00], it is a good candidate to be used as a common model in our approach.
3. *Administration of CBAC Should be Decentralized and Remain in the Hands of the Resource Owners.* Resource owners can best understand the risks of unauthorized access and should make the decisions about control.

Addressing the security issues in the area of dynamic coalitions is relatively new. Philips et al. [PTD02a] have described the dynamic coalition problem by providing several motivating scenarios in a defense and disaster recovery settings, and have developed a prototype that controls access to APIs and software artifacts [PTD02b]. Cohen et al. [CWTS02] have proposed a preliminary model that captures the entities involved in coalition resource sharing and identifies the interrelationships among them. [BB03, KGBK03] have addressed the issue of automating the negotiation of policy between coalition members in a dynamic coalition. However, none of the prior work in coalition based access control addresses the issue of automatic translation of coalition level policies to the implementation level policies, and vice versa. Our work can be viewed as complementary to the above work.

This paper is organized as follows. Section 2 provides an overview of our CBAC model approach. Section 3 presents the required definitions. Section 4 details our approach. Section 5 summarizes our conclusions and describes future work.

2 Overview of Our Approach

We propose a formal framework that enables automatic translation of *coalition-level security policies* so that users from one coalition entity gain access to objects residing at another coalition entity. This is accomplished by translating coalition-level security policies to *implementation level security policies* and vice versa. Specifically our approach assumes that there exist three levels: *coalition, role* and *user-object level.*

Imagine a scenario where entities A and B are part of a coalition. They have agreed to share some of their data objects. When users from A request access to the data of B, the access request at the user level needs first to be translated into an equivalent request compatible with access control policies at B. In order to accomplish this, we propose to translate the user-object level access request, say ⟨user-object request⟩, into role level so that when the request is sent to B, the role level at B is able to interpret it and decide whether to allow or deny it based on B's internal security policies. To this effect, A appends the *role segment* to the user request, thereby forming ⟨role segment ⟨user-object request⟩⟩. At the coalition level, the request is augmented with the *coalition segment*: ⟨coalition segment ⟨role segment ⟨user-object request⟩⟩⟩. When B receives the request on the other end, the coalition level first interprets the coalition segment and sends ⟨role segment ⟨user-object request⟩⟩ to the role level at B. The role level interprets the role segment and sends the ⟨user-object request⟩ to the user-object level. The process resembles the layers of the TCP/IP protocol in terms of lower levels serving upper levels, as shown in Figure 1.

We assume each user in a coalition possesses a finite set of credentials and they are assigned to appropriate roles based on their credentials. Under the RBAC model, roles represent organizational agents who perform certain job functions within the organization. Users in turn are assigned appropriate roles based on their qualifications. In this paper, we exploit the credential mechanism to help assign users to roles based on the credential attributes possessed by users. Unlike roles, credentials are characterized by a set of attributes, which allows one to specify permissions based on the user credentials that satisfy certain conditions. Therefore, a user may only be assigned to a certain role if they have the required credentials.

We assume that every member of a dynamic coalition employs RBAC as the access control policy (if not, the policies are translated and represented in RBAC), and that there exists a universal set of credential types and object types. Suppose user u from agency B wishes to access an object o of agency A. According to A's access

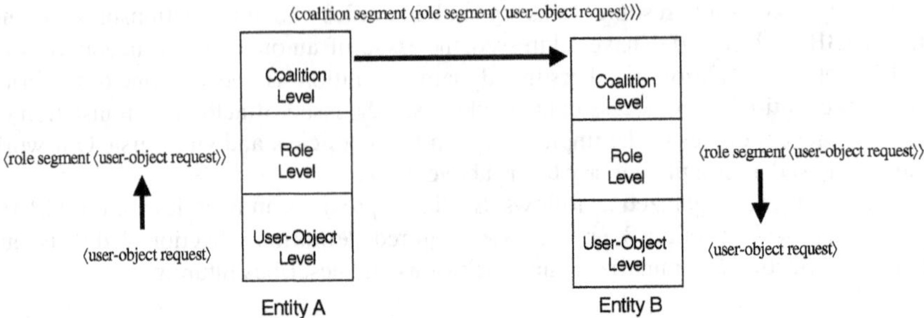

Fig. 1. Illustration of Different Layers in the CBAC Model

policy over *o*, only certain roles are allowed access and therefore, only the users who are assigned to these roles are allowed to access *o*. We compute the set of credentials (i.e. their attribute values) possessed by all these users at A. Taking a conservative approach, we assume these are the required set of credentials to access *o*. We allow a user *u* to access *o*, only if *u*'s credential attributes are equivalent or a superset of the set of required credential attributes. At B's end, we take the most authoritative set of credentials attributes possessed by user *u* to present with a request for object *o*.

3 Preliminaries

We briefly present the necessary formalism required to describe our approach. Specifically, we define our models use of objects, credentials and the RBAC model.

Objects:
Each organizational entity maintains a set of *objects*, *OBJS*, that can be shared with other organizational entities within a coalition. Each object belongs to an *object-type*, organized in *an object-type hierarchy*.

Definition 1. [Object-Type] An object-type *ot* is a pair (*ot_id, OA*), where $ot\_id \in OT$ is a unique object-type identifier; and *OA* is the set of attributes associated with *ot_id*. Each $oa_i \in OA$ is denoted by an attribute name.

Definition 2. [Object] An object *obj* is a triple (*ot_id, obj_id, obj-attr-values*), where $ot\_id \in OT$, $obj\_id \in OBJS$, $obj\text{-}attr\text{-}values = \langle oa: v_1, \ldots, oa: v_n)$, where $\{oa_1, .. oa_n\} \subseteq OA(ot)$. *OA(ot)* denotes the set of attributes associated with *ot*.

We use *obj*(*obj_id*), *obj*(*ot_id*) and *obj*(*obj-attr-values*) to denote the object id, the object-type id, and the set of attribute values of the object *obj*, respectively. The set of object attributes describe the objects such as keywords or concepts.

The RBAC Model:
In our work, we adopt the NIST standard of the RBAC model [FERR01]. For the sake of simplicity, we do not consider sessions or separation of duties constraints.

Definition 3. [RBAC]

- *U, ROLES, OPS, and OBJS* are the set of users, roles, operations, and objects.
- $UA \subseteq U \times ROLES$, a many-to-many mapping user-to-role assignment relation.
- *PRMS, (the set of permission)* $\subseteq \{(op, obj) \mid op \in OPS$ and $obj \in OBJS\}$.
- $PA \subseteq PRMS \times ROLES$, a many-to-many mapping of permission-to-role assignments.
- *assigned-users*$(r) = \{u \in U \mid (u, r) \in UA\}$, the mapping of role r onto a set of users.
- *assigned-roles*$(u) = \{ r \in ROLES \mid (u, r) \in UA\}$.
- *assigned-permissions*$(r) = \{ p \in PRMS \mid (p, r) \in PA\}$, the mapping of role r onto a set of permissions.
- *assigned-objects*$(r, p) \rightarrow \{obj \subseteq OBJS\}$, the permission-to-object mapping, which gives the set of objects associated with permission p for a given role. Formally, assigned-objects(r, p) $= \{ obj \in OBJS \mid p = (op, obj)\}$.
- $RH \subseteq ROLES \times ROLES$ is a partial order on *ROLES,* called the role hierarchy.

Due to the role hierarchy, there exists an inheritance relation, written as $\geq$ where $r_1 \geq r_2$ only if all permissions of r_2 are also permissions of r_1, and all users of r_1 are also users of r_2. Formally: $(r_1 \geq r_2) \Rightarrow$ assigned-permissions$(r_2) \subseteq$ assigned-permissions(r_1) Λ assigned-users$(r_1) \subseteq$ assigned-users(r_2). We assume that a comparison between roles can always be made. Parallel, incomparable role hierarchies are not allowed.

Credentials:

We assume that each subject is associated with one or more *credentials*. Credentials are assigned when a user is created and are updated according to the profile of the user. To make the task of credential specifications easier, credentials with similar structures are grouped into *credential-types*. Credential-types are typically organized as *credential-type hierarchy*. We denote the set of credential-type identifiers with *CT*, the set of credential identifiers with *CI*, and the set of user identifiers with *U*. A credential-type can be formally defined as follows.

Definition 4. [Credential-Type] A credential-type *ct* is a pair (*ct_id, A*), where $ct\_id \in CT$ is a unique identifier and *A* is the set of attributes belonging to *ct_id*. Each $a_i \in A$ has an attribute name and *A*(*ct*) is the set of attributes belonging to *ct*.

Example 1: The credential type "doctor" can be (doctor, {affiliation, specialty}).

Definition 5. [Credential] A credential *c*, an instance of a credential-type *ct,* is a 4-tuple (*ct_id, c_id, user_id, user-profile*), where $ct\_id \in CT$, $c\_id \in CI$, $user\text{-}id \in U$ and $user\text{-}profile = (a_1 : v_1, \ldots., a_n : v_n)$, where $\{a_1, .. a_n\} \subseteq A(ct)$.

The set of credentials associated with users in the system is denoted by the *credential base* (CB). We use *c*(*c_id*), *c*(*user-id*), *c*(*ct_id*) and *c*(*user-profile*) to denote the credential id of *c*, the user to which *c* is assigned, the credential type id of *c* and the set of attribute values of the user *u (the user profile)* for *c*, respectively.

Example 2: An example of a credential for credential type "doctor" is as follows: (doctor, c-1, Roberts, (affiliation: Doctors without Borders, Specialty: immunology)).

The attribute values of the credentials can be specified similarly to attribute certificates. Such certificates can be issued to users within coalition entities.

4 Coalition Based Access Control (CBAC) Model

In this section, we present the proposed CBAC model, the coalition policy translation protocol, and an example that illustrates the working of our protocol.

Definition 6. [Coalition] A *coalition C*, is a tuple (*coalition_id, E*) where *coalition_id* is a unique identifier of a coalition and $E = \{e_1, e_2, \ldots\}$ is a set of coalition entities that have unique identifiers, *entity_id*s.

Example 3: In a natural disaster, the International Red Cross is often on site providing shelter, food and protection to displaced persons. Doctors without Borders may provide services to combat the spread of infectious diseases. The two organizations could benefit from a coalition system that allows them to access each other's information in a secure manner. Throughout this paper we will expand on an instance of this example where both organizations respond to an emergency in Turkey. In our example, Doctors without Borders has noticed a large number of infected wounds and wants to determine whether the problem is localized and if so, the source of the infection. Thus they enter a coalition agreement to obtain the necessary data from the Red Cross. Treatment case records from the emergency in Turkey and prior information on diseases or injuries in Turkey are to be shared.

Coalition Level Policy Specification: This is a high level agreement between the members of the coalition on the types of objects they will share. We assume the objects of one coalition member, called the *source_entity*, are shared with another coalition member, the *destination_entity*.

A coalition level policy *p* is stated as follows: *p* = (*coalition_id, source_entity_id, destination_entity_id, source_object_type*). A *coalition_id* is a unique identifier for the coalition, *source_entity_id* is a unique identifier for the coalition member who will share its data objects, *destination_entity_id* is a unique identifier for the coalition member who is granted access to the objects belonging to the source entity and *source_object_type* is the set of object types that can be shared. We use *p.coalition_id, p.destination_entity_id, p.source_entity_id*, and *p.source_object_type* to identify these parameters of policy *p*. The specification of object types in the coalition policy, as opposed to object ids, allows the policy to be stated at a more abstract level, facilitating the dynamic addition of new objects without having to change the coalition level policy specification.

Example 4: In our example, the International Red Cross has agreed to provide access to its emergency response information system as it applies to the earthquake emergency in Turkey. The agreed upon high-level coalition policy among these two coalition members can be specified as follows: *Coalition level policy, p_1*: (Turkey-0704, RedCross, DrswoBorders, {Concept: Location = "Turkey"}).

Definitions that follow are required for our policy translation protocol. Note that, unlike prior approaches, users are not mapped to a specific role at the source entity. Instead, their credential attributes are matched with those required to access an object.

Definition 7. [Assigned-User-Credentials] Given a user *u* and a credential base *CB*, the set of credentials assigned to a user are *assigned-credentials*(*u*) = $\{c \in C \mid c(\textit{user-id}) = u\}$.

Definition 8. [Assigned-Role-Credentials] Given a role *r* and a set of users *U,* we define the set of credentials assigned to a role *r, assigned-credentials*(*r*) = $\cup\{\textit{assigned-credentials}(u) \mid u \in \textit{assigned\_users}(\mathrm{r})\}$.

Definition 9. [Assigned-Role-Credential-Attributes] Given a role *r* and a set of users *U,* we define the set of credential attributes assigned to a role *r, assigned-credential-attributes*(*r*) = $\cup\ \{c(\textit{user-profile}) \mid c \in \textit{assigned- credentials}(r)\}$.

Definition 10. [Required-Object-Credentials] Given a role *r,* an object *obj* and a set of permission-role assignments PA, we define the set of required credentials to access an object *obj, required-credentials*(*obj*) = $\cup\{\textit{assigned-credentials}(r) \mid obj \in \textit{assigned-objects}(r, p) \wedge (p, r) \in PA\}$.

Definition 11. [Required-Object-Credential-Attributes] Given a role *r,* an object *obj* and a set of users *U,* the set of credential attributes required to access an object *obj* is, *required-credential-attributes(obj)*=$\cup\{c(\textit{user-profile}) | c \in \textit{required-credentials}(obj)\}$.

The ***policy translation protocol*** uses coalition segment, role segment and user-object segment in its request/response messages. The format of these segments are:

Coalition Segment: ⟨coalitionid, sourceentityid, destinationentityid ⟩
Role Segment: ⟨assigned-credential-attributes(r)⟩
User-Object Segment: ⟨userid, object ⟩, where object can either be *obj_id* or *ot_id*.

```
Algorithm[Coalition Policy Translation Protocol]
  Object Request:
  Input: user-object request (user_id, object_type)
  request_object(destination_user_id, source_object_type){
  if user_id ∈ U,
       {destination-role-id-set ← assigned-roles(destination-user-id)
       RA ← assigned-credential-attributes(destination-role-id) such
       that destination-role-id ∈ destination-role-id-set;
       if (there exists a policy p such that object_type ∈
           p.source_object_type)
            request_message ← ⟨p.coalition_id, p.source_entity_id,
            p.destination_entity_id, ⟨RA ⟨user_id, p.source_object_type⟩⟩}
  else return error message "Invalid user"}
  Response:
  Input: request_message
  respond_object (source_entity_id, destination_entity_id,
    source_object){
  if there exists a policy p′ such that
     (p.source_object_type ∈ p′.source_object_type) ∧
     (p.destination_entity_id = p′.destination_entity_id)
        for every obj such that p.source_object_type∈obj(obj-attr-values)
             if RA ⊇ required-credential-attributes(obj)
                  allow access to obj by destination_user_id}
             else
                  return_error_message("No credential match")}
  else return_error_message("Invalid request")}
```

In the following, we present the detailed steps of the protocol:

Step 1: At the destination coalition entity, a user requests an object by specifying the user-object segment: ⟨*destination_user_id, source_object*⟩. The user-object segment identifies the requesting user and the requested object or set of objects.
Step 2: The user-object segment is mapped at the role level to a role and the *user_id* is removed from the user-object segment. If the user is a member of more than one role, the highest level role in the hierarchy is selected. The role segment is comprised of the credential attributes associated with the assigned-role. The resulting message is: ⟨*assigned-credential-attributes*(*destination-role-id*) ⟨ *source-object*⟩⟩.
Step 3: The combined role and user-object segments are sent to the coalition level. The request is mapped to a coalition instance. Then the coalition layer determines which coalition member shares the specified object type, appends the coalition segment to the request and delivers it to the appropriate coalition member. The coalition message is: ⟨*coalition_id, source_entity_id, destination_entity* ⟨*assigned-credential-attributes*(*destination-role-id*) ⟨*source-object*⟩⟩⟩.
Step 4: The message is sent to the source coalition entity which validates it.
Step 5: The role level at the source coalition entity examines the credential attributes specified in the role segment and tests if (*assigned-credential-attributes*(*destination_role_id*) ⊇ *required- credential-attributes*(*source-object*).
Step 6. If the above condition is satisfied, then access is granted to the objects associated with the source object id.

A system architecture for the CBAC system consists of a Coalition Control System (CCS) and an RBAC module. The CCS is the key component. It accomplishes the translation of coalition policies and controls external access to internal resources by entity members at other coalition member sites. It has three sub-components – coalition level policy interpreter, role interpreter, and user-object access controller. Although the example given in this paper is for the simplest case of two entities involved in a coalition, the approach is applicable to coalitions or partnerships with multiple entities. When there are multiple entities, we assume that there exists a coalition level policy instance among each pair of coalition entities. As a result, a pair-wise handshaking is required to enforce the agreed upon policy. This is recommended because: (i) it allows the coalition members to provide different levels of access to different partners based on level-of-trust. (ii) It facilitates the members to join and leave a coalition, without having to dissolve a coalition.

Example 5: Dr. Roberts, a member of Doctors Without Borders, wishes to access data on infectious diseases in the area of the earthquake maintained by the International Red Cross. Figure 2 illustrates the steps described below:

1. He sends a request to his organizational system, which is handled by its coalition control system. The access request is in the form: ⟨user-object segment⟩ = ⟨roberts, (concept: infectious diseases, location = Turkey)⟩. The user-object access controller validates Dr. Roberts and passes the request to the role interpreter.
2. The role interpreter selects the role played by Roberts, doctor, and retrieves the credentials associated with this roleid by computing the *assigned-credential-attributes*(doctor). The retrieved credential is of type medical-doctor and has the attributes affiliation and specialty. It appends the role segment to the user-object

segment: ⟨medical-doctor, (affiliation: Doctors without Borders, specialty: immunology) ⟨roberts, (concept: infectious diseases, location =Turkey) ⟩⟩ and passes it to the coalition level policy interpreter.

3. The coalition level policy interpreter determines the appropriate coalition and coalition member for the requested object based on the object-type, and appends the coalition segment to the role and object segments: ⟨Turkey-0704, RedCross, Doctors without Borders, ⟨medical-doctor, (affiliation: Doctors without Borders, specialty: immunology) ⟨roberts, (concept: infectious diseases, location = Turkey)⟩⟩⟩. The message is then passed to the International Red Cross system.
4. The Red Cross system validates the destination member and coalition id. It passes the valid request to its role interpreter after removing the coalition level segment.
5. The role-interpreter at this end attempts to test if someone with the received credential attributes could access objects of the specified types. It identifies the objects and computes the *required-credential-attributes*(*obj*) such that (concept: infectious diseases, location =Turkey $\in$ *obj*(*obj-attr-values*). If *assigned-credential-attributes*(medical-doctor) $\supseteq$ *required-credential-attributes*(*obj*), the set of objects are then passed to the user-object access controller: ⟨517,730⟩.
6. The user-object access controller retrieves the objects and makes them available to Dr. Roberts.

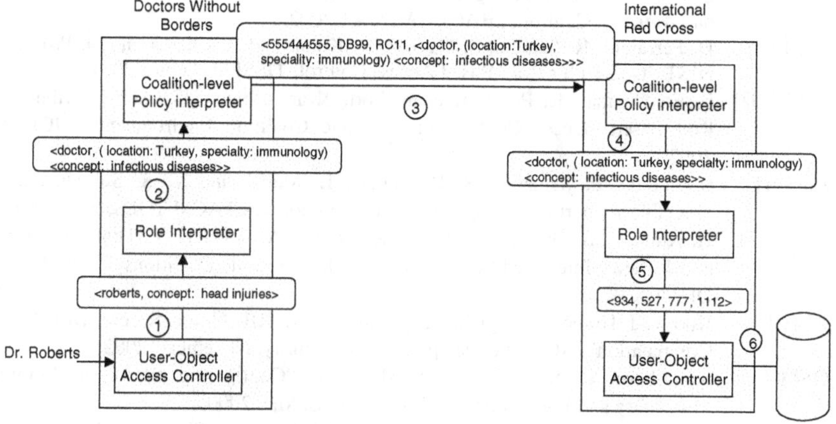

Fig. 2. The Different Steps of Object Request and Response

5 Conclusions and Future Research

In this paper, we have proposed a *coalition-based access control model* (CBAC) comprising of multiple layers – coalition, role, and user-object (or implementation) layer. Our model enables translation of coalition level policies to implementation level access control in a manner similar to that performed by the layers in the TCP/IP network protocol. The CBAC framework described in this paper allows for dynamic, ad-hoc formations of information sharing systems for coalitions that share objects based on object attributes and credential attributes.

We plan to undertake several research tasks in this area. (1) We have assumed that objects are owned by only one member of the coalition. However, there may be the need to have object ownership shared by several entities. We intend to extend our approach to facilitate such cooperative environments similar the work on cooperative role-based administration in [WL03]. (2) We have assumed that coalition member entities agree on high-level policies before there is any flow of information, making the coalition formation not completely ad-hoc. We plan to extend our approach to allow organizational entities to publish their policies and services. Coalitions could then be formed based on the compatibility and adherence to the published policies. (3) We have not considered static and dynamic separation of duties constraints and plan to extend our CBAC model to incorporate these constraints as well. Moreover, delegation is an important feature, which must be supported in coalition-based systems [FPPKK02]; and we intend to include this support as well. (4) We intend to implement our approach using the OASIS XACML specification, XML specification of attribute certificates, and registry service similar to that of UDDI registry.

References

[BB03] V. Bharadwaj and J. Baras, "A Framework for Automated Negotiation of Access Control Policies", Proceedings of DISCEX III, 2003.

[CWTS02] E. Cohen, W. Winsborough, R. Thomas and D. Shands, "Models for Coalition-based Access Control (CBAC), SACMAT 2002.

[FERR01] D. Ferraiolo, R. Sandhu, S. Gavrila, D. Kuhn, and R. Chandramouli, Proposed NIST Standard for Role-Based Access Control, TISSEC, August 2001.

[FPPKK02] P. Freudenthal, K. Pesin, Keenan, Port, &Karamcheti, "dRBAC: Distribute d Role-Based Access Control for Dynamic Coalition Environments", ICDCS, 2002.

[JSSS01] S. Jajodia, P. Samarati, S. Pierangela, L. Maria, and V. S. Subrahmanian, "Flexible support for multiple access control policies," ACM TODs, June 2001.

[KGBK03] H. Khurana, S. Gavrila, R. Bobba, R. Koleva, A. Sonalker, E. Dinu, V. Gligor and J. Baras, Integrated Security Services for Dynamic Coalitions 'Proc. of th e DISCEX III, 2003.

[KH02] Kuo and Humenn, "Dynamically Authorized RBAC for Secure Distributed Computation", ACM Workshop for XML Security, November, 2002

[OSM00] S. Osborn, R. Sandhu and Q. Munawer, "Configuring RBAC to Enforce Mandatory and DAC Policies, ACM TISSEC, May 2000.

[PTD02a] C. Philips, T.C. Ting, and S. Demurjian, "Information Sharing and Security in Dynamic Coalitions", SACMAT 2002.

[PTD02b] C. Philips, E. Charles, T. Ting, and S. Demurjian, "Towards Information Assurance in Dynamic Coalitions", IEEE IAW, USMA, February 2002

[WL03] H. F. Wedde and M. Lischka, "Cooperative Role-Based Administration", SACMAT 2003.

Implementing Consistency Checking in Correlating Attacks

Kaushal Sarda[1], Duminda Wijesekera[2] and Sushil Jajodia[2]

[1] Capgemini, Pirojshanagar, Vikhroli, Mumbai 400 079, India
[2] The Center for Secure Information Systems,
George Mason University, Fairfax VA 22030, USA
kaushal.sarda@capgemini.com
{dwijsek, jajodia}@gmu.edu

Abstract. Static analysis of attack sequences (a.k.a. topological vulnerability analysis -TVA) studies sequences of attacks that can eventually lead to exploitable vulnerabilities in a network. In models where the attacks are specified in terms of their preconditions and post conditions, the sequences that can be launched are those in which the post condition of the antecedent attack implies the precondition of the precedent attack. We show a method of doing so, and show the drawbacks in omitting these checks in the CRIM [5]) model.

Introduction

Topological Vulnerability Analysis (TVA) statically analyses sequences of exploitable vulnerabilities existing in a given network configuration so that no sequence of them can be systematically exploited in order to drive the network to an undesirable state. Steps taken during this process are called *attacks*, and networks states appearing immediately before and after are referred to as *preconditions* and *post conditions* of the attack. Thus, an attack chain or an attack tree is one in which all attacks launched Consequently, in the predicate-based model, these translate to a collection of post conditions of the precedent before the one in question prepares the environment in which it can be launched. attacks implying the pre conditions of their successors. However the inconsistency of such pre conditions results in a modeling error, as it symbolizes an unachievable network state. The CRIM model [5] and some other [7] that use its definitions do not check for this latter condition. As a remedy we offer a set of definitions that rectify this problem and some Prolog code that can compute attack sequences as proposed here.

The structure of the rest of paper is as follows. The next section describes the terminology and concepts used there after. We then formulate them in SWI Prolog, as we have implemented them. The subsequent section compares our correlation definitions with prior definitions. The final section concludes the paper.

Terminology and Concepts

Many tools such as [1], [2], and [3] determine vulnerabilities of individual hosts, although they do not compute vulnerabilities caused due to their interactions. Thus, if

R.K. Ghosh and H. Mohanty (Eds.): ICDCIT 2004, LNCS 3347, pp. 379–384, 2004.

only these tools are used to fix security holes of a network, applications that are secure when used in isolation, may become vulnerable when used in combination. An example is a file transfer utility (ftp) and an http service being hosted on a single machine. If an attacker uses ftp to load a program on a host and execute it by employing hosted web server to exploit a system. TVA is used to determine such chains of attacks that can lead to undesirable state.

There are at least two kinds of approaches to TVA. The first [4] uses a state based model of the network to discover all possible state transition paths that end in an undesirable one. The major disadvantages of this model are the well-known state explosion problem. The second approach uses logic to sequence the network states by joining them with atomic attacks. The Cooperative Module for Intrusion detection system (CRIM) [5] cluster, merge and correlate attacks. CRIM uses the following definitions to do so where A and B be two attacks with pre( ) and post( ) denoting pre and post conditions as a conjunction of literals.

`post(A) = expr`$_{A1,}$ `expr`$_{A2}$`, ..., expr`$_{Am}$
`pre(B) = exprB1, exprB2, ..., exprBn` where *expr* can be p or not(p) for a predicate p.

Definition 1. (Direct and Indirect Correlation and Attack Paths Ala CRIM)
Attack A and B are directly correlated if one of the following conditions is satisfied:

1. `exprAi` and `exprBj` has the most general unifier (mgu) θ for some iε[1,m] and jε[1,n], or
2. `exprAi` and `knows(user,exprBj)` has mgu θ for some iε[1,m] and jε[1,n] where knows( ) expresses the attackers knowledge about the vulnerability.

They can also be correlated are indirectly correlated through rules $R_1, \ldots, R_n$ of the form p $\rightarrow$q. The correlation definition used in [5] has some limitations. The key aspect of two attacks being correlated is that the launch of the attack A must make the network state such that attack B can be launched. For this to happen it is imperative that no subset of the post condition set of attack A would negate any of the preconditions of attack B. Thus, the post conditions of attack A must be consistent with preconditions of attack B for them to be correlated. For otherwise, attack B cannot be performed after attack A.

The correlation definition in [5] verifies if there exists any expression in *post(A)* that can either directly or indirectly be unified to an expression in *pre(B)* list. Now suppose $expr_{A1}$ unifies with $expr_{B1}$ directly and $expr_{A2}$ and $expr_{A3}$ imply $not(expr_{B2})$, the conditions expressed using $expr_{A2}$, $expr_{A3}$, and $expr_{B2}$ cannot exist at the same state. By the CRIM definition the attacks A and B will still be correlated, resulting in creating many attack paths that cannot be launched. This is an inaccuracy in the modeling presented in [5] and other work using the same correlation definition such as [7]. The same argument also holds true for the indirect correlation definition. Our definition of attack correlations and paths follow.

Definition 2. (Explicit and Semi-explicit Correlations)
If *post(A)* $\rightarrow$ *pre(B)*, then we say that attack B is explicitly related to attack A If there is another predicate C such that *post(A)^C* $\rightarrow$ *pre(B)* then we say that B is semi-explicitly correlated to , provided that C does not imply *Pre(B)* by itself and *post(A)^C* is consistent. An attack path is sequence of correlated attacks.

Attack Correlations in SWI Prolog

This section, we use SWI prolog [6] to implement both definitions and show the difference by means of an example. In order to do so we use the following predicates: We use lower case letters predicates and upper case letters for their lists.

1. `present(k,P)`: k unifies with at least one element in P. For example, `present(k, [p,t,k])`.
2. `different(A,P)`: An element in A does not unify with some element in P, defined as `different(A,P):- present(X,P),not(present(X,A))`.
3. `subset(K,T)`: any element of T unifies with some element of K.
4. `conflict(H,T)`: An element in T appears negated in H. For example, `conflict([q,not(p)],p)`.
5. `inconsistent(C,D)`: An element in C conflicts with some element in D, defined as `inconsistent(PreL,PostL):present(H,PreL),conflict(H,T),subset (T,PostL)`.
6. `correlated(C,D)`: Every element in C unifies with some element in D, defined as `correlated(A,B):-not(different(A,B)),not(inconsistent(A,B))`.

This is an auxiliary predicate stating that the group of elements in D falsifies no element in C.

For example, consider the two attacks and a rule given below:

```
post(attack1,[a, s, t]).
pre(attack2,[s,t]).
conflict(A,s):- istrue(A,p),istrue(A,m).
```

Here `correlated([s,t],[a,s,t])` holds because `not(different([s,t],[a,s,t]))` and `not(inconsistent([s,t],[a,s,t])` hold. Note that `istrue(A,p)` is true if p in A.

The not predicate in SWI Prolog [6], implements negation as failure defined as usual the cut-fail combination given as

```
not(Goal).
not(Goal) :- Goal, !, fail.
```

The following example based on our implementation illustrates the above definitions.

```
post(attack1,[p,y,n,z,s,t])
Pre(attack2,[s,t,z])
Conflict(A,s):- istrue(A,p), istrue(A,m)
conflict(R,t):- istrue(R,g)
```

Our implementation gave the following results:

```
?- correlated([s,t,z], [p,y,n,z,s,t]).
Yes
```

We then modified the example as follows:

```
post(attack1, [p,y,n,z,s,t])
Pre(attack2, [s,t,z])
Conflict(A, s):- istrue(A, p),istrue(A, n)
conflict(R, t):- istrue(R, g)
```

The result we obtain for the same query now is:

```
?- correlated([s,t,z], [p,y,n,z,s,t]).
No
```

We now define attack chains using the following predicates and rules, some of these are available in Prolog.

1. `nth(n,Q,T)`: the nth element of the list Q is T.
2. `composed([R],Q,P)`: list P is generated by pre-pending R to Q.
3. `length(S,N)`: the cardinality of S is N.
4. `union(P,T,S)`: S unifies with the union of lists P and T.
5. `pre(D,Prelist)`: Prelist is the precondition for attack D.
6. `post(C,Postlist)`: Postlist is the post condition of attack C.
7. `alist(W,Prelist,Postlist)`: Prelist and Postlist are respectively the collections of preconditions and post conditions of the list W of atomic attacks.
8. `chain(P)`: P is a list of correlated and consistent attack lists (i.e. alists), defined as follows:

```
chain(S):- length(S,1), present(X,S),
alist(X,Prelist2,Postlist2).
chain(P):-composed([R],Q,P),
            alist(R,Prelist,Postlist),chain(Q),nth1(1,Q,T),
            alist(T,Prelist1,Postlist1),
            correlated(Prelist,Postlist1).
```

Here P is defined as a chain if every element of the chain is an attack list, and each attack list element is correlated to the next attack element.

An attack path it is an attack chain that causes the network to reach an exploited state. Thus attack paths are special attack chains that are harmful and must be avoided. The attack path definition is built using the predicates and rules listed below.

1. `network(n,P)`: all predicates in P are initially true for network n.
2. `exploits(n,A)`: list of attacks A cause network n to reach an undesirable state.
3. `last(x,L)`: x is the last element of L.
4. `totalcorrelation(P1,P2)`: there is no element unifying with some element of P2 but with none in P1 and there is no (group of) element(s) in P1 conflicting with some element of P2, defined as

```
totalcorrelation(P1,P2):-not(different(P1,P2)),
                          not(inconsistent(P2,P1)).
```

5. `attackpath(N,A,X)`: an attack chain given by the list A can be launched on network N to accomplish the exploited state caused by attack X, defined as follows:

```
attackpath(N,A,X):- network(N, Initconditions), chain(A),
                    pre(X, Prelistc), exploits(N, Exploit),
                    present(X,Exploit),
                    last(X,A),prechain(A,Prelistd),
                  totalcorrelation(Initconditions,Prelistd).
```

Table 1. Attack Information

Attack Name	*Attack Preconditions*	*Attack Post conditions*
Attack 4	pre(attack4,[u])	post(attack4,[a])
Attack 5	pre(attack5,[v,w])	post(attack5,[b,c])
Attack 6	pre(attack6,[x])	post(attack6,[d])
Attack 7	pre(attack7,[e,f])	post(attack7,[u,v,w])
Attack 8	pre(attack8,[g,h])	post(attack8,[x])
Attack 9	pre(attack9,[c,d])	post(attack9,[q,r,i])

We now consider an example using these predicates with the configuration given in Table 1.

```
network(N,[e,f,g,h]), exploits(N,[attack1]).
conflict(A,t):- istrue(A,i).
```

When these facts were provided to the model, the output obtained on using the attack path definition was as follows:

```
?- attackpath(N, [[attack1], [attack2,attack3],
[attack4,attack5,attack6], [attack7,attack8]], attack1).
Yes
```

We now show that this attack path can be realized as a consequence of stated facts. The attacker eventually needs to launch attack1. He initially launches attack7 and attack8 in parallel. This can be done as the union of their preconditions e,f,g and h are initially satisfied in n because of `network(N,[e,f,g,h])`. Consequently, their post conditions u, v, w and x become true. As a result the attacker can launch attack4, attack5 and attack6 simultaneously. This is because the union of the post conditions of attack7 and attack8 are correlated to the union of the preconditions of attack4, attack5 and attack6. This group of attacks allows simultaneous launching of attack2 and attack3. Their post conditions validate the preconditions of attack1. Hence the attack path

'`[[attack1],[attack2,attack3],[attack4,attack5,attack6],[attack7,attack8]]`' can be taken.

Comparing Results

We now show the difference between our attack correlation and that of CRIM [5] using an example. To do so, consider a network n with an initial set of vulnerabilities "e, f, g, h" with the set of attacks given in Table 2.

Table 2. Information of Attacks used in this example

Attack Name	*Attack Preconditions*	*Attack Post conditions*
Attack 1	pre(attack1,[p,q,r,t]).	post(attack1,[m,n]).
Attack 2	pre(attack2,[a,b]).	post(attack2,[p,t]).
Attack 3	pre(attack3,[c,d]).	post(attack3,[q,r]).
Attack 4	pre(attack4,[u]).	post(attack4,[a]).
Attack 5	pre(attack5,[v,w]).	post(attack5,[b,c]).
Attack 6	pre(attack6,[x]).	post(attack6,[d]).
Attack 7	pre(attack7,[e,f]).	post(attack7,[u,v,w]).
Attack 8	pre(attack8,[g,h]).	post(attack8,[x]).
Attack 9	pre(attack9,[c,d]).	post(attack9,[q,r,I]).

Attack1 causes the exploit represented in the model as exploits(N,[attack1]). Another condition specified in this scenario is that predicate i will violate t, expressed as conflict(A,t):- istrue(A,i). According to the CRIM attack correlation definition in [5], the only requirement is that preconditions of the precedent and post condition of the antecedent attacks must unify. We have implemented this as:

```
correlated(C,D):- pre(D,Prelist), post(C,Postlist),
                  present(X,Postlist), present(X,Prelist).
```

where C and D represent correlated attacks. When we used this modified attack correlation definition, we get results as follows:

```
?- chain([[attack1],[attack2,attack9],
    [attack4,attack5,attack6],[attack7,attack8]]).
Yes
```

For the same example our definition gives:

```
?-
   chain([[attack1],[attack2,attack9],[attack4,attack5,attac
   k6], [attack7,attack8]]).
No
```

When the CRIM attack correlation definition is used, the model accepts the occurrence of attack chain `[[attack1], [attack2, attack9], [attack4, attack5, attack6], [attack7, attack8]]`. The post condition for attack9 is [q,r,i]. Thus t is not satisfied, preventing occurrence attack1. Because our definition checks the consistency between the two attacks, we are able to recognize that [attack1] and [attack2, attack9] are not correlated, as they are inconsistent, thereby removing the modeling inaccuracy of [5].

Conclusions

Correlating attacks is an important in TVA. We have demonstrated a limitation in the correlation definition used in the CRIM model [5], which leads to non-executable attack paths. We have proposed new correlation definitions that overcome this limitation by using consistency checking between the post conditions of an antecedent attack and the preconditions of a precedent attack correctly. As shown, although expensive, omitting this consistency checking causes inaccurate attack path computations.

References

1. Computer Oracle and Password System (COPS) information and software on the web at <ftp.cert.org/pub/tools/cops>
2. Internet Security Systems, System Scanner information at <http://www.iss.net>
3. Network Associates, CyberCop Scanner information at <http://www.nai.com/ aspset/products/tns/ccscannerintro.asp>
4. Ronald W. Ritchey and Paul Ammann. "Using model checking to analyze network vulnerabilities." In Proceedings 2000 IEEE Computer Society Symposium on Security and Privacy, pages 156-165, Oakland, CA, May 2000.
5. F. Cuppens et A. Miège, "Alert correlation in a cooperative intrusion detection framework." IEEE Symposium on Research in Security and Privacy, Oakland, Mai 2002.
6. http://www.swi-prolog.org
7. Peng Ning, Yun Cui, Douglas S. Reeves, "Analyzing Intensive Intrusion Alerts Via Correlation," in Proceedings of the 5th International Symposium on Recent Advances in Intrusion Detection (RAID 2002), LNCS 2516, pages 74--94, Zürich, Switzerland, October 2002.

LSAD: Lightweight SYN Flooding Attack Detector

Seung-won Shin, Ki-young Kim, and Jong-soo Jang

Electronics and Telecommunications Research Institute,
161Gajeong-dong, Yusung-gu, Daejon, Korea
{swshin, kykim, jsjang}@etri.re.kr
http://www.etri.re.kr/

Abstract. Currently, there are lots of approaches to detect SYN flooding, but they require too many resources to manage most of ongoing traffic. We propose a simple and robust approach to detect SYN flooding attacks by observing essential network information. Instead of managing all ongoing traffic on the network, our approach only monitors SYN count and ratio between SYN and other TCP packets. To make the detection mechanism robustly and easily, we use EWMA (exponentially weight moving average) approach in SPC (statistical process control) [3] [10] [11]. It makes the detection mechanism much more generally applicable and easier to implement. The trace-driven simulation results demonstrate that our proposal is efficient and simple to implement and prove that it detects SYN flooding accurately and finds attack in a very short detection time.

Keywords: network security, network intrusion detection system, SYN flooding.

1 Introduction

To defend SYN flooding attacks [1], a lot of defense mechanisms have been presented, for example Syn cookies[5], Syn cache[7], SynDefender[6], Syn proxying[8] and Synkill[9]. All of these approaches should be installed at the firewall of the victim server or inside the victim itself. Above approaches defend victims efficiently, but they do not prevent network from lots of wasted SYN packets, because the defense line is close to the victim and network resources are wasted by huge amount of SYN packets. To compensate these, Haining W et al proposed new technique defending SYN flooding attack at the leaf router. Their approach protects network resources from exhaustion with very simple and robust mechanism [2].

We also made our focus like Haining W et al, because it protects victim and also avoids network resources consumption. However, although their approach is efficient to detect SYN flooding and protect network resources, it has a problem to maintain all incoming TCP session information. We examined our traffic traces and found that hundred thousands sessions have to be maintained. To overcome this, researches about session management are proposed using timeout or other threshold value, but these makes decrease the possibility to detect all suspicious flows. For this reason, we tried to find method to detect SYN flooding without storing huge amount of sessions.

R.K. Ghosh and H. Mohanty (Eds.): ICDCIT 2004, LNCS 3347, pp. 385–390, 2004.

In this paper, we present and evaluate LSAD (Lightweight SYN flooding Attack Detector) system for detecting SYN flooding efficiently. Our main focus is to solve problem mentioned above paragraph and detect SYN flooding without too much burden. LSAD system detects SYN flooding by simple statistical approach. Instead of monitoring all ongoing packets on the network or the victim server itself, LSAD system only watches the TCP SYN packets and other TCP packets (TCP packets without SYN flag). If SYN flooding attacks happen and SYN number increases, then LSAD finds it by these. The first parameter of SYN count shows us dynamic behavior of TCP SYN. However, it presents energetic changes in most periods [4], so we add the ratio value between SYN packets and other TCP packets to our consideration. Because the ratio does not change seriously in normal status [4], it can compensate the instability of SYN count. If serious change happens in both parameters, LSAD system finds that it is possible to occur SYN flooding.

The rest of this paper is organized as follows. In Section 2, we describe the LSAD system and explain statistical approaches that we used. Section 3 shows the simulation environment and analysis results and our discussions are also provided. Finally, future works and conclusion are drawn in Section 4.

2 LSAD

The main goal of LSAD system is to detect SYN flooding attack without high cost. The simple statistical detection approach of LSAD system makes this possible. Unlike the other approaches, LSAD system does not monitor the entire flows on the network.

2.1 EWMA Algorithm

The performance of EWMA control chart is approximately equivalent to that of the cumulative sum chart (CUSUM chart) [3] [10] [11], and in some ways it is easier to set up and operate. As with the CUSUM, the EWMA is typically used with individual observations and this chart was introduces by Roberts. The exponentially weighted moving average is defined as like followings.

$$z_i = \lambda x_i + (1-\lambda) z_{i-1} \tag{1}$$

Where $0 < \lambda \leq 1$ is a constant and the starting value (required with the first sample at i =1) is the process target, so that $\mathbf{z}_0 = \mu_0$ (μ_0 is the target value).

Sometimes the average of preliminary data is used as the starting value of the EWMA, so that $z_0 = \bar{x}$. To demonstrate that the EWMA z_i is a weighted average of all previous sample means, we may substitute for z_{i-1} on the right-hand side of equation (1) to obtain

$$\begin{aligned} z_i &= \lambda x_i + (1-\lambda)[\lambda x_{i-1} + (1-\lambda) z_{i-2}] \\ &= \lambda x_i + \lambda(1-\lambda) x_{i-1} + (1-\lambda)^2 z_{i-2}] \end{aligned}$$

Continuing to substitute recursively for z_{i-j}, j =2,3,, t, we obtain

$$z_i = \lambda \sum_{j=0}^{i-1} (1-\lambda)^j x_{i-j} + (1-\lambda)^i z_0 \tag{2}$$

Since the EWMA can be viewed as a weighted average of all past and current observations, it is very insensitive to the normality assumption. It is therefore an ideal control chart to use with individual observations. If the observations x_i are independent random variables with variance σ^2, then the variance of z_i is;

$$\sigma_{z_i}^2 = \sigma^2 \left(\frac{\lambda}{2-\lambda}\right)[1-(1-\lambda)^{2i}] \tag{3}$$

Therefore, the EWMA control chart would be constructed by plotting z_i versus the sample number *i* (or time). The center line and upper and lower specification limits (***USL*** and ***LSL***) for the EWMA control chart are as follows.

$$USL = \mu_0 + L\sigma\sqrt{\frac{\lambda}{(2-\lambda)}[1-(1-\lambda)^{2i}]} \tag{4}$$

Center Line = μ_0

$$LSL = \mu_0 - L\sigma\sqrt{\frac{\lambda}{(2-\lambda)}[1-(1-\lambda)^{2i}]} \tag{5}$$

In equations (4) and (5), the factor $\boldsymbol{L}$ is the width of the control limit [10] [11].

2.2 How to Feel the Sign of SYN Flooding

To detect SYN flooding, we used received SYN number and ratio between SYN packets and other TCP packets information. The parameters that LSAD has are like followings.

- ✓ Received number of SYN packets **[*Parameter A*]**
- ✓ $\dfrac{\text{Received SYN packets}}{\text{Received TCP packets except SYN packets}}$ **[*Parameter B*]**

LSAD system applies EWMA method into both parameters to find change. This testing approach is similar to the algorithm as we mentioned in above section 2.1. To find the change of each Parameter, we used EWMA like followings. From the equation of (2), we match the variables of equation (2) to our data. The x_i means both Parameters and λ means the parameter that controls how much current prediction is influenced by past observations. For Equation (4) and (5), we applied 20 into the target value μ_0, because we know that the received number of SYN packets in 10 ms does not exceed the 20 in most cases from our previous research [4]. For Parameter B, we chose the value larger than 0.2, because it does not exceed 0.2 in our previous research [4]. Based on above assumptions, we make equation (2) and (4) reality (because we are just interested in increasing traffic, we only consider ***USL***). Consequently, we just check whether EWMA results of test traffic traces are larger than ***USL***.

3 Simulation and Results

To evaluate and validate the LSAD system, we have made trace driven simulation experiments. We have collected traces from ***E*** Research Institute. Our simulation program is written in C language and matlab script language and running on Linux platform and Matlab program.

3.1 Traffic Traces

For this analysis, we have used traces collected on ***E*** Research Institute in Korea. These traces were taken on a 150 Megabit Ethernet connecting ***E*** Research Institute to the Internet. We think there is only few malicious packets in our traces, because its internal network is protected by high performance IDS (Intrusion Detection System) and Firewall. We also made attack traffic by IXIA traffic generator. We made 4 SYN flooding attack traces with changing sending rate from 500 to 1200. And our attack traces have 4 target victims.

3.2 Detect SYN Flooding Attack

To detect SYN flooding Attack, we have applied proposed EWMA approach on all the normal traffic traces. Figure 1 and Figure 2 represent the normal traffic behavior for captured normal network. The test statistics, EWMA results of each parameter, for all traces are plotted in following Figures. In Figure 1, EWMA test results of Parameter A are represented and EWMA results of Parameter B, are shown in Figure 2. We selected λ as 0.45 and L (the width of control limit) as 4 in Equation (4) and (5). And, we chose μ_0 as 25 for Parameter A and 0.25 for Parameter B. Because our previous research [4] showed that the received SYN number in every 10ms does not exceed 20 and ratio value does not exceed 0.2 (we give μ_0 a margin – 5 and 0.5 to each parameter - to alleviate false-positive).

We also applied our proposed scheme on the attack traces. The simulation results are plotted in Figure 3, showing that the EWMA results exceed the flooding threshold "***USL***" for both Parameters at attack time. The test values suddenly increase when the SYN flooding attack comes about. Once the flooding attack is detected, LSAD system can send alarm to other security appliance or security administrator. At this point, we have to think about other important issue of detection time. In some sense, the detection time becomes another question, because it can affect to the performance of defense system. If detection system did not find SYN flooding attack for a long time, it could not protect victims from the attack (it was already damaged by attack). Because of this, defending system has to detect attack as soon as possible. LSAD finds attack very quickly, because our proposed scheme is very sensitive to abrupt change.

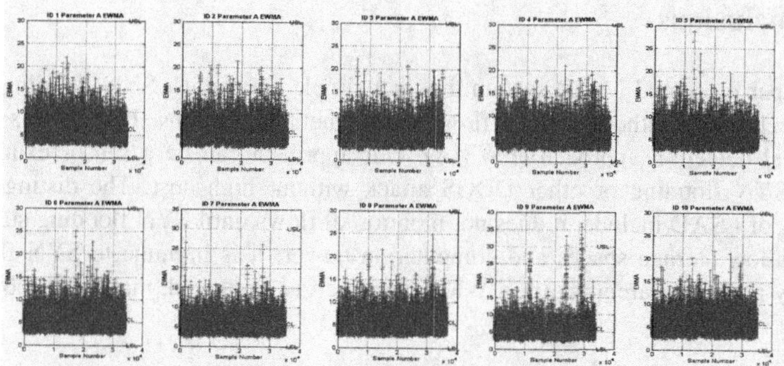

Fig. 1. EWMA test results of Parameter A (Normal Traffic)

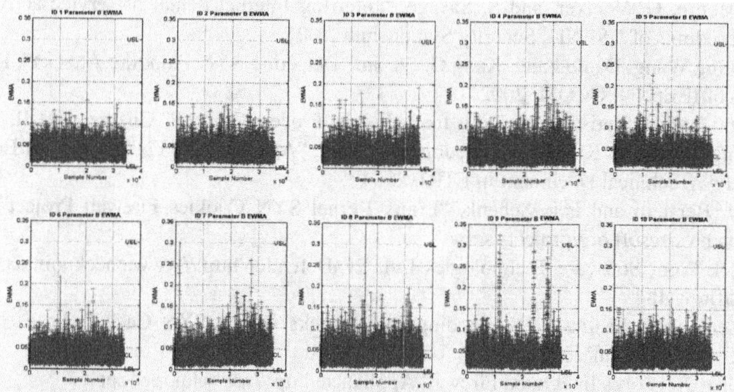

Fig. 2. EWMA test results of Parameter B (Normal Traffic)

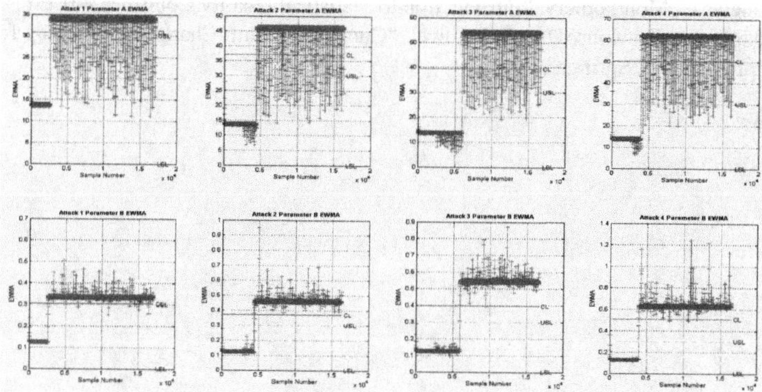

Fig. 3. EWMA test results of Parameter A(top) and B(bottom) (Attack Traffic)

4 Conclusions

This paper presented LSAD system that is a simple and robust SYN flooding detection mechanism without serious flow management algorithms. LSAD uses simple statistical detection approach (EWMA). Our approach can be a sensor example to detect SYN flooding or other DDOS attack without high cost. The distinguishing features of LSAD include, it does not monitor all flows until SYN flooding starts and requires low storage spaces and computation power; it is immune to SYN flooding itself by its simple architecture; EWMA approach is employed, making it robust and simple.

References

1. D. Moore, G. Voelker, and S. Savage, "Inferring Internet denial of service activity", In Proceedings of USENIX Security Symposium, 2001
2. Haining Wang, Danlu Zang, Kang G. Sh in, "Detecting SYN Flooding Attacks", Proceedings of IEEE INFOCOM, 2002
3. David Drain, "Statistical Methods for Industrial Process Control", Chapman &Hall, 1997
4. Seung-won Shin, Ki-young Kim, Jong-soo Jang, "Analysis of SYN Traffic: An Empirical Study", Technical Document in ETRI, 2004
5. D. J. Berstein and Eric Schenk, "Linux Kernel SYN Cookies Firewall Project", http://www.bronzesoft.org/projects/scfw
6. Check Point Software Technologies Ltd. SynDefender http://www.checkpoint.com/products/firewall-1
7. J. Lemon, "Resisting SYN Flooding Dos Attacks with a SYN Cache", Proceedings of USENIX BSDCon'2002, 2002
8. Juniper Networks Integrated Firewall Appliance, http://www.juniper.net
9. C. L. Schuba, I. V. Krsul, M. G. Kuhn, E. H. Spafford, A. Sundaram and D. Zmboni, "Analysis of a Denial of Service Attack on TCP", Proceedings of IEEE Symposium on Security and Privacy, 1997
10. Douglas C. Montgomery, "Introduction to Statistical Quality Control", WILEY, 2001
11. Douglas M. Hawkins, David H. Olwel, "Cumulative Sum Charts and Charting for Quality Improvement", Springer, 1998

UGSP: Secure Key Establishment Protocol for Ad-Hoc Networks*

Neelima Arora[1] and R.K. Shyamasundar[2]

[1] Currently at: Intel Technology Pvt. Ltd, India
neel@iitbombay.org
[2] School of Technology and Computer Science, Tata Institute of Fundamental Research, Mumbai, India
shyam@tcs.tifr.res.in

Abstract. In this paper, we propose a secure key establishment protocol, called UGSP, for wireless ad-hoc networks using tamper proof hardware (TPH). UGSP results in creating a secure communication channel between two nodes without any third party involvement and hence is suitable for ad-hoc networks. UGSP is robust to man-in-the-middle attack, passive eavesdropping, active impersonation attacks ensuring source authentication, data confidentiality and data integrity for communication. The system is amenable to dynamic addition of new members. A comparative evaluation of UGSP with other approaches along with issues of scalability and cost-effectiveness are discussed.

1 Introduction

The salient features of ad-hoc networks pose both challenges and opportunities in achieving security goals characterized by attributes like availability, confidentiality, integrity, source authentication and nonrepudiation [13]. Nodes, roaming in hostile environment (e.g., a battlefield) with relatively poor physical protection, have non-negligible probability of being compromised. Therefore, we should not only consider malicious attacks from outside a network, but also take into account the attacks launched from within the network by compromised nodes.

One of the largely investigated areas of ad-hoc network security research is devoted to secure routing protocols [11]. However, most of the routing schemes known neglect the crucial challenge in ad-hoc security: key establishment and key distribution. Protocols such as Ariadne[3], SPINS[9], TESLA[10], SEAD [4] and SRP [8] all assume the pre-existence and pre-sharing of secret and/or public keys for all the nodes. Recently some attempts for key distribution in ad-hoc networks have been proposed [13, 6, 12, 2] using variants of threshold certificates and trust. However, these do not address resource limitations of devices and

* The work was done under the Futuristics Technologies: Computer and Network sponsored by Ministry of Information Technology, New Delhi, India. The authors thank Prof A. Perrig (CMU) for many suggestions.

R.K. Ghosh and H. Mohanty (Eds.): ICDCIT 2004, LNCS 3347, pp. 391–399, 2004.

further, it must be noted that while threshold cryptography is attractive, it is expensive. Resurrecting Duckling paradigm [12] proposed for ubiquitous computing environment requires different types of hardware, master-slave notions and needs close proximity of the entities. While the technique [2] is interesting, it needs experimental validation.

Our aim is to arrive at a peer to peer protocol, for communication among a dynamic user group (DUG), that is resilient against the above mentioned attacks while maintaining confidentiality, integrity and authenticity. Even if the node gets compromised, it should not allow the attacker to gain access to any useful secret of the network. Typical examples of DUG include employees of a company, mobile cell-phone users of a particular network etc. Our protocol referred to as UGSP (User Group Security Protocol) uses a cheap uniform TPH, and overcomes a majority of the deficiencies mentioned above.

Rest of the paper is organized as follows: section 2 describes the structure of DUG and system architecture for UGSP followed by UGSP protocol in section 3. Security and performance analysis are provided in section 4 and 5 respectively. The paper concludes with section 6.

2 System Architecture for UGSP

One of the characteristics of ad-hoc networks is that the topology and membership is dynamic. In view of this, we shall first show how dynamic groups can be constructed and communication can be achieved among them in a secure way. Such a scenario is general and can overcome the drawback of explicit distribution of keys a priori. We shall call a typical dynamic group to be user group (UG) that can be authenticated using some information. To achieve secure communication among members of UG, we assume the following characteristics:

1. GroupName (GN): Each group will have a GroupName, it will be used by the user to access the right authentication information at the time of communication.
2. Group Access Code (GAC): For each UG, there will be a GAC and will be used during imprinting users of the group and for authentication at the time of communication.
3. UG owner: has the following functions: (a) assign a GAC for the UG, call it $My - GAC$ ($MGAC$), (b) assign a GroupName for the UG, and (c) dynamically imprint nodes that want to be a part of UG. Any node can create its own group and be the owner. After the nodes are imprinted by the UG owner node, that node comes on par with any other node in the UG and has no special privilege during communication.

The structure of TPH for UGSP shown in Fig. 1 has:

1. Access Module: contains (i) an universally unique, unalterable *id*, (ii) write only memory for hardware access code (HAC) (attempt to overwrite the

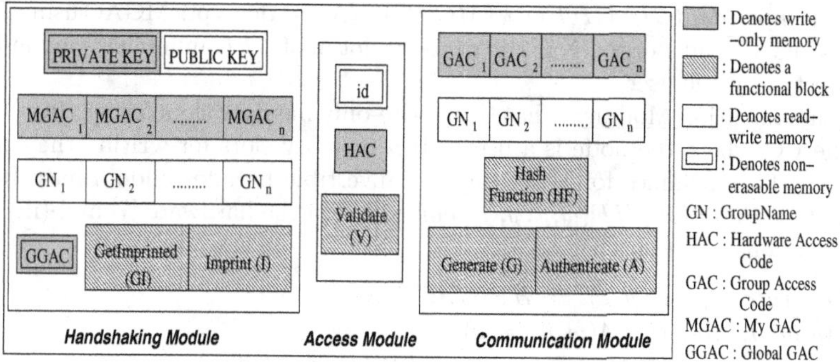

Fig. 1. TPH Hardware for UGSP Node

HAC will reset all other memory locations to $null$), and function $Validate$, V, for local authentication of the user with the hardware. If HAC' is the value given by the user, then

$V(HAC') = \ if\ HAC' \ = \ HAC\ then\ TRUE\ elseFALSE$

Only after the user correctly enters the HAC, access to hardware is granted; otherwise the TPH will remain in locked state.

2. Handshaking Module: (i) has n write-only memory slots for writing My-GAC $(MGAC)$ for the UG where the node is the owner, (ii) has n memory slots for writing the corresponding GroupNames for UGs. The reason that we store GN on TPH does not enhance security but makes the data more portable, (iii) has a write-only memory slot where Global-GAC $(GGAC)$ will be written by the manufacturer of the TPH (same for all the hardware pieces), and (iv) has memory for private key (PRK) that is not accessible to others, and has Memory slot for the corresponding public key (PUK) (these two values are unique for all the hardware pieces and will be determined by the manufacturer of the hardware). The module realizes two functions:

(i) $Imprint(I)$: When invoked, user will be asked whether he wants to set up a new UG or imprint the other node for any of the existing UGs. In case of a new UG, the function prompts the user to input a $MGAC$ value and a GroupName for the group. The value is then encrypted using the other node's public key and sent to the other node. The $MGAC$ and GroupName are then written in their memory slots in this module. If UG already exists, the user inputs GroupName, the corresponding $MGAC$ is encrypted and sent. That is,
If node i creates a new UG and adds node j as a member:

$Imprint(MGAC, GN, PUK(j)) \ =$
$HF(GGAC, id(i), E_{PUK}(MGAC), GN), E_{PUK}(MGAC), GN$

If node i already owns a UG and adds node j as a member:

$Imprint(GN, PUK(j)) =$
$HF(GGAC, id(i), E_{PUK}(MGAC), GN), E_{PUK}(MGAC), GN$

(ii) GetImprinted(GI): $GI(E_{PUK}(MGAC), GN, m)$ decrypts MGAC using PRK, writes MGAC and stores GN in the memory slot m of the communication module as directed by the user.
3. Communication Module: It has (i) n write-only memory slots for writing GAC for the UG where the node is a user, (ii) n memory slots for writing the corresponding GroupNames for UGs, (iii) non invertible pseudo random hash function, $HashFunction$, $HF(w, x, y, z)$, embedded in the hardware [7] and (iii) has two functions:

(i) $\underline{Generate(G)}: \; G(y, z) \;=\; HF(GAC, id, y, z)$
(ii) $\underline{Authenticate(A)}: \; A(w, id', y, z) \;=$
$\quad if\ w \;=\; HF(GAC, id', y, z)\ then\ TRUE\ else\ FALSE$

The hardware is tamper resistant in the following way: (i) Codes of functions (GI, I, V, HF, G, A) and id cannot be accessed directly, and (ii) inputs coming from write-only memory to hardware functions are hidden and cannot be changed during the evaluation.

3 UGSP: User Group Security Protocol

The user will carry the TPH with him as a token (just as a ATM user carries ATM card with him). In order to use the hardware, the user will be required to interface it with his mobile device and to enter the HAC correctly, which will be locally authenticated within the hardware. Only after successful authentication, hardware can be used subsequently.

Notation:

- *id(j)* denotes the identity of node j, GN refers to the GroupName of the UG in context, N denotes the *nonce*, K_{sy} denotes the symmetric session key established between the pair of communicating nodes and $(M_1 \;, M_2)$ denotes concatenation of M_1 with M_2.
- *HF(w,x,y,z)*referred to as MAC denotes the pseudo random hash function in the TPH, having four input parameters w, x, y, z.
- PUK, PRK are hard coded public and private keys of the node from *Handshaking Module*; $E_{K_j}(N)$ denotes N encrypted with K_j.

Operational Steps: The protocol consists of two phases. Phase I corresponds to bootstrapping of valid nodes while Phase II is session specific and happens when nodes want to communicate with each other.

Phase I (Network formation): In Step 1, user inputs the HAC when prompted to do so, which will be compared with the HAC stored on the TPH. In Step 2, the communicating nodes, which have been authenticated in step 1, will exchange RSA public keys. Nodes use function G to generate the packet for transmitting and every node on receiving the data invokes function A to evaluate the authenticity of the packet against id of the sender node, GAC, and data received. If that fails, the receiver aborts; otherwise it proceeds to the next step (cf. Fig. 3).

Phase II (Communication among UG): will be invoked when any node wants to communicate with some other node in the network. During step 3, the two communicating nodes establish a symmetric key. Directly using the private-public key pair will be bandwidth and computation expensive. Hence, we establish a symmetric key which ensures the establishment of a secure channel between two nodes. The trasitions are as shown in Fig. 5.

The following scenarios capture the functions of UGSP:

1. Creating a new UG and adding members: As already mentioned, when two nodes want to communicate they first check (using GroupName) whether they are already a part of the same UG or one of the nodes own an UG and wants to add the other node. If not, one of the nodes creates a new UG and imprints the other node using function I. Packet description and algorithm is given in Figure 2 and 4. Node i is creating a new UG and is adding a new member j to the UG. In Step 1, both users authenticate to the hardware using valid HAC. This can be thought of as if the smart card PIN is stored on the smart card and which can only be read by the smart card reading machine. Hence, user authentication can be done by a standalone ad-hoc smart card machine, not connected to the bank's back-end server, by comparing the PIN stored on the card with the PIN entered by the user. In Step 2, node j sends his PUK to node i. Node i validates the authenticity of PUK by invoking the function A in its hardware. Node i is able to generate the same MAC using his hardware because he has the same GGAC in his *Handshake Module*. After validation, i creates a new UG by invoking function I and assigning a GroupName and a $MGAC$ to the UG. Function I encrypts $MGAC$ with PUK of node j, generates MAC of the data and sends it across. Node j now authenticates the MAC, and passes the encrypted $MGAC$ to its GI function, which decrypts $MGAC$ and writes it to the *Communication Module* of the hardware along with the GroupName. Thus, node j is imprinted dynamically.

2. Joining an already existing UG: The packet and protocol description will be the same as given in Figure 2 and 4. The only difference will be that in this no new UG is created.

3. Communication among members of a UG: Here, node i is the sender and node j is the receiver. GAC for the UG is matched with various GACs by the GroupName. After one of the nodes has imprinted the other node dynamically, the communication takes place as described in Phase II (cf. Fig. 5).

Most previous work on secure ad-hoc network relies on asymmetric cryptography for establishing security parameters every time. However, computing such signatures on resource-constrained nodes is expensive and hence, may not be the ideal solution. A protocol with shared key is the most generic option, as it is not expensive both in terms of bandwidth and computation. UGSP uses the Public Key operations in a limited way as compared to other protocols.

4 Security Analysis

Creating a UG is a local operation between the owner and the TPH, protected by *HAC*. Thus, we analyze in detail the security properties of UGSP while adding a user and during communication between two nodes.

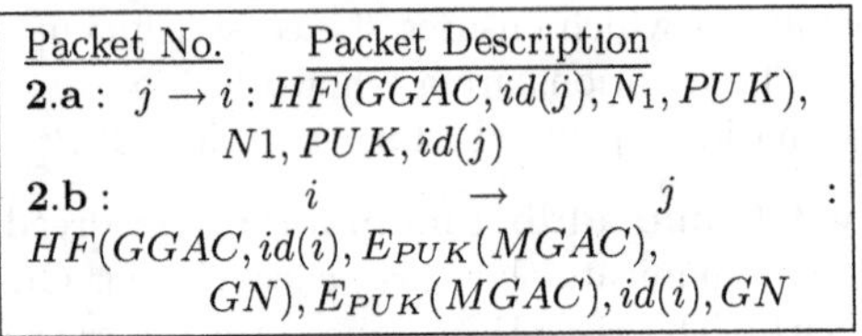

Packet No.	Packet Description
2.a :	$j \rightarrow i : HF(GGAC, id(j), N_1, PUK), N1, PUK, id(j)$
2.b :	$i \rightarrow j : HF(GGAC, id(i), E_{PUK}(MGAC), GN), E_{PUK}(MGAC), id(i), GN$

Fig. 2. Description of packets when Node i is imprinting Node j

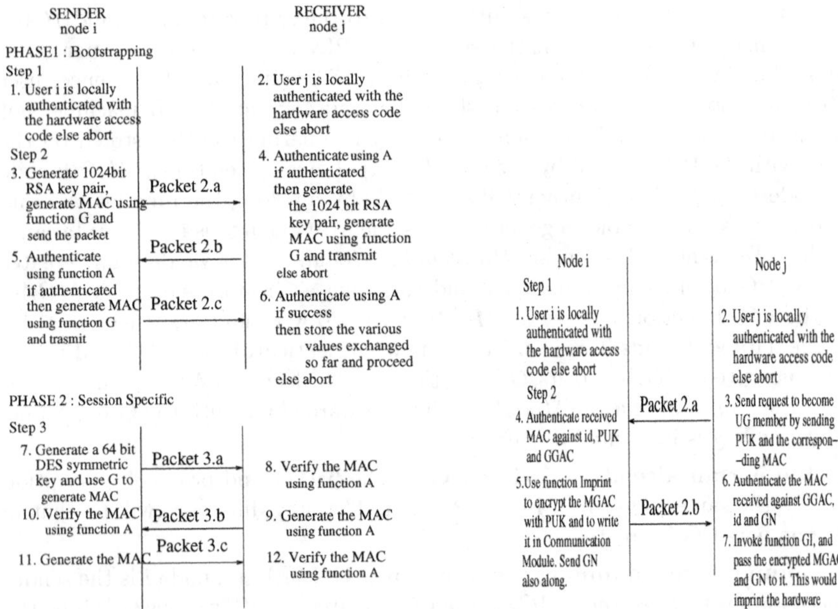

Fig. 3. Communication Between Nodes (cf. labels to Fig. 5)

Fig. 4. Imprinting algorithm at nodes (Packets as in Fig. 2)

Security while adding a user: While adding an user to any UG, GGAC and GAC of the UG are both needed; otherwise a valid MAC in packet 2.b (refer Figure 4) cannot be formed and hence, will be rejected by the *GI* function of the

PHASE I : Bootstrapping
Step 2 : exchange public keys

2.a : $i \rightarrow j : HF(GAC, id(i), N_1, K_i), N_1, K_i, id(i), GN$
2.b : $j \rightarrow i : HF(GAC, id(j), E_{K_i}(N_1), K_j), N_2, K_j, id(j)$
2.c : $i \rightarrow j : HF(GAC, id(i), E_{K_j}(N_2), *)$

PHASE II : Session specific
Step 3 : establish a shared symmetric key using the established public key
3.a : $i \rightarrow j : HF(GAC, id(i), N_3, E_{K_j}(K_{sy})), N_3, E_{K_j}(K_{sy})$
3.b : $j \rightarrow i : HF(GAC, id(j), E_{K_{sy}}(N_3), E_{K_i}(K_{sy}))$
3.c : $i \rightarrow j : HF(GAC, id(i), E_{K_{sy}}(id(i)), *)$

Fig. 5. Communication between i & j

node. GAC is known only to the UG owner and hence will not be accessible to the attacker even from a compromised UG member. *GGAC* is written in the write-only memory, and hence, cannot be known outside the TPH. Generating hash digest (MAC) with *GGAC* as a common input at both the nodes is equivalent to making the hash function unknown – similar to those envisaged in [1].

Security while imprinting: In this case, when the attacker gets the packet during the transition 2.b (cf. Fig. 4),*MGAC* cannot be decrypted as *PRK* is not known outside the TPH (decryption happens inside *GI*). Thus, an adversary cannot get the *GAC* of the UG.

Security while communication

1. Attack from outside the network: A node outside the network means that it does not have the TPH token configured with the *GAC* for that group. An attacker node from outside the network will generate a MAC corresponding to transition packet 2.a (cf. Fig. 3), that cannot be authenticated at receiving node due to the non-availability of *GAC* for the UG. If the attacker is at receiving end then it will fail to authenticate itself to the sender as it fails to form a valid *Packet 2.b* (cf. Fig. 3) due to a different *GAC*.

2. Attack from a compromised node: The attacker is assumed to have the TPH configured with the group access code for that group. Here, two level of attacks are possible:
(i) Attacker does not know the HAC: The authentication will fail during Step 1 (cf. Fig. 3). Hence, the attacker will not be able to use the hardware token. While if the attacker tries to overwrite the *HAC*, the other authentication information (such as *GGAC* and *GAC*s, *PRK* etc.) are reset to *null* (property of TPH) and hence, earlier analysis holds. *(ii) Attacker knows the HAC:*The attacker

can send valid packets to the network, but with his own *id*. It cannot actively impersonate any other node in the network (because of the properties of G). The attacker cannot simulate the hardware behavior and try to pass any other *id* to the model, as GAC is not known outside TPH. Thus, software simulation of the TPH will also not work. When nodes realize that some node is compromised then they can block that particular node from any further communication as the compromised node can participate in communication using its own identity.

Note that as compared to a PKI based system, when the node gets compromised, the attacker could get the keys and will be able to actively impersonate the user. Even though the keys may be password protected but should be accessible through brute-force methods (such as bit by bit reading of the hard disk), to which the TPH is resistant.

5 Performance Analysis

Scalability: In UGSP, the user could get an imprinted TPH from a UG owner (an employee could get it from his company, or buy a blank TPH from the market configured with HAC). In either case a user can either become a member of other groups or initiate his own group. Under UGSP, nodes can securely communicate if they are members of the same UG. If not, one of the nodes can imprint the other node to become part of the same UG. After this, the key establishment and data transfer can be initiated as per the ad-hoc network requirements. The nodes can form a communication network with other nodes in DUG securely without having to maintain either a database or a trusted third party; also, no other authentication is needed for data transfer. Thus, UGSP is suitable for ad-hoc wireless network security and is quite scalable.

Let us analyze UGSP with a PKI-based security from a scalability perspective. Under PKI each node will have a public-private key pair from a PKI and uses the certificate for authentication. To verify a certificate the node has to either go to a trusted third party (which is not possible in ad-hoc network) or maintain its own database of public keys of the other nodes (security is not guaranteed). The requirement of on-line authentication is not only costly but also infeasible for ad-hoc networks.

Cost-effective Implementation: UGSP has been implemented using *iButton* [5] which is off-the-shelf chip enclosed in a 16mm stainless steel costing less than ten dollars in retail. It has an on-board 512-bit SHA-1 engine that can compute 160-bit MACs in less than 0.0005 seconds as compared to 0.5 seconds for a typical micro-controller. *iButton* can be interfaced with a host system via serial/parallel port or USB. It is tamper proof, quite rugged and can be mounted virtually anywhere either indoor or outdoor. Our protocol has been tested with *iButton*. Mobility of the nodes was also emulated and multi-hop routing scenarios were evaluated against performance and energy cost. Note that, *iButton* offers the functionality of write-only memory, laser etched *id* and function G- more than that needed for UGSP. To provide a cheaper solution, we have completed the design of the required TPH and are in the process of testing it on a FPGA board.

6 Conclusion

To sum up, the proposed UGSP is resilient to attacks in ad-hoc networks forming a DUG. UGSP is based on mutual authentication rather than only one sided. The protocol provides dual security as we are using a TPH token and access code for using the TPH. Thus, even if the configured hardware token is stolen, an attacker cannot use the token without knowing HAC. Thus, it achieves security using the paradigm of *"Something you know, and something you get"* providing dual security to the network. The concept is similar to that used in ATMs (a combination of card and PIN is required to access the account). Once a secure communication channel is established among nodes, any of the existing protocols, for instance TESLA [10], can be used to run the application. Tamper proof nature of the hardware also makes UGSP secure against brute force attacks on compromised nodes. Based upon our experience of using the prototype, we have found that implementation of UGSP can be done in cost-effective way. UGSP is scalable and robust to addition of new members in the User Group.

References

1. M. Bellare, R. Canetti, H. Krawczyk, *Keyed Hash Functions and Message Authentication*, Proc. of Crypto, LNCS 1109, pp. 1-15, 1996.
2. S. Capkun, J-P. Hubaux, L. Buttyan, *Mobility Helps Security in Ad Hoc Networks*, ACM MobiHoc 2003.
3. Y.C. Hu, A. Perrig, D.B. Johnson, *Ariadne: A Secure On-Demand Routing Protocol for Ad Hoc Networks*, Mobicom, 2002.
4. Y.C. Hu, D. Johnson, A. Perrig, *SEAD: Secure Efficient Distance Vector Routing for Mobile Wireless Ad Hoc Networks*, IEEE Workshop on Mobile Computing Systems and Applications, June 2002.
5. iButton Details: *www.ibutton.com.*
6. A. Khalili, W. Arbaugh, *Toward Secure Key Distribution in Truly Ad-Hoc Networks*, IEEE Workshop on Security and Assurance in Ad-Hoc Networks, 2003
7. L. Lamport, *Password Authentication with Insecure Communication*, CACM, 24, pp. 770-771, 1981.
8. P. Papadimitratos, Z. Haas, *Secure Routing for Mobile Adhoc Networks*, Communication Networks and Distributed Systems Modeling and Simulation Conference, Jan 2002.
9. A. Perrig, R. Szewczyk, J.D. Tygar, V. Wen, D.E. Culler, *SPINS: Security Protocols for Sensor Networks*, Wireless Networks, 2002.
10. A. Perrig, R. Canetti, J.D. Tygar, D. Song *TESLA Broadcast Authentication Protocol*, RSA Cryptobytes, 2002.
11. E. M. Royer, C. K. Toh, *A Review of Current Routing Protocols for Ad Hoc Mobile Wireless Networks*, IEEE Pers. Comm., Apr. 1999.
12. F. Stajano, R. Anderson, *Resurrecting Duckling: Security Issues for Ad-hoc Wireless Networks*, 3rd AT & T Software Symp., Oct. 1999.
13. L. Zhou, Z. Haas, *Securing Ad Hoc Networks*, IEEE Networks, 13(6), 1999.

Tracing Attackers with Deterministic Edge Router Marking (DERM)

Shravan K Rayanchu[1] and Gautam Barua[2]

[1] Samsung India Software Operations,
Bangalore 560052, India
shravan.kr@samsung.com

[2] Dept. of CSE, IIT Guwahati,
Guwahati 781039, India
gb@iitg.ernet.in

Abstract. Tracing the attackers in a distributed denial-of-service (DDoS) attack is particularly difficult since attackers spoof the source addresses. We present a novel approach to IP Traceback - Deterministic Edge Router Marking (DERM). The proposed scheme is scalable to thousands of attackers, is very simple to implement at the routers, has no bandwidth overhead and needs minimal processing and storage requirements at the victim. As each complete mark fits into a single packet, our scheme can also be used for per-packet filtering and as a congestion signature in a pushback protocol. The traceback procedure requires a small number of packets and can be performed during the post-mortem analysis of an attack. Only limited co-operation is required from Internet Service Providers (ISP). They do not have to reveal the topology of their internal networks.

1 Introduction

DDoS attacks are among one of the hardest security problems to address because they are simple to implement, hard to prevent, and difficult to trace. Ideally, the network traffic of an attack should include information identifying the sources. The Internet protocol (IP) specifies a header field in all packets that contains the source IP address, which would seem to allow for identifying every packet's origin. However, the lack of security features in TCP/IP specifications facilitates IP spoofing - the manipulation and falsification of the source address in the header. Thus, an attacker could generate offending IP packets that appear to have originated from almost anywhere. IP traceback methods provide the victim with the ability to identify the address of the true source of the packets causing a DoS attack. A perfect solution to this problem is complicated especially because of the use of zombies and reflectors [1]. The exact origin of the attack may never be revealed as even the MAC source addresses may be spoofed. Hence, the traceback schemes try to solve the more limited problem of *identifying the closest router(s) to the attacker(s)*.

R.K. Ghosh and H. Mohanty (Eds.): ICDCIT 2004, LNCS 3347, pp. 400–409, 2004.

2 Evaluation Metrics and Assumptions for Traceback Schemes

We now present some of the important evaluation metrics essential in comparing IP Traceback approaches. These were originally proposed in [2].

ISP Involvement: An ideal traceback scheme must be inserted with little infrastructure and operational changes and the actual traceback process must involve little or no burden on the ISP. *Number of attack packets needed for traceback:* Once the attack has been identified, the traceback scheme should require very few packets to identify the attacker. *Post-mortem Analysis:* It must be possible to initiate the traceback procedure and identify the attacker after the attack as the victim might not be in a position to perform the analysis during the attack. *Processing, Bandwidth and Memory requirements:* Processing and memory overhead on routers must be minimal for the practical deployment of the scheme. Since bandwidth is one of the bottlenecks during flooding attacks, the scheme must not introduce additional bandwidth overhead. *Ease of evasion:* It must be very difficult for an attacker who is aware of the scheme to orchestrate an attack that is untraceable. *Ability to handle major DDoS attacks:* This reflects how well a scheme can perform traceback under severe circumstances. An ideal scheme should be able to identify all the attackers involved. *Scalability:* An ideal scheme should be easily scalable.

Assumptions mentioned here are largely borrowed from the previous schemes [3, 4]. The following are the basic assumptions for DERM:

1) An attacker may generate any packet, 2) Attackers may be aware that they are being traced, 3) Packets may be lost or reordered, 4) An attack may consist of just a few packets, 5) Packets of an attack may take different routes, 6) Routers are both CPU and memory limited, 7) Routers are not compromised.

We first propose a basic scheme which we term Basic Deterministic Edge Router Marking (Basic DERM) and then improve the scheme by introducing multiple hash functions.

3 Basic Deterministic Edge Router Marking

The 16 bit packet ID field and the 1 bit RF in the IP header are used for marking packets.Each and every packet that enters the network is marked; this removes the problem of an attacker spoofing any mark. The packet is marked by the edge ingress router to which the source is connected. Every incoming packet is marked whereas outgoing packets are not marked.

3.1 Marking Procedure for Basic DERM

In order to identify an attacker, the victim needs to know the IP address of the attacker which is 32 bits long. But all we have is the 16 bit ID field and the 1 bit RF field. The problem with other packet marking schemes which try to construct the IP address of the attacker (or the router nearest to the attacker) in multiple packets is that the markings cannot be used for filtering purposes as the victim cannot make out anything from the information available in a single packet. Hence, we must try to convey the information about the IP address of the attacker in a single packet. Instead of marking the packets with the IP address of the attacker which is 32 bits long, it would suffice if we send a 16 bit representation of the IP address. Of course, this would mean that there might be some collisions. In Basic DERM, each incoming packet on the ingress router is marked with a 16 bit hash of its own IP address. The ID field is used for this purpose. The RF bit is kept aside as of now. The hash mark (HM(IP)) serves as the representation of the IP address of the edge router. It is assumed that the hash function HM is known to everyone including the DERM enabled routers, all the destinations which would utilize HM and the attackers. It is further assumed that HM is an ideal hash. An ideal hash function minimizes the number of collisions.

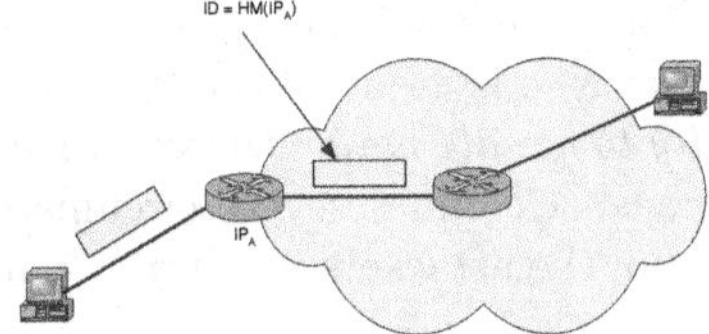

Fig. 1. Marking procedure for Basic DERM

3.2 Reconstruction by the Victim in Basic DERM

The victim has a table RecordTbl, each entry of which consists of the tuple $< HashMark, RECV\ bit, IngressAddList >$, where $HashMark$ is a possible hash mark and IngressAddList is the list of all ingress edge router addresses that have this hash mark. *RECV bit* is initialized to zero before the attack. This bit indicates whether the victim has received a particular HashMark. The reconstruction by the victim has two phases. One is the filtering phase and the other is the Attacker Identification phase. The filtering phase starts when the victim detects that it is under an attack. As with all the schemes, we assume that there is an intrusion detection system (IDS) which helps us identify the attack packets. Whenever an attack packet is identified, the HashMark of the packet is noted and the corresponding RECV bit in the RecordTbl is marked as 1.

Filtering Phase in Basic DERM: One of the aims of the traceback schemes is to aid the victim during the attack by helping it in filtering out the attack traffic. We note down the HashMarks in the RecordTbl for which the corresponding RECV bit is 1. These HashMarks can be used to identify the attack packets and to filter them. Thus, unlike other schemes, the victim itself can filter the packets without relying on the upstream routers to filter the traffic. Also wherever possible, the upstream routers can use these HashMarks to filter the traffic before the entire bandwidth at the victim is consumed. Protocols like Pushback [5] need some kind of a congestion signature which it uses to identify attack packets. In this case the HashMarks can be used as a congestion signature. Once an attack packet is identified, the Hashmark can be used to filter further attack packets which are now not sent to the IDS, whose load now decreases. The filtering simply consists of checking whether the RECV bit corresponding to the HashMark is 1. If so, the packet may be an attack packet and hence can be dropped. However, there may be collisions with legitimate packets which will also get dropped. These are called *false positives.*

Attacker Identification Phase in Basic DERM: In basic DERM, this involves noting the list of ingress IP addresses corresponding to each HashMark which has the RECV bit set to 1. This may result in many false positives as there will be more than one ingress address corresponding to each HashMark. It is however to be noted that only one packet from the attacker is enough to carry out the Attacker Identification Phase. This is one of the advantages of DERM against schemes like PPM[3].

3.3 Analysis

False positives during the Attacker Identification phase: Here we calculate the number of legitimate user IP addresses that we falsely identify as an attacker. Let M be the number of edge routers and d (=16) be the length of the HashMark. Let N be the number of attackers. If there is only one ingress address corresponding to each HashMark, then there will be no false positives because of the properties of the assumed ideal hash function HM. Hence, the rate of false positives is 0, when M is less than or equal to the number of possible HashMarks, 2^d. Suppose that M is greater than 2^d. The expected number of different HashMarks, $E(HashMarks)$ which have $RECVbit = 1$ after the Filtering phase can be thought of as the expected number of faces turning up on a 2^d sided die after N throws. This is a special case of the classical occupancy problem which is discussed in [7]. The expected number of different HashMarks is given by

$$E(HashMarks) = 2^d - 2^d(1 - 1/2^d)^N$$

Let the number of ingress addresses that match a particular HashMark be $N_d = M/2^d$. Thus the number of false positives would be

$$E(false\ positives) = (2^d - 2^d(1 - 1/2^d)^N) * N_d - N$$

False positives during the Filtering Phase: Here we calculate the number of legitimate user packets that might get discarded during the filtering phase, as a result of falsely identifying them as attackers. In Basic DERM, the number of false positives during the Filtering Phase is the same as the number of false positives during the Attacker identification Phase.

Storage requirements for RecordTbl: The amount of storage required for *IngressAddList* is $N_d * 32$ bits and one bit for storing the *RECV* bit. Hence, the total amount of storage required is $(N_d * 32 + 1) * 2^d$ bits.

4 Multiple Hash DERM

In order to reduce the false positives that arise while identifying attackers, we modify the scheme to use multiple hash functions of an IP address, HM_1, HM_2 .. HM_f. As before all these are assumed to be ideal hash functions. The 16 bit field now consists of a d bit HashMark and a log(f) bit Hash function identifier, where f is the number of Hash functions used. Hence, $d + log(f) = 16$.

4.1 Marking Procedure for Multiple Hash DERM

At startup, each DERM enabled router calculates f HashMarks by hashing its IP address with the functions HM_1, HM_2, .. HM_f. The router deterministically marks the packets with any one of these f HashMarks. The processing required for each packet would be limited to generating a small random number from 1 to f and then inserting the corresponding d bit HashMark in the packet along with the $log(f)$ bit hash function identifier.

4.2 Reconstruction by the Victim in Multiple Hash DERM

Instead of having a single *RecordTbl*, each victim must have f tables $RecordTbl_1$, $RecordTbl_2$, .. $RecordTbl_f$. Each of the tables will have as entries the tuple $< HashMark$, *RECV bit*, *IngressAddList* $>$ which have the same meaning as stated before. As before, the reconstruction will consist of two phases, the Filtering Phase and the Attacker Identification Phase.

Filtering Phase in Multiple Hash DERM: As already stated, we assume that there is an attack identifying algorithm that gives us the identified attack packets. Whenever the victim gets such a packet, the hash function identifier is noted and then the corresponding *RecordTbl* is identified. Then, the *RECV bit* corresponding to the HashMark in the packet is set to 1. These HashMarks are then used for aiding the victim in filtering the attack traffic. It is important to note that the number of false positives in this case would more than Basic DERM; in fact it would be multiplied by f times. This is because of the fact that during filtering the victim has to decide whether to drop the packet or not depending on the HashMark of the packet and nothing else. As the number of different HashMarks would now be multiplied by f, the false positives would also increase f times.

Attacker Identification Phase in Multiple Hash DERM: In this phase, the victim first collects all the ingress IP addresses in $RecordTbl_1$ for which the corresponding *RECV bit* is set to 1. Then it takes one IP address at a time and calculates HM_2, HM_3 .. HM_f for that IP address. Now if the *RECV* bits corresponding to the HashMarks in the respective *RecordTbls* are set i.e. if the *RECV bit* for $HashMark_2$ is set in $RecordTbl_2$, *RECV bit* for $HashMark_3$ is set in $RecordTbl_3$, .. *RECV bit* for $HashMark_f$ is set in $RecordTbl_f$, then that IP address is identified as the attacker's, else it is discarded. Because of these additional checks, the number of false positives now decrease.

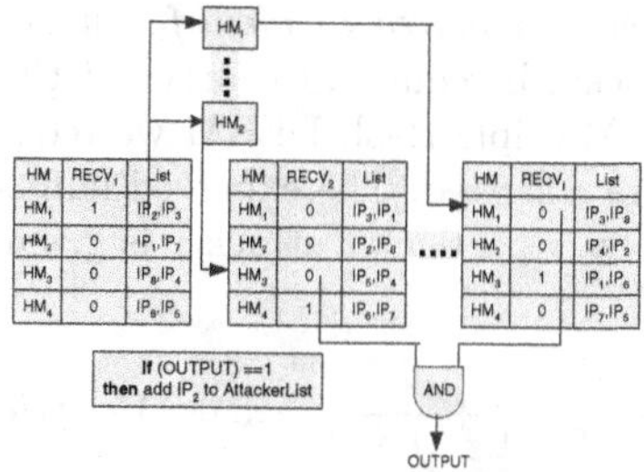

Fig. 2. Attacker Identification in Multiple Hash DERM

4.3 Analysis

False positives during the Attacker Identification phase: From the previous analysis, the expected number of false positives in *RecordTbl*$_1$ is:

$$E(false\ positives) = (2^d - 2^d(1 - 1/2^d)^N) * N_d - N$$

Consider *RecordTbl*$_2$, the expected number of different HashMarks which have *RECV bit* set to 1 for this table is:

$$E(HashMarks) = 2^d - 2^d(1 - 1/2^d)^N$$

Consider one of the false positives generated in *RecordTbl*$_1$. For this to still be a false positive it must match one of the above HashMarks. Thus the probability that HM_2 of this IP address will be accepted as a false positive after taking *RecordTbl*$_2$ into consideration is $E(HashMarks)/2^d$ Therefore, the probability that a particular false positive of *RecordTbl*$_1$ would still be a false positive after considering all the remaining $f - 1$ tables is:

$$(E(HashMarks)/2^d)^{f-1}$$

Hence, the number of false positives that arise while identifying the attacker is given by,

$$falsepos = ((E(HashMarks)N_d - N)(\frac{E(HashMarks)}{2^d})^{f-1}$$

Thus, the maximum number of attackers N_{MAX} (actually attacking networks) that we can afford such that, the number of false postives are less than 1% of N can be obtained by setting $falsepos$ to $0.01N$ and solving for N.

False Positives During the Filtering Phase: The number of false positives during the filtering phase of Multiple Hash DERM would simply be f times the number of false positives during the filtering phase of Basic DERM: $(E(HashMarks) * N_d - N) * f$.

Storage Requirements for the Tables: Storage requirements would be simply be f times the storage required for each table i.e. $((N_d * 32) + 1 + d) * 2^d * f$ bits.

Expected number of packets required to identify an attacker: In case of Basic DERM, only a single packet is required to carry out the Attacker Identification procedure. However, in Multiple Hash DERM we require that the HashMarks of all the f functions are collected. The expected number of packets $E(f)$ that are required to be sent by a particular attacker is given by a Coupon Collector problem discussed in [7]:

$$E(f) = f(\frac{1}{f} + \frac{1}{f-1} + \frac{1}{f-2} + ... + 1) \approx f(log(f) + 0.577)$$

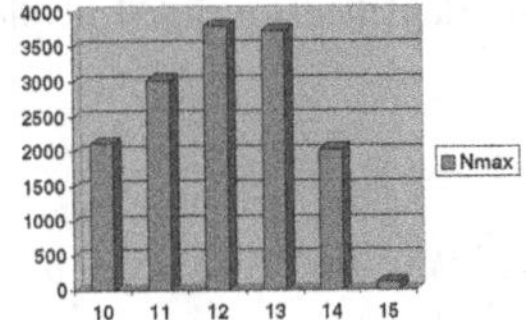

Fig. 3. Plot of N_{MAX} against d for $M = 2^{17}$

Figure 3 shows the plot of the maximum number of attackers N_{MAX} that we can afford against the length of the HashMark d. If we assume that there can be 128,000 ingress edge router addresses, then the maximum value of $N_{MAX} = 3800$ occurs when $d = 12$ (and so there are 16 hash functions). The storage requirement at the victim end for this value of d is found to be 8 MB and the expected number of packets required to be sent by an attacker for it to be identified, $E(f)$, is found to be 54. This shows that the algorithm can handle a large number of attackers with reasonable space and time requirements. The identification of attackers can also be done with a relatively small number of packets.

On Low Volume Attacks

As stated earlier, Multiple Hash DERM requires only $E(f)$ number of packets to get all the f HashMarks of the attacker. In this section we discuss how DERM fares for attacks constituting less than $E(f)$ packets. Let N be the number of attackers and let each attacker send m packets, where $m \leq E(f)$. Now, the expected number of different HashMarks that the victim would receive from a particular attacker is given by,

$$f' = f(1 - (1 - \frac{1}{f})^m)$$

The expected number of different HashMarks that have $RECV$ set to 1 in each RecordTbl is,

$$E(HashMarks) = 2^d(1 - (1 - \frac{1}{2^d})^{\frac{f'N}{f}})$$

In order to identify the attackers, we carry out the attacker identification procedure as before. Since all the f HashMarks are not received, we cannot identify the attackers by checking if the corresponding $RECV$ bit is set to one in the remaining $f-1$ RecordTbls. Instead, we identify the attackers by checking if the $RECV$ bit is set in atleast $f'-1$ RecordTbls. However, this would result in the increase of false positives. The number of false positives is given by,

$$(E(HashMarks) * N_d - N)\left(\frac{E(HashMarks)}{2^d}\right)^{f'-1}$$

5 Related Work and Comparison

5.1 The Pushback Protocol

The main idea behind the pushback protocol [5] is that if routers can detect packets belonging to an attack, they can then drop only those packets and thus the DDoS problem would be solved. Bad traffic is characterized by an *attack signature* which we strive to identify; what can be really identified is the *congestion signature*, which is the set of properties of a subset of traffic identified as causing problems. The authors in [8] use the destination address (victim's address) as the congestion signature. Thus even legitimate traffic destined for the victim is automatically dropped. One of the advantages of DERM is that it can be used as an effective congestion signature in the pushback protocol.

5.2 Packet Marking Schemes

In these schemes, basically some traceback data is inserted in each packet so that a victim can use this information to identify the attacker. To be effective, packet marking should not increase a packets' size. Furthermore, packet-marking methodologies must be secure enough to prevent attackers from generating false markings.

Probabilistic Packet Marking (PPM): In this scheme [3], the routers enroute probabilistically mark packets. As with DERM, the 16 bit ID field in the IP header is used for this purpose. Partial address information of the edges of a router are marked. A victim reconstructs the attack path with these marked packets. There are many advantages of DERM over PPM. The number of packets required in DERM in order to identify the attacker is much less (1 packet for Basic DERM and $E(f)$ packets for Multiple Hash DERM) as compared to PPM which requires a large number of packets. In PPM, the victim can reconstruct the path to the attacker based on multiple packet markings, but there is no guarantee that an individual packet will contain a marking that can identify an attacker. One of the major disadvantages of PPM is *Mark Spoofing*. If an attacker injects a packet with erroneous information and no router on the path marks the packet, then the spoofed marks from the attacker would also reach the victim.

Deterministic Packet Marking (DPM): In DPM ([4, 9]), only the edge routers participate in the marking procedure. As in DERM, interfaces are used as atomic units of traceback. DPM tries to construct the ingress address of the router closest to the source by fragmenting the IP address and sending it in two packets. The ID field is used to carry one half of an IP address and the RF bit is used to denote whether it is the first half or the second half of the IP address. A hash of the IP address is also sent along with the fragmented IP address to aid the victim in the reassembly procedure. Constructing an IP address from fragments would require trying out all the possible permutations. This results in a high number of false positives while assembling the fragments, especially in the case of a DDoS attack where multiple fragments from multiple attackers are collected. Per-packet filtering is not possible in DPM.

Pi and StackPi : Path Identification Mechanisms: In these schemes ([10, 6]), each packet is marked deterministically by the enroute routers. The StackPi mark created by a router is a 2 *bit* message digest of the concatenation of the IP addresses of the previous router and the current router. Only the last eight marks ($16/2 = 8$) made by the routers along the path reach the destination. In any case, the packets travelling along the same path will have the same marking so that the victim needs only to identify the StackPi marks of the attack packets and filter out all further packets with the same marking. As multiple routes may exist from a source to a destination, multiple sets of marks will have to be handled. All routers need to participate in the scheme rather than only edge routers and this is a restriction. As is the case with StackPi, DERM also requires constructing a table (RecordTbl) which consists of mapping the HashMarks with the IP addresses. This task is much easier in DERM as we have to collect the edge router IP addresses and simply hash them to get the corresponding HashMarks. Also, since these marks are only dependent on the edge routers we can have the table constructed at a particular location and distribute them. But in StackPi, the marks from a particular source will be different for two different hosts. Hence, each host has to construct its own table. Moreover, in StackPi we are dealing with addresses of hosts (not edge routers) which will be much more difficult to maintain.

6 Conclusion and Future work

In this paper, we have presented Deterministic Edge Router Marking (DERM), a technique to defend against DDoS attacks. The marking procedure for the routers is simple and can easily be implemented. The processing overhead at the victim during reconstruction is also very little. The reconstruction by a victim is done in two phases, a filtering phase and an attacker identification phase. The filtering phase involves setting a flag in a table based on marks in incoming packets to help identify attack traffic and the using of these marks for filtering the attack traffic. The Attacker Identification Phase consists of noting down the IP addresses of ingress packets and checking them against filter table entries to see whether the corresponding flag bits are set to 1. Analysis shows that about 3800 attackers can be handled with less than 1% false positives. This compares favourably with other known techniques and where scaling is a major issue. The storage requirements on the victim side are not very high. The expected number of packets required to identify an attacker is also small. Further work involves dealing with reflector attacks, where victim sites are used to *reflect* attack packets to camouflage the actual sources. The issue of compatibility of the scheme with IP fragmentation is another task for the future.

References

1. Paxson, V.: An Analysis of Using Reflectors for Distributed Denial-of-Service Attacks. Computer Communication Review 31(3) (2001)
2. Belenky, A., Ansari, N.: On IP Traceback. IEEE Communications Magazine 41(7) (2003) 142–153
3. Savage, S., Karlin, A.: Practical Network Support for IP Traceback. ACM SIGCOMM (2000) 295–306
4. Belenky, A., Ansari, N.: IP Traceback with Deterministic Packet Marking. IEEE Communication Letters, 7, (2003)
5. Ioannidis, J., Bellovin, S.M.: Implementing Pushback: Router-based Defense against DDoS Attacks. Proceedings of the Symposium on NDSS 2002, San Diego, CA. (2002)
6. Yaar, A., Perrig, A., Song, D.: StackPi: A New Defense Mechanism against IP Spoofing and DDoS Attacks. Technical Report, Carnegie Mellon University (2003)
7. Feller, W.: An Introduction to Probability Theory and Its Applications (2nd edition). Vol 1 (1966)
8. Mahajan, R., et. al: Controlling High Bandwidth Aggregates in the Network. Computer Communication Review 32(3), (2002) 62-73
9. Belenky, A., Ansari, N.: Tracing Multiple Attackers with Deterministic Packet Marking (DPM). Proceedings of the IEEE PACRIM '03, Victoria, B.C., Canada. (2003)
10. Yaar, A., Perrig, A., Song, D.: Pi: A path identification mechanism to defend against DDoS attacks. IEEE Symposium on Security and Privacy (2003)

Distributing Key Updates in Secure Dynamic Groups*

Sandeep S. Kulkarni and Bezawada Bruhadeshwar

Department of Computer Science and Engineering, Michigan State University, East Lansing MI 48824 USA Tel: +1-517-355-2387, Fax: 1-517-432-1061
{sandeep, bezawada}@cse.msu.edu

Abstract. We focus on the problem of distributing key updates in secure dynamic groups. Due to changes in group membership, the group controller needs to change and distribute the keys used for ensuring encryption. However, in the current key management algorithms the group controller broadcasts these key updates even if only a subset of users need them. In this paper, we describe a key distribution algorithm for distributing keys to only those users who need them. Towards this end, we propose a descendent tracking scheme. Using our scheme, a node forwards an encrypted key update only if it believes that there are descendents who know the encrypting key. We also describe an identifier assignment algorithm which assigns closer logical identifiers to users who are physically close in the multicast tree. We show that our identifier assignment algorithm further improves the performance of our key distribution algorithm as well as that of a previous solution. Our simulation results show that a bandwidth reduction of upto 55% is achieved by our algorithms.

Keywords: Secure Multicast, Key Distribution, Descendent Tracking, Identifier Assignment.

1 Introduction

In group oriented applications, such as conferencing, networked gaming and news dissemination, it is necessary to secure the data from intruders as the data is confidential or it has monetary value. In the algorithms for secure group communication (e.g., [1–6]), a group controller distributes a cryptographic key, called the group key, to all the group users. The group membership is dynamic. To protect privacy of the current users, the group controller changes and securely distributes the group key at each membership change. This rekeying is especially needed when a user leaves the group and should no longer understand the group communication.

* This work is partially sponsored by NSF CAREER 0092724, ONR grant N00014-01-1-0744, DARPA contract F33615-01-C-1901, and a grant from Michigan State University.

R.K. Ghosh and H. Mohanty (Eds.): ICDCIT 2004, LNCS 3347, pp. 410–419, 2004.

In the algorithms in [1–4], the group controller distributes additional keys which are shared by different subsets of users. These shared keys reduce the number of group key update messages the group controller needs to transmit. The group controller encrypts the new group key with a minimum subset of the shared keys and transmits it to the current users. To reflect current group membership, the group controller changes and securely transmits the shared keys known to the leaving user. Although each of the new shared keys needs to be transmitted to only a subset of the users, the current key management algorithms assume a broadcast primitive. Hence, *all* the current users receive *all* the key update messages. Of course, users cannot decrypt the key update messages that are not intended for them since they do not have the necessary keys.

From the above discussion, we observe that the current key management algorithms only focus on *what* key update messages are sent but do not emphasize on *how* they are distributed. This results in wastage of bandwidth as users receive key update messages for keys that they do not need. This wastage increases further if retransmission is required for any lost messages and such retransmission is done using a broadcast. Although solutions for reducing the number of retransmissions in secure group communication have been proposed in [7,8], the group controller still needs to broadcast them. Thus, efficient distribution of key updates is an important problem in secure dynamic groups.

In this paper, we propose an algorithm for the distribution of key update messages in secure dynamic groups. In our key distribution algorithm, we integrate the key management algorithms in [1, 2] with appropriate forwarding functionality. We assume that the users are arranged in a multicast tree which can be built using any of the IP [9–12] or overlay [13–15] multicast protocols. Depending on the multicast protocol used, an intermediate node in the multicast tree can be a router (IP multicast) or an overlay node. Hence, we only focus on the actions of an intermediate node as the implementation details are beyond the scope of this paper. The contributions of our paper are as follows:

- We describe a compact descendant tracking scheme to track the descendants of the intermediate nodes. The memory required at the intermediate nodes for our scheme is small and scales logarithmically in the group size. The advantage of our descendant tracking scheme is that this information can either be updated periodically or after the group communication has resumed.
- We describe the forwarding mechanisms used by the intermediate nodes to forward the key update messages.
- We describe a user identifier assignment algorithm. Using our assignment algorithm, the group controller assigns closer logical identifiers to users who are located close to each other in the multicast tree. We show that our assignment algorithm improves the performance of our key distribution algorithm as well as that of a previous solution in [16].

Organization of the Paper. The paper is organized as follows. In Section 2, we describe the notations used in our key distribution algorithm and describe a previous solution. In Section 3, we describe our key distribution algorithm and our user identifier assignment algorithm. In Section 4, we present the simulation results. Finally, in Section 5, we conclude and discuss some future work.

2 Notations

In this section, we describe the various components in our algorithms, i.e., the key management algorithms, the multicast tree and the problem of key distribution. We also briefly describe a previous solution to the problem of key distribution.

Key Management Algorithms. In the key management algorithms from [1,2], the group controller arranges the users and the keys in a key tree. The leaf nodes in this key tree correspond to the users in the group (cf. Figure 1). Based on this arrangement of users and keys, we number them according to their location in the tree. For example, in a key tree of height h, the user $u_{i_1 i_2 .. i_h}$ denotes the user obtained by taking the i_1^{th} child at level 1, i_2^{th} child at level 2, and so on. The keys are also numbered likewise. Each node in the key tree is associated with a key from the logical key hierarchy [1] or a key from the complementary key hierarchy [2] or both. We use $k_{i_1 i_2 .. i_l}$ to denote the logical key at node $i_1 i_2 .. i_l$. And, we use $c_{i_1 i_2 .. i_l}$ to denote the complementary key at node $i_1 i_2 .. i_l$. For the levels where the group controller uses logical keys, the user obtains the keys on the path to the root. For the levels where the group controller uses complementary keys, the user gets the keys associated with the siblings of its ancestors. For example in Figure 1, user u_{1112} gets the group key (k_g), the logical keys (k_1, k_{11} and k_{1112}), and the complementary keys ($c_{112}, c_{113}, c_{114}, c_{1111}, c_{1113}$ and c_{1114}). Finally, we use $k(m)$ to denote that message m is encrypted using the key k and, hence, only users that have the key k can obtain m.

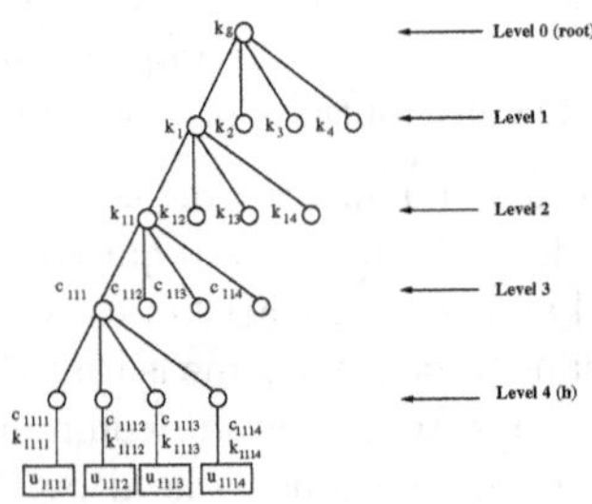

Fig. 1. Partial view of key tree

Multicast Tree. In our key distribution algorithm, we assume that the group controller distributes data and key update messages to the users and, hence the root of the multicast tree is the group controller. Any multicast protocol IP [9–12] or overlay [13–15] can be used to build the multicast tree; our approach is independent of the protocol used to build the multicast tree. We define the *parent* of a user x, say *parent.x*, as the next hop node on the path from x to the group controller. For an intermediate node, we consider its children and all other nodes reachable through its children as its descendents. Each intermediate node performs reverse path forwarding, i.e., a message from the group controller is replicated on all outgoing links except on the link on which the message was received. We define a Key Distribution (KD) aware intermediate node as a node which supports our key distribution algorithm. Unless otherwise specified, in our paper, we assume that all intermediate nodes in the multicast tree are Key Distribution (KD) aware.

Problem of Key Distribution. In the current key management algorithms [1,2], when group membership changes, the group controller changes the keys in the key tree and securely broadcasts the new keys. Since all users do not need all the keys, this mode of key distribution is not efficient. Hence, we focus on the key distribution in algorithms where each user receives only a small subset of keys that includes all the keys it needs.

Previous Solution for Key Distribution. In [16], to distribute the changed keys in the key tree, the group controller encrypts the keys at the higher levels using changed keys at the lower levels. For example, when u_{1111} leaves, to distribute a new key k'_1, the group controller generates the messages $k'_{11}(k'_1)$, $k_{12}(k'_1)$, $k_{13}(k'_1)$ and $k_{14}(k'_1)$, where the key k'_{11} is already distributed using keys further down in the key tree. Before transmitting these messages, the group controller broadcasts the identifier of the leaving user to the current users. Using this information and knowledge of the structure of the key tree, each user calculates the level numbers of the changed keys it needs. This information is propagated towards the group controller. Upon reception of replies, the group controller transmits the key update messages and includes the level number, at which the key is changed, in each message. When an intermediate node receives a key update message with a level number l, it forwards the message to its descendants only if some descendant of l had requested that key. The main shortcoming of this key distribution algorithm is that, it is executed for every membership change which causes delay at the users for receiving key updates.

3 Proposed Improvements for Key Distribution

In this section, we identify our approach for reducing the cost of key distribution. In Section 3.1, we describe our descendant tracking scheme that enables the intermediate nodes to approximately track its descendants. In Section 3.2, we describe our algorithm for assigning identifiers to users. This algorithm can be used to improve the performance of the key distribution algorithms in Section 3.1 and in [16].

3.1 Descendant Tracking Scheme

A simple method to track descendents is to store the identity of each descendant user and forward the key update message only if any descendant user needs this key. However, this straightforward solution requires each intermediate node to store a large amount of information, especially in large groups.

To describe our scheme, first, we define the steady state configuration of the multicast tree. Then, we describe the technique used at the intermediate nodes to update the descendant tracking information to account for group membership changes. Finally, we describe how keys are forwarded by the intermediate nodes.

Steady State Configuration. At each intermediate node, we store a h x d matrix called DT (Descendant Tracker), where h and d are, respectively, the height and degree of the key tree. Each element in DT is a single bit. Thus, the information kept in DT is very small, even for large groups. For example, for a group of 1024 users, where the group controller maintains a key tree of degree 4 and height 5, each intermediate node stores only 20 bits of information in DT. To track a descendant user with identifier $u_{i_1 i_2 .. i_h}$, at an intermediate node, we set the elements, $DT[1, i_1], DT[2, i_2], ..DT[h, i_h]$, to 1.

When the group is initialized, the group controller assigns each user a unique identifier based on its location in the key tree. The users who are leaves in the multicast tree record their identifiers in their DT matrices. The intermediate nodes request their children for the DT information. The DT entries of a parent are the disjunction (binary OR) of the corresponding entries of its children. As an illustration, in Figure 2, we show the DT entries at a leaf node, R_1 with users U_{2211}, U_{3311} and U_{3111}, and the disjunction of these entries by its parent node, R_2 with user U_{2111}. Although, the descendants identified in a DT matrix are a superset of the actual descendant users, the DT matrix provides sufficient information about the descendants to reduce traffic.

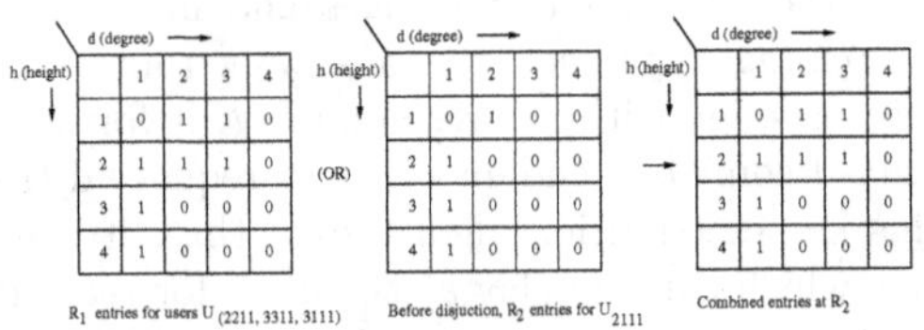

Fig. 2. DT entries at intermediate nodes R_1 and R_2

Tasks for Join. When a new user joins the group, the group controller distributes any keys, the new user needs, using a secure unicast channel. Also, the group controller distributes the new keys to the current users, where the intermediate nodes perform appropriate forwarding using the existing DT entries. The new user receives its identifier from the group controller and provides this information to its local intermediate node. The local intermediate node updates its DT matrix. Further, if the DT matrix has changed, it propagates this information to its ancestors in the multicast tree.

Tasks for Leave. When a user leaves the group, we do not update the DT entries at the intermediate nodes immediately. We perform an update of the DT

entries only when the number of group membership changes exceeds a threshold level. Although this could cause some messages to traverse extra links, updating the DT matrix periodically allows us to achieve a tradeoff between the processing overhead and the amount of bandwidth reduced.

Forwarding Key Update Messages Encrypted with Logical Keys. In a key tree with only logical keys [1], each user knows all the keys associated with its ancestors. Thus, based on the naming scheme of the key tree from Section 2, the label of every key a user knows is a prefix of the user's identifier. Now, consider the case when some user, say u_{1112}, leaves the group. The group controller changes all the keys known to u_{1112} and distributes them to the remaining users who need these keys.

To determine if a key update is needed by any descendants of an intermediate node, we need to determine whether the label of the encrypting logical key is a prefix of at least one descendant in the intermediate node's DT matrix. To allow the intermediate nodes to make this identification, the group controller includes the label of the encrypting logical key in the key update message and transmits it to the users. For example, to send $k_{12}(k_1')$, the group controller appends the label 12, to the encrypted message. To identify if the label $l_1, ..l_k$ of the encrypting logical key is a prefix to any descendant user, an intermediate node checks whether the DT elements, $DT[1,\ l_1]$,..,$DT[k,\ l_k]$ are all set to 1.

Forwarding Key Update Messages Encrypted with Complementary Keys. We note that, in a key tree with only complementary keys [2], each user knows the keys associated with the siblings of its ancestor. Thus, the labels of these keys differ in the last position from any prefix of the user's identifier.

To determine if a key update is needed by a descendant of an intermediate node, we need to determine whether the label of the encrypting complementary key differs in the last position from a prefix of a descendant's identifier. As in the case of transmitting keys encrypted with logical keys, the group controller appends the label of the encrypting complementary key to the key update message. Thus, to distribute $c_{112}'(c_{12}')$, the group controller appends the label 112 to the message. To verify that the label $l_1,\ l_2$,.., l_k of the encrypting complementary key is matched, an intermediate node checks whether the entries, $DT[1,\ l_1]$, $DT[2,\ l_2]$ .., $DT[k-1,\ l_{k-1}]$ and any entry $DT[k,\ l_p]$ where $p \neq k$, are set to 1.

3.2 User Identifier Assignment Algorithm

The key distribution algorithms we described in Sections 2 (from [16]) and 3.1, route the key update messages based on the identity of the descendants. The performance of these algorithms can be improved if the distribution of leaf nodes (group users) in the multicast tree corresponds to the distribution of the leaf nodes in the key tree. In this ideal scenario, users close to each other in the multicast tree will need almost the same key update messages and hence, the cost of key distribution would be low. While such a scenario is not always possible, one heuristic to achieve a near ideal scenario is to assign a joining user a logical identifier that is closer to the logical identifiers of users who are close to this user in the multicast tree. In this section, we use this heuristic to describe a user identifier assignment algorithm.

When a user sends a join request, the group controller communicates with this user using a secure unicast channel and learns about the location of the user in the multicast tree. Now, the group controller can use a program such as *mtrace* [17] to identify other nearby users in the multicast tree and record their logical identifiers. The group controller selects a user $u_{i_1 i_2 .. i_t}$, at the first intermediate node which is closest to the joining user. To assign an identifier to the joining user, the group controller selects an identifier $u_{i_1 i_2 .. i_p}$ such that $i_p \neq i_t$ and $1 \leq p, t \leq d$, i.e., the identifiers differ in the last position. The group controller assigns this identifier to the joining user, if it is not already assigned to any other user. If this attempt fails, the group controller repeats this process with another user at the first intermediate node. As an illustration, consider that the group controller selects the user u_{1111} at the first intermediate node. The group controller generates the identifiers 1112, 1113, 1114, which differ in the last position with 1111. If any of these identifiers are still available, the group controller assigns one of them to the joining user. If no more users exist at the first intermediate node, the group controller selects users at the second intermediate node and so on.

In our assignment algorithm, as the intermediate nodes are further away from the joining user, the group controller successively moves up the position at which the identifiers differ. For example, the group controller selects a user, $u_{i_1 i_2 .. i_k i_l}$, at the second intermediate node, and tries to assign the joining user, $u_{i_1 i_2 .. i_p i_l}$, such that $i_p \neq i_k$, i.e., the identifiers now differ in the second last position. The group controller repeats this process until it successfully assigns an identifier or stops, if the only users found are very close to itself.

In case the group controller finds that the only intermediate nodes with users are very close to itself, the group controller assigns the next available identifier to the joining user. We do not select the logical identifiers of users close to the group controller due to two reasons. The first reason is that these users are not in the proximity of the joining user. The second reason is that these users, being close to the group controller, receive almost all of the key update traffic anyway and, thus, there would be no performance gain if the joining user is logically closer to these users.

4 Simulation Results and Analysis

We simulated our algorithms using the NS2 network simulator [18]. We performed experiments on randomly generated network topologies for groups of 256, 512 and 768 users. We used the CBT [9] protocol to build the multicast tree with the group controller as the root node. For each experiment, we selected a random set of users to join or leave the group and recorded the number of messages in the multicast tree over the entire multicast session. We measure the total bandwidth reduction achieved in our algorithms using the formula: $TBRR = \frac{BW_{broadcast} - BW_{optimised}}{BW_{broadcast}}$, where BW stands for bandwidth and $TBRR$ stands for total bandwidth reduction ratio. We also measure the hopwise breakup of the $TBRR$ for a given network topology, termed $PBRR$, which gives an overview of the performance of our algorithms as a function of the network distance away from the group controller.

We conducted experiments on three key management algorithms. The first algorithm is the logical key hierarchy algorithm, referred as LKH, in [1]. The second and third algorithms are from our earlier work which appears in [2]. In the second algorithm, the group controller uses complementary keys at every level in the key tree. In the third algorithm, the group controller uses both logical and complementary keys at every level in the key tree. We refer to these algorithms, respectively, as CKH and $LKH + CKH$. For comparison purposes we also simulated the previous key distribution solution [16] we described in Section 2. We refer to the various key distribution algorithms as follows: (a) *Id-based* – our key distribution algorithm from Section 3.1, (b) *Id-based-cluster* – combination of algorithms in Sections 3.1 and 3.2, (c) *Level-based* – the key distribution algorithm from [16] that is described in Section 2, and (d) *Level-based-cluster* – combination of algorithms in [16] and 3.2.

In Figure 3, we plot the $TBRR$ for a group of 512 users. The $TBRR$ achieved is in the range of 20-45%. We observe that using our identifier assignment algorithm improves the $TBRR$ of our key distribution algorithm as well as that of the level based key distribution algorithm.

In Figure 4, we plot the $PBRR$ for a group of 768 users. The $PBRR$ value for *Hop Number* 1 indicates the $TBRR$ observed between hop 0 (group controller) and hop 1 (immediate children of group controller) and so on. From Figure 4,

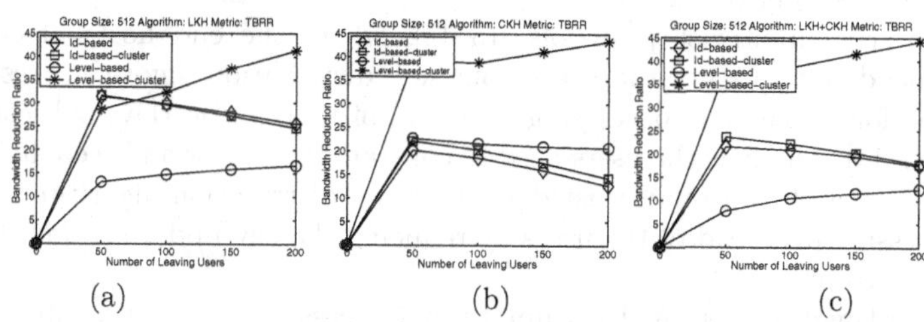

Fig. 3. TBRR for a group of 512 users using (a) LKH (b) CKH and (c) LKH+CKH

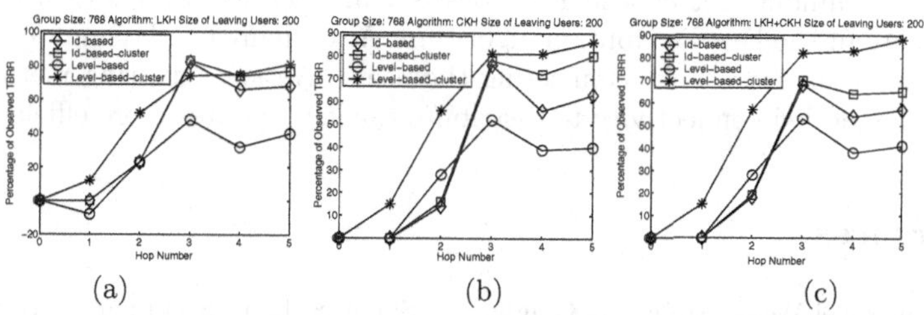

Fig. 4. PBRR for a group of 768 users using (a) LKH (b) CKH and (c) LKH+CKH

we observe that the *Level-based* algorithm causes more link stress near the group controller due to the responses by the users for each membership change. We note that, this problem is remedied by using our identifier assignment algorithm which reduces the link stress near the group controller in this algorithm.

5 Conclusion

In this paper, we addressed the problem of distributing key updates to users in secure dynamic groups. Towards this end, we described a descendant tracking scheme to track the descendants of the intermediate nodes in the multicast tree. In our descendant tracking scheme, each intermediate node stores a small information about its descendants. Next, we described the forwarding mechanisms used by the intermediate nodes based on the descendant tracking information. Each intermediate node forwards an encrypted key update message only if it believes that its descendants know the encrypting key. Using simulation results we showed that our key distribution algorithms reduce the bandwidth needed for distributing key updates in the key management algorithms in [1, 2] by upto 55% when compared to the broadcast of key updates.

Also, we described an algorithm for assigning identifiers to group users so that users who are physically close in the multicast tree are assigned logically close identifiers. We showed that our assignment algorithm improves the performance of our key distribution algorithm as well as that of the previous solution in [16]. Our key distribution algorithm can also be used to distribute data messages in secure interval multicast [19] where the group controller needs to send a message securely to a subset of the users.

For overlay multicast protocols [13–15], where the end hosts attempt to reduce bandwidth usage, the use of our key distribution algorithm results in better performance. The processing overhead of users in overlay multicast protocols [13–15] is high as the users need to constantly monitor and reconfigure the overlay links and route multicast data. Our key distribution algorithm reduces the processing overhead of the users by reducing the key update traffic that the users need to process.

For our key distribution algorithm it is not necessary that all the intermediate nodes store the DT matrices. We note that, a few selected nodes at appropriate points in the multicast tree are sufficient. We are currently exploring the selection techniques for choosing the best set of intermediate nodes which will participate in the key distribution algorithm. Also, many overlay multicast protocols maintain more links connecting the users. We are exploring methods to exploit the added connectivity to distribute the key updates more efficiently.

References

[1] Chung Kei Wong, Mohamed Gouda, and Simon S. Lam. Secure group communications using key graphs. *IEEE/ACM Transactions on Networking*, 2000.

[2] Sandeep S. Kulkarni and Bezawada Bruhadeshwar. Adaptive rekeying for secure multicast. *IEEE/IEICE Special issue on Communications: Transactions on Communications*, E86-B(10):2948–2956, October 2003.

[3] Debby M. Wallner, Eric J. Harder, and Ryan C. Agee. Key management for multicast: Issues and architectures. RFC 2627.

[4] D.McGrew and A.Sherman. Key establishment in large dynamic groups using one-way function trees. Manuscript.

[5] H.Harney and C.Muckenhirn. Group key management protocol (GKMP) specification. RFC 2093, July 1997.

[6] S.Mittra. Iolus: A framework for scalable secure multicasting. In *Proc. ACM SIGCOMM'97*, pages 277–288, 1997.

[7] Sanjeev Setia, Sencun Zhu, and Sushil Jajodia. A comparative performance analysis of reliable group rekey transport protocols for secure multicast. In *Performance Evaluation, special issue on the Proceedings of Performance 2002*, volume 49, pages 21–41, Rome, Italy, 2002.

[8] Y. Richard Yang, X. Steve Li, X. Brian Zhang, and Simon S. Lam. Reliable group rekeying: A performance analysis. In *Proceedings ACM SIGCOMM 2001*, San Diego, August 2001.

[9] A.J.Ballardie, P.F.Francis, and J.Crowcroft. Core based trees. In *Proceedings of the ACM SIGCOMM*, October 1993.

[10] T.Pusateri. Distance vector multicast routing protocol. IETF Draft, update to RFC 1075, draft-ietf-idmr-dvmrp-v3-06.txt, June 1998.

[11] S.Deering et al. Protocol independent multicast, sparse mode protocol: Specification. IETF Draft, work in progress, 1995.

[12] S.Deering et al. Protocol independent multicast (pim), dense mode protocol: Specification. IETF Draft, work in progress, 1995.

[13] Y.-H.Chu, S.G.Rao, S.Seshan, and H.Zhang. A case for end system multicast. *IEEE Journal on Selected Areas in Communications*, 20(8):1456–1471, October 2002.

[14] B.Zhang, S.Jamin, and L.Zhang. Host multicast: A framework for delivering multicast to end users. In *IEEE INFOCOM*, March 2000.

[15] J.Liebeherr, M.Nahas, and W.Si. Application-layer multicasting with delaunay triangulation overlays. *IEEE Journal on Selected Areas in Communications*, 20(8):1472–1488, October 2002.

[16] Di Pietro, L. V. Mancini, Y. W. Law, S. Etalle, and P. J. M. Havinga. Lkhw: A directed diffusion-based secure multicast scheme for wireless sensor networks. In *32nd Int. Conf. on Parallel Processing Workshops (ICPP)*, pages 397–406, October 2003.

[17] Bill Fenner and Steve Casner. A traceroute facility for ip multicast. Internet Draft, July 2000.

[18] Ns. ucb/lbnl/vint network simulator - ns (version 2). http://www-mash.cs.berkeley.edu/ns.

[19] Mohamed G. Gouda, Chin-Tser Huang, and E.N.Elnozahy. Key trees and the security of interval multicast. In *22nd International Conference on Distributed Systems*, pages 467–468, 2002.

Succinct and Fast Accessible Data Structures for Database Damage Assessment*

Jing Zhou, Brajendra Panda, and Yi Hu

Compuer Science and Computer Engineering Department,
University of Arkansas, Fayetteville, AR 72701, USA
{bpanda, jzhou, yhu}@uark.edu

Abstract. This paper presents methods for assessing damage in a database system after an attack is identified and a malicious transaction is detected. By using pre-developed data structures our protocols identify all affected transactions and also damaged data items without requiring any log access. These data structures are built using bit-vectors and are manipulated using logical AND and OR operations to achieve faster damage assessment.

1 Introduction

Database management systems (DBMS)s have the ability to recover from system, media, transaction, and communication failures. But when an attacker corrupts a data item, the DBMS itself cannot identify the malicious activity and recover. An intrusion detection system can be employed to recognize malicious activities in the database system and catch all malicious transactions. Once a malicious transaction is identified, damage assessment and recovery must be carried out immediately to restore the database to a safe state.

In this research, we focus on fast and precise damage assessment after the identification of a malicious transaction. We have presented two damage assessment models. The first one is the base model that uses dependency relationships among transactions to identify all affected transactions and then checks their operations to determine all damaged data items. The second method utilizes the base model to offer parallelism in the damage assessment process. This is required to further accelerate the process and can be utilized best when affected transactions form multiple clusters based on their dependency relationships.

The rest of the paper is organized as follows. The next section presents necessary background and motivations for this work. Sect. 3 and 4 discuss our base model and the parallel damage assessment model respectively. Sect. 5 concludes the paper.

* This work has been supported in part by US AFOSR under grant F49620-01-10346.

R.K. Ghosh and H. Mohanty (Eds.): ICDCIT 2004, LNCS 3347, pp. 420–429, 2004.

2 Background and Motivations

Defending data from illegal access is extremely important for survivability of any critical information system [10]. Since prevention mechanisms do not always succeed, intrusion detection systems are critical for discovering system misuse. Unfortunately, most of the detections are at the operating system level; detections at the DBMS level are limited [6],[2],[3] and cannot guarantee prompt detection of malicious database modification. Once the attacking transaction is commited, the database system will make the transactions effect permanent and those corrupted data items will be made available to other valid transactions. Thus, the damage will spread quickly through the database by legitimate users as they update other data items after reading any damaged data [1]. So it is extremely important to perform fast damage assessment and recovery [8] to stop further contamination and make the database system available as soon as possible. Ammann et al. presented an approach based on marking damage to maintain database consistency [1]. Liu et al. [7] reordered transactions for efficient recovery. Zuo and Panda [11] also developed other protocols for distributed database damage assessment. But in all these approaches, log was accessed and significant I/Os were involved. Lala and Panda [5] reduced the damage assessment time by saving the dependency relationships to avoid frequent log access. However, the shortcoming with that model is that data items were not made available before the entire recovery work was completed.

The main goal of this research is to provide a fast and accurate damage assessment model, which limits the amount of damage by hiding the affected data items from other transactions until recovery is complete, and at the same time, reduces denial-of-service by releasing unaffected data items for access. Our model, unlike previous models, does not access the log during the damage assessment process. Rather it processes pre-developed bit-matrices using simple logic (AND and OR) operations to identify affected transactions. Following damage assessment, all unaffected data items can be made available to users immediately and the recovery work can be carried out to restore legitimate values of all damaged data items.

3 The Base Model

Both the models presented in this paper are based on the assumptions that the malicious transaction has been identified, the scheduler produces a rigorous history, the database log cannot be corrupted, a data item will not be updated twice by one transaction, and that the dependency relationships among transactions will not change during recovery. The data structures developed for the base model is presented below.

3.1 Data Structures

First we define some of the terms that are essential for this model. Definition 1 is taken from [9] and Def. 2 is taken from [5].

Definition 1. *A write operation $w_i[x]$ of a transaction T_i is dependent on a read operation $r_i[y]$ of T_i if x is computed using the value obtained from $r_i[y]$.*

Definition 2. *A write operation $w_i[x]$ of a transaction T_i is dependent on a set of data items I if $x = f(I)$, i.e., the values of data items in I are used in calculating the new value of x. There are the following three cases for the set of data items I. (previous value of x is the value before current operation)*

Case 1: $I = \emptyset$. This means that no data item is used in calculating the new value of x. We denote such an operation as a fresh write. If $w_i[x]$ is a fresh write and if the previous value of x is damaged, the value of x will be refreshed after this write operation.

Case 2: $x \notin I$. Then $w_i[x]$ is called a blind write. If $w_i[x]$ is a blind write and if the previous value of x is damaged and none of the data items in I are damaged, then the value of x will be refreshed after this write operation.

Case 3: $x \in I$. If the previous value of x is damaged, then x remains damaged. Otherwise, if any other item in I is damaged, x is damaged.

Definition 3. *A transaction T_i is dependent on another transaction T_j if any of the data item(s) in T_i has been updated based on a data item that has been modified by T_j.*

Definition 4. *A legitimate write operation $w_i[x]$ of T_i is either a fresh write or a write operation that does not use any damaged data in its calculation.*

Definition 5. *The legitimate write that has refreshed the damaged data is called a valid write.*

Read_Matrix: This matrix is created to store information on data items that all updating type committed transactions have read. The first column records transaction IDs and the other columns represent all data items in the database. Each row represents a transaction. The corresponding columns that represent the data items that have been read by the transaction are set to 1s, other columns that have not been read are set to 0s. If all the updates made by a transaction are *fresh writes*, then a 0-vector is stored in the corresponding row.

Write_Matrix: This matrix stores information on all the data items that updating type committed transactions have written. Like the *Read_Matrix*, the first column records the transaction IDs, while remaining columns represent all data items in the database, and each row represents a transaction. In a vector of a transaction, the bits corresponding to the data items written by the transaction are set to 1s, and the rest of the bits are set to 0s.

Damaged_Data_Vector(DDV): This vector, which is a zero-vector initially, represents all data items that have been marked as damaged during the damage assessment procedure. In this vector, if the value at the position of data item d_i is 1 then d_i has been identified as damaged; otherwise, d_i has a consistent value.

Damaged_Transaction_List(DTL): This list shows all transactions that have been marked as damaged.

3.2 Damage Assessment Procedure

The *Read_Matrix* and *Write_Matrix* are constructed by scanning the database log and extracting information about the committed transactions. The order of the transactions in the matrices must remain the same as the order of commit sequence of the transactions in the log. Upon identification of a malicious transaction, the damage assessment procedure begins. Our damage assessment method is based exclusively on *Read_Matrix* and *Write_Matrix* instead of the database log. We will explain the damage assessment procedure using following example.

Example 1. *Let a history H consist of the following operations:* $H = r_1[B]r_1[D]$ $r_1[E]r_3[E]w_1[C]r_1[D]w_1[D]c_1r_2[C]r_2[D]r_2[E]w_2[B]w_2[A]c_2w_3[A]w_3[B]c_3r_4[A]w_4$ $[D]r_4[C]w_4[E]c_4$

The transaction dependency relationships in H can be established based on the definition of transaction dependency (see Def. 3). A directed acyclic graph is used to represent the dependency as in Fig. 1. A directed edge indicates that the transaction that the arrow points to is dependent on the transaction where the edge starts. For example, in Fig. 1, T_2 is dependent on T_1, T_4 is dependent on both T_1 and T_3.

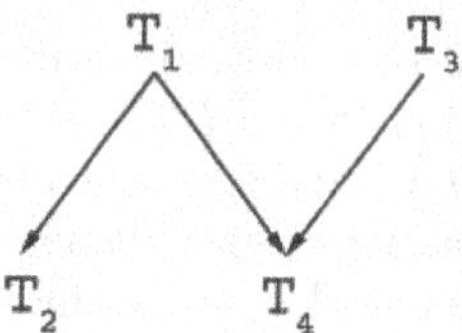

Fig. 1. Transaction Dependency Graph

The *Read_Matrix* and *Write_Matrix* for H based on the commit sequence of the transactions are constructed. A data item that a transaction have read or written is indicated by a 1 against the column representing the data item in the matrices. The matrices for H are depicted in Table 1 and Table 2.

Table 1. *Read_Matrix* for H

ID	A	B	C	D	E
T_1	0	1	0	1	1
T_2	0	0	1	1	1
T_3	0	0	0	0	1
T_4	1	0	1	0	0

Table 2. *Write_Matrix* for H

ID	A	B	C	D	E
T_1	0	0	1	1	0
T_2	1	1	0	0	0
T_2	1	1	0	0	0
T_4	0	0	0	1	1

Following is the damage assessment using the matrices.

1. Identify the corresponding row in the *Write_Matrix* that represents the data items written by the malicious transaction. For example, suppose transaction T_1 is the malicious transaction. Add transaction T_1 to the DTL. Then locate the position of transaction T_1 in the matrix (say m).
2. Do the logical OR operation (DDV OR *Write_Matrix[m]*). Positions of 1-bits in the *Write_Matrix* indicate that the corresponding data items have been damaged. Initially the DDV is set to 0s, that is, nothing is identified as damaged. For the previous example, after the OR operation, the DDV becomes: 0 0 1 1 0 . This indicates that data items C, D are damaged.
3. To find out the transactions that have read the damaged data items, first increase m by 1. Then carry out the logical AND operation (*Read_Matrix[m]* AND DDV). If the resulting vector is not zero, then the corresponding transaction has read one or more damaged data and, thus, has been affected. Add the transaction to the DTL. Moreover, perform the operation (*Write_Matrix[m]* OR DDV) and store the result as the new DDV. Here we assume that once a transaction reads a damaged data, all data items written in this transaction are damaged. Since T_2 has read $\{C, D, E\}$ and $\{C, D\} \in DDV$, the data items written by T_2, i.e., A and B, are damaged, too. The new DDV becomes: 1 1 1 1 0 .

   If a transaction has a valid write on any data item, those data items are removed from the DDV. For example, since T_3 has read $\{E\}$ and E is not damaged by the malicious transaction, so what T_3 has written, $\{A, B\}$ in this case, will be refreshed if they have been damaged before. The corresponding value for these data items in the DDV will become 0s.
4. Repeat step 3 until all the transactions in the *Read_Matrix* and *Write_Matrix* are processed. For the above example, it can be observed that transactions T_2, T_4 are all damaged, which is consistent with the transaction dependency relationship depicted in Fig. 1. DDV shows that the damaged data items include $\{C, D, E\}$.

After damage assessment work is completed, the damaged transactions are located and damage data items are marked, undamaged data items can be available to the legitimate user right away. Consequently recovery work can be performed. We will not discuss the recovery algorithm in detail. Researchers have developed several models such as in [4] and [8] to perform recovery work.

4 Parallel Damage Assessment

In a large database management system, some transactions have little or no relationship with each other. In order to do the damage assessment and recovery more efficiently, transactions can be partitioned into clusters based on their relationships with each other. Clusters that have no dependency relationships can be processed simultaneously. During damage assessment, only the cluster that contains the malicious transaction and the clusters depending on the former are considered. This further reduces damage assessment time.

Definition 6. *A cluster C_i is a group of transactions that have dependency relationships.*

Definition 7. *A cluster C_i is dependent on another cluster C_j if any of the transaction(s) in C_i reads the data item that has been modified by transaction(s) in C_i to perform write operation.*

Before discussing the method, first let us look at an example. We assume that the scheduler has produced a serializable history and the subscripts of the transactions denote the serialization order, i.e. T_1 is scheduled before T_2, T_2 before T_3, so on and so forth.

Example 2

$T_1 : a = 10;$	$T_2 : x = 30;$	$T_3 : b = a * x;$	$T_4 : a = b;$
$T_5 : c = a * 100;$	$T_6 : y = 200;$	$T_7 : x = y - 10;$	$T_8 : m = x;$
$T_9 : m = x/2;$	$T_{10} : n = c - m;$	$T_{11} : m = n * n;$	

Fig.2. shows the transaction dependency graph for H_c. It also shows the transactions in each cluster and the relationships among the clusters. A dotted square represents a cluster and a dotted edge represents the cluster dependency. The cluster that the dotted edge points to depends on the cluster from which the dotted edge starts. If a transaction that is located in C_1, is found to be a malicious transaction, then only the transactions in C_1 and C_3 are checked to perform the damage assessment. After they are processed, all other clusters depending on them can be processed. Similarly, if some clusters do not depend on each other and are determined to have affected transactions, they can be processed in parallel. This would accelerate the processing time.

4.1 Clustering Procedure

The *Read_Matrix* and *Write_Matrix*, as discussed in Sect. 3, are modified to capture the cluster information. One more column is added in both matrices to store the cluster that the transaction belongs to. Another matrix, *Write_Cluster*, is developed for recording the data items updated by transactions in a cluster. Each of the remaining columns represents a data item. An additional column is used to store the number of transactions in the cluster. This information is used to decide if two clusters need to be merged when a transaction depends

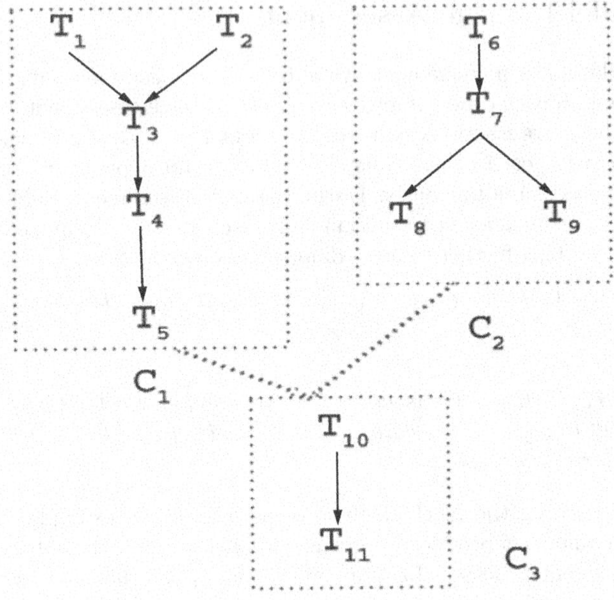

Fig. 2. Clusters and their dependencies

on both. They are initialized to all 0s at first. Not all the data items that have been updated by the transactions in a cluster will be marked as 1, rather only those data items that are most up to date are recorded. For example, after T_2 in C_1 updated data item D, a transaction in another cluster updated D, then the corresponding position for data item D in *Write_Cluster* of C_1 should be marked as 0. Other than this, two lists, *Dependent_Cluster_List*(DCL) and *Ancestor_Cluster_List*(ACL) for each cluster are used to store important information to do damage assessment. DCL is used to store all the dependent clusters for one cluster. ACL stores all the clusters it depends on. For example, if C_1 depends on C_2, and C_2 depends on C_3, the information is stored as illustrated by Table 3.

Table 3. Dependent and Ancestor Clusters

Cluster ID	Dependent_Cluster	Ancestor_Cluster
C_1		C_2C_3
C_2	C_1	C_3
C_3	C_1C_2	

The procedure for construction of clusters and matrices for the clusters are as follows:

A variable, say *Cluster_Position*, is assigned to the cluster ID for the first transaction. Another variable, *Scan_Position*, records the corresponding position for this transaction in the *Read_Matrix* and *Write_Matrix*. Update the *Write_Cluster*[*Cluster_Position*] by performing the logical *OR* operation with *Write_Matrix*[*Scan_Position*]. Update the *transaction_number* value for the cluster.

For every transaction that follows, first increment *Scan_Position* by 1. Check if it has dependency relationship with existing clusters by performing logical *AND* operation (*Read_Matrix*[*Scan_Position*] *AND* *Write_Cluster*[*Position*]) for *Position* from 1 to *Cluster_Position*.

If the result contains only 0s, this transaction is independent of any existing cluster. Increment *Cluster_Position* by 1, assign *Cluster_Position* as the new cluster ID to this transaction. Add a row for the new cluster in *Write_Cluster*. The value for the corresponding data items is the same as this transactions corresponding row in *Write_Matrix*. This can be obtained by performing the logical *OR* operation. Update the *transaction_number* value for the new cluster. Update the rows representing other clusters in the *Write_Cluster* by performing logical operation *NOT*(*Write_Matrix*[*Scan_Position*])*AND* *Write_Cluster*[*Position*] for *Position* from 1 to *Cluster_Position*-1.

If it depends on one of the clusters, add this transaction into this cluster. Update the corresponding row in the *Write_Cluster* by performing logical *OR* operation. Similarly, update all other clusters *Write_Cluster* by performing logical operation *NOT*(*Write_Matrix*[*Scan_Position*])*AND* *Write_Cluster*[*Position*] for *Position* from 1 to *Cluster_Position*-1. Update the *transaction_number* value for this cluster. Store the *Cluster_Position* as the cluster ID in the *Read_Matrix* and *Write_Matrix* for the transaction.

Otherwise, it is dependent on more than one cluster. There are two solutions for this situation. One solution is to merge all the clusters that it depends on into one cluster; the other is to form a new cluster that depends on several clusters. If we want to merge the clusters, restrictions can be set so that the size of the cluster will not grow too big. The whole idea of clustering is to perform damage assessment and recovery in parallel to achieve efficiency. But if we partition the database log based only on the dependency relationships without any restriction, the cluster can become too large, in the worst case one cluster for the whole log. The disadvantage is that the parallelism will be reduced. In that case, we can restrict the number of transactions, page size, and execution time to limit the cluster sizes. In the following discussion, we adopt number of transactions in any cluster as the restriction and assume that a variable N_t will store this value.

Before clusters are merged, see if the number of transactions after merging is less than N_t. Then these clusters can be merged together with the new transaction. Corresponding rows in the *Write_Cluster* have to be updated at the same time . The cluster ID information for each transaction that belongs to the merged clusters has to be modified too.

Otherwise, a new cluster will be generated. First add a new row to the *Write_Cluster* with the corresponding transactions information of what data items have been updated. Then update the *DCL* for all the clusters the transaction depends on to include the new cluster. Update the *ACL* of this cluster to include all the clusters it depends on too.

The above process is repeated until all transactions that follow in the log have been processed.

4.2 Parallel Damage Assessment Procedure

The parallel damage assessment starts by identifying affected clusters. The clusters containing the malicious transactions are located first. Following their *DCL*, the clusters that are dependent on the malicious clusters can be determined. Then in all the affected clusters, similar procedure as in the *Base Model* can be used to find the affected transactions. Clusters of which all ancestors have been processed can now be checked for damaged assessment. Several of such clusters can be processed simultaneously if they have no dependency relationships. The steps for checking clusters for damage assessment are enumerated below.

1. From the modified *Write_Matrix* or *Read_Matrix*, find the cluster ID of the malicious transaction. Then find the dependent clusters of the affected cluster from *DCL* and put them into *Affected_Cluster*. Repeat this procedure until all the affected clusters are found.
2. For all the affected clusters, if their ancestors in *ACL* fulfill one of the following conditions, perform damage assessment the same way as in the *Base Model* for the transactions in this cluster to identify affected transactions.
   (a) *ACL* is null
   (b) The cluster does not belong to the *Affected_Cluster*
   (c) The cluster belongs to the *Affected_Cluster*, but it has already been checked for affected transactions
3. If several clusters satisfy the above conditions, they can be processed concurrently if they have no dependency relationships.
4. Repeat steps 2 and 3 until all clusters in the *Affected_Cluster* are processed.

5 Conclusion

In this paper, we have focused on damage assessment in a database affected by committed malicious transactions. Two damage assessment models have been presented. These models use succinct auxiliary data structures to identify all affected transactions without requiring any log access. Since these data structures are built using bit-vectors and are manipulated using logical operations, damage assessment can be done very quickly. After affected transactions are identified, unaffected data items can be made available to users while the recovery phase continues.

The base model provides fundamental structures for the later approach. Considering that transactions in a big database system may have little or no relationship with each other, parallel damage assessment procedure is presented to further reduce the damage assessment time. In this approach, transactions are clustered based on the dependency relationships. Damage assessment is performed by finding the cluster that contains the malicious transaction and all other clusters that depend on the former. All clusters whose ancestor clusters are either unaffected or already checked can be processed in parallel. In future we wish to carry out simulation analysis to study performance of these models.

Acknowledgment. We are thankful to Dr. Robert L. Herklotz for his support, which made this work possible.

References

1. P. Ammann, S. Jajodia and C.D. McCollum, B.T. Blaustein, Surviving Information Warfare Attacks on Databases, In proceedings of the 1997 IEEE Symposium on Security and Privacy.
2. D. Barbara, R. Goel, and S. Jajodia, Mining Malicious Data Corruption with Hidden Markov Models, In Proceedings of the 16th Annual IFIP WG 11.3 Working Conference on Data and Application Security, Cambridge, England, July 2002.
3. Y. Hu and B. Panda, A Data Mining Approach for Database Intrusion Detection, In Proceedings of the 2004 ACM Symposium on Applied Computing, Special Track on Database Theory, Technology, and Applications, Nicosia, Cyprus, March 2004.
4. S. Jajodia, C. D. McCollum, and P. Amman, Trusted Recovery, Communications of the ACM, 42(7), pp. 71-75, July 1999.
5. C. Lala and B. Panda, Evaluating Damage from Cyber Attacks: A Model and Analysis, IEEE Transactions on System, Man, and Cybernetics Part A: Systems and Humans, Vol. 31, No. 4, July 2001.
6. V.C.S. Lee, J.A. Stankovic, S.H. Son, Intrusion Detection in Real-time Database Systems Via Time Signatures, In Proceedings of the Sixth IEEE Real Time Technology and Applications Symposium, 2000.
7. P. Liu, P. Ammann and S. Jajodia, Rewriting histories: recovering from malicious transactions, Distributed and Parallel Database, vol. 8, no.1, pp.7 40, January 2000.
8. B. Panda and R. Yalamanchili, Transaction Fusion in the Wake of Information Warfare, In Proceedings of the 2001 ACM Symposium on Applied Computing, Special Track on Database Systems, Las Vegas, Nevada, March 2001.
9. S. Patnaik and B. Panda, Dependency Based Logging for Database Survivability from hostile transactions, In Proceedings of the 12th International Conference Computer Application and Industry Engineering, Atlanta, GA, November 1999.
10. Defending Americas Cyberspace: National plan for information system protection, version 1.0. The White House, Washington, DC, 2000.
11. Y. Zuo and B. Panda, Damage Assessment Models For Distributed Database Systems, In Proceedings of the 18th Annual IFIP WG 11.3 Working Conference on Data and Application Security, Sitges, Spain, July 25-28, 2004.

A Secure Checkpointing Protocol for Survivable Server Design

Vamsi Kambhampati, Indrajit Ray, and Eunjong Kim

Department of Computer Science,
Colorado State University
{vamsi, indrajit, kimeu}@cs.colostate.edu

Abstract. Secure checkpointing appears to be a useful technique for designing survivable systems. These are fault-tolerant systems that are robust against malicious security attacks. Secure checkpointing, however, is not easily done. Without adequate protection, the checkpointing process can be attacked and compromised. The checkpointing data can be subjected to malicious attacks and be a source of security breach. In this paper, we present a new secure checkpointing scheme that is robust against malicious attacks. Our approach uses strong cryptographic techniques for data confidentiality and integrity, Byzantine agreement protocols for compromised peer detection and information dispersal techniques for reliability and availability.

1 Introduction

Businesses around the world are increasingly relying on the Internet for their daily operation. However, the open nature of the Internet makes it vulnerable to different types of security related attacks. Over the last few years business around the world has lost enormous amounts of money owing to these attacks. Thus organizations that use networked computer systems are clamoring to find effective ways to defend their networks against cyber attacks. The ideal approach to defense is, of course, to prevent the attacks from happening in the first place. However, distributed denial-of-service attacks are extremely difficult to prevent. Even with today's sophisticated intrusion detection technologies the best that can be hoped for is to detect such an attack in a timely manner, then rely on system administrators to launch mitigating actions to recover from the effects of such an attack. For denial-of-service types of attacks the mitigating actions take the form of isolating the attacked server from the network, stopping the services it provides, patching up the vulnerability that was exploited to launch the attack and possibly waiting till such times as the symptoms of the attack subside to restart the server. Unfortunately, almost always these steps require human intervention, which can be slow. Until the server can be adequately isolated, it can do damage to any other machine that it is connected to. Further, the clients that are currently receiving services from the attacked server, encounter a disruption of services; future clients are denied service till such time as the server is back up.

We believe that instead of relying solely on attack prevention technologies, systems should also be able to survive attacks and continue to provide services, even

R.K. Ghosh and H. Mohanty (Eds.): ICDCIT 2004, LNCS 3347, pp. 430–440, 2004.

if in a somewhat degraded manner. Our network survivability project addresses this problem of survivability of servers facing denial-of-service attacks. We adopt a three-pronged approach - (i) Predict network attacks and establish a multi-layered defensive framework in real time. (ii) Automatically migrate compromised (or to be compromised) services to other safer parts of the network. This is done without affecting the clients that were being served during the occurrence of the attack; the clients are continued to be provided with the services as usual as if nothing happened. (iii) Isolate and confine the network attack to the already compromised servers so as to prevent it from spreading.

This paper reports on one aspect of our efforts to re-distribute system services in the face of attacks. In order to migrate an affected server, we need to keep track of the process state of the server immediately before it was affected. This process state is then restored on a new machine and recovered. The process of saving process states is known as checkpointing. It has been well studied by fault-tolerant researchers and is mature. However, a malicious environment as ours throws a number of challenges to checkpointing techniques that have not yet been addressed by researchers. If a server is compromised, any checkpointing data that it stores needs to be considered malicious. To begin wit, therefore, we cannot store a server's checkpoint data on the same machine. It needs to be stored in remote locations. This creates a second problem. Any of these remote locations can itself be attacked and compromised. Thus, we need to disperse the checkpoint information over a number of locations such that compromise of one (or even a few) does not affect the quality of checkpoint data. The third problem that needs to be solved is how to distribute securely the checkpoint data to these remote locations. The current paper addresses these issues. We propose a secure checkpointing scheme that is robust against malicious attacks. Our approach uses strong cryptographic techniques for data confidentiality and integrity, Byzantine agreement protocols for compromised peer detection and information dispersal techniques for reliability and availability.

The rest of the paper is organized as follows. Section 2 provides some background information about checkpointing, information dispersal and byzantine agreement. Section 3 describes our checkpointing protocol. It begins with a description of our system model. Section 3.2 presents our consensus algorithm that is used by a group of servers to determine if some of them have been compromised. Section 3.3 describes the checkpointing and dispersing process. Section 3.4 describes the secure group communication scheme that is used by the servers to distribute checkpoint data in a secure manner. Finally, section 5 concludes the paper.

2 Background and Related Work

Checkpointing is a well-known technique used in fault-tolerant systems design. Checkpointing periodically saves the state of a running process to stable storage. After a failure, the recovery process uses this checkpointing data to restore the system to a consistent state before the failure. In the most general setting, simplistic checkpointing (called sequential checkpointing) periodically dumps the entire process state to stable storage at each checkpoint. However, its simplicity forsakes efficiency in terms of storage space and communication overhead. Several checkpointing schemes [1, 2, 3, 4, 16, 17] have been proposed in the literature to improve efficiency of checkpointing and to reduce overhead. Some of these include incremental checkpointing, compression, buffering, copy-on-write, compiler assistance and diskless checkpointing.

Quintessential to designing survivable storage systems is a mechanism for dispersing information on multiple physical storage media to improve reliability and to reduce storage space consumption. Rabin proposed an efficient Information Dispersal Algorithm (IDA) for security, fault-tolerance and load-balancing [6]. The idea is to divide a file F into n number of pieces and during reconstruction any m pieces ($m \leq n$) from the n pieces would suffice to successfully reconstruct the original file F. Any such (m -1) pieces would not reveal any information about the contents of the original file.

Central to our problem is determining if a process has become faulty. Software errors and adversary attacks targeted towards a specific process running on a node, forces the process to behave arbitrarily (Byzantine manner) [10]. Our approach for detecting process failures follows that of Byzantine Agreement (BA) [12, 13]. In general, solving Byzantine Agreement reduces to solving binary consensus problem in a distributed environment [13]. However, it has been proven that reaching consensus is impossible in an asynchronous environment that is subject to even a single crash fault [18]. Synchronous systems do not suffer from this problem because computations or communications are expected to finish within a bounded time. In contrast, partial synchrony places bounds on processing and message transmission times but the bounds are not known. Further, they hold only after some unknown time, called the global stabilization time (GST) [11]. Chandra and Toueg [11] introduced the concept of *unreliable failure detectors* to augment the asynchronous system model with an external detector that can make mistakes. They define failure detectors in terms of abstract properties. Unreliable fault detectors in an asynchronous environment can make mistakes by erroneously adding a non-faulty process to their suspect list and later remove them when they receive a response from the suspected process. Unreliable fault detectors are classified by the number of mistakes they make i.e., their *accuracy* and their ability to detect faulty processes i.e., their *completeness*. Several classes of Byzantine fault detectors were defined by Chandra et al. using the above properties. In addition, Chandra and Toueg give a transformation algorithm that transforms an eventual weak completeness detector D to an eventual strong completeness detector D'.

Malkhi and Reiter [12] suggested using an unreliable fault detector from the $\Diamond S(bz)$ class for solving consensus in an asynchronous Byzantine environment subjective to malicious attacks. Their detector is able to detect *quiet* processes and any process which sends *non-well-formed* messages. Further randomization techniques applied to the $\Diamond S(bz)$ detector result in a hybrid protocol that guarantees termination even if eventual weak accuracy does not hold.

Kihlstrom et al. [9] further improved the completeness properties proposed by Chandra et al. by defining fault detectors in terms of deviation from Algorithm A that is used for solving consensus. Two new completeness properties namely eventual strong Byzantine completeness for algorithm A and eventual weak Byzantine (k + 1)-completeness for algorithm A. These two properties combined with the existing [11] accuracy properties form a new set of unreliable Byzantine fault detectors that are capable of capturing some of the Byzantine behavior unattended by earlier approaches [11, 12].

3 The Secure Checkpointing Protocol

Our secure checkpointing scheme assumes the following environment. The system consists of pool of similar servers all providing the same service. The servers communicate with each other over an open network, which is susceptible to eavesdropping, message modification and replay. Any server can potentially be attacked and compromised. Servers periodically run the secure checkpointing algorithm to generate checkpoint data about their process states. To minimize the storage overhead we use compressed differences with incremental checkpointing.

To make the checkpoint information readily available we distribute the checkpoint data of each server to some (or all) of its peers. In case of failure of the current server, the checkpoint data is still available at some other location. Two security issues arise here. First, if the original server is attacked instead of simply failing the checkpoint data is compromised. To prevent this we delete the generated checkpoint data from the source as soon as it is safely distributed to other servers. Second, simple replication of checkpoint data at other servers increases the vulnerability of the data. We address this problem by dispersing the checkpoint data to a set of servers instead of replicating the same. The dispersion process breaks down the data into n segments such that any k segments can be used to re-create the data but no k-1 can do the same.

To disperse the data in a secure manner over open networks we establish secure channels between the peers. We employ secure group communication. Most of the secure group key schemes suggested in literature [14, 15] have considerable overhead in terms of re-keying for group membership events and keeping track of consistent view of the group. To solve this particular problem we develop a RSA-type keying scheme based on the theory proposed earlier by one of the authors [8]. The proposed group key has a simple re-keying method by which each member individually and independently computes the new group key in a completely distributed manner. While the group key guarantees the confidentiality of the dispersed data, integrity is ensured by the use of RSA based digital signatures.

A major problem that still needs to be addressed is determining if a server has been attacked and compromised. To do this, however, we cannot, rely on a single source of information. This is because that particular source may itself be compromised. Thus, we propose a consensus approach by which a coterie of peers determines if some sibling has been compromised. Our solution to the problem comes from the domain of unreliable fault detectors suggested by Chandra and Toueg [11].

3.1 System Model

We consider an asynchronous distributed environment with $n \geq 2$ processes. Each process has a unique logical identifier associated with it. All processes are connected to all other processes by communication channels and processes communicate with each other by passing messages. No bounds are placed on communication times for such messages. Each process has access to a local clock, but the clocks themselves are not synchronized. Message passing primitives include *send*, *recv*, *broadcast-send*, and *broadcast-recv*. Communication failures are modeled as process failures and for simplicity we consider communication faults as process faults.

Processes may behave correctly according to their algorithmic specification or they may show arbitrary (Byzantine) behavior. Crash faults due to software errors or hardware failures are modeled as Byzantine faults and hence receive no special treatment. We denote $k \leq \left\lfloor \frac{(n-1)}{3} \right\rfloor$ to be the maximum number of Byzantine processes and require at least $\left\lceil \frac{(2n+1)}{3} \right\rceil$ processes to be correct.

3.2 Byzantine Fault Detector

We propose a new algorithm for solving consensus in an asynchronous environment using a weak fault detector D_1 in $\Diamond W(bz)$. As part of the algorithm D_1 is transformed to a stronger detector D_2 in class $\Diamond S(bz)$. $Output(D_2)_p$ emulates the output of D_2 i.e., the eventual strong fault detector $\Diamond S$. The consensus algorithm presented here uses techniques from Chandra and Toueg [11], Kilhstrom et al. [9] and Malkhi and Reiter [12]. This scheme involves a revolving *coordinator* and proceeds in asynchronous *rounds*. All processes have *a priory* knowledge that during round *r*, the coordinator is process $c \equiv (r \bmod n + 1)$, where *n* is the number of processes in the system. Communication failures are counted towards process failures. The algorithm as follows.

ALGORITHM 1: ConsensusUsingByzantineFaultDetectors

Input: v_p is *p*'s estimate of input value.

D_{1_p} is a fault detector in class $\Diamond W$

$suspect_p$ is a local variable (vector) of suspected processes.

Output: $OutputD_{2_p}$ is the list of current failed processes.

decide(*v*) is the decided estimate.

Steps:

```
/* All processes execute the following in parallel */
/* Initialization */
    estimate_p ← v_p
    decide(v) ← ⊥
    ∀_i : Suspect_p[i] ← ⊥
    r_p ← 0
repeat forever
Phase 1
    r_p ← r_p + 1
    c_p ← (r_p mod n) + 1                /* c_p is the current coordinator */
    broadcast-send(ESTIMATE, r_p, estimate_p, p)
Phase 2
    /* coordinator */
    if [ p = c_p ] then
        wait until [ for ⌈(2n+1)/3⌉ distinct processes q : p broadcast-received
            well-formed-messages of type (ESTIMATE, r_p, estimate_p, q) from q]
```

```
∀_q : if [ received (ESTIMATE, r_p , estimate_p , q) ] then
        V_p[q] ← estimate_q
      else V_p[q] ← ⊥
    if [ for ⌊(n−1)/3⌋+1 estimate_q : estimate_i = estimate_j in V_p[i][j] ] then
        select_p ← estimate_q
    else select_p ← estimate_p
    broadcast-send(SELECT, r_p , select_p , c_p )
Phase 3  wait until [ received well-formed-message (SELECT, r_p , select_{c_p} , c_p )
            from c_p or c_p ∈ D_{1_p} ]        /* p queries its local fault detector D_{1_p} */
         if [ received (SELECT, r_p , select_{c_p} , c_p ) well-formed-message
            from c_p ] then
              estimate_p ← select_{c_p}
              send(ACK, r_p , p) to c_p
         else send((NACK, r_p , p) to c_p
Phase 4  if [ p = c_p ] then
           wait until [ for ⌈(2n+1)/3⌉ distinct processes q: p broadcast-received
                 well-formed-messages of type (ACK/NACK, r_q , q) from q ]
         if [ ⌊(n−1)/3⌋+1 of these messages are of type (ACK, r_q , q ] then
            decide(v) ← select_p
            broadcast-send(DECIDE, r_p , p, select_p )
Phase 5  if not [ received well-formed-message of type
                        (DECIDE, r_q , c_p , select_{c_p} ) from c_p ] then
           suspect_p ← c_p                  /* c_p is added to D_1 suspect list */
         broadcast-send(DECIDE, r_p , p, suspect_p )
Phase 6  wait [ receive well-formed-message(s) of type
                        (SUSPECT, r_p , q, suspect_q ) from q ]
           foreach [ r in suspect_q ]
             Suspect_p[r] ← Suspect_p[r]+1
         until [ for ⌈(2n+1)/3⌉ distinct processes q ]
         foreach [ r in Suspect_p[r] ]
```

$$\texttt{if [} Suspect_p[r] \geq \left\lfloor \frac{(n-1)}{3} \right\rfloor + 1 \texttt{] then}$$

$$OutputD_{2_p} \leftarrow r$$

$$suspect_p \leftarrow OutputD_{2_p}$$

$$\forall_i : Suspect_p[i] \leftarrow \perp$$

3.3 Checkpoint Data Generation and Dispersion

We adapt the technique of incremental checkpointing with compression differences suggested by Plank et al. [2]. A major advantage of Plank et al.' s scheme is that it is more successful than other in reducing the storage overhead for saving checkpoints. Moreover, it does not suffer from the aliasing problem discussed earlier. We assume that the entity computing checkpoint data for dispersion is a member of a group and has access to a group key K_g that has been previously generated using the group key protocol (described in section 4.4). The group periodically determines by executing algorithm 1 if a member is malicious. If so the other members of the group discard the malicious member by changing the group key for the other members.(described in the keying algorithm). It is possible that the current server is the malicious one in the group. However, since it does not have the most recent group key, the data it sends to others will not be available to those group members for all practical purposes. The last checkpoint data available to the peers before the current server was determined to be malicious will be the one use if needed.

ALGORITHM 2: Secure Checkpoint
Input: Checkpoint data
Output: Compressed checkpoint data split into n portions of partial checkpoint data and dispersed to n peers.

Steps:

(1) The check pointer allocates appropriate buffers to hold checkpointing data.
(2) After each checkpoint, the address space of the program is protected with *read-only* bit. Every time the program tries to change a read-only page, a page fault is generated and detected. Checkpointing application puts the fault-page number into a modified page list and it is copied to the checkpoint buffer.
(3) The page protection bit is then modified to *read-write.*
(4) At each checkpoint, new content of the page is written and the modified page list is cleared. The address space is protected with *read-only* again.
(5) Return control to the program
(6) At the next checkpoint, the two copies of each page (one is a current page ($page_i$) and the other is previous page which is in checkpoint buffer (buf_i)) are compared and the difference ($diff_i$) between them calculated by using bitwise Exclusive-OR operator ($\oplus$).
(7) Any word that is not changed in $page_i$ is *zero*ed in $diff_i$ due to the Exclusive-OR operation. In addition, any compression algorithm with a small compression ratio is enough to reduce the checkpointing information further.

(8) The *diff*'s are concatenated to form F which is then segmented into sequences of length m (with padding in the end as needed) as follows: $F = (b_1,\ldots,b_m),\ldots,(b_{N-m+1},\ldots,b_N)$. That is $F = S_1 \parallel S_2 \parallel \ldots \parallel S_{N/m}$ where $S_i = \left(b_{(i-1)m+1},\ldots,b_{im}\right)$, $1 \le i \le N/m$.

(9) Choose a set of n vectors $\bar{a}_i = (a_{i1},\ldots a_{im})$, $1 \le i \le n$ such that every subset of m different vectors is linearly independent. Using the set of vectors $\bar{a}_i = (a_{i1},\ldots a_{im})$, $1 \le i \le n$, F is processed and divided into n pieces $F_1' \ldots F_n'$ as follows: $F_i' = \left(\bar{a}_i \bullet S_k\right) = \left(a_{i1} \times b_{(k-1)\cdot m} + \ldots + a_{im} \times b_{k\cdot m}\right)$

(10) Concatenate the ith chunk F_i' obtained in step 9 with the ith vector $\bar{a}_i$. Compute the digital signature of the concatenated information and append. Encrypt the entire piece of information using the group key K_g.

(11) Distribute the ith-encrypted chunk to the ith group member.

3.4 Group Key Generation

We develop a new asymmetric key group key protocol based on the theory proposed earlier by Ray et al. [8]. The cryptographic scheme is similar to RSA. There is a single encryption key $K_g = \langle e, N_1 \times N_2 \times \ldots N_n \rangle$ where $N_1, N_2 \ldots, N_n$ are pairwise relatively prime integers and n is the number of members in the group.

Each member M_i has a public key/private key pair given by $K_i = \langle e, N_i \rangle / K_i^{-1} = \langle d_i, N_i \rangle$, where $e \bullet d_i \equiv 1 \bmod N_i$. The property of this scheme is such that any message that is encrypted with the key K_g can be decrypted by any one of the keys K_i^{-1} and only one of these keys.

We define three operations for group key management. These are *member join, member leave*, and *forced member delete*. Member *join* operation occurs when a new member wants to join a group, for example, when a new node is added to the network or some node, which has left the group, wants to re-join. However, nodes suspected by the group are never allowed to join the group unless the entire distributed protocol restarts. Also, note that a malicious node might attempt to join a different group in the network, in which case it might be accepted by that group for a short period and later deleted due to its Byzantine behavior. Member leave operation occurs when a member wants to leave the group. Lastly, if $(k + 1)$ members from the group agree upon a certain member to be malicious (through Byzantine fault detection) then a forced member *delete* operation occurs.

3.4.1 Member Join Operation

When a new member M_{i+1} wants to join the group, it broadcasts a *join-request* message to all group members $\{M_1,\ldots, M_i\}$ with its public key $K_{i+1} = <e, N_{i+1}>$ and keeps its private key $K'_{i+1} = <d_{i+1}, N_{i+1}>$ as secrete. For consistent behavior, all group members wait before responding until the current run of consensus algorithm finishes. This makes sure that all group members end up with the same suspect list of Byzantine processes.

Step1: A new member M_{i+1} broadcasts a *join-request* message to all group members with its public key $K_{i+1} = <e, N_{i+1}>$.

Step2: Each member checks its local suspected processes list and sends a *deny-join*/*grant-join* message to the new member.

Step3: Upon *grant-join,* each member computes the new group key using the new group member's public key.

$$K_{new} = K_{previous} \times K_{i+1} = K_1 \times K_2 \times \ldots \times K_i \times K_{i+1},$$
$$= <e, N_1 \times N_2 \times \ldots \times N_i \times N_{i+1}>.$$

3.4.2 Member Leave Operation

When a member $M_m \mid M_m \in [M_1, M_i]$, wants to leave the group, it broadcasts a *leave-request* message to all group members $\{M_1, \ldots, M_i\}$. To prohibit invalid group member M_m to decrypt the encrypted message *m'* with the invalid decryption key $K^{'}_{m} = <d_m, N_m>$, the group key K has to be changed.

Step1: A member M_m broadcasts a *leave-request* message to all group members.

Step2: Every member updates the list of other group members' public key information.

Step3: Every member computes the new group key using updated group members' public key list.

$$K_{new} = K_{previous} / K_m$$
$$= <e, N_1 \times N_2 \times \ldots \times N_{m-1} \times N_{m+1} \times \ldots \times N_{i-1} \times N_i>.$$

3.4.3 Forced Member Delete Operation

Upon completion of a consensus protocol run, each process ends up with a list of suspected processes. These processes should be removed from the group and a new group key should be re-keyed, as some of them could be malicious. All processes execute the following:

Step1: Start a new run of consensus solving algorithm (Algorithm ConsensusUsingByzantineFaultDetectors) and wait until completion.

Step2: Find if any group members are added to the suspect list.

Step3: For each member in suspect list, compute a new group key by deleting the suspected group member from the old key.

$$K_{new} = K_{previous} / K_m$$
$$= <e, N_1 \times N_2 \times \ldots \times N_{m-1} \times N_{m+1} \times \ldots \times N_{i-1} \times N_i>.$$

4 Conclusions and Future Work

In this paper, we propose a new secure checkpointing protocol that is suitable for an active intruder environment. We make three major contributions. First, we develop a consensus protocol based on Byzantine fault detectors. Using this protocol a group of servers can determine if some member of the group has been attacked and compromised. Second, we develop the main checkpointing protocol in which the checkpoint data is split into *n* chunks and dispersed securely among *n* recipient; this is done in such a manner that any k of those n recipients can get together and re-create the checkpoint information however, no k-1 or lesser number of recipients can. Moreover, no checkpoint information is dispersed to a server that has been determined as malicious. The third contribution is the development of a simple yet elegant group encryption scheme. This scheme provides the usual member join and leave operations. In addition, the group key allows a member to be kicked out if a quorum of the group determines that the member is malicious. To our knowledge, this is the first secure checkpointing protocol to offer this rich array of feature.

The protocol is still in its early phase of development. While individual modules have been implemented and tested we still do not have an integrated whole. Our next step will be to integrate these individual modules into a working proof-of-concept. A natural extension of this work is to develop the corresponding secure recovery protocol. This will ultimately contribute to our bigger effort in developing secure process migration techniques.

Acknowledgement

The work of Indrajit Ray was partially supported by the U.S. National Science Foundation under grant IIS-0242258. The opinion reflected in this paper is that of the authors and does not necessarily represent that of the NSF.

References

[1] S.I. Feldman and C.B. Brown, "Igor: A system for program debugging via reversible execution," ACM SIGPLAB Notices, Workshop on Parallel and Distributed Debugging, vol.24(1), Jan. 1989.

[2] J. Plank, J. Xu, and R. Netzer. "Compressed differences: An algorithm for fast incremental checkpointing." Technical Report CS-95-302, University of Tennessee, August 1995.

[3] H. Nam, J. Kim, S.J. Hong, and S. Lee, "Probabilistic checkpointing," In Proceedings of the 27th International Symposium on Fault-Tolerant Computing, Seattle, WA, June 1997.

[4] E.N. Elnozahy, "How safe is probabilistic checkpointing?," In Proceedings of the 28th International Symposium on Fault-Tolerant Computing, Munich, Germany, June 1998.

[5] M. Rabin, "Fingerprinting by random polynomials." Technical Report TR-15-81. Center for Research in Computing Technology. Harvard University, Cambridge, MA 1981.

[6] M. Rabin, "Efficient dispersal of information for security, load balancing, and fault tolerance." *Journal of the ACM*. vol. 36(2), April 1989.

[7] H. Nam, J. Kim, S.J. Hong, and S. Lee, "Secure checkpointing." In Proceedings of the 2001 Pacific Rim International Symposium on Dependable Computing, Seoul, Korea, December 2001.

[8] I. Ray, I. Ray and N. Narasimhamurthi, "A fair exchange e-commerce protocol with automated dispute resolution." In Proceedings of the 14th Annual IFIP WG 11.3 Working Conference on Database Security, Schoorl, The Netherlands, August 2000.

[9] K. P. Kihlstrom, L. E. Moser, P. M. Melliar-Smith, "Byzantine Fault Detectors for Solving consensus." *The Computer Journal* vol 46(1), 2003.

[10] L. Lamport et al., "The Byzantine generals problem," *ACM Transactions on Programming Languages and Systems,* vol. 4(3), July 1982.

[11] T. Chandra and S. Toueg, "Unreliable failure detectors for reliable distributed systems." *Journal of the ACM,* vol. 43(2), March 1996.

[12] D. Malkhi, D. M. Reiter, "Unreliable intrusion detection in distributed computations." In Proceedings of the 10th Computer Security Foundations Workshop, Rockport, MA, June, 1997.

[13] P. Feldman and S. Micali. "Optimal algorithms for byzantine agreement." In Proceedings of the 20th Annual ACM Symposium on Theory of Computing, Chicago, IL, May 1988.

[14] M. Steiner, G. Tsudik and M. Waidner, "CLIQUES: A new approach to group key agreement," Proceedings of the 18th International Conference on Distributed Computing Systems, Amsterdam, The Netherlands, May 1998.

[15] Y. Kim, A. Perrig and G. Tsudik, "Simple and fault-tolerant key agreement for dynamic collaborative groups." In Proceedings of the 7th ACM Conference on Computer and Communications Security, Athens, Greece, November 2000.

[16] J. S. Plack, Kai Li and Michael A. Puening, "Diskless checkpointing." *IEEE Transaction on Parallel and Distributed System*, vol 9(10), October, 1998

[17] J. S. Plank, M. Beck, G. Kingsley, and K. Li, "Libckpt: Transparent checkpointing under Unix." In Proceedings of the USENIX Winter 1995 Technical Conference, New Orleans, January 1995.

[18] M. J. Fisher, N. A. Lynch and M. S. Paterson, "Impossibility of distributed consensus with one faulty process," *Journal of the ACM*, vol. 32(2), April 1985

MobiCoin: Digital Cash for M-Commerce

Ranjit Abbadasari[1], Ravi Mukkamala[1], and V. Valli Kumari[2]

[1] Old Dominion University, Norfolk VA 23529, USA
mukka@cs.odu.edu,
http://www.cs.odu.edu/~mukka
[2] S.R.K.R Engineering College, Bhimavaram AP 524204, India

Abstract. Advances in mobile device technology have given rise to applications that rely on trusted hardware. These have also made the once only virtually possible ideas into real applications. One such application is transforming the mobile phone into a mobile wallet with digital cash that supports both anonymity (as in real cash) and security. In this paper, we introduce MobiCoin, a protocol to support M-commerce transactions. It employs SIM cards for data protection and active certificates for distributed trust. MobiCoin is secure, durable, fair, atomic and accountable. It may be used as a digital cash protocol with a mobile digital wallet without the trade-off for anonymity. In addition, it is an offline protocol, thus increasing the efficiency and availability of m-commerce transactions. The paper describes the model, the infrastructure, and the details of the protocol. It also discusses some implementation issues and security implications of using the protocol.

1 Introduction

While e-commerce is still the major boom in the global business scenario, new applications and technologies are beginning to focus on mobile commerce or m-commerce [22]. As the use of mobile devices becomes cheaper and convenient, more will the commerce through mobile devices. At present, a majority of the applications that exist require users to use credit cards to pay for commercial transactions through mobile phones. This requires the user to carry a mobile phone as well as his wallet. More convenience is achieved if we could add the functionality of the wallet into the mobile phone. The stedy improvement in the hardware side of mobile devices is one of the catalysts for efforts in this direction. For instance, the SIM card used in a mobile phone has changed from a memory chip to a smart card, which can perform several tasks [8]. The main objective of this paper is to show that the advances in mobile technology can be utilized to transform a mobile phone into an electronic wallet that contains digital cash.

The major inhibitor of m-commerce is the perception that it is not secure. However, many protocol standards are now trying to make m-commerce more secure and reliable [21]. An ideal m-commerce transaction system supports atomicity, fairness, accountability, privacy, and security [19]. Most often it is seen that the user privacy is given little or no importance compared to other features.

R.K. Ghosh and H. Mohanty (Eds.): ICDCIT 2004, LNCS 3347, pp. 441–451, 2004.

Traditional physical cash (or currency note) provides the user a high degree of privacy, as it is not traceable to a single user, when used for purchases. Our idea is to develop a protocol that replicates this cash using mobile phone as an electronic wallet.

Our protocol, MobiCoin, is based on PayCash [14], an e-commerce protocol. Primarily, our protocol is designed to work offline, without involving a third-party broker for every transaction. This change makes it all the more efficient because the communication overhead previously needed to contact the third-party is eliminated. On the other hand, none of the advantages offered by PayCash are lost. The hardware capability of SIM cards [17] and the feature-rich active certificates [13] enable MobiCoin to function in an offline fashion offering the much-needed efficiency for m-commerce transactions. While the SIM card is used as a storage medium for the digital cash and as a secure foundation for active certificates, active certificates implement distributed trust between various parties in an m-commerce transaction.

The paper is organized as follows. Section 2 provides the background for the technologies employed in MobiCoin. Section 3 describes MobiCoin's overall architecture. Section 4 describes the protocol in detail. Section 5 provides a detailed analysis of the protocol and proves some properties that MobiCoin satisfies. Finally, section 6 summarizes the contributions of the paper and describes our plans for future work.

2 Background

In this section, we provide a brief background of the technologies underlying the proposed MobiCoin protocol.

M-commerce has been defined as the use of handheld wireless devices to communicate, interact, and transact via high-speed connection to the Internet. A number of issues arise when we try to port the current e-commerce protocols and applications to M-commerce [22]. Mobile phone devices differ from desktops in many ways [7, 20]. Secure transmission is yet another issue [11]. While developments are taking place in each of these areas, this paper is mainly concerned with developing an M-commerce transaction protocol that supports authentication, authorization, fairness, privacy, non-repudiation, and efficiency.

Active Certificates expand the domain of digital certificate applicability to dynamic authorization, privilege management, and access control [13]. In MobiCoin, we primarily use active certificates to facilitate access control (for read/update) to the data that is stored in the SIM card and also to perform some simple operations such as checking the validity of data.

Smart cards are introduced in wireless networks as *SIM cards* [1]. They provide superior fraud protection since they were specifically designed to secure data against physical and logical attacks [16, 17]. MobiCoin employs SIM cards for their programmability and security [6].

An M-commerce transaction protocol may be called off-line or on-line based on the necessity for its interaction with a third-party during a transaction [15].

Some of the well-known on-line payment protocols are NetBill [6], PayCash [14], CyberCoin (http://www.cybercoin.com), and DigiCash [5]. Off-line protocols, on the other hand, do not involve a third party during the payment part of the transaction. The problem with off-line protocols is the issues of double spending and overspending [5, 24]. However, it is an efficient system. In MobiCoin, we employ off-line protocols and yet avoid overspending and double spending.

A good M-commerce payment protocol should be both convenient and secure [24]. One such protocol is the Wireless Payment Protocol (WPP). The shortcoming of WPP is that it does not actually address security. SWPP [24] is proposed to make up for WPP's security deficiencies. MobiPay (www.mobipay.com) is another system for mobile payments.

3 MobiCoin: Architecture

As stated in the introduction, the proposed protocol, MobiCoin, is targeted at offering security, efficiency, and privacy to m-commerce transactions. It is an offline mobile payment system offering a high level of privacy and anonymity to a mobile user. In addition, it offers features to prevent double spending and overspending, addressing the concerns of brokers. In this section, we describe the overall architecture and approach of MobiCoin.

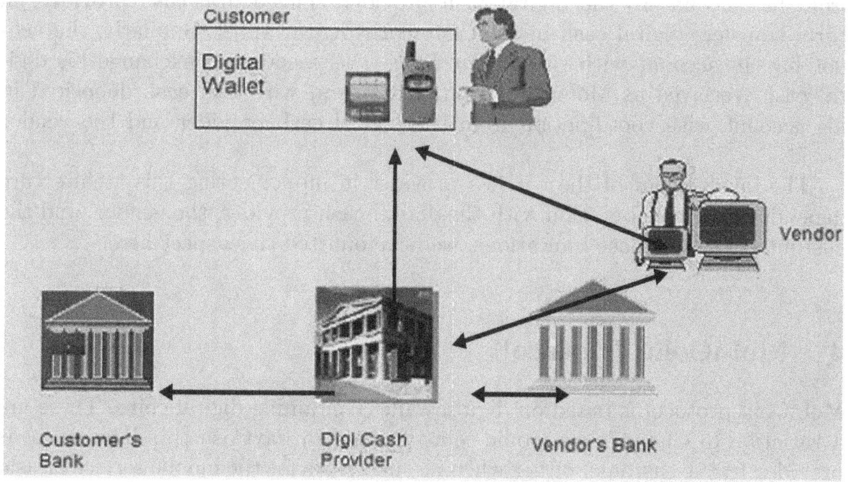

Fig. 1. Overall Architecture

As shown in Figure 1, six primary entities are involved in the protocol. The *customer* (or the user) owns a mobile phone. He/she is supported by a *wireless provider* (e.g., Verizon, T-Mobile, etc.) through a mobile phone. In addition to its basic functionality as a telephone, the mobile phone also offers several other internet-based services. In this paper, we are primarily interested in its role as a tool for enabling M-commerce.

The *digital cash provider* (or broker) is responsible for digital cash. It is the one that supplies a *digital wallet* to mobile phone customers to use M-commerce transaction services. The digital wallet is installed on a secure SIM card. (In cooperation with the wireless provider, it is also possible for the digital cash provider to install the wallet on wireless provider's SIM card as an added functionality.)

The *digital wallet* (implemented as an active certificate, in our work), in addition to containing digital cash in the form of MobiCoins, also contains code to support its interactions with the digital cash provider, the customer, and the vendor. As explained in the next section, it may optionally contain an audit of earlier transactions. The digital wallet is assumed to be secure and reliable, and hence its data and code are tamper-proof.

The *vendor* (or the merchant) sells electronic goods such as E-books, MP3 downloads, software, and results from digital library searches. He participates in the digital cash provider's network. So his system has an installation of secure software provided by the digital cash provider. The software has the ability to securely interact with the customer as well as the digital cash provider.

The customer has an account with a bank (*customer bank*). This is a traditional bank (e.g., Bank of America). Whenever a customer wants to enrich his digital wallet with more money, he can authorize his bank to transfer money from his account to the digital cash provider. The digital cash provider, in turn, transfers digital cash to the customer's digital wallet. Similarly, the vendor has an account with the *vendor bank*. The vendor can exchange his digital cash (received as MobiCoins from customers) with real cash deposited in his account with coordination from the digital cash provider and the vendor bank.

The involvement of the wireless provider in implementing this architecture depends on its collaboration with the digital cash provider, the vendor, and the customer. Due to space limitations, we have omitted this aspect here.

4 MobiCoin: Protocol

MobiCoin protocol is based on digital wallet containing digital coins. These are a variation of Chaum's electronic coins [3] used in PayCash [14]. The wallet is provided to the customer either when he subscribes for the mobile service or as a special subscription service with a monthly fee. The digital wallet is installed on a SIM card provided either by the wireless provider or the digital cash provider. The protocol has the following five primary operations.

(i) Blank Wallet Creation. Initially, the customer receives an inactive blank wallet. If the customer chooses to use the MobiCoin wallet, the wallet (the code part of it) handles subscription by executing the relevant code on the SIM card. It asks the customer for some subscription details and contacts the digital cash provider with the details to customize the account. The subscription process consists of the following steps:

1. Associating the customer's bank account with customer's MobiCoin account with the digital cash provider.
2. Providing information such as username, password, or pin, in an encrypted form, to authorize the digit al cash provider to interact with the customer bank.
3. Providing options such as using credit or debit to create the coins.

The details provided by the customer are encrypted and formatted by the wallet and sent as a message to the digital cash provider. Once the registration is successful, the wallet is considered active and ready for m-commerce transactions. The *value* of the wallet is initially set to zero. The *value* is maintained as a secure data field in the digital wallet showing the amount of digital cash in the wallet.

(ii) Coin Creation. This primarily involves an interactions between the customer and the digital cash provider through messages M0 and M1 (Fig. 2). The details are as follows.

1. Customer decides the amount of electronic cash (say n) to be purchased from the digital cash provider and interacts with his digital wallet. The digital wallet (implemented as an active certificate) generates a key pair <public key P, secret key S>. (Optionally, the pair can be generated by the customer and provided to the digital wallet.) Depending on the degree of anonymity required, the customer can choose to use the same key pair or different key pair every time he wants to create a new MobiCoin. The digital wallet now creates message **M0** sent to the digital cash provider:

   M0: {cusID, n, blind(f(P))}signed by customer

   f(.) and g(.) are two well-known functions published by the digital cash provider and stored in the digital wallet as code. $g^{-1}(.)$ is kept as a secret by the broker, and cannot be computed from g(.). blind() is a blinding function [4]. Thus, the digital cash provider never gets to see either P or f(P). This makes the coin anonymous.
2. Once the digital cash provider gets M0, it identifies the customer using the customer ID and the digital signature of the customer. Further authentication can be done by interacting with the digital wallet. It then debits "n" from the customer's bank account and hence has the prepayment for the MobiCoin to be minted. It applies g^{-1}(blind(f(P))) function to obtain a minted coin. This is like a stamp made by the third party because only the digital cash provider knows g^{-1}. He sends message M1 to the customer's digital wallet.

   M1: {n, g^{-1} (blind (f(P)))}signed by digital cash provider

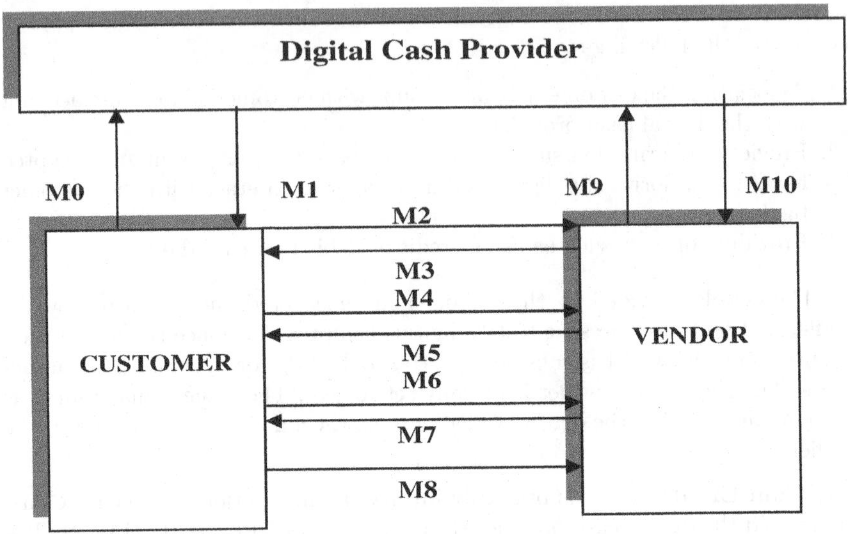

Fig. 2. Interactions in MobiCoin

3. The digital wallet unblinds the above function to obtain $g^{-1}(f(P))$. At this stage, the customer h as his newly minted MobiCoin, which can be used for M-commerce. Additionally, the digital wallet has a field called expenditure "e". This is initially set to zero when the certificate is issued.

(iii) Negotiation. This operation takes place between the customer and the vendor when customer decides to purchase an item. Referring to Fig. 2, the step-by-step flow of this operation is as follows.

1. The customer selects the item he wants to purchase and sends it as message **M2**.
2. The vendor makes two electronic documents, *record-1* and *record-2*, and sends them to the customer. Record-1 contains the description of the product and the details such as the price agreed for the transaction. Record-2 is an electronic payment form that contains an authorization for the third-party to transfer funds from the customer's account to the vendor's account. Record-1 and Record-2 contain a unique serial number for the transaction. The vendor signs both the records and sends M3 to the customer.

$$\textbf{M3: } \{\{\textbf{record-1}\}_{vendor}, \{\textbf{record-2}\}_{vendor}\}$$

3. Customer's digital wallet signs the record-1 and sends it to the vendor as message **M4**.

$$\textbf{M4:}\{\textbf{record-1}\}_{vendor+customer}.$$

4. Vendor sends the goods in an encrypted form to the customer as message **M5**. The decryption key is still with the vendor. Thus, the customer gets the goods before payment but then actual goods are not transferred.

$$\mathbf{M5{:}\{goods}_{(encrypted)}\mathbf{\}}$$

(iv) Payment. Here, customer pays the vendor. Like the PayCash protocol, functions *sign()* and *verify()* are used for payment. The *sign()* is used to encrypt some information with a secret key. For example *sign(S, Z)* encrypts message Z with the secret key S. The function *verify()* is used to decrypt the *sign()* value with the public key. For example *verify* (P, sign (S, Z)) = Z. Both the functions are well known to all three parties. It has the following steps.

1. The digital wallet computes ***sign*(S, record-1)** and sends the message M6. The record-1 is also encrypted using the secret key chosen by the customer and appended to the message. It should be noted that the message is sent only when the condition **n >= k+e,** where k is the cost of goods, and e is the amount expended so far, is met.

M6:{record-1, *sign* (S, record-1), k, P, g^{-1} (f(P))}signed by customer

2. The vendor computes f(P) from **P**. It then applies g() to the **g^{-1} (f(P))** field. If the computed f(P) tallies with the result of the previous computation, it can be sure that the coin is valid and also that "P" is a legal key. It applies *verify*(***sign*(S, record-1)**) using P and gets the value of record-1. It then compares the result of the previous computation with that of **record-1.** If they both tally, it can be sure that the message is from the customer. At this stage, the vendor can be sure about the customer and also that the coin is valid because record-1 is valid and also f(P) which is valid is also minted by the digital cash provider. It sends the decryption key to the customer in the form of M7. The key is encrypted using the customer's public key P. Later the customer can use his secret key to decrypt the key.

$$\mathbf{M7{:}\{record\text{-}1\ +Key}_{(signedbyvendor+EncryptedusingP)}\mathbf{\}}$$

3. Customer's digital wallet sends M8 in acknowledgement of the decryption goods and hence the acknowledgement for the goods. **M8:{record-2} vendor, customer.**

(v) Coin Cashing. Occasionally, the vendor may want to convert the digital cash (MobiCoins) into real cash. This involves the following steps.

1. The vendor presents **M9** containing record-2, which authorizes payment, to the digital cash provider. Record-2 is signed by the customer and by the vendor. So transfer of funds cannot take place without the notice of any of the parties. Also a time stamp is given for record-2. The vendor is expected to cash the coin within this time period. Even though the digital cash provider knows that the customer is transferring funds to the vendor, it never gets to know why the transfer is taking place.

2. The digital cash provider transfers the funds to the vendor's account basing on record-2 and sends a reply as **M10**.

5 Protocol Analysis

In this section, we try to analyze the proposed protocol and see how it satisfies different properties expected of an M-commerce protocol.

Claim 1: MobiCoin Supports Offline M-Commerce Transactions.
In this protocol, the digital coin (MobiCoin) of any value may be generated prior to customer's M-transaction. Customer can even recharge his mobile wallet and use the coin at a later time. So the customer-vendor transaction does not involve the digital cash provider, and hence it is offline. Similarly, the vendor can transact with the digital cash provider anytime prior to the digital cash's expiration time. So the vendor-digital cash provider transaction is also offline.

Claim 2: MobiCoin Allows Only Authorized User to Take Part in M-Commerce.
This transactional objective is achieved because only customers who are members with the digital cash provider (following MobiCoin protocol) can get a minted coin. The digital cash provider checks whether a customer ID (cusId in M0) is valid prior to processing a request for digital cash creation. This also enhances a vendor's trust in M-transactions since he knows that he is transacting with a customer who is also known to digital cash provider.

Claim 3: MobiCoin Prevents Double Spending of Digital Cash.
In the protocol, the digital wallet is maintained on a tamper-proof SIM card. In fact, the code in MobiCoin ensures that it is only residing at the digital wallet to which it is initially assigned at the time of its creation by the digital cash provider. The fields in the MobiCoin such as its current value, total expenditure, etc., are stored in an encrypted form on the SIM card. These are only accessible to the digital wallet. For this reason, there is no danger of a customer (or a hacker) making multiple copies of a MobiCoin.

Claim 4: MobiCoin Prevents Over Spending of Digital Cash.
Prior to approval of a purchase, the digital wallet ensures that the current value of MobiCoin is at least as much as the purchase amount. Unless this condition is satisfied, the digital wallet does not approve a transaction. In fact, the digital wallet maintains an up-to-date value of a MobiCoin by updating its current value after every transaction (credit or debit). Prior to any subtractions due to purchases, it ensures that the amount being subtracted is identical to that mentioned in the corresponding record-1 of the transaction. Record-1 is stored for later audits. In addition, except for the digital wallet, no other entity has access to the code or data fields of MobiCoin. These are stored in an encrypted manner. Thus, no illegal updates are possible on MobiCoin.

Claim 5: MobiCoin Prevents Non-repudiation.

The protocol keeps track of every interaction between the parties. Let us consider repudiation in different point of views.

1. *The customer claims that the goods received were not what he asked or the vendor sends wrong goods.* The vendor stores the description of the goods in an EPO (Electronic Purchase Order), record-1. The vendor signs the EPO and the customer also has to sign the EPO when he pays the vendor. So a mutually signed record of what the customer and vendor agreed is present. Thus, the parties cannot repudiate on the issue of the order.
2. *The customer or vendor dispute the price.* Again the price of a purchase is agreed and is recorded in the EPO that is signed by the customer and the vendor. So neither the vendor nor the customer can claim an incorrect amount.
3. *Customer does not pay for the goods after receiving it.* Here, with only informational goods, the vendor gives the decryption key only after receiving the payment from the customer.
4. *Vendor and customer collude to cheat digital cash provider by specifying a higher redeeming value from digital cash provider but deducting a lesser amount from MobiCoin.* The digital wallet and MobiCoin code will not allow such transactions to take place. They have sufficient code to compare the agreed amount and deducting only that amount. Only when digital wallet/Mobicoin code are satisfied that the amount being sent is equal to the amount in record-1, they send the signed record-2 to vendor. The customer has no way to alter the process.

Claim 6: MobiCoin Is Resistant to Replay Attacks.

Every message that is exchanged between the parties contains a unique order number either in record-1 or record-2. This can be used to keep track of duplicate messages that are replayed either due to network problems or by a malicious person tapping into the messages. If the vendor receives more than one message, say M6, he just ignores all the other messages with the same order number. Also, even if the malicious person interrupts the message in which the goods are received, he will not be able to decrypt it because the key is encrypted and can be decrypted only using the secret key.

6 Conclusion and Future Work

In this paper, we have introduced the MobiCoin wallet and have shown that M-Commerce can indeed have digital cash. Previous protocols had a trade-off with anonymity for efficiency, introducing vulnerabilities of double spending and overspending. In the case of MobiCoin, we have eliminated the need for a centralized agency during payment making the system both fast and inexpensive. MobiCoin is secure in terms of preventing customer fraud, double spending, non-repudiation and allows for partial and full anonymity. This paper just explains a theoretical basis for the proposed system with some infrastructural and implementation details. Our main task after this would be to implement the above model. Support for multiple currencies is another aspect that can be incorporated into the system. Micro payments are also possible with the above scheme but a more simple system, which also preserves all the advantages of MobiCoin, would be desirable.

References

1. Carrara, J., Legaspi, L. E.: SIM Cards: At the Heart of Digital Wireless Security. Annual Review of Communications, (2001), Vol. 54, 1-10
2. Chan, S.-C: An Overview of Smart Card security. http://home.hkstar.com/~alanchan/ papers/smartCardSecurity/, (1997)
3. Chaum, D., Fiat, A., Naor, N: Transaction Systems To Make Big Brother Obsolete. Communications of the ACM, (1985), Vol. 28, No. 5, 1030-1044
4. Chaum, D.: Blinding for Unanticipated Signatures. Advances in Cryptology EUROCRYPT '87, Springer-Verlag, (1987), 227-233
5. Chaum, D.: An introduction to ecash: DigiCash. http://www.digicash.com, (1995)
6. Cox, B. J.D., Tygar, Marvin, S.: Netbill Security and Transaction Protocol. First USENIX Workshop on Electronic Commerce, (1995), 77-88
7. De Bruijn, O., Spence, R., Chong, M. Y.: RSVP Browser: Web Browsing on Small Screen Devices. Personal and Ubiquitous Computing, (2002), 1-4
8. Dhem, J., Feyt, N.: Hardware and Software Symbiosis Helps Smart Card Evolution. IEEE MICRO, (2001), 14-25
9. Gemmell, P. S.: Traceable E-cash. IEEE Spectrum, (1997), Vol. 34, No. 2, 35-37
10. Gordon, P., Gebauer, J.: M-Commerce: Revolution + Inertia = Evolution. IM Information Management and Consulting, (2001), Vol. 2
11. Juul, N. C., Jørgensen, N.: Security Issues in Mobile Commerce using WAP. 15th Bled Electronic Commerce Conference, (2002), 6-13
12. Medvinsky, G., Clifford B.: Netcash: A design for practical electronic currency on the internet. First ACM Conference on Computer and Communications Security, (1993), 102-106
13. Mukkamala, R., Balusani,S.: Active Certificates: A New Paradigm in Digital Certificate Management. International Conference on parallel Processing Workshops (ICPPW'02), (2002), 30-37
14. Peha, M., Khamitov, M.: PayCash: A Secure Efficient Internet Payment System. 5th international conference on Electronic commerce, (2003), 125-130
15. Poutanen, T., Hinton, H., Stumm, M.: NetCents: A Lightweight Protocol for Secure Micropayments. Third USENIX Workshop on Electronic Commerce, (1998)
16. Shelfer, K. M., Procaccino, J. D.: SmartCard Evolution. Communications of the ACM, (2002)
17. SmartTrust: SIM - software shift. http://www.smarttrust.com/sim/default.asp, (2004)
18. Stefan, B.: Untraceable Off-line Cashing Wallet with Observer. Crypto'93, LNCS 773, Springer-Verlag, (1994), 302-318
19. Steves, D. V., Yurkanan, C. E.,Gouda, M.: An ACID Framework for Electronic Commerce. http://www.cs.utexas.edu/users/dhs/papers/ictec_98/forum.html, (1998)

20. Tandon, R., Mandal, S., Saha, D.: M-commerce-Issues and Challenges. International conference on High performance Computing, (2003)
21. Tarasewich, P.: Mobile commerce opportunities and challenges: Designing mobile commerce applications. Communications of the ACM, (2003), 46(12), 57-60
22. Tsalgatidou, A., Veijalainen, J.: Mobile Electronic Commerce: Emerging Issues. Proceedings of EC-We, (2000), 477-486
23. Varshney, U., Vetter, R.: Mobile Networks and Applications. Mobile Networks and Applications (MONET), (2002), 7(3), 185-198
24. Wang, H., Kranakis, E.: Secure Wireless Payment Protocol. Proceedings of ICT, (2001)

Cellular Automata: An Ideal Candidate for a Block Cipher

Debdeep Mukhopadhyay* and Dipanwita RoyChowdhury**

Indian Institute of Technology, Kharagpur, India

Abstract. Confusion and diffusion are two important requirements of the round of a block cipher. In the present paper Cellular Automata (CA) has been identified as a mathematical tool to achieve these. The analytical framework of the automata has been used to characterize a new class of linear CA and to implement the non-linearity through a non-linear reversible CA. A generalized ideal structure of the block cipher round have been developed and has been shown to perform both encryption and decryption.

Keywords: Cellular Automata, Block Ciphers, Cycle Structure, Non-linearity, Self-invertibility.

1 Introduction

With the ever increasing growth of data communication, the need for security and privacy has become a necessity. CA based pseudorandom generator has been studied in ([1, 2, 3, 4, 5, 6]). Quality of randomness has been evaluated as per the criterion set by Knuth [7]. The advent of wireless communication and other handheld devices like Personal Digital Assistants and smart cards have made the implementation of cryptosystems a major issue. Modern day ciphers require the scope of area minimization. The CA can be a good choice to develop algorithms which are compact.

Research have been carried out to use the CA for encryption as the automata has been known to have remarkable pseudorandom property. However the current implementations face the following problems. The maximal group CA (that is the CA in which all the non-zero elements lie in one cycle) used by several researchers to implement ciphers has the advantage of cyclic nature in its state transitions. This cyclic behavior of the CA helps in performing both encryption and decryption using the same cipher. But for the maximal group CA the length of the CA grows exponentially with the number of cells. Thus the number of clock cycles required to encrypt/decrypt grows exponentially with the number of cells. The other problem of CA based ciphers is the affine nature, which makes

* Debdeep Mukhopadhyay is a Phd student in the Department of Computer Sc. and Engg, IIT Kharagpur. debdeep@vlsi.iitkgp.ernet.in

** Dipanwita RoyChowdhury is Associate Professor in the Department of Computer Sc. and Engg, IIT Kharagpur. drc@cse.iitkgp.ernet.in

R.K. Ghosh and H. Mohanty (Eds.): ICDCIT 2004, LNCS 3347, pp. 452–457, 2004.

the modules amenable to cryptanalysis. The cipher systems based on Cellular Automata proposed by Nandi et al. [8] were proved to be affine and insecure [9]. Thus non-linearity is an essential feature of ciphers. However non-linearity should be introduced such that the cycle structure of the CA is not altered [10]. The present paper provides a viable solution to the above problems.

The outline of the paper is as follows: *Section 2* gives an overview on the proposed block structure. The linear and non-linear transformations of the round are constructed in *sections 3* and *4* respectively. *Section 5* presents the final round of the block cipher and also describes the properties of the overall round structure. The work is concluded in *section 6.*

2 Present Work

Research have been carried out to use the Cellular Automata (CA) for development of ciphers. The designs use maximal group CA because the cyclic nature helps in obtaining structures which can be used to both encrypt and decrypt data. However such structures have the lengths growing exponentially with the number of cells and hence with the number of bits of data. The number of bits inturn decides the security of the scheme. Also non-linearity should be introduced to the affine nature of linear CAs. However the non-linearity should not disturb the cyclic nature of the CA cipher.

In the following sections a structure of the block cipher is proposed which solves the above problems. The block cipher round is composed of a linear transformation T_1 and a non-linear part f. The linear (T_1) and the non-linear (f) parts are composed together to form a structure (T_2), where $T_2 = f.T_1.f^{-1}$ (refer figure 1). Thus non-linearity is introduced into the cipher and it has been proved that such a structure does not disturb the cyclic nature of the linear CA. It has

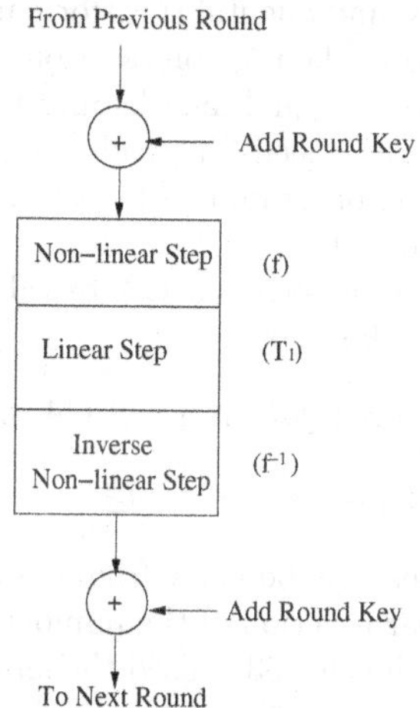

Fig. 1. The Proposed Structure of a Block Cipher Round

been shown that the transformation T_2 is self-invertible and fast (as the number of clock cycles required to operate are lesser). Also the fast-forwardness property of the structure helps in obtaining low cost and high-speed implementations.

In the following sections the linear and non-linear parts of the cipher are constructed with Cellular Automata.

3 Construction of the Linear Transformation (T_1)

The linear part of the cipher is constructed with the help of Cellular Automata. The transform must be a group CA as the cyclic nature of the state space helps in devising architectures which can both be used to encrypt and decrypt data. However in contrast to the maximal group CA (which is being used widely) the cycles of the new transform must grow linearly with the size of the automata. This makes the cipher faster inspite of having a larger block size, that is the speed of the cipher does not interfere with the security of the scheme. In the following subsection a Cellular Automata constructed out of the rule 153 have been characterized. It has been analytically shown that the automata forms cycles of equal dimension which grows linearly with the number of cells.

3.1 Characterization of the Fundamental Transformations and Its State Spaces

One of the rules of fundamental transformations ($\overline{T}$) is the rule 153, [11]. The present section characterizes the CA with rule 153. It is known that if a cellular automata with rule 153 is fed with an initial seed of X, then the cellular automata produces an output $\overline{T}(X) = T(X) + IF$, where I is a unit matrix and F is all one vector. Hence, we have $X, \overline{T}(X)$ and $\overline{T}^2(X)$ members of the same cycle. Physically, an n-cell uniform CA having rule 153 evolves with equal number of cyclic states. This fundamental transformation $\overline{T}$ is used as the linear transformation T_1 mentioned in the previous section. The CA has some remarkable properties. The CA evolves equal lengths and the length for an n-cell CA grows linearly with the number of cells. The advantage of such a structure is to obtain a module which can be programmed to perform both an encryption and decryption module at a faster rate.

The following theorem characterizes a CA based on the rule $\overline{T}$. The proof has been ommitted for the lack of space.

Theorem 1. *The length of cycle for an n-cell CA, having rule $\overline{T}$, is*

$$l = 2^{\lfloor log n \rfloor + 1}, n \geq 2 \tag{1}$$

The following observations may be made from the above theorem. The length of the proposed CA is a linear function of the number of cells. Thus if the length of the complemented CA with rule 153 is used the length of the cycles (l) formed may be obtained from equation 3. Thus $\overline{T}^l = I$. Thus $\overline{T}^{l/2} = \overline{T}^{-l/2}$. Thus using the automata self-invertible transforms can be constructed. Also the number of clock cycles required are less compared to a maximal group CA where the length of the cycles depend exponentially on the block size. Also the proposed CA does not have any fixed point compared to the maximal group CA. Thus the ciphers developed out of the 153 rule CA are fast and also hardware efficient.

4 Construction of the Non-linear Transformation (f)

Non-linearity to the block cipher should be introduced such that the cyclic nature of the embedded CA is not disturbed. The block cipher is thus self-invertible and thus is amenable to efficient implementation. The implementation of the non-linear function is also a major challenge. In the following subsections first it has been shown how to introduce non-linearity to the round of the block cipher. It has been proved that the non-linearity does not hamper the cyclic nature achieved by the linear transform described in the previous section. The total structure with both the linear and non-linear parts have been found to be self-invertible. Subsequently a non-linear CA has been suggested to implement the non-linear part. The CA has been shown to be reversible. Some of the properties for which the CA is a good candidate for a one-way function has also been discussed.

4.1 Introducing Non-linearity to the CA Transformation

Theorem 2. *The cycle structure of a transformation* T_1 *is the same as* $T_2 = f.T_1.f^{-1}$.

Proof. Let the length of T_1 be l, thus $T_1^l(X) = T_1^l(X)$.

Let us evaluate $Y = T_2^l(X) = (f.T_1.f^{-1})(f.T_1.f^{-1})\ldots(ltimes)(f.T_1.f^{-1})(X)$
$= (f.T_1^2.f^{-1}).(f.T_1.f^{-1})\ldots(f.T_1.f^{-1})(X)$
$= (f.T_1^l.f^{-1})(X)$
$= (f.f^{-1})(X)$ [since, $T_1^l(f^{-1}(X)) = f^{-1}(X)$]
$= f.f^{-1}(X)$
$= X$.

Thus the cycle structure of T_1 and T_2 are same.

It may be easily observed that the fields generated by T_1 and $f.T_1.f^{-1}$ are one-one. The new transformation can thus be used instead of the Cellular Automata alone. It may be noted that the transformation f is used to introduce non-linearity in the block ciphers. The following subsection shows a possible means to implement the non-linear part of the cipher using a reversible Cellular Automata.

4.2 Development of the Non-linear Part

The other feature required is that the Cellular Automata should have a non-linear rule. The update rule that has been used is: $x_{t+1}^i = x_t^i \oplus (x_t^{i+1} + x_t^{i+2})$.

The inverse rule for the non-linear CA may be obtained. The large radius of the inverse rule may be readily observed from the equations, thus making the rule a candidate for a "one-way" function. The resulting automata displays much the same behavior as rule 30 would if it was skewed sideways. The rule 30 automata is known to exhibit good randomness property but the rule is not reversible. The following section sums up the construction of the round of the block cipher.

5 The Resulting CA Based Cipher Structure

The previous sections identify a non-linear CA (f) and characterizes a linear CA (T_1) which can be the basic building components of the round of an ideal block cipher. Present section deals with the construction of a generalized cipher structure which employs the above transformations. It shows how the properties like self-invertibility, non-linearity and fast forwardness can be achieved by the proposed CA based cipher round.

The transformation T_2 has the advantage of fast forwardness. This may be observed as follows:

$$\begin{aligned} T_2^m(X) &= (f.T_1.f^{-1})^m \\ &= f(T_1(f^{-1}(f(T_1(f^{-1}(\ldots(mtimes)f(T_1(f^{-1})))\ldots)(X) \\ &= fT_1^m f^{-1}(X). \end{aligned}$$

Thus the transformation T_2 can be made to iterate without requiring the non-linear function to be iterated. Since the non-linear function is more computation intensive this reduces the cost of the operation and is amenable to efficient implementations. Also the transformation T_2 is self invertible. Thus the same round can be used for encryption and decryption.

The figure 2 shows the final constructed cipher round of a block cipher. The round operates on a block of data, which may be conceptualised to be made of bytes. For example a block of 128 bits is made up of 16 bytes. The non-linear reversible CA operates with the 16 bytes as input. Thus the function f is implemented. The fundamental Transformation is applied on each bytes. Thus the length of the state space is 16. Thus inorder to make the encryption and decryption blocks identical the 153 CA is cycled only 8 times. Instead if a

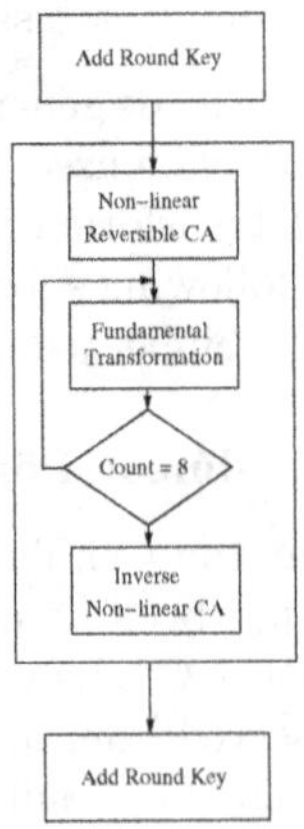

Fig. 2. Structure of a round of the Block Cipher

maximal group CA is used and it is required that the same structure be used for encryption and decryption then the number of clock cycles would have been $2^8/2$ = 128. The advantage of the present structure thus lies in making the cipher faster.

6 Conclusion

The present paper develops a generalized ideal block cipher round through the use of Cellular Automata. The analytical framework of the automata has been used to characterize a special class of null boundary CA, which forms the linear part of the block cipher round. It has been shown that the cycle structure of the linear CA leads to self-invertibe structures which can both encrypt and decrypt data. Also the cycle length grows linearly with the block size thus requiring less number of clock cycles. A non-linear CA has been identified to introduce non-linearity to the round without disturbing the cyclic nature of the cipher.

References

[1] Ph. Tsalides, "Cellular Automata based Built-In Self-Test Structures for VLSI Systems," *Elect. Lett.*, vol. 26, no. 17, pp. 1350–1352, 1990.

[2] Ph. Tsalides, T. A. York, and A. Thanailakis, "Pseudo-random Number Generators for VLSI Systems based on Linear Cellular Automata," *IEE Proc. E. Comput. Digit. Tech.*, vol. 138, no. 4, pp. 241–249, 1991.

[3] P. D. Hortensius et al., "Cellular automata based pseudo-random number generators for built-in self-test," vol. 8, pp. 842–859, August 1989.

[4] D. Roy Chowdhury, *Theory and Applications of Additive Cellular Automata for Reliable and Testable VLSI Circuit Design*, Ph.D. thesis, I.I.T. Kharagpur, India, 1992.

[5] D. Roy Chowdhury and P. Pal Chaudhuri, "Parallel memory testing : a BIST approach," in *Proc. 3rd Intl. Workshop on VLSI Design*. Bangalore, India, 1989, pp. 373–377.

[6] A. K. Das, *Additive Cellular Automata : Theory and Application as a Built-in Self-test Structure*, Ph.D. thesis, I.I.T. Kharagpur, India, 1990.

[7] D. E. Knuth, *The Art of Computer Programming – Seminumerical Algorithms*, Addison-Wesley, 1981.

[8] B.K. Kar, S. Nandi, and P. Pal Chaudhuri, "Theory and applications of cellular automata in cryptography," *IEEE Trans. Comp*, vol. 43, no. 12, pp. 1346–1357, December 1994.

[9] S. Murphy, S.R. Blackburn, and K.G. Paterson, "Comments on theory and applications of cellular automata in cryptography," *IEEE Trans. Comp.*, vol. 46, no. 5, pp. 637–638, 1997.

[10] Moni Naor and Omer Reingold, "Constructing pseudo-random permutations with a prescribed structure," *Journal of Cryptology*, vol. 14, pp. 97–102, 2001.

[11] P. Pal Chudhuri, D. Roy Chowdhury, Sukumar Nandi, and Santanu Chattopadhyay, *Additive Cellular Theory and its Application*, vol. 1, chapter 4, pp. 200–300, IEEE Computer Society Press, 1997.

NFD Technique for Efficient and Secured Information Hiding in Low Resolution Images

S.N. Sivanandam[1], C.K. Gokulnath[1], K. Prasanna[2], and S. Rajeev[2]

[1] Department of Computer Science & Engineering, PSG College of Technology, Coimbatore, India
profsns@hotmail.com, goki_pras@yahoo.co.in
[2] Department of Electronics & Communication Engineering, PSG College of Technology, Coimbatore, India
prasan_psg@yahoo.com, rajeev@ece.psgtech.ac.in

Abstract. A new steganography algorithm that supports transmission of huge information with minimal embedding is proposed. This approach uses the Newton's Forward Difference (NFD) Technique for mapping the text file/s onto a low resolution image file. A polynomial function is derived to represent the mapping of the text bits with the bit positions on the host image file. This polynomial is represented as bits and is embedded in the image file that is transmitted. The bit replacements made in the host image file are negligible compared to those in the existing embedding techniques.

1 Introduction

New approaches to data hiding open wide prospects in content management and secure communications. The text message hidden in a image (cover) medium may be plain text, cipher text, or any data/file that can be represented as a bit stream. To embed data onto an image, the following prevailing issues are worth noting:

Recent data hiding techniques indicate that bit-replacement or bit-substitution is inherently insecure with safe capacities far smaller than previously thought. Further these techniques demand lesser data to be embedded into the cover image so that probability of introducing detectable artifacts by the embedding process is less (i.e. the size of the text data to be embedded is strictly restricted to a fraction of the cover image file).

The proposed technique using NFD overcomes these issues by considering:

- The cover image data should not be significantly degraded by the embedded text data and the embedded data should be as imperceptible as possible.
- The embedded data should directly be encoded into the media rather than into a header or wrapper to maintain data consistency formats.
- The embedded data should be as immune as possible to modifications from intelligent attacks or anticipated manipulations such as filtering and re-sampling.

R.K. Ghosh and H. Mohanty (Eds.): ICDCIT 2004, LNCS 3347, pp. 458–467, 2004.

The proposed technique is designed to meet the above requirements and to overcome the disadvantages faced by other embedding techniques.

2 NFD Steganography Algorithm

The text data file to be hidden on to the image and the cover image file are read as bits. A table is constructed for all the bits in the text data file and the bit positions are correspondingly tabulated (taken as x-values). For each bit in the text file, a traversal is made on the image file and when a bit match is found an entry of corresponding bit position of the matched image bit is made as $f(x_i)$ against the text bit position x_i. The search for subsequent bits of text file is performed such that the $f(x_i)$ values for $i=1 \; to \; M$, yield a forward difference table in which the Pth differences of $f(x)$ are constant (typically $P=$ 2, 3 or 4) such that $P<M$, where M is the number of bits of the text file, thus generating a polynomial of degree P. In other words, the polynomial generated is going to perfectly correspond to the $(x_i, f(x_i))$ values for all $i=1 \; to \; M$ so that this provides lossless encoding. The forward difference table is constructed using the following formula.

The jth-order forward difference of f evaluated at x_k is

$$\Delta^j f(x_k)=\sum_{i=0}^{j}(-1)^i \binom{j}{i} f(x_{k+j-i}) \tag{1}$$

Where $\binom{j}{m}$ represents a binomial coefficient for a fixed value of m.

The final polynomial is constructed after the Pth differences in the forward difference table become constant.

$$f(x) = (1+xC_1\,\Delta+xC_2\,\Delta^2+...+xC_p\Delta^P)\,f(x_0) \tag{2}$$

This final polynomial with its highest degree and coefficients is partitioned into bits. This bit pattern can be considered as yet another data file and by applying the procedure a still reduced bit pattern can be obtained.

The data flow diagram of the NFD Stego algorithm is given below. The various blocks in the diagram are intended to represent the logical steps involved in the algorithm.

The image file (the cover) and the data file to be hidden are represented in binary format and sent to the Optimal Bit Mapper block which sequentially maps the bits in the data file to the matched bits in the image file such that for each bit in the former there is a positive integer value based on the bit position in the latter. The OBM chooses the matches in such a way that the higher order differences in the difference table vanish thus ensuring convergence and a polynomial function of a smaller degree. These set of positive integer values form an increasing trend so that the set of

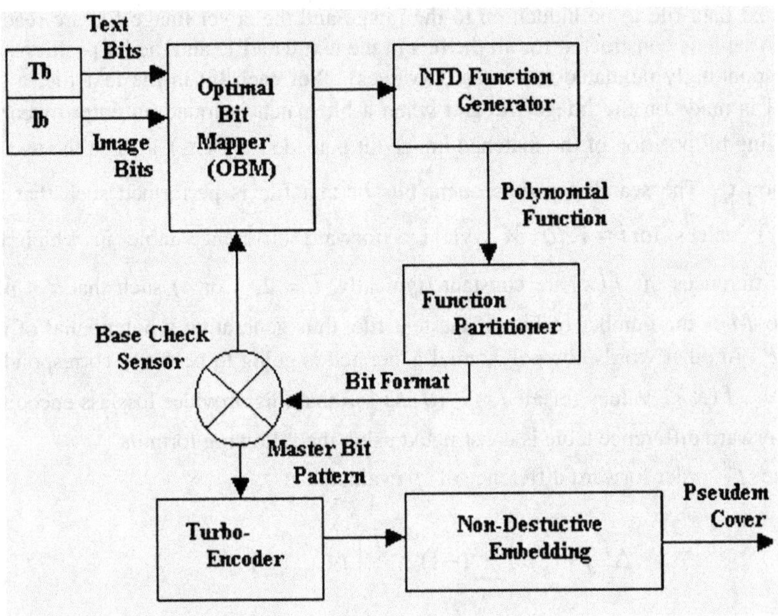

Fig. 1. Process Flow cycle of NFD Stego Algorithm

pairs of bit positions in the text x and position indexed values in the cover $f(x)$ generated can be applied to the Working Function Generator block which uses Newton's Forward Difference to construct the appropriate polynomial to fit the data set.

The position indexed values $f(x_i)$ can exceed the maximum number of bits N in the image file wherein bit mapping actually made indicates that bit in the position given by the following hypothesis:

$$f(x) = F_c(x) + N \times R \tag{3}$$

where $F_c(x)$ indicates the actual position of the bit in the cover and R, the number of recursions on the image file.

The working function i.e. the polynomial $f(x)$ generated is then partitioned as bit pattern in the Function Partitioner. This bit pattern is checked in the Base Check

Sensor for basis function requirement which includes the final size of the message bits which could be safely embedded without causing any perpetual degradation in the host image. If the polynomial obtained is not to the expected less degree then the bit pattern is fed into the OBM where it is considered as another text data file and the above procedure is recursively performed until the basis function requirement is met as indicated by the Base Check Sensor.

Once the basis function is obtained, it is partitioned into bit format storing the degree and the coefficients of the polynomial. This bit pattern is appended with the range of x, the number of recursions (r) of the procedure to give the Master Bit Pattern or the Basic Builder Set. If this Master Bit Pattern is brought down to 'm' bits, we embed just the 'm' bits instead of the M bits of the text file (M>>m).

The Master Bit Pattern thus obtained has to be safely guarded since any bit change in the MBP would lead to distorted retrieval of the hidden bits .Hence the obtained bit pattern is coded using Turbo Code .

The MBP is copied to encoder1 and encoder2. Before entering the encoder2, The MBP bits are scrambled by the interleaver. Each encoder generates a string of error-correction bits (parity bits) by performing a series of calculation on the data bits it receives. The original data and the two strings of parity bits are combined in to a single block are embedded on to the image in the embedding area. This final turbo encoded message is embedded using an existing efficient embedding technique gives the 'pseudem cover file' as the output.

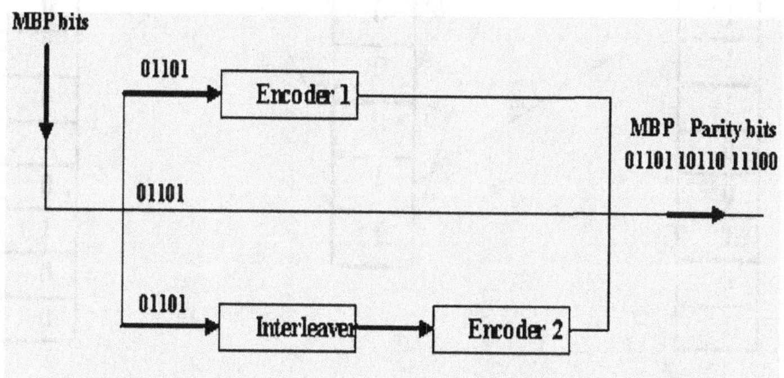

Fig. 2. Turbo encoder block with sample Master Bit Pattern

This NFD Stego embedding technique leads to two important aspects\

1. Image file is seldom distorted.
2. For maximum utility multiple data files can be pseudo-embedded till the maximum safe limit.

An Illustration of the NFD Stego Algorithm is given below

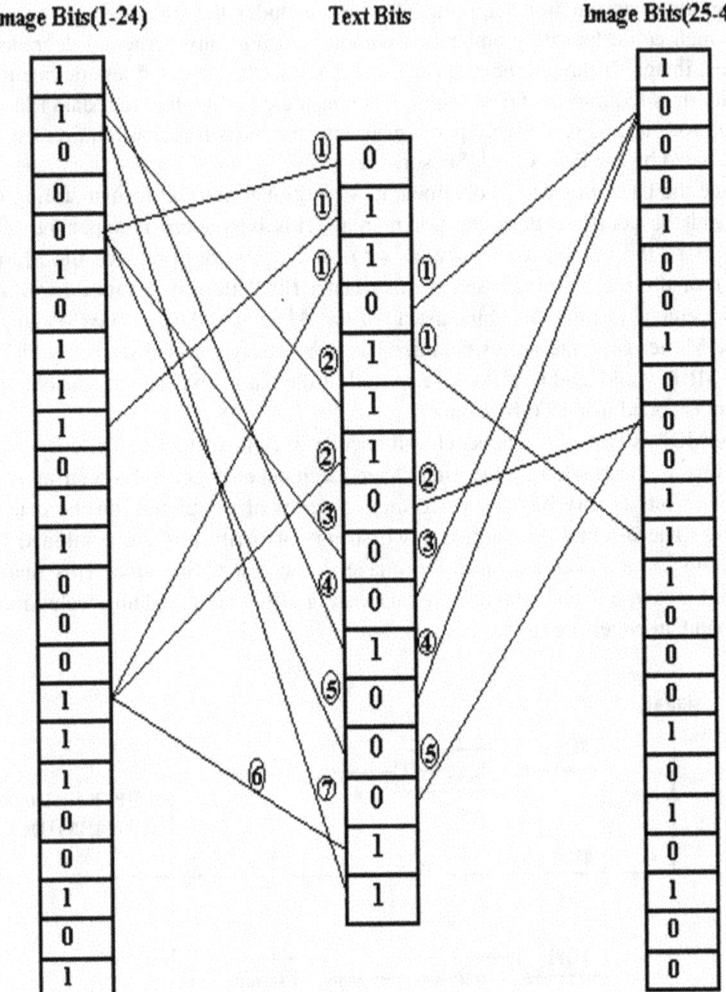

Fig. 3. Mapping of text bits with the image bits

Where (i) in the Fig. 3 indicates i[th] iteration on the image needed for providing mapping for the particular text bit.

Thus the difference table for the above mapping is provided below.

Applying the Newton's forward difference formula, the polynomial we get is

$$f(x)=x^2+2x+2 \tag{4}$$

X	F(X)
1	5
2	10
3	17
4	26
5	37
6	50
7	65
8	82
9	101
10	122
11	145
12	170
13	197
14	226
15	254
16	290

ΔF(x)
5
7
9
11
13
15
17
19
21
23
25
27
29
31
33

Δ²F(x)
2
2
2
2
2
2
2
2
2
2
2
2
2
2

Fig. 4. Difference table for the mapping of text bits with the image

Therefore the Master Bit Pattern is constructed as follows, two bits for each co efficient of the polynomial obtained and this would be turbo encoded for lossless recovery of the pattern in presence of channel noise.

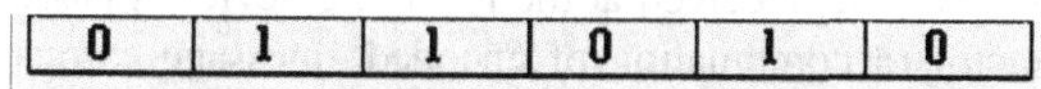

0	1	1	0	1	0

MBP for the obtained polynomial

3 Extraction Algorithm

The extraction process is reasonably simple. From the agreed bit locations (both at the transmitting and receiving ends) in the image, the turbo encoded message is extracted which is decoded to get the Master Bit Pattern. The decoding operation is as follows:

The received analog signal corresponding to the secure MBP is sampled and assigned integers indicating how likely it is a '0' or a '1'. For example, -7 means a bit is certainly a zero +7, a certain '1'. Note that an error occurred in the 5th bit in the block as highlighted. Originally a '1', it now has a negative value, which suggests it is a logical zero which is the error that has occurred.

Each Decoder takes noisy data and respective parity information and computes how confident it is about each decoded bit. The two decoders exchange this confidence information repeatedly and after a number of iteration, typically around 4 to

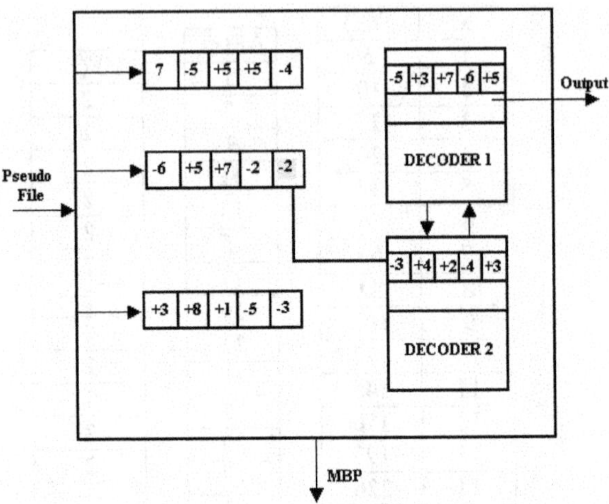

Fig. 5. Turbo decoder block for extraction of the Master Bit Pattern

10, they begin to agree on the decoded bits. The decoded data is the sum of noise and data plus the two strings of confidence value. The output is converted back to binary digits.

Once the Master Bit Pattern has been got by after decoding, the polynomial is framed with the power and the co-efficient bits and the size of the text file. The polynomial is evaluated for x: 1 to M and the necessary bits are extracted from the image bit positions generated by the polynomial and hence the data file is retrieved.

The pseudem cover file, received at the receiving device is passed into the Master Bit Pattern Extractor (a combination of encoded message extractor and turbo decoder) that retrieves the Basic Builder Set. This set enters the Bits to Function Converter, which converts the bits in to well-defined polynomial function and range of x the function should take. The higher level bit pattern is obtained in the Mapper and Reader block. Here the function is evaluated for each value of x and the bit at the position depicted by the function value is read from the image file. If the function value is found greater than the maximum size of the image, then a cyclic back-trace on the image file is made to read the required bit.

The actual position in the image is given by

$$F_c(x) = f(x) \bmod N \tag{5}$$

The obtained higher level bit pattern is sent as input to the Bits to Function Converter and after similar procedures we get the next higher level bit pattern and the recursion continues until the final text data is obtained. This recursion ends when the Recursion Null Comparator returns a 'Null' (this occurs when the decrement operation on the recursion counter results a null value).This final text data is driven to the output along with the image file.

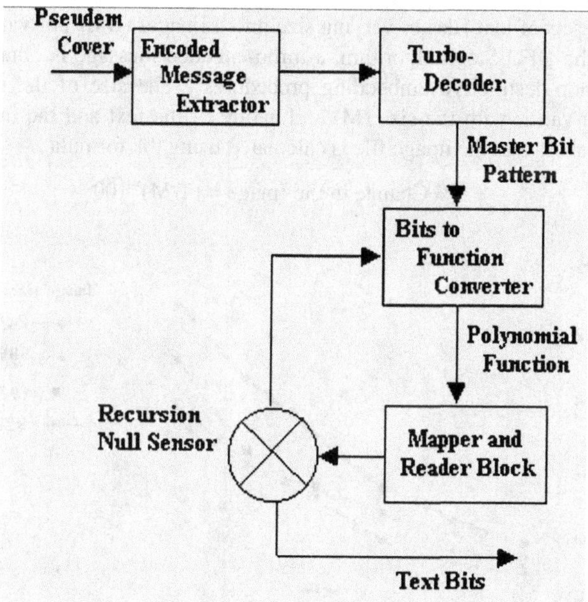

Fig. 6. Data flow diagram for the extraction algorithm

An Illustration of the Extraction Algorithm is given below.

From agreed locations in the Pseudem cover file the necessary bits to construct the Turbo-Encoded Message is taken and decoded to get the Master Bit Pattern. Once the polynomial (**$x^2 + 2x + 2$**) is constructed, it is evaluated for $x = 1 \ to \ M$, (16 in this case) and from the positions generated by the polynomial, the text file bits are retrieved from the mapped area in the received file.

Bit Locations in Image After Performing Modulo Operation:

X:	1	2	3	4	5	6	7	8	9	10	11	12	13	14	15	16
F(x):	5	10	17	26	37	2	17	34	5	26	1	26	5	34	17	2

Thus Bits Extracted from Mapping Area are:

0	1	1	0	1	1	1	0	0	0	1	0	0	0	1	1

4 Simulation Results

The NFD-Stego Algorithm has been simulated in MATLAB environment and the simulation results have been shown graphically. The graph gives the % Change in the image file after hiding the information from the text file. The results have been given for hiding 6 sets of text files of varying size into 4 images (BMP) of varying sizes. At the end of the NFD-Stego algorithm, a turbo-encoded message is obtained which is hidden by non-destructive embedding procedures. The size of the turbo-encoded message (T) varies with the size (M) and nature of the text and the image files. Finally the % change in the image file is calculated using the formula:

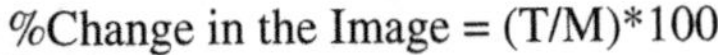

$$\%\text{Change in the Image} = (T/M)*100$$

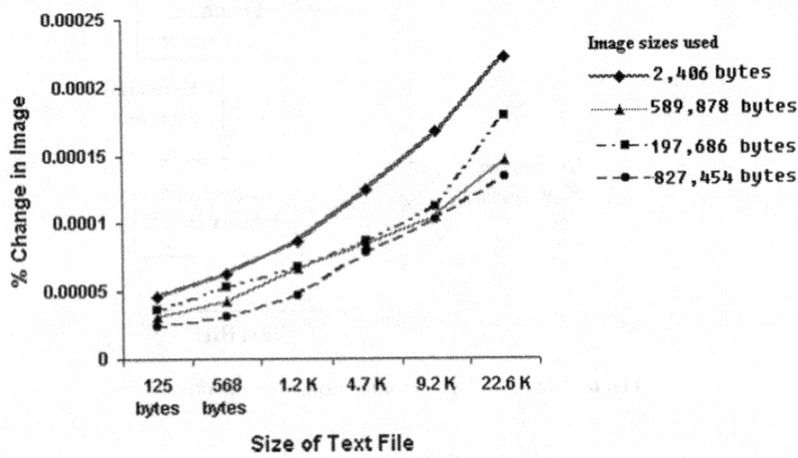

5 Conclusion

The main objective of this work is to hide large volume of data (text) in the host causing minimal perceptual distortion on the image. Further to ensure reliability the proposed model uses the turbo code which is one of the best possible error correction and detection encoding schemes available in digital communications. This concept of mapping is designed to represent a large text file with a polynomial achieving appreciable reduction in number of bits required to be embedded. Thus the size of the data to be hidden can be as high as or even more than the size of the image because actual data that is embedded is much lesser than the stego embedded information.

References

1. Y. Wang and P. Moulin, "Steganalysis of Block-Structured Stegotext," *Proc. SPIE Conf.*, Vol. 5306, San Jose, CA, Jan. 2004.
2. J. L. Cannons and P. Moulin, "Design and Statistical Analysis of a Hash-Aided Image Watermarking System," to appear in *IEEE Trans. on Image Processing*, 2004.
3. P. Moulin and J. A. O'Sullivan, "Information-Theoretic Analysis of Information Hiding," Sep. 1999 [Sep. 99 postscript] ; revised, Sep. 2002. *IEEE Trans. on Information Theory*, Vol. 49, No. 3, pp. 563-593, March 2003

4. P. Moulin, "A Mathematical Approach to Watermarking and Data Hiding," *ICASSP Tutorial*, Orlando, FL, May 13, 2002
5. Moulin and E. J. Delp, "A Mathematical Approach to Watermarking and Data Hiding," *ICIP Tutorial*, Thessaloniki, Greece, October 7, 2001
6. J. A. O'Sullivan and P. Moulin, "Some Properties of Optimal Information Hiding and Information Attacks," *Proc. 39th Allerton conference* , Monticello, IL, Oct. 3--5, 2001
7. Neil F. Johnson and Sushil Jajodia, "Steganalysis: The investigation of hidden information", proceedings of the 1998 ieee information technology conference, syracuse, new york, usa, september 1st - 3rd, 1998.
8. N.F. Johnson, S. Jajodia, "Steganalysis of images created using current steganography software", proceedings of information hiding workshop, portland, oregon, usa, april 1998.
9. F. A. P. Petitcolas, "Attacks on Copyright Marking Systems,"*Information Hiding: Second International Workshop*, D. Aucsmith,Editor, Lecture Notes in Computer Science **1525**,Springer-Verlag, Portland,OR(April 15–17, 1998), pp. 219–239.

Improving Feature Selection in Anomaly Intrusion Detection Using Specifications

Yanxin Wang[1], Andrew Miner[1], Johnny Wong[1], and Prem Uppuluri[2]

[1] Department of Computer Science,
Iowa State University, Ames, Iowa, 50011
{wangyx, asminer, wong}@iastate.edu

[2] Dept. of Computer Science and Electrical Engineering,
University of Missouri-Kansas City, MO, 64110
uppulurip@umkc.edu

Abstract. In the paper we discuss the intergration of an support vector machine (SVM) based anomaly detection system with an specification based intrusion detection system (IDS), where the specification based IDS improves the feature-selection function of the SVMs. We demonstrate through experimental results, that extended finite state machine (EFSA) based anomaly detectors performs better than either the EFSA and SVM anomaly detectors individually. Specifically the accuracy of detection improved and the time and space required for SVM learning reduced using the feature reduction based on EFSAs.

R.K. Ghosh and H. Mohanty (Eds.): ICDCIT 2004, LNCS 3347, p. 468, 2004.

Towards Automatic Learning of Valid Services for Honeypots

Vishal Chowdhary, Alok Tongaonkar, and Tzi-cker Chiueh

State University of New York, Stony Brook, NY 11794

Abstract. Honeypots have emerged as an important tool in the field of *Intrusion Detection Systems.* Honeypots are decoy machines whose sole purpose is to be compromised by network attackers, in order to gain information about the attack techniques. The biggest challenge in deploying honeypots is their configuration and maintenance compounded with the fact that they either *emulate* a few services or provide the real services. The emulated services, which are usually implemented using scripts, are restricted by the responses given to the attacker. This limits the amount of information that can be gathered. The scipts are also much easier to be detected by the attacker. On the other hand, the drawback of providing real services is the greater risk associated with their use.

In this paper, we describe *service-mining*, a machine learning approach to learn and emulate behavior of real-world services. Given large enough traces of the real-service interactions and some basic information about the service, we propose a scheme whereby we can learn the semantics of its various commands and then effectively emulate the service. This service may then be deployed on a honeypot to capture attack signatures without posing a threat to the complete network.

Our initial experience in trying to emulate the popular FTP service is promising. We are able to learn the FTP service and then intelligently and consistently respond to user queries with our emulated FTP service.

R.K. Ghosh and H. Mohanty (Eds.): ICDCIT 2004, LNCS 3347, p. 469, 2004.

Author Index

Lecture Notes in Computer Science

For information about Vols. 1–3241

please contact your bookseller or Springer

Vol. 3356: G. Das, V.P. Gulati (Eds.), Intelligent Information Technology. XII, 428 pages. 2004.

Vol. 3347: R.K. Ghosh, H. Mohanty (Eds.), Distributed Computing and Internet Technology. XX, 472 pages. 2004.

Vol. 3340: C.S. Calude, E. Calude, M.J. Dinneen (Eds.), Developments in Language Theory. XI, 431 pages. 2004.

Vol. 3339: G.I. Webb, X. Yu (Eds.), AI 2004: Advances in Artificial Intelligence. XXII, 1272 pages. 2004. (Subseries LNAI).

Vol. 3338: S.Z. Li, J. Lai, T. Tan, G. Feng, Y. Wang (Eds.), Advances in Biometric Person Authentication. XVI, 707 pages. 2004.

Vol. 3337: J.M. Barreiro, F. Martin-Sanchez, V. Maojo, F. Sanz (Eds.), Biological and Medical Data Analysis. XI, 508 pages. 2004.

Vol. 3336: D. Karagiannis, U. Reimer (Eds.), Practical Aspects of Knowledge Management. X, 523 pages. 2004. (Subseries LNAI).

Vol. 3334: Z. Chen, H. Chen, Q. Miao, Y. Fu, E. Fox, E.-p. Lim (Eds.), Digital Libraries: International Collaboration and Cross-Fertilization. XX, 690 pages. 2004.

Vol. 3333: K. Aizawa, Y. Nakamura, S. Satoh (Eds.), Advances in Multimedia Information Processing - PCM 2004. XXXV, 785 pages. 2004.

Vol. 3332: K. Aizawa, Y. Nakamura, S. Satoh (Eds.), Advances in Multimedia Information Processing - PCM 2004. XXXVI, 1051 pages. 2004.

Vol. 3331: K. Aizawa, Y. Nakamura, S. Satoh (Eds.), Advances in Multimedia Information Processing - PCM 2004. XXXVI, 667 pages. 2004.

Vol. 3329: P.J. Lee (Ed.), Advances in Cryptology - ASIACRYPT 2004. XVI, 546 pages. 2004.

Vol. 3323: G. Antoniou, H. Boley (Eds.), Rules and Rule Markup Languages for the Semantic Web. X, 215 pages. 2004.

Vol. 3322: R. Klette, J. Žunić (Eds.), Combinatorial Image Analysis. XII, 760 pages. 2004.

Vol. 3321: M.J. Maher (Ed.), Advances in Computer Science - ASIAN 2004. XII, 510 pages. 2004.

Vol. 3321: M.J. Maher (Ed.), Advances in Computer Science - ASIAN 2004. XII, 510 pages. 2004.

Vol. 3320: K.-M. Liew, H. Shen, S. See, W. Cai (Eds.), Parallel and Distributed Computing: Applications and Technologies. XXIV, 891 pages. 2004.

Vol. 3316: N.R. Pal, N.K. Kasabov, R.K. Mudi, S. Pal, S.K. Parui (Eds.), Neural Information Processing. XXX, 1368 pages. 2004.

Vol. 3315: C. Lemaître, C.A. Reyes, J.A. González (Eds.), Advances in Artificial Intelligence – IBERAMIA 2004. XX, 987 pages. 2004. (Subseries LNAI).

Vol. 3312: A.J. Hu, A.K. Martin (Eds.), Formal Methods in Computer-Aided Design. XI, 445 pages. 2004.

Vol. 3311: V. Roca, F. Rousseau (Eds.), Interactive Multimedia and Next Generation Networks. XIII, 287 pages. 2004.

Vol. 3309: C.-H. Chi, K.-Y. Lam (Eds.), Content Computing. XII, 510 pages. 2004.

Vol. 3308: J. Davies, W. Schulte, M. Barnett (Eds.), Formal Methods and Software Engineering. XIII, 500 pages. 2004.

Vol. 3307: C. Bussler, S.-k. Hong, W. Jun, R. Kaschek, D.. Kinshuk, S. Krishnaswamy, S.W. Loke, D. Oberle, D. Richards, A. Sharma, Y. Sure, B. Thalheim (Eds.), Web Information Systems – WISE 2004 Workshops. XV, 277 pages. 2004.

Vol. 3306: X. Zhou, S. Su, M.P. Papazoglou, M.E. Orlowska, K.G. Jeffery (Eds.), Web Information Systems – WISE 2004. XVII, 745 pages. 2004.

Vol. 3305: P.M.A. Sloot, B. Chopard, A.G. Hoekstra (Eds.), Cellular Automata. XV, 883 pages. 2004.

Vol. 3303: J.A. López, E. Benfenati, W. Dubitzky (Eds.), Knowledge Exploration in Life Science Informatics. X, 249 pages. 2004. (Subseries LNAI).

Vol. 3302: W.-N. Chin (Ed.), Programming Languages and Systems. XIII, 453 pages. 2004.

Vol. 3299: F. Wang (Ed.), Automated Technology for Verification and Analysis. XII, 506 pages. 2004.

Vol. 3298: S.A. McIlraith, D. Plexousakis, F. van Harmelen (Eds.), The Semantic Web – ISWC 2004. XXI, 841 pages. 2004.

Vol. 3295: P. Markopoulos, B. Eggen, E. Aarts, J.L. Crowley (Eds.), Ambient Intelligence. XIII, 388 pages. 2004.

Vol. 3294: C.N. Dean, R.T. Boute (Eds.), Teaching Formal Methods. X, 249 pages. 2004.

Vol. 3293: C.-H. Chi, M. van Steen, C. Wills (Eds.), Web Content Caching and Distribution. IX, 283 pages. 2004.

Vol. 3292: R. Meersman, Z. Tari, A. Corsaro (Eds.), On the Move to Meaningful Internet Systems 2004: OTM 2004 Workshops. XXIII, 885 pages. 2004.

Vol. 3291: R. Meersman, Z. Tari (Eds.), On the Move to Meaningful Internet Systems 2004: CoopIS, DOA, and ODBASE. XXV, 824 pages. 2004.

Vol. 3290: R. Meersman, Z. Tari (Eds.), On the Move to Meaningful Internet Systems 2004: CoopIS, DOA, and ODBASE. XXV, 823 pages. 2004.

Vol. 3289: S. Wang, K. Tanaka, S. Zhou, T.W. Ling, J. Guan, D. Yang, F. Grandi, E. Mangina, I.-Y. Song, H.C. Mayr (Eds.), Conceptual Modeling for Advanced Application Domains. XXII, 692 pages. 2004.

Vol. 3288: P. Atzeni, W. Chu, H. Lu, S. Zhou, T.W. Ling (Eds.), Conceptual Modeling – ER 2004. XXI, 869 pages. 2004.

Vol. 3287: A. Sanfeliu, J.F. Martínez Trinidad, J.A. Carrasco Ochoa (Eds.), Progress in Pattern Recognition, Image Analysis and Applications. XVII, 703 pages. 2004.

Vol. 3286: G. Karsai, E. Visser (Eds.), Generative Programming and Component Engineering. XIII, 491 pages. 2004.

Vol. 3285: S. Manandhar, J. Austin, U.B. Desai, Y. Oyanagi, A. Talukder (Eds.), Applied Computing. XII, 334 pages. 2004.

Vol. 3284: A. Karmouch, L. Korba, E.R.M. Madeira (Eds.), Mobility Aware Technologies and Applications. XII, 382 pages. 2004.

Vol. 3283: F.A. Aagesen, C. Anutariya, V. Wuwongse (Eds.), Intelligence in Communication Systems. XIII, 327 pages. 2004.

Vol. 3282: V. Guruswami, List Decoding of Error-Correcting Codes. XIX, 350 pages. 2004.

Vol. 3281: T. Dingsøyr (Ed.), Software Process Improvement. X, 207 pages. 2004.

Vol. 3280: C. Aykanat, T. Dayar, İ. Körpeoğlu (Eds.), Computer and Information Sciences - ISCIS 2004. XVIII, 1009 pages. 2004.

Vol. 3278: A. Sahai, F. Wu (Eds.), Utility Computing. XI, 272 pages. 2004.

Vol. 3275: P. Perner (Ed.), Advances in Data Mining. VIII, 173 pages. 2004. (Subseries LNAI).

Vol. 3274: R. Guerraoui (Ed.), Distributed Computing. XIII, 465 pages. 2004.

Vol. 3273: T. Baar, A. Strohmeier, A. Moreira, S.J. Mellor (Eds.), <<UML>> 2004 - The Unified Modelling Language. XIII, 454 pages. 2004.

Vol. 3271: J. Vicente, D. Hutchison (Eds.), Management of Multimedia Networks and Services. XIII, 335 pages. 2004.

Vol. 3270: M. Jeckle, R. Kowalczyk, P. Braun (Eds.), Grid Services Engineering and Management. X, 165 pages. 2004.

Vol. 3269: J. Lopez, S. Qing, E. Okamoto (Eds.), Information and Communications Security. XI, 564 pages. 2004.

Vol. 3268: W. Lindner, M. Mesiti, C. Türker, Y. Tzitzikas, A. Vakali (Eds.), Current Trends in Database Technology - EDBT 2004 Workshops. XVIII, 608 pages. 2004.

Vol. 3267: C. Priami, P. Quaglia (Eds.), Global Computing. VIII, 377 pages. 2004.

Vol. 3266: J. Solé-Pareta, M. Smirnov, P.V. Mieghem, J. Domingo-Pascual, E. Monteiro, P. Reichl, B. Stiller, R.J. Gibbens (Eds.), Quality of Service in the Emerging Networking Panorama. XVI, 390 pages. 2004.

Vol. 3265: R.E. Frederking, K.B. Taylor (Eds.), Machine Translation: From Real Users to Research. XI, 392 pages. 2004. (Subseries LNAI).

Vol. 3264: G. Paliouras, Y. Sakakibara (Eds.), Grammatical Inference: Algorithms and Applications. XI, 291 pages. 2004. (Subseries LNAI).

Vol. 3263: M. Weske, P. Liggesmeyer (Eds.), Object-Oriented and Internet-Based Technologies. XII, 239 pages. 2004.

Vol. 3262: M.M. Freire, P. Chemouil, P. Lorenz, A. Gravey (Eds.), Universal Multiservice Networks. XIII, 556 pages. 2004.

Vol. 3261: T. Yakhno (Ed.), Advances in Information Systems. XIV, 617 pages. 2004.

Vol. 3260: I.G.M.M. Niemegeers, S.H. de Groot (Eds.), Personal Wireless Communications. XIV, 478 pages. 2004.

Vol. 3259: J. Dix, J. Leite (Eds.), Computational Logic in Multi-Agent Systems. XII, 251 pages. 2004. (Subseries LNAI).

Vol. 3258: M. Wallace (Ed.), Principles and Practice of Constraint Programming – CP 2004. XVII, 822 pages. 2004.

Vol. 3257: E. Motta, N.R. Shadbolt, A. Stutt, N. Gibbins (Eds.), Engineering Knowledge in the Age of the Semantic Web. XVII, 517 pages. 2004. (Subseries LNAI).

Vol. 3256: H. Ehrig, G. Engels, F. Parisi-Presicce, G. Rozenberg (Eds.), Graph Transformations. XII, 451 pages. 2004.

Vol. 3255: A. Benczúr, J. Demetrovics, G. Gottlob (Eds.), Advances in Databases and Information Systems. XI, 423 pages. 2004.

Vol. 3254: E. Macii, V. Paliouras, O. Koufopavlou (Eds.), Integrated Circuit and System Design. XVI, 910 pages. 2004.

Vol. 3253: Y. Lakhnech, S. Yovine (Eds.), Formal Techniques, Modelling and Analysis of Timed and Fault-Tolerant Systems. X, 397 pages. 2004.

Vol. 3252: H. Jin, Y. Pan, N. Xiao, J. Sun (Eds.), Grid and Cooperative Computing - GCC 2004 Workshops. XVIII, 785 pages. 2004.

Vol. 3251: H. Jin, Y. Pan, N. Xiao, J. Sun (Eds.), Grid and Cooperative Computing - GCC 2004. XXII, 1025 pages. 2004.

Vol. 3250: L.-J. (LJ) Zhang, M. Jeckle (Eds.), Web Services. X, 301 pages. 2004.

Vol. 3249: B. Buchberger, J.A. Campbell (Eds.), Artificial Intelligence and Symbolic Computation. X, 285 pages. 2004. (Subseries LNAI).

Vol. 3246: A. Apostolico, M. Melucci (Eds.), String Processing and Information Retrieval. XIV, 332 pages. 2004.

Vol. 3245: E. Suzuki, S. Arikawa (Eds.), Discovery Science. XIV, 430 pages. 2004. (Subseries LNAI).

Vol. 3244: S. Ben-David, J. Case, A. Maruoka (Eds.), Algorithmic Learning Theory. XIV, 505 pages. 2004. (Subseries LNAI).

Vol. 3243: S. Leonardi (Ed.), Algorithms and Models for the Web-Graph. VIII, 189 pages. 2004.

Vol. 3242: X. Yao, E. Burke, J.A. Lozano, J. Smith, J.J. Merelo-Guervós, J.A. Bullinaria, J. Rowe, P. Tiňo, A. Kabán, H.-P. Schwefel (Eds.), Parallel Problem Solving from Nature - PPSN VIII. XX, 1185 pages. 2004.